Lecture Notes in Computer Science 8094

Commenced Publication in 1973
Founding and Former Series Editors:
Gerhard Goos, Juris Hartmanis, and Jan van Leeuwen

Editorial Board

David Hutchison
  Lancaster University, UK
Takeo Kanade
  Carnegie Mellon University, Pittsburgh, PA, USA
Josef Kittler
  University of Surrey, Guildford, UK
Jon M. Kleinberg
  Cornell University, Ithaca, NY, USA
Alfred Kobsa
  University of California, Irvine, CA, USA
Friedemann Mattern
  ETH Zurich, Switzerland
John C. Mitchell
  Stanford University, CA, USA
Moni Naor
  Weizmann Institute of Science, Rehovot, Israel
Oscar Nierstrasz
  University of Bern, Switzerland
C. Pandu Rangan
  Indian Institute of Technology, Madras, India
Bernhard Steffen
  TU Dortmund University, Germany
Madhu Sudan
  Microsoft Research, Cambridge, MA, USA
Demetri Terzopoulos
  University of California, Los Angeles, CA, USA
Doug Tygar
  University of California, Berkeley, CA, USA
Gerhard Weikum
  Max Planck Institute for Informatics, Saarbruecken, Germany

Florian Daniel   Jianmin Wang
Barbara Weber (Eds.)

Business Process Management

11th International Conference, BPM 2013
Beijing, China, August 26-30, 2013
Proceedings

Volume Editors

Florian Daniel
University of Trento
Department of Information Engineering and Computer Science
38123 Povo, Italy
E-mail: daniel@disi.unitn.it

Jianmin Wang
Tsinghua University
School of Software
Beijing 100084, China
E-mail: jimwang@tsinghua.edu.cn

Barbara Weber
University of Innsbruck
Business Process Management Research Cluster
6020 Innsbruck, Austria
E-mail: barbara.weber@uibk.ac.at

ISSN 0302-9743　　　　　　　　　　　　e-ISSN 1611-3349
ISBN 978-3-642-40175-6　　　　　　　　e-ISBN 978-3-642-40176-3
DOI 10.1007/978-3-642-40176-3
Springer Heidelberg Dordrecht London New York

Library of Congress Control Number: 2013944577

CR Subject Classification (1998): F.3, D.2, J.1, H.3.5, H.4, K.4.3, K.6

LNCS Sublibrary: SL 3 – Information Systems and Application,
incl. Internet/Web and HCI

© Springer-Verlag Berlin Heidelberg 2013
This work is subject to copyright. All rights are reserved by the Publisher, whether the whole or part of the material is concerned, specifically the rights of translation, reprinting, reuse of illustrations, recitation, broadcasting, reproduction on microfilms or in any other physical way, and transmission or information storage and retrieval, electronic adaptation, computer software, or by similar or dissimilar methodology now known or hereafter developed. Exempted from this legal reservation are brief excerpts in connection with reviews or scholarly analysis or material supplied specifically for the purpose of being entered and executed on a computer system, for exclusive use by the purchaser of the work. Duplication of this publication or parts thereof is permitted only under the provisions of the Copyright Law of the Publisher's location, in its current version, and permission for use must always be obtained from Springer. Permissions for use may be obtained through RightsLink at the Copyright Clearance Center. Violations are liable to prosecution under the respective Copyright Law.
The use of general descriptive names, registered names, trademarks, service marks, etc. in this publication does not imply, even in the absence of a specific statement, that such names are exempt from the relevant protective laws and regulations and therefore free for general use.
While the advice and information in this book are believed to be true and accurate at the date of publication, neither the authors nor the editors nor the publisher can accept any legal responsibility for any errors or omissions that may be made. The publisher makes no warranty, express or implied, with respect to the material contained herein.

Typesetting: Camera-ready by author, data conversion by Scientific Publishing Services, Chennai, India

Printed on acid-free paper

Springer is part of Springer Science+Business Media (www.springer.com)

Preface

BPM 2013 was the 11th conference in a series that provides a prestigious forum for researchers and practitioners in the field of business process management (BPM). The conference was organized by Tsinghua University, China, and took place during August 26–30, 2013, in Beijing, China. In response to the call for papers, we received 118 submissions. Each paper was evaluated by at least three Program Committee members and by one senior Program Committee member. We accepted 17 regular papers (14.4% acceptance rate) and eight short papers with an overall acceptance rate of 21.2%. Compared to previous editions of BPM, this year we noted a lower focus by authors on topics like process modeling, while we also observed a considerable growth of submissions regarding areas like process mining, conformance/compliance checking, and process model matching. The integrated consideration of processes and data remains popular, and novel viewpoints focus, among others, on data completeness in business processes, the modeling and runtime support of event streaming in business processes, and business process architectures.

The conference's resulting scientific program consisted of seven research sessions, including sessions on Process Mining, Process Models, Conformance Checking, Process Data, Process Model Matching, Process Architectures and Collaboration, and Alternative Perspectives, as well as one Industry Paper Session.

According to its tradition, the conference also hosted three invited keynote presentations. Tom Baeyens, founder and CEO of Effektiv.com, architect of several running BPM engines worldwide, and founder of the open-source process engines jBPM and Activiti, talked about the expected tremendous impact of cloud computing on BPM. Xiang Gao, General Manager of the Department of Management Information Systems at China Mobile Communication Corporation, outlined how next-generation intelligent BPM (iBPM) in the era of big data might look like. Noshir Contractor, Jane S. & William J. White Professor of Behavioral Sciences in the School of Engineering, School of Communication and the Kellogg School of Management at Northwestern University, USA, and Director of the Science of Networks in Communities (SONIC) Research Group at Northwestern University, contributed with enlightening insights into the formation and success of software development teams.

Next to the main scientific program of the conference, BPM 2013 also hosted 11 workshops, which attracted a very good number of participants and enriched the overall offering of the conference with attractive venues for the discussion of early results and ongoing works. We would like to thank the BPM Workshop Chairs, Niels Lohmann, Minseok Song and Petia Wohed, as well as the workshop organizers for their professional work and commitment. Similarly, we are grateful to Anne Rozinat, Hagen Voelzer and Liang Zhang, for the management of the

Industry Paper Track, Jianxun Liu and Chun Ouyang for the organization of the Doctoral Consortium, Boudewijn van Dongen and Marie Christine Fauvet for the organization of the Demo Track, Jian Yang and Zhaoxia Wang for the selection of the tutorials, and Massimo Mecella and Michael zur Muehlen for the professional publicity.

Our biggest thanks, of course, go the authors and presenters, whose contributions made BPM 2013 a success. We appreciate the senior Program Committee members, the Program Committee members, and the external reviewers for their thorough reviews and the serious discussions of the submitted papers. We thank the BPM Steering Committee for their valuable guidance.

We also thank the conference sponsors, Bizagi (Platinum) and IBM Research (Doctoral Consortium sponsor), and Mu Qiao, our Sponsorship Chair, as well as Lijie Wen, the Organization Chair. Our thanks also go to Springer, the publisher of the BPM proceedings, for the continuous support of BPM. Finally, the use of EasyChair was also much appreciated and made our lives so much easier.

August 2013

Florian Daniel
Jianmin Wang
Barbara Weber

Organization

BPM 2013 was organized in Beijing, P.R. China, by Tsinghua University.

Steering Committee

Boualem Benatallah	University of New South Wales, Australia
Fabio Casati	University of Trento, Italy
Peter Dadam	University of Ulm, Germany
Jörg Desel	Fernuniversität in Hagen, Germany
Marlon Dumas	University of Tartu, Estonia
Schahram Dustdar	Vienna University of Technology, Austria
Arthur Ter Hofstede	Queensland University of Technology, Australia
Wil van der Aalst	Eindhoven University of Technology, The Netherlands
Mathias Weske	HPI, University of Potsdam, Germany
Michael zur Mühlen	Stevens Institute of Technology, USA

Executive Committee

Honorary Chair

Jiaguang Sun	Tsinghua University, China

General Chair

Jianmin Wang	Tsinghua University, China

Program Chairs

Florian Daniel	University of Trento, Italy
Jianmin Wang	Tsinghua University, China
Barbara Weber	University of Innsbruck, Austria

Organization Chair

Lijie Wen	Tsinghua University, China

Industrial Chairs

Anne Rozinat	Fluxicon
Hagen Voelzer	IBM Research Zurich, Switzerland
Liang Zhang	Fudan University, China

Workshop Chairs

Niels Lohmann — University of Rostock, Germany
Minseok Song — Ulsan National Institute of Science and Technology, South Korea
Petia Wohed — Stockholm University, Sweden

Doctoral Consortium Chairs

Jianxun Liu — Hunan University of Science and Technology, China
Chun Ouyang — Queensland University of Technology, Australia

Demo Chairs

Boudewijn van Dongen — Eindhoven University of Technology, The Netherlands
Marie Christine Fauvet — University of Joseph Fourier, France

Publicity Chairs

Massimo Mecella — University of Rome, Italy
Michael zur Muehlen — Stevens Institute of Technolog, USA

Tutorial Chairs

Jian Yang — Macquarie University, Australia
Zhaoxia Wang — Logistical Engineering University, China

Sponsorship Chair

Mu Qiao — IBM Almaden Research Center, USA

Senior Program Committee

Boualem Benatallah — University of New South Wales, Australia
Peter Dadam — University of Ulm, Germany
Jörg Desel — Fernuniversität in Hagen, Germany
Schahram Dustdar — Vienna University of Technology, Austria
Stefan Jablonski — University of Bayreuth, Germany
Frank Leymann — University of Stuttgart, Germany
Jan Mendling — Vienna University of Economics and Business, Austria
Manfred Reichert — University of Ulm, Germany
Hajo A. Reijers — Eindhoven University of Technology, The Netherlands
Michael Rosemann — Queensland University of Technology, Australia
Arthur Ter Hofstede — Queensland University of Technology, Australia
Wil van der Aalst — Eindhoven University of Technology, Australia
Mathias Weske — HPI, University of Potsdam, Germany

Program Committee

Rafael Accorsi	University of Freiburg, Germany
Ahmed Awad	Cairo University, Egypt
Claudio Bartolini	HP Labs, United States
Boualem Benatallah	University of New South Wales, Australia
Christoph Bussler	Voxeo Labs, Inc., United States
Fabio Casati	University of Trento, Italy
Francisco Curbera	IBM Research, United States
Peter Dadam	University of Ulm, Germany
Jörg Desel	Fernuniversität in Hagen, Germany
Alin Deutsch	University of California, USA
Remco Dijkman	Eindhoven University of Technology, The Netherlands
Marlon Dumas	University of Tartu, Estonia
Schahram Dustdar	Vienna University of Technology, Austria
Johann Eder	University of Klagenfurt, Germany
Gregor Engels	University of Paderborn, Germany
Dirk Fahland	Eindhoven University of Technology, The Netherlands
Kathrin Figl	Vienna University of Economics and Business, Austria
Hans-Georg Fill	University of Vienna, Austria
Piero Fraternali	Politecnico di Milano, Italy
Avigdor Gal	Technion, Israel
Luciano García-Bañuelos	University of Tartu, Estonia
Holger Giese	HPI, University of Potsdam, Germany
Claude Godart	University of Lorraine, France
Thomas Hildebrandt	IT University of Copenhagen, Denmark
Marta Indulska	The University of Queensland, Australia
Stefan Jablonski	University of Bayreuth, Germany
Sonja Kabicher-Fuchs	University of Vienna, Austria
Leonid Kalinichenko	Russian Academy of Science, Russia
Gerti Kappel	Vienna University of Technology, Austria
Dimka Karastoyanova	University of Stuttgart, Germany
Ekkart Kindler	Technical University of Denmark
Marite Kirikova	Riga Technical University, Latvia
Jana Koehler	Hochschule Luzern, Switzerland
Agnes Koschmider	Karlsruher Institute of Technology, Germany
John Krogstie	Norwegian University of Science and Technology, Norway
Jochen Kuester	IBM Research, Switzerland
Akhil Kumar	Penn State University, USA
Frank Leymann	University of Stuttgart, Germany
Niels Lohmann	University of Rostock, Germany
Peter Loos	Saarland University, Germany

Heiko Ludwig	IBM Research, United States
Massimo Mecella	Sapienza Università di Roma, Italy
Ana Karla Medeiros	Capgemini Consulting, The Netherlands
Jan Mendling	Vienna University of Economics and Business, Austria
Hamid Motahari	HP Labs, United States
Bela Mutschler	University of Applied Sciences Ravensburg-Weingarten, Germany
Alex Norta	University of Helsinki, Finland
Markus Nüttgens	Universität Hamburg, Germany
Andreas Oberweis	Universität Karlsruhe, Germany
Hervé Panetto	CRAN, University of Lorraine, CNRS, France
Oscar Pastor Lopez	Universitat Politecnica de Valencia, Spain
Cesare Pautasso	University of Lugano, Italy
Artem Polyvyanyy	Queensland University of Technology, Australia
Frank Puhlmann	inubit AG, Germany
Manfred Reichert	University of Ulm, Germany
Hajo A. Reijers	Eindhoven University of Technology, The Netherlands
Stefanie Rinderle-Ma	University of Vienna, Austria
Michael Rosemann	Queensland University of Technology, Australia
Domenico Saccà	University of Calabria, Italy
Shazia Sadiq	The University of Queensland, Australia
Erich Schikuta	University of Vienna, Austria
Heiko Schuldt	University of Basel, Switzerland
Pnina Soffer	University of Haifa, Israel
Minseok Song	Ulsan National Institute of Science and Technology, South Korea
Mark Strembeck	Vienna University of Economics and Business, Austria
Harald Störrle	Danmarks Tekniske Universitet, Denmark
Jianwen Su	University of California at Santa Barbara, USA
Stefan Tai	Karlsruher Institute of Technology, Germany
Samir Tata	Institut TELECOM; TELECOM SudParis; CNRS UMR Samovar, France
Arthur Ter Hofstede	Queensland University of Technology, Australia
Farouk Toumani	Blaise Pascal University, France
Alberto Trombetta	University of Insubria, Italy
Aphrodite Tsalgatidou	National and Kapodistrian University of Athens, Greece
Wil Van Der Aalst	Eindhoven University of Technology, The Netherlands
Boudewijn Van Dongen	Eindhoven University of Technology, The Netherlands
Hagen Voelzer	IBM Research, Switzerland
Matthias Weidlich	Technion, Israel

Lijie Wen   Tsinghua University, China
Mathias Weske   HPI, University of Potsdam, Germany
Michael Westergaard   Eindhoven University of Technology,
                                The Netherlands
Petia Wohed   Stockholm University, Sweden
Karsten Wolf   University of Rostock, Germany
Andreas Wombacher   University of Twente, The Netherlands
Liang Zhang   Fudan University, China

Demo Track Program Committee

Henrik Leopold   Humboldt-Universität zu Berlin, Germany
Diogo R. Ferreira   Technical University of Lisbon, Portugal
Nick Russell   Eindhoven University of Technology,
                                The Netherlands
Agnès Front   Grenoble University, France
Michael Westergaard   Eindhoven University of Technology,
                                The Netherlands
Laurent D'Orazio   Blaise Pascal University, France
Ingo Weber   NICTA, Australia
Matthias Weidlich   Technion - Israel Institute of Technology
Gero Decker   Signavio
Sherif Sakr   The University of New South Wales, Australia
António Rito Silva   Technical University of Lisbon
Hye-Young Paik   The University of New South Wales, Australia
Marcelo Fantinato   University of São Paulo USP, Brazil
Christian Gierds   Humboldt-Universität zu Berlin, Germany
Jan Claes   Ghent University, Belgium
Barbara Weber   University of Innsbruck, Austria
Howard Foster   City University London, UK
Marcello La Rosa   Queensland University of Technology, Australia
Michael Adams   Queensland University of Technology, Australia
Oliver Kopp   University of Stuttgart, Germany
Simon Moser   IBM Deutschland Research & Development
                                GmbH, Germany
Anne Rozinat   Fluxicon, The Netherlands
Sandy Kemsley   Kemsley Design Ltd., Canada
Vishal Saxena   Oracle, United States
Luciano García-Bañuelos   University of Tartu, Estonia
Stefanie Rinderle-Ma   University of Vienna, Austria
Hajo A. Reijers   Eindhoven University of Technology,
                                The Netherlands
Remco Dijkman   Eindhoven University of Technology,
                                The Netherlands
Christoph Bussler   Voxeo Labs, Inc., United States

Artem Polyvyanyy   Queensland University of Technology, Australia
Jorge Cardoso   University of Coimbra, Portugal
Heiko Ludwig   IBM Research, United States

Additional Reviewers

Agostinho, Carlos
Amziani, Mourad
Aubry, Alexis
Bergmayr, Alexander
Boettcher, Boris
Bokermann, Dennis
Buijs, Joos
Chinosi, Michele
Daeuble, Gerald
De Masellis, Riccardo
Di Ciccio, Claudio
Dunkl, Reinhold
El Haouzi, Hind
Engel, Robert
España, Sergio
Fazal-Baqaie, Masud
Fdhila, Walid
Fehling, Christoph
Fischer, Robin
Furfaro, Angelo
Gaaloul, Walid
Garro, Alfredo
Gerth, Christian
Gierds, Christian
Guedria, Wided
Guermouche, Nawal
Guzzo, Antonella
Görlach, Katharina
Helal, Iman
Hellfeld, Stefan
Hildebrandt, Tobias
Hipp, Markus
Huma, Zille
Keuter, Björn
Koutrouli, Eleni
Kovalev, Dmitry
Kriglstein, Simone
Kucherbaev, Pavel
Köpke, Julius

Lakshmanan, Geetika
Leitner, Maria
Lezoche, Mario
Li, Ying
Liu, Weiwei
Loures, Eduardo
Mach, Werner
Mangler, Juergen
Mans, Ronny
Marrella, Andrea
Matijacic, Michel
Michelberger, Bernd
Mukhi, Nirmal
Muthusamy, Vinod
Müller, Richard
Nagel, Benjamin
Panach, Jose Ignacio
Pichler, Christian
Pontieri, Luigi
Rodriguez, Carlos
Rose, Mirko
Rozsnyai, Szabolcs
Ruiz, Marcela
Schoknecht, Andreas
Schultz, Martin
Schuster, Nelly
Schuster, Thomas
Serra, Edoardo
Sun, Yutian
Tsagkani, Christina
Ullrich, Meike
Valverde, Francisco
Verbeek, Eric
Vukojevic, Karolina
Weippl, Edgar
Werner, Michael
Wittern, Erik
Zdravković, Milan
Zugal, Stefan

Table of Contents

Keynotes

Moneyball for nanoHUB: Theory-Driven and Data-Driven Approaches to Understand the Formation and Success of Software Development Teams 1
    Noshir Contractor

Towards the Next Generation Intelligent BPM – In the Era of Big Data 4
    Xiang Gao

BPM in the Cloud 10
    Tom Baeyens

Process Mining

Bridging Abstraction Layers in Process Mining by Automated Matching of Events and Activities 17
    Thomas Baier and Jan Mendling

Mining Configurable Process Models from Collections of Event Logs 33
    Joos C.A.M. Buijs, Boudewijn F. van Dongen, and Wil M.P. van der Aalst

Slice, Mine and Dice: Complexity-Aware Automated Discovery of Business Process Models 49
    Chathura C. Ekanayake, Marlon Dumas, Luciano García-Bañuelos, and Marcello La Rosa

Business Process Mining from E-Commerce Web Logs 65
    Nicolas Poggi, Vinod Muthusamy, David Carrera, and Rania Khalaf

Discovering Data-Aware Declarative Process Models from Event Logs 81
    Fabrizio Maria Maggi, Marlon Dumas, Luciano García-Bañuelos, and Marco Montali

Enhancing Declare Maps Based on Event Correlations 97
    Rantham Prabhakara Jagadeesh Chandra Bose, Fabrizio Maria Maggi, and Wil M.P. van der Aalst

Conformance Checking

Aligning Event Logs and Process Models for Multi-perspective
Conformance Checking: An Approach Based on Integer Linear
Programming... 113
    Massimiliano de Leoni and Wil M.P. van der Aalst

Conformance Checking in the Large: Partitioning and Topology........ 130
    Jorge Munoz-Gama, Josep Carmona, and Wil M.P. van der Aalst

On Enabling Compliance of Cross-Organizational Business Processes ... 146
    *David Knuplesch, Manfred Reichert, Walid Fdhila, and
    Stefanie Rinderle-Ma*

Process Data

Verification of Query Completeness over Processes 155
    Simon Razniewski, Marco Montali, and Werner Nutt

Modeling and Enacting Complex Data Dependencies in Business
Processes 171
    Andreas Meyer, Luise Pufahl, Dirk Fahland, and Mathias Weske

Event Stream Processing Units in Business Processes 187
    *Stefan Appel, Sebastian Frischbier, Tobias Freudenreich, and
    Alejandro Buchmann*

Process Model Matching

Predicting the Quality of Process Model Matching 203
    *Matthias Weidlich, Tomer Sagi, Henrik Leopold, Avigdor Gal, and
    Jan Mendling*

Increasing Recall of Process Model Matching by Improved Activity
Label Matching.. 211
    *Christopher Klinkmüller, Ingo Weber, Jan Mendling,
    Henrik Leopold, and André Ludwig*

A Visualization Approach for Difference Analysis of Process Models
and Instance Traffic 219
    Simone Kriglstein, Günter Wallner, and Stefanie Rinderle-Ma

Process Architectures and Collaboration

Business Process Architectures with Multiplicities: Transformation and
Correctness 227
    Rami-Habib Eid-Sabbagh, Marcin Hewelt, and Mathias Weske

Optimal Resource Assignment in Workflows for Maximizing
Cooperation 235
  Akhil Kumar, Remco Dijkman, and Minseok Song

Accelerating Collaboration in Task Assignment Using a Socially
Enhanced Resource Model 251
  Rong Liu, Shivali Agarwal, Renuka R. Sindhgatta, and
  Juhnyoung Lee

Alternative Perspectives

Splitting GSM Schemas: A Framework for Outsourcing of Declarative
Artifact Systems 259
  Rik Eshuis, Richard Hull, Yutian Sun, and Roman Vaculín

Composing Workflow Activities on the Basis of Data-Flow Structures... 275
  Han van der Aa, Hajo A. Reijers, and Irene Vanderfeesten

Mixing Paradigms for More Comprehensible Models 283
  Michael Westergaard and Tijs Slaats

Industry Papers

An Agile BPM Project Methodology 291
  Christian Thiemich and Frank Puhlmann

Declarative Modeling—An Academic Dream or the Future for BPM? ... 307
  Hajo A. Reijers, Tijs Slaats, and Christian Stahl

Investigating Clinical Care Pathways Correlated with Outcomes 323
  Geetika T. Lakshmanan, Szabolcs Rozsnyai, and Fei Wang

Exformatics Declarative Case Management Workflows as DCR
Graphs 339
  Tijs Slaats, Raghava Rao Mukkamala, Thomas Hildebrandt, and
  Morten Marquard

Author Index 355

Moneyball for nanoHUB: Theory-Driven and Data-Driven Approaches to Understand the Formation and Success of Software Development Teams

Noshir Contractor

Jane S. & William J. White Professor of Behavioral Sciences
Northwestern University
Evanston IL 60201
nosh@northwestern.edu

"Your goal shouldn't be to buy players. Your goal should be to buy wins. In order to buy wins, you need to buy runs." (Bakshi, M., & Miller, B. (2011). Moneyball, Motion picture. USA: Columbia Pictures.

Keynote Abstract

The same principle that transformed baseball may hold the key to building more innovative scientific teams. In 2002, Billy Beane changed baseball when he fielded a $41 million baseball team for the Oakland Athletics that successfully competed with the $125 million New York Yankees. We increasingly turn to teams to solve wicked scientific problems from sequencing the human genome to curing cancer. Building scientific dream teams who produce breakthrough innovations at minimal cost is not unlike choosing the players who will go on to win the World Series. Like pre-Beane baseball, much of the selection of scientific dream teams currently rests on an assessment of the caliber of the individual scientists, with far less attention paid to the relationships that gel the team together, and the factors that determine how those pivotal relationships come about.

Given the increasing importance of teams in producing high-impact innovations, it is important for success in all of the domains in which teams are critical that we understand how to assemble innovation-ready teams. While there is considerable research on how to make teams more effective once they are formed, there is growing evidence that the assembly of the team itself influences the range of possible outcomes. Most prior work on teams is based on the premise that the team has been "formed" and fails to investigate the mechanisms that influence the assembly of teams and their impact on team processes and outcomes. This paper seeks to understand and enable the assembly of innovative scientific teams. We use theory-driven (social science theories) as well as data-driven (data/text mining and machine learning algorithms) to discern factors that explain/predict assembly of innovative scientific teams.

We define team assembly as the set of principles that jointly determine how a team is formed. Team assembly is a multilevel construct, capturing the sets of factors occurring at four levels of emergence that determine how teams come together. The theoretical mechanisms of team assembly can be categorized at four levels of emergence: compositional, relational, task-based, and ecosystem. All four approaches are well-captured using network approaches, with the aim of understanding the impact of these four sets of factors on the likelihood that a team-assembly edge (or, in network parlance, a hyperedge) will form.

The first level of compositional emergence considers each team as an aggregation of people and uses the composition of individual attributes and team attributes to explain individuals' motivations to join teams. The second level of relational emergence also considers prior relations (such as prior collaboration or friendship) among team members to explain why members assemble into a team. A third level of task-based emergence adds attributes of the task (such as the development of open source versus proprietary software) to attributes of individuals and the relations among them to explain why people join teams. Individuals joining a certain project are represented as a bipartite graph with linkages between individuals and their project. The fourth level of ecosystem emergence captures how the larger intellectual ecosystem might explain the emergence of successful scientific teams. For instance, an ecosystem surrounding a software development team would include prior or current collaborators of those who are on the team, and collaborators of their collaborators and so on. The ecosystem approach is a novel theoretical advance in research on teams by focusing on the explanatory power of, rather than discounting as a "bug," the fact that individuals belong simultaneously to multiple teams that have overlapping members.

We conducted this research in the context of nanoHUB (`http://nanohub.org`), a cyberinfrastructure developed as part of the NSF-funded Network for Computational Nanotechnology. nanoHub offers a platform where teams assemble to develop software, documents, presentations and tutorials for education and research. These materials are published on nanoHUB and then rated, tagged, downloaded and utilized in ways that provide objective metrics of team outcomes. Over the past 10 years of operation nanoHUB has served a community of users that has grown to more than 250,000 annually from 172 countries worldwide. These visitors come from all of the Top 50 engineering graduate schools and from 21% of all available educational (.edu) domains, and they access more than 3,000 seminars, tools, tutorials, courses, and teaching materials posted on the site. During the past 12 months, more than 12,500 registered users have accessed over 269 simulation tools through nanoHUB's unique, web-based simulation infrastructure, and they have launched some 430,357 simulation runs. Hence nanoHUB is uniquely suited for us to observe teams engaged in the creation of scientific products – both basic and applied. In nanoHUB, scientists can self assemble and we can observe the choices that they make with self-assembly.

We developed a theory-driven approach by elucidating factors that influence team assembly at the compositional level (attributes of individuals on the team), relational level (prior collaboration, co-authorship and citations between individuals), task level (attributes of the task, such as development of open vs closed software), and ecosystem level (their prior and current membership in the landscape of all teams). We also developed a data-driven approach by using machine learning techniques to identify which of a set of features were the best predictors of team assembly and success. We offer substantive interpretations of the results of the data-driven models by eliciting specific decision trees that predicted high probabilities of team formation and success. Interpretations of decisions trees from data-driven approaches offer new insights that can in turn be used to guide the development of new social science theories about the team assembly. As such this paper argues for a new iterative computational social science methodology that combines both theory and data driven approaches.

Results of the research described here will help (i) individual researchers assemble their own dream team, (ii) university administrators to help organize interdisciplinary initiatives for research and education, (iii) leaders of cyberinfrastructure such as the NSF-funded nanoHUB, use a dashboard and recommender system, to monitor and enable high performing virtual collaboration within the nanoHUB community, (iv) program officers at funding agencies who make decisions about the likely payoff of scientific teams, and (v) science policy makers on how to design and fund research programs that incentivize the assembly of dream teams.

Towards the Next Generation Intelligent BPM – In the Era of Big Data

Xiang Gao

Department of Management Information System,
China Mobile Communications Corporation, Beijing 100033, China
gaoxiang@chinamobile.com

Abstract. Big data opens a new dimension, space, to offer the advantage of gleaning intelligence from data and translating that into business benefits. It will lead to knowledge revolution in all sectors, including Business Process Management (BPM). This paper sheds light on key characteristics of intelligent BPM (iBPM) from an industrial point of view. A big data perspective on iBPM is then proposed, showing the challenges and potential opportunities in attempt to catalyze ideas from insight to application. China Mobile Communications Corporation's (CMCC) exploring and practice are provided, which also elicit the future research directions for enterprise applications.

Keywords: big data, intelligent BPM.

1 From BPM to Intelligent BPM

Business Process Management (BPM) is recognized as a holistic management approach that promotes business effectiveness and efficiency while striving for innovation, flexibility, and integration with technology. It is growing as a discipline, where new technologies are rapidly emerging, keeping BPM center stage in both business and technology domains [11].

Recently, intelligent BPM (iBPM) has been given new impetus by integrating analytical technologies into orchestrated processes. It is enabling leading organizations to make their business operations more intelligent, and giving process participants better real-time situational awareness and the ability to tailor their responses appropriately. Gartner considers it the next stage in the evolution of BPM for the following reasons [7]. Firstly, it will meet the ongoing need for process agility, especially for regulatory changes and more-dynamic exception handling. Secondly, it will aim at leveraging the greater availability of data from inside and outside the enterprise as input into decision making. Thirdly, it will facilitate interactions and collaboration in cross-boundary processes.

From an application infrastructure and middleware (AIM) point of view, an iBPM Suite inherits all the features of traditional BPM Suite, complemented with more-advanced technologies, summarized from 10 areas of functionalities by Gartner [7]. From enterprise application and consolidation point view, the difference of next generation iBPM from the current one can be summarized as the following "4As".

- **Analytical**: The most prominent feature of iBPM is the capability of advanced analytics. It integrates with state-of-the-art analytic technologies, including both pre-analytics and post-analytics. The former mainly concentrates on process model based analysis, such as model decomposition [6], clone detection [5], similarity search [4] etc. The latter makes use of the historical log and other information, and refers to automatic business process discovery (i.e., process mining [15, 16]), social analysis [17], intelligent recommendation, prediction and so on.
- **Automatic**: The enormous volumes of data require automated or semi-automated analysis techniques to detect patterns, identify anomalies, and extract knowledge. Take business processes consolidation for example. It is always an extremely arduous task for large organizations with more than thousands of process models. The iBPM should be designed to facilitate the procedure that automatically reduces duplications and makes the differences between process models explicit, instead of manual operation.
- **Adaptive**: The dynamic changing of business processes and external data inside and outside should be flexibly captured and responded by resorting to not only the adaptive adjusting of the analysis algorithm parameters, but also the on-demand selection of appropriate algorithms in a configuration way.
- **Agile**: There is always a big gap: business analysts have deep understanding of business but cannot design the process models independently without the support of IT staffs, even though notation based modeling language is exploited. The iBPM is expected to simplify the procedure. For example, by incorporating process fragments with business semantics into design tool, the efficiency of modeling can be significantly improved and most of the procedures can be implemented by business analysts with the least IT efforts.

It is worth noticing that achieving of the "4As" features will be given new opportunities in the era of big data.

2 A Big Data Perspective on iBPM

The birth and growth of big data was the defining characteristic of the 2000s. As obvious and ordinary as this might sound to us today, we are still unraveling the practical and inspirational potential of this new era [13].

What does big data really mean in the evolution of BPM? Just one thing, elegantly stated by the founding father and pioneer long before the introduction of the big data concept. "In God we trust; all others must bring data," – W. Edwards Deming. Before the existence of big data, we could only treat these words as maxims. However, now, we must consider them as achievable technical criteria for our work, where big data brings unprecedented impetus and vitality for BPM. Driven by process data and other related data, it can be a new platform for the R&D of intelligence based on big data, making Deming's maxims a reality for the operation of future iBPM systems.

To find the needle in the big data iBPM haystack, one must first clarify what the "Big Data" is in business process field. In common sense, mobile sensors, social media services, genomic sequencing, and astronomy are among myriad applications that have generated an explosion of abundant data, which are naturally treated as big data. However, it is very important that the biggest misnomer actually comes from the name itself. When we talk about big data, we must put its size in relation to the available resources, the question asked, and the kind of data. To some extent, large numbers of historical log and instances data generated by running business processes can all be treated as "big data" for their high variety and heterogeneity, especially in a large-scale organization. Furthermore, from a generalized point of view, data with the following features can be recognized as process data [8]: 1) composed of events; 2) on multiple units and levels of analysis with ambiguous boundaries; 3) of variable temporal embeddedness; and 4) eclectic. Then, the web search query log, data of product ordering by customers, and so many other kinds of data all belongs to process big data.

On the path from insight to action, one must pay much attention to the following perspectives.

- **Sparsity Vs. Redundancy**. The widespread use of traditional data mining and artificial intelligence algorithms has usually exposed their limitations on data sparsity in large-scale data set or problems associated with high dimensionality [2]. For example, user-based collaborative filtering systems have been very successful in the past, but their weakness has been revealed for large, sparse databases [12]. However, the large amount of process data always exhibits redundancy instead of sparsity. A real scenario is investigated in China Mobile Communications Corporation (CMCC) Office Automation (OA) systems. There are totally more than 8000 processes running in these systems, independently maintained and evolved by subsidiary organizations themselves. Due to individual management requirements, these processes, even expressing the same business behavior, are usually not exactly the same while having a high degree of similarity. The technology for automatic fragmentation of process models and identification of highly reusable fragments are required in iBPM.
- **Sample Vs. Population**. Sample based analysis is usually conducted to infer the whole behavior of population. However, in the age of big data, one turns to put emphasis on population but not sample, since collecting and processing large amount of data are feasible now. Take the process mining scenario for example, where the completeness of event log plays an extremely important role. For limited event log (i.e., recognized as sample), the global completeness needs to be evaluated by resorting to distribution fitting or at least bound estimation. However, for complete event log (i.e., recognized as population), the global completeness is definitely guaranteed. It seems that the discovery problem becomes easier and the result will be more accurate! However, much more attention should be further paid to the special cases and quality of event log. Free control is fairly particular in CMCC to describe

the behavior that allows administrator to adjust a normal routine as what he wants. It seldom appears in the complete event log for very special cases. Actually, it almost cannot be automatically discovered due to its flexibility. The data quality can also affect the efficiency of mining algorithms, while it suffers from data missing and noise infection for population data.
- **Individual Vs. Network**. The observation of a large variety of complex systems often reflects individual data sets and decentralized links, which can be further integrated and consolidated together into a data network. Big data is often associated with such kind of complex data network, so that it is offering a fresh perspective, rapidly developing into a new network science discipline [1]. It also has exerted a subtle influence on the BPM research and applications. Web Ontology Language (OWL) has been introduced to serve the annotation of process models, and then, a set of mapping strategies are developed to conduct the annotation by considering the semantic relationships between model artifacts to facilitate process knowledge management and semantic interoperability [9]. Moreover, the business network management (BNM) can strive to make business network, joined up by collaborating business processes, visible within network views and combine automatic discovery, mining and inference capabilities with expert knowledge in complex, dynamic and heterogeneous enterprise domains [10].
- **Causality Vs. Correlation**. A major issue of concern in big data research is that correlation plays much more important role than causality. For example, Google's founding philosophy is that we don't know why this page is better than that one: If the statistics of incoming links say it is, that's good enough. No semantic or causal analysis is required. However, we would like to mention that causality and correlation are equally important in BPM field. Obviously, process mining is strongly based on the rigorous deduction of activity causality from event log. Correlation also attracts much attention, in the scenario that some clustering based technologies are taken into consideration. In this situation, not only the business behavior and structure but also ontology based business semantics should be treated to describe the process features.

3 Embrace the Idea of iBPM in the Era of Big Data

CMCC is committing itself to the exploring and practice of iBPM in the era of big data, aiming at facilitating process consolidation and improving analytical intelligence.

First of all, CMCC is concentrating on the key problems of business understanding & raw process reconstruction, complex business logic & recessive rules, flexible modeling based on business semantics, as well as redundancy removal & process repository. Several existing algorithms, such as process mining, process models decomposition, similarity search, clustering and merging, are well considered and exploited. These algorithms are further implemented and integrated into a tailor made process model configuration tool, in order that the advanced analysis is appropriately integrated into the BPM life-cycle. Empirical study also discovers some problems to be further considered. For example, the refined process structure tree (RPST) [18] and its extension mainly focus on the structure instead of business logics. It suggests that business analysts may not easily reuse these fragments directly obtained by RPST for modeling, where involving business semantics into the fragmentization algorithms is of much interest. The current mining algorithms provide efficient procedure to reconstruct mostly the control flow, while the information from e-forms, rules and organizational relationship are also needed to elaborately consider in real scenario. Besides, the business behavior of processes is always restricted by specifying constraints on allowed actions, which are usually recessive and need to be modeled semantically.

Secondly, most of the big data surge is data in the wild–unruly stuff like words, images and videos. Similar phenomenon partially happens in heterogeneous process data. It is not typically grist for traditional databases. The NoSQL databases based on distributed storage technology exhibit obvious advantages in CRUD, which gains benefits regarding to extensibility, data model flexibility, economical efficiency, accessibility and so on. Based on YCSB benchmark [3] and analysis framework, CMCC developed a novel distributed cloud storage benchmark, initially consisted of 15 x86s (IBM 3650M3). Function, performance, scalability, consistency are designed as the main test metrics for the mainstream distributed file systems (e.g., HDFS, Swift, GPFS and so on) and NOSQL databases (e.g., Hbase, Cassandra, MongoDB and so on). By testing them, we found distributed file systems also have exactly the same standard read & write interface, and thus, is ready to conveniently replace traditional storage mode. MongoDB has the most familiar operation interface with RDBM and balanced performance and reliability in most cases. However, open source frameworks need detailed parameter selection and optimization.

Thirdly, several related analyses are also conducted in CMCC. We have established an open source based big data analytics platform. It implements several time series analysis models for CMCC's operations indicators predictions. By combining Hadoop and Mahout, an efficient recommendation engine is constructed for Mobile Market (CMCC's App Store, like Apple App Store), using Parallel FP-Growth algorithm and taking advantages of the platform. Besides, social network analysis (SNA) is applied and improved to analyze users' behavior, public feeling, employee emotion and so many topics, using internal social network data and external internet micro-blog data. These technologies will be further adjusted and transformed to BPM field to discover new value.

As mentioned in the previous conference keynote by Prof. Van der Aalst, the "Big Data" wave is providing new prospects for BPM research [14]. We do believe that big data will provide advancing trends in technology that open the door to a new approach to promptly improve the theory and application level of iBPM.

References

[1] Barabászló, A.L.: The Network Takeover. Nature Physics 8(1), 14–16 (2011)
[2] Billsus, D., Pazzani, M.J.: Learning Collaborative Information Filters. In: Proc. of ICML 1998, pp. 46–53 (1998)

3. Cooper, B.F., Silberstein, A., Tam, E., et al.: Benchmarking Cloud Serving Systems with YCSB. In: Proc. of the 1st ACM Symposium on Cloud Computing, pp. 143–154. ACM (2010)
4. Dijkman, R.M., Dumas, M., Dongen, B., Uba, R., Mendling, J.: Similarity of Business Process Models: Metrics and Evaluation. Information Systems 36(2), 498–516 (2011)
5. Ekanayake, C.C., Dumas, M., García-Bañuelos, L., La Rosa, M., ter Hofstede, A.H.M.: Approximate Clone Detection in Repositories of Business Process Models. In: Barros, A., Gal, A., Kindler, E. (eds.) BPM 2012. LNCS, vol. 7481, pp. 302–318. Springer, Heidelberg (2012)
6. Gschwind, T., Koehler, J., Wong, J.: Applying patterns during business process modeling. In: Dumas, M., Reichert, M., Shan, M.-C. (eds.) BPM 2008. LNCS, vol. 5240, pp. 4–19. Springer, Heidelberg (2008)
7. Janelle, B.H., Roy Schulte, W.: BPM Suites Evolve into Intelligent BPM Suites, Gartner G00226553 (2011)
8. Langley, A.: Strategies for Theorizing from Process Data. Academy of Management Review, 691-710 (1999)
9. Lin, Y.: Semantic Annotation for Process Models. Diss. Trondheim, Norway (2008)
10. Ritter, D.: Towards a Business Network Management. Enterprise Information Systems of the Future, pp. 149–156. Springer, Heidelberg (2013)
11. Samantha, S.: Research Index: New BPM Technologies Lead the Way to Achieving Process Adaptability. Gartner 00228461 (2012)
12. Sarwar, B., Karypis, G., Konstan, J., Riedl, J., et al.: Item-based Collaborative Filtering Recommendation Algorithms. In: Proc. International Conference on World Wide Web 2001, pp. 285–295. ACM (2001)
13. Tawny, S., Brian, D.J.: Entertainment in the Age of Big Data. Proceedings of the IEEE 100(5), 1404–1408 (2012)
14. van der Aalst, W.M.P.: A Decade of Business Process Management Conferences: Personal reflections on a Developing Discipline. In: Barros, A., Gal, A., Kindler, E. (eds.) BPM 2012. LNCS, vol. 7481, pp. 1–16. Springer, Heidelberg (2012)
15. van der Aalst, W.M.P., Weijters, T., Maruster, L.: IEEE Transactions on Knowledge and Data Engineering 16(9), 1128–1142 (2004)
16. van der Aalst, W.M.P., Dongen, B., Herbst, J., Maruster, L., Schimm, G., Weijters, A.: Workflow mining: A Survey of Issues and Approaches. Data & Knowledge Engineering 47(2), 237–267 (2003)
17. van der Aalst, W.M.P., Song, M.S.: Mining Social Networks: Uncovering Interaction Patterns in Business Processes. In: Desel, J., Pernici, B., Weske, M. (eds.) BPM 2004. LNCS, vol. 3080, pp. 244–260. Springer, Heidelberg (2004)
18. Vanhatalo, J., Völzer, H., Koehler, J.: The Refined Process Structure Tree. In: Dumas, M., Reichert, M., Shan, M.-C. (eds.) BPM 2008. LNCS, vol. 5240, pp. 100–115. Springer, Heidelberg (2008)

BPM in the Cloud

Tom Baeyens

Effektif GmbH
Nürnbergerstraße 8, 10787 Berlin, Germany
tom@effektif.com
http://effektif.com

Abstract. When Salesforce started delivering software in the cloud, they started a big shift in the CRM space. In the meantime, Software as a Service has become the preferred form to deliver software. Now, Business Process Management (BPM) products are starting to make their way to the cloud and they cause a big impact. Here we explore the benefits of cloud computing applied to BPM products. Basically the cloud is making BPM easier, faster and cheaper.

Keywords: BPM, business, process, management, cloud, SaaS, case, social, collaboration, BPMN, IT, enterprise.

1 Hardware, Installation and Hosting

At first SaaS was mostly known for the fact that no client software needs to be installed on laptops and PCs. In the last ten years, the primary end user interface for most BPM systems already were web clients. From that technological aspect, it's not a big change for BPM. The change will be much more significant when looking at the product design as we'll discuss throughout this paper.

The cloud also removes the need for server software installation. No hardware needs to be selected, bought, installed and operated. This is normally done by the company's IT department. The IT department has loads of other tasks beyond just hosting that single BPM product. So in house IT personnel can never be as specialized in hosting a particular BPM product then the vendor of that product itself. The quality of service and responsiveness that companies get from in-house IT departments is a lot less than from a cloud vendor. And on top of that, the cost of hosting and maintenance is transferred from the buyer to the cloud vendor.

In typical on premise BPM purchase scenarios, a manager sees the benefits of a BPM system and becomes the promoter within the organization. It takes dedication from that manager to organize several meetings with IT to push the purchase of a BPM product. There are many managers that see the benefit, but don't have that perseverance. Cloud BPM services eliminate that lengthy BPM purchase process. On the cloud, managers can just register an account themselves and get started without depending on the IT department. This way, getting started with BPM on the cloud is a lot faster and lowers the threshold so that managers can take an individual decision to get started with BPM.

2 Security, Firewall and Tenants

Same specialization reasoning holds for security. Cloud software providers are in the business of software and IT. Their existence directly depends being honest, open and secure. SaaS vendors are far more specialized in security compared to IT staff in a brick-and-mortar company.

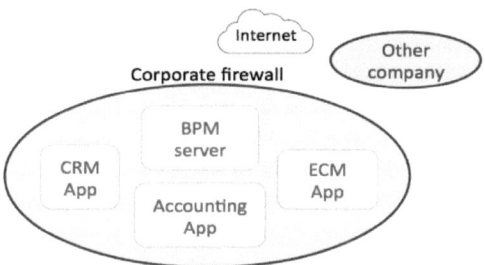

Fig. 1. The corporate firewall shields a company's internal network from the outside

Over the last two decades, a feeling of security was obtained by placing a firewall fence around the company's network. Internal applications are then deployed within the VPN. The downside of this approach is accessibility. People need a VPN to access internal systems and that is not available everywhere. Also for B2B integration this is a pain as it is often a difficult procedure to get the corporate IT department to open access to a certain system.

For all those on premise applications, new cloud services have appeared in recent years. All enterprise services like Google Apps have the notion of a tenant. A tenant represents the boundaries of the company and replaces the function of the firewall within a service.

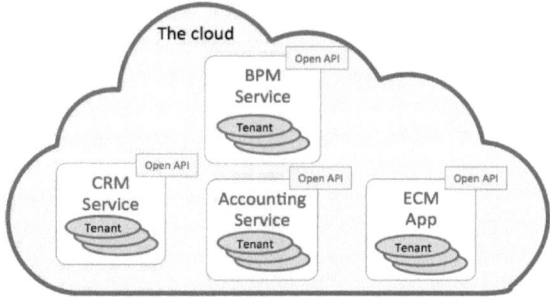

Fig. 2. Multi-tenancy in cloud computing environments

In the past, there has been a bit of reluctance to put corporate data outside of the firewall. But nowadays tenant policies replace the function of the firewall. A tenant is the space in a cloud service that is reserved for single company. Typically those services have the capability to specify advanced security policies. In a cloud BPM system an example of such a policy would be: No documents from our Google Drive can be shared by with people outside our company. And the advantage is that documents and other items living in a cloud services are accessible from anywhere and easier to share.

3   Easier B2B Collaboration

Cloud services are ideal to facilitate B2B collaboration. It's easy to see when comparing how people collaborate on a Google Document versus the alternative of emailing Word document versions around. When collaborating with people in other companies, internal corporate systems behind a firewall are hard to use at best.

For BPM services in the cloud this means it's easy to share cases, tasks and other forms of collaboration spaces with people from other companies.

4   Eliminating the Upfront Investment

The server purchase and installation efforts combined with the typical high cost of an on-premise BPM product form a big financial investment that has to be done upfront before actual use of the system can start.

For many smaller scale deployments, this investment is just not feasible. Even in large organizations, a lot of managers initially have just one process where a BPM system would be a good fit. This initial investment prevents them to get started for a single process. Without this upfront investment, managers can get started even with a single process.

The big upfront investment also implies that decision makers face a big risk. What if the benefits don't turn out the way people have hoped for? In the cloud, the pay per use models remove the need for facing such uncertainty. A pilot process can be put in operation knowing that the cost for this process will remain low.

5   New Category of Clients: End Users

People in IT departments are primarily the drivers of BPM product purchases. When looking at cloud BPM, these people still take initiative to purchase a product. But because anyone can register an account, also end users can now become the drivers for purchasing a cloud BPM solution. This leads to Bring You Own BPM system. Meaning that individual employees can take initiative and choose their own solution to deal with a problem.

This may look insignificant, but for the cloud in general, this is the root cause of a big shift in terms of product design. This is the reason that SaaS services excel in simplicity and user experience. In the past, the focus was on features. The IT department selection process often involves a request for proposal (RFP). Such an RFP contains a big list of features with checkboxes for each product in the comparison. Of course, this is a big driver to BPM vendors to add more features.

In BPM, this effect is reinforced by big analyst firms. The intelligent BPMS definition of Gartner is a good example of this. It highlights all components and functions that can be included in a BPM product. These are totally valid, but what is missing is the tradeoff in terms of simplicity and user experience. How much training is required to make use of all those features and functions? Can people outside the company be involved at all? That's a hidden cost often overlooked. Both RFPs and analyst firms have pushed BPM products to include ever more features and functions without taking those hidden costs for end users into account.

When selling to end users, user experience exceeds the importance of the number of features. End users require that they become productive without assistance or training. And they have an attention span that is often just five minutes. That puts a totally different perspective on how cloud products are designed.

Let's look at cloud services like zapier.com or ifttt.com. These are based on a 2 step process. Essentially these services allow users select a trigger and bind it to an action. For example, when a new contact is added to my Salesforce account, add it to my Google account. It could be seen as the simplest form of process. They succeeded in making the simplest form of a process available to everyone. That's a good example of the other end of the tradeoff between features and simplicity.

The end users as a new category of clients will require BPM products in the cloud to take user experience to new levels, even when this comes at the expense of some advanced features.

6   Changing Dynamics between Business and IT

A major unique selling point for BPM systems has been their agility. It's often demonstrated how easy it is to change arrows in a process diagram and instantly publish that change into a running system. In practice on the other hand, the processes implemented with BPM systems tend to have many integrations with other systems. The main reason for this is lack of an iterative approach. The whole process is typically analysed upfront and all there is a high degree of feature creep.

For example at some point in a seminar process, the participants might be pushed to the company's Salesforce account as contacts. Those integrations require data to be exchanged between the BPM system and the external system. So there is a dependency between the activities in a process producing a certain data item and other activities consuming the data. This aspect is usually not modeled as it would clutter the process diagram. In those processes it's not possible for non-technical business people to change the diagram freely without being aware of those data dependencies.

So from the moment when IT people start to include integrations with other systems, data dependencies start to appear. It's those data dependencies that prevent business people from changing the process diagram freely.

This aspect also leads to a clear split between end users and IT people. Managers should be able to create processes that handle the coordination of people. For the people coordination aspect, no system integration is required so managers can keep changing the process until it is stable, measured and proven to be valuable. It makes sense to postpone technical system integrations until that point.

This means that in the first phase, managers on their own can publish the complete process that deals with handovers, approvals and escalations. With only those aspects in the process it remains agile and managers can change and optimize it freely on their own. As they don't need to coordinate changes with IT, these iterations can be published fast and frequently. The process is kept agile a lot longer and many costly, time consuming IT cycles are prevented.

7 From Collaboration to Processes

The last five years, a clear trend has been to add Advanced Case Management (ACM) to BPM. Where BPM is historically focused on predefined flows, ACM is focused on supporting ad hoc work.

In the cloud, services like asana.com, basecamp.com and do.com show the same features as found in ACM. Basically they have tasks that can be shared with other people. Tasks are shared with a group of people, they can be discussed and contain a list of documents and links. I will refer to this type of service as social collaboration service.

The mentioned social collaboration services are created with a primary focus on user experience. Any employee that works online regular can learn these services without special training. These examples show that collaboration is the more general term used in the cloud for ACM features.

Social collaboration is an essential component of a cloud BPM service. It's the incubation ground for processes. A large portion of the work and tasks that people perform is done only once. When users spot patterns in the work they do, then a template or a process is a natural next step.

Tasks in the process execution can then be offered inside the social collaboration environment. That creates consistency between dynamic work and predefined work. And more important, it allows process owners to release early. That's because all aspects not yet part of the process can be handled in each case individually as ad hoc collaboration.

8 The Lifecycle of a Process

A process can start in a very basic form of a checklist. This just takes one or two minutes to produce. The process only contains a list of tasks and some of them can be assigned. When this is proven to be helpful and after some more experience is obtained with the process, then the process can be elaborated in a subsequent iteration. That could be to put tasks in sequence or add forms to tasks. Typically it only makes sense to include custom coded integrations and exception paths in later stages.

This shows the lifecycle of a process. A process can start off as a checklist or simple template. This only models a fraction of the whole process and the social collaboration features complement the predefined process. Going forward it's easy to publish improvements to that process. Typically it only makes sense to add integrations in later stages as the data dependencies can impact the agility. So at that point, the process should be fairly stable.

9 Capture the Experience

In the BPM community and in most BPM systems, there seems to be an assumption that processes need to be analysed and then they can be automated. I believe this originates from BPM projects being seen as IT projects. As analysts dive deep into the process, they spot a lot of opportunities for automation and this leads to feature creep. Feature creep means that feature requests keep being added so that the scope becomes bigger than originally intended. The result is that processes often become very large IT projects.

But this actually implies a big unnecessary overhead. Interviewing people and figuring out how the pieces of the process puzzle fit together is often one of the hardest parts of BPM. It's often surprising how people get things done when it's so hard to find out how people work together. So even the quality of those type of analysis can be questioned. When capturing the experience on the spot, the idea is that the big upfront analysis is skipped.

As a side note, there is an unwritten law in the cloud stating that users must see instant value for the actions they perform. Doing an upfront theoretical analysis can hardly be called direct. Instead this should be replaced with capturing the experience that is obtained by doing.

Taking the lifecycle of the process in mind, it's clear that in the early stages, the process is still very agile. When a process is only a checklist of tasks, it's very easy to add or remove a task and republish the process. So rather than performing that upfront analysis and try to capture the full process in one go, let's start simple and make it easy to apply improvements in small increments.

The main advantage of this iterative approach is that real world experience can be captured. When a manager discovers that an employee has bought a personal laptop with the company credit card, an approval could be added to the process for purchases above $1000.

The experience that is captured while process owners are dealing with concrete cases of the process, is much better quality compared to the theoretic knowledge produced by an analyst. On top of that, all the effort done to produce the lower quality upfront analysis is eliminated.

10 Adding Custom Code into a Cloud Process

On the cloud, there needs to be a scalable and simple way to include integration and custom coded logic into a process. Amazon Simple Workflow Service introduced a robust pattern for this purpose. Similar to a task list for people, the cloud workflow system maintains an activity instance list each time an activity is to be performed. External activity workers can initiate a request to obtain instances of an activity they have to perform. Typically external workers perform only instances of a specific activity in process.

This is a great pattern because it activity workers can be hosted on anywhere: on premise behind the firewall, on a private cloud or on public cloud infrastructure. It's great for scaling because for high throughput activities, as many activity workers can be started as necessary to cope with that load.

This pattern is also great because it supports polyglot programming. Nowadays, it's quite normal to have multiple programming languages in use in a single organization. Developers can choose their favorite language to implement the task logic and the communication is standardized with HTTP and REST web services.

The open APIs for obtaining and completing activity instances allows for any cloud service to offer actions in their service as activities in a process. For example, Salesforce or any other party could create an activity worker to add a lead to Salesforce as an activity in the process. This will enable a marketplace for activity types.

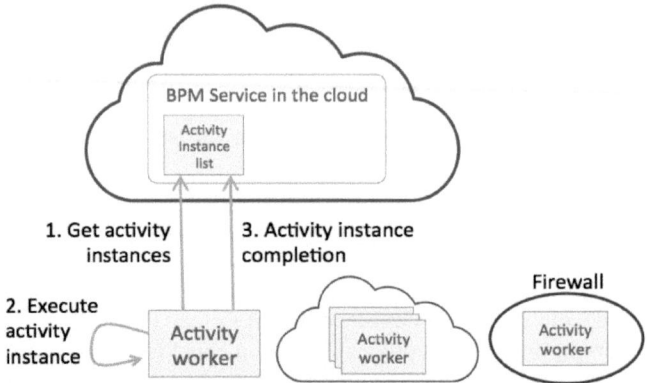

Fig. 3. The role of activity workers in cloud-based BPM

11   Conclusion

The cloud will make BPM simpler, faster and cheaper. The pay per use model on the cloud removes upfront investment of money and resources. Because end users are added as the new clients in that model, user experience becomes essential. This means that employees don't need training and can learn BPM services by trying and exploring. Instead, individual managers can start practicing BPM on their own. The lifecycle of the process will shift to become a natural path from social collaboration over simple checklists to fully automated processes. An iterative approach allows real world experience to be captured often removing the need for upfront analysis. Because of the open APIs to complete system tasks, a marketplace will ensure a broad range of activity types that can be used in processes.

On premise BPM technology has proven its value and already has a significant market size. The cloud will enable usage of BPM in many situations where it wasn't affordable before. Especially the reduction of investment in time and money will enable individuals to start with process automation. That shift from company wide to personal initiatives will cause mainstream adoption and put BPM as a central technology in small, medium and large enterprises.

Bridging Abstraction Layers in Process Mining by Automated Matching of Events and Activities

Thomas Baier[1] and Jan Mendling[2]

[1] Hasso Plattner Institute at the University of Potsdam
Prof.-Dr.-Helmert-Str. 2-3, D-14482 Potsdam, Germany
thomas.baier@hpi.uni-potsdam.de
[2] Wirtschaftsuniversität Wien, Augasse 2-6, 1090 Vienna, Austria
jan.mendling@wu.ac.at

Abstract. While the maturity of process mining algorithms increases and more process mining tools enter the market, process mining projects still face the problem of different levels of abstraction when comparing events with modeled business activities. Current approaches for event log abstraction most often try to abstract from the events in an automated way which does not capture the required domain knowledge to fit business activities. This can lead to misinterpretation of discovered process models. We developed an approach which aims to abstract an event log to the same abstraction level which is needed by the business. We use domain knowledge extracted from existing process documentation in order to automatically match events and activities. Our proposed abstraction approach is able to deal with n:m relations between events and activities and also supports concurrency. We evaluated our approach in a case study with a German IT outsourcing company.

Keywords: Process Mining, Abstraction, Event Mapping.

1 Introduction

Process mining is an emerging research field which is increasingly applied in practice. Using the event data logged by IT systems, process mining algorithms discover and enhance process models or check whether the execution of a process conforms to specification [1]. Looking at conformance checking and enhancement, it is obvious that the events stemming from the IT system have to be mapped to the activities defined in the process models. However, the events are typically more fine-granular than the activities defined by business users. This implies that different levels of abstraction need to be bridged in order to conduct a conformance analysis. Furthermore, such a mapping is not only necessary for conformance checking and process model enhancement, but also for discovery. The benefit of a discovered process model can only be fully exploited if the presented results are on an abstraction level which is easily understandable for the business user. Nevertheless, most of current process mining techniques assume that there is a 1:1 mapping between events and activities. There are some abstraction approaches which try to close this gap by preprocessing the event log and automatically finding clusters of events which can be bundled into activities. Yet, these techniques have limited capabilities in dealing with complex mappings between events and activities. Also, they provide no or only limited support for correctly refining these mappings based on domain knowledge.

The contribution of this paper, which builts on our former work [2], is a mapping approach which suggests relations between events and activities in an automated manner using existing process documentation as e.g. work instructions. Having suggested a set of potential event-activity relations, we furthermore define means to dissolve n:m relations. In contrast to existing approaches, the method introduced in this paper is designed to deal with concurrency and to handle n:m relations between events and activities. Our event log abstraction approach can be used as a preprocessing for every process mining technique. Furthermore, we conducted a case study in order to evaluate our approach. The results show the benefits of our approach and emphasize the sensitivity of conformance checking to the defined mapping problem.

The paper is structured as follows. Section 2 describes the problem of different abstraction levels in event logs and process models and introduces the preliminaries for our approach. Section 3 introduces the strategies to overcome the gap between abstraction levels of event log and process model. In section 4, we show the results from a case study of a German outsourcing provider where we benchmarked our approach against a manually created mappping and outline the implications on conformance testing. Related work is discussed in section 5 and section 6 concludes the work.

2 Background

2.1 Problem Description

In this section we illustrate the problem at hand. In order to illustrate the different abstraction layers on design and event log level, Fig. 1 shows a simple process model with a sequence of activities A, B and C. For each activity we find a set of related events in the event log. Hence, the activities and events are in a 1:n relation which is due to the fact, that the event log is on a lower level of abstraction compared to the designed model. Thus, there has to be a bridging model in between which is on the same level as the event log and shows the relations between the events and their relations to the high-level activities defined in the process model. Yet, this model is typically not available and too complicated to be created. One possible model of these sub activities is shown in Fig. 1. Here, we assume that all events are mandatory and occur in a strict sequence. Nevertheless, every other order of these events is possible and could also include loops, parallelism or exclusions. Furthermore, certain events might not be mandatory. Note that Fig. 1 also shows that events with the same name might not always belong to the same activity because they represent some shared functionality which is used in different activities. An example of such a shared activity is the writing of protocols during the execution of an activity. This is often done for several activities in a process. The bridging model would specify

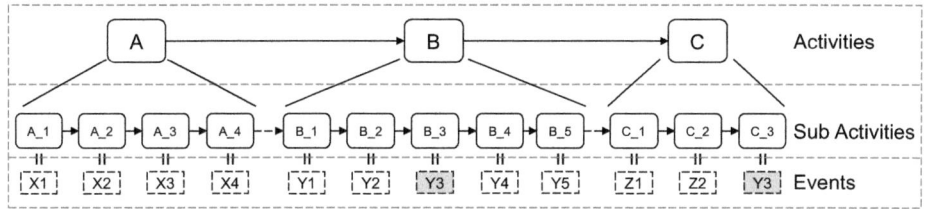

Fig. 1. Abstraction levels with shared functionality: From design to event log

the process in that detail that each sub activity could be identified with an event. In the absence of this bridging model, the relationship between events belonging to the same activity remains unspecified.

In order to make the problem more comprehensive, we will use the Incident Management process as defined in the IT Infrastructure Library (ITIL) as a running example. Figure 2 shows the process model of the Incident Management process at a very abstract level similar to the definition which can be found in the ITIL reference books [3]. At the bottom of Fig. 2, an excerpt of six example cases from a corresponding event log is displayed. Here, the difference between the abstraction levels as well as between the execution sequences can be seen. Activities designed as sequence run in parallel in reality which confuses current abstraction approaches relying on pattern extraction and close co-occurrence as e.g. proposed in [4]. The problem of shared activities is also clearly depicted. The event "Select CI" (configuration item, e.g. a harddisk) is executed between zero and 3 times per process instance. Depending on when in the process execution the event occurs, it belongs to different activities. When happening at the beginning of the process execution the event reflects the activity "Initial diagnosis" executed by the first level team. Later it occurs if the configuration item is changed by the 2nd level team or if somebody changes a wrong configuration item during the quality checks of the incident closure.

2.2 Preliminaries

In this section we introduce the preliminaries on which we ground our work. This includes the definition of a process model, a process execution and an event log. Definition 1 formalizes a process model as a tuple of activities, control nodes and flow relation. Based on this, we introduce the notion of a process execution in Definition 2. Note that this definition also includes process executions which do not conform to the process model.

Definition 1. *(Process model) A process model is a triplet $P = (A, F, C)$, with*

- *A as a non-empty set of activities, each having different attributes (attr $\in$ AT). For each attribute $\#_{attr}(a)$ refers to the value of the attribute attr for the activity $a \in A$.*

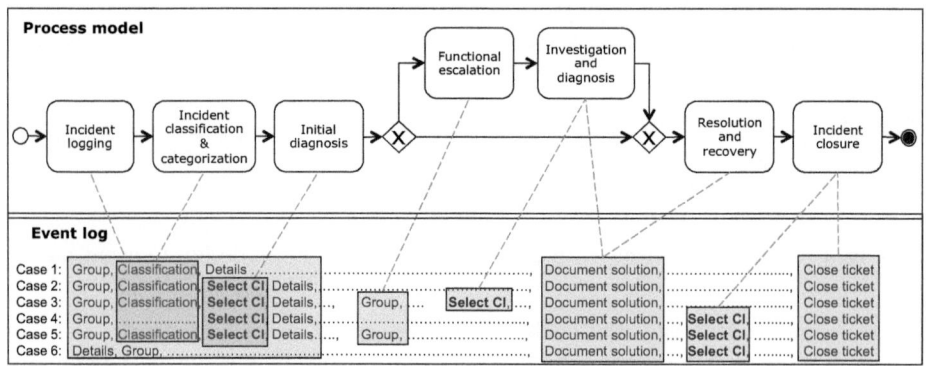

Fig. 2. Example of event to activity relations: Incident Management process model and low level event log with shared functionalities and concurrency

- C as a set of control nodes which is disjoint to set A.
- $F \subseteq (A \cup C) \times (A \cup C)$ as the flow relation, which connects activities with each other and with control nodes to build a directed graph.

We require each activity to have at least the following two attributes:

- $\#_{name}(a)$ refers to the activity name.
- $\#_{id}(a)$ refers to the unique identifier of the activity.

It has to be noted that $\#_{name}(a) = \#_{id}(a)$ is also a valid case, iff $\forall a \in A \; \nexists a' \in A : \#_{name}(a) = \#_{name}(a')$.

Definition 2. *(Process execution, process instance, activity instance)* Let P be a process model and A the set of defined activities within this model. A process execution is any sequence of activity instances $\hat{a} \in \hat{A}^*$.

An IT system which supports process executions typically records events in an event log. Definition 3 presents the basic concepts of an event log.

Definition 3. *(Event class, event instance, event attributes, trace, event log)* Let E be the non-empty set of event classes and $\hat{E}$ the set of event instances. Each event instance has different attributes (attr $\in AT$) assigned to it. For each attribute $\#_{attr}(\hat{e})$ refers to the value of the attribute attr for the event $\hat{e}$. A trace is a list of the form $\hat{E}^*$. An event log L is a multi-set of traces over $\hat{E}$, i.e., $L \in \mathbb{B}(\hat{E}^*)$.

We assume that an event has the following standard attributes (cf. [1]):

- $\#_{name}(\hat{e})$, which refers to the event name and thus, to the event class.
- $\#_{time}(\hat{e})$, which refers to the time when the event occurred.

Furthermore, each trace in an event log is related to a process execution. Note that the formerly described attributes are only the mandatory attributes we assume for every event. Other attributes may contain role information or values of changed database field which might also be used for defining the mapping.

3 Abstracting Event Logs Using Automatic Matching

This section introduces our approach for relating events to process model activities. The approach consists of four distinct phases:

1. Annotation of process model activities,
2. Matching of activities and events on type level,
3. Definition of context-sensitive mappings, and
4. Clustering of event instances to activity instances.

3.1 Annotation of Process Model Activities

As a major challenge in event-activity matching is the diverging level of abstraction, we utilize annotations. These annotations serve the purpose of enriching the coarse-granular activities of the process model with detailed information that helps to link to events. Typically, organizations maintain such detailed textual documentation of a process, which extends the information provided in the model, e.g. to serve different stakeholder groups [5]. Such documentation is often used as work instructions.

In modern business process modeling tools, process models and activities can be connected with such work instructions, such that the annotation of the activities is readily available. In the companies we have worked with, we often found work instructions in a tabular form consisting of columns for the activity name and the detailed description. In the following, we assume that such a description is available or can be directly linked to an activity. Note, that the annotation is not mandatory for each activity. Yet, it is likely to significantly improve the automated matching result.

Definition 4. *(Process description, activity description) Let P be a process model and A the set of defined activities within this model. A process description is a set of activity descriptions which are triplets of the form $(\#_{id}(a), \#_{name}(a), \text{textual description})$.*

3.2 Automatic Matching of Events and Activities

Having established the connection between activities and their textual description, this second phase deals with the derivation of mappings between events and activities. To this end, we have to inspect each combination of event class names and activity descriptions for potential correspondences. In order to check for a potential correspondence, we extract business objects from the event class name, the activity name and description using the Stanford Part-of-Speech (POS) tagger [6,7]. This allows us to use not only string comparison, but also semantic relationships between terms on the event and on the activity level. We also use stemming and word decomposition [8], e.g. to find correspondences between singular and plural words and between different derived forms. For the decomposition of compound words in our case study, we use a language independent, lexicon-based approach developed by Abels and Hahn [9]. It generates possible splittings of words and checks whether the generated parts are covered in a lexicon. In our approach we use JWordSplitter, an open source implementation of this approach with an integrated German lexicon[1].

Algorithm 1. Check activity description for potential event-activity relation

```
 1: checkRelation(eventClass, text)
 2: Set eventObjects = extractNouns(eventClass)
 3: Set textObjects = extractNouns(text)
 4: for all eventObject ∈ eventObjects do
 5:    for all textObject ∈ businessObjects do
 6:       if eventObject==textObject then
 7:          return true
 8:       else
 9:          if checkPartialWordMatch(eventObject, textObject) then
10:             return true
11:          end if
12:       end if
13:    end for
14: end for
15: return false
```

Hence, we compare all business objects in two ways. First, we do a simple string match and second, we decompose the business objects into their smallest semantic components and compare these with one another. The comparison of decomposed word parts is done with simple string comparison and comparison of word stems. In this way, we are able to relate words like "Fachgruppe" (professional group) and "Skillgruppen" (skill groups). The result of this phase is an automatically provided list of potential event-activity relations on type level, which can be refined and extended by a domain expert.

3.3 Building Context-Sensitive Event-to-Activity Mappings

Based on the approach reported above, we find potential event-activity relations. This section describes the necessary steps to get from the potential relations to a concrete event-to-activity mapping which can be used to abstract the event log.

In order to lift an event log to the abstraction level of a corresponding set of activities, we define a mapping relation which assigns every event instance $\hat{e} \in \hat{E}$ to an activity instance $\hat{a} \in \hat{A}$. Hence, all events in an event log have to be either mapped onto their corresponding activity or removed from the log. The challenge in this context is to identify the condition that helps to decide when one event class matches one of alternative activities. To this end, we consider the context of an event, either as defined over the event attributes or the surrounding

---

[1] See http://www.danielnaber.de/jwordsplitter/

event instances. First, the role that is related to an event might be important to distinguish different activities in the process model. For example, a the selection of a configuration item (CI) in Figure 2 belongs to the activity "Initial diagnosis" when executed by a first level agent while the same event class refers to the activity "Investigation and diagnosis" when executed by a second level supporter. Second, the relation of an event instance to an activity might also depend on the context in terms of preceding or succeeding event instances. While the selection of a CI normally happens during the activities "Initial diagnosis" or "Investigation and diagnosis", depending on the executing role, it can also be performed as a quality improvement step during the closure of the incident ticket. As shown in Figure 2, this is always the case if the solution has been documented before. Third, an event might be interpreted differently if it occurs for the first time or if it has been preceded by earlier executions. In the example in Figure 2, the working group is always set in the beginning where it simply refers to the logging of the incident while every other change of the working group refers to the functional escalation of the ticket. In order to use such domain knowledge, we have to encode it in a formal way. Definitions 5 and 6 introduce the formalization of meta data conditions and event context conditions.

Definition 5. *(Meta data condition) Let O be the set of comparison operators, e.g. $O = \{equals, contains, startswith\}$, and let V be the set of values that an event attribute $attr \in AT$ should be tested against. Then, a meta data condition is a tupel $mdc \subseteq AT \times V \times O$.*

Definition 6. *(Event context condition) An event context condition is defined by a tupel $ecc = (f, r)$, where f is a condition defined as linear temporal logic formula [10] and $r \in \{before, after\}$ refers to the part of an event context $\hat{EC}$ in which this formula should be tested. The event context $\hat{EC}$ is a tupel (t_{before}, t_{after}) where t_{before} and t_{after} are subtraces of a trace t such that $t = t_{before}\|\hat{e}\|t_{after}$.*

When shared functionalities are discovered in the suggestion phase, the user needs to define the necessary meta data or context conditions in order to dissolve the assignment problem. Having these conditions, we define an event class to activity mapping EAM based on event classes and conditions that have to be fulfilled for a corresponding event instance in order to be mapped to a specific activity. The conditions can be meta data conditions as well as event context conditions.

Definition 7. *(Event class to activity mapping) An event to activity mapping is a function $EAM : E \times MDC \times ECC \to A$, which relates an event class to an activity class based on a set of meta data conditions and a set of event context conditions.*

Definition 7 gives the mapping between activities from a process model and event instances found in an event log. For our examples the role based mapping could be defined as
('Select CI', $\{('role', \text{'first level'},' equals')\}, \{\}) \to$ 'Initial diagnosis'

('Select CI', $\{('role', \text{'second level'}, 'equals')\}, \{\}) \to$ 'Investigation & diagnosis' and the occurrence based mapping could be defined as
('Select CI', $\{\}, \{(<> ("Document solution"), 'before')\}) \to$ 'Incident closure'.

3.4 Clustering Events to Activity Instances

Having established the relations between event classes and activities on the type level, we still need to identify relations between events and implicit activity instances. Therefore, we specify a function $\hat{E}AM$ which maps event instances surrounded by an event context to an activity.

Definition 8. *(Event instance to activity mapping)* $\hat{E}AM : \hat{E} \times \hat{E}C \times EAM \to A$ *is the function which maps an event instance $\hat{e}$ to an activity class A based on the event context EC and the given event class to activity mapping.*

Having a mapping function $\hat{E}AM$, the next step is to define how to map event instances belonging to the same activity class to activity instances. As there might be multiple activity instances for one activity in a process execution, i.e. in a loop, the question is, which criteria are used to map an event instance $\hat{x}_i$ to an activity instance $\hat{a}_j$. In this case, we need to define the border between events belonging to two or more instances of the same activity. Definition 9 therefore introduces the notion of instance border conditions.

Definition 9. *(Instance border condition)* *An instance border condition defines under which conditions two event instances, which are mapped to the same activity a, cannot belong to the same activity instance $\hat{a}_i$ and thus, correspond to two different activity instances $\hat{a}_i, \hat{a}_j$. It is defined as a boolean function $BC : \hat{E} \times \hat{E} \to \{true, false\}$.*

Instance border definitions relate to two levels: intra sub-activity structure and inter sub-activity structure. Concerning the intra sub-activity structure, we have to decide whether there are loops in sub-activities or not. While the assumed sub-activity model might not contain loops, this does not imply that there are no loops on the inter sub-activity level. The latter have to be lifted to activity level if we assume there should not be any loops on sub-activity level. In line with this assumption, an activity instance border is marked by the repetition of source events from the same event class, i.e. the repetition of a source event class signals that a new activity instance has started. Thus, for example two protocol events could indicate rework and therefore two instances of the corresponding activity.

Using recurring source event classes as instance border definition works only if there are no loops in the assumed sub-activity model. If there are loops on the intra sub-activity level and in the process model, multiple event instances from the same event class might belong to one activity instance. A typical example for this is a loop over the order items in an order list where different activities like "Choose supplier" and "Sent order" have to be performed for each order item and are modeled in the process model on activity level. The activity "Choose supplier" might contain different activities which have to be executed for each supplier, like e.g. "Check prices". Thus, we have a loop on activity level and a loop on sub-activity level. In order to find the correct instance borders, we need to extend the instance border definition to also use different business objects, e.g. the order line, as instance border markings. Thus, instance borders can be defined over any attributes attached to an event.

If such meta data is not available or if it is not possible to make such statements about the assumed sub-activity model, we need to use heuristics in order to be able to identify different activity instances. As a first heuristic for instance border definition builds on the assumptions of a maximum number of events that belong to one activity instance. This is simple, if we can exclude the occurrence of loops on sub-activity level, but might be difficult otherwise. A second heuristic is defined based on a threshold for the maximum distance between two events which belong to one activity instance. This distance can be specified using the time perspective, i.e. defining how long the time frame between two events of the same activity instance can be. For example one might limit the time distance between two events of the same activity instance, e.g. two edit events for a protocol belong to different activity instances if there are more than 24 hours between them. Another way to specify the distance is to use a maximal number of events which are allowed to occur between two events of the same activity instance.

Definition 10 specifies the function $\hat{E}\hat{A}M$ which uses the previously defined event instance to activity correlation provided by $\hat{E}AM$ and maps these pairs of the form $(\hat{e}, a)$ to activity instances using defined instance border conditions.

Definition 10. *(Event instance to activity instance mapping) The function $\hat{E}AM$ provides a set of event instances mapped to activity classes which is a subset of $\hat{E} \times A$. Then $\hat{E}\hat{A}M : \hat{E} \times A \times BC \rightarrow \hat{A}$ is the function which assigns a previously mapped event instance to its corresponding activity instance $\hat{a}$. For each $a \in A$ there is a set of instance border conditions $bc \subset BC$. An event instance $\hat{e}$ which is mapped to an activity instance $\hat{a}$ is referred to as source event of $\hat{a}$.*

Definition 10 covers 1:1 and 1:n relations on the instance level. A 1:1 mapping on instance level only occurs for events and activities which are on the same abstraction level. Looking at different abstraction levels it is most likely that an activity instance on a higher level subsumes multiple event instances representing different sub activities. Thus, in most cases we face a 1:n mapping on instance level and event instance will be clustered to activity instances. Nevertheless, it can be the case that one event instance reflects multiple activities. Coming again back to our protocol example, it might happen that the protocol does not only contain the analysis results but also the planning of the next steps. This might be recognized by scanning the content of the protocol which is attached to the event instance as meta data. To solve this n:1 relation problem, we can simply duplicate the event instance to create a 1:1 or 1:n mapping on instance level.

In order to transform a given event log to a higher abstraction level, we iterate over the traces in a log and rename the event instances with the names

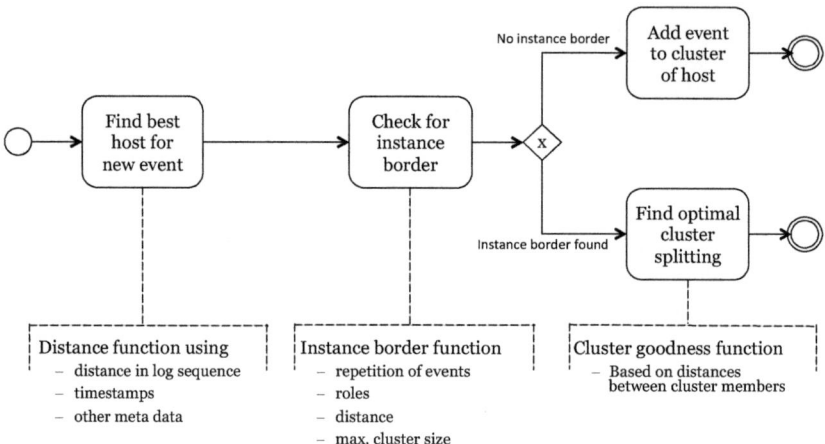

Fig. 3. 4-step instance clustering algorithm

of the activities assigned by the function $\hat{E}AM$. The source events are kept as attributes to the abstracted events. Next, the events assigned to the same activity class need to be clustered to activity instances using the instance border definitions as defined by the function $\hat{E}\hat{A}M$. The algorithm we propose for the clustering of events to activity instances is grounded on a tree-based incremental clustering algorithm known from classical data mining [11]. For every activity class the clustering forms a tree with the event instances as leaves and the activity instances on the next higher level. The clustering starts with an empty tree for each activity class consisting of the root alone. Next, the event instances are incrementally inserted into the tree. Updating the tree is done by finding the right place to put the new leaf. This may also cause the restructuring of the part of tree that is affected by the new instance. The algorithm consists of 4 main steps as depicted in Figure 3. The best host for a new event is the event with the minimal distance which can be expressed by a distance function using e.g. the time stamps of the events or other meta data. Having found the optimal host, we have to check for all events belonging to the same activity instance as the host event, that these do not fulfill any border condition in combination with the event that has to be inserted into the cluster. If no instance border is found, the event is added to the activity instance cluster of the determined host event. Once an instance border is found, we need to determine where the new activity instance starts as this might already have happened before the occurence of the event that signaled the border. This is done using a goodness function based on the summation of distances within a cluster. The goal is to find the optimal clustering with the minimal sum of distances between events belonging to the same activity instance cluster. For further explanations of the instance clustering algorithm, we refer the reader to our previous work [2].

4 Evaluation

In order to validate how well our approach works with real life data, we conducted a case study using data from the incident process of a large German IT outsourcing project. The process model specifying the designed process has 41 activities and the corresponding event log contains 17,209 cases, 31 event classes and a total of 479,408 event instances for a selected month. Within the case study we evaluated all four phases of our approach. We pay special attention to the automated matching of events to activities and to the clustering of event instances as these are the critical parts of our approach. We therefore compare (1) the automated matching with a manual matching and evaluate the gain retrieved by using external domain knowledge. Moreover, we compare (2) the produced activity instances by our proposed clustering algorithm with manually build activity instances. To further highlight the importance of a correct abstraction, we (3) show the impact of different clustering parameters on conformance analysis. For the purpose of evaluation, our approach has been implemented as a set of two plugins in the process mining workbench ProM.[2]

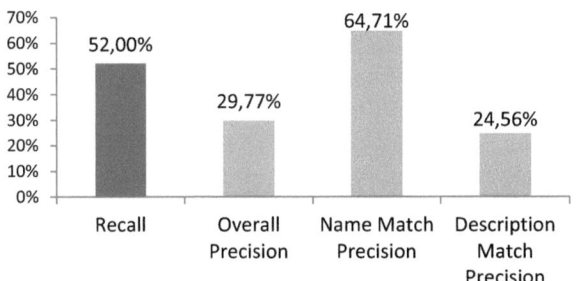 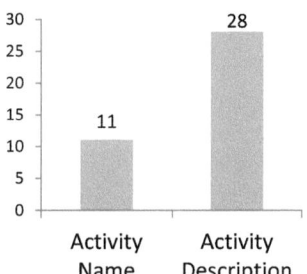

Fig. 4. Recall and precision for automated matching

Fig. 5. Correct matches by source

In the first phase, we annotated the activities from the given process model with descriptions from two provided work instruction documents with a total of 238 activity descriptions. The matching algorithm annotated 32 process model activities with 66 description. Thus, for many of the activities we even found multiple descriptions in the provided process description. Yet, not all process model activities could be annotated due to missing descriptions in the process documentation. This already provides valuable information for the process manager of the process. Looking at the result of the second phase, the automated matching of events to activities on type level, we measure (1) the *precision* (number of correctly matched event-activity pairs divided by all matched pairs) and the *recall* (number of correctly matched event-activity pairs divided by all manually matched event-activity pairs). Figure 4 presents the overall results for these two

---

[2] See http://processmining.org for more information on ProM.

measures. The not very high overall precision of 29,77 %, is mainly caused by matches which are based on the additional activity descriptions. Here, we only retrieve a precision of 24,56 % while the precision of matches on the activity names is quite high with 64,71 %. Nevertheless, the additional descriptions account for 28 correct matches while there are only 11 correct matches on activity names. Thus, the matching of activity descriptions contributes a much higher share to the overall recall of 52 % than the matching of activity names. This shows that our approach of annotating the activities with additional data is beneficial.

Still, the gap in recall has to be further analyzed. The main reason for about 85 % of the event-activity relations that could not be found in this setting, is that these steps where simply not documented in the given work instructions. Some of these are simply missed out and need to be updated in the description. Here the approach already helped in identifying gaps in the process documentation. The other fraction of the undocumented relations are steps which are automatically done by the system and are therefore missing in the documentation for the people executing the process. Here, future research needs to investigate whether such relations could be retrieved from existing software documentations. Beside the undocumented relations, there are two other minor reasons why relations could not be found. First, some relations can only be found looking at the meta data of the events. For example there is an event "Neues Kommunikationsprotokoll" (new communication protocol) which contains all events for sent e-mail messages. Looking at the subjects of these messages which are most often standardized, one could derive further relations. What is more, we also encountered one case where the relation could have been established using a verb instead of a business object. Further research is needed to evaluate whether verbs could be included in the matching without a dramatic decrease of precision. Furthermore, we encountered some mappings which could have been found using synonym relations. Yet, these synonyms are domain specific an could only be found in a domain specific ontology which would have to be build first.

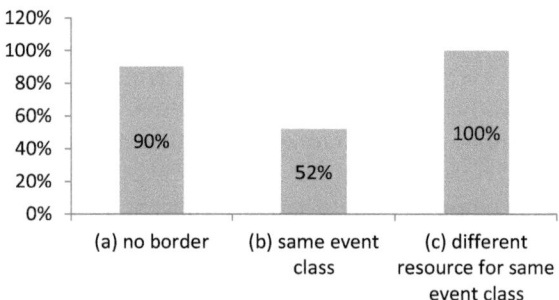

Fig. 6. Fraction of correct traces for different instance border definitions

In order to evaluate (2) the produced activity instances by our proposed clustering algorithm, the mapping has been provided with context-sensitive mapping conditions and has been completed manually by the domain expert (third phase). The domain expert furthermore manually mapped the event instances of 152 cases to activity instances to provide a benchmark for our algorithm.

Looking at the fourth phase of our approach, we want to compare the abstraction results for different activity instance border definitions. We differentiate between merging (a) and not merging (b) event instances stemming from the same event class and hence, either allow for loops on sub activity level or not. As a third option, we consider that a single resource might do things iteratively and thus, events from the same event class and same resource belong to one activity instance while this is not the case if they are created by different resources (c). Option (b) returns with 52 % the least percentage of correct traces when compared to the gold standard. When allowing for loops on the sub-activity level (a) this results in 90 % of all traces being correctly abstracted. The option which only allows loops executed by a single resource performs best and even yields 100 % correct cases. The reason for this is e.g. the iterative filling of fields in the web mask of the used ticketing tool. If a service agent writes down the problem description and pushes the save button several times during this activity, there will be a new event for every saving. These events obviously belong to the same activity instance. In contrast, when a different service agent picks up the ticket and needs to update the problem description, this is seen as rework and thus, as a new activity instance.

To further assess the (3) impact of different instance border definitions we investigated their influence on conformance analysis using the constraint-relative behavioral profile conformance metric as defined in [12]. We analyzed the results for the heuristic activity instance border definition over event distances and found that there is a difference of 17 % points in the conformance metric between the lowest and highest result. Thus, there is a quite big influence of the correct activity instance clustering on conformance checking.

Summing up, we showed in this section that the presented approach performs well in a practical setting and that the use of additional domain knowledge is beneficial. Furthermore, we showed influences of instance border conditions on the abstracted result as well as on conformance analysis. It has to be noted that there is still a significant part of manual work to be done in order to encode missing domain knowledge into the required mapping definitions. Other approaches for event log abstraction require less manual work or are even fully automated, but in return are not able to fully capture the introduced concepts and thus, will lead to inferior abstraction results. We will discuss these approaches in the next section.

5 Related Work

Research related to this paper can be subdivided into three specific areas: clustering in process mining, event log abstraction and automatic process model matching.

In the area of process mining, there are several works focusing on clustering events to activities. An approach similar to the one used in this paper clusters events to activities using a distance function based on time or sequence position [13]. These clusters can be refined by the help of modified data types and originators. Due to performance issues with this approach, a new means of abstraction on the level of event classes is introduced in [14]. These event classes are clustered globally based on co-occurrence of related terms, yielding better performance but lower accuracy. A similar approach introducing semantic relatedness, n:m relations and context dependence is defined in [4]. However, it has an inflexible definition of activity instance borders, leading to problems when dealing with concurrency. In contrast to these works, the approach presented in this paper is able to deal with concurrency and n:m relations from shared activities without exhibiting the discussed performance limitations. Although it requires more manual intervention, it provides a transparent and simple means for the user to influence the abstraction result and has proven suitable in a practical case study.

The importance of event log abstraction is emphasized among others in [15]. The approach reported in [16] clusters process instances with similar behavior in order to abstract behavior which is different between these clusters. While this is an interesting approach for exploratory analysis, it is not able to abstract events that always occur together. A different means of abstracting event logs is to simply remove insignificant behavior. Together with the fuzzy miner, an approach is defined to abstract a mined process model by removing and clustering less frequent behavior [17]. Furthermore, there are different approaches that apply behaviour abstraction in process discovery and trace alignment [18,19,20]. The technique proposed in this paper provides preprocessing for these approaches.

Our work also relates to automatic matching for process models. While matching has been partially addressed in various works on process similarity [21], there are only a few papers that covers this topic as their major focus. The work on ICoP defines a generic framework for process model matching [22]. This framework is extended with semantic concepts and probabilistic optimization in [23], adapting general concepts from ontology matching [24]. The implications of different abstraction levels for finding correspondences is covered in [25,26,27]. However, all these works focus on finding matches between two process models, not between events and activities. Also related to this paper is research on event correlation, e.g. in [28]. The main objective of event correlation techniques is to connect events belonging to the same process instance using event attributes. Still, these approaches typically only consider 1:1 mappings. Against this background, our approach can be considered as a new area of process model matching, which takes the instance level into account.

6 Conclusion

In this paper we presented a novel approach to tackle the abstraction of event logs. Our approach distinguishes from current works by explicitly targeting a specific abstraction level and by allowing for n:m relations and concurrency. We therefore explicitly encode domain knowledge into the mapping function in order to get the same level of abstraction as used in the defined business activities. We do this in a semi-automated manner by automatically matching events and activities using existing process descriptions and by allowing for the specification of activity instance borders. Our approach can be used as preprocessing of event logs to lift the results of process mining techniques to a business level. We have successfully evaluated our approach and could thereby show the influence of incorrect abstractions on conformance analysis results.

Future work should seek for possibilities to automatically propose context conditions and should include further techniques to derive event-activity relations, e.g. by combining our approach with the one proposed in [4]. Looking at the low level events, it should been studied how further semantics could be integrated into the abstraction approach in order to leverage life-cycle transitions such as start and end of an activity in a semi-automatic way.

References

1. van der Aalst, W.M.P.: Process Mining: Discovery, Conformance and Enhancement of Business Processes, 1st edn. Springer Publishing Company, Incorporated (2011)
2. Baier, T., Mendling, J.: Bridging abstraction layers in process mining: Event to activity mapping. In: Nurcan, S., Proper, H.A., Soffer, P., Krogstie, J., Schmidt, R., Halpin, T., Bider, I. (eds.) BPMDS 2013 and EMMSAD 2013. LNBIP, vol. 147, pp. 109–123. Springer, Heidelberg (2013)
3. Cannon, D., Wheeldon, D.: ITIL – Service Operation. TSO (May 2007)
4. Li, J., Bose, R.P.J.C., van der Aalst, W.M.P.: Mining context-dependent and interactive business process maps using execution patterns. In: Muehlen, M.z., Su, J. (eds.) BPM 2010 Workshops. LNBIP, vol. 66, pp. 109–121. Springer, Heidelberg (2011)
5. Scheer, A.-W.: ARIS - Modellierungsmethoden, Metamodelle, Anwendungen, 4th edn. Springer (2001)
6. Jurafsky, D., Martin, J.: Speech and language processing. Prentice Hall (2008)
7. Toutanova, K., Manning, C.D.: Enriching the Knowledge Sources Used in a Maximum Entropy Part-of-Speech Tagger. EMNLP, 63–70 (2000)
8. Braschler, M., Ripplinger, B.: How Effective is Stemming and Decompounding for German Text Retrieval? Information Retrieval 7(3/4), 291–316 (2004)
9. Abels, S., Hahn, A.: Pre-processing Text for Web Information Retrieval Purposes by Splitting Compounds into their Morphemes. In: OSWIR 2005 (2005)
10. Pnueli, A.: The Temporal Logic of Programs. In: Foundations of Computer Science, pp. 46–57 (1977)
11. Witten, I.H., Frank, E.: Data Mining: Practical Machine Learning Tools and Techniques, 2nd edn. Morgan Kaufmann (2005)
12. Weidlich, M., Polyvyanyy, A., Desai, N., Mendling, J., Weske, M.: Process compliance analysis based on behavioural profiles. Information Systems 36(7), 1009–1025 (2011)
13. Günther, C.W., van der Aalst, W.M.P.: Mining activity clusters from low-level event logs. In: BETA Working Paper Series, vol. WP 165, Eindhoven University of Technology (2006)
14. Günther, C.W., Rozinat, A., van der Aalst, W.M.P.: Activity mining by global trace segmentation. In: Rinderle-Ma, S., Sadiq, S., Leymann, F. (eds.) BPM 2009. LNBIP, vol. 43, pp. 128–139. Springer, Heidelberg (2010)

15. Smirnov, S., Reijers, H.A., Weske, M., Nugteren, T.: Business process model abstraction: a definition, catalog, and survey. Distributed and Parallel Databases 30(1), 63–99 (2012)
16. Greco, G., Guzzo, A., Pontieri, L.: Mining taxonomies of process models. Data & Knowledge Engineering 67(1), 74–102 (2008)
17. Günther, C.W., van der Aalst, W.M.P.: Fuzzy mining: adaptive process simplification based on multi-perspective metrics. In: Alonso, G., Dadam, P., Rosemann, M. (eds.) BPM 2007. LNCS, vol. 4714, pp. 328–343. Springer, Heidelberg (2007)
18. Polyvyanyy, A., Smirnov, S., Weske, M.: Process Model Abstraction: A Slider Approach. In: EDOC, pp. 325–331. IEEE (2008)
19. Fahland, D., van der Aalst, W.M.P.: Simplifying discovered process models in a controlled manner. Inf. Syst. 38(4), 585–605 (2013)
20. Bose, R.P.J.C., van der Aalst, W.M.P.: Process diagnostics using trace alignment: Opportunities, issues, and challenges. Inf. Syst. 37(2), 117–141 (2012)
21. Dijkman, R.M., Dumas, M., van Dongen, B.F., Käärik, R., Mendling, J.: Similarity of Business Process Models: Metrics and Evaluation. Information Systems 36(2), 498–516 (2011)
22. Weidlich, M., Dijkman, R.M., Mendling, J.: The ICoP Framework: Identification of Correspondences between Process Models. In: Pernici, B. (ed.) CAiSE 2010. LNCS, vol. 6051, pp. 483–498. Springer, Heidelberg (2010)
23. Leopold, H., Niepert, M., Weidlich, M., Mendling, J., Dijkman, R., Stuckenschmidt, H.: Probabilistic optimization of semantic process model matching. In: Barros, A., Gal, A., Kindler, E. (eds.) BPM 2012. LNCS, vol. 7481, pp. 319–334. Springer, Heidelberg (2012)
24. Euzenat, J., Shvaiko, P.: Ontology Matching. Springer (2007)
25. Weidlich, M., Dijkman, R., Weske, M.: Behaviour Equivalence and Compatibility of Business Process Models with Complex Correspondences. ComJnl (2012)
26. Klinkmüller, C., Weber, I., Mendling, J., Leopold, H., Ludwig, A.: Improving the recall of process model matching. In: Business Process Management - 11th International Conference, BPM 2013, Proceedings. LNCS. Springer (2013)
27. Weidlich, M., Sagi, T., Leopold, H., Gal, A., Mendling, J.: Making process model matching work. In: Business Process Management - 11th International Conference, BPM 2013, Proceedings. LNCS. Springer (2013)
28. Pérez-Castillo, R., Weber, B., de Guzmán, I.G.R., Piattini, M., Pinggera, J.: Assessing event correlation in non-process-aware information systems. Software and Systems Modeling, 1–23 (2012)

Mining Configurable Process Models from Collections of Event Logs

J.C.A.M. Buijs, B.F. van Dongen, and W.M.P. van der Aalst

Eindhoven University of Technology, The Netherlands
{j.c.a.m.buijs,b.f.v.dongen,w.m.p.v.d.aalst}@tue.nl

Abstract. Existing process mining techniques are able to discover a *specific* process model for a given event log. In this paper, we aim to discover a *configurable* process model from a *collection* of event logs, i.e., the model should describe a *family of process variants* rather than one specific process. Consider for example the handling of building permits in different municipalities. Instead of discovering a process model per municipality, we want to discover one configurable process model showing commonalities and differences among the different variants. Although there are various techniques that merge individual process models into a configurable process model, there are no techniques that construct a configurable process model based on a collection of event logs. By extending our ETM genetic algorithm, we propose and compare four novel approaches to learn configurable process models from collections of event logs. We evaluate these four approaches using both a running example and a collection of real event logs.

1 Introduction

Different organizations or units within a larger organization may need to execute similar business processes. Municipalities for instance all provide similar services while being bound by government regulations [6]. Large car rental companies like Hertz, Avis and Sixt have offices in different cities and airports all over the globe. Often there are subtle (but sometimes also striking) differences between the processes handled by these offices, even though they belong to the same car rental company. To be able to share development efforts, analyze differences, and learn best practices across organizations, we need *configurable process models* that are able to describe families of process variants rather than one specific process [8, 16].

Given a collection of event logs that describe similar processes we can discover a process model using existing process mining techniques [1]. However, existing techniques are not tailored towards the discovery of a *configurable* process model based on a *collection* of event logs. In this paper, we compare four approaches to mine configurable models. The first two approaches use a combination of existing process discovery and process merging techniques. The third approach uses a two-phase approach where the fourth approach uses a new, integrated approach. All four approaches have been implemented in the ProM framework [18].

The remainder of the paper is organized as follows. In Section 2, we discuss related work on process discovery, configurable process models and current model merging techniques. In Section 3 we describe the four different approaches to mine configurable

F. Daniel, J. Wang, and B. Weber (Eds.): BPM 2013, LNCS 8094, pp. 33–48, 2013.
© Springer-Verlag Berlin Heidelberg 2013

process models in more detail. There we also describe how our genetic process discovery algorithm (ETM) has been extended to perform each of the four different approaches. Then we apply each of the approaches on a running example in Section 4. In Section 5 we apply the four approaches on a real-life event log collection to demonstrate the applicability of each of the approaches in practice. Section 6 concludes the paper and suggests directions for future work.

2 Related Work

The goal of *process discovery* in the area of process mining is to automatically discover process models that accurately describe processes by considering only an organization's records of its operational processes [1]. Such records are typically captured in the form of *event logs*, consisting of cases and events related to these cases. Over the last decade, many such process discovery techniques have been developed. For a complete overview we refer to [1]. However, until now, no process mining technique exists that is able to discover a single, configurable, process model that is able to describe the behavior of a *collection of event logs*.

A *configurable process model* describes a family of process models, i.e., variants of the same process. A configuration of a configurable process model restricts its behavior, for example by *hiding* or *blocking* activities. Hiding means that an activity can be skipped. Blocking means that a path cannot be taken anymore. Most formalisms allow operators to be made more restrictive (e.g., an OR-split is changed into an XOR-split). By configuring the configurable process model a (regular) process model is obtained. A configurable process model aims to show commonalities and differences among different variants. This facilitates reuse and comparison. Moreover, development efforts can be shared without enforcing a very particular process. Different notations and approaches for process configuration have been suggested in literature [4, 8, 11, 15–17]. In this paper we use a representation based on [17].

Configurable process models can be constructed in different ways. They can be designed from scratch, but if a collection of existing process models already exist, a configurable process model can be derived by merging the different variants. The original models used as input correspond to configurations of the configurable process model.

Different approaches exist to merge a collection of existing process models into a configurable process model. A collection of EPCs can be merged using the technique presented in [9]. The resulting configurable EPC may allow for additional behavior, not possible in the original EPCs. La Rosa et al. [12] describe an alternative approach that allows merging process models into a configurable process model, even if the input process models are in different formalisms. In such merging approaches, some configurations may correspond to an unsound process model. Li et al. [13] discuss an approach where an existing reference process model is improved by analyzing the different variants derived from it. However, the result is not a configurable process model but an improved reference process model, i.e., variants are obtained by modifying the reference model rather than by process configuration. The CoSeNet [17] approach has been designed for merging a collection of block structured process models. This approach always results in sound and reversible configurable process models.

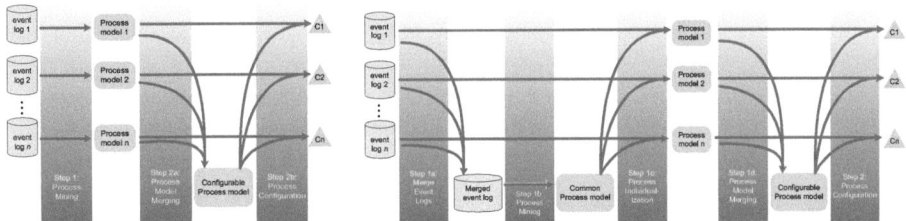

(a) Approach 1: Merge individually discovered process models

(b) Approach 2: Merge similar discovered process models

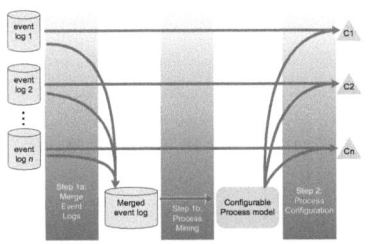
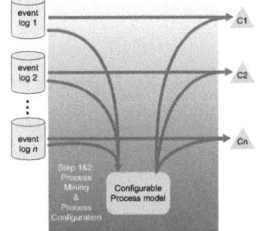

(c) Approach 3: First discover a single process model then discover configurations

(d) Approach 4: Discover process model and configurations at the same time

Fig. 1. Creating a configurable process model from a collection of event logs

Another way of obtaining a configurable process model is not by merging process models but by applying process mining techniques on a collection of event logs. This idea was first proposed in [10], where two different approaches were discussed, but these were not supported by concrete discovery algorithms. The first approach merges process models discovered for each event log using existing process model merge techniques. In the second approach the event logs are first merged and then a combined process model is discovered and individualized for each event log.

3 Mining a Configurable Process Model

In this section we present different approaches to mine a configurable process model from a collection of event logs. We also present the algorithm used for the discovery of process models.

3.1 Approaches

As mentioned in Section 1, we consider four approaches to discover a configurable process model from a collection of event logs.

The first approach, as is shown in Figure 1a, applies process discovery on each input event log to obtain the corresponding process model. Then these processes models are merged using model merge techniques. This approach was first proposed in [10].

Since the process models of the first approach are discovered independently of each other, they might differ significantly hence merging them correctly becomes more difficult. Therefore we propose a second approach as an improvement of the previous approach. The overall idea is shown in Figure 1b. From the input event logs first one process model is discovered that describes the behavior recorded in all event logs. Then the single process model is taken and individualized for each event log. For this we use the work presented in [7] to improve a process model within a certain edit distance. In the next step these individual process models are merged into a configurable process model using the approach of [17]. By making the individual process models more similar, merging them into a configurable process model should be easier.

The third approach, as shown in Figure 1c, is an extension of the second approach presented by Gottschalk et al. in [10]. A single process model is discovered that describes the behavior of all event logs. Then, using each individual event log, configurations are discovered for this single process model. In this approach the common process model should be less precise than other process models since we can only restrict the behavior using configurations, but not extend it. Therefore the process discovery algorithm applied needs to put less emphasis on precision.

The fourth approach is a new approach where the discovery of the process model and the configuration is combined, see Figure 1d. This approach is added to overcome the disadvantages of the other three approaches. By providing an integrated approach, where both the process model and the configuration options are discovered simultaneously, better trade-offs can be made.

The third and fourth approaches require an algorithm that is able to balance trade-offs in control flow, and optionally in configuration options. In previous work we presented the ETM-algorithm [5] that is able to seamlessly balance different quality dimensions. Therefore, in this paper the ETM-algorithm is extended such that it can discover a single process tree using a collection of event logs. Together with the process tree a configuration for each of the event logs is also discovered. In order to be able to compare the results of the different approaches, the ETM-algorithm is used as the process discovery algorithm in all four approaches.

3.2 The ETM Algorithm

In this section we briefly introduce our evolutionary algorithm first presented in [5]. The ETM (*Evolutionary Tree Miner*) algorithm is able to discover tree-like process models that are sound and block-structured. The fitness function used by this genetic algorithm can be used to seamlessly balance different quality dimensions. In the remainder of this section we only discuss the ETM-algorithm on a high-level together with the extensions made, to prevent repetition. All details of the ETM-algorithm can be found in [5].

Overall the ETM algorithm follows the genetic process shown in Figure 2. The input of the algorithm is one or more event logs describing the observed behavior and, optionally, one or more reference process models. First, different quality dimensions for each candidate currently in the population are calculated, and using the weight given to each quality dimension, the *overall fitness* of the process tree is calculated. In the next step certain stop criteria are tested such as finding a tree with the desired overall fitness, or exceeding a time limit. If none of the stop criteria are satisfied, the candidates in the population are changed and the fitness is again calculated. This is continued until at least one stop criterion is satisfied and the best candidate (highest overall fitness) is then returned.

The ETM-algorithm works on process trees, which are a tree-like representation of a process model. The leafs are activities and the other nodes represent one of several predefined control-flow constructs.

To measure the quality of a process tree, we consider one metric for each of the four main quality dimensions described in literature [1–3] (see Fig. 3). We have shown in [5] that the *replay fitness* dimension is the most important of the four in process discovery. The replay fitness dimension expresses how much of the observed behavior in the event log can be replayed in the process model. The *precision* dimension indicates how much additional behavior is possible in the process model but is not observed in the event log. The *simplicity* dimension assesses how simple the process model description of the behavior is. The *generalization* dimension is added to penalize "overfitting", i.e., the model should allow for unseen but very likely behaviors.

For the simplicity dimension we use a slightly different metric than in previous work. Simplicity is based on Occam's razor, i.e., the principle that says that when all other things are equal the simplest answer is to be preferred. Size is one of the simplest measures of complexity [14] since bigger process models are in general more complex to understand. Unfortunately, the ideal size of the process tree cannot directly be calculated, as control flow nodes can have multiple children. Furthermore, it might be beneficial for other quality dimensions, such as replay fitness or precision, to duplicate certain parts. Therefore, in the genetic algorithm, we use the fraction of the process tree that consists of 'useless' nodes as a simplicity metric since it does not influence the other quality dimensions. A node is useless if it can be removed without changing the behavior of the tree. Useless nodes are operators with only one child, τ leafs in a $\rightarrow$ or $\wedge$ construct, non-first τ's in an $\vee$ construct and $\circlearrowleft$'s consisting of one $\circlearrowleft$ as a child and two τ's as other children.

Each of the four metrics is computed on a scale from 0 to 1, where 1 is optimal. Replay fitness, simplicity and precision can reach 1 as optimal value. Generalization can only reach 1 in the limit, i.e., the more frequent nodes are visited, the closer the value gets to 1.

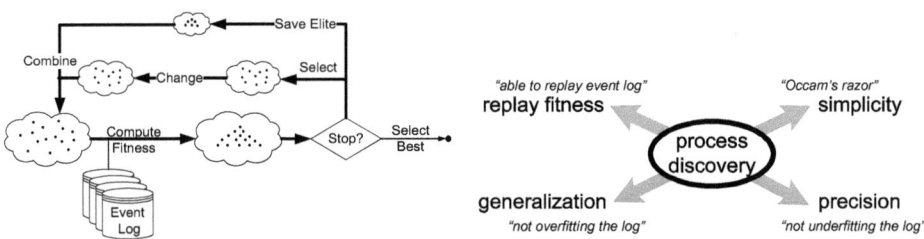

Fig. 2. The phases of the genetic algorithm

Fig. 3. Quality dimensions for Discovery [1, 2]

3.3 Configuring Process Trees

In this paper, we extend process trees [5] with configuration options. A node in a process tree can be not configured, blocked, hidden or 'downgraded' for each of the input event logs. The blocking and hiding operations are as specified in existing configuration languages [8, 16, 17] (see Section 2) and either *block* a path of execution or *hide* a part of the process. However, we add the configuration option that operators can be *downgraded*. By downgrading an operator, the behavior of the operator is restricted to a subset of the initially possible behavior. The $\circlearrowleft$ operator for instance can be downgraded to a $\rightarrow$. This is done by removing the 'redo' part of the $\circlearrowleft$ operator and putting the 'do' and 'exit' children of the loop in a sequence.

Another operator that can be downgraded is the $\vee$ operator which can be downgraded to an $\wedge$ (forcing all children to be executed), $\times$ (only allowing for one child to be executed), and a $\rightarrow$ (executing all its children in a particular order). However, since in one configuration the order of the children might be different than in another, we also added the $\leftarrow$ operator, representing a *reversed sequence*, which simply executes the children in the reversed order, i.e. from right to left. Finally, also the $\wedge$ can be downgraded to an $\rightarrow$ or $\leftarrow$ operator.

The *quality of the configuration perspective* should also be incorporated in the fitness function of the ETM-algorithm. This is partly done by applying the configuration options on the overall (i.e. configurable) process tree before evaluating the main four quality dimensions. For instance, when an activity that is not present in an event log is hidden from the process tree, this is reflected by replay fitness. The four quality dimensions are calculated for each individual event log and then a weighted average is calculated using the size of each event log. However, as part of the quality of the configuration, the number of nodes that have a configuration option set should be considered (otherwise all nodes can be made configurable without any penalty). Therefore, we add a new quality dimension for configuration that simply measures the fraction of nodes in the process tree for which no configuration option exist. The other four quality dimensions are more important than the configuration fitness, but if a configurable process tree exists with fewer configuration options and the same quality in the other dimensions, then the latter process tree is preferred.

4 Running Example

Our running example [7] is based on four variants of the same process describing a simple loan application process of a financial institute, providing small consumer credit through a webpage. The four BPMN process models describing the variants are shown in Figure 4. The event logs that were obtained through simulation are shown in 1.

In the *first variant* the process works as follows: when a potential customer fills in a form and submits the request on the website, the process is started by activity A which is sending an e-mail to the applicant to confirm the receipt of the request. Next, three activities are executed in parallel. Activity B is a check of the customer's credit history with a registration agency. Activity C is a computation of the customer's loan capacity and activity D is a check whether the customer is already in the system. This check is

Table 1. Four event logs for the four different variants of the loan application process of Figure 4

Trace	#
A B C D E G	6
A B C D F G	38
A B D C E G	12
A B D C F G	26
A B C F G	8
A C B E G	1

(a) Event log for variant 1

Trace	#
A D C B F G	4
A C D B F G	2
A D B C F G	1
A D B C E G	1
A C B F G	1

Trace	#
A B1 B2 C D2 E G	20
A B1 B2 C D2 F G	50

(b) Event log for variant 2

Trace	#
A C B E	120
A C B F	80

(c) Event log for variant 3

Trace	#
A B1 D B2 C E	45
A B1 D2 B2 C F	60

(d) Event log for variant 4

skipped if the customer filled in the application while being logged in to the personal page, since then it is obsolete. After performing some computations, a decision is made and communicated to the client. The loan is accepted (activity E, covering about 20% of the cases) or rejected (activity F, covering about 80% of the cases). Finally, activity G (archiving the request) is performed.

The second loan application variant is simpler than the first process. Most notable is the absence of parallelism. Furthermore, activity B has been split into the activities B1 (send credit history request to registration agency) and B2 (process response of registration agency). Activity D of the original process has been replaced by D2 which is checking the paper archive.

The third variant of the loan application process is even simpler where after sending the confirmation of receipt (activity A) the capacity is calculated (activity C) and the credit is checked (activity B). Then the decision is made to accept (activity E) or reject (activity F) the application. The application is not archived; hence no activity G is performed.

In the fourth and final variant of this process, after sending the confirmation of receipt (activity A), the request for the credit history is sent to the agency (activity B1). Then either the system archive (activity D) or paper archive (activity D2) is checked. Next the response of the credit history check is processed (activity B2) and next the capacity is

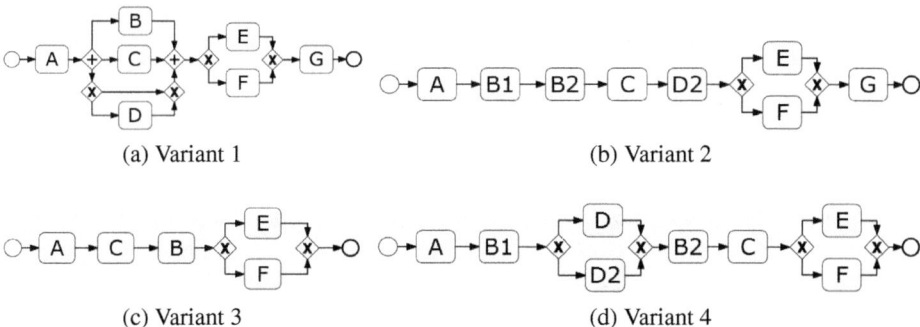

Fig. 4. Four variants of a loan application process. (A = send e-mail, B = check credit, B1 = send check credit request, B2 = process check credit request response, C = calculate capacity, D = check system, D2 = check paper archive, E = accept, F = reject, G = send e-mail).

calculated (activity C). Then the decision is made to accept (activity E) or reject (activity F) the application. The application is not archived (i.e., no activity G in model).

Although the four variations of the loan application process seem similar, automatically discovering a configurable process model is far from trivial.

4.1 Experimental Setup

In the remainder of this section we use the ETM algorithm as our discovery technique to construct a process model, in the form of a process tree, from an event log. We ran the experiments for 20, 000 generations on each individual event log for approaches 1 and 2. Because in approaches 3 and 4 we consider all four event logs at once, we increased the number of generations to 80, 000 to get a stable result. Each generation contained a population of 20 trees out of which the best six were kept unchanged between generations, i.e. the elite. The quality dimensions of replay fitness and simplicity were given a weight of ten, since we want a small process model with a good relation to the event log. A weight of five for precision makes sure the model does not allow for too much additional behavior and a weight of one-tenth for generalization makes the models more general.

4.2 Approach 1: Merge Individually Discovered Process Models

The results of applying the first approach on the running example are shown in Figure 5. Each of the individual process models (see Figures 5a through 5d) clearly resemble each of the individual event logs. The combined configurable process model however is nothing more than a choice between each of the individual input process models. In this configurable process model those nodes that are configured have a grey 'callout' added, indicating for each configuration whether that node is not configured ('-'), hidden ('H') or blocked ('B'). The table shown in Figure 5f shows the different quality scores for both the configurable process models as well as for each of the configurations. Moreover, the simplicity statistics of size, number of configuration points (#C.P.) and similarity of the configured process model w.r.t. the configurable process model is shown. The fact that the four configuration options block a big part of the process model is reflected in the low similarity of the configured process models with the configurable process model. This is also shown by the relatively large size of the process tree.

4.3 Approach 2: Merge Similar Discovered Process Models

In the second approach we try to increase similarity by discovering a common process model from all event logs combined, of which the result is shown in Figure 6a. This process model has difficulties to describe the combined behavior of the four variants. The four individual process models derived from this common process model are shown in Figures 6b through 6e. Each individual process model has a high similarity with the common process model, while some changes are made to improve the overall fitness for that particular event log. For the first three variants the discovered process models are identical to the one of approach 1. The process of the fourth variant however differs too much from the common model, hence the similar process model is not as good as the one found in approach 1. The combined process tree is shown in Figure 6f. Despite the

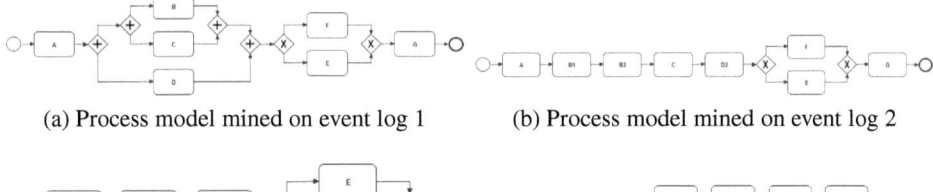

(a) Process model mined on event log 1

(b) Process model mined on event log 2

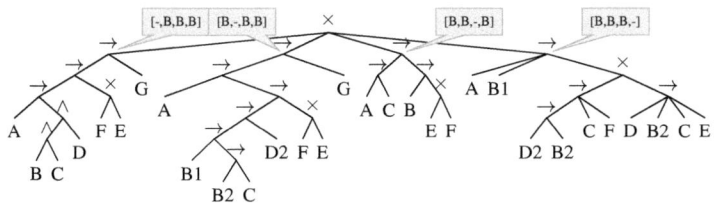

(c) Process model mined on event log 3

(d) Process model mined on event log 4

(e) Configurable process model obtained after merging models (a) through (d)

	Overall	Fitness	Precision	Simplicity	Generalization	Size	#C.P.	Similarity
Combined	0.989	0.999	0.999	0.981	0.220	53	4	-
Variant 0	0.986	0.995	0.995	0.981	0.235	14	3	0.418
Variant 1	0.989	1.000	1.000	0.981	0.263	16	3	0.464
Variant 2	0.989	1.000	1.000	0.981	0.174	10	3	0.317
Variant 3	0.989	1.000	1.000	0.981	0.264	16	3	0.464

(f) Quality statistics of the configurable process model of (e)

Fig. 5. Results of merging seperate discovered process models on the running example

similarity of the individual process models, the combined configurable process model is still a choice of the four input process models. The overall fitness of this model is slightly worse than that of approach 1, mainly due to the process model of variant 4. Similar to the previous approach, the number of configuration points is low. Unfortunately, also the similarity between the configured process model and the configurable process model is low.

4.4 Approach 3: First Discover a Single Process Model Then Discover Configurations

The resulting configurable process model is shown in Figure 7. From this model it can be seen that we relaxed the precision weight, in order to discover an 'overly fitting' process model. Then, by applying configurations, the behavior is restricted in such a way that the model precisely describes each of the variants, as is indicated by the perfect replay fitness. This process model also scores relatively high for precision and simplicity. The process tree however has a similar large size as the two previous approaches. Nonetheless, the similarity of each of the individual process models to the configurable

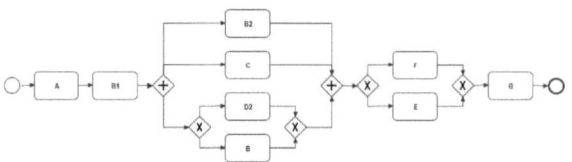

(a) Process model discovered from combined event log

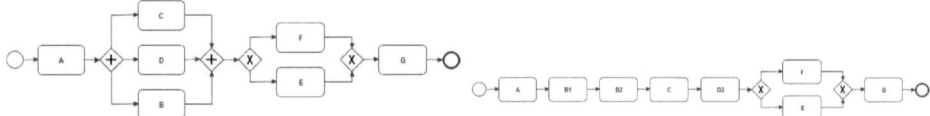

(b) Process model individualized for event log 1 (c) Process model individualized for event log 2

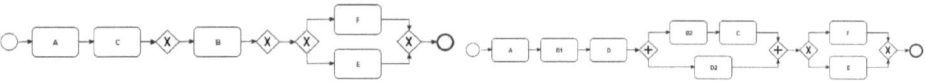

(d) Process model individualized for event log 3 (e) Process model individualized for event log 4

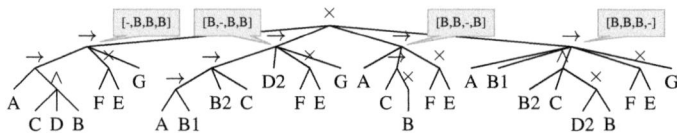

(f) Configurable process model obtained after merging models (b) through (e)

	Overall	Fitness	Precision	Simplicity	Generalization	Size	#C.P.	Similarity
Combined	0.958	0.974	0.921	0.968	0.212	46	4	-
Variant 0	0.981	0.995	0.995	0.968	0.232	12	3	0.414
Variant 1	0.984	1.000	1.000	0.968	0.246	13	3	0.441
Variant 2	0.984	1.000	1.000	0.968	0.180	10	3	0.357
Variant 3	0.869	0.886	0.649	0.968	0.232	14	3	0.467

(g) Quality statistics of the configurable process model of (f)

Fig. 6. Results of merging the similar process models on the running example

process model is higher than in the previous two approaches since only small parts are configured.

4.5 Approach 4: Discover Process Model and Configurations at the Same Time

The result of applying the fourth, integrated approach is shown in Figure 8. This process model is smaller and therefore simpler than previous models, a result of the weight of ten for the simplicity dimension. Moreover, it clearly includes the common parts of all variants only once, e.g. always start with A and end with a choice between E and F, sometimes followed by G. This process model correctly hides activities that do not occur in certain variants, for instance G for variants 3 and 4 and the B, B1 and B2 activities. Moreover, it correctly discovered the parallelism present in variant one, where the other variants are configured to be sequential. As a trade-off, it did not include activity D2, which is the least occurring activity in the event logs, and occurs in different locations in the process.

The discovered configurable process model can be further improved by increasing the replay fitness, making sure that all behavior can be replayed. This results in the configurable process model as shown in 9. This process model is able to replay all behavior, something that only was achieved in the two-phase mining approach. However, this results in a process model with a lot of ↻ and ∨ constructs, which are then blocked for particular configurations. Moreover, the resulting process model is rather large, contains many configuration points and has mediocre similarity scores. This is a clear trade-off of aiming for a higher replay fitness value. However, the two-phase approach produced a better model with perfect replay fitness.

4.6 Comparison of the Four Approaches

The results of applying the four different approaches on the running example are very different. All discovered models have similar scores for replay fitness and precision and there are (almost) no useless nodes. However, there are noticeable differences in generalization, size and similarity between the configurable and the configured models. The first two approaches score relatively poor on generalization, because the merge operator used introduces specific submodels for each log, which limits the number of visits per node during replay. Also, due to duplication, the models are significantly larger, and because in the configuration large parts are blocked, the configured models are dissimilar to the configurable one. Mining a process model and then mining configurations improves the similarity, but still the configurable model remains larger than necessary. Furthermore, the number of configuration points is very high. However, it is easier to aim for higher replay fitness values The final approach, where the configurations are

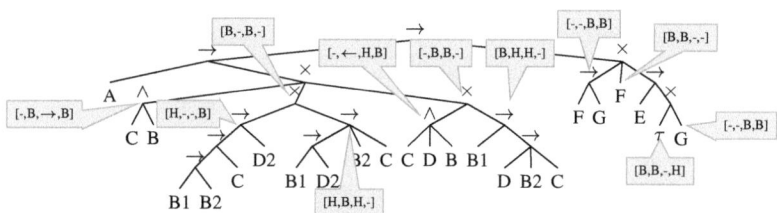

(a) Configurable process model discovered using the two-phase approach

	Overall	Fitness	Precision	Simplicity	Generalization	Size	#C.P.	Similarity
Combined	0.988	1.000	0.981	0.986	0.374	42	11	-
Variant 0	0.990	1.000	0.990	0.986	0.400	20	6	0.645
Variant 1	0.992	1.000	1.000	0.986	0.408	20	7	0.645
Variant 2	0.992	1.000	1.000	0.986	0.285	13	8	0.473
Variant 3	0.977	1.000	0.922	0.986	0.496	24	6	0.727

(b) Quality statistics of the configurable process model of (a)

Fig. 7. Results of the two-phase mining approach on the running example

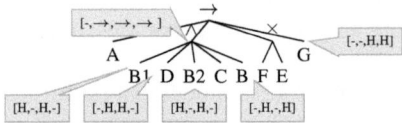

(a) Configurable process model discovered using the integrated discovery approach

	Overall	Fitness	Precision	Simplicity	Generalization	Size	#C.P.	Similarity
Combined	0.983	0.962	0.999	1.000	0.684	12	6	-
Variant 0	0.996	0.995	0.994	1.000	0.738	10	2	0.909
Variant 1	0.957	0.894	1.000	1.000	0.723	10	3	0.909
Variant 2	0.998	1.000	1.000	1.000	0.614	8	5	0.800
Variant 3	0.961	0.905	1.000	1.000	0.741	10	3	0.909

(b) Quality statistics of the configurable process model of (a)

Fig. 8. Results of the integrated mining approach on the running example

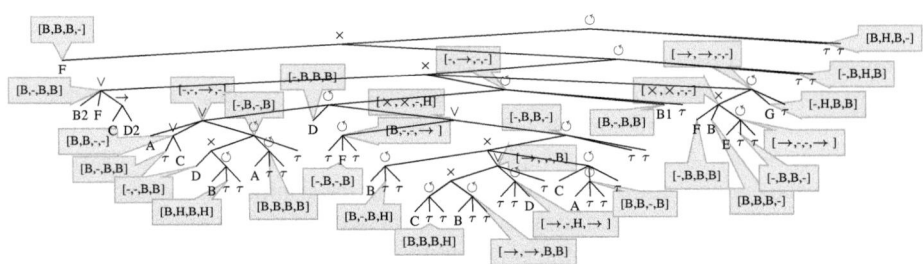

(a) Configurable process model discovered with more weight on replay fitness

	Overall	Fitness	Precision	Simplicity	Generalization	Size	#C.P.	Similarity
Combined	0.980	1.000	0.767	0.993	0.345	82	31	-
Variant 0	0.985	1.000	0.826	0.993	0.534	54	20	0.794
Variant 1	0.974	1.000	0.696	0.993	0.306	30	21	0.527
Variant 2	0.986	1.000	0.850	0.993	0.349	31	20	0.549
Variant 3	0.973	1.000	0.680	0.993	0.261	24	21	0.453

(b) Quality statistics of the configurable process model of (a)

Fig. 9. Result of the integrated mining approach when improving replay fitness

discovered simultaneously with the configurable model reduces the size significantly, thus improving the similarity score. However, this comes at a minor cost of replay fitness.

The first two approaches seem to struggle with merging process models based on their behavior. Because they only focus on the structure of the model, the frequencies of parts of the process model being visited are not considered during the merge. The third and fourth approach both directly consider the behavior and frequencies as recorded in the event log. This seems to be beneficial for building a configurable process model since these latter two approaches outperform the first two. In the next section we apply all four approaches on a collection of real-life event logs to validate these findings.

Table 2. Case study event log statistics

	#traces	#events	#activities
Combined	1214	2142	28
L1	54	131	15
L2	302	586	13
L3	37	73	9
L4	340	507	9
L5	481	845	23

Table 3. Statistics of merging the separate process models on the case study event logs

	Overall	Fitness	Precision	Simplicity	Generalization	Size	#C.P.	Similarity
Combined	0.979	0.973	0.962	0.997	0.560	1555	5	-
Variant 0	0.977	0.977	0.949	0.996	0.362	581	4	0.544
Variant 1	0.973	0.967	0.944	0.998	0.617	201	4	0.229
Variant 2	0.991	1.000	0.993	0.988	0.234	72	4	0.089
Variant 3	0.984	0.978	0.974	0.998	0.690	455	4	0.453
Variant 4	0.978	0.971	0.964	0.997	0.480	250	4	0.277

5 Case Study

To validate our findings we use a collection of five event logs from the CoSeLoG project[1], each describing a different process variant. The main statistics of the event logs are shown in Table 2. The event logs were extracted from the IT systems of five different municipalities. The process considered deals with objections related to building permits.

The result of both the first (individually discovered process models that are then merged) and the second approach (making sure the models are similar) result in process trees with more than 200 or even 1,500 nodes. Both process models however again consist of an × operator as the root with each of the five original models as its children that are then blocked, similar to the running example results. We therefore only show the statistics in Table 3 and 4 since the process models are unreadable.

The third approach, where the ETM-algorithm first discovers a common process model that is not very precise, and then applies configuration options, results in the process tree as shown in Fig. 10a. The statistics for this process model are shown in Table 10b. This process tree is rather compact and has reasonable scores for replay fitness, precision and simplicity.

The fourth approach, where the control flow and configuration points are discovered simultaneously, results in the process tree as shown in Fig. 11a. The statistics are shown in Table 11b. With only 4 configuration points, and similar quality scores as the previous result, this process tree is even smaller and hence simpler.

The application of the different approaches on the real-life event logs show similar results as on the running example. The first two approaches seem to have difficulties in merging the process models based on the behavior of the process model.

---

[1] More information can be found at http://www.win.tue.nl/coselog/wiki/start

Table 4. Statistics of merging the similar process models on the case study event logs

	Overall	Fitness	Precision	Simplicity	Generalization	Size	#C.P.	Similarity
Combined	0.980	0.989	0.936	0.998	0.540	236	5	-
Variant 0	0.973	0.992	0.894	0.999	0.337	65	4	0.432
Variant 1	0.977	0.969	0.958	0.998	0.598	34	4	0.252
Variant 2	0.966	0.991	0.863	0.998	0.533	24	4	0.185
Variant 3	0.991	0.999	0.968	0.999	0.461	48	4	0.338
Variant 4	0.977	0.994	0.909	0.998	0.582	69	4	0.452

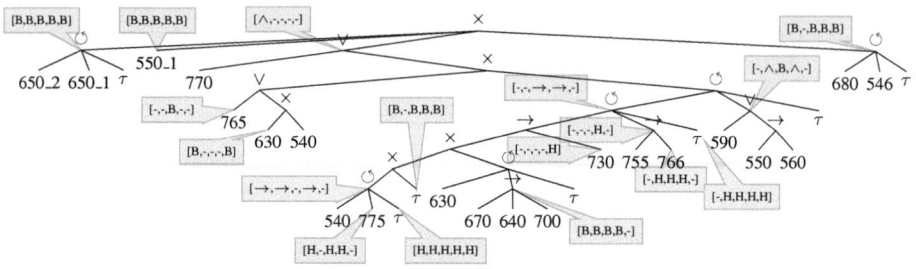

(a) Results of the two-phase mining approach

	Overall	Fitness	Precision	Simplicity	Generalization	Size	#C.P.	Similarity
Combined	0.973	0.965	0.951	0.999	0.451	46	17	-
Variant 0	0.947	0.943	0.862	0.999	0.319	31	10	0.792
Variant 1	0.979	0.968	0.971	0.999	0.452	36	8	0.878
Variant 2	0.961	0.932	0.958	0.999	0.267	25	12	0.690
Variant 3	0.980	0.990	0.934	0.999	0.390	30	13	0.763
Variant 4	0.970	0.950	0.961	0.999	0.522	34	8	0.850

(b) Statistics of the two-phase mining result

Fig. 10. Results of the two-phase mining approach on the real-life event logs

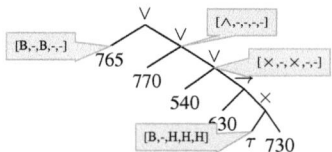

(a) Result of the integrated mining approach

	Overall	Fitness	Precision	Simplicity	Generalization	Size	#C.P.	Similarity
Combined	0.966	0.952	0.929	1.000	0.839	11	4	-
Variant 0	0.945	0.866	1.000	1.000	0.622	9	4	0.900
Variant 1	0.970	0.958	0.935	1.000	0.861	11	0	1.000
Variant 2	0.955	0.920	0.942	1.000	0.651	10	3	0.952
Variant 3	0.974	0.975	0.923	1.000	0.845	11	1	1.000
Variant 4	0.962	0.945	0.921	1.000	0.860	11	1	1.000

(b) Statistics result

Fig. 11. Results of the integrated mining approach on the real-life event logs

6 Conclusion

In this paper we presented and compared four approaches to construct a *configurable* process model from a *collection* of event logs. We applied all four approaches on both a running example and a real-life collection of event logs. Our results show that the naive approach of first discovering a process model for each event log separately and then merging the discovered models yields large configurable models to which the individual configurations are not very similar. It is slightly better to first discover a process model on the combination of the event logs and then configure this model for each log. However, both of these approaches struggle with merging the modeled behavior of the input process models into a configurable process model. The other two approaches that directly discover a configurable process model from the event log seem to be able to use the recorded behavior to better generalize the behavior into a configurable process model. The approach where both the control flow and the configuration options are changed together seems to have more flexibility than the approach where first a control flow is discovered which is then configured.

Using the results presented in this paper we can improve model merging techniques by considering the actual intended behavior instead of the process model structure. We also plan to develop more sophisticated techniques for the ETM-algorithm to directly mine configurable models from collections of event logs. For example, we plan to add configuration-specific mutation operators and learn good parameter settings (using large collections of real-life event logs from the CoSeLoG project). Moreover, we plan to consider other perspectives (e.g., data-, resource- and time-related aspects) and further develop the new area of cross-organizational mining [6]. The ultimate goal is to support organizations in selecting a suitable configuration based on their recorded behavior.

References

1. van der Aalst, W.M.P.: Process Mining: Discovery, Conformance and Enhancement of Business Processes. Springer (2011)
2. van der Aalst, W.M.P., Adriansyah, A., van Dongen, B.: Replaying History on Process Models for Conformance Checking and Performance Analysis. WIREs Data Mining and Knowledge Discovery 2(2), 182–192 (2012)
3. Adriansyah, A., van Dongen, B., van der Aalst, W.M.P.: Conformance Checking using Cost-Based Fitness Analysis. In: Proceedings of EDOC, pp. 55–64. IEEE Computer Society (2011)
4. Becker, J., Delfmann, P., Dreiling, A., Knackstedt, R., Kuropka, D.: Configurative Process Modeling–Outlining an Approach to increased Business Process Model Usability. In: Proceedings of the 15th IRMA International Conference (2004)
5. Buijs, J.C.A.M., van Dongen, B.F., van der Aalst, W.M.P.: On the Role of Fitness, Precision, Generalization and Simplicity in Process Discovery. In: Meersman, R., Panetto, H., Dillon, T., Rinderle-Ma, S., Dadam, P., Zhou, X., Pearson, S., Ferscha, A., Bergamaschi, S., Cruz, I.F. (eds.) OTM 2012, Part I. LNCS, vol. 7565, pp. 305–322. Springer, Heidelberg (2012)
6. Buijs, J.C.A.M., van Dongen, B.F., van der Aalst, W.M.P.: Towards Cross-Organizational Process Mining in Collections of Process Models and their Executions. In: Daniel, F., Barkaoui, K., Dustdar, S. (eds.) BPM Workshops 2011, Part II. LNBIP, vol. 100, pp. 2–13. Springer, Heidelberg (2012)

7. Buijs, J.C.A.M., La Rosa, M., Reijers, H.A., Dongen, B.F., van der Aalst, W.M.P.: Improving Business Process Models using Observed Behavior. In: Proceedings of the Second International Symposium on Data-Driven Process Discovery and Analysis. LNBIP, Springer (to appear, 2013)
8. Gottschalk, F., van der Aalst, W.M.P., Jansen-Vullers, M.H., La Rosa, M.: Configurable Workflow Models. International Journal of Cooperative Information Systems (IJCIS) 17(2) (2008)
9. Gottschalk, F., van der Aalst, W.M.P., Jansen-Vullers, M.H.: Merging Event-driven Process Chains. In: Meersman, R., Tari, Z. (eds.) OTM 2008, Part I. LNCS, vol. 5331, pp. 418–426. Springer, Heidelberg (2008)
10. Gottschalk, F., van der Aalst, W.M.P., Jansen-Vullers, M.H.: Mining Reference Process Models and their Configurations. In: Meersman, R., Tari, Z., Herrero, P. (eds.) OTM-WS 2008. LNCS, vol. 5333, pp. 263–272. Springer, Heidelberg (2008)
11. Hallerbach, A., Bauer, T., Reichert, M.: Capturing Variability in Business Process Models: The Provop Approach. Journal of Software Maintenance 22(6-7), 519–546 (2010)
12. La Rosa, M., Dumas, M., Uba, R., Dijkman, R.: Business Process Model Merging: An Approach to Business Process Consolidation. ACM Transactions on Software Engineering and Methodology 22(2) (2012)
13. Li, C., Reichert, M., Wombacher, A.: The MINADEPT Clustering Approach for Discovering Reference Process Models Out of Process Variants. International Journal of Cooperative Information Systems 19(3-4), 159–203 (2010)
14. Mendling, J., Verbeek, H.M.W., van Dongen, B.F., van der Aalst, W.M.P., Neumann, G.: Detection and Prediction of Errors in EPCs of the SAP Reference Model. Data and Knowledge Engineering 64(1), 312–329 (2008)
15. La Rosa, M., Gottschalk, F., Dumas, M., van der Aalst, W.M.P.: Linking Domain Models and Process Models for Reference Model Configuration. In: Becker, J., Delfmann, P. (eds.) Informal Proceedings of the 10th International Workshop on Reference Modeling (RefMod 2007), pp. 13–24. QUT, Brisbane (2007)
16. Rosemann, M., van der Aalst, W.M.P.: A Configurable Reference Modeling Language. Information Systems 32(1), 1–23 (2007)
17. Schunselaar, D.M.M., Verbeek, E., van der Aalst, W.M.P., Raijers, H.A.: Creating Sound and Reversible Configurable Process Models Using CoSeNets. In: Abramowicz, W., Kriksciuniene, D., Sakalauskas, V. (eds.) BIS 2012. LNBIP, vol. 117, pp. 24–35. Springer, Heidelberg (2012)
18. Verbeek, H.M.W., Buijs, J.C.A.M., van Dongen, B.F., van der Aalst, W.M.P.: XES, XESame, and ProM 6. In: Soffer, P., Proper, E. (eds.) CAiSE Forum 2010. LNBIP, vol. 72, pp. 60–75. Springer, Heidelberg (2011)

Slice, Mine and Dice: Complexity-Aware Automated Discovery of Business Process Models

Chathura C. Ekanayake[1], Marlon Dumas[2], Luciano García-Bañuelos[2], and Marcello La Rosa[1]

[1] Queensland University of Technology, Australia
{c.ekanayake,m.larosa}@qut.edu.au
[2] University of Tartu, Estonia
{marlon.dumas,luciano.garcia}@ut.ee

Abstract. Automated process discovery techniques aim at extracting models from information system logs in order to shed light into the business processes supported by these systems. Existing techniques in this space are effective when applied to relatively small or regular logs, but otherwise generate large and spaghetti-like models. In previous work, trace clustering has been applied in an attempt to reduce the size and complexity of automatically discovered process models. The idea is to split the log into clusters and to discover one model per cluster. The result is a collection of process models – each one representing a variant of the business process – as opposed to an all-encompassing model. Still, models produced in this way may exhibit unacceptably high complexity. In this setting, this paper presents a two-way divide-and-conquer process discovery technique, wherein the discovered process models are split on the one hand by variants and on the other hand hierarchically by means of subprocess extraction. The proposed technique allows users to set a desired bound for the complexity of the produced models. Experiments on real-life logs show that the technique produces collections of models that are up to 64% smaller than those extracted under the same complexity bounds by applying existing trace clustering techniques.

1 Introduction

Process mining is concerned with the extraction of knowledge about business processes from information system logs [17]. Process mining encompasses a vast array of techniques, including techniques for automated discovery of business process models. Numerous algorithms for automated process discovery have been developed, which strike various tradeoffs between accuracy and comprehensibility of the discovered models.

One key limitation of the bulk of techniques for automated process discovery is that they fail to scale to processes with high levels of variance, i.e. high number of distinct traces. This is mainly because traditional process discovery techniques aim at producing a single model covering all traces in the log, leading to large and spaghetti-like models as the variance increases. A common divide-and-conquer approach to address this issue is by means of trace clustering [2,4,9,15]. The idea is to slice the log into separate clusters, each one grouping similar traces, and to discover (via standard mining techniques) one process model per cluster. Accordingly, the output is a collection of process models, each covering a subset of the traces, as opposed to a single model encompassing all traces. The underlying assumption is that each model in this collection has lower complexity than a single all-encompassing model mined from all traces. In this context, complexity can be measured in terms of size (number of nodes or edges) or in terms of structural complexity metrics such as control-flow complexity or average connector degree, which have been shown to be correlated with model comprehensibility [11,13].

While process discovery techniques based on trace clustering produce smaller individual models than single-model techniques, they do not seek to minimize the overall size of the discovered collection of models. On the contrary, these techniques generally yield models that share duplicate fragments. This duplication entails that collectively, a set of models produced via trace clustering can be much larger and not necessarily easier to comprehend as a whole than a single model mined from all traces.

In this setting, this paper presents a two-way divide-and-conquer process discovery technique, wherein discovered process models are split on the one hand by variants via trace clustering (an operation we term "slicing"), but also hierarchically via shared subprocess extraction and merging ("dicing"). Slicing enables high-complexity mined models to be split into lower-complexity ones at the expense of duplication. Dicing, on the other hand, reduces duplication by refactoring shared fragments. By slicing, mining and dicing recursively, the technique attempts in a best-effort way to produce a collection of models each with size or structural complexity below a user-specified threshold, while minimizing the overall size of the discovered collection of models and without affecting accuracy. The technique is termed SMD (Slice, Mine and Dice) in reference to the steps performed at each level of the recursion.

SMD can be applied as a post-processing phase on top of any automated discovery technique based on (hierarchical) trace clustering. The paper reports on experiments using three real-life logs that put into evidence the improvements achieved by SMD on top of three existing trace clustering methods.

The rest of the paper is structured as follows. Section 2 provides an overview of related work on process mining and trace clustering, and introduces techniques for clone detection and process model merging, upon which SMD builds. Next, Section 3 presents and illustrates the algorithms behind SMD. Section 4 discusses the experimental setup and results, and Section 5 draws conclusions and spells out directions for future work.

2 Background and Related Work

SMD builds upon techniques for: (i) automated process discovery; (ii) hierarchical trace clustering; (iii) clone detection in process models; and (iv) process model merging. This section introduces these techniques in turn and discusses how they are used by SMD.

2.1 Automated Process Discovery Techniques

Numerous techniques for discovering a single (flat) process model from a process execution log have been proposed in the literature [17,21]. For example, Weijters et al. [22] propose the *Heuristics Miner*, which is based on an analysis of the frequency of dependencies between events in a log. In essence, frequency data is extracted from the log and used to construct a graph of events, where edges are added based on different heuristics. Types of splits and joins in the resulting event graph can be determined by analyzing the frequency of events associated to those splits and joins. This information can be used to convert the output of the Heuristics Miner into a Petri net. The Heuristics Miner is robust to noise in the event logs due to the use of frequency-based thresholds, which makes it suitable for use with real-life event logs. Meantime, van der Werf et al. [18] proposed a discovery method where relations observed in the logs are translated to an Integer Linear Programming (ILP) problem. The ILP miner is independent of the number of events in the log, making it applicable in practical scenarios.

Process discovery techniques can be evaluated along four dimensions: fitness (recall), appropriateness (precision), generalization and complexity [17]. Fitness measures the extent to which the traces in a log can be parsed by the discovered model. Appropriateness is a measure of additional behavior allowed by a discovered model, that is not found in the log. A model with low appropriateness is one that can parse a proportionally large number of traces that are not in the log from which the model is discovered. Generalization captures how well the discovered model generalizes the behavior found in a log. For example, if a model can be discovered using 90% of the traces of the log and this model can parse the remaining 10% of traces in the logs, it can be said the model generalizes well the log. The complexity of a model can be measured using several metrics proposed in the literature [11]. A simple complexity metric is the size the model, measured by the total number of nodes in the model (or alternatively number of edges). Empirical studies, e.g. [11], have shown that process model size is strongly correlated with model comprehensibility and error probability. Other (structural) complexity metrics correlated with comprehensibility include:

- CFC (Control-Flow Complexity): sum of all connectors weighted by their potential combinations of states after a split.
- ACD (Average Connector Degree): average number of nodes a connector is connected to.
- CNC (Coefficient of Network Connectivity): ratio between arcs and nodes.
- Density: ratio between the number of arcs and the maximum possible number of arcs for the same number of nodes.

An extensive empirical evaluation [21] of automated process discovery techniques has shown that Heuristics Miner offers a good tradeoff between precision and recall with satisfactory performance. The ILP miner achieves high recall – at the expense of some penalty on precision – but it does not scale to larger logs due to memory requirements. The SMD technique presented in this paper abstracts from the mining algorithm used to extract a model from a collection of traces. However, due to its scalability, we specifically use the Heuristics Miner as a basis for the evaluation of SMD.

2.2 Hierarchical Trace Clustering

Several approaches to trace clustering have been proposed [1, 2, 4, 9, 15, 16, 20]. Some of these techniques produce a flat collection of trace clusters, e.g. [20], though most produce hierarchical collections of trace clusters from which models can be mined. Specifically, hierarchical trace clustering methods construct a so-called *dendrogram*. The dendrogram is a tree wherein the root corresponds to the entire log. The root is decomposed into N (typically 2) disjoint trace clusters of smaller size, each of which is split again into N clusters and so on recursively.

A trace cluster is a set of "similar" traces. The notion of trace similarity varies between approaches and is generally defined with respect to a feature space. For instance, if traces are seen as strings on the alphabet consisting of the set of activity labels, the feature space corresponds to the set of all possible permutations of activity labels. With such a feature space, similarity of traces can be assessed by means of standard string similarity functions, such as Hamming distance or Levenshtein edit distance. However, mappings to other feature spaces have been used in the literature, such as the count of occurrences of activities, the count of motifs over such activities (e.g. n-grams), etc.

In addition to differing by the choice of similarity notion, trace clustering techniques also differ in terms of the underlying clustering technique. Hierarchical clustering techniques can be divided in two families: agglomerative and divisive clustering. In agglomerative clustering, pairs of clusters are aggregated according to their proximity following a bottom-up approach. In divisive clustering, a top-level cluster is divided into a number of sub-clusters and so on recursively until a stop condition is fulfilled.

The techniques of Song et al. [15, 16] and Bose et al. [1, 2] both use agglomerative hierarchical clustering. Song et al. also consider other clustering techniques, such as k-means and self-organizing maps. The main difference between the approaches of Song et al. and Bose et al. lie in the underlying feature space. Song et al. map traces into a set of features such as count of occurrences of individual activities, or count of occurrences of pairs of activities in immediate succession. On the other hand, Bose et al. evaluate the occurrence of more complex motifs such as repeats (i.e., n-grams observed at different points in the trace). Meanwhile, the DWS method of Medeiros et al. [4, 9] adopts divisive hierarchical clustering with k-means for implementing each division step. They use a similarity measure based on the count of occurrences of n-grams.

The above techniques produce a collection of models by applying single-model process mining techniques (e.g. Heuristics Miner) to each cluster at the lowest level of the dendrogram. Thus, the output is a flat collection of models of different levels of complexity. Accordingly, SMD does not take as input the collection of models produced by these techniques, but instead it takes the dendrogram. The dendrogram is traversed top-down to extract models at the required level of complexity.

To the best of our knowledge only two methods have been proposed aimed at mining hierarchies of process models. Bose et al. [3] presents a method that mines a single root process and a set of subprocesses that correspond to the factorization of motifs observed in the traces (a.k.a. conserved patterns). The method is hence intended to work on a single process model and not on a collection thereof. Meanwhile, Greco et al. [8, 9] use trace clustering to mine hierarchies of process models. In these hierarchies, the models associated to leaf nodes correspond to "concrete" models. In contrast, the models associated to inner nodes correspond to generalizations, resulting from the abstraction of multiple activities observed in models of descendant nodes. Thus the end result is a generalization-specialization hierarchy of models. In contrast, SMD aims at producing a collection of process models with (shared) sub-processes, thus the relation between lower-level and higher-level models is a part-of relation.

2.3 Clone Detection in Process Models

SMD relies on techniques for detecting duplicate fragments (a.k.a. clones) in process models. The idea is that these clones will be refactored into shared subprocess models in order to reduce the overall size and possibly also the complexity of discovered process models. Given that subprocess models must have a clear start point and a clear end point[1] we are interested in extracting single-entry, single-exit (SESE) fragments. Accordingly, SMD makes use of a clone detection technique based on a decomposition of process models into a tree representing all SESE fragments in the model, namely the Refined Process Structure Tree (RPST) [19]. Each node in an RPST corresponds to a SESE fragment in the underlying process model. The root node corresponds to the entire process model. The child nodes of a node N correspond to the SESE fragments that are contained directly under N. In other words, the parent-child relation in the RPST corresponds to the containment relation between SESE fragments. A key characteristic of the RPST is that it can be constructed for any model captured in a graph-oriented process modeling notation (e.g. BPMN or EPC).

For the purpose of exact clone detection, we make use of the RPSDAG index structure [6]. Conceptually, an RPSDAG of a collection of models is the union of the RPSTs of the models in the collection. Hence, a node in the RPSDAG corresponds to a SESE fragment whereas edges encode the containment relation between SESE fragments. Importantly, each fragment appears only once in the RPSDAG. If a SESE fragment appears multiple times in the collection of process models (i.e. it is a clone), it will have multiple parent fragments in the RPSDAG. This feature allows us to efficiently identify duplicate clones: a duplicate clone is simply a fragment with multiple parents.

In addition to allowing us to identify exact clones, the RPSDAG provides a basis for approximate clone detection [7]. Approximate clone detection is achieved by applying clustering techniques on the collection of SESE fragments of an RPSDAG, using one minus the graph-edit distance as the similarity measure (as defined in [5]). Two clustering techniques for approximate clone detection based on this principle are presented in [7]. The first is an adaptation of the Density-Based Spatial Clustering of Applications with Noise (DBSCAN) algorithm, the second is an adaptation of the Hierarchical Agglomerative Clustering (HAC) algorithm. Both of these techniques take as input a collection of process models and return a set of approximate clone clusters – each cluster representing a set of SESE fragments that are similar within a certain similarity threshold. To evaluate SMD, we adopted the DBSCAN approach to approximate clone clustering due to it being more scalable.

2.4 Process Model Merging

Approximate clone detection allows us to identify clusters of similar SESE fragments in a collection of process models. Having done so, we can replace each of the identified approximate clones with references to a single subprocess model representing the union of these similar fragments, so as to reduce the overall size of the collection of process

---

[1] Note that top-level process models may have multiple start and end events, but subprocess models must have a single start and end event in order to comply with the call-and-return semantics of subprocess invocation.

models. It can be argued that this single subprocess should represent the collective behavior of all the SESE fragments in a cluster, otherwise some behavior would be lost when replacing the approximate clones with the single shared subprocess.

The technique for process model merging presented in [14] allows us to achieve this property. This technique takes as input a collection of process models (or SESE fragments) and returns a single merged process model, such that the set of traces of the merged model is the union of the traces of the input models. Thus, applying this technique on fragments of automatically discovered process models does not affect the fitness, appropriateness or generalization of the particular discovery technique used. An experimental evaluation reported in [14] shows that, if the input process models (or fragments) are similar, the size of the merged process model is significantly lower than the sum of the sizes of the input models. Also, the more similar the merged models are, the more significant is the size reduction achieved during merging.

This merging technique is applicable to any graph-oriented process modeling language that includes the three connectors XOR, AND and OR (e.g EPCs and BPMN).

3 The SMD Technique

The idea of SMD is to traverse the dendrogram produced by hierarchical trace clustering in a top-down manner (breadth-first), attempting at each level of the traversal to produce models of complexity below a certain user-defined threshold. This threshold can be placed on the size of a model or on its structural complexity measured in terms of CFC, density or other complexity metrics. For example, the user can specify an upper-bound of 50 for the number of nodes in a model or a maximum control flow complexity of 20 per model. At each level of the traversal, the algorithm applies subprocess extraction and merging in order to reduce duplication. The traversal stops at a given cluster d in the dendrogram – meaning that its child clusters are not visited – if a single model can be mined from d that after subprocess extraction meets the complexity threshold, or if d is a leaf of the dendrogram, in which case the model mined from d is returned.

The detailed description of SMD is given in Algorithm 1. Hereafter we illustrate this algorithm by means of the example dendrogram shown in Fig. 1 and we use size 12 as the complexity threshold. Observe that the root cluster $L1$ of the dendrogram is the log used as input to generate the dendrogram. As we traverse the dendrogram D, we mark the current position of the dendrogram with the clusters from which process models need to be mined. At the beginning, the root cluster is the only marked cluster (line 2). While there are marked trace clusters, we perform the following operations (lines 3–16). First, we mine a set of process models from marked trace clusters in D (line 4). As only $L1$ is marked at the beginning, a single process model $m1$ is mined. Let us assume that the model mined from $L1$ is that shown in Fig. 2. If we reach a leaf trace cluster of D at any stage, we cannot simplify the process model mined from that trace cluster anymore by traversing D. Thus, when a leaf of D is reached, we add the process model mined from that leaf to the set of leaf level process models M_l (line 5). As $L1$ is not a leaf, we do not update M_l at this stage. We then unmark all the clusters in M_l to avoid mining a process model again from these clusters, in next iterations of the while cycle (line 6). Then we extract subprocesses using Algorithm 2 (line 7) from the union of all

Algorithm 1. Discover process model collection

Input: Dendrogram D, complexity threshold k
Output: Set of root process models M_s, set of subprocesses S

1. Initialize M_l with $\varnothing$
2. Mark the root trace cluster of D
3. **while** *there are marked trace clusters in D* **do**
4.   Mine a set of process models M from all marked trace clusters in D
5.   Add to M_l the set of models from M mined from marked leaves of D
6.   Unmark all trace clusters used to mine models in M_l
7.   Invoke Algorithm 2 to extract subprocesses from $M \cup M_l$ and obtain a simplified set of root process models M_s and a set of subprocesses S
8.   Let M_c be the process models in M_s that do not satisfy k
9.   Let S_c be the subprocesses in S that do not satisfy k
10.   Let P be the process models of M_s containing subprocesses in S_c
11.   Add all models in P to M_c
12.   Remove M_l from M_c
13.   **if** M_c *is empty* **then** Unmark all trace clusters in D
14.   **foreach** *model m_c in M_c* **do**
15.   Get the trace cluster d used to mine m_c
16.   Mark child trace clusters of d in D and unmark d
17. **return** M_s and S

mined models so far and all models mined from leaves M_l. In our example, we extract subprocesses only from $m1$, as M_l is empty.

In Algorithm 2, we first construct the RPSDAG from the set of process models in input (line 3). Then we identify sets of exact clones using the technique in [6] (line 4). For each set of exact clones, we create a single subprocess and replace the occurrence of these clones in their process models with a subprocess activity pointing to the subprocess just created (lines 6-7). Once exact clones have been factored out, we identify clusters of approximate clones using the technique in [7] (line 8). For each fragment cluster, we merge all approximate clones in that cluster into a configurable fragment (line 11) using the technique in [14]. If this fragment satisfies the threshold, we embed it into a subprocess (line 14) and replace all occurrences of the corresponding approximate clones with a subprocess activity pointing to this subprocess (lines 15–16).

A cluster of approximate clones may contain the parent or the child of a fragment contained in another cluster. As a fragment that has been used to extract a subprocess does no longer exist, we need to also remove its parent and child fragments occurring in other clusters (lines 17–18). We use the RPSDAG to identify these containment relationships efficiently. One or more fragment clusters may be affected by this operation. Thus, we have to order the processing of the approximate clones clusters based on some *benefit-cost-ratio* (BCR), so as to prioritize those clusters that maximize the number of process models satisfying the threshold after approximate clones extraction (line 10). If we set our threshold on size, we can use the BCR defined in [7], which is the ratio

Algorithm 2. Extract subprocesses

Input: Set of process models M, complexity threshold k
Output: Set of root process models M_s, set of subprocesses S

1. Initialize M_s with M
2. Initialize S with $\varnothing$
3. Let F_s be the set of SESE fragments of M_s
4. Let F_e in F_s be the set of exact clones
5. Add F_e to S
6. **foreach** *fragment f in F_e* **do**
7.   Replace all occurrences of f in models of $M_s \cup S$ with a subprocess activity pointing to f
8. Apply approximate clone detection on $F_s \setminus F_e$ to identify fragment clusters C
9. **while** *C is not empty* **do**
10.   Retrieve the cluster c with highest BCR from C
11.   Merge fragments in c to obtain a merged fragment f_m
12.   Remove c from C
13.   **if** *f_m satisfies k* **then**
14.   Add f_m to S
15.   **foreach** *fragment f in c* **do**
16.   Replace all occurrences of f in models of M_s with a subprocess activity pointing to f_m
17.   Remove all ascendant and descendant fragments of f from all clusters in C
18.   Remove all clusters that are left with less than 2 fragments from C
19. **return** M_s and S

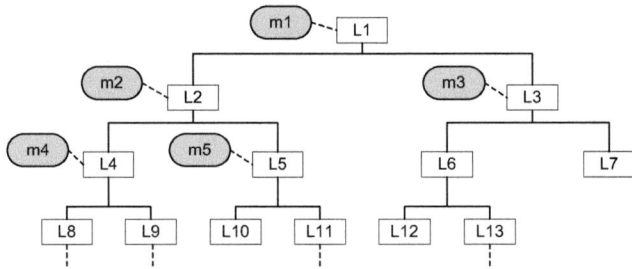

Fig. 1. A possible dendrogram generated by hierarchical trace clustering

between overall size reduction (benefit) and distance between approximate clones within a cluster (cost). Similar BCRs can be defined on other complexity metrics.

Coming back to our example, we can see there are two exact clones ($f6$ and $f8$) and two approximate clones ($f4$ and $f9$) in $m1$, as highlighted in Fig. 2. After applying Algorithm 2 we obtain the process model collection in Fig. 3, where we have two subprocesses ($s1$ and $s2$) with $s2$ being a configurable model. In particular, we can observe that $s2$ has two configurable gateways – the XOR-split and the XOR-join represented with a thicker border – so that the selection of outgoing edges of the XOR-split (incoming edges of the XOR-join) is constrained by the annotated fragment identifiers. In addition, $s2$ has an annotated activity to keep track of the original labels for that activity in $f4$ and $f9$. For example, if we want to replay the behavior of $f4$, only the top and bottom branches of this merged model will be available with the bottom branch bearing activity "Perform external procurements".

Once subprocesses have been extracted, we add all models that have to be further simplified to set M_c (lines 8–12 of Algorithm 1). M_c contains all non-leaf models not satisfying the threshold and all non-leaf models containing subprocesses not satisfying the threshold. Algorithm 1 terminates if M_c is empty (line 13). Otherwise, for each model in M_c, we mark the respective cluster (lines 14–16) and reiterate the while loop.

In our example, the size of $m1$ after subprocess extraction is 19, which does not satisfy the threshold 12. Thus, we discard $m1$ and mine two process models $m2$ and $m3$ from $L2$ and $L3$, which are shown in Fig. 4. $m2$ and $m3$ contain two exact clones ($f24$ and $f31$) and two approximate clones ($f22$ and $f34$). Now we apply Algorithm 2 on $m2$ and $m3$ and obtain the process model collection shown in Fig. 5. The sizes of $m2$ and $m3$ after subprocess extraction are 14 and 11 respectively. Thus, $m3$ satisfies our threshold while $m2$ has to be further simplified. We then discard $m2$ and mine two fresh models $m4$ and $m5$ from $L4$ and $L5$ and so on.

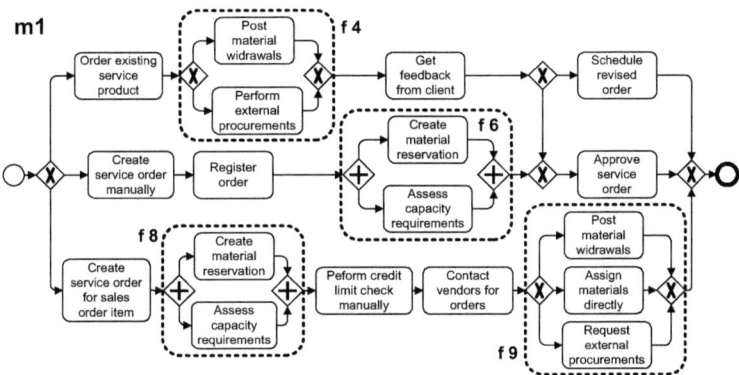

Fig. 2. Process model $m1$ with similar fragments

The complexity of Algorithm 1 depends on four external algorithms which are used to i) discover process models from the clusters of the dendrogram (line 4), ii) detect exact clones (line 4 of Algorithm 2), iii) detect approximate clones (line 8 of Algorithm 2) and iv) merge approximate clones (line 11 of Algorithm 2). Let c_1, c_2, c_3 and c_4 be the respective costs of these algorithms. The complexity of exact clone detection is determined by the insertion of fragments into the RPSDAG, which dominates the complexity of deleting fragments [6]. The complexity of approximate clone detection is dominated by that of computing the graph-edit distance between fragments [7]. Let F be the set of all SESE fragments of the process models that can be discovered from all trace clusters of dendrogram D, i.e. F is the union of all F_s. In the worst case, we need to discover

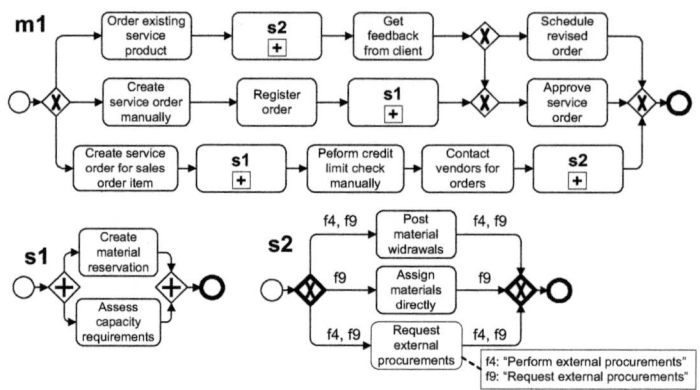

Fig. 3. Process model $m1$ and subprocess $s1$ after subprocess extraction

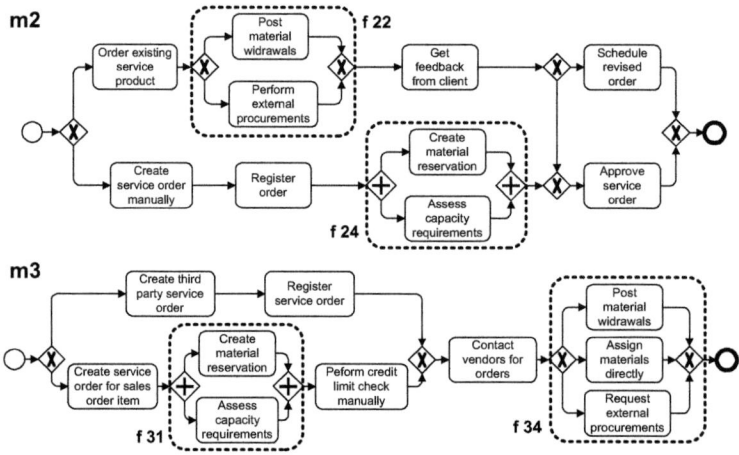

Fig. 4. Process models $m2$ and $m3$ mined from trace clusters $L2$ and $L3$

a process model from each cluster of the dendrogram, which is $O(|D|c_1)$; insert all fragments in the RPSDAG, which is $O(|F|c_2)$; compute the graph-edit distance of all pairs of fragments, which is $O(|F|^2 c_3)$; and merge $|F|/2$ fragments, which is $O(|F|c_4)$. Thus, the worst-case complexity of Algorithm 1 is $O(|D|c_1 + |F|(c_2 + c_4) + |F|^2 c_3)$. c_1 depends on the specific discovery technique used. For example, the Heuristic Miner is quadratic on the number of event classes in the log. Theoretically, c_2 is factorial in the number of nodes with the same label inside a single SESE fragment, though in practice this number is often very small or equal to zero thanks to various optimizations of exact clone detection [6]. Thus in practice c_2 is linear on $|F|$ [6]. c_3 is cubic on the size n of the largest fragment if using a greedy algorithm [5], as in the experiments reported in this paper. Finally, c_4 is $O(n \log(n))$.

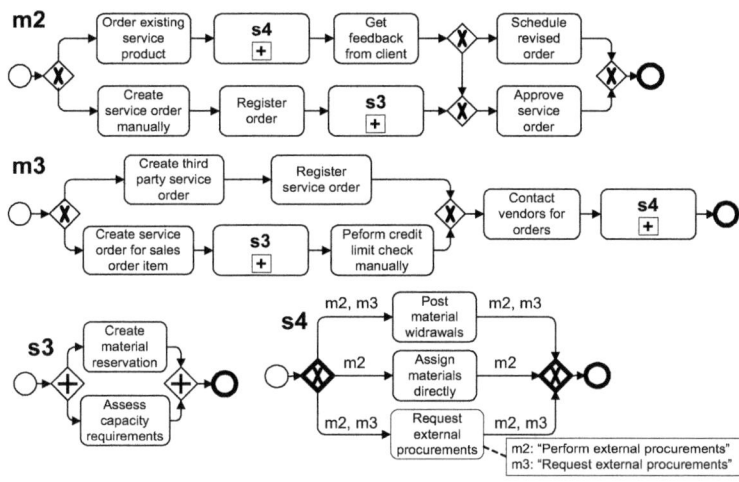

Fig. 5. Process models and subprocesses after subprocess extraction from $m2$ and $m3$

As with any process mining technique, the outcome of SMD is affected by the quality of the logs used as input. However, as SMD can work with different process discovery and hierarchical trace clustering algorithms, quality requirements on the logs depend on the specific algorithms used.

4 Evaluation

We implemented the SMD technique on the Apromore [10] platform.[2] We then used this tool to evaluate the technique on two event logs extracted from a large insurance company and on the log of the BPI challenge 2012[3] (hereafter called BPI Log). The first log of the insurance company was taken from a motor insurance claims handling process for windscreen claims (called Motor Log). The second log was taken from a commercial insurance claims handling process (called Commercial Log). We extracted completed traces from the first two months of each log, leading to a total of 4,300 to 5,300 traces. As we can see from Tab. 1, the three logs exhibit different characteristics despite the similar number of traces. In particular, there is a substantial difference in duplication ratio (i.e. the ratio between events and event classes).

Using these logs, we measured the reductions in overall size and number of models achieved by SMD on top of three hierarchical trace clustering techniques: Song et al. [15, 16], Bose et al. [1, 2] and the DWS technique by Medeiros et al. [4, 9]. These techniques were integrated in our tool. In particular, we used the DWS technique with K=2 and adapted it to split clusters until the process models mined from all trace clusters have complexity lower than or equal to the threshold, so that irrelevant clusters are not generated. For consistency, we used the Heuristics Miner [22] to

---
[2] The tool is available at www.apromore.org/platform/tools
[3] http://www.win.tue.nl/bpi2012/doku.php?id=challenge

Table 1. Characteristics of event logs used in the experiments

Log	Traces	Events	Event classes	Duplication ratio
Motor	4,293	33,202	292	114
Commercial	4,852	54,134	81	668
BPI	5,312	91,949	36	2,554

discover process models from the clusters retrieved by all three techniques. For clone detection we used the implementation described in [6] while for approximate clone clustering, we used the implementation of the DBSCAN algorithm described in [7] with graph-edit distance threshold of 0.4. These implementations, as well as that of the technique for merging process models described in [14], were also integrated into our tool.

In this evaluation, we set the user-defined complexity threshold on the process model size, as it has been shown that size has the largest impact on perceived process model complexity [11]. There is an *implicit limit* on the minimum size each mined process model can have. This limit, which is a lower-bound for the user-defined threshold, depends on the number and size of the clones we can identify in the process model collection mined from the dendrogram of the trace clusters. The risk of choosing a threshold lower than this limit is that we may end up with a proliferation of process models, many of which still with size above the threshold. This high number of models is due to the fact that the technique would explore the dendrogram as deep as possible. To discover this implicit limit we would need to run SMD using a size threshold of 1, so as to fully explore the dendrogram, and measure the size of the largest process model we obtain. This would be inefficient. However, we empirically found out that a good approximation of this implicit limit, which can be computed in a matter of seconds, is given by the size of the largest process model that can be mined from a single trace.

We set the size threshold to this approximate implicit limit, which is 37 for the Motor log, 34 for the Commercial log and 56 for the BPI log.[4] The results of the experiments are shown in Fig. 6 (Motor Log), Fig. 7 (Commercial Log) and Fig. 8 (BPI Log), where "S", "B" and "M" stand for the technique by Song et al., Bose et al. and Medeiros et al., respectively, while "SMD_S", "SML_B" and "SMD_M" indicate their respective SMD extensions.

As we can observe from the histograms, SMD consistently yields a significant reduction in the overall size across all three logs and all three trace clustering techniques used. This reduction ranges from 14.2% (with SMD_M on the Motor log) to 63.9% (with SMD_M on the BPI log), as evidenced by Tab. 2. In particular, we can observe that despite the technique of Medeiros et al. always produces the lowest overall size while that of Bose et al. produces the highest one among the trace clustering techniques, these differences are thinned out by SMD. This is because SMD compensates for the redundancies between clusters that may be introduced by a trace clustering technique as the number of clusters increases.

Similarly, we can observe significant reductions in the number of models, ranging from 22% (with SMD_M on the Commercial log) to 65.8% (with SMD_M on the BPI

---

[4] It turns out that these values correspond to the actual implicit size limits of the three logs.

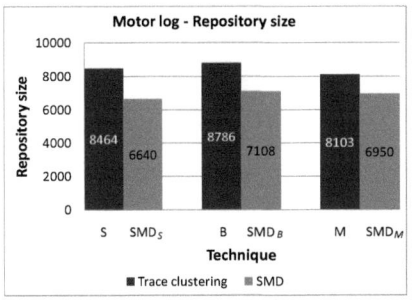 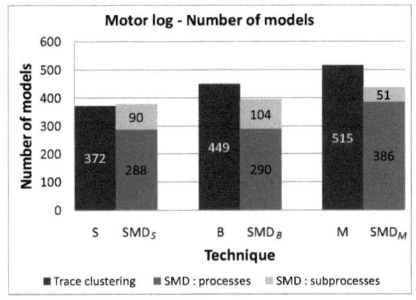

Fig. 6. Overall size and number of models obtained from the Motor log

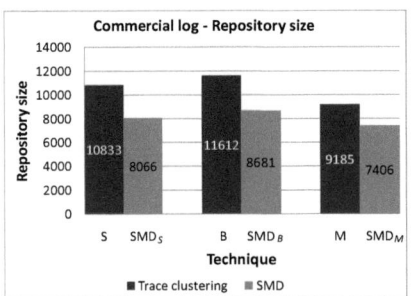 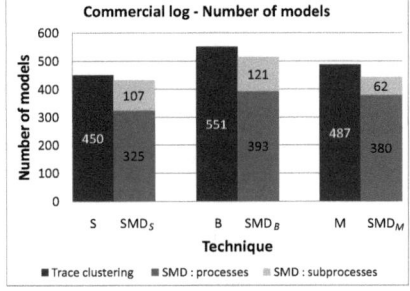

Fig. 7. Overall size and number of models obtained from the Commercial log

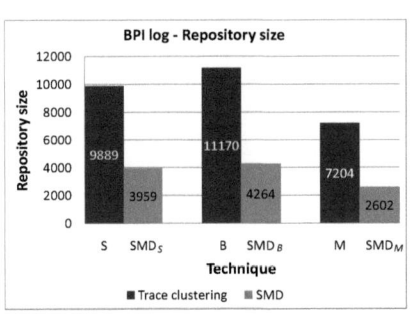 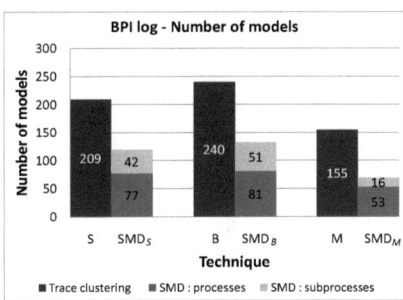

Fig. 8. Overall size and number of models obtained from the BPI log

log) if considering root models only (see Tab. 2). Adding subprocesses to the count, the extent of this reduction is clearly diminished (there is even a slight increase of 1.6% in the total number of models in the case of SMD_S on the Motor log). These results should be interpreted as an indication that SMD can often achieve the complexity threshold with less process models (particularly less root process models) compared to the three baseline trace clustering techniques used in the experiments.

Table 2. Savings in the overall size and number of models yielded by SMD

Log	Method	Size savings (%)	(Root) models number savings (%)
Motor	SMD_S	21.6	(22.6) -1.6
	SMD_B	19.1	(35.4) 12.2
	SMD_M	14.2	(25.0) 15.1
Commercial	SMD_S	25.5	(27.8) 4.0
	SMD_B	25.2	(28.7) 6.7
	SMD_M	19.4	(22.0) 9.2
BPI	SMD_S	60.0	(63.2) 43.1
	SMD_B	61.8	(66.3) 45.0
	SMD_M	63.9	(65.8) 55.5

Table 3. Size and structural complexity metrics for model collections mined with SMD

Log	Method	Size				CFC	ACD	CNC	Density
		avg	min	max	savings (%)	avg	avg	avg	avg
Motor	S	22.75	4	37	22.8	12.07	2.71	1.26	**0.07**
	SMD_S	**17.57**	4	37		**10.07**	**2.34**	**1.21**	0.11
	B	20.01	4	37	9.8	9.97	2.51	1.2	**0.08**
	SMD_B	**18.04**	4	37		10.05	**2.38**	1.2	0.11
	M	15.73	3	49	-1.1	7.36	2.14	**1.12**	**0.11**
	SMD_M	15.9	4	49		8.34	**2.12**	1.14	0.12
Commercial	S	24.07	6	34	22.4	13.65	2.96	1.32	**0.06**
	SMD_S	**18.67**	2	34		**11.34**	**2.49**	**1.24**	0.1
	B	21.11	2	34	20.3	11.04	2.65	1.23	**0.07**
	SMD_B	**16.82**	2	34		**9.73**	**2.29**	**1.18**	0.12
	M	18.86	2	40	11.1	10.18	2.47	1.22	**0.09**
	SMD_M	**16.76**	2	34		9.71	**2.38**	**1.21**	0.11
BPI	S	47.32	15	56	29.7	20.77	**2.34**	**1.24**	**0.03**
	SMD_S	**33.27**	4	56		**20.18**	2.41	1.28	0.07
	B	46.54	13	56	30.6	20.48	2.35	**1.23**	**0.03**
	SMD_B	**32.3**	4	56		**19.29**	**2.33**	1.27	0.07
	M	46.48	21	61	18.9	**21.16**	**2.34**	**1.24**	**0.03**
	SMD_M	**37.71**	7	56		25.29	2.38	1.3	0.04

From Tab. 2 we can also observe that the extent of the improvement, both for size and models number, increases with the increase of the log's duplication ratio (from the Motor log to the BPI log – see Tab. 1). This is confirmed by the strong correlation between the duplication ratio and the percentage of size savings produced by SMD (0.99), and the strong correlation between the duplication ratio and the percentage of models number savings (0.95). Thus, we can conclude that the amount of improvement achieved by SMD depends on the amount of duplication in the log.

Further, the average size and structural complexity of individual models reported in Tab. 3, indicate that SMD achieves the size threshold on individual models without affecting structural complexity. The table shows that the average values for structural complexity measures remain largely unchanged after applying SMD (the increase in density is due to the inverse correlation of density and size). It is also worth noting that in most cases, the average model size is reduced after applying SMD (up to 30.6% savings in the case of the BPI log).

In most of the experiments, SMD took more time than the corresponding baseline trace clustering technique. This is attributable to the reliance on graph-edit distance for process model comparison. In the worst case, SMD took double the time required by the baseline (e.g., 58 mins instead 28 mins of Medeiros et al. on the Commercial log). However, in other cases, SMD took less time than the baseline (e.g., 17 mins instead of 22 mins of Bose et al. on the BPI log). This is because if SMD mines less models relative to its baseline trace clustering technique, the time saved by the mining steps can compensate for the time taken to compute graph-edit distances.

5 Conclusion

SMD advances the state-of-the-art in automated process discovery along two directions. First, it is to the best of our knowledge the first complexity-aware automated process discovery method, insofar as it seeks to produce models that meet user-specified complexity thresholds. Second, SMD provides significant reductions in overall size relative to existing process discovery techniques based on hierarchical trace clustering, while preserving the fitness, appropriateness and generalization of process models mined from trace clusters. The experimental evaluation based on three large real-life logs shows size reductions of up to 64%, with little impact on structural complexity metrics of individual process models – barring an increase in density attributable to the dependency of this complexity metric on size.

While complexity metrics have been shown to be correlated with comprehensibility [13], it is unclear how exactly to tune the thresholds used by SMD so as to produce models that users would best comprehend. While methods for determining complexity thresholds on individual models have been put forward [12], the interplay between overall size of a collection of process models, size of individual models and their structural complexity is less understood. Building an understanding on how to set complexity thresholds for automated process discovery is a direction for future work. Another direction for future work is to optimize SMD in order to reduce its execution time. For example, an option is to parallelize divisive trace clustering, as well as process discovery, for sibling nodes of the dendrogram. The GED matrix computation can also be parallelized by dividing the fragment collection into multiple groups that are processed in parallel.

Acknowledgments. This work is funded by the Smart Services Cooperative Research Centre (CRC) under the Australian CRC Program and EU Regional Development Funds via the Estonian Centre of Excellence in Computer Science.

References

1. Bose, R.P.J.C.: Process Mining in the Large: Preprocessing, Discovery, and Diagnostics. PhD thesis, Eindhoven University of Technology, Eindhoven (2012)

2. Bose, R.P.J.C., van der Aalst, W.M.P.: Trace clustering based on conserved patterns: Towards achieving better process models. In: Rinderle-Ma, S., Sadiq, S., Leymann, F. (eds.) BPM 2009 Workshops. LNBIP, vol. 43, pp. 170–181. Springer, Heidelberg (2010)
3. Bose, R.P.J.C., Verbeek, E.H.M.W., van der Aalst, W.M.P.: Discovering hierarchical process models using prom. In: Nurcan, S. (ed.) CAiSE Forum 2011. LNBIP, vol. 107, pp. 33–48. Springer, Heidelberg (2012)
4. de Medeiros, A.K.A., Guzzo, A., Greco, G., van der Aalst, W.M.P., Weijters, A.J.M.M., van Dongen, B.F., Saccà, D.: Process mining based on clustering: A quest for precision. In: ter Hofstede, A.H.M., Benatallah, B., Paik, H.-Y. (eds.) BPM Workshops 2007. LNCS, vol. 4928, pp. 17–29. Springer, Heidelberg (2008)
5. Dijkman, R.M., Dumas, M., van Dongen, B.F., Käärik, R., Mendling, J.: Similarity of business process models: Metrics and evaluation. Inf. Syst. 36(2), 498–516 (2011)
6. Dumas, M., García-Bañuelos, L., La Rosa, M., Uba, R.: Fast detection of exact clones in business process model repositories. Inf. Syst. 38(4), 619–633 (2012)
7. Ekanayake, C.C., Dumas, M., García-Bañuelos, L., La Rosa, M., ter Hofstede, A.H.M.: Approximate clone detection in repositories of business process models. In: Barros, A., Gal, A., Kindler, E. (eds.) BPM 2012. LNCS, vol. 7481, pp. 302–318. Springer, Heidelberg (2012)
8. Greco, G., Guzzo, A., Pontieri, L.: Mining taxonomies of process models. Data Knowl. Eng. 67(1), 74–102 (2008)
9. Greco, G., Guzzo, A., Pontieri, L., Saccà, D.: Discovering expressive process models by clustering log traces. IEEE Trans. Knowl. Data Eng. 18(8), 1010–1027 (2006)
10. La Rosa, M., Reijers, H.A., van der Aalst, W.M.P., Dijkman, R.M., Mendling, J., Dumas, M., García-Bañuelos, L.: APROMORE: An Advanced Process Model Repository. Expert Syst. Appl. 38(6) (2011)
11. Mendling, J., Reijers, H.A., Cardoso, J.: What Makes Process Models Understandable? In: Alonso, G., Dadam, P., Rosemann, M. (eds.) BPM 2007. LNCS, vol. 4714, pp. 48–63. Springer, Heidelberg (2007)
12. Mendling, J., Sánchez-González, L., García, F., La Rosa, M.: Thresholds for error probability measures of business process models. J. Syst. Software 85(5), 1188–1197 (2012)
13. Reijers, H.A., Mendling, J.: A study into the factors that influence the understandability of business process models. IEEE T. Syst. Man Cy. A 41(3), 449–462 (2011)
14. La Rosa, M., Dumas, M., Uba, R., Dijkman, R.: Business process model merging: An approach to business process consolidation. ACM T. Softw. Eng. Meth. 22(2) (2013)
15. Song, M., Günther, C.W., van der Aalst, W.M.P.: Improving process mining with trace clustering. J. Korean Inst. of Industrial Engineers 34(4), 460–469 (2008)
16. Song, M., Günther, C.W., van der Aalst, W.M.P.: Trace clustering in process mining. In: Ardagna, D., Mecella, M., Yang, J. (eds.) BPM 2008 Workshops. LNBIP, vol. 17, pp. 109–120. Springer, Heidelberg (2009)
17. van der Aalst, W.M.P.: Process Mining - Discovery, Conformance and Enhancement of Business Processes. Springer (2011)
18. van der Werf, J.M.E.M., van Dongen, B.F., Hurkens, C.A.J., Serebrenik, A.: Process discovery using integer linear programming. Fundam. Inform. 94(3-4), 387–412 (2009)
19. Vanhatalo, J., Völzer, H., Koehler, J.: The Refined Process Structure Tree. Data Knowl. Eng. 68(9), 793–818 (2009)
20. Veiga, G.M., Ferreira, D.R.: Understanding spaghetti models with sequence clustering for prom. In: Rinderle-Ma, S., Sadiq, S., Leymann, F. (eds.) BPM 2009. LNBIP, vol. 43, pp. 92–103. Springer, Heidelberg (2010)
21. De Weerdt, J., De Backer, M., Vanthienen, J., Baesens, B.: A multi-dimensional quality assessment of state-of-the-art process discovery algorithms using real-life event logs. Inf. Syst. 37(7), 654–676 (2012)
22. Weijters, A.J.M.M., Ribeiro, J.T.S.: Flexible heuristics miner (fhm). In: CIDM, pp. 310–317. IEEE (2011)

Business Process Mining from E-Commerce Web Logs

Nicolas Poggi[1,2], Vinod Muthusamy[3], David Carrera[1,2], and Rania Khalaf[3]

[1] Technical University of Catalonia (UPC) Barcelona, Spain
[2] Barcelona Supercomputing Center (BSC) Barcelona, Spain
[3] IBM T. J. Watson Research Center Yorktown, New York, USA

Abstract. The dynamic nature of the Web and its increasing importance as an economic platform create the need of new methods and tools for business efficiency. Current Web analytic tools do not provide the necessary abstracted view of the underlying customer processes and critical paths of site visitor behavior. Such information can offer insights for businesses to react effectively and efficiently. We propose applying Business Process Management (BPM) methodologies to e-commerce Website logs, and present the challenges, results and potential benefits of such an approach.

We use the Business Process Insight (BPI) platform, a collaborative process intelligence toolset that implements the discovery of loosely-coupled processes, and includes novel process mining techniques suitable for the Web. Experiments are performed on custom click-stream logs from a large online travel and booking agency. We first compare Web clicks and BPM events, and then present a methodology to classify and transform URLs into events. We evaluate traditional and custom process mining algorithms to extract business models from real-life Web data. The resulting models present an abstracted view of the relation between pages, exit points, and critical paths taken by customers. Such models show important improvements and aid high-level decision making and optimization of e-commerce sites compared to current state-of-art Web analytics.

1 Introduction

To remain competitive, online retailers need to adapt in an agile, non-structured way, resulting in large, unstructured websites and rapidly changing server resource demands [14]. Moreover, Conversion Rates (CR), the fraction of users that reach a certain goal, such as buying a product on the site, are decreasing: less than 2% of visits result in a purchase on most sites [14]. A low CR is influenced by factors including affiliation programs, changes in user habits such as comparing different sites at the same time [15], and meta-crawling. For example, *Kayak.com* and similar meta-crawlers present the user the best results gathered from several sites, thereby lowering the visits to each site and the CR.

Most online businesses rely on free Web analytic tools to inform their Web marketing campaigns and strategic business decisions. However these tools currently do not provide the necessary abstracted view of the customer's actual behavior on the site. Without the proper tools and abstractions, site owners have a simplified and incorrect understanding of their users' real interaction patterns on the site, and how they evolve.

In this paper we apply Business Process Management (BPM) methodologies to e-commerce Website logs. Structured formal models of user behavior can provide insights on potential improvements to the site. In particular, providing a high-level abstracted view of the workflows leading to purchases and most common exit pages in order to make decisions on site optimization. BPM concerns the management of business processes including the modeling, design, execution, monitoring, and optimization of processes [8]. While loosely-structured to completely ad-hoc processes have not traditionally not been considered by BPM, we (and others [7]) see this is part of a spectrum [19].

Unlike Web analytics [9], process analytics is concerned with correlating events [20], mining for process models [24,26,18], and predicting behavior [25]. We propose treating a user's web clicks as an unstructured process, and use process mining algorithms to discover user behavior. The mined process model captures the causality and paths of user interactions that lead to certain outcomes of interest, such as buying a product. Such insights can be difficult to extract from traditional Web analytic tools.

We use the Business Process Insight (BPI) platform, a collaborative process intelligence toolset [19]. BPI includes the knowledge-based process miner, which differs from traditional process mining in its initial search structure and the set of activities considered for edge operations.

We use a real data set from Atrapalo, an online travel and booking agency (OTA) that includes popular services such as flight and hotel reservation systems. The data set includes the HTTP requests made by customers to the site over a three month period, captured using Real User Monitoring techniques. We apply process analytics to this dataset, and make three main contributions:

1. We outline how to transform web clicks into tasks suitable for analysis and modeling with BPM tools. In particular, we classify the URLs that correspond to web clicks into high level tasks. We compare both a manual classification approach with knowledge from a domain expert, and an automatic classification algorithm. The tasks are then grouped into web sessions representing a particular customer's interaction with the site.
2. We describe how to mine business processes that includes how regular web visitors and customers behave. A challenge here is that, by design, most process mining algorithms capture only the most common behavior in order to keep the resulting mined process model simple enough for a human to understand. However, in web commerce data, the behaviors of interest, such as a customer buying a product, are infrequent. We address this issue with techniques such as saturating the dataset with low frequency behavior we wish to observe, clustering the process instances to extract patterns of behavior, and using a knowledge-based processing mining algorithm.
3. We evaluate the use of the knowledge-based mining algorithm under a variety of conditions, and explain its suitability to extract process models that

abstract a complete over-view of user navigation from real, noisy data. Our evaluation is notable for using real web logs, and unique in applying BPM techniques to an e-commerce site.

2 Background and Related Work

Business Process Management. Business processes can be strongly structured (as in BPEL), loosely-structured (as in Case Management tools), or entirely unstructured. The latter are common with ad-hoc human tasks. For example, a party planning process may be carried out by phone, e-mail, and faxes by people not following any predefined process. Such unstructured processes are an important part of the spectrum of processes in the wild [7,19]. Process mining automates the discovery of process models from event logs, and we propose treating e-commerce web interactions as business processes.

Business Process Insight. The Business Process Insight (BPI) system [19] detects relationships among events, and outputs a set of correlation rules. The correlation engine applies these rules to create *process traces* that group related events that belong to the same process instance. The process traces can then be used to discover different process models or to train predictive models for making live predictions on future behavior. Similar to Process Spaceship [11], BPI is a process intelligence solution that simplifies the understanding of business process executions across heterogeneous systems, as well as provide a foundation for process-aware analytics for both historical and live events. The BPI architecture supports plugging in different process mining algorithms, such as the alpha and heuristic mining algorithms in the ProM process mining tool [26].

Process Mining. Process mining aims to extract a business process model from a set of execution logs [1,26,23,4,13,17,25]. Process mining algorithms typically find all activities (nodes) in the process model, constructing a dependency graph with no edges, and then search through the space of process models by adding, deleting, and reversing edges. However, many algorithms restrict the activities that can be considered for these edge operations by observing activity adjacency in the execution log. For instance, only if activities A and B are adjacent in the log will they be considered for an edge operation. The *knowledge-based miner* developed at IBM Research can leverage domain knowledge by initializing its search with a predefined process model. The algorithm also considers a larger search space of process model structures by considering edge operations on both log-adjacent and log non-adjacent activities. This larger search space enables the discovery of process models that more accurately represent the process execution log. The knowledge-based miner constructs an activity precedence graph that encodes statistically significant activity dependencies among the execution logs, as well as dependency and independency graphs [16] augmented with the confidence levels of edges specified by a domain expert. The algorithm first extracts activity dependencies and independencies from the process logs and expert knowledge, partially using some of the techniques developed by Agrawal *et al.* [2]. It then discovers the split/join semantics based on some of the ideas in [16].

ProM is a prominent process mining tool that serves as a front-end for various process mining techniques [26]. How data attributes influence the choices made in a process based on past process executions by leveraging decision trees has been investigated in [18]. The focus of [18] is to correctly identify decision points in the presence of duplicate and invisible tasks in a log. There are also a number of probabilistic models proposed for modeling business processes [13,17,25]. In [5] Ferreira et al. proposes a probabilistic approach implementing Expectation-Maximization for discovering process models from unlabeled event logs. In Section 4 we propose a similar approach to cluster clicks into events, both by manual and automatic methods.

Web Analytics. Web analytics deals with the collection, measurement, and analysis of user navigational data. One way to classify the analytics techniques is by the method of data collection: page tagging through Javascript, web server log analysis, beaconing by inserting a remote object on the page, packet sniffing, and hybrid approaches [27]. The main metrics analyzed include the number of unique and returning visits, URL access frequency, geolocation, client web browser and version, and statistics around these metrics. Newer tools from Google and Yahoo also support tracking of marketing campaigns and conversion goals, such as users subscribing to the site's newsletter or purchasing a product. The latter platforms are Javascript-based implementations of page tagging. Page tagging can be manually tuned to group different tasks on the website logically; by default tools follow the traditional URL analysis. The objective of web analytics it to provide feedback for website owners on user behavior in order to improve site navigation and conversion goals [9]. However, improvements are only possible when there is a clear understanding on the underlying site structure and user needs.

Web Mining. There are few published studies on real e-commerce data, mainly because web logs are considered sensitive data. In [21] web mining is classified into usage, content, and structure web mining. The main purpose for structure mining is to extract previously unknown relationships between Web pages. While this paper falls within the scope of structure web mining, most of the literature in this topic focus on recommendation systems and web personalization [3]. In [22] authors presented a comparative study of the navigation behavior of customers and non-customers to assess and improve the quality of a commercial web site; while in this work we aim to build a process model that shows the complete interactions of most users in the site that includes customer sessions.

Customer Behavior Model Graphs (CBMG) can be used to provide an abstracted view on web navigation [10]. The CBMG is built using the k-means clustering algorithm that creates a probability matrix for the possible path transitions from a state. In this paper, we do not focus on predicting the user's next click, but seek to extract the most relevant critical paths occurring in the site and build the process model. In particular, we are interested in the important events and workflows that lead to a user buying a product.

Web analytics has evolved from those that analyzed web server access logs to generate reports and evaluations based on URL, IP address, and browser agent grouping and frequency analysis, to newer tools such as Google's or Yahoo's analytics. These tools, however, do not extract the user behavior at an abstraction level that is appropriate to understand the actual critical paths taken by consumers. The experimental results in this paper lead us to believe that web analytics can benefit from BPM modeling. We are not aware of any other literature on applying BPM techniques to an e-commerce site.

3 Application Scenario and Dataset

Online Travel E-commerce Market. Online travel agencies (OTAs) are a prominent sector in the online services market. A Nielsen report on global online shopping found airline ticket reservations represented 24% of online shopping purchases, hotel reservations 16%, and event tickets 15%, for a combined 55% of global online sales [12]. Conversion Rates (CR) are usually not made public as they reveal the success of a business strategy, but we have confirmed that for the OTA industry CR of less than 2% is a common figure when taking into account all web requests [14]. Our study considers Atrapalo, an international online travel agency and booking site representative of the OTA industry. It features popular e-commerce applications found in the Web and over twelve years of online presence. We have been given access to a three month dataset from 2012 featuring several million HTTP requests of site visits.

Atrapalo's Application. Atrapalo's online application follows a typical travel site structure, offering the following products: flights, hotels, cars, restaurants, activities, cruises, vacation packages, and ticket bookings. Some product inventories are maintained internally, such as restaurant bookings, some are completely external, such as flights, and some products such as hotels contain a mix of internal and external providers. The company's main presence and clientele include Spain and Italy from Europe; Peru, Colombia, Brazil and Chile in South America; and a few visitors from elsewhere. Each country is served by a separate top level domain and has differentiated products enabled. It is important to remark that the site has over 12 years of online presence, and its structure has been in constant update and optimization including a recently added mobile version, but it retains an important legacy code base.

Dataset Used for the Experiments. The dataset provided by Atrapalo contains click-stream information from visitors and customers of the different products offered in their domains presented in the previous section. The dataset contains more than four million user clicks representing about 850 000 full user sessions. The average navigation time per user is four minutes and eight seconds, and there are 4.36 clicks per session. The dataset was collected by sampling over a period of three months from June to September 2012.

The novelty of the presented dataset is that it was produced using Real User Monitoring (RUM) techniques, in contrast to typical server logs collected by the web server. Every time a page is loaded in Atrapalo—for a sample of web sessions—an asynchronous AJAX request is sent from the user browser to the server. This information is used by Atrapalo to monitor and optimize the performance of web pages from the user's perspective.

RUM log files are useful in this study. First, the dataset is cleaner, as it only contains data from web browsers that can process Javascript, thereby avoiding most crawler and bot traffic. Crawler behavior is particularly different from user traffic and can account for over 20% of total requests [15] and distort results. Second, it only contains information about pages that the user actually clicks. In our previous work [15] we have performed workload characterization of web server generated datasets and among other findings found that less than 50% of requests corresponded to user clicks. The rest of the request traffic was composed of automatic AJAX requests for autocomplete controls or the RUM request, dynamically generated Javascript and CSSs, HTTP redirections, and backend requests for the user session. Third, cached web pages, either in the customer browser or any intermediate proxy are present in the RUM log. With this, the complete user navigation can be reconstructed. Having complete data sets is important for any mining or prediction algorithms, as most are susceptible to noise to different degrees. The next section presents our approach to convert web sessions into process models.

4 Web Sessions as Process Models

Among the characteristics and challenges in process mining [24] is having to deal with noisy event data. Noise is common in web logs as web proxies and caches can alter content. Moreover, web browsers behave differently, and browser plugins can affect navigation patterns. Furthermore some requests can get lost, due to dropped connections, users roaming over a mobile network, and users altering the normal flow with refresh, back, and forward browser buttons. Also, a user's web session can expire. We have observed in our preliminary work that weblogs are indeed noisier than typical event logs for BPM systems.

Another set of important characteristics is the presence of *loops*, *duplicate activities* and *parallel* tasks. Web sessions also exhibit these properties to different degrees. For example, when a user is searching for hotels, he might try different dates, looping over the search page, or he might click on a hotel deal, see the details, go back to the search page, click on another deal and so forth. The user might have also opened different hotel deals in different tabs of his browser, creating *parallel* tasks. He might have also been searching for flights to the same destination, or to rent a car from the airport in parallel. Parallel tasks, duplicate activities and loops are present in most web navigations of more than a couple of clicks. Current research detecting loops and having loop aware algorithms can be substantially beneficial for mining web navigation and performing predictions on the user's navigation.

While Web sessions are also time constrained as typical BPM activities, *time* is also major difference. As mentioned in the previous section, the average web navigation is only of about four minutes, while BPM processes, such as supply chain management, can span days. As BPM processes can require human intervention, in the web the process is completely automatic. This difference has several implications as there is no time for manual interpretation and modification of an executing process. BPM tools, if applied to web navigation need to be automatic, free of human intervention and deployed in real-time.

While on this study we only target web content, we advocate that user navigation be included in process models of companies that involve both web interaction and traditional processes. The next section looks at how to abstract web clicks into logical tasks to be consumed by a BPM system.

4.1 Classifying URLs into Logical Tasks

The first challenge analyzing web logs is to classify the URLs of the site. For the dataset used in the experimentation several URL rewriting techniques were implemented for security, dynamic page generation, search engine optimization, and localization. There were 949 532 unique URL in the dataset, if we take the query string out of the URL, the number of distinct pages reduces to 375 245.

In order to extract the *action* —type of process and output of a page— from a URL in Atrapalo's dataset, we had to implement the rewrite engine used for the page classification. Rewrite engines usually perform regular expression matching to URLs. In Atrapalo's URLs, the first element in the URL path indicates the name of the product, such as flights, hotels, cars, or events. Each product had custom implementations of the rewrite engine and how regular expressions were performed. About 20% of the URLs didn't match any regular expression, and for these URLs query string classification was performed by looking for a custom parameter "pg", which specified the page *action*. Using the query string approach we were left with 5% of unclassified URLs that were manually analyzed and classified using string search and replace.

Table 1. Classification of URLs into logical tasks

Tag	Description
Home	Main home page
ProductHome	Home page for each product
Landing	Search engine landing pages
Promo	Special promotional pages
Search	General site search
Results	Product search and results
Details	Product detailed information
Opinions	Opinions about a product
Info	Site help or general information
CartDetails	Shopping cart details
CartPurchase	Shopping cart purchase forms
Confirmation	Confirmation page of a sale
UserAdmin	User self reservation management

After the URLs where translated we were left with 533 different page actions or type of pages. However some of the page names occurred only once, a problem we attribute to noise and errors in the rewrite engine implementation. We then filtered the pages that did not have more than one occurrence, and ended with

233 page names. This means that across the products of the site there were 233 different types of pages. Some of the pages serve the same logical function, such as the search page for hotels, flights or cars, or the different home pages for each product. After a manual analysis on the site structure and URLs, we decided to classify them in 14 logical types of pages detailed in Table 1.

Although the classification in Table 1 is particular to Atrapalo's dataset, many e-commerce sites share similar structures especially for sites implementing travel and booking products. It is important to remark that through the classification of pages no data is lost. Page classification is added as extra columns to the dataset. The URL and page types are kept in the dataset, so we can later use them to filter or to extract better path predictions. The next section presents a proposal for automating page classification.

4.2 Automating Page Classification

Classification of types of pages into logical groups is necessary to map user clicks occurring in a website to abstracted logical tasks to be consumed both by BPM algorithms and final reports to humans. We noticed while reviewing the results that many page actions had similar names. There was at least a search page per product and different types of search pages, including flightsSearch, hotelsSearch, flightsCalendarSearch, hotelsSearchCity. To aid classification, we have tested the clustering of the page names using the WEKA open source machine learning framework [6]. WEKA contains several popular ready to use algorithms for classification and clustering among other tools. As we had previously decided that the classification has 14 logical types of pages, K-means clustering was our first natural choice to test, as it performs in general scenarios with known number of clusters. We have used WEKA's SimpleKMeans implementation and setting the number of clusters to 14 and the "classes to clusters" evaluation option. SimpleKMeans yielded an error of 39.90% in classifying the 233 names into 14 clusters. We have also experimented with the EM (Expectation-Maximisation) algorithm both with automated and manual numbers of clusters yielding 76.93% and 41.88% of classification errors, respectively. Table 2 summarizes the clustering results. If the number of classifications is known, K-means clustering can reduce the manual work needed to simplify page classification. The next section details our experiments with process mining.

Table 2. Classifier Evaluation

Algorithm	Clusters	Error
SimpleKmeans	14	39.90%
EM	14	41.88%
EM	Automatic	76.93%

5 Process Mining for Customers

This section details our experiments mining the business processes of customers in Atrapalo's dataset with the page classification from the previous section. Three new events were added to each web session: Start, End, and BuyerEnd.

These events are helpers to the mining algorithms and to their visualizations to show where sessions start—as there are different starting points—and exit. Exit events were marked BuyerEnd if the session ended in a purchase, to differentiate them from regular sessions. This distinction is not only used for visualization purposes, but for path prediction algorithms as well for our ongoing research.

As mentioned in Section 3, only a small fraction of visits to the site ended buying a product. The conversion rate for the site is less than 2% of the total number of visits. Having such a small percentage is a problem for most mining algorithms, as these low-frequency traces (web sessions) will be filtered out by most implementations producing an incomplete model. In our study we present three different approaches to this problem creating three new different datasets: saturating the data set (*saturated*), clustering (*clustered*), and *biasing* toward a previously set model with the knowledge-based miner. We call the original dataset the *normal* dataset.

5.1 Saturating the Dataset with Customers

The first strategy to mine customer models was saturating the dataset. This entailed producing a new dataset where the percentage of buying customers is higher by removing sessions that did not purchase. We have chosen the ratio 1/3 of customers to just visitors. This ratio is choosen as customer sessions are longer in average, leaving us with and even dataset of about half of the entries belonging to customer sessions. With this ratio, we have created a new dataset including the entire customer sessions present in the normal dataset, and 2/3 more sessions from regular visits from the top of the dataset. This dataset having about 8% of the total entries of the normal dataset, but including all the purchasing sessions.

This approach was tested with the process mining algorithms implemented in BPI, and allowed us to test the different algorithm implementations. As mentioned previously, the alpha miner is not suited for event logs with noise or incompleteness, as is typical in real logs [4]. Results for alpha miner are omitted for the saturated dataset as it produced incomplete results.

Knowledge-Based Miner. Figure 1 shows the resulting models by applying our knowledge based miner with default noise and window parameters to the *normal* (Figure 1(a)) and *saturated* (Figure 1(b)) datasets. The general workflow of events can be seen from the figures, with the main distinction being that the *normal* dataset does not contain the *Confirmation* and *BuyerEnd* events and edges. The *CartDetails* event is present in both. This means that while there are many users that add a product to the shopping cart and see its details, few ultimately purchase the product. In these cases the buying events are being discarded as noise, while on the *saturated* dataset they are being kept. Loops can also be seen in both models, but the loops are from the same originating event to itself, such as users iterating over the *Results* event.

Another insight from the knowledge-based miner models is that the *Promo* event is not linked to any other event; almost all users that get to the site through a promotional page leave the site without any further navigation. On the *normal*

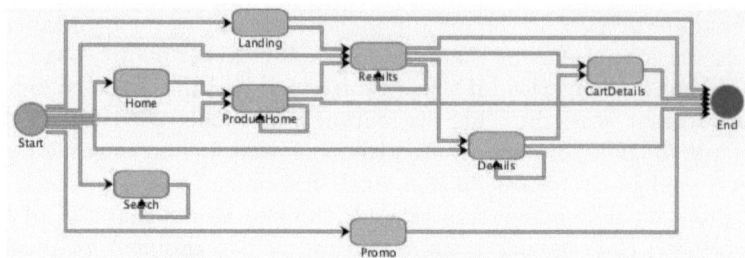

(a) Knowledge-based miner process model for the normal dataset

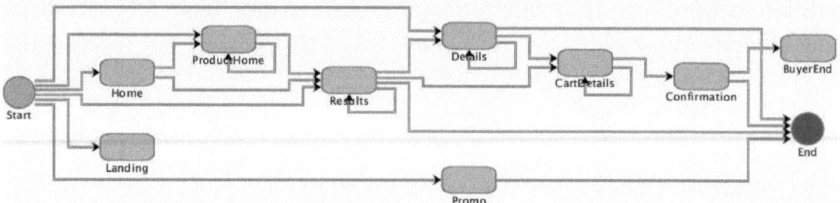

(b) Knowledge-based miner process model for the buyers saturated dataset

Fig. 1. Knowledge-based miner process models for the *normal* and *saturated* datasets

dataset, some users from the *Landing* event get to the results. In the *saturated* dataset, however, the landing page event doesn't have any outbound links. The same can be observed with the *Search* event in the *normal* dataset: it's only link is a self-loop. The *Search* event is not present in the *saturated* model, because it is a low frequency event and not used by most customers. We have verified that most results pages were directly reached from each product home pages. *Search* events represent the general site search feature that searches all products at the same time, and results show they are not very effective and were reported back for optimization. Further details about the knowledge-based miner are given later in this Section.

Heuristic Miner. Figure 2 shows the model generated by the heuristic miner. The heuristic miner model included all of the events from the *saturated* dataset, presenting the same behavior for the *Search*, *Promo*, and *Landing* events as the knowledge-based miner. One addition is the *UserAdmin* event, discarded by the knowledge-based miner as noise. There is however one main difference with the knowledge-based miner: most events are shown as independent from another, except for a few with one edge and the combination *Details-Info-ProductHome*. This is the main difference with the knowledge-based miner, and from our tests it makes it less applicable to web logs and similar datasets where an end to end path is required.

Another disadvantage is that it overfits the model. If we had more events, as we did prior to applying the classification in Section 4, the algorithm would not highlight the critical paths in the web navigation. While the heuristic miner is very well regarded [4], as mentioned in Section 2, the same study also questions

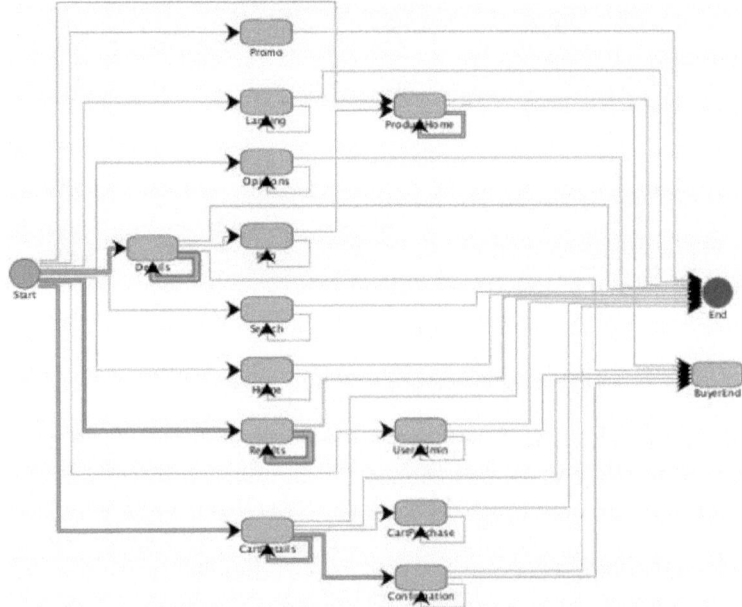

Fig. 2. Heuristic miner with saturated dataset

traditional process mining algorithms and advocates for new methods for real data. Results with the *normal* dataset were almost identical, except for the thickness (significance) of the edges between activities, as the frequency was different between both datasets.

Fuzzy Miner. The Fuzzy Miner in PRoM [26] can visually cluster events, and can be useful when working with a large number of activities and unstructured behavior. The fuzzy miner gave good results mining the *saturated* dataset. The main difference with the knowledge-based miner is that it doesn't remove noise from the dataset, but it can simplify and group the model to the desired level of abstraction. However, the generated clusters do not necessarily group events logically; the clusters included unrelated event types as compared to our manual classification. It, therefore, does not seem that fuzzy mining can be used to aid or avoid the URL classification performed in Section 4.

5.2 Clustering Sessions

The next tested approach to mine for customer sessions was clustering. BPI implements the string distance algorithm to cluster imported traces. By clustering similar sessions, we can run the process mining directly on individual clusters through the BPI interface. This feature is very helpful as clustering can help remove noise and allows the ability to mine specific customer clusters or target groups without the need to saturate the dataset. For example, with clustering, the alpha miner could be applied to small clusters if required.

Fig. 3. Process model of a customer cluster for Heuristic and knowledge-based miners

Figure 3 shows the model produced by both Heuristic and knowledge-based miner to a specific small cluster of customers, representative of the most common buying process. It shows the critical path (the most important pages) for buyers on the website, and thus, the most important pages to keep optimized. It also shows that the most typical buying process consists of three main pages: *Details*, specific product information; *CartDetails*, final costs details and payment options; and *Confirmation*, the reservation confirmation page. This would mean that most buying sessions go strait to purchasing without much searching, probably performed at a previous time and different session.

The disadvantage of clustering, besides not having the complete process in the output model, is that models cannot be combined directly without manual work. The knowledge-based miner allows us to use prior knowledge, such as the model produced by clustering as shown in Figure 3, to assign more weight for these events and edges. This particular feature is detailed in the next subsection as a different strategy.

5.3 Prior Knowledge

The knowledge-based miner, besides being able to keep longer paths and be parameterized by the amount of noise (fitting) and window size, can use another model as prior knowledge with a tunable confidence. This feature can be used not only to mine for customer models without saturating the dataset, but also to include certain clusters or behavior, such as the effect of improving the promotional page, or a marketing campaign targeting a certain product.

Figure 4 shows both the model produced by the knowledge-based miner miner on the *normal* dataset, and the output when the model from Figure 3 is applied to the knowledge-based miner. Results are the same in both, except that when the prior knowledge is applied, the output includes the *CartPurchase*, *Confirmation*, and *BuyerEnd* events.

Figure 4 also shows the use of the knowledge miner parameters. Compared to Figure 1 it shows the *UserAdmin* event and more edges and loops between events. The reason is that both figures were executed with lower *window* and *noise* parameters. This shows how models can be abstracted and fitted using these parameters in the knowledge-based miner algorithm.

6 Discussion of Results

The previous section presented three strategies to mine process models to include customer navigation behavior besides general user behavior, as well as a comparison of the mining algorithms. As we are dealing with real web user navigation of a large site, there is no correct process model we can compare our results against.

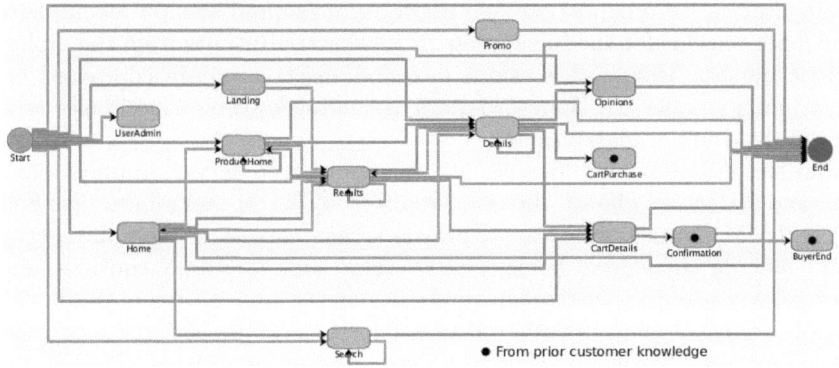

Fig. 4. Knowledge-based miner process models on the normal dataset

The main reasons for this are that there are about one million different pages, most pages can be reached from search engines or link sharing directly and the combinations of pages are too large to generate or validate manually. Rather, we rely on domain knowledge of the site and previous works characterizing the site and generating CBMGs [10].

The first strategy to generate the process models consisted in *saturating* the supplied dataset—in our case with customers—to be able to work with most mining implementations. The alpha miner gave incomplete results in the *saturated* dataset. The heuristic miner process model did not show the relation between the different pages, but displayed them as independent from one another (see Figure 2) except for one combination of pages. The second strategy consisted in *clustering* sessions before applying process mining. *Clustering* enabled mining directly on a specific group of interest, such as customer clusters, but required human intervention to select the target cluster and only represent sessions contained in the selected cluster. A benefit of *clustering*, is that it allowed the alpha miner to produce results on small clusters of similar sessions, and can be used for tools that need a model produced by the alpha miner. The heuristic miner also gave coherent results for clusters. The last strategy, particular to our implementation, was the use of *prior knowledge*, a specific feature of our knowledge-based miner implementation that can use a previously generated model, such as from a customer's clustering as taken from Figure 3. The knowledge-based miner was able to produce process models our domain experts were expecting, as it was able to filter non-critical events, bias towards a particular group, and keep longer paths between edges. Furthermore, the size of the output model can be altered through its parameters to control the noise and trace window size.

Lessons Learned. While applying techniques described in previous sections enabled us to produce meaningful process models, process mining on real logs, including the datasets presented in this study, demonstrates the need for new algorithms that can work with noisy event logs, a large number of events, and underrepresented groups, such as buyer sessions. As with [4], we also quickly found that the alpha miner was not able to produce the process models we and domain experts were expecting. We attribute noise and session incompleteness as the main reasons for the incomplete or incoherent outputs from the alpha and heuristic miners. Most web sessions in our datasets are only composed of one click, while a smaller fraction of visitors, including buyers, have longer sessions which mislead miner classification.

From the different web logs we had available: web server, application, analytics, and RUM; we choose the one produced by RUM techniques (see Section 3). The RUM dataset was free of crawlers that cannot process Javascript, it doesn't include automated background actions such as AJAX controls, and includes pages cached by intermediary proxies or the user browser. While cleaner and more complete than the other available logs, they were still not clean enough for some mining algorithms. Having a large number of activities (pages), was a problem for most of the mining algorithms which failed to produce coherent results and required excessive computational resources. We tested the fuzzy miner in ProM with success as a suitable option to process a large numbers of events and unstructured activities. The fuzzy miner can also group events into clusters for visualization though ProM's interface. However a pre-classification of events into categories is needed not only for miners, but for models to have a clear abstraction level for human consumption. As from our previous experience, we also found that only a small sample of sessions—a few thousand—are needed to produce meaningful process models. However, while this is true for a general process model, for process models that need to reflect seasonal trends, larger datasets are needed. Processing larger datasets requires the mining implementations to be efficient in computational resources as well as parallelizable.

User Feedback. The Atrapalo.com Web Analytics team provided some feedback about the results in this paper. They noted that for a data analyst to use the discovered models, BPM tools need to be integrated into their familiar day-to-day products such as their current Web analytics tools stack. Since the time our results were presented, the general site search feature, which our process models showed as not contributing to the sale process, has been redesigned. With the added features we have been reported that the conversion rate of visitors using the search feature has improved up to 46% and the bounce rate (users that leave the site after visiting this particular page) lowered by 22% for a particular product. Page classification as performed in Section 4.1 was also mentioned to be very useful, as the site contains over a million different URLs and the number of different pages keeps growing making it difficult to get a clear understanding of the site. In general we have found that while larger models are needed for automated processing such as path prediction, simpler, more abstracted models are appropriate for informing business decisions.

7 Conclusions

This paper applied process mining techniques, and in particular the Business Process Insight platform, to analyze web user behavior. We found that web navigation shares characteristics with traditional BPM activities such as loops and parallel tasks. However, sessions only span a few minutes on average and include no human intervention. We also discovered that any analysis of web logs required the classification of URLs to higher level logical tasks. Otherwise, the number of unique URLs—almost a million in our case study—is impractical for human consumption and traditional mining algorithms. Manual URL rewriting rules reduced the number of unique URLs substantially in our case study. We also showed that clustering algorithms can automatically classify URLs, requiring only that each cluster be named. The above classification of URLs allowed web logs to be mined for processes that represent the navigation behavior of users. We found that a knowledge-based process mining algorithm performed the best, generating process models that most resemble the behavior we were expecting in our dataset. We hypothesize that this mining algorithm may perform well in other real web applications, but this will require further study to validate. There are several insights from the obtained process models, such as the low conversion of the *Promo* page, and the ineffectiveness of the general site search feature. Since our first results and feedback, the company redesigned the general site search, improving the conversion rate of visitors using the search feature by up to 46%, and lowering the bounce rate by 22% for a particular product.

Process mining algorithms are designed to extract the dominant behavior observed and filter out noise to keep the resulting mined process manageable. However, in our case study the interesting behavior—those that result in a user buying a product—seldom occur. We expect this to be the case in many web applications. To avoid losing this behavior, we took the approach of saturating the dataset with more traces that result in the outcome of interest. This simple strategy worked well in producing a complete process model that includes both the most common behavior on the site, and also includes the behavior of users that buy a product. An alternate strategy is to provide an expected process model—for example from clustering—as input to the mining algorithm. However, this option is only available with the knowledge-based miner, and requires some domain knowledge. Web sites can be complex to model, but the insights derived from mining the actual behaviors were extremely valuable in our case study for site optimization. We feel that BPM tools and techniques can complement and improve current Web Analytic tools by giving them abstracted views of the most important paths taken by types of visitors. This understanding of their navigation behavior can be used to inform business and IT decisions and improve sales as from the results of this study.

Acknowledgements. We thank Atrapalo.com for the datasets, feedback, and domain knowledge for this study. We also acknowledge Aubrey Rembert who developed and offered support on the knowledge-based miner. This work is partially supported by the Ministry of Science and Technology of Spain under contract TIN2012-34557.

References

1. Aalst, W., et al.: Process mining manifesto. In: Business Process Management Workshops, vol. 99, Springer, Heidelberg (2012)
2. Agrawal, R., Gunopulos, D., Leymann, F.: Mining process models from workflow logs. In: Schek, H.-J., Saltor, F., Ramos, I., Alonso, G. (eds.) EDBT 1998. LNCS, vol. 1377, pp. 469–483. Springer, Heidelberg (1998)

3. Bhushan, R., Nath, R.: Automatic recommendation of web pages for online users using web usage mining. In: ICCS (2012)
4. De Weerdt, J., et al.: A multi-dimensional quality assessment of state-of-the-art process discovery algorithms using real-life event logs. Inf. Syst. 37(7) (2012)
5. Ferreira, D.R., Gillblad, D.: Discovering process models from unlabelled event logs. In: Dayal, U., Eder, J., Koehler, J., Reijers, H.A. (eds.) BPM 2009. LNCS, vol. 5701, pp. 143–158. Springer, Heidelberg (2009)
6. Hall, M., Frank, E., Holmes, G., Pfahringer, B., Reutemann, P., Witten, I.H.: The weka data mining software: an update. SIGKDD Explorations 11(1) (2009)
7. Kemsley, S.: It's not about BPM vs. ACM, it's about a spectrum of process functionality, http://www.column2.com/2011/03/its-not-about-bpm-vs-acm-its-about-a-spectrum-of-process-functionality/
8. Koehler, J.: Business process modeling
9. Kumar, L., Singh, H., Kaur, R.: Web analytics and metrics: a survey. In: ACM ICACCI (2012)
10. Menascé, D.A., Almeida, V.A., Fonseca, R., Mendes, M.A.: A methodology for workload characterization of e-commerce sites. In: ACM EC (1999)
11. Nezhad, H.R.M., Saint-Paul, R., Casati, F., Benatallah, B.: Event correlation for process discovery from web service interaction logs. VLDB J. 20(3) (2011)
12. Nielsen. Trends in online shopping, a Nielsen Consumer report. Technical report, Nielsen (February 2008)
13. Pfeffer, A.: Functional specification of probabilistic process models. In: AAAI (2005)
14. Poggi, N., Carrera, D., Gavald, R., Ayguad, E., Torres, J.: A methodology for the evaluation of high response time on e-commerce users and sales. In: ISF (2012)
15. Poggi, N., et al.: Characterization of workload and resource consumption for an online travel and booking site. In: IEEE IISWC (2010)
16. Rembert, A.J., Ellis, C.S.: Learning the control-flow of a business process using icn-based process models. In: ACM ICSOC, pp. 346–351 (2009)
17. Rozinat, A., Mans, R.S., Song, M., van der Aalst, W.M.P.: Discovering colored petri nets from event logs. STTT 10(1) (2008)
18. Rozinat, A., van der Aalst, W.M.P.: Decision mining in ProM. In: Dustdar, S., Fiadeiro, J.L., Sheth, A.P. (eds.) BPM 2006. LNCS, vol. 4102, pp. 420–425. Springer, Heidelberg (2006)
19. Rozsnyai, S., et al.: Business process insight: An approach and platform for the discovery and analysis of end-to-end business processes. In: IEEE SRII (2012)
20. Rozsnyai, S., Slominski, A., Lakshmanan, G.T.: Discovering event correlation rules for semi-structured business processes. In: ACM DEBS (2011)
21. Sharma, K., Shrivastava, G., Kumar, V.: Web mining: Today and tomorrow. In: ICECT, vol. 1 (2011)
22. Spiliopoulou, M., Pohle, C., Faulstich, L.C.: Improving the effectiveness of a web site with web usage mining. In: Masand, B., Spiliopoulou, M. (eds.) WebKDD 1999. LNCS (LNAI), vol. 1836, pp. 142–162. Springer, Heidelberg (2000)
23. van der Aalst, W.M.P.: Process Mining - Discovery, Conformance and Enhancement of Business Processes. Springer (2011)
24. van der Aalst, W.M.P.: et al. Workflow mining: a survey of issues and approaches. Data Knowl. Eng., 47(2) (November 2003)
25. van der Aalst, W.M.P., Schonenberg, M.H., Song, M.: Time prediction based on process mining. Inf. Syst. 36(2), 450–475 (2011)
26. van der Aalst, W.M.P., van Dongen, B.F., Gunther, C.W., Rozinat, A., Verbeek, E., Weijters, T.: ProM: The process mining toolkit. In: BPM (Demos) (2009)
27. Waisberg, D., et al.: Web analytics 2.0: Empowering customer centricity (2009)

Discovering Data-Aware Declarative Process Models from Event Logs

Fabrizio Maria Maggi[1], Marlon Dumas[1], Luciano García-Bañuelos[1], and Marco Montali[2]

[1] University of Tartu, Estonia
{f.m.maggi,marlon.dumas,luciano.garcia}@ut.ee
[2] KRDB Research Centre, Free University of Bozen-Bolzano, Italy
montali@inf.unibz.it

Abstract. A wealth of techniques are available to automatically discover business process models from event logs. However, the bulk of these techniques yield procedural process models that may be useful for detailed analysis, but do not necessarily provide a comprehensible picture of the process. Additionally, barring few exceptions, these techniques do not take into account data attributes associated to events in the log, which can otherwise provide valuable insights into the rules that govern the process. This paper contributes to filling these gaps by proposing a technique to automatically discover declarative process models that incorporate both control-flow dependencies and data conditions. The discovered models are conjunctions of first-order temporal logic expressions with an associated graphical representation (Declare notation). Importantly, the proposed technique discovers underspecified models capturing recurrent rules relating pairs of activities, as opposed to full specifications of process behavior – thus providing a summarized view of key rules governing the process. The proposed technique is validated on a real-life log of a cancer treatment process.

Keywords: Automated Process Discovery, Predicate Mining, Linear Temporal Logic, Declare.

1 Introduction

Business processes in modern organizations are generally supported and controlled by information systems. These systems usually record relevant events, such as messages and transactions, in the form of event logs. Process mining aims at exploiting these event logs in order to model and analyze the underlying processes. One of the most developed family of process mining techniques is automated process discovery. Automated process discovery aims at constructing a process model from an event log consisting of traces, such that each trace corresponds to one execution of the process. Each event in a trace consists as a minimum of an event class (i.e., the task to which the event corresponds) and generally a timestamp. In some cases, other information may be available such as the originator of the event (i.e., the performer of the task) as well as data produced by the event in the form of attribute-value pairs.

The Process Mining Manifesto [9] argues that one of the open challenges in process mining is *to find a suitable representational bias (language) to visualize the resulting models*. The suitability of a language largely depends on the level of standardization and the environment of the process. Standardized processes in stable environments (e.g., a process for handling insurance claims) are characterized by low complexity of collaboration, coordination and decision making. In addition, they are highly predictable, meaning that it is feasible to determine the path that the process will follow. On the other hand, processes in dynamic environments are more complex and less predictable. They comprise a very large number of possible paths as process participants have considerable freedom in determining the next steps in the process (e.g., a doctor in a healthcare process).

As discussed in [24,20,23], procedural languages, such as BPMN, EPCs and Petri nets, are suitable for describing standardized processes in stable environments. Due to their predictability and low complexity, these processes can be described under a "closed world" assumption, meaning that it is feasible to explicitly represent all the allowed behavior of the process. In contrast, the use of procedural languages for describing processes in dynamic environments leads to complex and incomprehensible models. In this context, declarative process modeling languages are more appropriate [23]. Unlike their procedural counterparts, declarative models describe a process under an "open world" assumption, such that everything is allowed unless it is explicitly forbidden. Accordingly, a declarative model focuses on capturing commitments and prohibitions that describe what must or must not occur in a given state of the process.

Previous work on automated discovery of declarative process models [16,14] has focused on mining control-flow dependencies, such as "the execution of a task entails that another task must eventually be executed". This prior work, as well as the bulk of process discovery techniques for procedural languages, ignores data attributes attached to events, besides the event class. Hence, the resulting models lack insights into the role of data in the execution of the process.

The importance of data in business processes, particularly dynamic ones, is paramount as it is often data that drives the decisions that participants make. In dynamic processes, the fact that a task A is executed often tells us little about what must or must not happen later. It is only when considering the data produced by task A and other data associated to the process that we can state that something must or must not happen later. This holds in particular for healthcare processes, which according to Rebuge et al. [21] involve numerous variables that determine how a specific patient should be treated (e.g., age, gender, type of disease).

This paper addresses the above gap by presenting a technique to discover data-aware declarative process models, represented using an extension of the *Declare* notation [17]. Declare is a declarative language that combines a formal semantics grounded in Linear Temporal Logic (LTL) on finite traces,[1] with a graphical representation. In essence, a Declare model is a collection of LTL rules, each capturing a control-flow dependency between two activities. Declare itself

---

[1] For compactness, we will use the LTL acronym to denote LTL on finite traces.

is not designed to capture data aspects of a process. Accordingly, for the sake of discovering data-aware models, we extend Declare with the ability to define data conditions (predicates). The extended (data-aware) Declare notation is defined in terms of LTL-FO (First-Order LTL) rules, each one capturing an association between a task, a condition and another task. An example of such rule is that if a task is executed and a certain data condition holds after this execution, some other task must eventually be performed.

The proposed approach relies on the notion of *constraint activation* [3]. For example, for the constraint "every request is eventually acknowledged" each request is an activation. This activation becomes a fulfillment or a violation depending on whether the request is followed by an acknowledgement or not. In our approach, we first generate a set of candidate constraints considering the constraints that are most frequently activated. Then, we apply an algorithm to replay the log and classify activations (with their data snapshots) into fulfillments and violations. Given the resulting classification problem, we use invariant discovery techniques to identify the data conditions that should hold for a constraint activation to be fulfilled.

The paper is structured as follows. Section 2 introduces the basic Declare notation as well as the techniques used to discover data conditions. Next, Section 3 introduces the proposed data-aware extension of Declare and the technique for automated discovery of data-aware Declare models. In Section 4, we validate our approach in a real-life scenario. Finally, Section 5 discusses related work and Section 6 concludes and spells out directions for future work.

2 Background

In this section, we introduce some background material needed to present our proposed approach. In Section 2.1, we give an overview of the Declare language and introduce the notion of activation, fulfillment and violation for a Declare constraint. We describe the data condition discovery technique we use in our discovery algorithm in Section 2.2.

2.1 Declare: Some Basic Notions

Declare is a declarative process modeling language first introduced by Pesic and van der Aalst in [18]. A Declare model is a set of constraints that must hold in conjunction during the process execution. Declare constraints are equipped with a graphical notation and an LTL semantics. Examples of Declare constraints are $response(A, B)$ (formally: $\Box(A \rightarrow \Diamond B)$), $responded\ existence(A, B)$ (formally: $\Diamond A \rightarrow \Diamond B$) and $precedence(A, B)$ (formally: $(\neg B \sqcup A) \vee \Box(\neg B)$). We refer the reader to [19] for a complete overview of the language.

Constraint $response(A, B)$ indicates that if A occurs, B must eventually follow. Therefore, this constraint is satisfied for traces such as $t_1 = \langle A, A, B, C \rangle$, $t_2 = \langle B, B, C, D \rangle$ and $t_3 = \langle A, B, C, B \rangle$, but not for $t_4 = \langle A, B, A, C \rangle$ because, in this case, the second A is not followed by a B.

Note that, in t_2, $response(A,B)$ is satisfied in a trivial way because A never occurs. In this case, we say that the constraint is *vacuously satisfied* [11]. In [3], the authors introduce the notion of *behavioral vacuity detection* according to which a constraint is non-vacuously satisfied in a trace when it is activated in that trace. An *constraint activation* in a trace is an event whose occurrence imposes, because of that constraint, some obligations on other events in the same trace. For example, A is an activation for $response(A,B)$ because the execution of A forces B to be executed eventually.

A constraint activation can be classified as a *fulfillment* or a *violation*. When a trace is perfectly compliant with respect to a constraint, every constraint activation in the trace leads to a fulfillment. Consider, again, constraint $response(A,B)$. In trace t_1, the constraint is activated and fulfilled twice, whereas, in trace t_3, the same constraint is activated and fulfilled only once. On the other hand, when a trace is not compliant with respect to a constraint, a constraint activation in the trace can lead to a fulfillment but also to a violation (and at least one activation leads to a violation). In trace t_4, for example, $response(A,B)$ is activated twice, but the first activation leads to a fulfillment (eventually B occurs) and the second activation leads to a violation (the target event class B does not occur eventually).

In [3], the authors define two metrics to measure the conformance of an event log with respect to a constraint in terms of violations and fulfillments, called *violation ratio* and *fulfillment ratio* of the constraint in the log. These metrics are valued 0 if the log contains no activations of the considered constraint. Otherwise, they are evaluated as the percentage of violations and fulfillments of the constraint over the total number of activations.

2.2 Discovery of Data Conditions

Given a set of Declare constraints extracted from an event log, a key step of the proposed technique is to generate a set of data-aware constraints, meaning constraints that incorporate conditions based on data attributes found in the logs. This problem can be mapped to a classification problem as follows. Given a Declare constraint and a set of traces, we can determine by "replaying" the log, the points in each trace of the log where the constraint is fulfilled or violated. In other words, we can construct a set of *trace snapshots* where the constraint is fulfilled and another set where the constraint is violated, where a snapshot is an assignment of values to each attribute appearing in the log (possibly including "null" values). Given these two sets, classification techniques, such as decision tree learning, can be used to discover a condition on the data attributes that discriminates between fulfillments and violations. The discovered condition is then used to enrich the initial (control-flow) Declare constraint.

A similar principle is used in ProM's Decision Miner [22] for the purpose of discovering conditions that can be associated to branches of a decision point of a business process model. ProM's Decision Miner applies decision tree learning to discover conditions consisting of atoms of the form 'variable op constant', where 'op' is a relational operator (e.g., =, <, or >). Given the capabilities of standard decision tree learning techniques, this approach does not allow us to discover expressions of the form 'variable op variable' or conditions involving linear combinations of variables. This limitation is lifted in our previous work [5], where we combine standard decision tree learning with a technique for the discovery of (likely) invariants from execution logs, i.e., Daikon [7]. Daikon allows us to discover invariants that hold true at a given point in a program, where a program point may be a method call, a field access or some other construction of the target programming language. The execution logs that serve as input to Daikon are commonly generated by instrumented code that monitors the program's points of interest, but they can also come from other sources. Given such execution logs, Daikon discovers invariants consisting of linear expressions with up to three variables as well as expressions involving arrays.

The technique described in [5] uses Daikon as an oracle to discover conditions that, given a decision point (e.g., XOR-split), discriminates between the cases where one branch of the decision point is taken and those where the other branch is taken. In a nutshell, this technique works as follows: given a set of traces S, a process model M discovered from S and a task T in this process model, Daikon is used to discover invariants that hold true before each execution of task T. Given a decision point between a branch starting with task $T1$ and a branch starting with task $T2$, the invariants discovered for branch $T1$ and those discovered for branch $T2$ are combined in order to discover a conjunctive expression that discriminates between $T1$ and $T2$. In order to discover disjunctive expressions, decision tree learning is employed to first partition the observation instances where $T1$ (or $T2$) are executed into disjoint subsets. One conjunctive expression is then discovered for each subset.

In this paper, this technique is employed to discover conditions that discriminate between violations and fulfillments of a constraint as detailed in Section 3.2.

3 Discovering Data-Aware Declare Models

In this section, we first define a semantics to enrich Declare constraints with data conditions based on First-Order Linear Temporal Logic (LTL-FO). Then, we present an algorithm for discovering Declare models with data.

3.1 LTL-FO Semantics for Declare

We now define a semantics to extend the standard Declare constraints with data conditions. To do this, we use First-Order Linear Temporal Logic (LTL-FO), which is the first-order extension of propositional LTL. While many reasoning tasks are clearly undecidable for LTL-FO, this logic is appropriate to unambiguously describe the semantics of the data-aware Declare constraints we can generate by using our algorithm.

The defined semantics (shown in Table 1) is quite straightforward. In particular, the original LTL semantics of a Declare constraint is extended by requiring an additional condition on data, $Cond$, to hold when the constraint is activated.

Table 1. LTL-FO semantics and graphical representation for some Declare constraints extended with data conditions

constraint	description	formalization	notation
responded existence(A,B,Cond)	if A occurs and Cond holds, B must occur before or after A	$\Diamond(A \wedge Cond) \to \Diamond B$	A —Cond→ B
response(A,B,Cond)	if A occurs and Cond holds, B must occur afterwards	$\Box((A \wedge Cond) \to \Diamond B)$	A —Cond→ B
precedence(A,B,Cond)	if B occurs and Cond holds, A must have occurred before	$(\neg(B \wedge Cond) \sqcup A) \vee \Box(\neg(B \wedge Cond))$	A —Cond→ B
alternate response(A,B,Cond)	if A occurs and Cond holds, B must occur afterwards, without further As in between	$\Box((A \wedge Cond) \to \bigcirc(\neg A \sqcup B))$	A —Cond→ B
alternate precedence(A,B,Cond)	if B occurs and Cond holds, A must have occurred before, without other Bs in between	$((\neg(B \wedge Cond) \sqcup A) \vee \Box(\neg(B \wedge Cond))) \wedge \Box((B \wedge Cond) \to \bigcirc(\neg B \sqcup A))$	A —Cond→ B
chain response(A,B,Cond)	if A occurs and Cond holds, B must occur next	$\Box((A \wedge Cond) \to \bigcirc B)$	A —Cond→ B
chain precedence(A,B,Cond)	if B occurs and Cond holds, A must have occurred immediately before	$\Box(\bigcirc(B \wedge Cond) \to A)$	A —Cond→ B
not resp. existence(A,B,Cond)	if A occurs and Cond holds, B can never occur	$\Diamond(A \wedge Cond) \to \neg \Diamond B$	A —Cond‖→ B
not response(A,B,Cond)	if A occurs and Cond holds, B cannot occur afterwards	$\Box((A \wedge Cond) \to \neg \Diamond B)$	A —Cond‖→ B
not precedence(A,B,Cond)	if B occurs and Cond holds, A cannot have occurred before	$\Box(A \to \neg \Diamond(B \wedge Cond))$	A —Cond‖→ B
not chain response(A,B,Cond)	if A occurs and Cond holds, B cannot be executed next	$\Box((A \wedge Cond) \to \neg \bigcirc B)$	A —Cond‖→ B
not chain precedence(A,B,Cond)	if B occurs and Cond holds, A cannot have occurred immediately before	$\Box(\bigcirc(B \wedge Cond) \to \neg A)$	A —Cond‖→ B

$Cond$ is a closed first-order formula with the following structure: $\exists x_1, \ldots, x_n$. $curState(x_1, \ldots, x_n) \wedge \Phi(x_1, \ldots, x_n)$, where $curState/n$ is a relation storing the n data available in the system (considering both case attributes and event attributes in the log) and Φ/n is a first-order formula constraining such data by means of conjunctions, disjunctions and relational operators.

For example, $response(A, B, Cond)$ specifies that whenever A occurs and condition $Cond$ holds true, then a corresponding occurrence of B is expected to eventually happen. Constraint $precedence(A, B, Cond)$ indicates that whenever B occurs and $Cond$ holds, then an occurrence of A must have been executed beforehand. The semantics for negative relations is also very intuitive. For example, $not\ responded\ existence(A, B, Cond)$ indicates that if an instance of A occurs and $Cond$ holds, then no occurrence of B can happen before or after A. Note that some Declare constraints derive from the conjunction of other constraints. For example, the $succession$ constraint is the conjunction of $response$ and $precedence$. In this case, we have a condition on the attribute values of A and a condition on the attribute values of B. These two conditions can be, in principle, different.

Based on this semantics, the notion of constraint activation changes. Activations of data-aware Declare constraints are all those constraint activations (according to the standard definition) for which $Cond$ is true. For example, $response(A, B, Cond)$ is activated when A occurs and, also, $Cond$ is valid. On the other hand, $precedence(A, B, Cond)$ is activated when B occurs and $Cond$ is valid. The definitions of fulfillments and violations are also adapted accordingly.

3.2 Discovery Algorithm

In a nutshell, our approach aims at *discovering data-aware Declare constraints with fulfillment ratio close to 1 from an event log*. We thus start from event logs where the process execution traces and their events are equipped with data, modeled as attribute-value pairs.

More specifically, the algorithm takes as input an event log, which is a set of execution traces. Each execution trace represents, as usual, the sequence of events characterizing a specific instantiation of the process. Our focus is on *case data*, i.e., we consider data to be attached to the case and their values to be manipulated by the corresponding events. For this reason, a case can be associated to a set of key-value pairs defining the initial values for some of the data. These can be extracted by applying the caseAtts/1 function to a trace. The other data mentioned in the events of the log are implicitly considered to have an initial null value.

Events are meant to manipulate such case data. Specifically, each event ev is associated to: *(i)* a *class* that represents the task to which the event refers to and that can be extracted with evClass(ev); *(ii)* a *timestamp*; *(iii)* a set of attribute-value pairs that denotes the impact of the event in terms of case data and that can be extracted with evAtts(ev). We follow the classical *commonsense law of inertia*: given a data attribute a, its value remains constant until it is explicitly overridden by an event that provides a new value for a.

The discovery of data-aware Declare constraints is based on a supervised learning approach. Before discussing the details of the algorithm, we introduce a short example that summarizes its key aspects. The algorithm requires the user to choose the constraint types she is interested in. In the following, we assume that *response* is selected. Consider an event log constituted by the following execution traces (we use triples to represent the events):

$\{(A, 1, \{x = 1, y = 1\}), (B, 5, \{x = 2, y = 2\}), (C, 8, \{x = 3, y = 3\})\}$
$\{(A, 1, \{x = 1, y = 2\}), (B, 3, \{x = 1, y = 2\})\}$
$\{(A, 1, \{x = 2, y = 1\}), (C, 7, \{x = 2, y = 4\})\}$

The event log contains three event classes: A, B and C. Therefore, in principle, all possible pairs of event classes could be involved in response constraints: response from A to B, from A to C, from B to A, from B to C, from C to A and from C to B. Among all these possibilities, only those that are "relevant" are considered to be candidate constraints. Relevance is measured in terms of number of activations, which, in the case of response, correspond to the execution of the source activity.

For example, response constraints with source A are activated once in each trace present in the log above, whereas response constraints with source B or

C are activated in only two traces out from three. Assuming to filter away those constraints with number of activations < 3, only response constraints with source A are kept. For each of those, the activations are classified as fulfillments or violations, depending on whether there is an event that refers to the target activity and occurs after it.

In the case of $response(A, B)$, the activations in the first two traces are marked as fulfilled, whereas the one for the third trace is not (in fact, no B is present in the third trace). This means that this constraint is not fully supported by the log. The classification of activations into fulfillments and violations is used as input of the approach discussed in Section 2.2. With this approach, we try to improve the support of a constraint by discovering finer-grained data conditions, used to restrict the context of application for the constraint. For example, we could learn that $response(A, B)$ is fully supported by the log whenever at the time A is executed, the value for attribute x is 1.

The full algorithm is shown in Fig. 1. It takes as input an event log, a set of constraint types userTypes previously selected by the user, a threshold minRatio representing the minimum expected fulfillment ratio for a constraint to be discovered and a threshold minActivations representing the minimum number of activations for a constraint to be considered as a candidate.

All the information needed for the discovery is collected by traversing the log twice. In the first iteration, the event classes and the (event and case) attributes with their types are collected (lines 2-9). To start the second iteration, we invoke function generateConstraints to generate the set of possible candidate constraints given the required minimum level of activation support, minActivations (line 10). This function produces all possible constraints of the form $Constr(A, B)$, where $Constr$ is one of the constraint types in userTypes and A and B are event classes in eClasses (the one corresponding to the constraint activation with at least minActivations occurrences).

In the second iteration (lines 14-28), we process each event in the log with a twofold purpose: constructing a snapshot that tracks the values of data obtained after the event execution and classifying constraint activations into fulfillments and violations. These two sources of information are used to select the final constraints and decorate them with data-aware conditions. In particular, when we start replaying a trace trace, we create a set $state_0$ of pairs (attribute,value), where each event/case attribute is firstly initialized to null (line 15) and each case attribute present in trace is then associated to the corresponding value (line 16). Given a trace/event x and an attribute a, we use function value(x,a) to extract the corresponding value. When an event occur at position p, the value of each event attribute is replaced by the new value attached to the event just occurred (through the update of curState, line 20), so as to reconstruct the effect of the event in terms of data values update. In this way, we associate each event occurring in trace at position p to snapshot[p], calculated by updating the previous state with the contribution of that event (line 21).

In parallel with the construction of snapshots, constraint activations are classified into fulfillments and violations. For every trace, each candidate constraint

Fig. 1. Discovery algorithm for data-aware Declare

```
Algorithm Discovery
Input: log, an event log
       userTypes, a set of Declare constraint types
       minRatio, the minimum expected fulfillment ratio for a constraint to be discovered
       minActivations, the minimum number of activations for a constraint to be considered as a candidate
 1: eClasses = ∅; cAtts = ∅; model = ∅; prunedModel = ∅;
 2: for each trace in log do
 3:     cAtts = cAtts ∪ caseAtts(trace);
 4:     for each trace in log do
 5:         for each ev in trace do
 6:             cAtts = cAtts ∪ evAtts(ev); eClasses = eClasses ∪ evClass(ev);
 7:         end
 8:     end
 9: end
10: constraints = generateConstraints(userTypes,eClasses,minActivations);
11: for each c in constraints do
12:     fulfSnapshots(c) = ∅; violSnapshots(c) = ∅;
13: end
14: for each trace in log do
15:     state₀ = {(a, null) | a ∈ cAtts};
16:     for each a in caseAtts(trace) do state₀ = (state₀ \ {(a, null)}) ∪ {(a, value(trace, a))};
17:     curState = state₀;
18:     snapshot = new Array(length(trace));
19:     for (p=0; p < length(trace); p++) do
20:         for each a in evAtts(trace[p]) do curState = (curState \ {(a, _)}) ∪ {(a, value(trace[p], a))};
21:         snapshot[p] = curState;
22:         for each c in constraints do classifyActivations(candidate, id(trace), p);
23:     end
24:     for each c in constraints do
25:         for each fp in getFulfPositions(c) do fulfSnapshots(c) = fulfSnapshots(c) ∪ snapshot[fp];
26:         for each vp in getViolPositions(c) do violSnapshots(c) = violSnapshots(c) ∪ snapshot[vp];
27:     end
28: end
29: for each c in constraints do
30:     if (min{|fulfSnapshots(c)|, |violSnapshots(c)|} ≥ 10 × |cAtts|)
31:         dataCondition= callDaikon(fulfSnapshots(c),violSnapshots(c));
32:         model= model ∪ (c, dataCondition);
33:     end
34: end
35: for each c in model do complianceCount(c) = 0;
36: for each trace in log do
37:     for each c in model do
38:         if (checkCompliance(trace, c)) complianceCount(c)++;
39:     end
40: end
41: for each c in model do
42:     if ($\frac{complianceCount(c)}{|log|}$ ≥ minRatio) prunedModel = prunedModel ∪ c; 42
43: end
44: return prunedModel;
```

is associated to a set of activations. Internally, every activation is a quadruple (candidate, id(trace), p, curState) indicating that in position p of the trace identified by id(trace), an event occurs activating constraint candidate and that snapshot(id(trace), p) = curState in the same position. These quadruples are classified into fulfillments and violations by leveraging on function classifyActivations (line 22). This function depends on the constraint type.

In particular, there is a difference when we are processing an event for a constraint looking at the past (e.g., *precedence*) and for constraints looking at the future (e.g., *response*). For constraints looking at the past, we store each scanned event as possible target in a sorted list. The same event will be an activation for some candidate constraints. In particular, it will be a fulfillment if the list of the events already occurred contains a possible target and a violation if the list does not contain such an event. For constraints looking at the future, we process an event by considering it as a "pending" activation waiting for a possible target to be classified as a fulfillment. The same event can be, on the other hand, a target for a pending activation. All the activations that are still pending when the trace has been completely replayed are classified as violations (indeed, no further events can occur to fulfill them). Note that undirected constraints (e.g., *responded existence*) use an hybrid approach. Furthermore, for each negative constraint the same algorithm used for the corresponding positive constraint is adopted, by substituting fulfillments with violations and vice-versa.

As an example, consider constraint (response, A, B). Activation ((response,A,B), 123, 4, curState) is added to the list of pending activations whenever in trace 123 at position 4, activity A is executed. This activation is pending, since it expects a consequent execution of B. If B occurs in 123 at a later position, say, 12, then the activation at position 4 is classified as a fulfillment. On the other hand, if we evaluate constraint (not response, A, B) on the same trace, ((not response,A,B), 123, 4, curState) would be classified as a violation (indeed, *not response* would forbid the presence of B after A).

When the processing of a trace is completed, the aforementioned functions have calculated, for each constraint c, the set of positions at which an activation for c was classified as a fulfillment or as a violation. These two sets can then be retrieved by respectively calling function getFulfPositions(c) and getViolPositions(c). Starting from these positions, we can in turn obtain the corresponding snapshots, globally accumulating them into two sets fulfSnapshots(c) and violSnapshots(c) (lines 24-27).

With the information collected in fulfSnapshots(c) and violSnapshots(c), we proceed with the discovery of data-aware conditions using the approach discussed in Section 2.2 (lines 29-34). It is well known that the quality of decision trees is sensible to the amount of the observations for each class being considered and so is the method used for discovering data conditions. To filter cases with not enough observations, we use a common heuristic as described in [10]. According to this heuristic, the number of samples for classifier learning should be at least 10 times the number of features. Hence, we filter out candidate constraints that have a number of fulfillments and a number of violations (i.e., number of positive and negative samples) lower than 10 times the number of attributes in the log.

Finally, the resulting data-aware Declare model can be further pruned by means of threshold minRatio, i.e., the minimum expected fulfillment ratio for a discovered data-aware constraint. Function checkCompliance/2 is called to check whether the aforementioned ratio is above minRatio or not. If so, the constraint is maintained in the final model and discarded otherwise (lines 41-43).

Table 2. Discovered response constraints

A	B	data condition
Milk acid dehydrogenase LDH kinetic	squamous cell carcinoma using eia	(((Diagnosis code == "M13") || (Diagnosis code == "822")) || (Diagnosis code == "M12"))
First outpatient consultation	teletherapy - megavolt photons bestrali	(((org:group == "Radiotherapy") || (Treatment code == "113")) || ((Diagnosis == "Gynaecologische tumoren") || (Diagnosis == "Maligne neoplasma cervix uteri") || (Diagnosis == "maligniteit cervix")))
bilirubin- total	squamous cell carcinoma using eia	((Diagnosis code == "M13") || (Diagnosis code == "822"))
gammaglutamyl- transpeptidase	squamous cell carcinoma using eia	(((Diagnosis code == "M13") || (Diagnosis code == "822")) || (Diagnosis code == "M12"))
unconjugated bilirubin	squamous cell carcinoma using eia	(((Diagnosis code == "M13") || (Diagnosis code == "822"))|| (Diagnosis code == "M12"))
outpatient follow-up consultation	differential count automatically	(Specialism code == "13")
CEA - tumor marker using meia	squamous cell carcinoma using eia	(((((Diagnosis == "Maligne neoplasma cervix uteri") || (Diagnosis == "maligniteit cervix")) || (Diagnosis code == "M13")) || ((Diagnosis == "Plaveiselcelca. vagina st II") || (Diagnosis == "maligniteit vagina"))) || ((Diagnosis == "Plav.celcarc. vulva: st II") || (Diagnosis == "maligne melanoom van de vulva")))

Table 3. No. of activations, fulfillments and fulfillment ratio (response)

A	B	# activ no data	# activ data	# fulf. no data	# fulf. data	fulf. ratio no data	fulf. ratio data
Milk acid dehydrogenase LDH kinetic	squamous cell carcinoma using eia	1282	474	420	315	0.32	0.66
First outpatient consultation	teletherapy - megavolt photons bestrali	1200	646	530	452	0.44	0.69
bilirubin- total	squamous cell carcinoma using eia	1253	499	419	321	0.33	0.64
gammaglutamyl- transpeptidase	squamous cell carcinoma using eia	1442	595	479	372	0.33	0.62
unconjugated bilirubin	squamous cell carcinoma using eia	967	406	361	284	0.37	0.69
outpatient follow-up consultation	differential count automatically	6860	2575	2096	1345	0.30	0.52
CEA - tumor marker using meia	squamous cell carcinoma using eia	465	132	145	103	0.31	0.78

Table 4. Discovered not response constraints

A	B	data condition
rhesus factor d - Centrifuge method - email	ABO blood group antigens other than rhesu	(Age >= 46)
rhesus factor d - Centrifuge method - email	cde phenotyping	(Age >= 46)
Milk acid dehydrogenase LDH kinetic	teletherapy - megavolt photons bestrali	((((((Diagnosis code == "M16") || (Diagnosis code == "821")) || ((Diagnosis == "Maligne neoplasma adnexa uteri") || (Diagnosis == "Maligne neoplasma vulva") || (Diagnosis == "maligniteit vulva"))) || (Diagnosis code == "823")) || ((Diagnosis == "Plaveiselcelca. vagina st II") || (Diagnosis == "maligniteit vagina"))) || (Diagnosis code == "M11"))
bilirubin - total	teletherapy - megavolt photons bestrali	((((((Diagnosis code == "M16") || (Diagnosis code == "821")) || ((Diagnosis == "Maligne neoplasma adnexa uteri") || (Diagnosis == "Maligne neoplasma vulva") || (Diagnosis == "maligniteit vulva"))) || (Diagnosis code == "823")) || (Diagnosis code == "M11")) || (Diagnosis == "maligniteit myometrium"))
unconjugated bilirubin	teletherapy - megavolt photons bestrali	(((((Diagnosis code == "M16") || (Diagnosis code == "821")) || (Diagnosis code == "M11")) || ((Diagnosis code == "M13") && (Diagnosis == "maligniteit cervix"))) || (Diagnosis code == "839")) || (Treatment code == "503"))
alkaline phosphatase-kinetic-	teletherapy - megavolt photons bestrali	(((((Diagnosis code == "M16") || (Diagnosis code == "821")) || ((Diagnosis == "Maligne neoplasma adnexa uteri") || (Diagnosis == "Maligne neoplasma vulva") || (Diagnosis == "maligniteit vulva"))) || (Diagnosis code == "823")) || (Diagnosis code == "M11"))
ABO blood group and rhesus factor	ABO blood group antigens other than rhesu	(Age >= 46)
ABO blood group and rhesus factor	cde phenotyping	(Age >= 46)

Table 5. No. of activations, fulfillments and fulfillment ratio (not response)

A	B	# activ no data	# activ data	# fulf. no data	# fulf. data	fulf. ratio no data	fulf. ratio data
rhesus factor d - Centrifuge method - email	ABO blood group antigens other than rhesu	1558	1071	1271	1041	0.81	0.97
rhesus factor d - Centrifuge method - email	cde phenotyping	1558	1071	1273	1043	0.81	0.97
Milk acid dehydrogenase LDH kinetic	teletherapy - megavolt photons bestrali	1191	541	908	528	0.76	0.97
bilirubin - total	teletherapy - megavolt photons bestrali	1166	518	880	504	0.75	0.97
unconjugated bilirubin	teletherapy - megavolt photons bestrali	909	457	676	441	0.74	0.96
alkaline phosphatase-kinetic-	teletherapy - megavolt photons bestrali	1326	557	1001	544	0.75	0.97
ABO blood group and rhesus factor	ABO blood group antigens other than rhesu	1558	1071	1271	1041	0.81	0.97
ABO blood group and rhesus factor	cde phenotyping	1558	1071	1273	1043	0.81	0.97

4 Validation

We implemented the approach as a plug-in of the process mining tool ProM.[2] As a proof of concept, we validated the approach with the event log used in the BPI challenge 2011 [1] that records the treatment of patients diagnosed with cancer from a large Dutch hospital. The event log contains 1143 cases and 150,291 events distributed across 623 event classes. Moreover, the event log contains a total of 13 domain specific attributes, e.g., Age, Diagnosis Code, Treatment code, in addition to the standard XES attributes, i.e., concept:name, lifecycle:transition, time:timestamp and org:group. In our experiments, we take into consideration only the domain specific attributes.

In a first experiment,[3] we discovered data-aware *response* constraints from the event log, with a fulfillment ratio of at least 0.5. Since the log contains 13 data attributes, the candidate constraints must have at least 130 fulfillments and 130 violations (i.e., 10 times the number of attributes, as explained in Section 3.2). The execution time for this experiment was 9.6 minutes for the first traversal of the log (gathering of data snapshots, fulfillments and violations for each candidate constraint) and 15.3 minutes for the discovery of data-aware conditions. The constraints discovered are summarized in Table 2.

In Table 3, we compare the number of activations and fulfillments for the discovered constraints, first without considering the data conditions and then considering the data conditions (in bold). As expected, both the number of activations and the number of fulfillments decrease when the data conditions are considered. However, the decrease in the number of fulfillments is less pronounced than the decrease in the number of activations. If we interpret the fulfillment ratio as a measure of goodness of a constraint, we obtain better results when considering the data conditions (see the last two columns of Table 3).

---

[2] www.processmining.org
[3] The experiments were performed on a standard, 2.6 GHz dual-core processor laptop.

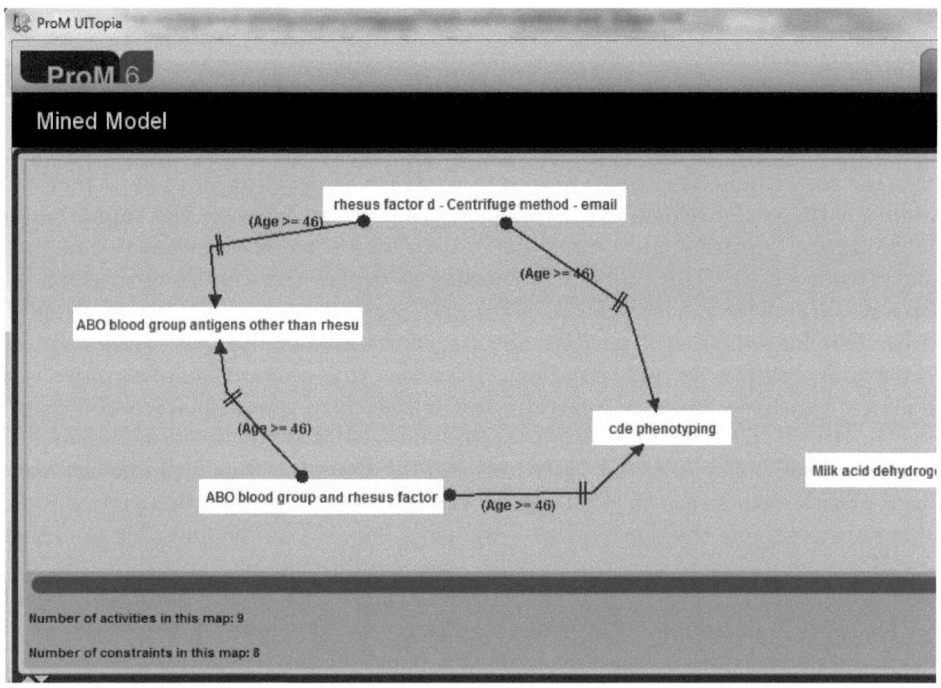

Fig. 2. Some of the discovered not response constraints in ProM

In a second experiment, we considered the discovery of *not response* constraints. It is worth noting that negative constraints are interesting because they specify forbidden scenarios that usually result in extremely complex representations when using procedural modeling languages. For this experiment, we decided to discover data-aware *not response* constraints with a fulfillment ratio of at least 0.95. The execution time for this experiment was 13.3 minutes for the first traversal of the log (to collect data snapshots and fulfillments and violations for each candidate constraint) and 14.1 minutes for the discovery of data conditions. The *not response* constraints discovered are summarized in Table 4. Interestingly, in this experiment we discovered more complex data conditions. For instance, the *not response* constraint between *unconjugated bilirubin* and *teletherapy - megavolt photons bestrali* has a data condition associated with a combination of conjunctions and disjunctions.

In Table 5, we compare the number of activations and the number of fulfillments for the constraints discovered in the second experiment. Similarly to the results obtained in the first experiment, we can clearly observe a lift in the fulfillment ratio when the data conditions are considered. In Fig. 2, we present a screenshot of ProM with the data-aware Declare model discovered in the second experiment. For example, the *not response* constraint between *rhesus factor d - Centrifuge method - email* and *ABO blood group antigens other than rhesu* indicates that, if the age of the patient is greater than or equal to 46, when *rhesus factor d - Centrifuge method - email* occurs, then *ABO blood group antigens other than rhesu* can no longer occur.

5 Related Work

Several algorithms have been proposed to discover declarative process models. Some of these algorithms [12,8,4] assume that every trace in the input log is labeled as a "positive" or a "negative" case, where a negative case is one that should not occur. The problem of mining a declarative model is mapped to one of discriminating between positive and negative cases. The assumption of a pre-existing labeling of positive and negative cases enables the separation of constraint fulfillments and violations. However, this assumption often does not hold as negative cases are generally not explicitly present in a real-life event log. In [16,14], LTL model checking techniques are used to classify negative and positive cases (i.e., constraint violations and fulfillments), thus avoiding the need for a preprocessing step to explicitly label the traces. The approach presented in this paper extends the one in [16,14] by using data attributes in order to enrich candidate control-flow constraints with data conditions. We have shown in the case study that this enrichment leads to constraints with higher fulfillment ratio.

The work reported in [6] provides an alternative approach to declarative process mining that does not assume explicit labeling of positive and negative cases. In this approach, each Declare constraint is mapped to a regular expression. The regular expressions are used to generate a set of matrices of fulfillments and these matrices are used to generate a Declare model. It would be worth investigating the combination of this approach with our data enrichment algorithm. To this end, the approach in [6] would first have to be extended to reconstruct the constraint activations and the corresponding fulfillments and violations.

Automated discovery of behavioral models enhanced with data conditions has been addressed recently in [13,22,5]. In [13], a technique is presented to mine finite state machines extended with data. This work builds on top of a well-known technique to mine finite state machines that incrementally merges states based on automata equivalence notions (e.g., trace equivalence). However, this approach is not suitable for discovering business process models, as automata do not capture concurrency and concurrency is common in business processes. ProM's decision miner [22] embodies a technique to discover data-aware procedural process models, based on existing techniques for discovering "control-flow" process models (e.g., Petri nets) and decision trees. [5] extends ProM's decision miner in order to discover more general conditions as discussed in Section 2.2.

6 Conclusion and Future Work

This paper has presented a technique to automatically discover data-aware declarative models consisting of LTL-FO rules from event logs. A validation on real-life logs from a cancer treatment process demonstrates that the technique can discover more precise rules (higher fulfillment ratio) compared to a technique for discovering declarative models without data conditions.

As future work, we will carry out a more extensive experimentation with new datasets. Furthermore, some optimizations of the presented technique are warranted. For example, it may be possible to prune the discovered models through transitive reduction. In [15], the authors use an algorithm for transitive reduction of cyclic graphs to prune a Declare model discovered from a log. This approach, however, can be used when the model only includes Declare constraints without data conditions. For data-aware Declare models different reduction algorithms should be used. For example, approaches for transitive reduction of weighted graphs like the one presented in [2] could be adopted.

Another avenue for future work is to optimize the performance of the proposed technique, for example by reducing the number of invocations made to Daikon. This could be achieved by caching some of the invariants discovered by Daikon for a given constraint and reusing them for other constraints. Such optimization should be based however on a case-by-case analysis of which invariants can be reused for a given constraint type.

Finally, we plan to extend the technique so that it can discover a larger set of LTL-FO rule templates such as the existence templates and the non-binary relation templates in Declare as well as templates beyond the standard set included in Declare.

Acknowledgment. This research is supported by the EU's FP7 Programme (ACSI Project).

References

1. 3TU Data Center. BPI Challenge, Event Log (2011), doi: 10.4121/uuid:d9769f3d-0ab0-4fb8-803b-0d1120ffcf54
2. Bonaki, D., Odenbrett, M.R., Wijs, A., Ligtenberg, W.P.A., Hilbers, P.A.J.: Efficient reconstruction of biological networks via transitive reduction on general purpose graphics processors. BMC Bioinformatics 13, 281 (2012)
3. Burattin, A., Maggi, F.M., van der Aalst, W.M.P., Sperduti, A.: Techniques for a Posteriori Analysis of Declarative Processes. In: EDOC, pp. 41–50 (2012)
4. Chesani, F., Lamma, E., Mello, P., Montali, M., Riguzzi, F., Storari, S.: Exploiting Inductive Logic Programming Techniques for Declarative Process Mining. In: Jensen, K., van der Aalst, W.M.P. (eds.) ToPNoC II. LNCS, vol. 5460, pp. 278–295. Springer, Heidelberg (2009)
5. de Leoni, M., Dumas, M., García-Bañuelos, L.: Discovering Branching Conditions from Business Process Execution Logs. In: Cortellessa, V., Varró, D. (eds.) FASE 2013 (ETAPS 2013). LNCS, vol. 7793, pp. 114–129. Springer, Heidelberg (2013)
6. Di Ciccio, C., Mecella, M.: Mining constraints for artful processes. In: Abramowicz, W., Kriksciuniene, D., Sakalauskas, V. (eds.) BIS 2012. LNBIP, vol. 117, pp. 11–23. Springer, Heidelberg (2012)
7. Ernst, M.D., Cockrell, J., Griswold, W.G., Notkin, D.: Dynamically discovering likely program invariants to support program evolution. IEEE Trans. Software Eng. 27(2), 99–123 (2001)
8. Goedertier, S., Martens, D., Vanthienen, J., Baesens, B.: Robust process discovery with artificial negative events. JMLR 10, 1305–1340 (2009)

9. IEEE Task Force on Process Mining. Process Mining Manifesto. In: Algebraic Semantics. LNBIP, vol. 99, pp. 169–194. Springer (2011)
10. Jain, A.K., Duin, R.P.W., Mao, J.: Statistical pattern recognition: A review. IEEE Trans. on Pattern Analysis and Machine Intelligence 22(1), 4–37 (2000)
11. Kupferman, O., Vardi, M.Y.: Vacuity Detection in Temporal Model Checking. Int. Journal on Software Tools for Technology Transfer, 224–233 (2003)
12. Lamma, E., Mello, P., Riguzzi, F., Storari, S.: Applying Inductive Logic Programming to Process Mining. In: Blockeel, H., Ramon, J., Shavlik, J., Tadepalli, P. (eds.) ILP 2007. LNCS (LNAI), vol. 4894, pp. 132–146. Springer, Heidelberg (2008)
13. Lorenzoli, D., Mariani, L., Pezzè, M.: Automatic generation of software behavioral models. In: Proc. of ICSE, pp. 501–510. IEEE (2008)
14. Maggi, F.M., Bose, R.P.J.C., van der Aalst, W.M.P.: Efficient discovery of understandable declarative models from event logs. In: Ralyté, J., Franch, X., Brinkkemper, S., Wrycza, S. (eds.) CAiSE 2012. LNCS, vol. 7328, pp. 270–285. Springer, Heidelberg (2012)
15. Maggi, F.M., Bose, R.P.J.C., van der Aalst, W.M.P.: A knowledge-based integrated approach for discovering and repairing declare maps. In: Salinesi, C., Norrie, M.C., Pastor, Ó. (eds.) CAiSE 2013. LNCS, vol. 7908, pp. 433–448. Springer, Heidelberg (2013)
16. Maggi, F.M., Mooij, A.J., van der Aalst, W.M.P.: User-guided discovery of declarative process models. In: Proc. of CIDM, pp. 192–199. IEEE (2011)
17. Pesic, M., Schonenberg, H., van der Aalst, W.M.P.: DECLARE: Full Support for Loosely-Structured Processes. In: Proc. of EDOC, pp. 287–300. IEEE (2007)
18. Pesic, M., van der Aalst, W.M.P.: A Declarative Approach for Flexible Business Processes Management. In: Eder, J., Dustdar, S. (eds.) BPM Workshops 2006. LNCS, vol. 4103, pp. 169–180. Springer, Heidelberg (2006)
19. Pesic, M.: Constraint-Based Workflow Management Systems: Shifting Controls to Users. PhD thesis, Beta Research School for Operations Management and Logistics, Eindhoven (2008)
20. Pichler, P., Weber, B., Zugal, S., Pinggera, J., Mendling, J., Reijers, H.A.: Imperative versus declarative process modeling languages: An empirical investigation. In: Daniel, F., Barkaoui, K., Dustdar, S. (eds.) BPM Workshops 2011, Part I. LNBIP, vol. 99, pp. 383–394. Springer, Heidelberg (2012)
21. Rebuge, A., Ferreira, D.R.: Business process analysis in healthcare environments: A methodology based on process mining. Inf. Syst. 37(2), 99–116 (2012)
22. Rozinat, A., van der Aalst, W.M.P.: Decision mining in ProM. In: Dustdar, S., Fiadeiro, J.L., Sheth, A.P. (eds.) BPM 2006. LNCS, vol. 4102, pp. 420–425. Springer, Heidelberg (2006)
23. van der Aalst, W.M.P., Pesic, M., Schonenberg, H.: Declarative Workflows: Balancing Between Flexibility and Support. Computer Science - R&D, 99–113 (2009)
24. Zugal, S., Pinggera, J., Weber, B.: The impact of testcases on the maintainability of declarative process models. In: BMMDS/EMMSAD, pp. 163–177 (2011)

Enhancing Declare Maps Based on Event Correlations

R.P. Jagadeesh Chandra Bose[1], Fabrizio Maria Maggi[2], and Wil M.P. van der Aalst[1]

[1] Eindhoven University of Technology, The Netherlands
[2] University of Tartu, Estonia

Abstract. Traditionally, most process mining techniques aim at discovering *procedural* process models (e.g., Petri nets, BPMN, and EPCs) from event data. However, the variability present in less-structured flexible processes complicates the discovery of such procedural models. The "open world" assumption used by declarative models makes it easier to handle this variability. However, initial attempts to *automatically discover declarative process models* result in cluttered diagrams showing misleading constraints. Moreover, additional data attributes in event logs are not used to discover meaningful causalities. In this paper, we use *correlations* to prune constraints and to disambiguate event associations. As a result, the discovered process maps only show the more meaningful constraints. Moreover, the data attributes used for correlation and disambiguation are also used to find *discriminatory patterns*, identify *outliers*, and analyze *bottlenecks* (e.g., when do people violate constraints or miss deadlines). The approach has been implemented in ProM and experiments demonstrate the improved quality of process maps and diagnostics.

1 Introduction

Processes executed in today's world are often supported and controlled by information systems, which record events, like messages and transactions, in so-called *event logs*. *Process mining* aims at discovering, monitoring and improving real-life processes by extracting knowledge from event logs. *Process discovery, conformance checking,* and *process enhancement* are three main process mining tasks [3]. In particular, process enhancement aims at enriching and extending existing process models with information retrieved from logs, e.g., a process model can be extended with performance-related information such as flow time and waiting time.

Choosing a suitable representational bias for process discovery, visualization, and analysis is one of the challenges in process mining [11]. Process characteristics play a significant role in the selection of a suitable representational bias. Processes working in stable environments are typically highly predictable, i.e., it is easy to determine in advance the way how processes execute and behave (e.g., a process for handling travel requests). Procedural languages, such as BPMN, UML ADs, EPCs, and Petri nets, are suitable for describing such processes because it is easy to explicitly represent all allowed behavior of the process at hand [4, 22]. In contrast, processes operating in flexible/turbulent environments are often more complex and less predictable. Here, process participants make decisions based on multiple (possibly conflicting) objectives and have a lot of freedom in the process execution (e.g., a doctor in a healthcare process).

F. Daniel, J. Wang, and B. Weber (Eds.): BPM 2013, LNCS 8094, pp. 97–112, 2013.
© Springer-Verlag Berlin Heidelberg 2013

Declarative process modeling languages like *Declare* [4] are more suitable for such environments. Declarative models describe a process as a list of constraints that must be satisfied during the process execution. In declarative languages, an "open world" is assumed where everything is allowed unless it is explicitly forbidden. Declarative models are widely used in domains and applications where processes cannot be "straightjacketed" into a procedural model [7, 15, 16, 25].

Declare is a declarative language introduced in [4] that combines a formal semantics grounded in Linear Temporal Logic (LTL) with a graphical representation for users.[1] A *Declare map* is a set of Declare constraints each one with its own graphical representation and LTL semantics (see [4] for a full overview of Declare). In recent years, approaches to discover Declare models from event logs [17–19] and approaches to check conformance of Declare models with respect to event logs [9, 13] have been proposed.

Although promising, these approaches face several challenges and limitations when being applied to real-life event logs. First of all, discovery approaches typically generate too many constraints resulting in incomprehensible Declare maps. Most of the generated constraints have no domain significance and are uninteresting for experts/analysts. Second, when evaluating the satisfaction of a constraint, one often faces ambiguities in connecting events that "activate" the constraint (activations) and events that "fulfill" it (target events). For example, consider trace $\mathbf{t} = \langle A, A, B, B \rangle$ and the constraint *response(A,B)*.[2] It is unclear which instance of activity B can be associated to the two instances of activity A. Such ambiguities inhibit a correct evaluation of constraints in terms of satisfaction/violation and the application of certain types of analysis such as performance analysis (e.g., computing the response time of constraints).

One of the main reasons for these ambiguities and incomprehensible maps is the exclusive focus on the *control-flow* perspective. Typically, event logs contain additional information in the form of attributes and values. Let $\mathbf{t} = \langle A(x = 1, y = 2), A(x = 2, y = 1), B(x = 2, y = 0), B(x = 1, y = 4) \rangle$ be the above trace with its data attributes. The additional information suggests that the first instance of A is related to the second instance of B and the second instance of A is related to the first instance of B because they share the same value for attribute x.

In this paper, we propose an approach to automatically discover significant event correlations between events involved in a constraint and use these correlations to (i) enhance (annotate) a discovered Declare map and improve its comprehensibility (see Fig. 1), (ii) prune discovered constraints that are uninteresting, (iii) disambiguate events so that correct events are correlated, (iv) extend a Declare map with meaningful performance information, and (v) improve the diagnostic abilities by finding discriminatory patterns (if any) between different classes of behavior (e.g., patterns that may discriminate between conformant and non-conformant activations of a constraint).

We evaluate the proposed approach using a real-life event log provided for the 2011 BPI Challenge [2], which pertains to the treatment of patients diagnosed with cancer in a large Dutch academic hospital. Fig. 2 depicts the Declare maps obtained using the hospital's event log for the *response* and *precedence* constraints with and without correlations (the correlations used are A.org:group = B.org:group and A.Producer

---

[1] In the remainder, LTL refers to the version of LTL tailored towards finite traces.
[2] *response(A,B)* = If A occurs, then eventually B follows after A.

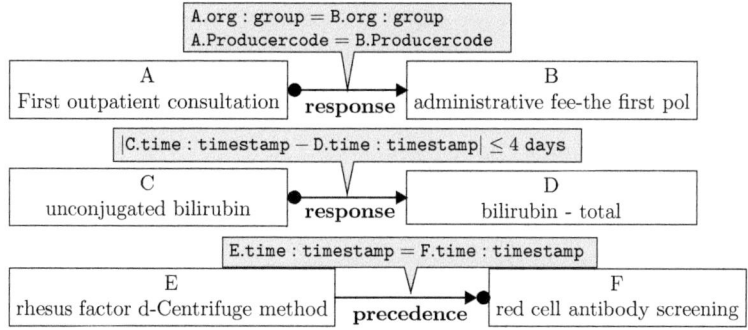

Fig. 1. A Declare map annotated with correlations

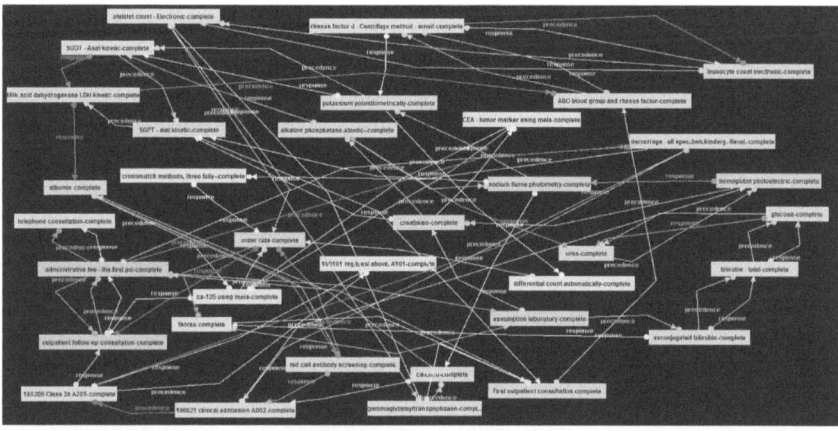

(a) without correlations

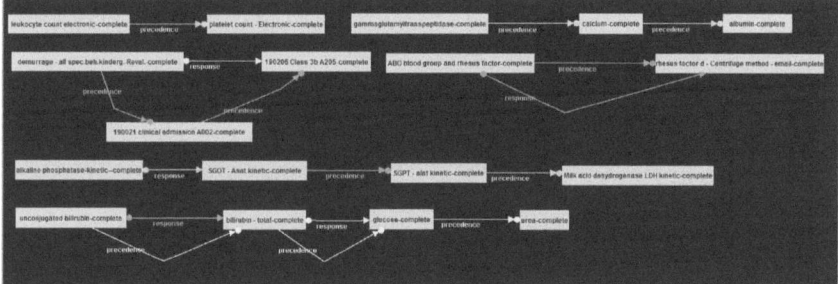

(b) with correlations

Fig. 2. Declare maps discovered for a hospital's event log [2] using the response and precedence constraints with and without correlations

code = B.Producer code). We can clearly see that the map obtained using correlations (Fig. 2(b)) is much simpler and more comprehensible than the map using the conventional approach (Fig. 2(a)).

The remainder of this paper is organized as follows. Section 2 presents some preliminaries on event logs and the Declare language. Section 3 presents some of the issues in contemporary approaches in the discovery of Declare maps and highlights how correlations can help address them. Section 4 presents our approach to discovering event correlations and discriminatory patterns between different classes of constraint behavior. Section 5 presents and discusses the experimental results. Related work is presented in Section 6. Finally, Section 7 concludes the paper.

2 Preliminaries

In this section, we introduce some preliminary notions. In particular, in Section 2.1, we summarize what an event log is and, in Section 2.2, we give an overview of the Declare language.

2.1 Event Logs

An event log captures the manifestation of events pertaining to the instances of a single process. A *process instance* is also referred to as a *case*. Each event in the log corresponds to a single case and can be related to an activity or a task. Events within a case need to be *ordered*. An event may also carry optional additional information like *timestamp*, *transaction type*, *resource*, *costs*, etc. For analysis, we need a function that maps any event e onto its *class* $\bar{e}$. In this paper, we assume that each event is classified based on its activity. We use the following notations:

- $\mathcal{A}$ denotes the set of *activities*. $\mathcal{A}^+$ is the set of all non-empty finite sequences of activities from $\mathcal{A}$.
- A *process instance* (i.e., a case) is described as a *trace* over $\mathcal{A}$, i.e., a finite sequence of activities. Examples of traces are $\mathbf{t}_1 = \langle A, B, C, D \rangle$ and $\mathbf{t}_2 = \langle A, B, B, B, A, D \rangle$.
- Let $\mathbf{t} = \langle \mathbf{t}(1), \mathbf{t}(2), \ldots, \mathbf{t}(n) \rangle \in \mathcal{A}^+$ be a trace over $\mathcal{A}$. $|\mathbf{t}| = n$ denotes the *length* of trace $\mathbf{t}$. $\mathbf{t}(k)$ represents the kth activity in the trace.
- An *event log*, $\mathcal{L}$, corresponds to a *multi-set* (or bag) of traces from $\mathcal{A}^+$. For example, $\mathcal{L} = [\langle A, B, C, D \rangle, \langle A, B, C, D \rangle, \langle A, B, B, B, A, D \rangle]$ is a log consisting of three cases. Two cases follow trace $\langle A, B, C, D \rangle$ and one case follows trace $\langle A, B, B, B, A, D \rangle$.

2.2 Declare: Some Basic Notions

Declare is a declarative process modeling language introduced by Pesic and van der Aalst in [4]. A *Declare map* is a set of constraints that must hold in conjunction during the process execution. Declare constraints are equipped with graphical notations and LTL semantics. The most frequently used Declare constraints are shown in Table 1. However, the language is extensible and new constraints can be added by providing a graphical representation and corresponding LTL semantics. The results discussed in this paper only refer to positive relation constraints and not to negative relations (last three rows in Table 1). Indeed, since negative relation constraints forbid the occurrence of events, it is less natural to define the notion of correlation for these constraints.

Table 1. Graphical notation and textual description of some Declare constraints

Constraint	Meaning	LTL semantics	Graphical notation
responded existence(A,B)	if A occurs then B occurs before or after A	$\Diamond A \to \Diamond B$	A •──── B
co-existence(A,B)	if A occurs then B occurs before or after A and vice versa	$\Diamond A \leftrightarrow \Diamond B$	A •──── • B
response(A,B)	if A occurs then eventually B occurs after A	$\Box(A \to \Diamond B)$	A •───▶ B
precedence(A,B)	if B occurs then A occurs before B	$(\neg B \sqcup A) \vee \Box(\neg B)$	A ───▶• B
succession(A,B)	for A and B both precedence and response hold	$\Box(A \to \Diamond B)$ $\wedge$ $(\neg B \sqcup A) \vee \Box(\neg B)$	A •───▶• B
alternate response(A,B)	if A occurs then eventually B occurs after A without other occurrences of A in between	$\Box(A \to \bigcirc(\neg A \sqcup B))$	A •═══▶ B
alternate precedence(A,B)	if B occurs then A occurs before B without other occurrences of B in between	$((\neg B \sqcup A) \vee \Box(\neg B))$ $\wedge$ $\Box(B \to \bigcirc((\neg B \sqcup A) \vee \Box(\neg B)))$	A ═══▶• B
alternate succession(A,B)	for A and B both alternate precedence and alternate response hold	$\Box(A \Rightarrow \bigcirc(\neg A \, U B)) \wedge$ $(((\neg B \sqcup A) \vee \Box(\neg B)) \wedge$ $\Box(B \to \bigcirc((\neg B \sqcup A) \vee \Box(\neg B))))$	A •═══▶• B
chain response(A,B)	if A occurs then B occurs in the next position after A	$\Box(A \to \bigcirc B)$	A •≡≡≡▶ B
chain precedence(A,B)	if B occurs then A occurs in the next position before B	$\Box(\bigcirc B \to A)$	A ≡≡≡▶• B
chain succession(A,B)	for A and B both chain precedence and chain response hold	$\Box(A \to \bigcirc B)$ $\wedge$ $\Box(\bigcirc B \to A)$	A •≡≡≡▶• B
not co-existence(A,B)	A and B cannot occur together	$\neg(\Diamond A \wedge \Diamond B)$	A •──╫──• B
not succession(A,B)	if A occurs then B cannot eventually occur after A	$\Box(A \to \neg(\Diamond B))$	A •──╫─▶• B
not chain succession(A,B)	if A occurs then B cannot occur in the next position after A	$\Box(A \to \bigcirc(\neg B))$	A •═╫═▶• B

Consider the *response* constraint $\Box(A \to \Diamond B)$. This constraint indicates that if A occurs, B must eventually *follow*. Therefore, this constraint is satisfied for traces such as $\mathbf{t}_1 = \langle A, A, B, C \rangle$, $\mathbf{t}_2 = \langle B, B, C, D \rangle$, and $\mathbf{t}_3 = \langle A, B, C, B \rangle$, but not for $\mathbf{t}_4 = \langle A, B, A, C \rangle$ because $\mathbf{t}_4(3)$, i.e., the second instance of A, is not followed by a B. Note that, in $\mathbf{t}_2$, the response constraint is satisfied in a trivial way because A never occurs. In this case, we say that the constraint is *vacuously satisfied* [12]. In [9], the authors introduce the notion of *behavioral vacuity detection* according to which a constraint is non-vacuously satisfied in a trace when it is activated in that trace. An *activation* of a constraint in a trace is an event whose occurrence imposes, because of that constraint, some obligations on other events in the same trace. For example, A is an activation for the response constraint because the execution of A forces B to be executed eventually.

An activation of a constraint results in either a *fulfillment* (the obligation is met) or a *violation* (e.g., A is not followed by B in a response constraint). A trace is perfectly compliant if there are no violations. Consider, again, the response constraint. In trace $\mathbf{t}_1$, the constraint is activated and fulfilled twice, whereas, in trace t_3, the same constraint is activated and fulfilled only once. When a trace is not compliant w.r.t. a constraint, at least one activation leads to a violation. In trace t_4, for example, the response constraint is activated twice (at $t_4(1)$ and $t_4(3)$): the activation at $t_4(1)$ leads to a fulfillment (eventually B occurs), but the activation at $t_4(3)$ leads to a violation (B does not occur subsequently). An algorithm to discriminate between fulfillments and violations for a constraint in a trace is presented in [9].

3 Correlations as a Means of Enhancing Declare Maps

Techniques for the automated discovery of Declare maps from event logs have been proposed in [17–19]. These approaches, although promising, typically generate *maps with too many constraints, have difficulties in correctly associating events, and do not provide diagnostic information.* This can be attributed to the fact that these techniques exploit only the control-flow perspective. Several of today's event logs contain rich information in the form of (event) attributes pertaining to the *data, resource,* and *time* perspectives.

In this paper, we advocate the use of these additional perspectives and investigate the correlations between event attributes as a means of addressing some of the above mentioned issues. Correlations are defined over event attributes and linked through *relationship operators* between them. For example, two events are correlated if they act upon common data elements of the process or if they are executed by the same resource etc. Such correlations can be used in conjunction to the control-flow relationship between events (defined in the form of Declare constraints) to further assess the relevance/significance of a constraint. Correlations can help us to:

- *prune uninteresting constraints:* we conjecture that constraints involving activities are interesting from a domain point of view only in cases where they share some common (data) elements of a process. For example, consider an insurance claim process where, apart from the handling of a claim application, applicants are asked to fill out a regular questionnaire. Clearly, in this process, the portion soliciting feedback does not interfere with the claim handling. Subsequently, the control-flow constraints between the activities involved in the claim handling and the activities involved in the questionnaire handling are less interesting to experts. This might be reflected in the activities in these two portions of the process sharing no or very few attributes (and thereby there are not significant correlations between them). Pruning such constraints will help reduce the number of uncovered constraints and improve the comprehensibility of a Declare map.
- *disambiguate events:* event associations that are ambiguous purely from a control-flow point of view can be disambiguated with additional conditions on their attributes. For example, consider trace $t_1 = \langle A, B, C, B \rangle$ and the *response* constraint $\Box(A \rightarrow \Diamond B)$. Let us assume that activities A and B have a common attribute x and that we have an additional condition $A.x = B.x$ correlating these attributes for this constraint, i.e., the constraint now reads as "if A occurs, then B eventually follows and the value of attribute x is the same for both A and B". Now let us assume that $t_1(1).x = 1$, $t_1(2).x = 2$, and $t_1(4).x = 1$. Using the correlation, we

can now clearly identify that the instance of B at $\mathbf{t}_1(4)$ is the one to be associated to the activation at $\mathbf{t}_1(1)$. Disambiguation of events facilitates a correct association of events involved in a constraint and thereby helps in performance analysis of a process (e.g., computing the response time more accurately).
- *improve diagnostic capabilities:* event correlations can be used for a plethora of diagnostic insights on process execution. One may use the discovered correlations to identify any potential exceptional executions/outliers. For example, let us assume that the correlation $A.x = B.x$ holds for 98% of the fulfillments of a response constraint $\Box(A \to \Diamond B)$. The 2% of the activations where the correlation does not hold (but considered as fulfillments purely from a control-flow perspective) may potentially be outliers or can be considered as a fulfillment due to wrong association of events for the constraint. Similarly, one may try to find if any discriminatory correlation patterns exist between different classes of behavior, e.g., between activations that are fulfillments and activations that are violations. For example, in an insurance claim, one may learn that a constraint is violated if the claim amount is greater than 1000 euros.

Furthermore, correlations can be used in defining conceptual groupings of activities. Different correlations between events can be used to define different conceptual groupings. For example, one may define equivalence classes based on a common attribute and consider all activities in that equivalence class as one conceptual group, e.g., the activities involving all events that are executed within the same department can be defined as one conceptual group. Such conceptual groupings of activities can be used for guiding the discovery of Declare maps towards results that are more significant from an application domain point of view [18].

For a categorization of correlations we refer to [6]. In this paper we use:

- *Property-based correlation*, i.e., events are classified based on a function operating on their attributes. For example, all claim applications referring to an amount greater than 1000 euros are grouped together.
- *Reference-based correlation*, i.e., two events are correlated if an attribute of the first event (identifier attribute) and an attribute of the second event (reference attribute) have the same value.
- *Moving time-window correlation*, i.e., two events are correlated if they occur within a given duration of one another (e.g., one hour).

We use an extended definition of reference-based correlation according to which two events are correlated if there is a function connecting an attribute of the first event with an attribute of the second event. This function can include not only equality but also operators such as *greater than*, *less than*, and *not equal to*. For example, an event of producing a document is correlated to an event of checking it if the resource that produces the document is different from the resource that checks it.

4 Discovering Correlations from Event Logs

Correlations can be provided by a domain expert, or alternatively, one can try to learn these correlations automatically from event logs. In this section, we focus on the automated discovery of correlations and discriminatory (correlation) patterns between different classes of behavior from event logs.

The XES standard [1] for event logs allows for events having attributes. XES supports data types such as string, date, boolean, int, and float (henceforth, we consider int and float types as *continuous*). Depending on the type, standard operators are supported. For example, we use the $\leq, \geq, <, >, =, \neq$ operators for continuous attributes and $=, \neq$ for string and boolean attributes. Timestamp (date) attributes are related using *before, after* operators in addition to all relation operations (i.e., $\leq, \geq, <, >, =, \neq$) over the time *difference* between two events.

We are interested in correlations between *comparable* attributes of different events, e.g., in an insurance claim process, attribute *amount claimed* is comparable to *amount issued*, but not to, say, *location*. If a priori knowledge about the domain is available, we can use that knowledge to identify/group attributes that are comparable. In the absence of prior domain knowledge, we consider *attributes having the same data type* to be comparable. Standard event attributes in XES are handled differently, e.g., although the attributes *concept:name* and *org:group* are of string type, they are not comparable.

Using the above correlation notion, we generate all feasible correlations for a given constraint. For discovering significant correlations, we partition the constraint activations into *ambiguous* activations and *non-ambiguous* activations. The definition of what constitutes an ambiguous activation is specific for each constraint type. We consider a fulfilled activation as non-ambiguous if there is only one possible target that can be associated to it. For example, for the *response* constraint $\Box(A \rightarrow \Diamond B)$, the activations in traces $t_1 = \langle A, C, B \rangle$ and $t_2 = \langle A, A, C, B \rangle$ are non-ambiguous whereas the activations in traces $t_3 = \langle A, B, C, B \rangle$ and $t_4 = \langle A, A, B, B \rangle$ are ambiguous. One may argue that the activations in trace t_2 are also ambiguous because B can be associated to either of the two A's. We consider the scenario in t_1 as *strongly non-ambiguous* and the scenario in t_2 as *weakly non-ambiguous*. For each feasible correlation, we evaluate its *support* considering only non-ambiguous activations. The support of a correlation is defined as *the ratio between the number of activations in which that correlation is true and the total number of non-ambiguous activations*. We consider a feasible correlation as *significant* if its support is greater than a (user-specified) threshold. For correlations involving an attribute and a constant value, e.g., $B.timestamp - A.timestamp < \delta$, δ is derived based on the mean μ and standard deviation σ time difference of all non-ambiguous activations (for example δ can be set to $\mu + \sigma$).

Significant correlations thus discovered from non-ambiguous activations of a constraint can then be used to address the issues highlighted before, e.g., to disambiguate ambiguous activations. For each significant correlation, its *degree of disambiguation* is defined as *the ratio between the number of ambiguous activations that can be disambiguated and the total number of ambiguous activations*. Furthermore, different correlations can be combined using conjunctions or disjunctions to form complex correlations. Fig. 3 depicts the block diagram of discovering constraint correlations.

Discovering Discriminant Correlations. An event log may exhibit several classes of behavior. For example, certain activations of a constraint may be eventually fulfilled while others may not. As another example, one may observe differences in the response time for different activations of a constraint (one may distinguish the activations into

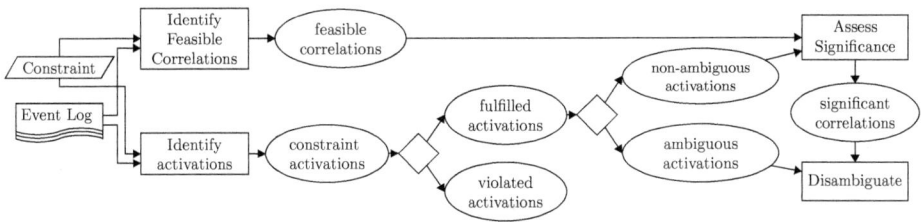

Fig. 3. Correlations are discovered for non-ambiguous activations and are subsequently used to disambiguate other (ambiguous) activations

slow, *medium*, and *fast* based on their response time). Such differences in behavior may be attributed to some of the characteristics of the events/traces, e.g., one may perceive differences in the response time of a constraint based on the resources involved in the execution of the activities or based on the attribute values (such as the claim amount or geography in a loan handling process). An analyst would be interested in uncovering any significant discriminatory correlations that can explain the different classes of behavior among the activations. We find such discriminatory correlations using the following three classification steps:

Step 1: Class Labeling. First, we select all the activations of a constraint and associate a class label to them. Different strategies for labeling can be adopted. For example, one can classify them as *conformant* or *non-conformant* based on whether they correspond to a fulfillment or to a violation. One can also consider all the *fulfilled* activations of a constraint and classify them as *slow*, *medium*, and *fast* based on their response time.

Step 2: Feature Extraction and Selection. The attributes of the events involved in a constraint and the process instance (case) attributes are considered as primitive features for finding discriminatory patterns. If all activations of a constraint (i.e., both fulfilled and violated) are selected in the previous step, then we only consider the correlations between attributes of the activations. If only fulfilled activations of a constraint are selected, then the correlations between attributes of the activations and attributes of the target events are also considered. This is due to the fact that a correlation involving an attribute of an activation and a target event can only be defined if the constraint is fulfilled (only in this case both activation and target event occur).[3]

Let $\mathcal{C} = \{c_1, c_2, \ldots, c_n\}$ be the set of feasible correlations for a constraint, $\mathcal{A} = \{a_1, a_2, \ldots, a_m\}$ be the set of attributes of the activation of a constraint, and $\mathcal{P} = \{p_1, p_2, \ldots, p_k\}$ be the set of case attributes corresponding to an activation. Each activation of a constraint can be translated into a vector where the dimensions correspond to $\mathcal{C} \cup \mathcal{A} \cup \mathcal{P} \cup \{C_l\}$; C_l is a special feature called the class label. The values of the features for each activation correspond to:

---

[3] This is true only for positive relation constraints (which are the ones considered in this paper). For negative relations the opposite applies (i.e., a correlation involving an attribute of an activation and a target event can only be defined if the constraint is violated because only in this case both activation and target event occur).

- *{true, false}* if the feature is a correlation feature. The value is *true* if the correlation holds in the activation and *false* if it does not hold,
- the value of the attribute in the event corresponding to the activation of the constraint if the feature corresponds to $a_i \in \mathcal{A}$,
- the value of the case attribute corresponding to the process instance of the activation if the feature corresponds to $p_i \in \mathcal{P}$, and
- the class label of the activation if the feature is the class label.

The set of all activations upon transformation into a vector space can be seen as a dataset as depicted in Table 2.

Table 2. A labeled dataset defined by features

Activation	c_1	c_2	...	c_n	a_1	a_2	...	a_m	p_1	p_2	...	p_k	C_l
1	true	false	...	true	50	xyz	...	1.5	1000	p	...	r	conformant
2	true	false	...	false	110	abc	...	3.25	500	q	...	s	non-conformant
3	false	true	...	true	64	ted	...	0.2	275	p	...	t	non-conformant
4	false	true	...	true	15	xyz	...	0.87	1255	u	...	s	conformant
⋮	⋮	⋮		⋮	⋮	⋮		⋮	⋮	⋮		⋮	⋮

Step 3: Discovering Discriminatory Patterns. Given a dataset as depicted in Table 2, the goal of this step is to discover the patterns over the features, which are strongly correlated to the class label (e.g., conformant and non-conformant). We adopt standard data mining techniques, i.e., decision tree learning [23] and association rule mining [5, 14]. For the association rule mining, we adopt the special subset called the *class association rules* [14], which is an integration of classification rule mining and association rule mining. The details of these algorithms are beyond the scope of this paper. The result of this step are rules such as:

> If $c_n = true$ AND $a_1 \leq 50$ AND $a_2 = $ xyz AND $p_1 \geq 1000$ then *conformant*;
> If $a_1 \geq 60$ AND $a_2 \neq $ xyz AND $p_1 \leq 500$ then *non-conformant*.

Each rule can be associated with metrics such as the number of true positives (TP), false positives (FP), support and confidence. The quality of the entire set of discriminatory patterns uncovered can be assessed using standard metrics such as *accuracy, sensitivity, specificity, precision*, and *F1-score*.

5 Experiments and Results

The concepts presented in this paper have been implemented as the **Extend Declare Map with Correlations** and **Extend Declare Map with Time Information** plug-ins in ProM[4]. The former deals with the discovery and evaluation of correlations while the latter deals with performance analysis of Declare constraints (e.g., computing the

---

[4] ProM is an extensible framework that provides a comprehensive set of tools/plug-ins for the discovery and analysis of process models from event logs. See www.processmining.org for more information and to download ProM.

response times). The plug-ins take a Declare map and an event log as input and produce an enhanced Declare map annotated with data correlations and/or performance information. The input Declare map can either be discovered using the **Declare Maps Miner** plug-in or provided by a domain expert.

We have applied the proposed approach to the BPI challenge 2011 event log [2] pertaining to the treatment of patients diagnosed with cancer in a large Dutch academic hospital. The event log contains 1143 cases and 150,291 events distributed across 623 event classes (activities). The event log contains domain specific attributes, e.g., *Producer code, Section, Activity code, Number of executions,* and *Specialism code* in addition to the standard XES attributes for events: *concept:name, lifecycle:transition, time:timestamp,* and *org:group*. We considered attributes with the same name to be *comparable* (i.e., an attribute x of the activation event is comparable only to attribute x of the target event) and explored the feasible correlations for various attributes.

We first generated a Declare Map from this event log using the **Declare Maps Miner** plug-in and considered constraints with a support of 50%. Activations that are fulfillments are further partitioned into ambiguous and non-ambiguous activations. Table 3 depicts the number of ambiguous and non-ambiguous activations for some constraints. Using the non-ambiguous activations we evaluated the support for the various correlations. Some significant correlations are depicted in Table 3 (refer columns correlation and support (correl.)).

From the table, we can see that for the response constraint $\Box(A \rightarrow \Diamond B)$ (where A corresponds to *First outpatient consultation* and B corresponds to *administrative fee - the first pol*), there are 559 ambiguous activations. Correlation *A.org:group* = *B.org:group* (i.e., both activities A and B are performed in the same department) holds for 94% of the 517 non-ambiguous activations. It is expected that the fee is decided and collected by the same department that performed the activation activity. However, it is interesting to see that 6% of the activations do not satisfy this correlation. It could be the case that by considering only the control-flow perspective, we have wrongly associated some administrative fee events thereby incorrectly evaluating the constraint as fulfillment for these activations. This correlation is able to disambiguate 57.96% of the 559 ambiguous activations. There exists another correlation *A.Producer code* = *B.Producer code* for this constraint, whose support is 93.61% in the non-ambiguous activations. This correlation is able to disambiguate 61.53% of the ambiguous activations.

For the response constraint $\Box(C \rightarrow \Diamond D)$ (where C corresponds to *unconjugated bilirubin* and D corresponds to *bilirubin - total*), we discover the correlation $|\,C.time:timestamp - D.time:timestamp\,| \leq 4$ days (i.e., activity D should be performed within 4 days of performing activity C). This event log exhibits coarse granular timestamps (recorded at the level of a day). The threshold of 4 days corresponds to $\mu + \sigma$ where μ and σ correspond to the mean and standard deviation time difference for all non-ambiguous activations of this constraint. This correlation holds in 99.63% of the non-ambiguous activations. The remaining 0.37% are most likely *outliers*. This correlation is able to disambiguate 81.61% of the ambiguous activations.

As another example, for the precedence constraint $(\neg F \sqcup E) \vee \Box(\neg F)$ (where E corresponds to *rhesus factor d - Centrifuge method* and F corresponds to *red cell antibody screening*), there are 603 and 932 non-ambiguous and ambiguous activations

Table 3. Correlations discovered for some constraints and their support and degree of disambiguation. The encoded activities correspond to A = First outpatient consultation, B = administrative fee - the first pol, C = unconjugated bilirubin, D = bilirubin - total, E = rhesus factor d - Centrifuge method, F = red cell antibody screening.

constraint	support (constr.) (%)	#non-ambig. inst.	#ambig. inst.	correlation		support (correl.) (%)	degree of disambig-uation(%)
response (A,B)	57.39	517	559	A.org:group B.org:group	=	94.00	57.96
				A.Producer code B.Producer code	=	93.61	61.53
response (C,D)	52.40	542	359	|C.time:timestamp − D.time:timestamp| 4 days	≤	99.63	81.61
precedence (E,F)	54.85	603	932	E.time:timestamp F.time:timestamp	=	100.00	96.45

respectively. We discover that the correlation *E.time:timestamp = F.time:timestamp* holds in all the non-ambiguous activations (i.e., both these activities are performed on the same day). Using this correlation, we are able to disambiguate 96.45% of the ambiguous activations.

Although we discussed the applicability of correlations in disambiguation for the response and precedence templates, correlations exhibit a similar behavior for other templates too. Table 4 depicts the average and maximum degree of disambiguation across various constraints (with a support of 50%) for different templates. From the table, we can see that the approach proposed above is able to assist in disambiguation significantly.

Table 4. Degree of disambiguation for different templates

Template	#Constraints	Avg #Activations per constraint		Deg. of Disamb.	
		non-ambi.	ambi.	Avg. (%)	Max. (%)
response	86	402	1321	51.68	95.76
precedence	250	842	1536	32.17	96.45
alternate response	53	733	601	70.67	100.00
alternate precedence	52	807	715	41.86	100.00
responded existence	584	682	2365	20.52	97.62

The discovered correlations can be used to reassess the fulfillment of constraint activations. For example, a response constraint $\Box(A \rightarrow \Diamond B)$ can be compounded with a correlation condition, *A.org:group = B.org:group* (i.e., in addition to *B* eventually following *A*, it is also required that they are executed by the same resource/department for an activation to be considered as fulfilled). Some activations that were deemed to be fulfilled when considering only the control-flow perspective, may no longer be fulfilled thereby impacting the *support* of the constraint, whose value, if less than a threshold, renders the constraint insignificant and a candidate for pruning. Table 5 illustrates how correlations assist in pruning constraints. The first row in each constraint type depicts the number of constraints for varying support thresholds and without considering correlations, e.g., 371 response constraints have a support of at least 30% in the event log. The subsequent rows show the effect of adding correlations. For example, by adding a correlation based on *org:group*, the number of response constraints with a support of at least 30% reduces from 371 to 229 (a reduction of 38.3%). Adding the correlation requirement *A.Producer code = B.Producer code* results in a reduction from 371 to 100 response constraints.

Table 5. Pruning of constraints using correlations. The number of constraints reported are without filtering transitive reductions.

constraint	correlation	#constraints			
		supp=30	supp=35	supp=40	supp=45
response(A,B)	⟨⟨ *no correlation* ⟩⟩	371	286	225	125
	A.org:group = B.org:group	229	180	163	114
	A.Producer code = B.Producer code	100	85	83	71
	|A.time:timestamp − B.time:timestamp| ≤ 4 days	226	172	139	112
precedence(A,B)	⟨⟨ *no correlation* ⟩⟩	458	403	352	261
	A.org:group = B.org:group	274	249	240	237
	A.Producer code = B.Producer code	113	106	104	104
	|A.time:timestamp − B.time:timestamp| ≤ 4 days	325	281	274	217

We further analyzed the log for discriminatory patterns that may exist between fulfillments and violations of some constraints. Here, we present one such example of the *response(A, B)* constraint (where A corresponds to *First outpatient consultation* and B corresponds to *administrative fee - the first pol*). The event log contains 517 (non-ambiguous) fulfillments and 60 violations of this constraint. We considered the event attributes of *First outpatient consultation*, correlations involving these attributes, and the case attributes pertaining to the traces involving these activations.

The event log contains several case level attributes such as diagnosis and treatment codes (the reader is referred to [8] for a detailed description on these case attributes). We have grouped different variants of similar case attributes into a single attribute (e.g., the 16 diagnosis code attribute values are captured as a set of values under a single attribute). We have transformed the 577 activations into vector space using these attributes and their correlations and applied the J48 [23] decision tree learning algorithm. Out of the 60 non-conformant activations, we could find discriminant patterns covering 23 activations using these features. For example, five of the six activations whose value of *A.Section* is *Section 5* and *C.DiagnosisCodeSet* is $\{106, 823\}$ are non-conformant, i.e., TP=5 and FP=1 (C signifies a case-level attribute). Similarly, three of the four activations whose value of *A.Section* is not equal to *Section 5* and *A.Producercode* is *SGSX* are non-conformant, i.e., TP=3 and FP=1.

Fig. 4 depicts the annotation of a Declare map with performance information using the **Extend Declare Map with Time Information** plug-in. The map is color coded to easily pin-point bottlenecks based on flow times and the plug-in allows for the interactive exploration of a wealth of diagnostic information e.g., #activations, #fulfillments, etc. on the constraints.

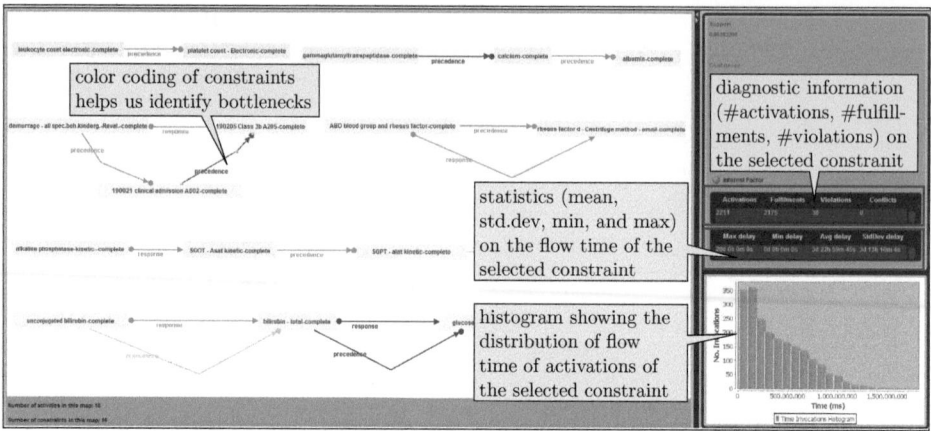

Fig. 4. Interactive visualization of a Declare map with diagnostic information such as flow time and bottlenecks

6 Related Work

Techniques for the automated discovery of Declare maps from event logs have been proposed in [17–19]. In [19], the authors rely on a combinatorial exploration of all feasible constraint activations and evaluate the constraints' goodness based on their activation ratio, i.e., the percentage of traces where a constraint is activated. In [17], the authors adopt the classic *apriori* algorithm [5] to find frequent item sets in data mining to identify significant activations and propose several metrics such as support and confidence to prune uninteresting constraints. In [18], the authors extend the work of [17] through the incorporation of domain knowledge and techniques for pruning redundant constraints to uncover interesting constraints. None of these approaches exploit the availability of rich information in the form of data attributes in event logs.

Correlation is a critical topic when applying process mining techniques to event data recorded by non-BPM/WFM systems. Indeed, these systems just generate a list of events without providing a properly structured event log. To generate an event log, it is necessary to correlate events into process instances. In [21], the authors present an event correlation algorithm to discover the best correlation conditions from a set of candidates. This algorithm is used to generate an event log from a set of uncorrelated events. A probabilistic approach based on the Expectation-Maximization (EM) principle has been proposed in [10] for correlating events from unlabeled event logs (where case ids are not available).

In [20], the authors identify different types of correlations and investigate the problem of discovering event correlation from data recorded by service oriented systems. The authors also introduce the concept of *process view* to represent the process resulting from a certain way of event correlation. They argue that correlation is subjective and that multiple views are possible. For example, in a process for customer order handling, in one view, orders can be considered from the viewpoint of order lines and, in another view, the same orders can be considered from the viewpoint of deliveries. A collection of process views is called the *process space*.

Rozsnyai et al [24] propose approaches for automatically deriving correlations from arbitrary sources of data. An interesting part of their work is the automatic identification of attributes that might be correlated based on properties such as their type, cardinality and the domain of values. In this paper, we used the heuristic of considering attributes of similar type as comparable. It would be interesting to explore the applicability of the concepts proposed in [24] for correlating events for Declare map discovery.

7 Conclusions and Future Work

Declarative process maps discovered from event logs without any consideration for event and case attributes tend to result in inaccurate and incomprehensible results. In this paper, we exploited the data present in event logs to discover process maps only showing relevant and accurate constraints. We proposed a means of discovering significant correlations that exist between events and use these correlations to *prune constraints*, to *disambiguate event associations*, and to provide additional *diagnostic information*. Our evaluation using real-life logs demonstrates that the proposed approach is very promising, e.g., we are able to disambiguate up to 96.45% of events in a hospital log. In this paper, we focused only on positive relation constraints involving two activities. In the future, we would like to extend this to also cover constraints involving multiple activities and negative relations (e.g., not co-existence and not succession in Table 1). Also, the proposed approach relies on some heuristics such as the use of $\mu \pm \sigma$ of time difference for temporal correlations and the correlations of *like* attribute types. As future work, we would like to study the trade-off between completeness and efficiency of mining. Furthermore, we would like to evaluate our approach using more case studies.

References

1. XES Standard Definition (2009), www.xes-standard.org
2. 3TU Data Center: BPI Challenge 2011 Event Log (2011), doi:10.4121/uuid:d9769f3d-0ab0-4fb8-803b-0d1120ffcf54
3. van der Aalst, W.M.P.: Process Mining: Discovery, Conformance and Enhancement of Business Processes. Springer (2011)
4. van der Aalst, W.M.P., Pesic, M., Schonenberg, H.: Declarative Workflows: Balancing Between Flexibility and Support. Computer Science - R&D, 99–113 (2009)
5. Agrawal, R., Srikant, R.: Fast Algorithms for Mining Association Rules. In: VLDB, pp. 487–499 (1994)
6. Barros, A., Decker, G., Dumas, M., Weber, F.: Correlation Patterns in Service-Oriented Architectures. In: Dwyer, M.B., Lopes, A. (eds.) FASE 2007. LNCS, vol. 4422, pp. 245–259. Springer, Heidelberg (2007)

7. Binder, M., Dorda, W., Duftschmid, G., Dunkl, R., Fröschl, K.A., Gall, W., Grossmann, W., Harmankaya, K., Hronsky, M., Rinderle-Ma, S., Rinner, C., Weber, S.: On Analyzing Process Compliance in Skin Cancer Treatment: An Experience Report from the Evidence-Based Medical Compliance Cluster (EBMC2). In: Ralyté, J., Franch, X., Brinkkemper, S., Wrycza, S. (eds.) CAiSE 2012. LNCS, vol. 7328, pp. 398–413. Springer, Heidelberg (2012)
8. Bose, R.P.J.C., van der Aalst, W.M.P.: Analysis of Patient Treatment Procedures: The BPI Challenge Case Study. Technical Report BPM-11-18, BPMCenter.org (2011)
9. Burattin, A., Maggi, F.M., van der Aalst, W.M.P., Sperduti, A.: Techniques for a Posteriori Analysis of Declarative Processes. In: EDOC, pp. 41–50 (2012)
10. Ferreira, D.R., Gillblad, D.: Discovering Process Models from Unlabelled Event Logs. In: Dayal, U., Eder, J., Koehler, J., Reijers, H.A. (eds.) BPM 2009. LNCS, vol. 5701, pp. 143–158. Springer, Heidelberg (2009)
11. IEEE Task Force on Process Mining: Process Mining Manifesto. In: Guessarian, I. (ed.) Algebraic Semantics. LNBIP, vol. 99, pp. 169–194. Springer, Berlin (1981)
12. Kupferman, O., Vardi, M.Y.: Vacuity Detection in Temporal Model Checking. International Journal on Software Tools for Technology Transfer, 224–233 (2003)
13. de Leoni, M., Maggi, F.M., van der Aalst, W.M.P.: Aligning Event Logs and Declarative Process Models for Conformance Checking. In: Barros, A., Gal, A., Kindler, E. (eds.) BPM 2012. LNCS, vol. 7481, pp. 82–97. Springer, Heidelberg (2012)
14. Liu, B., Hsu, W., Ma, Y.: Integrating Classification and Association Rule Mining. In: KDD, pp. 80–86. The AAAI Press (1998)
15. Ly, L.T., Indiono, C., Mangler, J., Rinderle-Ma, S.: Data Transformation and Semantic Log Purging for Process Mining. In: Ralyté, J., Franch, X., Brinkkemper, S., Wrycza, S. (eds.) CAiSE 2012. LNCS, vol. 7328, pp. 238–253. Springer, Heidelberg (2012)
16. Ly, L.T., Rinderle-Ma, S., Knuplesch, D., Dadam, P.: Monitoring Business Process Compliance Using Compliance Rule Graphs. In: Meersman, R., Dillon, T., Herrero, P., Kumar, A., Reichert, M., Qing, L., Ooi, B.-C., Damiani, E., Schmidt, D.C., White, J., Hauswirth, M., Hitzler, P., Mohania, M. (eds.) OTM 2011, Part I. LNCS, vol. 7044, pp. 82–99. Springer, Heidelberg (2011)
17. Maggi, F.M., Bose, R.P.J.C., van der Aalst, W.M.P.: Efficient Discovery of Understandable Declarative Models from Event Logs. In: Ralyté, J., Franch, X., Brinkkemper, S., Wrycza, S. (eds.) CAiSE 2012. LNCS, vol. 7328, pp. 270–285. Springer, Heidelberg (2012)
18. Maggi, F.M., Bose, R.P.J.C., van der Aalst, W.M.P.: A Knowledge-Based Integrated Approach for Discovering and Repairing Declare Maps. In: Salinesi, C., Norrie, M.C., Pastor, Ó. (eds.) CAiSE 2013. LNCS, vol. 7908, pp. 433–448. Springer, Heidelberg (2013)
19. Maggi, F.M., Mooij, A.J., van der Aalst, W.M.P.: User-Guided Discovery of Declarative Process Models. In: IEEE Symposium on Computational Intelligence and Data Mining, vol. 2725, pp. 192–199. IEEE Computer Society (2011)
20. Motahari-Nezhad, H.R., Saint-Paul, R., Casati, F., Benatallah, B.: Event Correlation for Process Discovery from Web Service Interaction Logs. The VLDB Journal 20(3), 417–444 (2011)
21. Perez-Castillo, R., Weber, B., Guzmn, I.R., Piattini, M., Pinggera, J.: Assessing Event Correlation in Non-Process-Aware Information Systems. Software & Systems Modeling, 1–23 (2012)
22. Pichler, P., Weber, B., Zugal, S., Pinggera, J., Mendling, J., Reijers, H.A.: Imperative Versus Declarative Process Modeling Languages: An Empirical Investigation. In: Daniel, F., Barkaoui, K., Dustdar, S. (eds.) BPM Workshops 2011, Part I. LNBIP, vol. 99, pp. 383–394. Springer, Heidelberg (2012)
23. Quinlan, J.R.: C4.5: Programs for Machine Learning. Morgan Kaufmann (1993)
24. Rozsnyai, S., Slominski, A., Lakshmanan, G.T.: Discovering Event Correlation Rules for Semi-structured Business Processes. In: DEBS, pp. 75–86 (2011)
25. Schulte, S., Schuller, D., Steinmetz, R., Abels, S.: Plug-and-Play Virtual Factories. IEEE Internet Computing 16(5), 78–82 (2012)

Aligning Event Logs and Process Models for Multi-perspective Conformance Checking: An Approach Based on Integer Linear Programming

Massimiliano de Leoni and Wil M.P. van der Aalst

Eindhoven University of Technology, Eindhoven, The Netherlands
{m.d.leoni,w.m.p.v.d.aalst}@tue.nl

Abstract. Modern organizations have invested in collections of descriptive and/or normative process models, but these rarely describe the actual processes adequately. Therefore, a variety of techniques for *conformance checking* have been proposed to pinpoint discrepancies between modeled and observed behavior. However, these techniques typically focus on the control-flow and *abstract from data, resources and time*. This paper describes an approach that aligns event log and model while taking *all* perspectives into account (i.e., also data, time and resources). This way it is possible to quantify conformance and analyze differences between model and reality. The approach was implemented using ProM and has been evaluated using both synthetic event logs and a real-life case study.

1 Introduction

Today's organizations are challenged to make their processes more efficient and effective; costs and response times need to be reduced in all of today's industries. Process models are used to guide people, discuss process alternatives, and to automate parts of critical business processes. Often these process models are not enforced and people can deviate from them. Such flexibility is often desirable, but still it is good to analyze differences between modeled and observed behavior. This illustrates the relevance of *conformance checking* [1]. Conformance checking techniques take an event log and a process model and compare the observed traces with the traces possible according to the model. There are different dimensions for comparing process models and event logs. In this paper, we focus of the *fitness* dimension: a model with good fitness allows for most of the behavior seen in the event log. A model has *perfect* fitness if all traces in the log can be replayed by the model from beginning to end. Other quality dimensions are *simplicity*, *precision*, and *generalization* [1].

Various conformance checking techniques have been proposed in recent years [1,2,3,4]. Unfortunately, they focus on the control-flow, i.e. the ordering of activities, thereby ignoring the other perspectives, such as data, resources, and time. In a process model, each case, i.e. a process instance, is characterized by its case variables. Paths taken during the execution may be governed by guards and conditions defined over such variables. Process models define the domain of possible values to assign to each variable, along with modeling the variables that each activity is prescribed to write or update. In addition, process models describe which resources are allowed to execute

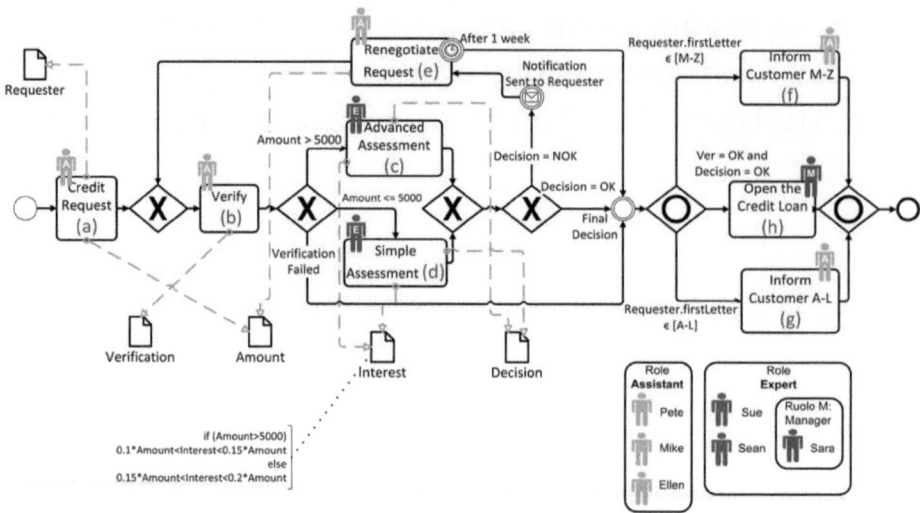

Fig. 1. BPMN diagram describing a process to handle credit requests. Besides the control-flow perspective, also the data perspective (see data objects and conditions), the resource perspective (see roles), and the time perspective (see timeout) are modeled. Dotted lines going from activities to data objects indicate the variables manipulated by each activity. Each activity requires a person having a particular role.

which activities. An activity is typically associated with a particular role, i.e., a selected group of resources. There may also be additional rules such as the "four-eyes principle" which does not allow for the situation where the same resource executes two related tasks for the same case. Finally, there may be time-related constraints, e.g., a registration activity needs to be followed by decision activity within 30 days.

Since existing conformance checking techniques abstract from data, resources, and time, many deviations remain undetected. Let us consider the process model in Figure 1 (taken from [5]). The model describes a process to deal with loans requested by clients to buy small home appliances. After the credit request, the requester's financial data are verified and, if the verification is positive, the request is assessed. In case of a positive assessment, the credit is provided and the requester is informed. In case of a negative assessment, requesters can try to renegotiate the credit within one week or, otherwise, the request is definitely rejected. In the remainder, data objects are simply referred with the upper-case bold initials, e.g., **V**=*Verification*, and activity names by the letter in boldface in brackets, e.g. **a**=*Credit Request*.

Let us also consider the following trace where variables are shortened with the initial letter and $\mathbf{E_x}$ and $\mathbf{T_x}$ denote the executor of x and the timestamp when x was executed:[1]

$\langle(\mathbf{a}, \{\mathbf{A} = 1000, \mathbf{R} = \text{Mary}, \mathbf{E}_a = \text{Pete}, \mathbf{T_a} = 03 \text{ Jan}\}), (\mathbf{b}, \{\mathbf{V} = OK, \mathbf{E_b} = \text{Sue}\}),$
$(\mathbf{c}, \{\mathbf{I} = 150, \mathbf{D} = OK, \mathbf{E_c} = \text{Sue}, \mathbf{T_b} = 4 \text{ Jan}\}), (\mathbf{e}, \{\mathbf{E_e} = \text{Pete}, \mathbf{A} = 1000, \mathbf{T_e} = 15 \text{ Jan}\}),$
$(\mathbf{c}, \{\mathbf{I} = 150, \mathbf{D} = NOK, \mathbf{E_c} = \text{Sue}, \mathbf{T_c} = 16 \text{ Jan}\}), (\mathbf{g}, \{\mathbf{E_g} = \text{Pete}, \mathbf{T_g} = 17 \text{ Jan}\}),$
$(\mathbf{h}, \{\mathbf{E_h} = \text{Sara}, \mathbf{T_h} = 18 \text{ Jan}\})\rangle.$

---

[1] Notation $(act, \{attr_1 = val_1, \ldots, attr_n = val_n\})$ is used to denote the occurrence of activity act in which variables $attr_1, \ldots, attr_n$ are assigned values $val_1, \ldots, val_n$, respectively.

Conformance checking techniques only considering the control-flow perspective cannot find the following conformity's violations: *(i)* the requested amount cannot be 1000: activity **d** should be executed, instead of **c**; *(ii)* for the considered credit loan, the interest is against the credit-institute's policy for large loans; *(iii)* 'Sue' is not authorized to execute activity **b** since she cannot play role *Assistant*; *(iv)* activity **e** is performed 11 days after the preceding **c** occurrence, whereas it should not be later than 7 days; *(v)* activity **h** has been executed and, hence, the last decision cannot be negative. The approach we propose is based on the principle of finding an *alignment* of event log and process model. The events in the log traces are mapped to the execution of activities in the process model. Such an alignment shows how the event log can be *replayed* on the process model. We allow costs to be assigned to every potential deviation: some deviations may be more severe than others.

This paper proposes a technique based on building a suitable ILP program to find a valid sequence of activities that is as close as possible to the observed trace, i.e., we aim to minimize the cost of deviations and create an optimal alignment. To assess the practical feasibility and relevance, the technique has also been implemented in ProM and tested using synthetic event logs and in a real-life case study. Experimental results show that conformance of the different perspectives can be checked efficiently.

When checking for conformance, pinpointing the deviations of every single trace is definitely useful, but it is not enough. Process analysts need to be provided with a helicopter view of the conformance of the model with respect to the entire log. Therefore, this paper also introduces some diagnostics to clearly highlight the most frequent deviations encountered during the process executions and the most common causes.

Our previous work [5] provides an initial approach for *multi-perspective conformance checking*. However, our previous technique could not deal with variables defined over infinite domains. The ILP-based approach presented in this paper also allows for numerical values. Our new approach is also several orders of magnitude faster. Finally, the work reported in [5] was limited to returning optimal alignments. In this paper, we provide enhanced diagnostics guiding the user in finding the root-cause of specific conformance problems.

Our conformance-checking technique is independent of the specific formalism used to describe the control-flow and data-flow perspectives. Therefore, BPMN, EPC or any other formalism can be employed to represent these perspectives. However, we need a simple modeling language with clear semantics to explain our technique. For this purpose we use *Petri nets with data*. The notation is briefly discussed in Section 2. Section 3 illustrates the basic concepts related to aligning a process and an event log. Section 4 details our new technique to compute optimal alignments and to provide enhanced diagnostics. Section 5 describes the implementation in ProM and reports on the experimental results. Finally, Section 6 concludes the paper, comparing this work with the state of the art and describing future research directions.

2 Petri Nets with Data

A *Petri net with data* (DPN-net) is a Petri net in which transitions can write variables. This formalism was introduced in [6] and, later, revisited in [7]. A transition modeling an activity performs *write operations* on a given set of variables and may have a data-dependent guard. A transition can fire only if its guard is satisfied and all input places are marked. A guard can be any formula over the process variables, using logical operators such as conjunction ($\land$), disjunction ($\lor$), and negation ($\neg$).

Definition 1 (DPN-net). *A Petri net with data (DPN-net) $N = (P, T, F, V, U, W, G)$ consists of:*

- *a Petri net (P, T, F);*
- *a set V of variables;*
- *a function U that defines the values admissible, i.e., for each variable $v \in V$, $U(v)$ is the domain of variable v;*
- *a write function $W : T \to 2^V$ that labels each transition with a set of write operations, i.e. with a s the set of variables whose value needs to be written/updated;*
- *a guard function $G : T \to \mathcal{G}_V$ that associates a guard with each transition.[2]*

When a variable $v \in V$ appears in a guard $G(t)$, it refers to the value just before the t occurrence. Nonetheless, if $v \in W(t)$, it can also appear as v' (i.e., with the prime symbol). In this case, it refers to the value after the t occurrence. Some transitions can be *invisible* and correspond to τ-steps: they do not represent actual pieces of work. Pictorially, they are represented as black boxes in the model.

Example 1. *Figure 2 shows the DPN-net that models the same process as that modeled in Figure 1 through the BPMN notation. In particular, Figure 2(a) depicts the control-flow and the write operations. In addition to the variables depicted in the figure, there exists a set of variables to model the resource and time perspective, i.e., for each transition t, there are two variables E_t and T_t. Moreover, these two variables are associated with a write operation of t. Figure 2(b) enumerates the data-perspective guards $G_d(t)$ for each transition t. When defining guards, we assume that string values can be lexicographically ordered and, hence, it is also possible to use inequality operators (i.e., $<$ and $>$) for strings.*

To also model the resource and time perspective, a second guard $G_r(t)$ can be associated with each transition t (see Figure 2(c)). Formally, only one guard $G(t)$ can be assigned to t and, hence, we set $G(t) = G_d(t) \land G_r(t)$. Note the atom $E'_c \neq E_c$ in the guard of transition Simple Assessment *in Figure 2(c): it models the resource constraint that the* Simple Assessment *cannot be performed the i-th time by the same resource that performed it the $(i - 1)$-th time within the same case (i.e., the "four-eyes" principle mentioned in Section 1). Formula $(T'_e \leq T_c + 7days \lor T'_e \leq T_d + 7days)$ in the guard of transition* Renegotiate Request *to model that it must occur within 7 days from the occurrence of the Assessment, Simple or Advanced. Conditions are never satisfied when involving variables that are not set.*

Space limitations prevent us from describing a complete operational semantics of DPN-net. Interested readers are referred to [7]. We only introduce the concepts needed later. The preset of a transition t is the set of its input places: $^\bullet t = \{p \in P \mid (p, t) \in F\}$. The postset of t is the set of its output places: $t^\bullet = \{p \in P \mid (t, p) \in F\}$. Definitions of pre- and postsets of places are analogous. A marking of a Petri net (with data) is a multiset of its places, i.e., a mapping $M : P \to \mathbb{N}$. We say the marking assigns to each place a

---

[2] The guard is defined over (a sub set of) variables in V. If a transition t has no guard, we set $G(t) = \text{true}$.

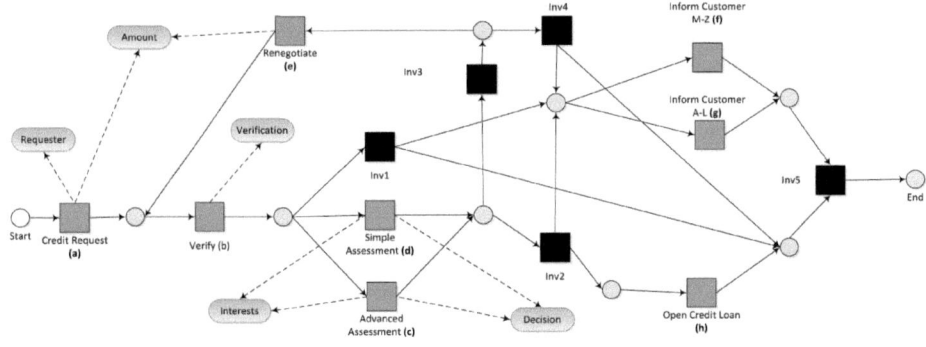

(a) The control-flow and write operations. Transitions and places are represented as squares and circles, respectively. Each rounded orange rectangle identifies a different process variable. A dotted arrow from a transition t to a variable v is a pictorial representation of the fact that $v \in W(t)$.

Transition	Guard
Advanced Assessment	$Verification = \text{true} \land Amount > 5000 \land 0.1 < Interest'/Amount < 0.15$
Inv1	$Verification = \text{false}$
Inv2	$Decision = \text{true}$
Inv3	$Decision = \text{false}$
Open Credit Loan	$Verification = \text{true} \land Decision = \text{true}$
Register Decision and Inform Customer M-Z	$Requester \geq \text{``M''}$
Register Decision and Inform Customer A-L	$Requester \leq \text{``L''}$
Renegotiate	$Amount' \leq Amount$
Simple Assessment	$Verification = \text{true} \land Amount \leq 5000 \land 0.15 < Interest'/Amount < 0.2$

(b) The guards to encode the data-perspective constraints.

Transition	Guard
Credit Request	$E'_a \in \{\text{``Pete''}, \text{``Mike''}, \text{``Ellen''}\}$
Verify	$E'_b \in \{\text{``Pete''}, \text{``Mike''}, \text{``Ellen''}\}$
Simple Assessment	$E'_c \in \{\text{``Sue''}, \text{``Sean''}, \text{``Sara''}\} \land E'_c \neq E_c$
Advanced Assessment	$E'_d \in \{\text{``Sue''}, \text{``Sean''}, \text{``Sara''}\} \land E'_d \neq E_d$
Renegotiate Request	$E'_e \in \{\text{``Pete''}, \text{``Mike''}, \text{``Ellen''}\}$ $\land (T'_e \leq T_c + 7\text{days} \lor T'_e \leq T_d + 7\text{days})$
Open Credit Loan	$E'_h = \text{``Sara''}$
Register Decision and Inform Customer M-Z	$E'_f \in \{\text{``Pete''}, \text{``Mike''}, \text{``Ellen''}\}$
Register Decision and Inform Customer A-L	$E'_g \in \{\text{``Pete''}, \text{``Mike''}, \text{``Ellen''}\}$

(c) The guards to encode the constraints over resources and time. $E_i \in \{a_1, \ldots, a_n\}$ is a shortcut for expression $E_i = a_1 \lor \ldots \lor E_i = a_n$.

Fig. 2. The DPN-net of the working example

number of tokens. A state is a pair (M, A) where M is a marking for Petri net (P, T, F) and A is a function that associates a value with each variable, i.e. $A : V \rightarrow D \cup \{\bot\}$, with $A(v) \in U(v) \cup \{\bot\}$.[3] Each DPN-net defines two special places $p_o, p_e \in P$, the initial and final place. The *initial state* is (M_0, A_0) where the initial place $p_0 \in P$ contains exactly one token, i.e. $M_0(p_0) = 1$, and any other $p \in P \setminus \{p_0\}$ contains no tokens, i.e. $M_0(p) = 0$. Moreover, $A_0(v) = \bot$ for each $v \in V$. A transition firing $s = (t, w)$ is *valid* in state (M, A) if each place in the preset of t contains at least one token, i.e. iff $\forall p \in {}^\bullet t$. $M(p) > 0$, t writes all and only the variables that it is prescribed to and $G(t)$ evaluates true with respect to assignment A. We introduce the following functions to access to the components of s: $\#_{vars}(s) = w$ and $\#_{act}(s) = t$. Function $\#_{vars}$ is also overloaded such that $\#_{vars}(s, v) = w(v)$ if $v \in \text{dom}(\#_{vars}(s))$, or $\#_{vars}(s, v) = \bot$ if $v \notin \text{dom}(\#_{vars}(s))$.[4]

---

[3] A special value $\bot$ is assigned to variables that have not been initialized.
[4] The domain of a function f is denoted with $\text{dom}(f)$.

Firing a transition s in a state (M, A) leads to a state (M', A') where M' assigns a token less than M to the t's input places $^\bullet t$ and a token more that M to t's output places $t^\bullet$; the number of tokens in the other places remains unchanged. Moreover, for each $v \in V$, $A'(v) = A(v)$ if $\#_{vars}(s,v) = \bot$, or, otherwise, $A(v') = \#_{vars}(s,v)$. The **set of valid process traces** of a DPN-net N is denoted with $\mathcal{P}_N$ and consists of all firing sequences $\sigma \in (T \times (V \nrightarrow U))^*$ that, from an initial state (M_0, A_0), lead to a state (M_F, A_F) where $M_F(p_e) > 0$.

A DPN-net is *data sound* iff, for each sequence of transitions yielding a token in the final place, there is a sequence of write operations for the transitions in the sequence such that the guard of every transition t in the sequence is satisfied when t fires.

Definition 2 (Data Soundness). *Let $N = (P, T, F, V, U, W, G)$ be a DPN-net. Let $N' = (P, T, F, \varnothing, U', W', G')$ be a DPN-net such that dom(U') = dom(W') = dom$(G') = \varnothing$. DPN-net N is data sound iff, for each $\langle s'_1, \ldots, s'_n \rangle \in \mathcal{P}_{N'}$, there exists a sequence $\langle s_1, \ldots, s_n \rangle \in \mathcal{P}_N$ where, for all $1 \leq i \leq n$, $\#_{act}(s_i) = \#_{act}(s'_i)$.*

3 Alignments of Event Logs and Process Models

An event log contains events associated to cases, i.e., process instances. Each case follows a trace of events. Each trace records the execution of a process instance. Different instances may follow the same trace. Let S_N be the set of (valid and invalid) firing of transitions of a DPN-net N with S_N. An **event log** is a multi-set of traces: $\mathcal{L} \in \mathbb{B}(S_N^*)$.[5]

Conformance checking requires an *alignment* of event log $\mathcal{L}$ and process model $\mathcal{P}$: the events in the event log need to be related to model elements and vice versa. Such an alignment shows how the event log can be replayed on the process model. This is far from being trivial since the log may deviate from the model and not all activities may have been modeled and recorded.

We need to relate "moves" in the log to "moves" in the model in order to establish an alignment between a process model and an event log. However, it may be the case that some of the moves in the log cannot be mimicked by the model and vice versa. We explicitly denote "no move" by $\gg$. For convenience, we introduce the set $S_N^\bot = S_N \cup \{\gg\}$.

One move in an *alignment* is represented by a pair $(s', s'') \in (S_N^\bot \times S_N^\bot) \setminus \{(\gg, \gg)\}$ such that

Table 1. A complete alignment

Event-Log Trace	Proc
a $\{A = 1000, R = \text{Mary}\}$	a $\{A = 5001, R = \text{Mary}\}$
b $\{V = OK\}$	b $\{V = OK\}$
c $\{I = 150, D = OK\}$	c $\{I = 650, D = NOK\}$
	Inv3
e $\{A = 1000\}$	e $\{A = 5001\}$
	b $\{V = OK\}$
c $\{I = 150, D = OK\}$	c $\{I = 650, D = OK\}$
	Inv2
g $\{\}$	g
h $\{\}$	h
	Inv5

- (s', s'') is a *move in log* if $s' \in S$ and $s'' = \gg$,
- (s', s'') is a *move in process* if $s' = \gg$ and $s'' \in S$,
- (s', s'') is a *move in both without incorrect write operations* if $s' \in S$, $s'' \in S$ and $\forall v \in V$ $\#_{vars}(s', v) = \#_{vars}(s'', v)$,
- (s', s'') is a *move in both with incorrect write operations* if $s' \in S$, $s'' \in S$ and $\exists v \in V$ $\#_{vars}(s', v) \neq \#_{vars}(s'', v)$.

$\mathcal{A}_N = (S_N^\bot \times S_N^\bot) \setminus \{(\gg, \gg)\}$ is the set of all *legal moves*.

---
[5] $\mathbb{B}(X)$ the set of all multi-sets over X.

The **alignment** of two execution traces $\sigma', \sigma'' \in S_N^*$ is a sequence $\gamma \in \mathcal{A}_N^*$ such that, ignoring all occurrences of $\gg$, the projection on the first element yields to σ' and the projection on the second yields σ''. In the remainder, σ' and σ'' are referred to as the log and the process projection of alignment γ. In particular, γ is a **complete alignment** if $\sigma'' \in \mathcal{P}_N$. Table 1 shows a complete alignment of the process model in Figure 2 and the log trace in Section 1.

In order to define the severity of a deviation, we introduce a cost function on legal moves: $\kappa \in S_A \to \mathbb{R}_0^+$. The cost of each legal move depends on the specific model and process domain and, hence, cost function κ needs to be defined ad-hoc for every specific case. The cost function can be generalized to an alignment γ as the sum of the cost of each individual move: $\mathcal{K}(\gamma) = \sum_{(s',s'') \in \gamma} \kappa(s', s'')$.

However, we do not aim to find any complete alignment. Given a log trace $\sigma_L \in \mathcal{L}$, our goal is to find a complete alignment of σ_L and $\mathcal{P}$ which minimizes the cost. We refer to it as an optimal alignment. Let $\Gamma_{\sigma_L, \mathcal{P}}$ be the multi-set of all complete alignments of σ_L and $\mathcal{P}$. The alignment $\gamma \in \Gamma_{\sigma_L, \mathcal{P}}$ is an **optimal alignment** if $\forall \gamma' \in \Gamma_{\sigma_L, \mathcal{P}} \; \mathcal{K}(\gamma) \leq \mathcal{K}(\gamma')$. Note that there may exist several optimal alignments, i.e. several complete alignments having the same minimal cost.

Regarding the complexity, in [8] we discuss a polynomial-time reduction of SAT problems (i.e., simply satisfiability problems) to problems of finding an optimal alignment. The existence of this reduction implies that finding an optimal alignment is an NP-hard problem. Therefore, while it is clear that no deterministic algorithm can guarantee an optimal alignment to be computed in polynomial time, this paper attempts to reduce the computation time for the average case.

4 The ILP-Based Technique and Diagnostics

In order to find an optimal alignment of a DPN net $N = (P, T, F, V, U, W, G)$ and a log trace σ_L, we rely on existing techniques to build an alignment that only considers the control-flow perspective. Later, we construct a problem of Integer Linear Programming (ILP) to obtain an optimal alignment which also takes the other process perspectives into account.

The approach assumes four functions to be provided by process analysts. Functions $\kappa^l(t)$ and $\kappa^p(t)$ return a non-negative cost associated with a move in log or process for transition t. Function $k^v(v)$ returns a non-negative cost relative to a variable v and a move in both (s_i^L, s_i^P) where $\#_{vars}(s_i^L, v) \neq \bot$ and $\#_{vars}(s_i^L, v) \neq \#_{vars}(s_i^P, v)$ (i.e., s_i^L assigns to v a value that is out of the domain or incompatible with some guard). Function $k^n(v)$ returns a non-negative cost relative to a variable v and a move in both (s_i^L, s_i^P) where $\#_{vars}(s_i^L, v) = \bot$ and $\#_{vars}(s_i^P, v) \neq \bot$ (i.e., s_i^L does not perform a prescribed write operation for v). These four functions can be suitably composed to obtain cost functions κ as defined in Section 3. Our ILP-based technique comprises of three phases:

1. We employ the off-the-shelf techniques described in [9] to build an alignment $\gamma_C = \langle (s_1^L, s_1^P), \ldots, (s_n^L, s_n^P) \rangle$ between the Petri net (P, T, F) and the log trace σ_L using the cost functions k^l and k^m. Since such techniques only take the control-flow into account, the process projection of γ_C does not contain write operations, i.e. if $s_i^P \neq \gg$, $\text{dom}(\#_{vars}(s_i^P)) = \emptyset$ for all $1 \leq i \leq n$. In the remainder, γ_C is called *control-flow alignment* and is not a complete alignment since its process projection is not a trace in $\mathcal{P}_N$.
2. We enrich the firings of transitions in the process projection σ_C of γ_C with the opportune write operations so as to minimize their difference with respect to the write operations observed in σ_L. Since it is a minimization problem, finding the opportune write operations can be formulated as solving a certain ILP problem: when a solution is found, the values of certain variables of the ILP-problem denote those to be assigned to variables in the writing operations of σ_C. The ILP-problem objective function f is the alignment cost.
3. We compute the fitness value $\mathcal{F}(\sigma_L) \in [0, 1]$. Adriansyah et al. [9] propose a fitness measurement where only the control-flow is considered. Let $\mathcal{F}_C(\sigma_L) \in [0, 1]$ be this measure. Here, we propose a fitness with respect to all perspectives: $\mathcal{F}(\sigma_L) = (\mathcal{F}_D(\sigma_L) + \mathcal{F}_C(\sigma_L))/2$ which is the mean of $\mathcal{F}_C(\sigma_L)$ and a certain quantity $\mathcal{F}_D(\sigma_L) \in [0, 1]$ that considers the fitness with respect to any of the non-control-flow perspectives (data, resource, time):

$$\mathcal{F}_D(\sigma_L) = \frac{f_{\min}}{\sum_{(s^L, s^P) \in \gamma_O \,:\, s^P \neq \gg} \sum_{v \in \#_{vars}(s^P)} \max(k^d(v), k^n(v))}$$

where $f_{\min}$ is the value of the objective function for the solution found of the ILP problem. The denominator corresponds to the highest cost in term of deviations, i.e. for each move (s^L, s^P) in both, the deviations between the write operations of s^L and s^P have the highest cost.

Section 4.1 discusses how to build an ILP problem to obtain optimal solutions. To keep the discussion simple, each guard is assumed to be atomic (e.g., $Amount > 5000$). However, this limitation can be easily addressed, as discussed in technical report [8]. The technical report also discusses how to convert date- and string-typed variables into integers and, hence, to support these types of variables. Section 4.2 discusses our proposal for a helicopter view where common deviations and their causes are shown.

4.1 Construction of the ILP Problem

Given a DPN-net N and a log trace σ_L, the outcome of the first phase is a control-flow alignment $\gamma_C = \langle (s_1^L, s_1^P), \ldots, (s_n^L, s_n^P) \rangle$.

Example 2. *In order to maintain the example of a reasonable size, in the remainder, we only consider the data perspective (i.e., we ignore the guards in Figure 2(c)). Let us assume $\kappa^l(t) = \kappa^p(t) = 1$ for each transition $t \in T \setminus \{Inv1, Inv2, Inv3, Inv4\}$ and $\kappa^l(t) = \kappa^p(t) = 0$ for each transition $t \in \{Inv1, Inv2, Inv3, Inv4\}$. The latter transitions are invisible and, hence, by definition, they never appear in the log. Therefore, they are always associated with moves in*

(a) Control-flow Alignment.

Event-Log Trace		Proc
a {A = 1000, R = Mary}		a
b {V = OK}		b
c {I = 150, D = OK}		c
		Inv3
e {A = 1000}		e
		b
c {I = 150, D = NOK}		c
		Inv2
g {}		g
h {}		h
		Inv5

(b) The ILP problem to find an optimal alignment.

$$\min 10 + \widehat{V_1} + \widehat{I_1} + \widehat{D_1} + \widehat{A_1} \\ + \widehat{A_2} + \widehat{I_2} + \widehat{D_2} + \widehat{R_1}$$
$$V_1 = 1$$
$$I_1 > 0.1\, A_1$$
$$I_1 < 0.15\, A_1$$
$$D_1 = 0$$
$$A_2 < 0.6\, A_1$$
$$I_2 > 0.1\, A_2$$
$$I_2 < 0.1\, A_2$$
$$I_2 < 0.15\, A_2$$
$$D_2 = 0$$
$$R_1 < \text{``}M\text{''}$$
$$\mathbf{A_1 = 1000} \Leftrightarrow \widehat{A_1} = 0$$
$$\mathbf{R_1 = \text{``Mary''}} \Leftrightarrow \widehat{R_1} = 0$$
$$\mathbf{I_1 = 150} \Leftrightarrow \widehat{I_1} = 0$$
$$\mathbf{A_2 = 1000} \Leftrightarrow \widehat{A_1} = 0$$
$$\mathbf{I_2 = 150} \Leftrightarrow \widehat{I_2} = 0$$
$$\mathbf{D_2 = 1} \Leftrightarrow \widehat{D_2} = 0$$

(c) Optimal Alignment obtained as solution of an ILP problem: v_i^* denotes the value assigned to variable v_i in the ILP-problem solution that is found.

Event-Log Trace		Proc
a {A = 1000, R = Mary}		a {A = A_1^*, R = R_1^*}
b {V = OK}		b {V = V_1^*}
c {I = 150, D = OK}		c {I = I_1^*, D = D_1^*}
		Inv3
e {A = 1000}		e {A = A_2^*}
		b {V = V_2^*}
c {I = 150, D = NOK}		c {I = I_2^*, D = D_2^*}
		Inv2
g {}		g
h {}		h
		Inv5

Fig. 3. The technique applied to the working example. First, a control-flow alignment is built, which, later, is used to build an ILP problem, whose solution allows for extending the control-flow alignment to obtain the write operations of the process projection. The constraints in bold in Figure 3(b) are non-linear. Nevertheless, as discussed in the text, each can be transformed into two equivalent linear constraints.

process, without them being real deviations. Figure 3(a) is a possible control-flow alignment $\overline{\gamma}$ for the trace considered in Section 1, which is returned by the technique reported in [9]. This is the output of the first phase, which needs to be extended to obtain an optimal alignment.

In order to build the ILP problem, we introduce a helper function $\#_V(\gamma, v)$ that returns the number of write operations that are prescribed to happen for variable v, considering the transitions fired in the process projection of γ.

For each write operation that is prescribed to happen for a variable $v \in V$, there exists an ILP variable v_i. The set of such variables is denoted with V_{ILP}: $V_{ILP} = \{v_i : v \in V \land 0 < i \leq \#_V(\gamma, v)\}$.

By analyzing the control-flow alignment, it is possible to determine whether the i-th write operation for v has or has not occurred. In remainder, constant $\underline{v_i}$ denotes the actual value observed in the log trace, with $\underline{v_i} = \bot$ if the i-th write operation has not been observed. For instance, considering the control-flow alignment in Figure 3(a) and, specifically, the first move, it can be observed that $\underline{A_1} = 1000$ and $\underline{R_1} = 1000$, whereas, considering the 6th move (i.e., for transition **b**), $\underline{V_2} = \bot$. In addition to the variables in V_{ILP}, the ILP problem also includes a boolean variable $\widehat{v_i}$, for each $v_i \in V_{ILP}$ such that $\underline{v_i} \neq \bot$. For the solution found for the ILP problem, variable $\widehat{v_i}$ is assigned value 1 if variable v_i is not assigned value $\underline{v_i}$, i.e. there is a deviation relative to the i-th write operation for variable v. Otherwise, $\widehat{v_i}$ is given value 0.

We create a set Φ_{γ_C} of ILP-problem constraints as follow. For each prefix $\gamma_C' = \langle (s_1^L, s_1^P), \ldots, (s_i^L, s_i^P) \rangle$ of control-flow alignment γ_C, there exists a constraint $\phi \in \Phi_{\gamma_C}$ if $s_i^P \neq \gg$. Constraint ϕ is obtained starting from $G(\#_{act}(s_i^P))$ and replacing, for each $v \in V$, all occurrences of v with $v_{k-1} \in V_{ILP}$ and all occurrences of v' (i.e., with the prime symbol) with $v_k \in V_{ILP}$, where $k = \#_V(\gamma_C', v)$.

Example 3. *By analyzing the control-flow in Figure 3(a), variables* **V, I, D** *need to be written twice each and variable* **R** *once. Therefore, following variables* $V_1, V_2, I_1, I_2, D_1, D_2$ *and* R_1 *are introduced to the ILP problem. Moreover, besides the write operation for* **V** *associated with the 6th move of the control-flow alignment (i.e., the second execution of transition* **b***), they have all occurred. Therefore the following boolean variables* $\widehat{V_1}, , \widehat{I_1}, \widehat{I_2}, \widehat{D_1}, \widehat{D_2}, \widehat{R_1}$ *needs to be introduced, i.e.* $\widehat{V_2}$ *is excluded. Figure 3(b) shows the ILP problem to find the optimal alignment: the constraints not in bold are those in* $\Phi_{\overline{\gamma}}$, *i.e. relative to the transitions' guards. Each occurrence* v *and* v' *is replaced with the respective variable* $\underline{v_{i-1}}$ *and* $\underline{v_i}$ *of ILP problem, as described above. To enhance the example's comprehension, string constants are not converted into their respective numeric representations. Nonetheless, the conversion is necessary to be able to solve the ILP problem.*

Once these elements are introduced, the structure of the entire ILP problem can be described. Let $CN(\gamma_C, k^n)$ be the cost relative to missing write operations:

$$CN(\gamma_C, k^n) = \sum_{(s_i^L, s_i^P) \in \gamma_C \text{ s.t. } s_i^P \neq \gg} \left(\sum_{v \in (\text{dom}(\#_{vars}(s_i^P)) \setminus \text{dom}(\#_{vars}(s_i^L)))} k^n(v) \right)$$

The objective function to minimize is the cost associated with deviations of any perspective different from the control-flow:

$$\min \left(CN(\gamma_C, k^n) + \sum_{v_i \in V_{ILP}: \underline{v_i} \neq \perp} \left(k^d(v) \cdot \widehat{v_i} \right) \right) \quad (1)$$

subject to the constraints in Φ_{γ_C} and the following ones:

$$\forall v_i \in V_{ILP} \text{ s.t. } \underline{v_i} \neq \perp. \ v_i = \underline{v_i} \Leftrightarrow \widehat{v_i} = 0 \quad (2)$$

and

$$\forall v_i \in V_{ILP}. \ v_i \in U(v); \quad \forall v_i \in V_{ILP} \text{ s.t. } \underline{v_i} \neq \perp. \ \widehat{v_i} \in [0, 1]$$

The constraints in Equation 2 are clearly not linear. Nonetheless, each of these constraints can also be written as a pair of linear constraints:

$$v_i - M\widehat{v_i} \leq \underline{v_i}; \quad -v_i - M\widehat{v_i} \leq -\underline{v_i}$$

where M is a sufficiently large number (e.g., the maximum machine-representable number). The equivalence of each pair of these constraints can be easily observed: in the solution of the ILP problem, if $\widehat{v_i} = 0$, then $v_i = \underline{v_i}$ must hold; otherwise any value can be assigned to v_i. Nonetheless, we aim to minimize the objective function in Equation 1; hence, $\widehat{v_i} = 1$ only if value $\underline{v_i}$ cannot be assigned to v_i.

Example 4. *Let us suppose that* $k^n(v) = 10$ *and* $k^d(v) = 1$ *for each* $v \in V$. *In Figure 3(b), the constraints in bold are those which are introduced to enforce that* $\widehat{v_i} = 0$ *iff* $v_i = \underline{v_i}$, *i.e. the constraints of the type described in Equation 2. Figure 3(c) shows the optimal alignment in function of the solution of the ILP problem. It contains write operations of form* $v = v_i^*$ *where* v_i^* *is the value assigned to variable* v_i *in the solution found for the ILP problem. Note the objective function has an added constant 10, which is relative to the only missing write operation, which is for* V.

The following theorem discusses the admissibility of the ILP problems constructed as described above (see [8] for a sketch of the proof):

Theorem 1 (Admissibility of the ILP problem). *Let $N = (P, T, F, V, U, W, G)$ be a data-sound DPN-Net and σ_L be a log trace. The ILP problem constructed as mentioned above to find an optimal alignment of σ_L and N is always admissible.*

4.2 A Helicopter View on the Optimal Alignments

Alignments can be projected on the process model to obtain a helicopter view. Transitions and variables are colored based on their *level of conformance*: a value between 0 and 1. Extreme values 1 and 0 identify the situations in which, according to the behavior in an event log $\mathcal{L}$, the executions of a transition or the write operations for a variable are always or never conforming with the model. When projecting deviations on the model, transitions and variables are colored according to their level of conformance: if the level is 1 or 0, a white or black color is used, with intermediate values associated with intermediate shades of color, including different intensities of yellow, orange, red, purple and brown. Readers are referred to [8] for more details on how levels of conformance are computed.

Each transition t is also associated with a decision tree that relates the deviations for t (e.g., moves in log) to the typical causes, e.g. the typical DPN-net states (M, A) when such deviations occurred. Decision trees classify instances by sorting them down in a tree from the root to some leaf node. Each non-leaf node specifies a test of some classification feature and each branch descending from that node corresponds to a range of possible values for the feature. Leaf nodes are relative to the value for the classification feature.

Decision trees are constructed starting from a set of training instances. In our case, a different training instance $\vec{o}$ is associated with each prefix $\gamma' = \langle (s_1^L, s_1^P), \ldots, (s_i^L, s_i^P) \rangle$ of every optimal alignment $\gamma \in \Gamma$. Instance $\vec{o}$ is used to train the decision tree for transition $\#_{act}(s_i^P)$, if $s_i^P \neq \gg$, or $\#_{act}(s_i^L)$, if $s_i^P = \gg$. The possible value of the classification feature in $\vec{o}$ corresponds to one of 4 types of moves, i.e. moves in process, in log, as well as moves in both with or without incorrect write operations. Let σ_L' be the log projection of alignment prefix $\langle (s_1^L, s_1^P), \ldots, (s_{i-1}^L, s_{i-1}^P) \rangle$, i.e., ignoring the last move in γ'. If γ occurs multiple times in Γ, i.e. $\#_\Gamma(\gamma) > 1$, each γ prefix generates $\#_\Gamma(\gamma)$ training instances, which are giving the same values to all classification features.

For each variable $v \in V$, there exist two classification features: v and v'. The value of the classification feature v is the value of the last write operation for v in log trace σ_L'. If there is no write operation for v in σ_L', no value is assigned to the feature. As a matter of fact, decision-tree construction algorithms can deal with missing values of features. The value of the classification feature v' is the value assigned to v by log event s_i^L, i.e. $\#_{vars}(v, s_i^L)$. If $s_i^L = \gg$ or $\#_{vars}(v, s_i^L) = \bot$, no value is assigned to the feature. We also add an additional feature $\#t$ for each transition $t \in T$. The value for feature $\#t$ is the number of firings of transition t in σ_L', i.e. the number of execution of t before the last move of γ'.

5 Implementation and Experiments on Real Life Event Logs

Our *multi-perspective conformance checking approach* is realized through two software plug-ins of ProM, a generic open-source framework for implementing process mining tools in a standard environment.[6] A first ProM plug-in, the *Data-aware Conformance Checker*, takes a process model in form of a DPN-net and an event log as input and operationalizes the techniques described in Section 4, including the extensions for non-atomic formulas. The output is a set of optimal alignments, one for each trace in the event log. A second plug-in, the *Data-aware Conformance Projector*, projects the optimal alignments onto the process model, operationalizing the approach described in Section 4.2. To solve ILP problems our implementation uses the *lp_solve* library, which is based on the revised simplex method combined with a branch-and-bound method for the integers.[7] To construct decision trees, we leverage on the implementation of the C4.5 algorithm in the *WEKA* toolkit.[8]

To assess the practical feasibility of the approach, the two ProM plug-ins have been tested on a real-life case study involving a Dutch insurance institute. We used an event log containing 12319 traces (i.e. process instances), where, on average, each trace is composed by around 7 events, with a minimum of 4 events and a maximum of 11 events. The event log has been generated through XESame, which is bundled in ProM. XESame allowed us to extract the event log from the database of the insurance institute. A control-flow process model has been designed in collaboration with a process analyst of the institute. Figure 5 shows the DPN-net for the case study. Each transition t modeling an activity t is associated with a guard $G(t) = G_r(t) \wedge G_d(t)$ where formulas $G_r(t)$ and $G_d(t)$ encode the constraints on the resource and data perspective, respectively. We have derived $G_r(t)$ for every transition t after a number of talks with the process analyst; formulas $G_d(t)$ have automatically been mined through the Decision Miner [7] and validated with the process analyst. Although the event log contains 32 data attributes, only five are actually involved in the guards of the activities. Therefore, we did not include the others in the process model to preserve the model's readability. These five attributes are written once with the *Start* activity when a insurance claim is submitted and never updated. Here, the *Data-aware Conformance Checker* plug-in is used to evaluate whether this process model is a good representation of the real behavior observed in the event log. The process analyst could not identify some deviations as more severe than others. Therefore, the four cost functions were defined so as to return 1 for any control-flow and data-flow deviation.

Visualization of the Optimal Alignments in ProM. Figure 4 shows how the optimal alignments are visualized in ProM: the optimal alignment of each log trace is shown as a sequence of triangles, each representing an alignment's move. Each triangle is colored according to the move that it represents. The green and white colors are used to identify moves in both without or with incorrect write operations, respectively; yellow and purple are for moves in the log or in the process, respectively. Finally, the gray is used for moves for invisible transitions. When the user passes over a triangle with the

---
[6] http://www.promtools.org/
[7] http://lpsolve.sourceforge.net/
[8] http://weka.sourceforge.net

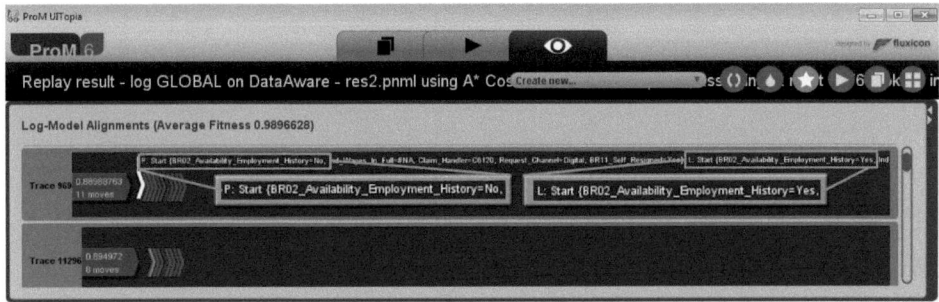

Fig. 4. The ProM User Interface to show the optimal alignments

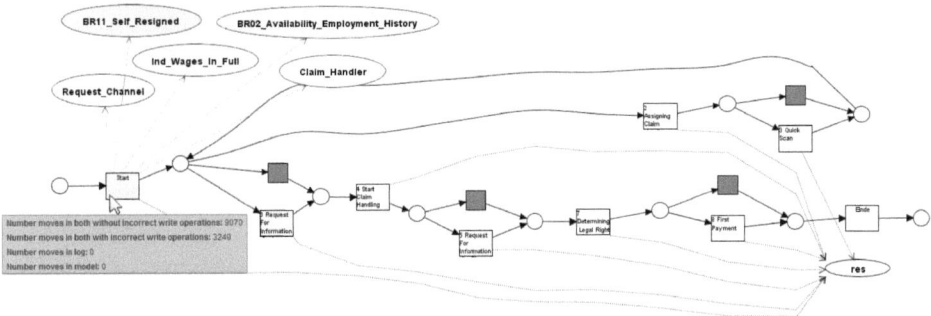

Fig. 5. The process model relative to the case study of a Dutch insurance institute. The alignments have been projected on the model to pinpoint where deviations occur more often.

mouse, the plug-in highlights the two transition firings s^L and s^P associated with the move (s^L, s^P). Specifically, the figure refers to a move in both with an incorrect write operation for variable *Availability_Employment_History*. The value next to the optimal alignment for every trace σ_L is the fitness value $\mathcal{F}(\sigma_L)$. On the top of the screen view, the average fitness of all traces is shown.

Enhanced Diagnostics in ProM. Figure 5 illustrates the output of the *Data-aware Conformance Projector* in ProM. Activities and variables are colored according to their level of conformance, as discussed in Section 4.2. Activity *Start* is the most involved in deviations, since the rectangle of respective transition is filled with the darkest color. Similarly, *BR11_Self_Resigner* is the variables for which there is the highest number of incorrect write operations. When passing over a transition/activity or variable with the mouse, more information is given: the figure shows that activity *Start* is 3249 moves in both with incorrect write operations and 9070 moves without incorrect write operations. It is worthy observing that variable *res* is filled with a white color, which implies activities are generally performed by authorized resources. When clicking on a transition's rectangle, as discussed in Section 4.2, an associated decision tree is shown which classifies the types of deviations relative to the transition as function of the process state when the deviations occurred. Figure 6 shows the decision tree associated with transition *Quick Scan*. In brackets, each tree leaf shows the number of moves in

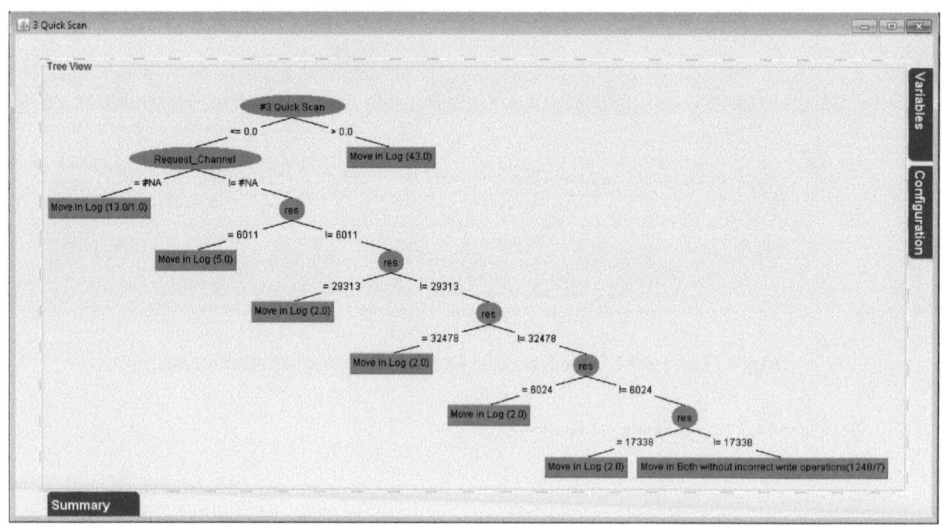

Fig. 6. The decision tree associated with activity/transition *Quick Scan*. Each tree leaf corresponds to one of the possible types of moves: in log, in process and in both, with or without incorrect write operations.

the computed optimal alignments that are classified in that leaf. Some moves can be incorrectly classified: the type of moves may be different from what the values of the classification features would suggest. In these cases, after the slash, a second number is shown, which is the number of wrongly classified moves. The labels around the decision tree, i.e. *Variables*, *Configuration* and *Summary*, allow users, on the one hand, to access information about the quality of the decision tree and, on the other hand, to set the configuration parameters and the classification features to consider when constructing the decision tree. By analyzing the tree in Figure 6, one can observe that activity *Quick Scan* is usually correctly executed if it has never been previously executed (i.e., $\#3QuickScan = 0$) and the claim's request channel is known and the previous activity is performed by any resource different from #6011, #29313, #32478, #6024, #17338. This statement is not confirmed in only 7 out of 1248 moves as indicated by the label "Move in Both without incorrect write operation (1248/7)" associated with the tree's leaf. In any different state of the DPN-net when *Quick Scan* was performed, a move in log is expected.

Table 2. Execution time comparison between the new technique and the technique in [5] for some log-model combinations. When unspecified, the time units are seconds.

Event Log & Model	New	Previous
Dutch Insurance Institute	3+7.02	> 2 hs
Synthetic Log ($n = 4$)	0.17+0.38	13.3
Synthetic Log ($n = 5$)	0.2+0.21	48
Synthetic Log ($n = 6$)	0.2+0.44	205

Execution-Time Analysis. As mentioned in the introduction, our new technique is several orders of magnitude faster than it predecessor described in [5]. To support this claim, we performed a number of experiments with different combinations of event logs and process models. The experimental results are summarized in Table 2: the second column is relative to the results for our new technique, i.e. the ILP-based technique described in this paper, whereas the third refers to the previous technique. For the new technique, the execution time is reported as $x+y$ where x and y are, respectively, the execution times to compute the control-flow alignments and to complement them to consider the other perspectives.

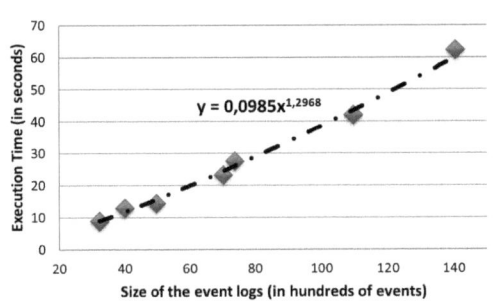

Fig. 7. Scalability of the approach with event logs of different sizes

The first row is relative to the real-life event log of the Dutch insurance institute used before to showcase the implementation. Along with the real-life event log, we have employed the same process models that were used for execution-time analysis reported in Section 5 of paper [5]. In particular, a process model has been considered with n parallel activities. Each of n parallel activities performs a write operation for a different integer variable, which can be assigned a value between 0 and 42. After the n activities, a different activity is performed which is associated with a guard involving the n variables. Further details on the model are given in [5]. To perform the comparison, we have conducted experiments for $n = 4, 5$ or 6. For each of these three values, we have generated an event log that contained 60 traces with data-related deviations on the write operations. Finally, we have employed both of techniques and compared the execution time to find the 60 optimal alignments. Comparing the results reported in Table 2, the improvements of the new ILP-based technique are evident.

As further evaluation, we performed detailed experiments to see how the approach scales up with logs of different sizes. To this purpose, we generated 7 events logs by simulating the model in Figure 2 with CPNTools[9]. Each event log contained a different number of events while the number of traces were always 3000 (i.e., the average length of traces was different in each of 7 event logs). To generate event logs of different sizes, we instructed the simulation in a way that, on average, each loan request required a different number of renegotiations (i.e., the loop was executed a large number of times in each trace). After the generation of the logs, 20% of events were moved to a different position in the respective trace to introduce deviations. Figure 7 shows the the execution time required to compute the optimal alignments for the traces in the 7 event logs. The dotted line indicates the general trend. This shows that optimal alignments can be computed efficiently (at least, for the considered example): the execution time grows almost linearly with event logs of increasing sizes.

6 Conclusion

Various conformance checking techniques have been proposed in recent years. As mentioned in Section 1, they only focus on the control-flow thereby ignoring, e.g., incorrect

---

[9] http://cpntools.org/

routing decisions, incorrect values assigned to variables, delayed activities, and unqualified resources executing activities.

This paper presents a technique that consider data, resources and time when checking for process conformance. The proposed technique using state-of-the-art techniques to first create control-flow alignments. Such alignments are extended to incorporate the other perspectives. To extend alignments with other perspectives, an additional ILP problem is constructed and solved for each log trace. The conformance-checking technique discussed in this paper has been implemented in ProM and was tested with various synthetic log-model combinations and, also, using a real-life case study. This way we were able to demonstrate the practical relevance and feasibility of the technique.

Our approach goes much further than existing techniques for data-aware behavioral compliance checking [10,11]. The setting considered in [10,11] is different from ours: a set of compliance rules rather than a multi-set of log traces is checked. There also exist efficient algorithms to perform sequence alignments (e.g., the algorithms of Needleman-Wunsch and Smith-Waterman). Similarly, in Process Mining, J.C. Bose et al. [12] have proposed techniques to efficiently align pairs of log traces. Unfortunately, they cannot be applied to find an alignment between a log trace and a process model. In our setting, we do not know a priori the process trace to align with the log trace; conversely, the process trace needs to be chosen, thus minimizing the severity of the deviations. Moreover, sequence and trace alignments only focus on the activity names, i.e. the control-flow perspective, ignoring the other perspectives.

Montali [13] developed some techniques to check the conformity of running process instances with respect to a set of temporal- and data-related constraints. Certainly, these techniques can also be applied for a-posteriori analysis, but they would not be able to pinpoint where the deviations exactly occur, which we aim to do. For this purpose, one could also leverage on existing techniques in the field of distributed systems for system debugging [14,15]. Unfortunately, they would also be limited to alert deviations, without highlighting where they actually occur.

References

1. van der Aalst, W.M.P.: Process Mining - Discovery, Conformance and Enhancement of Business Processes. Springer (2011)
2. Rozinat, A., van der Aalst, W.M.P.: Conformance Checking of Processes Based on Monitoring Real Behavior. Information Systems 33, 64–95 (2008)
3. Weidlich, M., Polyvyanyy, A., Desai, N., Mendling, J.: Process Compliance Measurement based on Behavioural Profiles. In: Pernici, B. (ed.) CAiSE 2010. LNCS, vol. 6051, pp. 499–514. Springer, Heidelberg (2010)
4. Cook, J., Wolf, A.: Software Process Validation: Quantitatively Measuring the Correspondence of a Process to a Model. ACM Transactions on Software Engineering and Methodology (TOSEM) 8, 147–176 (1999)
5. de Leoni, M., van der Aalst, W.M.P., van Dongen, B.F.: Data- and Resource-Aware Conformance Checking of Business Processes. In: Abramowicz, W., Kriksciuniene, D., Sakalauskas, V. (eds.) BIS 2012. LNBIP, vol. 117, pp. 48–59. Springer, Heidelberg (2012)
6. Sidorova, N., Stahl, C., Trčka, N.: Soundness Verification for Conceptual Workflow Nets With Data: Early Detection of Errors With the Most Precision Possible. Information Systems 36(7), 1026–1043 (2011)

7. de Leoni, M., van der Aalst, W.M.P.: Data-Aware Process Mining: Discovering Decisions in Processes Using Alignments. In: Proc. of the 28th ACM Symposium on Applied Computing (SAC 2013). ACM (2013)
8. de Leoni, M., van der Aalst, W.M.P.: Aligning Event Logs and Process Models for Multi-Perspective Conformance Checking: An Approach Based on Integer Linear Programming, BPM Center Report BPM-13-05 (2013)
9. Adriansyah, A., van Dongen, B.F., van der Aalst, W.M.: Conformance Checking Using Cost-Based Fitness Analysis. In: IEEE International Enterprise Distributed Object Computing Conference, pp. 55–64. IEEE Computer Society (2011)
10. Ly, L., Rinderle-Ma, S., Knuplesch, D., Dadam, P.: Monitoring business process compliance using compliance rule graphs. In: Meersman, R., Dillon, T., Herrero, P., Kumar, A., Reichert, M., Qing, L., Ooi, B.-C., Damiani, E., Schmidt, D.C., White, J., Hauswirth, M., Hitzler, P., Mohania, M. (eds.) OTM 2011, Part I. LNCS, vol. 7044, pp. 82–99. Springer, Heidelberg (2011)
11. Belardinelli, F., Lomuscio, A., Patrizi, F.: Verification of GSM-Based Artifact-Centric Systems through Finite Abstraction. In: Liu, C., Ludwig, H., Toumani, F., Yu, Q. (eds.) ICSOC 2012. LNCS, vol. 7636, pp. 17–31. Springer, Heidelberg (2012)
12. Jagadeesh Chandra Bose, R.P., van der Aalst, W.M.P.: Process Diagnostics Using Trace Alignment: Opportunities, Issues, and Challenges. Information Systems 37(2) (2012)
13. Montali, M.: Specification and Verification of Declarative Open Interaction Models. LNBIP, vol. 56. Springer, Heidelberg (2010)
14. Reynolds, P., Killian, C., Wiener, J.L., Mogul, J.C., Shah, M.A., Vahdat, A.: Pip: detecting the unexpected in distributed systems. In: Proceedings of the 3rd Conference on Networked Systems Design & Implementation, vol. 3, pp. 115–128. USENIX Association (2006)
15. Xu, W., Huang, L., Fox, A., Patterson, D., Jordan, M.I.: Detecting large-scale system problems by mining console logs. In: Proceedings of the ACM SIGOPS 22nd Symposium on Operating Systems Principles, pp. 117–132. ACM (2009)

Conformance Checking in the Large: Partitioning and Topology

Jorge Munoz-Gama[1], Josep Carmona[1], and Wil M.P. van der Aalst[2]

[1] Universitat Politecnica de Catalunya, Barcelona, Spain
[2] Eindhoven University of Technology, Eindhoven, The Netherlands
{jmunoz,jcarmona}@lsi.upc.edu, w.m.p.v.d.aalst@tue.nl

Abstract. The torrents of event data generated by today's systems are an important enabler for process mining. However, at the same time, the size and variability of the resulting event logs are challenging for today's process mining techniques. This paper focuses on "conformance checking in the large" and presents a novel decomposition technique that partitions larger processes into sets of subprocesses that can be analyzed more easily. The resulting topological representation of the partitioning can be used to localize conformance problems. Moreover, we provide techniques to refine the decomposition such that similar process fragments are not considered twice during conformance analysis. All the techniques have been implemented in ProM, and experimental results are provided.

Keywords: Process Mining, Conformance Checking, Process Diagnosis.

1 Introduction

The interest in process mining is increasing because of the widespread availability of event data and the desire to improve performance and compliance of operational processes. Process mining relates modeled behavior and observed behavior [1,2]. This novel discipline tackles three challenges relating event data (i.e., log files) and process models: the *discovery* of a process model from an event log, checking the *conformance* of a process model and a log, and the *enhancement* of a process model with the information extracted from a log. Process mining research resulted in a variety of algorithms that demonstrated to be of great value for undertaking small or medium-sized problem instances. However, real-life experiences show that most of the existing algorithms have difficulties dealing with industrial-sized problems (cf. Section 6).

This paper proposes a decomposition technique for determining the conformance of a Petri net with respect to a log (i.e., how good is the model describing the behavior of the log). Instead of trying to asses the conformance of the whole event log and the complete Petri net, we check conformance for selected subprocesses (subnets of the initial Petri net and corresponding sublogs). Subprocesses are identified as fragments of the Petri net that have a single-entry and a single-exit node (*SESE*), thus representing an isolated part of the model with a well-defined interface to the rest of the net [3].

In [4], we presented a conformance checking approach using the so-called *Refined Process Structure Tree* (RPST). The RPST [3] allows for the construction of hierarchy of SESEs. This paper extends the approach presented in [4] as follows: First of all, we present a new strategy to compute fitness (i.e., the dimension of conformance that focuses on analyze if the traces in the log are valid sequences of the model) by selecting a partitioning of the RPST. Then this partitioning is extended with a new set of fragments corresponding to the interface between place-bordered SESEs. With this extension, it is guaranteed that the fitness of the whole Petri net can be computed directly from the fitness of the fragments forming the partition. Experiments show a considerable reduction (orders of magnitude) in the fitness checking, and moreover the techniques allow for identifying those subnets that have fitness problems, allowing the process owner to focus on the problematic parts of a large model.

The RPST-based decomposition is not only used for efficiency reasons. We also use it to provide diagnostics that help the analyst in localizing conformance problems. We create a topological structure of SESEs in order to detect the larger connected components that have fitness problems. Moreover, problematic parts can be analyzed in isolation and independently of the rest of the model. Finally, the approach is refined to avoid considering the same problem multiple times. For example, it makes no sense to consider small or highly similar process fragments.

Related Work. Cook et al. [5] were among the first to quantify the relationship between event logs and process models. They compared event streams of the model with event streams generated from the event log. Several authors proposing process discovery algorithms also provide a quality metric (often related to fitness). For example, in [6] the authors define a fitness function for searching for the optimal model using a genetic approach.

The first comprehensive approach to conformance analysis was proposed in [7]. Two different types of metrics are proposed: (a) *fitness metrics*, i.e., the extent to which the log traces can be associated with valid execution paths specified by the process model, and (b) *appropriateness metrics*, i.e., the degree of accuracy in which the process model describes the observed behavior in the log, combined with the degree of clarity in which it is represented. One of the drawbacks of the approach in [7] and most other approaches that "play the token game", is that fitness is typically overestimated. When a model and log do not fit well together, replay will overload the process model with superfluous tokens. As a result, the model will allow for too much behavior. Approaches such as the one in [7] also have problems when the model has "invisible activities" (silent steps that are not recorded in the event log) or "duplicate activities" (multiple transitions bearing the same label). To deal with such phenomena state-space exploration and heuristics are needed to replay the event log. In fact, most conformance techniques give up after the first non-fitting event or simply "guess" the corresponding path in the model. Therefore, Adriansyah et al. formulated conformance checking problems as an optimization problem [8,9].

Lion's share of attention in conformance checking has been devoted to checking fitness. However, in recent papers researchers started to explore the other quality dimensions [1,8,10]. For example, Munoz-Gama et al. quantified the precision dimension [11,12].

In [13] various process mining decomposition approaches are discussed. In [14] the notion of passages is used to decompose a process model and/or event log into smaller parts that can be checked or discovered locally. This approach is generalized in [15] where it is shown that fitness-related problems can be decomposed as long as the different process fragments only share transitions having unique labels. This idea is used in this paper. However, unlike [14,15] we use an RPST-based decomposition that also allows for place-boundaries. Moreover, the refined RPST-based decomposition and the topological structure enable additional diagnostics not considered before.

Outline. Section 2 provides some preliminaries, before describing our partitioning approach (Section 3). Section 4 presents the notion of a topological graph to show conformance diagnostics. In Section 5 we discuss a refinement to avoid inspecting small or highly similar process fragments. Experimental results are presented in Section 6. Section 7 concludes the paper.

2 Preliminaries

To explain our conformance checking approach we introduce some basic notions. We use Petri nets (workflow nets to be precise) to model processes.

Definition 1 (Petri Net, Workflow Net). *A Petri net[16] is a tuple $PN = (P, T, A)$ having a finite set of places P and a finite set of transitions T where $P \cap T = \emptyset$, and a flow relation $A \subseteq (P \times T) \cup (T \times P)$.*[1] *The* preset *and* postset *of a node are defined as $^\bullet x = \{y | (y,x) \in A\}$ and $x^\bullet = \{y | (x,y) \in A\}$, respectively. The state of a Petri net is defined by its* marking, *i.e., a multiset over P. A* workflow net *(WF-net) $WN = (P, T, A, i, o)$ is a particular type of Petri net where the net has one source place i and one sink place o, and all the other nodes are in a path between them.*

Definition 2 (Workflow Graph). *Given a Petri net $PN = (P, T, A)$, we define its* workflow graph *simply as the structural graph $G = (V, E)$ with no distinctions between places and transitions, i.e., $V = P \cup T$ and $E = A$.*

Definition 3 (System Net, Full Firing Sequences). *A system net is a tuple $SN = (PN, m_i, m_o)$ where m_i and m_o define the initial and final marking of the net, respectively. $(PN, m_1)[\sigma\rangle(PN, m_2)$ denotes that a sequence of transitions $\sigma \in T^*$ is enabled in marking m_1 and executing σ in m_1 results in marking m_2. $\{\sigma \mid (PN, m_i)[\sigma\rangle(PN, m_o)\}$ are all full firing sequences of SN.*

An *event log* is a multiset of traces. Each *trace* is a sequence of activities (in this paper corresponding to the set of transitions T). Multiple cases may follow the same trace.

---

[1] Although the approach is valid also for weighted Petri nets, for the sake of clarity in this paper we restrict to the case with no weights on the arcs.

Definition 4 (Event Log). *An event log $L \in \mathbb{B}(T^*)$ is a multiset of traces.*

Fitness can be defined in various ways [1,8,10]. In this paper, we just classify traces into fitting or non-fitting. Fitting traces correspond to full firing sequences.

Definition 5 (Fitting Trace). *A trace $\sigma \in T^*$ fits $SN = (PN, m_i, m_o)$ if $(PN, [m_i])[\sigma\rangle(PN, [m_o])$, i.e., σ corresponds to a full firing sequence of SN. An event log $L \in \mathbb{B}(T^*)$ fits SN if $(PN, [m_i])[\sigma\rangle(PN, [m_o])$ for all $\sigma \in L$.*

To decompose conformance checking problems, we identify so-called *SESE components*. In the remainder, the following context is assumed: Let G be the workflow graph of a given WF-net WN, and let $G_S = (V_S, S)$ be a connected subgraph of G formed by a set of edges S and the vertexes $V_S = \Pi(S)$ induced by S.[2]

Definition 6 (Interior, Boundary, Entry and Exit nodes [3]). *A node $x \in V_S$ is interior with respect to G_S iff it is connected only to nodes in V_S; otherwise x is a boundary node of G_S. A boundary node y of G_S is an entry of G_S iff no incoming edge of y belongs to S or if all outgoing edges of y belong to S. A boundary node y of G_S is an exit of G_S iff no outgoing edge of y belongs to S or if all incoming edges of y belong to S.*

For example, given the model in Fig. 1a and its corresponding workflow graph in Fig. 1b, let consider the subgraph S_4 containing the arcs b, d, f, h and the vertexes induced by them. The nodes corresponding with t_1 and t_4 are boundary nodes, while p_2, t_2 and p_4 are interior nodes. Moreover, the node t_1 is an entry node, while t_4 is an exit.

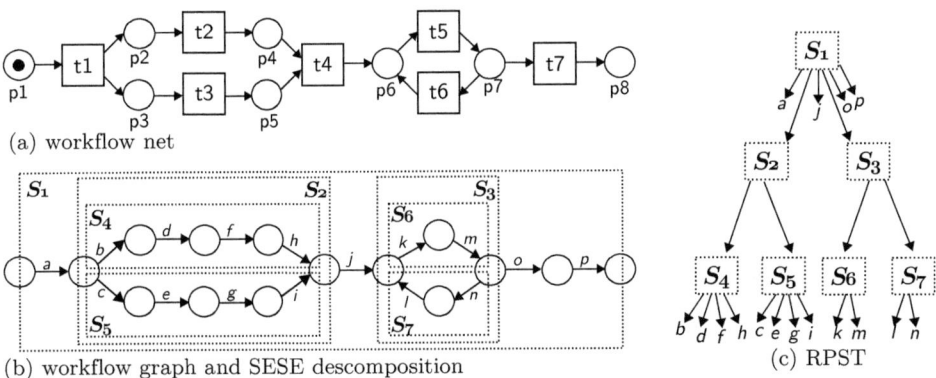

Fig. 1. A WF-net, its workflow graph and the RPST and SESE decomposition

Definition 7 (SESE, Trivial SESE and Canonical SESE [3]). *$S \subseteq E$ is a SESE (Single-Exit-Single-Entry) of graph $G = (V, E)$ iff G_S has exactly two boundary nodes: one entry and one exit. A SESE is trivial if it is composed of a*

---

[2] $\Pi(R) = \bigcup_{(a,b) \in R} \{a, b\}$ is the set of elements referred to by relation $X \subseteq A \times B$.

single edge. S is a canonical *SESE of G* if it does not partially overlap with any other *SESE* of G, i.e., given any other *SESE* S' of G, they are nested ($S \subseteq S'$ or $S' \subseteq S$) or they are disjoint ($S \cap S' = \emptyset$). By definition, the source of a WF-net is an entry to every fragment it belongs to and the sink of the net is an exit from every fragment it belongs to.

The decomposition based on canonical SESEs is a well studied problem in the literature, and can be computed in linear time. In [17], the authors proposed the algorithm for constructing the *Refined Process Structure Tree (RPST)*, i.e., an hierarchical structure containing all the canonical SESEs of a model. In [3], the computation of the RPST is considerably simplified and generalized by introducing a pre-processing step that reduces the implementation effort considerably.

Definition 8 (RPST-based Decomposition [3]). *Let G be the workflow graph of the WF-net WN.[3] The* Refined Process Structured Tree (RPST) *of G is the tree composed by the set of all its canonical SESEs, such that, the parent of a canonical SESE S is the smallest canonical SESE that contains S. The root of the tree is the entire graph, and the leaves are the trivial SESEs. The set of all the nodes of the tree is denoted as $\mathbb{S}$.*

Figure 1c shows the RPST for the given example. In the remainder of the paper, we will refer to canonical SESEs resulting from the RPST decomposition simply as SESEs. Also note that the SESEs are defined as a set of edges (i.e., S) over the workflow graph (not as subgraphs, i.e., G_S). However, for simplicity and when the context is clear, we will use the term SESE to refer also to the subgraph of the workflow graph or Petri net induced by those edges ($PN_S = (P \cap \Pi(S), T \cap \Pi(S), A \cap S)$). For example, the SESE S_4 of Fig. 1b containing the edges b, d, f and h, refers also to the Petri net composed by the transitions t_1, t_2 and t_4, the places p_2 and p_4, and the arcs between them in the WF-net of Fig. 1a.

3 Partitioning Conformance Diagnosis

In this section, we propose a divide-and-conquer approach for conformance checking, preserving the SESE decomposition's underlying semantics. Moreover, we show that a trace is fitting the overall model if and only if it is fitting the individual fragments. The proposed approach is based on selecting a set of RPST nodes that *partition* the set of arcs of the process model. The maximum size of the components to be analyzed can be limited in order to deal with computation time restrictions or to control the complexity of individual components. Formally:

Definition 9 (k-partitioning over a SESE decomposition). *Given the SESE decomposition $\mathbb{S}$ of a WF-net WN, we define $\mathbb{P} = \{S_1, \ldots, S_n\} \subseteq \mathbb{S}$:*

---
[3] Although the approach presented in this paper can be generalized to graphs with several sources and sinks, for the sake of clarity in this paper we restrict to the case with only one source and only one sink [3].

Algorithm 1. k-partitioning algorithm

procedure k-PART(RPST,k)
   $V = \{root(RPST)\}$
   $\mathbb{P} = \emptyset$
   while $V \neq \emptyset$ **do**
      $v \leftarrow pop(V)$
      if $|v.arcs()| \leq k$ **then** $\mathbb{P} = \mathbb{P} \cup \{v\}$
      else $V = V \cup \{children(v)\}$

a partitioning of SESEs such that each arc in WN is contained in exactly one S_i. A k-partitioning of $\mathbb{S}$ is a set of SESEs $\mathbb{P} = \{S_1, \ldots, S_n\} \subseteq \mathbb{S}$ where each S_i contains at most k arcs.

Proposition 1 (k-**partitioning existence**). *Given a SESE decomposition* $\mathbb{S}$ *over the WF-net* $WN = (P, T, A, i, o)$, *and given any* k *such that* $1 \leq k \leq |A|$, *there always exists a* k-*partitioning of* $\mathbb{S}$.

Proof. By definition, any edge is a SESE (and they appear as leaves of the RPST). Therefore, a trivial partitioning with all parts being trivial SESEs is always possible. □

Algorithm 1 shows how to compute a k-partitioning. The algorithm has linear complexity (with respect to the size of the RPST) and termination is guaranteed by the fact that fragments size is reduced with every iteration.

Given a partitioning, we use it to decompose conformance checking. Remember that SESEs only interface the rest of the net through the single entry and single exit nodes, which may be shared by different SESEs. The rest of nodes of a SESE (i.e., the interior nodes) have no connection with other SESEs. For the boundary nodes, we distinguish two cases: *transition bounded* and *place bounded*.

As proven in [15], transition bounded net fragments can be checked in isolation. For a partitioning into SESEs where all entry and single nodes are transitions the following holds: a trace perfectly fitting the whole WF-net will also fit all individual SESEs (projected trace on corresponding transitions) and vice versa. For example, consider the WF-net in Fig. 2a, and the partitioning shown in Fig. 2b. The existence of d in both S_1 and S_2 ensures that both subnets move synchronously when replaying a trace. For instance, trace *abcddefg* (non-fitting in the original net due the double d) is fitting on S_2 (on S_2, the preset of d is empty), but not in S_1. On the other hand, trace *abcefg* (also non-fitting in the original net) is fitting in neither S_1 nor S_2.

However, the case of *place bounded* SESEs (i.e., entry and/or exit nodes correspond to places) is completely different. Places, unlike transitions, have no reflection in the log, and therefore, cannot be used to synchronize the individual SESEs during replay. Consider, for example, the net in Fig. 3a, and the partitioning shown in Fig. 3b. There is a strong dependency between the execution of S_1 and the initial marking considered for S_2. For example, consider a marking of one token on p and the trace *abcdef*. Such trace fits the original model, but it

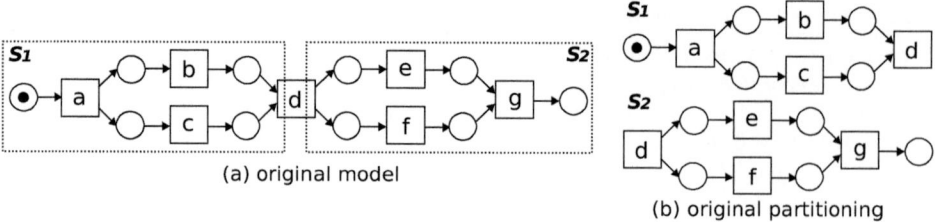

(a) original model

(b) original partitioning

Fig. 2. Example of partitioning with transition boundary

does not fit S_2 (i.e., it requires two tokens on p). On the other hand, considering an initial marking of S_2 with two tokens on p, the trace $abdecf$ fits S_1 and S_2 but does not fit the original net.

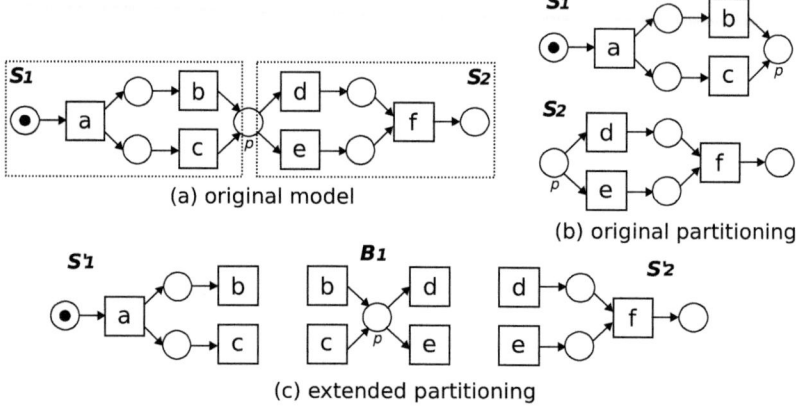

Fig. 3. Example of partitioning with place boundary

Thus, in case of place-boundaries, we extend the isolated fitness calculation by considering a new element that we call *bridge*. A bridge simply contains the pre and post sets of the boundary place. Bridges replicate the behavior on the boundary places thus synchronizing all components connected to such place. For example, given the place boundary of Fig. 3a, besides the two SESE components S'_1 and S'_2, a third component B_1 is constructed explicitly, containing the place p, its preset, and its postset (cf. Fig. 3c). Although bridges do not satisfy the SESE definition, their structure is very specific (i.e., nets with only one place). Given that the bridge makes the synchronization explicit on the boundary place, SESEs having this boundary place no longer need it, and therefore, it is removed from all the SESEs (cf. S'_1 and S'_2 on Fig. 3c). Note that the modified SESEs do not longer satisfy the SESE definition, but have a set of input and output transitions. Remarkably, the removal of boundary places in the original SESEs and the introduction of bridges ensures transition bounded fragments, and therefore, the results of [15] can be applied directly. We now formally define the so-called extended partitioning:

Definition 10 (Extended partitioning over a SESE decomposition). *Let $\mathbb{P} = \{S_1, \ldots S_n\}$ be a partitioning of the WF-net $WN = (P, T, A, i, o)$. Let $I_\mathbb{P} = \{i_1, \ldots, i_n\}$ and $O_\mathbb{P} = \{o_1, \ldots, o_n\}$ be the set of all entry and exit nodes of the SESEs in $\mathbb{P}$. $B = \{p_1, \ldots, p_k\} = ((I_\mathbb{P} \cup O_\mathbb{P}) \cap P) \setminus \{i, o\} = (I_\mathbb{P} \cap O_\mathbb{P}) \cap P$ is the set of boundary places, i.e., entry and exit nodes of the SESEs that are places but not the source or sink place of the WF-net WN. The extended partitioning $\mathbb{P}' = \{S'_1, \ldots S'_n, B_1 \ldots B_k\}$ of $\mathbb{P}$ is constructed as follows:*

- *For all $1 \leq i \leq n$: $S'_i = \{(x, y) \in S_i \mid \{x, y\} \cap B = \emptyset\}$ (boundary places are removed from the SESEs).*
- *For $1 \leq j \leq k$: $B_j = \{(x, y) \in A \mid p_j \in \{x, y\}\}$ (bridges are added).*

Note that, a bridge may not satisfy the *k-size* property. However, its size is limited because it contains a single place. Lemma 1 shows that, given any extended partitioning, fitness is preserved among its components, i.e., a trace fits the whole WF-net if and only if it fits all the parts of the extended partitioning.

Lemma 1 (Decomposed Fitness Checking). *Let L be a log and $SN = (WN, m_i, m_o)$ be a system net where $WN = (P, T, A, i, o)$ is a WF-net. Let $\mathbb{P}'$ be any extended partitioning over WN. A trace $\sigma \in L$ fits SN (i.e., $(WN, [m_i])[\sigma\rangle(WN, [m_o]))$ if and only if it fits all the parts, i.e., for all $S \in \mathbb{P}'$, $PN_S = (P_S, T_S, A_S) = (P \cap \Pi(S), T \cap \Pi(S), A \cap S)$: $(PN_S, [m_{i\downarrow P_S}])[\sigma_{\downarrow T_S}\rangle(PN_S, [m_{o\downarrow P_S}]))$.*[4]

Proof. Special case of the more general Theorem 2 in [15]. If the overall trace σ fits SN, then each of the projected traces $\sigma_{\downarrow T_x}$ fits the corresponding SESE. If this is not the case, then at least there exist one projected trace $\sigma_{\downarrow T_x}$ that does not fit. If the projected traces $\sigma_{\downarrow T_x}$ fit the corresponding SESEs, then these traces can be stitched back into a trace σ that fits SN.

Although the use of a partitioning makes it possible to decompose a complex problem as conformance checking into smaller subproblems, there are applications (e.g., process diagnosis) where a more fined-grained analysis is required. In other words, we need to be able to navigate zooming in and out of the model, to get a better understanding (see Chapter 13 in [1]). With this idea in mind, the theory proposed on this section can be combined with the properties of the RPST to obtain a hierarchy of fitness results based on SESEs. Therefore, given an RPST, an extension based on bridges is performed over each level of the tree, and the fitness is checked for the complete level. Unlike other techniques (like in [4]), this analysis guarantees the fitness for the complete level. Note that, the RPST contains the whole net as its root. Therefore, in those cases where the complete system cannot be checked due its complexity, this is also not possible with this technique. However, a greedy procedure can be developed, that starts processing the higher levels of the RPST hierarchy (root is at level 0), and goes up until it reaches a level non-computable due to complexity or time reasons. Algorithm 2 describes the resulting conformance checking technique.

---
[4] $\sigma_{\downarrow T}$ is the projection of sequence σ onto transitions T and $m_{\downarrow P}$ is the projection of marking m onto the multiset of places P.

Algorithm 2. Extended RPST Conformance algorithm

procedure CONFEXTRPST(RPST,log)
  $level \leftarrow heigth(RPST)$
  while $level \geq 0$ **and** $level$ computable **do**
    $\{S_1 \ldots S_n\} \leftarrow$ Find partitioning containing the SESEs in $level$ of the RPST
    $\{S'_1 \ldots S'_n, B_1 \ldots B_k\} \leftarrow$ Extend partitioning $\{S_1 \ldots S_n\}$ with bridges
    check fitness for the pairs $(S'_1, log_{\downarrow T_1}), \ldots, (B_k, log_{\downarrow T_k})$
    $level \leftarrow level - 1$

4 Topological Graph of a Partitioning

In this section we present the *topological graph* of a partitioning, and some techniques that can use it to improve the diagnosis. Given an extended partitioning, the topological graph is the directed graph that represents the connections via boundary nodes between the parts. Formally:

Definition 11 (Topological Graph of a Partitioning). *Let* $\mathbb{P} = \{S_1, \ldots S_n\}$ *be a partitioning of the WF-net* $WN = (P, T, A, i, o)$, *with boundary places* $\{p_1, \ldots, p_k\}$. *Given an extended partitioning* $\mathbb{P}' = \{S'_1, \ldots S'_n, B_1, \ldots B_k\}$ *(cf. Def. 10), we define its topological graph* $\mathbb{T} = (\mathbb{P}', C)$ *as the graph whose vertexes are the parts of* $\mathbb{P}'$, *and the set of edges is* $C = \{(S'_i, S'_j) | 1 \leq i, j \leq n \land (y, x) \in S_i \land (x, z) \in S_j\} \cup \{(S'_i, B_j) | 1 \leq i \leq n \land 1 \leq j \leq k \land (y, p_j) \in S_i\} \cup \{(B_j, S'_i) | 1 \leq i \leq n \land 1 \leq j \leq k \land (p_j, y) \in S_i\}$.

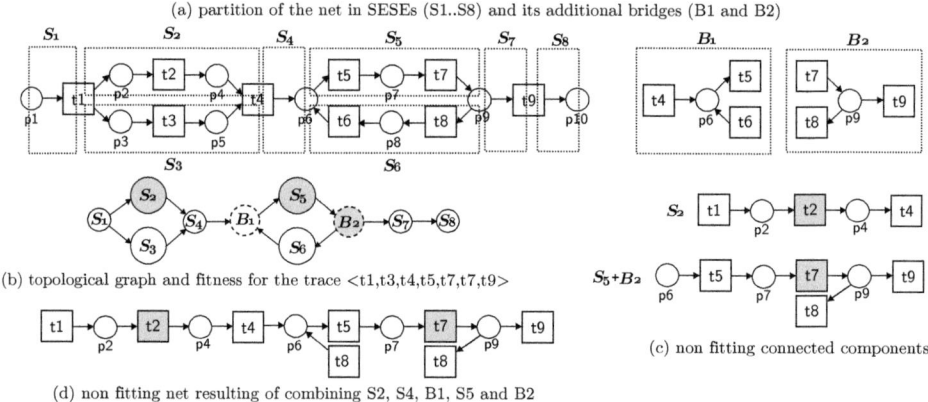

Fig. 4. Example of partitioning, topological graph, and its corresponding non-fitting connected components, and non-fitting net

Note that the topological graph has as vertexes the transition-bordered parts of the extended partitioning, but some arcs of this graph (those regarding connection to bridges) are defined over the parts of the original partitioning $\mathbb{P}$, since in the extended partitioning boundary places have been removed. One of the functions of the topological graph is to aid in the visualization of the extended partitioning resulting from applying the techniques developed in Sec. 3. For example, let us consider an extended partitioning that arises from a 4-partitioning of the WF-net in Fig. 4a (a slight modification of the model in Fig. 1). The resulting extended partitioning is composed by the SESEs $S'_1 \ldots S'_8$ and the two bridges B_1 and B_2 corresponding with the two boundary places p_6 and p_9. The corresponding topological graph is shown in Fig. 4b. Besides simply showing the connections through boundary nodes, the topological graph can be enhanced with other information. For instance, in this example, bridges are represented with dotted borders, while SESEs with solid borders. Moreover, the size of the nodes in the graph is directly related with the size of the corresponding parts, i.e., larger parts will have more importance in the representation and will appear larger than smaller parts. Finally, the graph can be enhanced with the conformance analysis results. In this example we have considered the fitness dimension of the model with respect to the log composed by only one trace $t_1 t_3 t_4 t_5 t_7 t_7 t_7$. Considering this trace, three parts contain fitness anomalies (filled in gray): in S'_2, t_4 is fired without firing t_2; in S'_5, t_7 is executed twice, but this requires the firing of t_5 also twice; finally, in the bridge B_2, t_7 is fired twice, but t_9 only once, leaving a token remaining in p_9.

Although the topological graph is an important aid for the process diagnosis by itself, it can also guide subsequent analysis. In the remainder of this section we present and motivate some ideas.

The topological graph extended with conformance information can be used to *identify maximal process fragments with fitness problems*. This allows us to focus on the problematic parts of a model, discarding those parts of the model perfectly fitting. Algorithm 3 describes a procedure that is based on detecting connected components on the graph induced by the non-fitting vertexes. First, the topological graph is filtered, leaving only non-fitting vertexes, and the edges connecting them. Then, for each set of weakly connected components (i.e., connected vertexes without considering the direction of the edges), we project the elements of the original net they refer to. Note that this algorithm prioritizes the connectivity among vertexes resulting in weakly connected components. However, alternative versions of the algorithm yielding strongly connected components are possible. For instance, given the example of Fig. 4b, two connected components are found as shown in Fig. 4c: S_2 and $S_5 + B_2$.

The topological graph extended with conformance information can also be used to create one complete subnet that includes all non-fitting parts of the extended partitioning. We use a heuristic based on the greedy expansion of the largest non-fitting connected component (based on Algorithm 3), to get connected with the second largest component, until all the non-fitting behavior is connected, trying to include as few fitting nodes as possible. A schema of the procedure is shown in Algorithm 4. Given the example of Fig. 4b, the net resulting (shown in Fig. 4d) contains the elements of S_2, S_4, B_1, S_5 and B_2. In Sec. 6 we provide experimental results on large models for the two techniques proposed in this section.

Algorithm 3. Non-Fitting Weakly Connected Components Algorithm

    function NFWCC($\mathbb{T}$,V)   ▷ Let V be the non-fitting vertexes
         $C_c = \emptyset$
         remove from $\mathbb{T}$ all arcs $c = \{x,y\}$ such that $x, y \notin V$ ▷ Graph induced by V
         remove from $\mathbb{T}$ all vertexes $z \notin V$
         while $\mathbb{T}$ has vertexes **do**   ▷ Find Weakly Connected Components
             $v_1 \leftarrow$ select random vertex on $\mathbb{T}$
             $\{v_1, \ldots v_n\} \leftarrow$ get vertexes weakly connected with v_1 using Depth-first search
             remove $\{v_1, \ldots v_n\}$ from $\mathbb{T}$
             $C_c = C_c \cup \{(\bigcup_1^n places(v_i), \bigcup_1^n trans(v_i), \bigcup_1^n arcs(v_i))\}$
         return C_c

Algorithm 4. Non-Fitting Subnet Algorithm

    function NFN($\mathbb{T}$,V)   ▷ Let V be the non-fitting vertexes
         while graph G induced by V on $\mathbb{T}$ is not connected **do**
             $c_1 \leftarrow$ get the largest connected component of G
             $c_2 \leftarrow$ get the second largest connected component of G
             $\{v_1 \ldots v_n\} \leftarrow$ shortest_path_vertexes($\mathbb{T}, c_1, c_2$)
             $V = V \cup \{v_1 \ldots v_n\}$.
         return Petri net induced by V

5 RPST Simplifications

Although the decomposition of a model based on SESEs and their RPST is intuitive and fine-grained, it remains different from the conceptual decomposition typically on the mind of the process analysts. In [4], the results of an experiment performed over 7 subjects identify three main differences between their manual decomposition and the one provided by the RPST: 1) predisposition of the analysts to *discard small components*, 2) to *not consider twice similar components*, and 3) to *not make grow the depth of the hierarchy unnecessarily*. In this section we formalize the two last items into a similarity metric between parent-child SESEs, enabling discarding child components when the similarity with the parent is above some threshold. Also we tackle 1) by defining a threshold on the minimal size of a SESE to consider. Note that in the case of 1), Lemma 1 may not be applicable (since a partitioning of the net may not be possible) and therefore these RPST simplifications can only be applied without any guarantee.

    In particular we present a metric (cf. Def.12) for estimating the *similarity* between a node S and its single child S' based on two factors: *size* and *simplicity*. The size factor is straightforwardly related with the number of arcs of S not included on S'. The more arcs shared by both components, the more similar they are. For instance, considering the component S_1 of Fig. 5a, all its arcs are included in S_2 except two, i.e., S_2 is in essence S_1. Therefore, a detailed conformance diagnosis over S_1 may be sufficient for understanding both subprocesses. The *simplicity* factor refers to the simplicity of part of the parent S not included on the child S'. When such part defines a simple behavior (e.g., the strictly sequential behavior of S_3 not included in S_4, in Fig. 5b), the analysis and understanding of the parent may again be enough. On the other hand, when the behavior not included in S' contains complex constructions (e.g., mixtures of concurrency and choice) it may be more advisable to analyze both subprocesses.

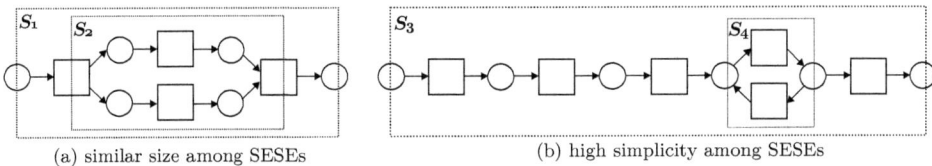

(a) similar size among SESEs (b) high simplicity among SESEs

Fig. 5. Example of cases with high similarity between nested SESEs

Definition 12 (Similarity Metric). *Let $S_P = (V_P, F_P)$ be an RPST node, and let $S_C = (V_C, F_C)$ be its only child. Let size define the difference on size between them, i.e., $size = |F_C|/|F_P|$. Let $F_O = F_P \setminus F_C$ be the set of non-intersecting arcs. Let F_O^* be the arcs in F_O that have a source vertex with only one outgoing edge, and a target vertex with only one incoming edge, i.e., $F_O^* = \{(x, y) \in F_O : |(x, v) \in F_O| = 1 \land |(w, y) \in F_O| = 1\}$. Let simplicity define the simplicity of the non-intersecting arcs, i.e., $simplicity = |F_O^*|/|F_O|$. The similarity between S_P and S_C is the harmonic mean between size and simplicity:*

$$similarity = 2 \cdot \frac{size \cdot simplicity}{size + simplicity}$$

Although the similarity merging is restricted to single-child nodes, our experimental results show that the reduction achieved on the tree may be considerable. Both simplification techniques (small components and similarity merging) have been implemented and tested. The next section shows the effects of their application on large models.

6 Experimental Results

All techniques presented in this paper have been implemented within ProM framework and are accessible through the *JorgeMunozGama* package.[5] To test performance we created various benchmarks generated by PLG tool [18][6] In this section we first highlight the empirical differences with related conformance checking approaches described in the literature and the partitioning-based proposed in this paper. Second, we provide some results on the application of the topological graph algorithms. Finally, we illustrate the effects of the simplification methods proposed on large models.

Table 1 shows the ability to handle conformance problems of industrial size using our approach. The experiment is composed of several large models (having

---

[5] Download from http://www.promtools.org/prom6/nightly/.
[6] http://dx.doi.org/10.4121/uuid:44c32783-15d0-4dbd-af8a-78b97be3de49

P places and T transitions), and their corresponding logs. For each benchmark, the table contains the fitness value (f) and the time required for analyzing their conformance using the approach proposed in [9,11] (t). Dashes denote the lack of results after 10 hours of computation. The rest of the table contains the results of applying the same conformance technique over a 50, 100 or 200 SESE-based extended partitioning, respectively. For each k-partitioning the table provides the number of parts (S SESEs and B bridges), the number of non-trivial small parts (> 5) containing more than 5 arcs (threshold extracted from the study in [4]), and the total time required for the fitness analysis (t). In addition, the table shows the number of parts with a fitness value lower than one (i.e., non-fitting nf) and the percentage of arcs they represent within the whole model. Remarkably, the time required to compute the RPST and the k-partitioning is negligible (i.e., never more than few seconds).

Table 1. Comparison between k-partitioning and [9,11]

	P	T	[9,11] f	t	S/B k=50	>5	nf	t	S/B k=100	>5	nf	t	S/B k=200	>5	nf	t
prAm6	347	363	0.92	75	129/57	29	7(3%)	423	62/27	14	1(9%)	323	27/12	7	1(10%)	180
prBm6	317	317	1	88	93/38	22	0(0%)	608	66/29	14	0(0%)	318	36/16	8	0(0%)	114
prCm6	317	317	0.57	2743	93/38	22	58(92%)	189	66/29	14	41(94%)	185	36/16	8	22(96%)	502
prDm6	529	429	-	-	105/34	33	5(8%)	1386	60/23	18	4(14%)	986	33/15	9	4(23%)	1284
prEm6	277	275	0.97	3566	82/35	20	2(5%)	529	35/13	11	2(5%)	343	15/7	5	2(6%)	211
prFm6	362	299	-	-	108/43	28	2(6%)	1667	57/23	15	2(21%)	863	21/9	5	1(23%)	562
prGm6	357	335	-	-	94/37	25	2(8%)	867	67/31	15	2(8%)	850	51/25	11	2(8%)	474

Table 1 shows that partitioning yields significant speedups in case event logs are not perfectly fitting the model [9,11]. In cases with a perfect fitting (e.g., prBm6) the time required for the proposed approach is higher, due the overhead caused by creating and storing in memory the generated parts. However, in real cases where the log is poorly fitting the model, the time needed for conformance checking is reduced in one order of magnitude using k-partitioning. More important, the proposed approach is able to tackle and provide conformance information for those cases where [9,11] is not able to provide a result (e.g., prDm6, prFm6 and prGm6).

Table 1 also shows the capability of the proposed approach to detect and isolate the subprocesses causing the fitness problems. In particular, the approach is able to identify those cases were all the fitness problems are located in only a few parts of the process, e.g., in prEm6, all the fitness problems of a net with 277 transitions can be restricted to 2 subprocesses that represent only the 5% of the model. Note that, although the number of parts generated by the approach can be considered high, most of them are trivial parts with less than 5 arcs. Importantly, the number of large parts remains low, and its maximum size can be controlled by the parameter k of Algorithm 1.

The second experiment aims at illustrating the role of the topological graph. Figure 6 shows a graphical example on how the techniques of Sec. 4 can be used for diagnosis: given a large model having conformance problems (denoted in red), Algorithms NFWCC and NFN can be used to identify one subprocess with conformance problems or a connected subnet including all the subprocesses with

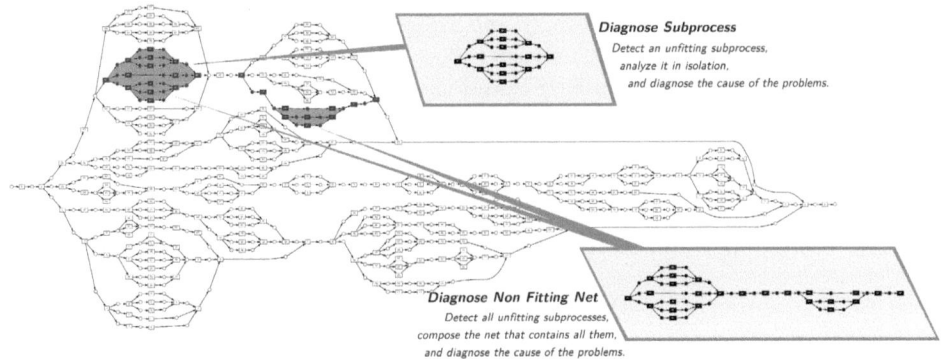

Fig. 6. The 50-partition as a diagnosis tool for the *prFm6* benchmark

Table 2. Results of NFWCC and NFN algorithms

	P	T	$|C_C|$	$|\bar{V}|$	$|\bar{P}|$	$|\bar{T}|$	$|V|$	$|P|$	$|T|$
			NFWCC				NFN		
prAm6	317	317	7	1	2.1	3	14	15	14
prCm6	317	317	38	1.5	8.2	9.5	113	315	317
prDm6	529	429	5	1	9.4	9.4	31	55	52
prEm6	277	275	2	1	1	2	31	29	40
prFm6	362	299	2	1	13	11	7	27	25
prGm6	357	335	2	1	16.5	14.5	5	34	29

conformance problems, respectively. Table 2 reports on the performance of these two algorithms using the examples of the previous experiment.[7] For the experiments, we have considered the topological graph resulting from the 50-partitioning for the different log-model combinations. For the NFWCC algorithm, the table contains the number of non-fitting weakly connected components ($|C_C|$), the average size (places $|\bar{P}|$ and transitions $|\bar{T}|$) and average number of vertexes ($|\bar{V}|$) whose connected components are composed of. For the NFN algorithm, the table provides the size of the derived non-fitting net ($|P|$ and $|T|$), and the number of topology vertexes it includes. The table illustrates the benefits of the proposed algorithms to detect and isolate the fitness mismatches. In case the fitness problems are spread all over the whole model, the resulting net is almost the original net (e.g., prCm6). However, when the fitness problems are local, the net that encloses all problem spots may be orders of magnitude smaller than the original net, thus easing the diagnosis.

The final experiment illustrates the effects of the simplification over the RPST decomposition on the number of components and hierarchy levels. Figure 7 shows the simplification of two models used in the previous experiments of this section. For each model, the figure provides the number of components (Y-axis) at each level of the RPST tree (being 1 the root of the RPST, and 14 the deepest level). The figure contains the number components for the original RPST, after removing the

---

[7] Only non-fitting models of Table 1 are considered in Table 2.

small components (less than 10 arcs), and after merging *similar* nested nodes (i.e., similarity degree over 0.8). Both charts reflect the difference between the number of components on the original RPST and the one after removing the small components, i.e., most of the RPST nodes are small. After removing small nodes the depth of the RPST only decreases two levels (from 14 to 13). On the other hand, the effect on the depth after merging similar nodes is high. In both cases, the number of levels of the tree is reduced significantly (from 12 to 6), providing a decomposition with less redundancy and more aligned with human perception [4].

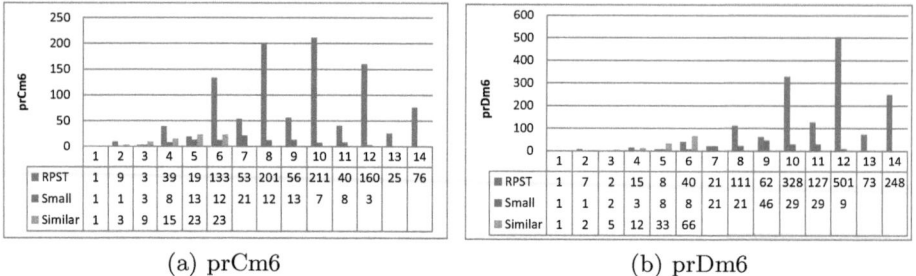

Fig. 7. Effect of the simplification techniques

7 Conclusions and Future Work

The practical relevance of process mining increases as more event data becomes available. More and more events are being recorded and already today's event logs provide massive amounts of process related data. However, as event logs and processes become larger, many computational challenges emerge.

In this paper, we presented an approach that makes use of the well-known SESE and RPST analysis to decompose the problem of conformance checking and process diagnosis. The approach makes it possible to discover conformance problems more efficiently both in terms of computation and diagnostics. Although our experimental results support these claims, more real-life case studies need to be conducted. For example, we would like to empirically show that the diagnostics based on the topological graph are indeed more insightful because the analyst can focus on the problem spots. Moreover, the inclusion of other conformance dimensions into the approach, together with the possibility of tackling invisible and duplicate transitions, is another direction for future work.

Acknowledgments. The authors would like to thank Dr. Artem Polyvyanyy for his comments and help. This work has been partially supported by the Ministerio de Educación (AP2009-4959) and by the projects TIN-2011-22484 and TIN-2007-66523.

References

1. van der Aalst, W.M.P.: Process Mining: Discovery, Conformance and Enhancement of Business Processes. Springer (2011)

2. IEEE Task Force on Process Mining: Process Mining Manifesto. In: Daniel, F., Barkaoui, K., Dustdar, S. (eds.) Business Process Management Workshops. LNBIP, vol. 99, pp. 169–194. Springer (2012)
3. Polyvyanyy, A., Vanhatalo, J., Völzer, H.: Simplified computation and generalization of the refined process structure tree. In: Bravetti, M. (ed.) WS-FM 2010. LNCS, vol. 6551, pp. 25–41. Springer, Heidelberg (2011)
4. Munoz-Gama, J., Carmona, J., van der Aalst, W.M.P.: Hierarchical Conformance Checking of Process Models Based on Event Logs. In: Applications and Theory of Petri Nets (2013), TR: http://www.lsi.upc.edu/~techreps/files/R13-5.zip
5. Cook, J., Wolf, A.: Software Process Validation: Quantitatively Measuring the Correspondence of a Process to a Model. ACM Transactions on Software Engineering and Methodology 8(2), 147–176 (1999)
6. de Medeiros, A.K.A., Weijters, A.J.M.M., van der Aalst, W.M.P.: Genetic Process Mining: An Experimental Evaluation. Data Mining and Knowledge Discovery 14(2), 245–304 (2007)
7. Rozinat, A., van der Aalst, W.M.P.: Conformance checking of processes based on monitoring real behavior. Inf. Syst. 33(1), 64–95 (2008)
8. van der Aalst, W.M.P., Adriansyah, A., van Dongen, B.: Replaying History on Process Models for Conformance Checking and Performance Analysis. WIREs Data Mining and Knowledge Discovery 2(2), 182–192 (2012)
9. Adriansyah, A., van Dongen, B.F., van der Aalst, W.M.P.: Conformance checking using cost-based fitness analysis. In: EDOC, pp. 55–64. IEEE Computer Society (2011)
10. Weerdt, J.D., Backer, M.D., Vanthienen, J., Baesens, B.: A Multi-Dimensional Quality Assessment of State-of-the-Art Process Discovery Algorithms Using Real-Life Event Logs. Information Systems 37(7), 654–676 (2012)
11. Adriansyah, A., Munoz-Gama, J., Carmona, J., van Dongen, B.F., van der Aalst, W.M.P.: Alignment Based Precision Checking. In: La Rosa, M., Soffer, P. (eds.) BPM Workshops 2012. LNBIP, vol. 132, pp. 137–149. Springer, Heidelberg (2013)
12. Munoz-Gama, J., Carmona, J.: Enhancing Precision in Process Conformance: Stability, Confidence and Severity. In: Chawla, N., King, I., Sperduti, A. (eds.) IEEE Symposium on Computational Intelligence and Data Mining (CIDM 2011), Paris, France, pp. 184–191. IEEE (April 2011)
13. van der Aalst, W.M.P.: Distributed Process Discovery and Conformance Checking. In: de Lara, J., Zisman, A. (eds.) FASE 2012. LNCS, vol. 7212, pp. 1–25. Springer, Heidelberg (2012)
14. van der Aalst, W.M.P.: Decomposing Process Mining Problems Using Passages. In: Haddad, S., Pomello, L. (eds.) PETRI NETS 2012. LNCS, vol. 7347, pp. 72–91. Springer, Heidelberg (2012)
15. van der Aalst, W.M.P.: Decomposing Petri Nets for Process Mining: A Generic Approach. BPMCenter.org BPM-12-20 (accepted for Distributed and Parallel Databases) (2012)
16. Murata, T.: Petri nets: Properties, analysis and applications. Proceedings of the IEEE **77**(4) () 77(4), 541–580 (1989)
17. Vanhatalo, J., Völzer, H., Koehler, J.: The refined process structure tree. Data Knowl. Eng. 68(9), 793–818 (2009)
18. Burattin, A., Sperduti, A.: Plg: A framework for the generation of business process models and their execution logs. In: Muehlen, M.z., Su, J. (eds.) BPM 2010 Workshops. LNBIP, vol. 66, pp. 214–219. Springer, Heidelberg (2011)

On Enabling Compliance of Cross-Organizational Business Processes[*]

David Knuplesch[1], Manfred Reichert[1], Walid Fdhila[2],
and Stefanie Rinderle-Ma[2]

[1] Institute of Databases and Information Systems, Ulm University, Germany
[2] Faculty of Computer Science, University of Vienna, Austria
{david.knuplesch,manfred.reichert}@uni-ulm.de,
{walid.fdhila,stefanie.rinderle-ma}@univie.ac.at

Abstract. Process compliance deals with the ability of a company to ensure that its business processes comply with domain-specific regulations and rules. So far, compliance issues have been mainly addressed for intra-organizational business processes, whereas there exists only little work dealing with compliance in the context of cross-organizational processes that involve multiple business partners. As opposed to intra-organizational processes, for a cross-organizational process, compliance must be addressed at different modeling levels, ranging from interaction models to public process models to private processes of the partners. Accordingly, there exist different levels for modeling compliance rules. In particular, we distinguish between local compliance rules of a particular partner and global compliance rules to be obeyed by all partners involved in the cross-organizational process. This paper focuses on checking the compliance of interaction models. For this purpose, we introduce the notion of *compliability*, which shall guarantee that an interaction model is not conflicting with a set of imposed global compliance rules.

1 Introduction

Business process compliance has been identified as one of the core challenges for process-aware information systems [1]. So far, the focus has been on intra-organizational business processes, and a variety of proposals for checking the compliance of a business process with domain-specific regulations and rules in different phases of the process life cycle have been made [2,3,4,5,6]. Besides few approaches (e.g., business contracts [7,8]), compliance checking for cross-organizational processes has been neglected so far, even though being crucial in collaborative settings [9,10]. Therefore, the consideration of compliance rules in the context of cross-organizational processes and the provision of techniques for checking them are indispensable. Compared to approaches checking the compliance of intra-organizational business processes, however, additional challenges

---

[*] This work was done within the research project C^3Pro funded by the German Research Foundation (DFG) under project number RE 1402/2-1, and the Austrian Science Fund (FWF) under project number I743.

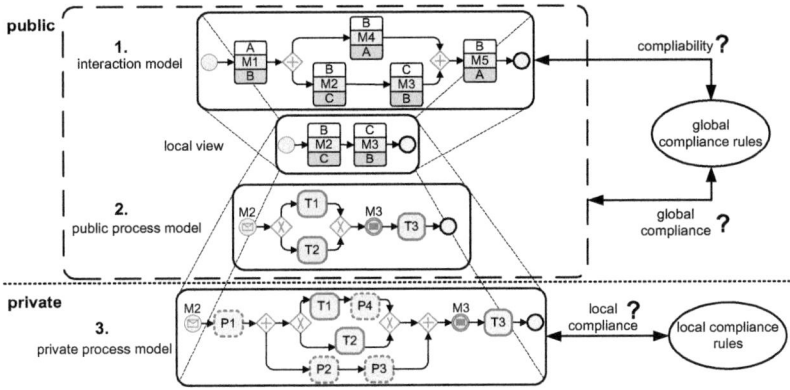

Fig. 1. Different levels of compliance rules in a cross-organizational setting

emerge [9]. In particular, process compliance must be ensured at different levels. Furthermore, compliance checking must cope with the fact that parts of cross-organizational processes are not known by all partners, e.g. due to privacy reasons.

Consider Fig. 1: Compliance rules relevant for setting up and running cross-organizational processes refer to different levels as known from interaction modeling [11]. First, the global view of the interactions (i.e. messages exchanged) between the partners of a cross-organizational process (i.e., the *interaction model*) provides the top level. Second, each partner defines a public model of its process taking its *local view* on the interaction model into account. Accordingly, a local view refers to the behavior of the interaction model from the viewpoint of a particular partner. Note that public models must *conform* with the behavior of the respective local view. Finally, each partner maintains its own *private process model*, which not only comprises activities for exchanging messages with the other partners, but also private activities not relevant for the interactions with the partners; i.e., due to privacy, a partner usually does not reveal all details about its private processes to the other partners. However, the *private processes* must *conform* with the public process model. Semantic constraints in respect to such private processes are denoted as *local compliance rules*. In turn, *global compliance rules* are imposed on interaction models and public process models. Altogether, the *public parts* of a cross-organizational process include the interaction model, public process models, and global compliance rules. In turn, private process models and local compliance rules constitute *private parts*.

As opposed to intra-organizational processes, in the context of cross-organizational processes we must consider three levels of compliance. First, we must deal with local compliance rules that constrain private partner processes. Second, we must support global compliance rules that constrain the public parts of a cross-organizational process scenario. Third, interaction models must enable the partners to model both public and private processes meeting the global compliance rules. This requires interaction models being not in conflict with the set of global compliance rules.

This paper focuses on the latter level of compliance and provides a novel correctness criterion, which we denote as *compliability* in the following. Compliability refers to the ability of an interaction model to comply with a given set of global compliance rules without knowing all details of the private and public process models of the partners. We denote an interaction model as *not compliabile*, if it conflicts with the given set of global compliance rules. In particular, we present an approach enabling automated compliability checking of interaction models against a given set of imposed global compliance rules. Note that compliability must be ensured before the partners specify their public and private process models. Therefore, our approach extends interaction models with additional control flow structures and activities to approximate the not yet specified behavior of partners. Furthermore, it merges and adapts the global compliance rules, before checking compliability through the application of model checking techniques.

Note that this paper focuses on compliability checking of interaction models at build time, but does not consider any other phase of the process life cycle (e.g., execution and change time). Furthermore, we focus on compliance rules related to control-flow and do not explicitly address data, resources, or time. Finally, our approach requires from the partners to publish the set of activities they use for specifying their public and private processes.

The remainder of this paper is structured as follows: Sect. 2 illustrates an example from the healthcare domain. Sect. 3 provides algorithms for compliability checking as the main contribution of this paper. Sect. 4 discusses related work and Sect. 5 closes with a discussion and outlook.

2 Example

Figs. 2 and 3 depict an example of a cross-organizational process from the healthcare domain using the BPMN 2.0 standard. This process involves three *partners*: gynecologist, laboratory, and hospital. In particular, Fig. 2 depicts the interactions (i.e., messages exchanged) between these partners. In turn, Fig. 3 shows their public process models. Note that the public process model of the hospital is simplified due to space limitations. Tab. 1 shows and classifies examples of compliance rules imposed on the cross-organizational process from Figs. 2 and 3.

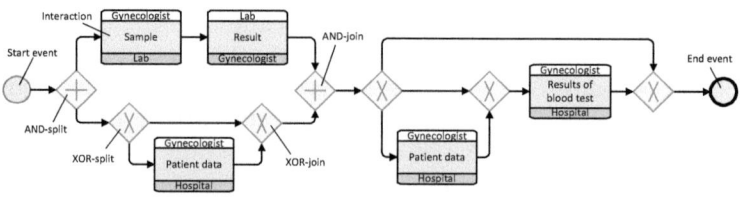

Fig. 2. Interaction model of a healthcare scenario [9]

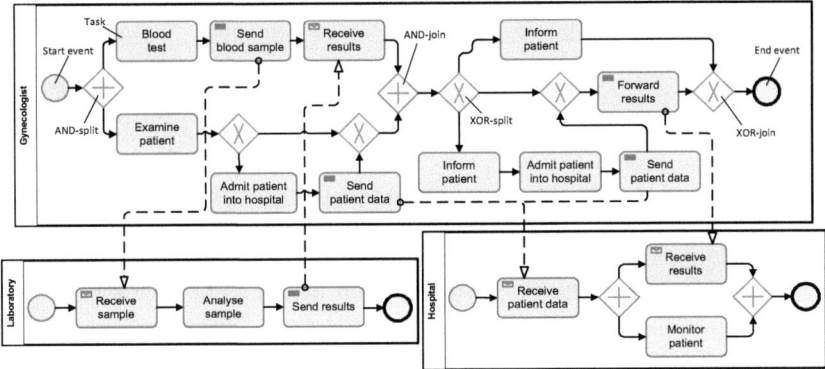

Fig. 3. Public models of a healthcare scenario [9]

Table 1. Examples of compliance rules

-	Classification	Compliance rule
r_1	Global compliance Rule	After a blood test, the blood sample has to be analyzed.
r_2	Global compliance rule	After the patient is admitted to the hospital, she must be monitored.
r_3	Local compliance rule of gynecologist	The patient must be informed about the results of a blood test.

The interaction model from Fig. 2 is compliable with the set of global compliance rules, which comprise r_1 and r_2. This can be easily shown, since the collaboration of the public processes (cf. Fig. 3) complies with r_1 and r_2. In general, however, public processes will not have been specified yet when verifying compliability (cf. Fig. 1).

3 Compliability Checking

When setting up a cross-organizational process, *compliability* constitutes a semantic correctness criterion to be considered when designing interaction models. It ensures that interaction models do not conflict with the set of imposed global compliance rules. Consequently, if an interaction model is not compliable, the involved partners are unable to implement their public and private processes in such a way that the overall cross-organizational process satisfies all imposed compliance rules. As input our approach takes the interaction model $\mathcal{I}$, the set of global compliance rules GR expressed in terms of linear temporal logic (LTL), the set of partners $\mathcal{P}$, and for each partner $p \in \mathcal{P}$ the set of activities A_p that p may execute.

Similar to approaches checking compliance of intra-organizational processes, we apply model checking to ensure compliability. As opposed to these intra-organizational approaches, however, we do not want to show that all possible executions of a model comply with all compliance rules in GR, but that there exists at least one execution satisfying all compliance rules in GR, and hence $\mathcal{I}$

and GR do not conflict. Furthermore, we cannot directly take the interaction model $\mathcal{I}$ as input for model checking, but must consider all tasks that might be additionally executed by partners. Thus, we cannot apply model checking directly, but have to add preprocessing steps.

Consider Fig. 4: We utilize the knowledge about the set of activities A_p to enrich interaction model $\mathcal{G}$ with parts simulating the behavior of the partners involved (cf. Alg. 1), and obtain an extended interaction model (EIM) as result (cf. Fig. 5). This enrichment is expressed through the following constructs: sequence (SEQ), parallelism (PAR), choice (CHC), and repeated loop (RPT). Note that this does not require the interaction model to be well-structured.

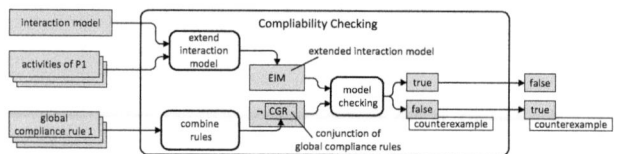

Fig. 4. Process of compliability checking

```
Algorithm 1: Extend interaction model
1  Function extendInteractionModel(I, P, A_p);
2  begin
3      PM := EMPTY;
4      foreach partner p ∈ P do
5          foreach activity a ∈ A_p do
6              PM := CHC(a, PM);
7          end
8      end
9      EIM := PAR(I, RPT(PM));
10 end
11 Output: EIM Extend interaction model
```

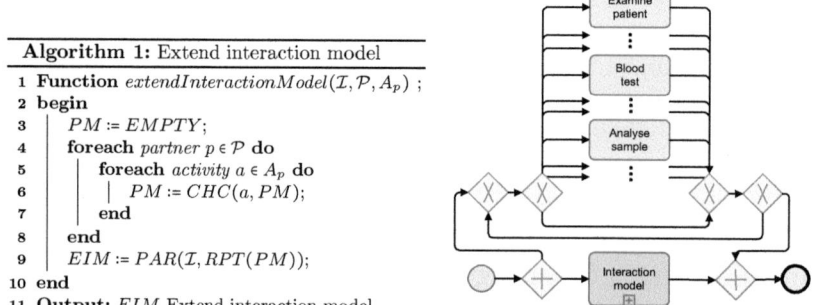

Fig. 5. Extended interaction model EIM

Next, we construct the conjunction of all global compliance rules CGR in Alg. 2. Finally, we apply LTL model checking to the extended interaction model EIM and the negation of CGR in Alg. 3. In case the enriched model EIM is compliable, at least one trace τ is producible through EIM satisfying all global compliance rules. Consequently, the negated conjunction of the global compliance rules does not hold. For this case, explicit LTL model checking returns false (and outputs τ as counter-example), which means that compliabily holds. Otherwise, all traces violate at least one of the global compliance rules, and EIM satisfies the negated formula. In this case, model checking returns true, but compliability is violated. Basically, our algorithm for compliability checking applies model checking over the enriched interaction model EIM and the negated conjunction of the global compliance rules, and then negates the result (cf. Alg. 3 and Fig. 4).

Algorithm 2: Combine global compliance rules	Algorithm 3: Compliability checking
1 **Function** $combineRules(GR)$; 2 **begin** 3 $CGR := true;$ 4 **foreach** global compliance rule $r \in GR$ **do** 5 $\mid CGR := CGR \wedge r;$ 6 **end** 7 **end** 8 **Output:** CGR the combined global compliance rules	1 **Function** $checkCompliability(GR, \mathcal{I}, \mathcal{P}, A_p)$; 2 **begin** 3 $EIM := extendInteractionModel(\mathcal{I}, \mathcal{P}, A_p);$ 4 $CGR := combineRules(GR);$ 5 $MC\_Result := LTLModelCecking(EIM, \neg CGR);$ 6 $compliability := \neg MC\_Result.propertyValid;$ 7 **end** 8 **Output:** $compliability$ the compliability of $\mathcal{I}$ with GR

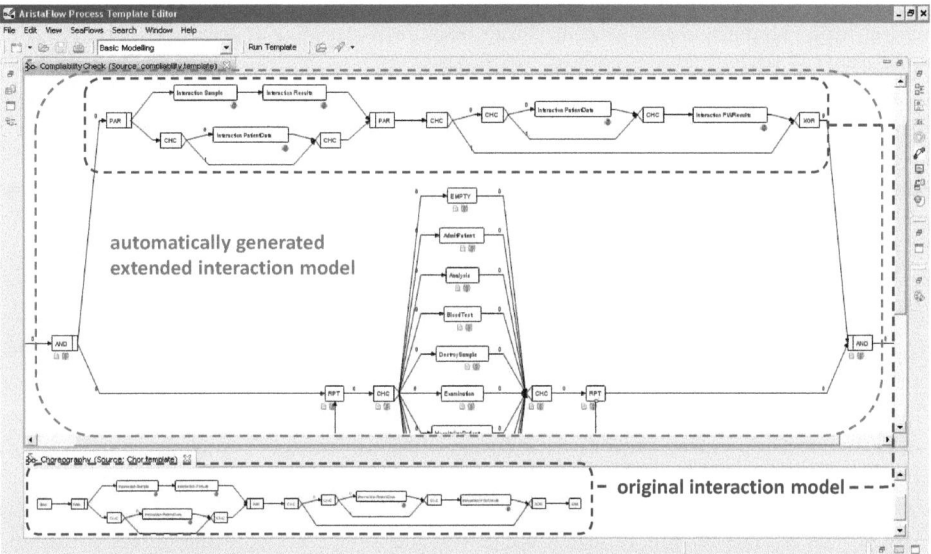

Fig. 6. Proof-of-concept prototype enabling compliability checking

We have demonstrated the feasibility of our approach by a proof-of-concept prototype. We applied this prototype to different application scenarios including the sketched healthcare example [9]. More precisely, the presented compliance checking techniques have been implemented as plug-in of the Aristaflow BPM Suite [12]. The upper part of Fig. 6 shows an automatically generated, extended interaction model for compliability checking, while the lower part depicts the original interaction model.

4 Related Work

In many domains, process execution is subject to compliance rules and restrictions that stem from laws, regulations, and guidelines (e.g. Basel or Sarbanes-Oxley-Act) [1]. Existing approaches differ with respect to the process lifecycle phase in which compliance is considered [13]. Compliance rules are often considered as restrictions to the order in which process activities may be executed.

In literature, there exist approaches formalizing these rules with temporal logic [2,14], patterns [15], or graphical notations [2,16]. To check whether compliance rules are fulfilled by a process model at build time, most approaches apply model checking [2,14,17,18]. Furthermore, business process compliance along the process lifecycle is discussed in [3,4].

Only little work exists, which deals with compliance of cross-organizational processes [7,8]. In particular, compliability of interaction models with a given set of compliance rules has not been addressed yet.

Various other issues related to the correctness of *cross-organizational* processes and complementing compliability have been addressed. For example, [19,20] discuss whether private processes are compatible with the public ones. In turn, [21,22] introduce the notion of *realizability* of interaction models, i.e., to check whether involved partners are able to model public and private processes compatible with a particular interaction model. [23] discusses changes and their propagation in cross-organizational scenarios.

5 Discussion and Outlook

To ensure compliance of business processes with existing guidelines, standards, and laws is crucial for both intra-organizational and cross-organizational settings. However, existing proposals have only dealt with intra-organizational processes so far [9]. This paper constitutes an important step towards enabling compliance of cross-organizational business processes at different levels. In particular, we introduced the notion of *compliability*, i.e., the general ability of an interaction model to not conflict with a given set of compliance rules independent from the concrete process models of the partners.

However, compliability does not guarantee that there exists a compliant realization of an interaction model; i.e., public and private process models that comply with the global compliance rules. For example, consider the interaction model from Fig. 7 and the global compliance rules r_4 and r_5 from Tab. 2. As indicated by the process log being the output of compliability checking (cf. Fig. 7), there exists no conflict between the model and r_4 and r_5. Nevertheless, the partners are not able to specify compliant private and public processes, because the `laboratory` is unable to determine, when the patient is notified. Thus, `laboratory` can not determine when activity *analyse sample* may be started without violating r_5. This is caused by a missing interaction. In the example, it is easy to enhance the interaction model with an additional interaction to enable the partners to specify compliant private and public processes (cf. Fig. 7). Generally, *compliability* remains a necessary, but not sufficient precondition for the ability of the partners to specify their public and private models in such a way that the overall cross-organizational process satisfies the set of imposed compliance rules.

In future work, we will present a comprehensive formal theory for compliance and related criteria (e.g., compliability) in cross-organizational processes. Further, we will present additional algorithms for checking compliability and global

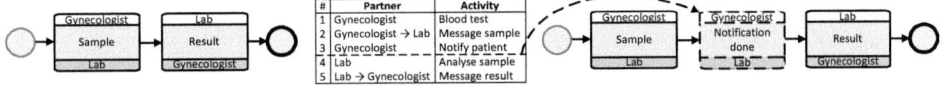

Fig. 7. An example indicating the limitations of compliability

Table 2. Examples of compliance rules

-	Classification	Compliance rule
r_4	Global compliance rule	After blood sample is sent to laboratory, the patient has to be notified.
r_5	Global compliance rule	The analysis must start after the notification of the patient, but before results are sent.

compliance as well as related semantic correctness criteria. Finally, we will consider additional process perspectives (e.g. data, time, resources) in the context of compliance and compliability checking.

References

1. Sadiq, W., Governatori, G., Namiri, K.: Modeling control objectives for business process compliance. In: Alonso, G., Dadam, P., Rosemann, M. (eds.) BPM 2007. LNCS, vol. 4714, pp. 149–164. Springer, Heidelberg (2007)
2. Awad, A., Decker, G., Weske, M.: Efficient compliance checking using BPMN-Q and temporal logic. In: Dumas, M., Reichert, M., Shan, M.-C. (eds.) BPM 2008. LNCS, vol. 5240, pp. 326–341. Springer, Heidelberg (2008)
3. Ly, L.T., et al.: On enabling integrated process compliance with semantic constraints in process management systems. Inf. Sys. Frontiers 14(2), 195–219 (2012)
4. Knuplesch, D., Reichert, M.: Ensuring business process compliance along the process life cycle. Technical Report 2011-06, University of Ulm (2011)
5. Maggi, F.M., Montali, M., Westergaard, M., van der Aalst, W.M.P.: Monitoring business constraints with linear temporal logic: an approach based on colored automata. In: Rinderle-Ma, S., Toumani, F., Wolf, K. (eds.) BPM 2011. LNCS, vol. 6896, pp. 132–147. Springer, Heidelberg (2011)
6. Ramezani, E., Fahland, D., van der Werf, J.M., Mattheis, P.: Separating compliance management and business process management. In: Daniel, F., Barkaoui, K., Dustdar, S. (eds.) BPM Workshops 2011, Part II. LNBIP, vol. 100, pp. 459–464. Springer, Heidelberg (2012)
7. Berry, A., Milosevic, Z.: Extending choreography with business contract constraints. Int. J. Coop. Inf. Sys. 14(2-3), 131–179 (2005)
8. Governatori, G., Milosevic, Z., Sadiq, S.: Compliance checking between business processes and business contracts. In: EDOC 2006, pp. 221–232 (2006)
9. Knuplesch, D., Reichert, M., Mangler, J., Rinderle-Ma, S., Fdhila, W.: Towards compliance of cross-organizational processes and their changes - research challenges and state of research. In: La Rosa, M., Soffer, P. (eds.) BPM Workshops 2012. LNBIP, vol. 132, pp. 649–661. Springer, Heidelberg (2013)
10. Leitner, M., Mangler, J., Rinderle-Ma, S.: Definition and enactment of instance-spanning process constraints. In: Wang, X.S., Cruz, I., Delis, A., Huang, G. (eds.) WISE 2012. LNCS, vol. 7651, pp. 652–658. Springer, Heidelberg (2012)

11. Decker, G., Weske, M.: Interaction-centric modeling of process choreographies. Inf. Sys. 35(8) (2010)
12. Dadam, P., Reichert, M.: The ADEPT project: a decade of research and development for robust and flexible process support. Computer Science-Research and Development 23(2), 81–97 (2009)
13. El Kharbili, M., et al.: Business process compliance checking: Current state and future challenges. In: MobIS 2008, pp. 107–113 (2008)
14. Ghose, A.K., Koliadis, G.: Auditing business process compliance. In: Krämer, B.J., Lin, K.-J., Narasimhan, P. (eds.) ICSOC 2007. LNCS, vol. 4749, pp. 169–180. Springer, Heidelberg (2007)
15. Dwyer, M.B., Avrunin, G.S., Corbett, J.C.: Property specification patterns for finite-state verification. In: FMSP 1998 (1998)
16. Ly, L.T., Rinderle-Ma, S., Dadam, P.: Design and verification of instantiable compliance rule graphs in process-aware information systems. In: Pernici, B. (ed.) CAiSE 2010. LNCS, vol. 6051, pp. 9–23. Springer, Heidelberg (2010)
17. Ly, L.T., et al.: Seaflows toolset–compliance verification made easy for process-aware information systems. Inf. Syst. Evolution, 76–91 (2011)
18. Knuplesch, D., Ly, L.T., Rinderle-Ma, S., Pfeifer, H., Dadam, P.: On enabling data-aware compliance checking of business process models. In: Parsons, J., Saeki, M., Shoval, P., Woo, C., Wand, Y. (eds.) ER 2010. LNCS, vol. 6412, pp. 332–346. Springer, Heidelberg (2010)
19. Decker, G., Weske, M.: Behavioral consistency for B2B process integration. In: Krogstie, J., Opdahl, A.L., Sindre, G. (eds.) CAiSE 2007. LNCS, vol. 4495, pp. 81–95. Springer, Heidelberg (2007)
20. Fdhila, W., Rouached, M., Godart, C.: Communications semantics for WS-BPEL processes. In: ICWS 2008 (2008)
21. Lohmann, N., Wolf, K.: Realizability is controllability. Web Services and Formal Methods, 110–127 (2010)
22. Knuplesch, D., Pryss, R., Reichert, M.: Data-aware interaction in distributed and collaborative workflows: modeling, semantics, correctness. In: CollaborateCom 2012, pp. 223–232. IEEE Comp. Press (2012)
23. Fdhila, W., Rinderle-Ma, S., Reichert, M.: Change propagation in collaborative processes scenarios. In: CollaborateCom 2012, pp. 452–461. IEEE Comp. Press (2012)

Verification of Query Completeness over Processes

Simon Razniewski, Marco Montali, and Werner Nutt

Free University of Bozen-Bolzano
Dominikanerplatz 3
39100 Bozen-Bolzano
{razniewski,montali,nutt}@inf.unibz.it

Abstract. Data completeness is an essential aspect of data quality, and has in turn a huge impact on the effective management of companies. For example, statistics are computed and audits are conducted in companies by implicitly placing the strong assumption that the analysed data are complete. In this work, we are interested in studying the problem of completeness of data produced by business processes, to the aim of automatically assessing whether a given database query can be answered with complete information in a certain state of the process. We formalize so-called *quality-aware processes* that create data in the real world and store it in the company's information system possibly at a later point. We then show how one can check the completeness of database queries in a certain state of the process or after the execution of a sequence of actions, by leveraging on query containment, a well-studied problem in database theory.

1 Introduction

Data completeness is an important aspect of data quality. When data is used in decision-making, it is important that the data is of good quality, and in particular that it is complete. This is particularly true in an enterprise setting. On the one hand, strategic decisions are taken inside a company by relying on statistics and business indicators such as KPIs. Obviously, this information is useful only if it is reliable, and reliability, in turn, is strictly related to quality and, more specifically, to completeness.

Consider for example the school information system of the autonomous province of Bolzano in Italy, which triggered the research included in this paper. Such an information system stores data about schools, enrolments, students and teachers. When statistics are computed for the enrolments in a given school, e.g., to decide the amount of teachers needed for the following academic year, it is of utmost importance that the involved data are complete, i.e., that the required information stored in the information system is aligned with reality.

Completeness of data is a key issue also in the context of auditing. When a company is evaluated to check whether its way of conducting business is in accordance to the law and to audit assurance standards, part of the external audit is dedicated to the analysis of the actual data. If such data are incomplete w.r.t. the queries issued during the audit, then the obtained answers do not properly reflect the company's behaviour.

There has been plenty of work on fixing data quality issues, especially for fixing incorrect data and for detecting duplicates [10,6]. However, some data quality issues cannot be automatically fixed. This holds in particular for incomplete data, as missing data cannot be corrected inside a system, unless additional activities are introduced to acquire them. In all these situations, it is then a mandatory requirement to (at least) detect data quality issues, enabling informed decisions drawn with knowledge about which data are complete and which not.

The key question therefore is how it is possible to obtain this completeness information. There has been previous work on the assessment of data completeness [12], however this approach left the question where completeness information come from largely open. In this work, we argue that, in the common situation where the manipulation of data inside the information system is driven by business processes, we can leverage on such processes to infer information about data completeness, provided that we suitably annotate the involved activities with explicit information about the way they manipulate data.

A common source of data incompleteness in business processes is constituted by delays between real-world events and their recording in an information system. This holds in particular for scenarios where processes are carried out partially without support of the information system. E.g., many legal events are considered valid as soon as they are signed on a sheet of paper, but their recording in the information system could happen much later in time. Consider again the example of the school information system, in particular the enrolment of pupils in schools. Parents enroll their children at the individual schools, and the enrolment is valid as soon as both the parents and the school director sign the enrolment form. However, the school secretary may record the information from the sheets only later in the local database of the school, and even later submit all the enrolment information to the central school administration, which needs it to plan the assignment of teachers to schools, and other management tasks.

In the BPM context, there have been attempts to model data quality issues, like in [7,14,2]. However, these approaches mainly discussed general methodologies for modelling data quality requirements in BPMN, but did not provide methods to asses their fulfilment. In this paper, we claim that process formalizations are an essential source for learning about data completeness and show how data completeness can be verified. In particular, our contributions are (1) to introduce the idea of extracting information about data completeness from processes manipulating the data, (2) to formalize processes that can both interact with the real-world and record information about the real-world in an information system, and (3) to show how completeness can be verified over such processes, both at design and at execution time.

Our approach leverages on two assumptions related to how the data manipulation and the process control-flow are captured. From the data point of view, we leverage on annotations that suitably mediate between expressiveness and tractability. More specifically, we rely on annotations modeling that new information of a given type is acquired in the real world, or that some information present in the real world is stored into the information system. We do not explicitly consider the evolution of specific values for the data, as incorporating full-fledged data without any restriction would immediately make our problem undecidable, being simple reachability queries undecidable in such a rich setting [9,3,4]. From the control-flow point of view, we are completely orthogonal to process specification languages. In particular, we design our data completeness algorithms over (labeled) transition systems, a well-established mathematical structure to represent the execution traces that can by produced according to the control-flow dependencies of the (business) process model of interest. Consequently, our approach can in principle be applied to any process modeling language, with the proviso of annotating the involved activities. We are in particular interested in providing automated reasoning facilities to answer whether a given query can be answered with complete information given a target state or a sequence of activities.

The rest of this paper is divided as follows. In Section 2, we discuss the scenario of the school enrolment data in the province of Bozen/Bolzano in detail. In Section 3, we discuss our formal approach, introducing quality-aware transition systems, process activity annotations used to capture the semantics of activities that interact with the real world and with an information system, and properties of query completeness over such systems. In Section 4, we discuss how query completeness can be verified over such systems at design time and at runtime, how query completeness can be refined and what the complexity of deciding query completeness is.

The proofs of Proposition 1 and 2 and of Lemma 1 and 2 are available in the extended version available at Arxiv.org [13].

2 Example Scenario

Consider the example of the enrollment to schools in the province of Bolzano. Parents can submit enrollment requests for their child to any school they want until the 1st of March. Schools then decide which pupils to accept, and parents have to choose one of the schools in which their child is accepted. Since in May the school administration wants to start planning the allocation of teachers to schools and take further decisions (such as the opening and closing of school branches and schools) they require the schools to process the enrollments and to enter them in the central school information system before the 15th of April.

A particular feature of this process is that it is partly carried out with pen and paper, and partly in front of a computer, interacting with an underlying school information system. Consequently, the information system does not often contain all the information that hold in the real world, and is therefore incomplete. E.g., while an enrollment is legally already valid when the enrollment sheet is signed, this information is visible in the information system only when the secretary enters it into a computerised form.

A BPMN diagram sketching the main phases of this process is shown in Fig. 1, while a simple UML diagram of (a fragment of) the school domain is reported in Fig. 2. These diagrams abstractly summarise the school domain from the point of view of the central administration. Concretely, each school implements a specific, local version of the enrolment process, relying on its own domain conceptual model. The data collected on a per-school basis are then transferred into a central information system managed by the central administration, which refines the conceptual model of Fig. 2. In the following, we will assume that such an information system represents information about children and the class they belong to by means of a *pupil(pname, class, sname)* relation, where *pname* is the name of an enrolled child, *class* is the class to which the pupil belongs, and *sname* is the name of the corresponding school.

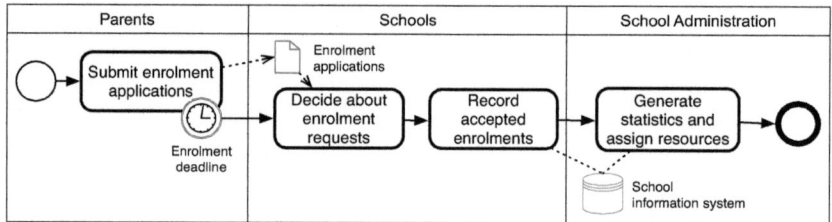

Fig. 1. BPMN diagram of the main phases of the school enrollment process

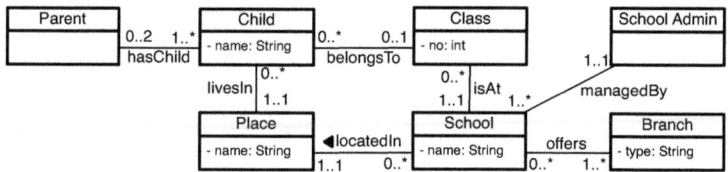

Fig. 2. UML diagram capturing a fragment of the school domain

When using the statistics about the enrollments as compiled in the beginning of May, the school administration is highly interested in having correct statistical information, which in turn requires that the underlying data about the enrollments must be complete. Since the data is generated during the enrollment process, this gives rise to several questions about such a process. The first question is whether the process is generally designed correctly, that is, whether the enrollments present in the information system are really complete at the time they publish their statistics, or whether it is still possible to submit valid enrollments by the time the statistics are published. We call this problem the *design-time verification*.

A second question is to find whether the number of enrollments in a certain school branch is already complete before the 15th of April, that is, when the schools are still allowed to submit enrolments (i.e., when there are school that still have not completed the second activity in the school lane of Fig. 1), which could be the case when some schools submitted all their enrollments but others did not. In specific cases the number can be complete already, when the schools that submitted their data are all the schools that offer the branch. We call this problem the *run-time verification*.

A third question is to learn on a finer-grained level about the completeness of statistics, when they are not generally complete. When a statistic consists not of a single number but of a set of values (e.g. enrollments per school), it is interesting to know for which schools the number is already complete. We call this the *dimension analysis*.

3 Formalization

We want to formalize processes as in Fig. 1, which both operate over data in the real-world (pen and paper) and record information about the real world in an information system. We therefore first introduce real-world databases and information system databases, and then annotate transition systems, which represent possible process executions, with effects to interact with the real-world or the information system database.

3.1 Real-World Databases and Information System Databases

As common in database theory, we assume a set of constants *dom* and a fixed set Σ of relations, comprising the built-in relations $<$ and $\leq$ over the rational numbers. We assume that *dom* is partitioned into the types of strings and rational numbers and that the arguments of each relation are typed. A database instance is a finite set of facts in Σ over *dom*. As there exists both the real world and the information system, in the following we model this with two databases: D^{rw} called the real-world database, which describes the information that holds in the real world, and D^{is}, called the information system database, which captures the information that is stored in the information system. We assume that the stored information is always a subset of the real-world information. Thus, processes actually operate over pairs (D^{rw}, D^{is}) of real-world database and information system database. In the following, we will focus on processes that create data in the real world and copy parts of the data into the information system, possibly delayed.

Example 1. Consider that in the real world, there are the two pupils John and Mary enrolled in the classes 2 and 4 at the Hofer School, while the school has so far only processed the enrollment of John in their IT system. Additionally it holds in the real world that John and Alice live in Bolzano and Bob lives in the city of Merano. The real-world database D^{rw} would then be {*pupil(John, 2, HoferSchool), pupil(Mary, 4, HoferSchool), livesIn(John, Bolzano), livesIn(Bob, Merano), livesIn(Alice, Bolzano)*} while the information system database would be {*pupil(John, 2, HoferSchool)*}.

When necessary, we annotate atoms with the database they belong to. So, $pupil^{is}$(*John*, 4, *HoferSchool*) indicates a fact stored in the information system database.

3.2 Query Completeness

For planning purposes, the school administration is interested in figures such as the number of pupils per class, school, profile, etc. Such figures can be extracted from relational databases via SQL queries using the COUNT keyword. In an SQL database with a table `pupil(name, class, school)`, a query asking for the number of students per school would be written as:

$$\text{SELECT school, COUNT(name) as pupils\_nr} \\ \text{FROM pupil} \\ \text{GROUP BY school.} \tag{1}$$

In database theory, conjunctive queries were introduced to formalize SQL queries. A *conjunctive query* Q is an expression of the form $Q(\bar{x}) := A_1, \ldots, A_n, M$, where $\bar{x}$ are called the distinguished variables in the head of the query, A_1 to A_n the atoms in the body of the query, and M is a set of built-in comparisons [1]. We denote the set of all variables that appear in a query Q by $Var(Q)$. Common subclasses of conjunctive queries are linear conjunctive queries, that is, they do not contain a relational symbol twice, and relational conjunctive queries, that is, queries that do not use comparison predicates. Conjunctive queries allow to formalize all single-block SQL queries, i.e., queries of the form "SELECT ... FROM ... WHERE ...". As a conjunctive query, the SQL query (1) above would be written as:

$$Q_{p/s}(schoolname, count(name)) :- pupil(name, class, schoolname) \qquad (2)$$

In the following, we assume that all queries are conjunctive queries. We now formalize query completeness over a pair of a real-world database and an information system database. Intuitively, if query completeness can be guaranteed, then this means that the query over the generally incomplete information system database gives the same answer as it would give w.r.t. the information that holds in the real world. Query completeness is the key property that we are interested in verifying.

A pair of databases (D^{rw}, D^{is}) satisfies *query completeness* of a query Q, if $Q(D^{rw}) = Q(D^{is})$ holds. We then write $(D^{rw}, D^{is}) \models \text{Compl}(Q)$.

Example 2. Consider the pair of databases (D^{rw}, D^{is}) from Example 1 and the query $Q_{p/s}$ from above (2). Then, $\text{Compl}(Q_{p/s})$ does not hold over (D^{rw}, D^{is}) because $Q(D^{rw}) = \{(HoferSchool, 2)\}$ but $Q(D^{is}) = \{(HoferSchool, 1)\}$. A query for pupils in class 2 only, $Q_{class2}(n) :- pupil(n, 2, s)$, would be complete, because $Q(D^{rw}) = Q(D^{is}) = \{John\}$.

3.3 Real-World Effects and Copy Effects

We want to formalize the real-world effect of an enrollment action at the Hofer School, where in principle, every pupil that has submitted an enrolment request before, is allowed to enroll in the real world. We can formalize this using the following expression: $pupil^{rw}(n, c, HoferSchool) \leftsquigarrow request^{rw}(n, HoferSchool)$, which should mean that whenever someone is a pupil at the Hofer school now, he has submitted an enrolment request before. Also, we want to formalize copy effects, for example where all pupils in classes greater than 3 are stored in the database. This can be written with the following implication: $pupil^{rw}(n, c, s), c > 3 \rightarrow pupil^{is}(n, c, s)$, which means that whenever someone is a pupil in a class with level greater than three in the real world, then this fact is also stored in the information system.

For annotating processes with information about data creation and manipulation in the real world D^{rw} and in the information system D^{is}, we use real-world effects and copy effects as annotations. While their syntax is the same, their semantics is different. Formally, a *real-world effect* r or a *copy effect* c is a tuple $(R(\bar{x}, \bar{y}), G(\bar{x}, \bar{z}))$, where R is an atom, G is a set of atoms and built-in comparisons and $\bar{x}, \bar{y}$ and $\bar{z}$ are sets of distinct variables. We call G the *guard* of the effect. The effects r and c can be written as follows:

$$r : R^{rw}(\bar{x}, \bar{y}) \leftsquigarrow \exists \bar{z}: G^{rw}(\bar{x}, \bar{z})$$
$$c : R^{rw}(\bar{x}, \bar{y}), G^{rw}(\bar{x}, \bar{z}) \rightarrow R^{is}(\bar{x}, \bar{y})$$

Real-world effects can have variables $\bar{y}$ on the left side that do not occur in the condition. These variables are not restricted and thus allow to introduce new values.

A pair of real-world databases (D_1^{rw}, D_2^{rw}) *conforms* to a real-world effect $R^{rw}(\bar{x}, \bar{y}) \leftsquigarrow \exists \bar{z}: G^{rw}(\bar{x}, \bar{z})$, if for all facts $R^{rw}(\bar{c}_1, \bar{c}_2)$ that are in D_2^{rw} but not in D_1^{rw} it holds that there exists a tuple of constants $\bar{c}_3$ such that the guard $G^{rw}(\bar{c}_1, \bar{c}_3)$ is in D_1^{rw}. The pair of databases conforms to a set of real-world effects, if each fact in $D_2^{rw} \setminus D_1^{rw}$ conforms to at least one real-word effect.

If for a real-world effect there does not exist any pair of databases (D_1, D_2) with $D_2 \setminus D_1 \neq \emptyset$ that conforms to the effect, the effect is called *useless*. Useless effects can be detected by checking whether the effect does not have unbound variables ($\bar{y}$ is empty) and whether $Q(\bar{x}) :- G(\bar{x}, \bar{z})$ is contained in $Q(\bar{x}) :- R(\bar{x})$. In the following we only consider real-world effects that are not useless.

The function $copy_c$ for a copy effect $c = R^{rw}(\bar{x}, \bar{y}), G^{rw}(\bar{x}, \bar{z}) \rightarrow R^{is}(\bar{x}, \bar{y})$ over a real-world database D^{rw} returns the corresponding R-facts for all the tuples that are in the answer of the query $P_c(\bar{x}, \bar{y}) :- R^{rw}(\bar{x}, \bar{y}), G^{rw}(\bar{x}, \bar{z})$ over D^{rw}. For a set of copy effects CE, the function $copy_{CE}$ is defined by taking the union of the results of the individual copy functions.

Example 3. Consider a real-world effect r that allows to introduce persons living in Merano as pupils in classes higher than 3 in the real world, that is, $r = pupil^{rw}(n, c, s) \leftsquigarrow c > 3, livesIn(n, Merano)$ and a pair of real-world databases using the database D^{rw} from Example 1 as $(D^{rw}, D^{rw} \cup \{pupil^{rw}(Bob, 4, HoferSchool)\}$. Then this pair conforms to the real-world effect r, because the guard of the only new fact $pupil^{rw}(Bob, 4, HoferSchool)$ evaluates to true: Bob lives in Merano and his class level is greater than 3. The pair $(D^{rw}, D^{rw} \cup \{pupil^{rw}(Alice, 1, HoferSchool)\}$ does not conform to r, because Alice does not live in Merano, and also because the class level is not greater than 3.

For the copy effect $c = pupil^{rw}(n, c, s), c > 3 \rightarrow pupil^{is}(n, c, s)$, which copies all pupils in classes greater equal 3, its output over the real-world database in Example 1 would be $\{pupil^{is}(Mary, 4, HoferSchool)\}$.

3.4 Quality-Aware Transition Systems

To capture the execution semantics of *quality-aware processes*, we resort to (suitably annotated) labelled transition systems, a common way to describe the semantics of concurrent processes by interleaving [5]. This makes our approach applicable for virtually every business process modelling language equipped with a formal underlying transition semantics (such as Petri nets or, directly, transition systems).

Formally, a *(labelled) transition system* T is a tuple $T = (S, s_0, A, E)$, where S is a set of states, $s_0 \in S$ is the initial state, A is a set of names of actions and $E \subseteq S \times A \times S$ is a set of edges labelled by actions from A. In the following, we will annotate the actions of the transition systems with effects that describe interaction with the real-world and the information system. In particular, we introduce *quality-aware transition systems* (QATS) to capture the execution semantics of processes that change data both in the real world and in the information system database.

Formally, a *quality-aware transition system* $\bar{T}$ is a tuple $\bar{T} = (T, re, ce)$, where T is a transition system and re and ce are functions from A into the sets of all real-world effects and copy effects, which in turn obey to the syntax and semantics defined in Sec. 3.3. Note that transition systems and hence also QATS may contain cycles.

Example 4. Let us consider two specific schools, the Hofer School and the Da Vinci School, and a (simplified version) of their enrolment process, depicted in BPMN in Fig. 3(a) (in parenthesis, we introduce compact names for the activities, which will be used throughout the example). As we will see, while the two processes are independent from each other from the control-flow point of view (i.e., they run in parallel), they eventually write information into the same table of the central information system.

Let us first consider the Hofer School. In the first step, the requests are processed with pen and paper, deciding which requests are accepted and, for those, adding the signature of the school director and finalising other bureaucratic issues. By using relation $request^{rw}(n, HoferSchool)$ to model the fact that a child named n requests to be enrolled at Hofer, and $pupil^{rw}(n, 1, HoferSchool)$ to model that she is actually enrolled, the activity pH is a real-world activity that can be annotated with the real-world effect $pupil^{rw}(n, 1, HoferSchool) \leftsquigarrow request^{rw}(n, HoferSchool)$. In the second step, the information about enrolled pupils is transferred to the central information system by copying all real-world enrolments of the Hofer school. More specifically, the activity rH can be annotated with the copy effect $pupil^{rw}(n, 1, HoferSchool) \rightarrow pupil^{is}(n, 1, HoferSchool)$.

Let us now focus on the Da Vinci School. Depending on the amount of incoming requests, the school decides whether to directly process the enrolments, or to do an entrance test for obtaining a ranking. In the first case (activity pD), the activity mirrors that of the Hofer school, and is annotated with the real-world effect $pupil^{rw}(n, 1, DaVinci) \leftsquigarrow request^{rw}(n, DaVinci)$. As for the test, the activity tD can be annotated with a real-world effect that makes it possible to enrol only those children who passed the test: $pupil^{rw}(n, 1, DaVinci) \leftsquigarrow request^{rw}(n, DaVinci), test^{rw}(n, mark), mark \geq 6$. Finally, the process terminates by properly transferring the information about enrolments to the central administration, exactly as done for the Hofer school. In particular, the activity rD is annotated with the copy effect $pupil^{rw}(n, 1, DaVinci) \rightarrow pupil^{is}(n, 1, DaVinci)$. Notice that this effect feeds the same *pupil* relation of the central information systems that is used by rH, but with a different value for the third column (i.e., the school name).

Fig. 3(b) shows the QATS formalizing the execution semantics of the parallel composition of the two processes (where activities are properly annotated with the previously discussed effects). Circles drawn in orange with solid line represent execution states where the information about pupils enrolled at the Hofer school is complete. Circles in blue with double stroke represent execution states where completeness holds for pupils enrolled at the Da Vinci school. At the final, sink state information about the enrolled pupils is complete for both schools.

3.5 Paths and Action Sequences in QATSs

Let $\bar{T} = (T, re, ce)$ be a QATS. A *path* π in $\bar{T}$ is a sequence $t_1, \ldots, t_n$ of transitions such that $t_i = (s_{i-1}, a_i, s_i)$ for all $i = 1 \ldots n$. An *action sequence* α is a sequence $a_1, \ldots, a_m$ of action names. Each path $\pi = t_1, \ldots, t_n$ has also a *corresponding action sequence* α_π defined as $a_1, \ldots, a_n$. For a state s, the set $Aseq(s)$ is the set of the action sequences of all paths that end in s.

Next we consider the semantics of action sequences. A *development* of an action sequence $\alpha = a_1, \ldots, a_n$ is a sequence $D_0^{rw}, \ldots, D_n^{rw}$ of real-world databases such that each pair (D_j^{rw}, D_{j+1}^{rw}) conforms to the effects $re(\alpha_{j+1})$. Note that D_0^{rw} can be arbitrary.

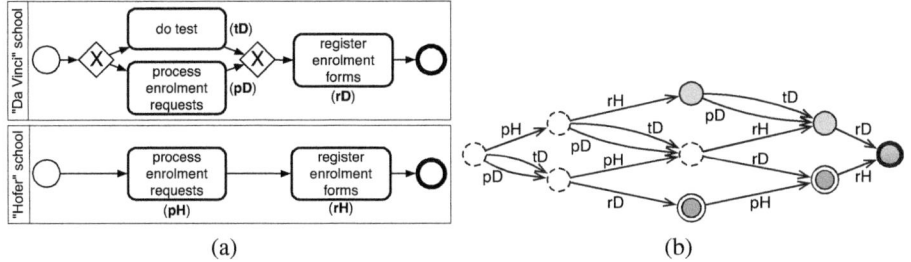

Fig. 3. BPMN enrolment process of two schools, and the corresponding QATS

For each development $D_0^{rw}, \ldots, D_n^{rw}$, there exists a unique trace $D_0^{is}, \ldots, D_n^{is}$, which is a sequence of information system databases D_j^{is} defined as follows:

$$D_j^{is} = \begin{cases} D_j^{rw} & \text{if } j = 0 \\ D_{j-1}^{is} \cup \text{copy}_{CE(t_j)}(D_j^{rw}) & \text{otherwise.} \end{cases}$$

Note that $D_0^{is} = D_0^{rw}$ does not introduce loss of generality and is just a convention. To start with initially different databases, one can just add an initial action that introduces data in all real-world relations.

3.6 Completeness over QATSs

An action sequence $\alpha = a_1, \ldots, a_n$ *satisfies* query completeness of a query Q, if for all developments of α it holds that Q is complete over (D_n^{rw}, D_n^{is}), that is, if $Q(D_n^{rw}) = Q(D_n^{is})$ holds. A path P in a QATS $\bar{T}$ satisfies query completeness for Q, if its corresponding action sequence satisfies it. A state s in a QATS $\bar{T}$ satisfies Compl(Q), if all action sequences in *Aseq(s)* (the set of the action sequences of all paths that end in s) satisfy Compl(Q). We then write $s \models \text{Compl}(Q)$.

Example 5. Consider the QATS in Figure 3(b) and recall that the action pH is annotated with the real-world effect $pupil^{rw}(n, 1, HoferSchool) \looparrowleft request^{rw}(n, HoferSchool)$, and action rH with the copy effect $pupil^{rw}(n, 1, HoferSchool) \to pupil^{is}(n, 1, HoferSchool)$. A path $\pi = ((s_0, \text{pH}, s_1), (s_1, \text{rH}, s_2))$ has the corresponding action sequence (pH, rH). Its models are all sequences $(D_0^{rw}, D_1^{rw}, D_2^{rw})$ of real-world databases (developments), where D_1^{rw} may contain additional pupil facts at the Hofer school w.r.t. D_0^{rw} because of the real-world effect of action a_1, and $D_2^{rw} = D_1^{rw}$. Each such development has a uniquely defined trace $(D_0^{is}, D_1^{is}, D_2^{is})$ where $D_0^{is} = D_0^{rw}$ by definition, $D_1^{is} = D_0^{is}$ because no copy effect is happening in action a_1, and $D_2^{is} = D_1^{is} \cup \text{copy}_{ce(a_1)}(D_1^{rw})$, which means that all pupil facts from Hofer school that hold in the real-world database are copied into the information system due to the effect of action a_1. Thus, the state s_2 satisfies Compl(Q_{Hofer}) for a query $Q_{Hofer(n)} := pupil(n, c, HoferSchool)$, because in all models of the action sequence the real-world pupils at the Hofer school are copied by the copy effect in action rH.

4 Verifying Completeness over Processes

In the following, we analyze how to check completeness in a state of a QATS at design time, at runtime, and how to analyze the completeness of an incomplete query in detail.

4.1 Design-Time Verification

When checking for query completeness at design time, we have to consider all possible paths that lead to the state in which we want to check completeness. We first analyze how to check completeness for a single path, and then extend our results to sets of paths.

Given a query $Q(\bar{z}) :- R_1(\bar{t}_1), \ldots, R_n(\bar{t}_n), M$, we say that a real-world effect r is *risky* w.r.t. Q, if there exists a pair of real-world databases (D_1^{rw}, D_2^{rw}) that conforms to r and where the query result changes, that is, $Q(D_1^{rw}) \neq Q(D_2^{rw})$. Intuitively, this means that real-world database changes caused by r can influence the query answer and lead to incompleteness, if the changes are not copied into the information system.

Proposition 1 (Risky effects). *Let r be the real-world effect $R(\bar{x}, \bar{y}) \leftsquigarrow G_1(\bar{x}, \bar{z}_1)$, Q be the query $Q :- R_1(\bar{t}_1), \ldots, R_n(\bar{t}_n), M$ and $\bar{v} = Var(Q)$. Then r is risky wrt. Q if and only if the following formula is satisfiable:*

$$G_1(\bar{x}, \bar{z}_1) \wedge \left(\bigwedge_{i=1\ldots n} R_i(\bar{t}_i) \right) \wedge M \wedge \left(\bigvee_{R_i = R} (\bar{x}, \bar{y}) = \bar{t}_i \right)$$

Example 6. Consider the query $Q(n) :- pupil(n, c, s), livesIn(n, Bolzano)$ and the real-world effect $r_1 = pupil(n, c, s) \leftsquigarrow c = 4$, which allows to add new pupils in class 4 in the real world. Then r_1 is risky w.r.t. Q, because pupils in class 4 can potentially also live in Bolzano. Note that without integrity constraints, actually most updates to the same relation will be risky: if we do not have keys in the database, a pupil could live both in Bolzano and Merano and hence an effect $r_2 = pupil(n, c, s) \leftsquigarrow livesIn(n, Merano)$ would be risky w.r.t. Q, too. If there is a key defined over the first attribute of $livesIn$, then r_2 would not be risky, because adding pupils that live in Merano would not influence the completeness of pupils that only live in Bolzano.

We say that a real-world effect r that is risky w.r.t. a query Q is *repaired* by a set of copy effects $\{c_2, \ldots, c_n\}$, if for any sequence of databases (D_1^{rw}, D_2^{rw}) that conforms to r it holds that $Q(D_2^{rw}) = Q(D_1^{rw} \cup copy_{c_1 \ldots c_n}(D_2^{rw}))$. Intuitively, this means that whenever we introduce new facts via r and apply the copy effects afterwards, all new facts that can change the query result are also copied into the information system.

Proposition 2 (Repairing). *Consider the query $Q :- R_1(\bar{t}_1), \ldots R_n(\bar{t}_n), M$, let $\bar{v} = Var(Q)$, a real-world effect $R(\bar{x}, \bar{y}) \leftsquigarrow G_1(\bar{x}, \bar{z}_1)$ and a set of copy effects $\{c_2, \ldots, c_m\}$. Then r is repaired by $\{c_2, \ldots, c_m\}$ if and only if the following formula is valid:*

$$\forall \bar{x}, \bar{y} : \left(\left(\exists \bar{z}_1, \bar{v} : G_1(\bar{x}, \bar{z}_1) \wedge \bigwedge_{i=1\ldots n} R_i(\bar{t}_i) \wedge M \wedge \bigvee_{R_i = R} (\bar{x}, \bar{y}) = \bar{t}_i \right) \implies \bigvee_{j=2\ldots m} \exists \bar{z}_j : G_j(\bar{x}, \bar{z}_j) \right)$$

This implication can be translated into a problem of query containment, a well-studied topic in database theory [11,8,15,12]. In particular, for a query

$Q(\bar{z}):- R_1(\bar{t}_1), \ldots, R_n(\bar{t}_n)$, we define the atom-projection of Q on the i-th atom as $Q_i^\pi(\bar{x}):- R_1(\bar{t}_1), \ldots, R_n(\bar{t}_n), \bar{x} = \bar{t}_i$. Then, for a query Q and a relation R, we define the R-projection of Q, written Q^R, as the union of all the atom-projections of atoms that use the relation symbol R, that is, $\bigcup_{R_i=R} Q_i^\pi$. For a real-world effect $r = R(\bar{x}, \bar{y}) \leftsquigarrow G(\bar{x}, \bar{z})$, we define its associated query P_r as $P_r(\bar{x}, \bar{y}):- R(\bar{x}, \bar{y}), G(\bar{x}, \bar{z})$.

Corollary 1 (Repairing and query containment). *Let Q be a query, $\alpha = a_1, \ldots a_n$ be an action sequence, a_i be an action with a risky real-world effect r, and $\{c_1, \ldots, c_m\}$ be the set of all copy effects of the actions $a_{i+1} \ldots a_n$.*
Then r is repaired, if and only if it holds that $P_r \cap Q^R \subseteq P_{c_1} \cup \ldots \cup P_{c_m}$.

Intuitively, the corollary says that a risky effect r is repaired, if all data that is introduced by r that can potentially change the result of the query Q are guaranteed to be copied into the information system database by the copy effects c_1 to c_n.

The corollary holds because of the direct correspondence between conjunctive queries and relational calculus [1].

We arrive at a result for characterizing query completeness wrt. an action sequence:

Lemma 1 (Action sequence completeness). *Let α be an action sequence and Q be a query. Then $\alpha \models \text{Compl}(Q)$ if and only if all risky effects in α are repaired.*

Before discussing complexity results in Section 4.4, we show that completeness entailment over action sequences and containment of unions of queries have the same complexity. A query language is defined by the operations that it allows. Common sublanguages of conjunctive queries are, e.g., queries without arithmetic comparisons (so-called relational queries), or queries without repeated relation symbols (so-called linear queries).

For a query language $\mathcal{L}$, we call *EntC($\mathcal{L}$)* the problem of deciding whether an action sequence α entails completeness of a query Q, where Q and the real-world effects and the copy effects in α are formulated in language $\mathcal{L}$. Also, we call *ContU($\mathcal{L}$)* the problem of deciding whether a query is contained in a union of queries, where all are formulated in the language $\mathcal{L}$.

Theorem 1. *Let $\mathcal{L}$ be a query languages. Then EntC($\mathcal{L}$) and ContU($\mathcal{L}$) can be reduced to each other in linear time.*

Proof. "$\Rightarrow$": Consider the characterization shown in Lemma 1. For a fixed action sequence, the number of containment checks is the same as the number of the real-world effects of the action sequence and thus linear.

"$\Leftarrow$": Consider a containment problem $Q_0 \subseteq Q_1 \cup \ldots \cup Q_n$, for queries in a language $\mathcal{L}$. Then we can construct a QATS $\bar{T} = (S, s_0, A, E, re, ce)$ over the schema of the queries together with a new relation R with the same arity as the queries where $S = \{s_0, s_1, s_2\}$, $A = \{a_1, a_2\}$, $re(a_1) = \{R^{rw}(\bar{x}) \leftsquigarrow Q_0(\bar{x})\}$ and $ce(a_2) = \bigcup_{i=1\ldots n}\{Q_i(\bar{x}) \rightarrow R^{is}(\bar{x})\}$. Now, the action sequence a_1, a_2 satisfies a query completeness for a query $Q'(\bar{x}):- R(\bar{x})$ exactly if Q_0 is contained in the union of the queries Q_1 to Q_n, because only in this case the real-world effect at action a_1 cannot introduce any facts into D_1^{rw} of a development of a_1, a_2, which are not copied into D_2^{is} by one of the effects of the action a_2. □

We discuss the complexity of query containment and hence of completeness entailment over action sequences more in detail in Section 4.4.

So far, we have shown how query completeness over a path can be checked. To verify completeness in a specific state, we have to consider all paths to that state, which makes the analysis more difficult. We first introduce a lemma that allows to remove repeated actions in an action sequence:

Lemma 2 (Duplicate removal). *Let* $\alpha = \alpha_1, \tilde{a}, \alpha_2, \tilde{a}, \alpha_3$ *be an action sequence with* $\tilde{a}$ *as repeated action and let Q be a query. Then α satisfies* $\text{Compl}(Q)$ *if and only if* $\alpha' = \alpha_1, \alpha_2, \tilde{a}, \alpha_3$ *satisfies* $\text{Compl}(Q)$.

The lemma shows that our formalism can deal with cycles. While cycles imply the existence of sequences of arbitrary length, the lemma shows that we only need to consider sequences where each action occurs at most once. Intuitively, it is sufficient to check each cycle only once. Based on this lemma, we define the *normal action sequence* of a path π as the action sequence of π in which for all repeated actions all but the last occurrence are removed.

Proposition 3 (Normal action sequences). *Let* $\bar{T} = (T, re, ce)$ *be a QATS, Π be the set of all paths of $\bar{T}$ and Q be a query. Then*
1. *for each path $\pi \in \Pi$, its normal action sequence has at most the length $|A|$,*
2. *there are at most $\sum_{k=1}^{|A|} \frac{|A|!}{(|A|-k)!} < (|A|+1)!$ different normal forms of paths,*
3. *for each path $\pi \in \Pi$, it holds that $\pi \models \text{Compl}(Q)$ if its normal action sequence α' satisfies* $\text{Compl}(Q)$.

The first two items hold because normal action sequences do not contain actions twice. The third item holds because of Lemma 2, which allows to remove all but the last occurrence of an action in an action sequence without changing query completeness satisfaction.

Before arriving at the main result, we need to show that deciding whether a given normal action sequence can actually be realized by a path is easy:

Proposition 4. *Given a QATS $\bar{T}$, a state s and a normal action sequence α. Then, deciding whether there exists a path π that has α as its normal action sequence and that ends in s can be done in polynomial time.*

The reason for this proposition is that given a normal action sequence $\alpha = a_1, \ldots, a_n$, one just needs to calculate the states reachable from s_0 via the concatenated expression $(a_1, \ldots, a_n)^+, (a_2, \ldots, a_n)^+, \ldots, (a_{n-1}, a_n)^+, (a_n)^+$. This expression stands exactly for all action sequences with α as normal sequence, because it allows repeated actions before their last occurrence in α. Calculating the states that are reachable via this expression can be done in polynomial time, because the reachable states S_n^{reach} can be calculated iteratively for each component $(a_i, \ldots, a_n)^+$ as S_i^{reach} from the reachable states S_{i-1}^{reach} until the previous component $(a_{i-1}, \ldots, a_n)^+$ by taking all states that are reachable from a state in S_{i-1}^{reach} via one or several actions in $\{a_i, \ldots, a_n\}$, which can be done with a linear-time graph traversal such as breadth-first or depth-first search. Since there are only n such components, the overall algorithm works in polynomial time.

Theorem 2. *Given a QATS $\bar{T}$ and a query Q, both formulated in a query language $\mathcal{L}$, checking "$s \not\models \text{Compl}(Q)$?" can be done using a nondeterministic polynomial-time Turing machine with a $\text{ContU}(\mathcal{L})$-oracle.*

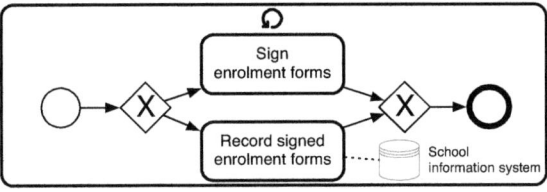

Fig. 4. Simplified BPMN process for the everyday activity of a secretary in a school

Proof. If $s \not\models \text{Compl}(Q)$, one can guess a normal action sequence α, check by Prop. 4 in polynomial time that there exists a path π from s_0 to s with α as normal action sequence, and by Thm. 1 verify using the $ContU(\mathcal{L})$-oracle that α does not satisfy $\text{Compl}(Q)$. □

We discuss the complexity of this problem in Section 4.4

4.2 Runtime Verification

Taking into account the concrete activities that were carried out within a process can allow more conclusions about completeness. As an example, consider that the secretary in a large school can perform two activities regarding the enrollments, either he/she can sign enrollment applications (which means that the enrollments become legally valid), or he/she can record the signed enrollments that are not yet recorded in the database. For simplicity we assume that the secretary batches the tasks and performs only one of the activities per day. A visualization of this process is shown in Fig. 4. Considering only the process we cannot draw any conclusions about the completeness of the enrollment data, because if the secretary chose the first activity, then data will be missing, however if the secretary chose the second activity, then not. If however we have the information that the secretary performed the second activity, then we can conclude that the number of the currently valid enrollments is also complete in the information system.

Formally, in runtime verification we are given a path $\pi = t_1, \ldots, t_n$ that was executed so far and a query Q. Again the problem is to check whether completeness holds in the current state, that is, whether all developments of π satisfy $\text{Compl}(Q)$.

Corollary 2. *Let π be a path in a QATS and Q be a query, such that both Q and the real-world effects and the copy effects in the actions of π are formulated in a query language $\mathcal{L}$. Then "$\pi \models \text{Compl}(Q)$?" and $ContU(\mathcal{L})$ can be reduced to each other in linear time.*

The corollary follows directly from Theorem 1 and the fact that a path satisfies completeness if and only if its action sequence satisfies completeness.

Runtime verification becomes more complex when also the current, concrete state of the information system database is explicitly taken into account. Given the current state D of the database, the problem is then to check whether all the developments of π in which $D_n^{is} = D$ holds satisfy $\text{Compl}(Q)$. In this case repairing of all risky actions is a sufficient but not a necessary condition for completeness:

Example 7. Consider a path $(s_0, a_1, s_1), (s_1, a_2, s_2)$, where action a_1 is annotated with the copy effect $request^{rw}(n, s) \rightarrow request^{is}(n, s)$, action a_2 with the real-world effect

school	pupils_nr
Hoferschule	217
"Da Vinci"	254
"Max Valier"	151
"Gherdena"	19

school	pupils_nr	Completeness
Hoferschule	217	Yes
"Da Vinci"	254	Yes
"Max Valier"	151	No
"Gherdena"	19	No
?	?	No

Fig. 5. Visualization of the dimension analysis of Example 8

$pupil^{rw}(n, c, s) \leftsquigarrow request^{rw}(n, s)$, a database D_2^{is} that is empty, and consider a query $Q(n) :- pupil(n, c, s), request(n, s)$. Then, the query result over D_2^{is} is empty. Since the relation *request* was copied before, and is empty now, the query result over any real-world database must be empty too, and therefore Compl(Q) holds. Note that this cannot be concluded with the techniques introduced in this work, as the real-world effect of action a_2 is risky and is not repaired.

The complexity of runtime verification w.r.t. a concrete database instance is still open.

4.3 Dimension Analysis

When at a certain timepoint a query is not found to be complete, for example because the deadline for the submissions of the enrollments from the schools to the central school administration is not yet over, it becomes interesting to know which parts of the answer are already complete.

Example 8. Consider that on the 10th of April, the schools "Hofer" and "Da Vinci" have confirmed that they have already submitted all their enrollments, while "Max Valier" and "Gherdena" have entered some but not all enrollments, and other schools did not enter any enrollments so far. Then the result of a query asking for the number of pupils per school would look as in Fig. 5 (left table), which does not tell anything about the trustworthiness of the result. If one includes the information from the process, one could highlight that the data for the former two schools is already complete, and that there can also be additional schools in the query result which did not submit any data so far (see right table in Fig. 5).

Formally, for a query Q a dimension is a set of distinguished variables of Q. Originally, dimension analysis was meant especially for the arguments of a GROUP BY expression in a query, however it can also be used with other distinguished variables of a query. Assume a query $Q(\bar{x}) :- B(\bar{x}, \bar{y})$ cannot be guaranteed to be complete in a specific state of a process. For a dimension $\bar{w} \subseteq \bar{x}$, the analysis can be done as follows:

1. Calculate the result of $Q'(\bar{w}) :- B(\bar{x}, \bar{y})$ over D^{is}.
2. For each tuple $\bar{c}$ in $Q'(D^{is})$, check whether $s, D^{is} \models \text{Compl}(Q[\bar{w}/\bar{c}])$. This tells whether the query is complete for the values $\bar{c}$ of the dimension.
3. To check whether further values are possible, one has to guess a new value $\bar{c}_{new}$ for the dimension and show that $Q[\bar{w}/\bar{c}_{new}]$ is not complete in the current state. For the guess one has to consider only the constants in the database plus a fixed set of new constants, hence the number of possible guesses is polynomial for a fixed dimension $\bar{v}$.

Query/QATS language $\mathcal{L}$	Complexity of $ContU(\mathcal{L})$ and $EntC(\mathcal{L})$ ("$\pi \models Compl(Q)$"?)	Complexity of "$s \models Compl(Q)$"?
Linear relational queries	PTIME	in coNP
Linear conjunctive queries	coNP-complete	coNP-complete
Relational conjunctive queries	NP-complete	in Π_2^P
Relational conjunctive queries over databases with finite domains	Π_2^P-complete	Π_2^P-complete
Conjunctive queries with comparisons	Π_2^P-complete	Π_2^P-complete
Relational conjunctive queries over databases with keys and foreign keys	in PSPACE	in PSPACE

Fig. 6. Complexity of design-time and runtime verification for different query languages

Step 2 corresponds to deciding for each tuple with a certain value in $Q(D^{is})$, whether it is complete or not (color red or green in Fig. 5, right table), Step 3 to deciding whether there can be additional values (bottom row in Fig. 5, right table).

4.4 Complexity of Completeness Verification

In the previous sections we have seen that completeness verification can be solved using query containment. Query containment is a problem that has been studied extensively in database research. Basically, it is the problem to decide, given two queries, whether the first is more specific than the second. The results follow from Theorem 1 and 2, and are summarized in Figure 6. We distinguish between the problem of runtime verification, which has the same complexity as query containment, and design-time verification, which, in principle requires to solve query containment exponentially often. Notable however is that in most cases the complexity of runtime verification is not higher than the one of design-time verification. The results on linear relational and linear conjunctive queries, i.e., conjunctive queries without selfjoins and without or with comparisons, are borrowed from [12]. The result on relational queries is reported in [15], and that on conjunctive queries from [11]. As for integrity constraints, the result for databases satisfying finite domain constraints is reported in [12] and for databases satisfying keys and foreign keys in [8].

5 Conclusion

In this paper we have discussed that data completeness analysis should take into account the processes that manipulate the data. In particular, we have shown how process models can be annotated with effects that create data in the real world and effects that copy data from the real world into an information system. We have then shown how one can verify the completeness of queries over transition systems that represent the execution semantics of such processes. It was shown that the problem is closely related to the problem of query containment, and that more completeness can be derived if the run of the process is taken into account.

In this work we focussed on the process execution semantics in terms of transition systems. The next step is to realize a demonstration system to annotate high-level business process specification languages (such as BPMN or YAWL), extract the underlying quality-aware transition systems, and apply the techniques here presented to check completeness. Also, we intend to face the open question of completeness verification at runtime taking into account the actual database instance.

Acknowledgements. This work was partially supported by the ESF Project 2-299-2010 "SIS - Wir verbinden Menschen", and by the EU Project FP7-257593 ACSI. We are thankful to Alin Deutsch for an invitation that helped initiate this research, and to the anonymous reviewers for helpful comments.

References

1. Abiteboul, S., Hull, R., Vianu, V.: Foundations of Databases. Addison-Wesley (1995)
2. Bagchi, S., Bai, X., Kalagnanam, J.: Data quality management using business process modeling. In: IEEE International Conference on Services Computing, SCC 2006 (2006)
3. Bagheri Hariri, B., Calvanese, D., De Giacomo, G., De Masellis, R., Felli, P.: Foundations of relational artifacts verification. In: Rinderle-Ma, S., Toumani, F., Wolf, K. (eds.) BPM 2011. LNCS, vol. 6896, pp. 379–395. Springer, Heidelberg (2011)
4. Bagheri Hariri, B., Calvanese, D., De Giacomo, G., Deutsch, A., Montali, M.: Verification of relational data-centric dynamic systems with external services. In: PODS (2013)
5. Baier, C., Katoen, J.P.: Principles of Model Checking. The MIT Press (2008)
6. Bilenko, M., Mooney, R.J.: Adaptive duplicate detection using learnable string similarity measures. In: ACM SIGKDD, pp. 39–48 (2003)
7. Bringel, H., Caetano, A., Tribolet, J.M.: Business process modeling towards data quality: A organizational engineering approach. In: ICEIS, vol. (3) (2004)
8. Calì, A., Lembo, D., Rosati, R.: Query rewriting and answering under constraints in data integration systems. In: IJCAI 2003, pp. 16–21 (2003)
9. Damaggio, E., Deutsch, A., Hull, R., Vianu, V.: Automatic verification of data-centric business processes. In: Rinderle-Ma, S., Toumani, F., Wolf, K. (eds.) BPM 2011. LNCS, vol. 6896, pp. 3–16. Springer, Heidelberg (2011)
10. Hernández, M.A., Stolfo, S.J.: Real-world data is dirty: Data cleansing and the merge/purge problem. Data Mining and Knowledge Discovery 2(1), 9–37 (1998)
11. van der Meyden, R.: The complexity of querying indefinite data about linearly ordered domains. In: PODS, pp. 331–345 (1992)
12. Razniewski, S., Nutt, W.: Completeness of queries over incomplete databases. In: VLDB (2011)
13. Razniewski, S., Montali, M., Nutt, W.: Verification of query completeness over processes [Extended version] (2013), http://arxiv.org/abs/1306.1689
14. Rodríguez, A., Caro, A., Cappiello, C., Caballero, I.: A BPMN extension for including data quality requirements in business process modeling. In: Mendling, J., Weidlich, M. (eds.) BPMN 2012. LNBIP, vol. 125, pp. 116–125. Springer, Heidelberg (2012)
15. Sagiv, Y., Yannakakis, M.: Equivalence among relational expressions with the union and difference operation. In: VLDB, pp. 535–548 (1978)

Modeling and Enacting Complex Data Dependencies in Business Processes

Andreas Meyer[1], Luise Pufahl[1], Dirk Fahland[2], and Mathias Weske[1]

[1] Hasso Plattner Institute at the University of Potsdam
{Andreas.Meyer,Luise.Pufahl,Mathias.Weske}@hpi.uni-potsdam.de
[2] Eindhoven University of Technology
d.fahland@tue.nl

Abstract. Enacting business processes in process engines requires the coverage of control flow, resource assignments, and process data. While the first two aspects are well supported in current process engines, data dependencies need to be added and maintained manually by a process engineer. Thus, this task is error-prone and time-consuming. In this paper, we address the problem of modeling processes with complex data dependencies, e.g., m:n relationships, and their automatic enactment from process models. First, we extend BPMN data objects with few annotations to allow data dependency handling as well as data instance differentiation. Second, we introduce a pattern-based approach to derive SQL queries from process models utilizing the above mentioned extensions. Therewith, we allow automatic enactment of data-aware BPMN process models. We implemented our approach for the Activiti process engine to show applicability.

Keywords: Process Modeling, Data Modeling, Process Enactment, BPMN, SQL.

1 Motivation

The purpose of enacting processes in process engines or process-aware information systems is to query, process, transform, and provide data to process stakeholders. Process engines such as Activiti [4], Bonita [5] or AristaFlow [12] are able to enact the control flow of a process and to allocate required resources based on a given process model in an automated fashion. Also simple data dependencies can be enacted from a process model, for example, that an activity can only be executed if a particular data object is in a particular state. However, when *m:n relationships* arise between processes and data objects, modeling and enactment becomes more difficult.

For example, Fig. 1 shows a typical *build-to-order process* of a computer manufacturer in which customers order products that will be custom built. For an incoming *Customer order*, the manufacturer devises all *Components* needed to build the product. Components are not held in stock, but the manufacturer on demand creates and executes a number of *Purchase orders* to be sent to various *Suppliers* to procure the Components required. To reduce costs, Components of multiple Customer orders are bundled in joint Purchase orders. The two subprocesses of Fig. 1 handle complex m:n relationships between the different orders: one Purchase order contains Components of multiple Customer orders and one Customer order depends on Components of multiple Purchase orders.

Widely accepted process modeling languages such as BPMN [17] do not provide sufficient modeling concepts for capturing m:n relationships between data objects, activities, and processes. As a consequence, actual data dependencies are often not derived from a process model. They are rather implemented manually in services and application code, which yields high development efforts and may lead to errors.

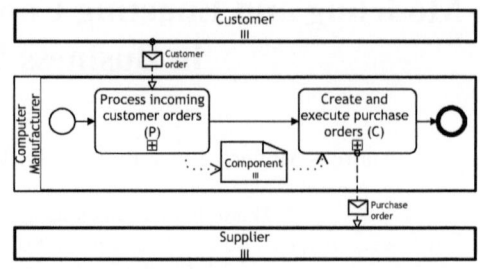

Fig. 1. Build-to-order process, where subprocess P collects multiple orders from several Customers in an internal loop and where C sends multiple Purchase orders to several Suppliers using a multi instance subprocess internally

Explicitly adding data dependencies to process models provides multiple advantages. In contrast to having data only specified inside services and applications called from the process, an integrated view facilitates *communication with stakeholders* about processes and their data manipulations; there are *no hidden dependencies*. With execution semantics one can *automatically enact* processes with complex data dependencies from a model only. Finally, an integrated conceptual model allows for *analyzing control and data flow combined* regarding their consistency [11, 24] and correctness. Also *different process representations can be generated automatically*, for instance, models showing how a data object evolves throughout a process [9, 13].

Existing techniques for integrating data and control flow follow the "object-centric" paradigm [3, 6, 10, 15]: a process is modeled by its involved objects; each one has a life cycle and multiple objects synchronize on their state changes. This paradigm is beneficial when process flow follows from process objects, e.g., in manufacturing processes [15]. However, there are many domains, where processes are rather "activity-centric" such as accounting, insurance handling, or municipal procedures. In these, execution follows an explicitly prescribed ordering of domain activities, not necessarily tied to a particular object life cycle. For such processes, changing from an activity-centric view to an object-centric view for the sake of data support has disadvantages. Besides having to redesign all processes in a new paradigm and training process modelers, one also has to switch to new process engines and may no longer be supported by existing standards. This gives rise to a first requirement (**RQ1-activity**): processes can be modeled in an activity-centric way using well-established industrial standards for describing process dynamics and data dependencies.

In this paper, we address the problem of modeling and enacting *activity-centric* processes with complex data dependencies. The problem itself was researched for more than a decade revealing numerous requirements as summarized in [10]. The following requirements of [10] have to be met to enact activity-centric processes with complex data dependencies directly from a process model:

(**RQ2-data integration**) The process model refers to data in terms of object types, defines pre- and post-conditions for activities (cf. requirements R01 and R14 in [10]), and

(**RQ3-object behavior**) expresses how data objects change (cf. R04 in [10])

(**RQ4-object interaction**) in relation and interaction with other data objects; objects are in 1:1, 1:n, or m:n relationships. Thereby, process execution depends on the state of its interrelated data objects (cf. R05 in [10]) and

(**RQ5-variable granularity**) an activity changes a single object, multiple related objects of different types, or multiple objects of the same type (cf. R17 in [10]).

In this paper, we propose a technique that addresses the requirements (RQ1)-(RQ5). The technique combines classical activity-centric modeling in BPMN [17] with relational data modeling as known from relational databases [21]. To this end, we introduce few extensions to BPMN data objects: Each data object gets dedicated life cycle information, an object identifier, and fields to express any type of correlation, even m:n relationships, to other objects with identifiers. We build on BPMN's extension points ensuring conformance to the specification [17]. These data annotations define pre- and post-conditions of activities with respect to data. We show how to automatically derive SQL queries from annotated BPMN data objects that check and implement the conditions on data stored in a relational database. For demonstration, we extended the Activiti process engine [4] to automatically derive SQL queries from data-annotated BPMN models.

The remainder of this paper is structured as follows. In Section 2, we discuss the current data modeling capabilities of BPMN including shortcomings. Then, in Section 3, we present our technique for data-aware process modeling with BPMN, which we give operational semantics in Section 4. There, we also discuss the SQL derivation and our implementation before we review related work in Section 5 and conclude in Section 6.

2 Data Modeling in BPMN

BPMN [17], a rich and expressive modeling notation, is the industry standard for business process management and provides means for modeling as well as execution of business processes. In this section, we introduce BPMN's existing capabilities for data modeling and its shortcomings with respect to the requirements introduced above.

So far, we used the term "data object" with a loose interpretation in mind. For the remainder, we use the terminology of BPMN [17], which provides the concept of *data objects* to describe different types of data in a process. Data flow edges describe which activities read or write which data objects. The same data object may be *represented* multiple times in the process distinguishing distinct read or write accesses. A data flow edge from a *data object representation* to an activity describes a read access to an *instance* of the data object, which has to be present in order to execute the activity. A data object instance is a concrete data entry of the corresponding data object. A data flow edge from an activity to a data object representation describes a write access, which creates a data object instance, if it did not exist, or updates the instance, if it existed before. Fig. 2 shows two representations of data object D, one is read by activity A and one is written. Data object representations can be modeled as a *single instance* or as a *multi instance* (indicated by three parallel bars) that comprises a set of instances of one data object. Further, a data object can be either *persistent* (stored in a database) or *non-persistent* (exists only while the process instance is active). Our approach focuses on persistent single and multi instance data objects.

The notion of an *object life cycle* emerged over the last years for giving data objects a behavior. The idea is that each data object D can be in a number of different states. A process activity A reading D may only get enabled if D is in a particular state; when A is executed object D may transition to a new state. To express this behavior, BPMN provides the concept of *data states*, which allows to annotate each data object with a *[state]*. Fig. 2 shows an example: Activity A may only be executed when the respective object instance is indeed in *state X*; after executing the activity, this object instance is in *state Y*.

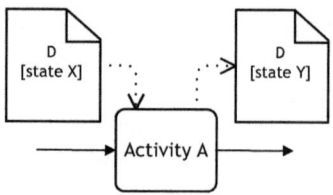

Fig. 2. Object life cycle of data object D with two representations

The BPMN semantics is not sufficient to express all data dependencies in a process model with respect to the following four aspects. The annotations to data object representations in Fig. 2 do not allow to distinguish different object instances of D in the same process instance, e.g., two different customer orders. Likewise, we cannot express how several instances of different data objects relate to each other. Further, the type of a write access on data objects, e.g., creation or update, is not clear from the annotations shown above. Finally, the correlation between a process instance and its object instances is not supported. Next, we propose a set of extensions to BPMN data objects to overcome the presented shortcomings.

3 Extending BPMN Data Modeling

In this section, we introduce annotations to BPMN data objects to overcome the shortcomings utilizing *extension points*, which allow to extend BPMN and still being standard conform. With these, we address requirements (RQ1)-(RQ5) from the introduction. In the second part, we illustrate the extensions on a build-to-order process.

3.1 Modeling Data Dependencies in BPMN

To distinguish and reference data object instances, we utilize proven concepts from relational databases: primary and foreign keys [21]. We introduce *object identifiers* as an annotation that describes the attribute by which different data object instances can be distinguished (i.e., primary keys). Along the same lines, we introduce attributes, which allow to refer to the identifier of another object (cf. foreign keys in [21]).

Fig. 3 shows annotations for primary key (pk) and foreign key (fk) attributes in BPMN data object representations. Instances of D are distinguishable by attribute d_id and instances of E by attribute e_id. In Fig. 3a, each instance of D is related to one instance of E by the fk attribute e_id, i.e., a 1:1 relationship. The activity A can only execute when one instance e of E is in *state Z* and one instance d of D is in *state X* that is related to e exist. Upon execution, d enters *state Y* whereas e remains unchanged. A *multi instance* representation of D expresses a 1:n relationship from E to D as shown in Fig. 3b, e.g., several computer components for one customer order. To execute activity A, *all* instances of D

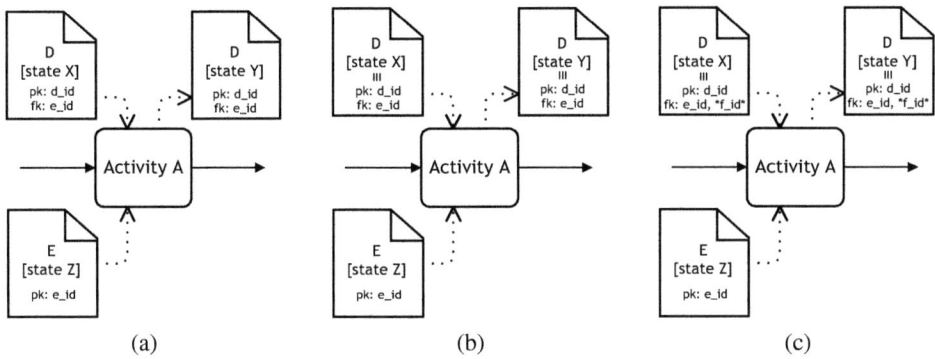

Fig. 3. Describing object interactions in (a) 1:1, (b) 1:n, and (c) m:n cardinality

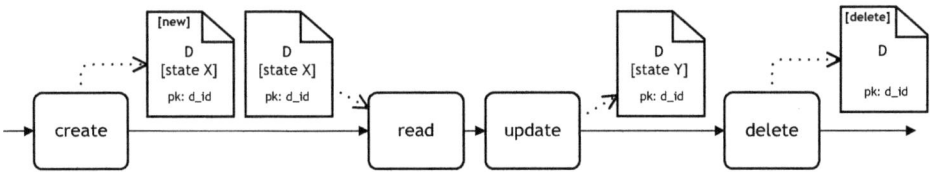

Fig. 4. Describing create, read, update, and delete of a data object

related to e have to be in *state X*; the execution will put all instances of D into *state Y*. We allow *multi-attribute foreign keys* to express m:n relationships between data objects as follows. Assume, data objects D, E, F have primary keys d_id, e_id, f_id, respectively, and D has foreign key attributes e_id, f_id. Each instance of D (e.g., a component) refers to one instance of E (e.g., a customer order it originated from) and one instance of F (e.g., a purchase order in which it is handled). Different instances of D may refer to the same instance e of E (e.g., all components of the same customer order) but to different instances of F (e.g., handled by different purchase orders) and vice versa. This yields an m:n relationship between E and F via D. We allow to *all-quantify* over foreign keys by enclosing them in asterisks, e.g., *$*f\_id*$* in Fig. 3c. Here, activity A updates *all instances* of D from *state X* to *state Y* if they are related to the instance e of E and to any instance of F, that is, we quantify over *$*f\_id*$*. A foreign key attribute can be *null* indicating that the specific reference is not yet set. A data object may have further attributes, however, these are not specified in the object itself but in a data model, possibly given as UML class diagram [18], accompanying the process model.

In order to derive all data dependencies from a process model, we need to be able to express the four major data operations: *create, read, update,* and *delete* for a data object instance (see Fig. 4). Read and update are already provided through BPMN's data flow edges. To express create or delete operations, we need to add two annotations shown in the upper right corner: *[new]* expresses the creation of a new data object instance having a completely fresh identifier and *[delete]* expresses its deletion. Note that one activity can apply several data operations to different data objects. For example, activity A in Fig. 3a reads and updates an instance of D and reads an instance of E.

The introduced extensions require that a data object contains a *name* and a set of attributes, from which one needs to describe a *data state*, an *object identifier* (primary key), and a *set of relations* to other data objects (foreign keys). Fig. 5 summarizes these extensions for a data object representation. Based on the informal considerations above, we formally define such extended representation of a BPMN data object as follows.

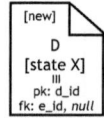

Fig. 5. Extended data object representation

Definition 1 (Data object representation). A *data object representation* $r = (name, state, pk, FK, FK^*, \eta, \omega)$ refers to the *name* of the data object, has a *state*, a *primary key* (pk), a finite set FK of *foreign keys*, a set $FK^* \subseteq FK$ of all-quantified foreign keys, and a data operation type $\eta \in \{new, delete, \bot\}$. $\omega \in \{singleInstance, multiInstance\}$ defines the instance multiplicity property. ◇

$\bot$ as element of set η refers to a blank data operation description for which the data access is derived from the data flow: an input data flow requires a read operation while an output data flow requires an update operation.

To let a specific *process instance* create or update specific data object instances, we need to link these two. For this, we adopt an idea from business artifacts [16] that each process instance is "driven" by a specific data object instance. We call this object *case object*; all other objects have to be related to it by means of foreign keys. This idea naturally extends to instances of subprocesses or multi-instance activities. Each of them defines a *scope* which has a dedicated instance id. An annotation in a scope defines which data object acts as case object. A case object instance is either freshly created by its scope instance based on a *new* annotation (the object instance gets the id of its scope instance as primary key value). Alternatively, the case object instance already exists and is passed to the scope instance upon creation (the scope instance gets the id of its case object instance). By all means, a case object is always *single instance*. For this paper, we assume that all non case objects are *directly* related to the case object; see our technical report [14] for the general case. We make data objects and case objects part of the process model as follows, utilizing a subset of BPMN [17].

Definition 2 (Process model). A *process model* $M = (N, R, DS, C, F, P, type_A, case, type_G, \kappa)$ consists of a finite non-empty set $N \subseteq A \cup G \cup E$ of *nodes* being *activities* A, *gateways* G, and *events* E, a finite non-empty set R of *data object representations*, and the finite set DS of *data stores* used for persistence of data objects (N, R, DS are pairwise disjoint). $C \subseteq N \times N$ is the *control flow* relation, $F \subseteq (A \times R) \cup (R \times A)$ is the *data flow* relation, and $P \subseteq (R \times DS) \cup (DS \times R)$ is the *data persistence* relation; $type_A : A \rightarrow \{task, subprocess, multiInstanceTask, multiInstanceSubprocess\}$ gives each activity a type; $case(a)$ defines for each $a \in A$ where $type_A(a) \neq task$ the case object. Function $type_G : G \rightarrow \{xor, and\}$ gives each gateway a type; partial function $\kappa : F \nrightarrow exp$ optionally assigns an expression exp to a data flow edge. ◇

An expression at a data flow edge allows to refer to data attributes that are neither state nor key attribute, as we show later. As usual, a process model M is assumed to be structural sound, i.e., M contains exactly one start and one end event and every node of M is on a path from the start to the end event. Further, each activity has at most one incoming and one outgoing control flow edge.

3.2 Example

In this section, we apply the syntax introduced above to model the build-to-order scenario presented in the introduction. The scenario consists of two interlinked process models and the corresponding data model. The scenario comprises the collection of customer orders, presented in Fig. 7, and the arrangement of purchase orders based on the customer orders received, presented in Fig. 8. Each customer order can be fulfilled by a set of purchase orders and each purchase order consolidates the components required for several customer orders. This m:n relationship is expressed in the data model in Fig. 6.

Data Model. The *processing cycle* (ProC) contains information about *customer orders* (CO) being placed by customers and *purchase orders* (PO) used to organize the purchase of components within a particular time frame. Data object *component* (CP) links CO

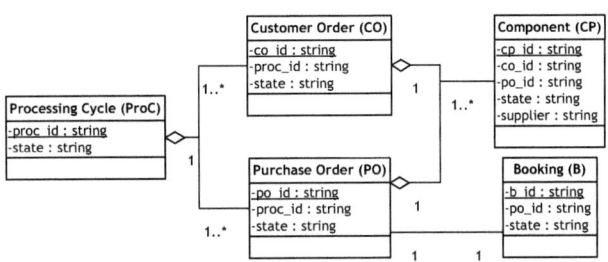

Fig. 6. Data model

and PO in an m:n-fashion, i.e., CP has two foreign keys, one to CO and one to PO. CO and PO each have one foreign key to ProC. Accounting of the manufacturer is performed utilizing data object *booking* (B). For simplicity, we assume that all data is persisted in the same data store, e.g., the database of the manufacturer, and omit representations of the data store in the process diagrams.

Customer Order Collection Process. In Fig. 7, the first task starts a new processing cycle allowing customers to send in orders for computers. By annotation *new*, a new ProC object instance is created for each task execution. As this is the case object of the process, the primary key *proc_id* gets the id of the process instance as value. Next, COs are collected in a loop structure until three COs have been successfully processed. Task *Receive customer order* receives one CO from a customer and correlates this CO instance to the ProC instance of the process instance (annotation *fk: proc_id*) before it is analyzed in a subprocess. CO is the case object of the subprocess, which gets its instance id from the primary key of the received CO instance. Task *Create component list* determines the components needed to handle the CO: several CP instances are

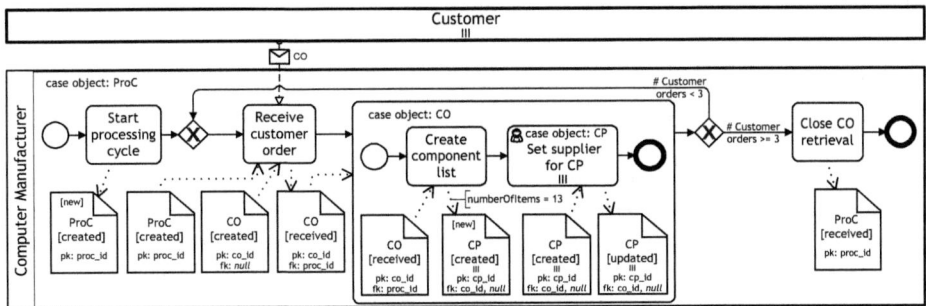

Fig. 7. Build-to-order scenario: customer order collection

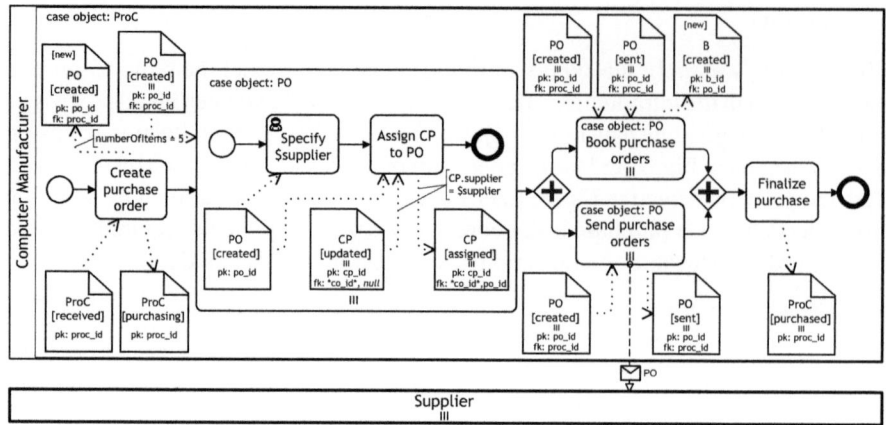

Fig. 8. Build-to-order scenario: purchase order arrangement

created (annotation *new* on a multi instance object representation). Each CP instance has a unique primary key value; the foreign key attribute *co_id* referring to CO is set to the current CO instance; the foreign key attribute referring to PO is still *null*. The number of CP instances to create is given in the expression on the data output flow edge. Here, we give an explicit number, but it could also be a process variable holding the result of the task execution (e.g., user input, result of a service invocation). Next, an user updates the attribute *CP.supplier* for each component (CP) to indicate where it can be purchased, e.g., by using a form. The loop structure is conducted for each received CO and repeated until three COs are collected. CO retrieval is closed by moving the current ProC to state *received*.

Purchase Order Arrangement Process. The second process model in Fig. 8 describes how components (extracted from different COs) are associated to purchase orders (POs), building an m:n relationship between POs and COs. Object ProC links both processes, the process in Fig. 8 can only start when there is a ProC object instance in state *received*.

Create purchase order creates multiple PO object instances correlated to the ProC instance. All PO instances are handled in the subsequent multi instance subprocess: for each PO instance one subprocess instance is created, having the PO instance as case object and the corresponding *po_id* value as instance identifier. Per PO, first, one supplier is selected that will handle the PO; here we assume that the task *Select supplier* sets a process variable *$supplier* local to the subprocess instance. Task *Assign CP to PO* relates to the PO *all* CP instances in state *updated* that have no *po_id* value yet and where attribute *CP.supplier* equals the chosen *$supplier*. The relation is built by setting the value of *CP.po_id* to the primary key *PO.po_id* of the case object. The update quantifies over all values of *co_id* as indicated by the asterisks.

The execution of the multi instance subprocess results in several CP subsets each being related to one PO. The POs along with the contained information about the CPs are sent to the corresponding supplier. In parallel, *Book purchase orders* creates a new booking for each PO; it may start when either all POs are in *created* or in *sent*.

Object Life Cycle. Altogether, our extension to BPMN data objects increases the expressiveness of a BPMN process model with information about process-data-correlation on instance level. As such, it does not interfere with standard BPMN semantics.

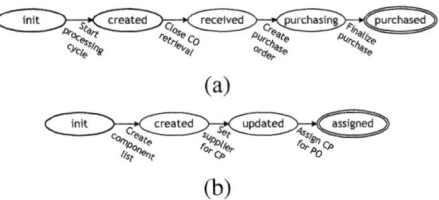

Fig. 9. Object life cycles of objects (a) *ProC* and (b) *CP* derived from the process model

In addition, our extension is compatible with the object life cycle oriented techniques allowing to derive object life cycles from sufficiently annotated process models [9,13]. Taking our build-to-order process, we can derive the object life cycles shown in Fig. 9.

4 Executing Data-Annotated BPMN Models

This section presents *operational execution semantics* for the data annotated process models defined in Section 3. Aiming at standardized techniques, we *refine* the standard BPMN semantics [17, Section 13] with SQL database queries (see Section 4.1) that are derived from annotated input and output data objects (see Section 4.2).

4.1 Process Model Semantics

Our semantics distinguishes control flow and data flow aspects of a process model M. A *state* $s = (C, \mathcal{D})$ of M consists of a control flow state C describing a distribution of tokens on sequence flow edges and activities and a database $\mathcal{D}$ storing the data objects of M in tables. To distinguish the states of different process instances, each token in C is an identifier id. The data model of the process is implemented in a relational database $\mathcal{D}$ (shared by all processes). Each data object is represented in $\mathcal{D}$ as a table; columns represent attributes, having at least columns for primary key, foreign keys (if any), and state. Each row in a table describes an instance of this data object with concrete values.

An activity A has several input and output data object representations, grouped into *input sets* and *output sets*; different input/output sets represent alternative pre-/postconditions for A. A representation R of an input object is *available* in instance id if the corresponding table in $\mathcal{D}$ holds a particular row. We can define a *select* query $Q_R(id)$ on $\mathcal{D}$ and a guard $g_R(id)$ that compares the result of $Q_R(id)$ to a constant or to another select query; $g_R(id)$ is *true* iff R is available in id. A representation R of an output object of A has to become available when A completes. We operationalize this by executing an *insert*, *update*, or *delete* query $Q_R(id)$ on $\mathcal{D}$ depending on R.

Activity A is *enabled* in instance id in state $s = (C, \mathcal{D})$ iff a token with id id is on the input edge of A and for some input set $\{R_1, \ldots, R_n\}$ of A, each guard $g_{R_i}(id)$ is *true*. If A is enabled in C, then A gets *started*, i.e., the token id moves "inside" A in step $(C, \mathcal{D}) \to (C', \mathcal{D})$ and depending on the type of activity services are called, forms are shown, etc. When this instance of A *completes*, the outgoing edge of A gets a token id and the database gets updated in a step $(C', \mathcal{D}) \to (C'', \mathcal{D}')$, where $\mathcal{D}'$ is the result of executing queries $Q_{R_1}(id), \ldots, Q_{R_m}(id)$ for some output set $\{R_1, \ldots, R_m\}$ of A. The semantics for gateways and events is extended correspondingly. If activity A is a subprocess with case object D, and A has D as data input object, then we create a *new instance* of subprocess A for each entry returned by query $Q_D(id)$. Each subprocess instance is identified by the primary key value of the corresponding row of D. Next, we explain how to derive queries from the data object representations.

4.2 Deriving Database Queries from Data Annotations

The annotated data object representations defined in Section 3 describe pre- and post-conditions for the execution of activities. In this section, we show how to derive from a data object representation R (and its context) a guard g_R or a query Q_R that realizes this pre- or post-condition.

In a combinatorial analysis, we considered the occurrence of a data object as *case object*, as single dependent object with 1:1 relationship to another object, and as multiple dependent object with 1:n or m:n relationship in the context of a *create, read, update,* and *delete* operation. Additionally, we considered process instantiation based on existing data and reading/updating object attributes other than state. Altogether, we obtained a complete collection of *43 parameterized patterns* regarding the use of data objects as pre- or post-conditions in BPMN [14]. For each of these patterns, we defined a corresponding database query or guard. During process execution, each input/output object is matched against the patterns. The guard/query of the matching pattern is then used as described in Section 4.1. Here, we present the five patterns that are needed to execute the subprocess in the model in Fig. 8; Tables 1 and 2 list the patterns and their formalization that we explain next. All 43 patterns and their formalization are given in our technical report [14].

As introduced in Section 3, we assume that each scope (e.g., subprocess) is driven by a particular case object. Each scope instance has a dedicated instance id. The symbol $ID refers to the instance id of the directly enclosing scope; $PID refers to the process instance id.

Read Single Object Instance. Pattern 1 describes a read operation on a single data object D1 that is also the case object of the scope. The activity is only enabled when this case object is in the given state s. The guard shown below P1 in Table 1 operationalizes this behavior: it is *true* iff table D1 in the database has a row where the state attribute has value 's' and the primary key $d1\_id$ is equal to the scope instance id.

Read Multiple Object Instances. Pattern 2 describes a read operation on multiple data object instances of D2 that are linked to the case object D1 via foreign key $d1\_id$. The activity is only enabled when all instances of D2 are in the given state t. This is captured by the guard shown below P2 in Table 1 that is *true* iff the rows in table D2 that are linked to the D1 instance with primary key value $ID are also the rows in table D2 where state = 't' (and the same link to D1); see [14] for the general case of arbitrary tables between D1 and D2. For example, consider the second process of the build-to-order scenario (see Fig. 8). Let us assume that activity *Create purchase order* was just executed for process instance 6 and the database table of the purchase order (PO) contains the entries shown in Fig. 10a. All rows with $proc\_id = 6$ are in state *created*, i.e., both queries of pattern 2 yield the same result and the subprocess gets instantiated.

Instantiate Subprocesses from Data. Pattern 3 deals with the instantiation of a multi instance subprocess combined with a read operation on the dependent multi instance

Table 1. SQL queries for patterns 1 to 3 for subprocess in Fig. 8

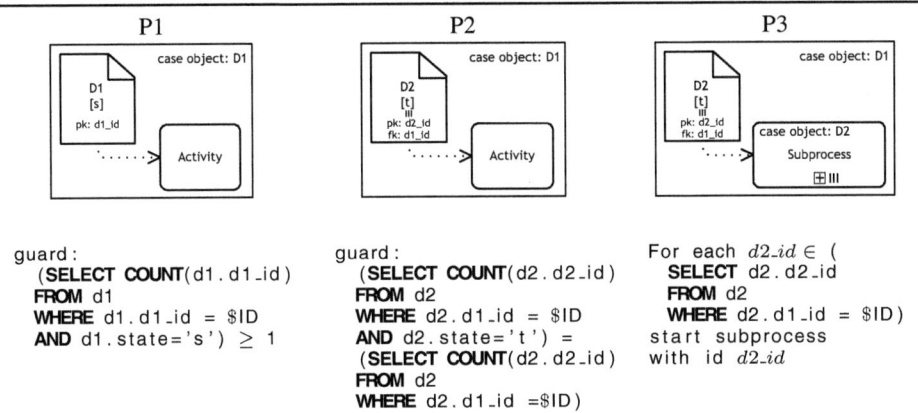

Table 2. SQL queries for patterns 4 and 5 for subprocess in Fig. 8

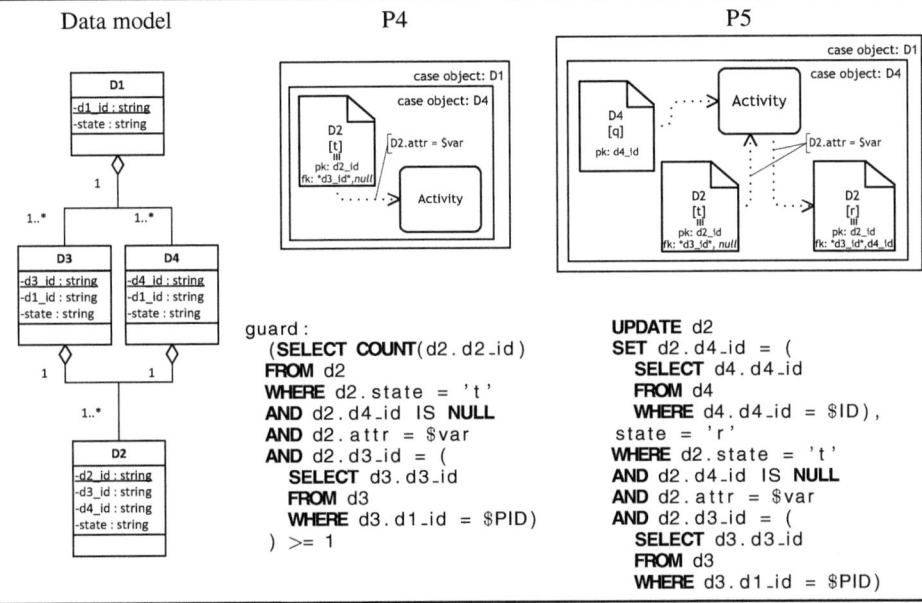

data object D2. As described in Section 4.1, we create a new instance of the subprocess for each id returned by the query shown below P3 in Table 1. For our example, where process instance 6 is currently executed, the subprocess having the PO as case object is instantiated twice, once with id 17 and once with id 18. In each subprocess instance, control flow reaches activity *Select supplier* for which pattern 1 applies. For the subprocess instance with id 17, the guard of Pattern 1 evaluates to true of the state in Fig. 10a: activity *Select Supplier* is enabled.

Transactional Properties. Patterns 4 and 5 illustrate how our approach updates m:n-relationships. Pattern 4 describes a read operation on multiple data object instances D2 that share a particular attribute value and are *not* related to the case object (in contrast

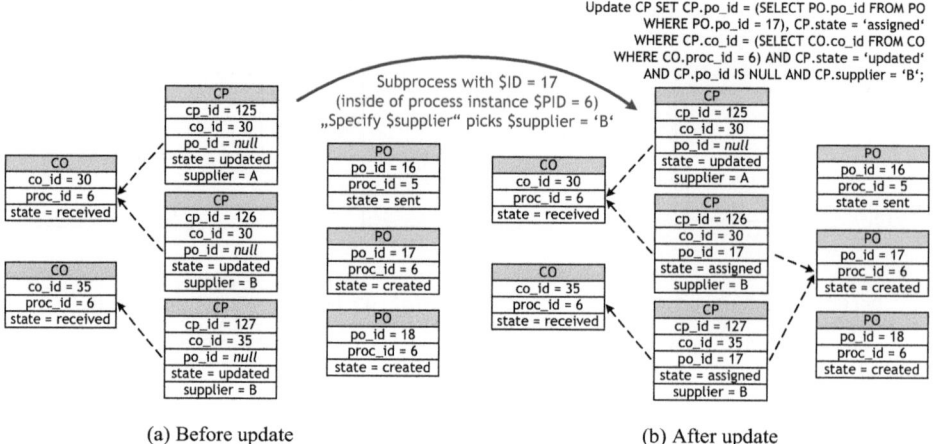

Fig. 10. Setting missing foreign key relation of m:n object *Component*: Concrete update statement of subprocess 17 to relate all CPs referring to supplier B to the PO with ID 17 indicated by arrows

to Pattern 2). We have to ensure that another process instance does not interfere with reading (and later updating) these instances of D2, that is, we have to provide *basic transactional properties*. We achieve this by accessing only those instances of D2 that are in some way related to the current process instance. Therefore, this read operation assumes a data model as shown in Table 2(left): D2 defines an m:n relationship between D3 and D4 via foreign keys d3_id and d4_id; D3 and D4 both have foreign keys to D1 which is the case object of the process; see [14] for the general case. The guard shown below P4 in Table 2 is true iff there is at least one instance of D2 in state t, with a particular attribute value, not linked to D4, and where the link to D3 points to an instance that itself is linked to the case object instance of the process (i.e., foreign key of D3 points to $PID). The link to D3 ensures that the process instance only reads D2 instances and no other process instance can read. In our example, the pattern occurs at task *Assign CP to PO* reading all instances of object component (CP), which are not yet assigned to a PO (i.e., *null* value as foreign key) and where $CP.supplier = \$supplier$. Assume the state shown in Fig. 10a and that $\$supplier = B$ was set by task *Select $supplier* for the subprocess instance with ID 17. In this state, the queries of pattern 4 return two rows having a *null* value for *po_id*, B as supplier value, and *updated* as state value: the activity is enabled.

Updating m:n Relationships. Finally, pattern 5 describes an update operation on multiple data object instances of D2, which sets the foreign key d4_id that is not set yet and moves them to state r. All instances of D2 get as value for d4_id the instance id of the current instance of case object D4. Semantically, this turns the select statement of pattern 4 into an update statement that sets attributes *d4_id* and *state* for all rows where the pre-condition holds; see the SQL query of pattern 5 in Table 2. In our example, pattern 5 occurs at task *Assign CP to PO* for assigning a specific set of components (CP) to a purchase order (PO) based on the chosen supplier. As assumed for the subprocess instance with ID 17, the process variable *$supplier* has the value B. The entire derived query is shown in Fig. 10b (top right); executing the query gives components with ID

126 and ID 127 concrete references to PO ($po\_id = 17$), and the state *assigned*. The resulting state of the database in Fig. 10b shows the m:n relationship that was set.

4.3 Implementation

We evaluated our approach for enacting process models with complex data dependencies by implementation. In the spirit of building on existing standards and techniques, we made the existing BPMN process engine Activiti [4] data-aware by only few additions to its control structures. Activiti enacts process models given in the BPMN XML format and supports standard BPMN control flow constructs.

We extended the BPMN XML specification with our concepts introduced in Section 3.1 using *extension elements* explicitly supported by BPMN [17]. The BPMN parser of Activiti was supplemented correspondingly. Finally, we adapted the actual execution engine to check for availability of input data objects when an activity is enabled, and to make output data objects available when an activity completes – both through the SQL queries presented in Section 4.2. Our extensions required just over 1000 lines of code with around 600 lines being concerned with classifying data objects to patterns and generating and executing SQL queries; see [14] for details.

With the given implementation, a user can model data annotated processes in BPMN, and directly deploy the model to the extended Activiti engine, which then executes the process *including* all data dependencies. No further hard-coding is required as all information is derived from the process model. The extended engine, a graphical modeling tool, examples, and a complete setup in a virtual machine are available for download together with the source code and a screencast at http://bpt.hpi.uni-potsdam.de/Public/BPMNData.

5 Related Work

In the following, we compare the contributions of this paper to other techniques for modeling and enacting processes with data; our comparison includes all requirements for "object-aware process management" described in [10] and three additional factors.

The requirements cover modeling and enacting of *data*, *processes*, *activities*, authorization of *users*, and support for *flexible* processes. (1) Data should be managed in terms of a data model defining object types, attributes, and relations; (2) cardinality constraints should restrict relations; (3) users can only read/write data they are authorized to access; and (4) users can access data not only during process execution. Processes manage (5) the life cycle of object types and (6) the interaction of different object instances; (7) processes are only executed by authorized users and (8) users see which task they may or have to execute in the form of a task list; (9) it is possible to describe the sequencing of activities independently from the data flow. (10) One can define proper pre- and post-conditions for service activities based on objects and their attributes; (11) forms for user-interaction activities can be generated from the data dependencies; (12) activities can have a variable granularity wrt. data updates, i.e., an activity may read-/write objects in 1:1, 1:n, and m:n fashion. (13) Whether a user is authorized to execute a task should depend on the role and on the authorization for the data this task accesses. (14) Flexible processes benefit from data integration in various ways (e.g., tasks that set mandatory data are scheduled when required, tasks can be re-executed, etc.).

Table 3. Comparison of data-aware process modeling techniques

	requirement [in [10]]	Proclets [3]	CorePro [15]	OPM [8]	Obj.-Cent. [19]	PBWS [22]	Artifacts [6]	CH [2]	BPMN [17]	PH.Fl. [10]	this
data	1: data integration [R1]	o	o	o	o	o	+	o	-	+	+ (RQ2)
	2: cardinalities [R2]	+	o	+	+	-	+	o	o	+	+
	3: data authorization [R10]	-	o	-	-	-	-	o	-	+	-
	4: data-oriented view [R8]	-	o	-	-	-	o	o	-	+	o
process	5: object behavior [R4]	o	+	+	+	-	o	o	o	+	+ (RQ3)
	6: object interactions [R5]	+	+	+	+	o	o	o	o	+	+ (RQ4)
	7: process authorization [R9]	+	+	+	+	+	o	+	o	+	o
	8: process-oriented view [R7]	+	+	+	+	+	+	+	+	+	+
	9: explicit sequencing of activities	+	o	o	o	-	-	-	+	o	+
activity	10: service calls based on data [R14]	+	+	+	+	+	+	o	o	+	+ (RQ2)
	11: forms based on data/flow in forms [R15/R18]	-	-	-	-	-	o/-	+/-	-	+	-
	12: variable granularity 1:1/1:n/m:n [R17]	-	-	-	-	-	-	o	o	-	o	+ (RQ5)
users flex	13: authorization by data and roles [R11/R12]	-	-	-	-	-	-	-	-	+	-
	14: flexible execution [R3/R6/R13/R16/R19]	-	o	-	-	o	o	o	-	+	-
factors	15: process paradigm	A	D	D	D	D	D	D	A	D	A (RQ1)
	16: standards	o	o	o	o	-	-	-	o	+	+ (RQ1)
	17: reusability of existing techniques	+	-	o	-	-	-	-	+	-	+

fully satisfied (+), partially satisfied (o), not satisfied (-), activity-centric (A), object-centric (D).

In addition to these requirements, we consider *factors* that influence the adaption of a technique, namely, (15) whether the process paradigm is activity-centric or object-centric, (16) whether the approach is backed by standards, and (17) to which extent it can reuse existing methods and tools for modeling, execution, simulation, and analysis. Table 3 shows existing techniques satisfy these requirements and requirements (RQ1)-(RQ5) given in the introduction.

Classical activity-centric techniques such as *workflows* [1] lack a proper integration of data. Purely data-based approaches such as *active database systems* [21] allow to update data based on event-condition-action rules, but lack a genuine process perspective. Many approaches combine activity-centric process models with *object life cycles*, but are largely confined to 1:1 relationships between a process instance and the object instances it can handle, e.g., [9, 13, 23] and also BPMN [17]; some of these techniques allow flexible process execution [20].

Table 3 compares techniques that support at least a basic notion of data integration. *Proclets* [3] define object life cycles in an activity-centric way that interact through channels. In [22], process execution and object interaction are derived from a product data model. *CorePro* [15], the *Object-Process Methodology* [8], *Object-Centric Process Modeling* [19], and the *Artifact-Centric* approach [6] define processes in terms of object life cycles with various kinds of object interaction. Only artifacts support all notions of variable granularity (12), though it is given in a declarative form that cannot always be realized [7]. In *Case Handling* [2], process execution follows updating data such that particular goals are reached in a flexible manner. *PHILharmonic Flows* [10] is the most advanced proposal addressing variable granularity as well as flexible process execution through a combination of *micro processes* (object life cycles) and *macro processes* (object interactions); though variable granularity is not fully supported for service tasks and each activity must be coupled to changes in a data object (limits activity sequencing). More importantly, the focus on an object-centric approach limits the reusability of existing techniques and standards for modeling, execution, and analysis.

The technique proposed in this paper extends BPMN with data integration, cardinalities can be set statically in the data model and dynamically as shown in Section 3.2; a data-oriented view is available by the use of relational databases and SQL. Object behavior and their interactions are managed with variable granularity. Our work did not focus on authorization aspects and forms, but these aspects can clearly be addressed in future work. Our approach, as it builds on BPMN, does not support flexible processes, and thus should primarily be applied in use cases requiring structured processes. Most importantly, we combine two industry standards for processes and data, allowing to leverage on various techniques for modeling and analysis. We demonstrated reusability by our implementation extending an existing engine. Thus, our approach covers more than the requirements (RQ1)-(RQ5) raised in the introduction.

6 Conclusion

In this paper, we presented an approach to model processes incorporating complex data dependencies, even m:n relationships, with classical activity-centric modeling techniques and to automatically enact them. It covers all requirements RQ1-RQ5 presented in the introduction. We combined different proven modeling techniques: the idea of object life cycles, the standard process modeling notation BPMN, and relational data modeling together make BPMN data-aware. This was achieved by introducing few extensions to BPMN data objects, e.g., an object identifier to distinguish object instances. Data objects associated to activities express pre- and post-conditions of activities. We presented a pattern-based approach to automatically derive SQL queries from depicted pre- and post-conditions. It covers all *create*, *read*, *update*, and *delete* operations by activities on different data object types so that data dependencies can be automatically executed from a given process model. Further, we ensure that no two instances of the same process have conflicting data accesses on their data objects. Through combining two standard techniques, BPMN and relational databases, we allow the opportunity to use existing methods, tools, and analysis approaches of both separately as well as combined in the new setting. The downside of this approach is an increased complexity of the process model; however, this complexity can be alleviated through appropriate tool support providing views, abstraction, and scoping.

The integration of complex data dependencies into process execution is the first of few steps towards fully automated process enactment from process models. We support operations on single data attributes beyond life cycle information and object identifiers in one step. In practice, multiple attributes are usually affected simultaneously during a data operation. Further, we assumed the usage of a shared database per process model. Multi-database support may be achieved by utilizing the concept of data stores. We focused on process orchestrations with capabilities to utilize objects created in other processes. Process choreographies with data exchange between different parties is one of the open steps. Fourth, research on formal verification is required to ensure correctness of the processes to be executed. In future work, we will address these limitations.

References

1. van der Aalst, W.M.P., ter Hofstede, A.H.M.: YAWL: Yet Another Workflow Language. Information Systems 30(4), 245–275 (2005)
2. van der Aalst, W.M.P., Weske, M., Grünbauer, D.: Case Handling: A New Paradigm for Business Process Support. Data & Knowledge Engineering 53(2), 129–162 (2005)
3. van der Aalst, W., Barthelmess, P., Ellis, C., Wainer, J.: Proclets: A Framework for Lightweight Interacting Workflow Processes. Int. J. Cooperative Inf. Syst. 10(4), 443–481 (2001)
4. Activiti: Activiti BPM Platform, https://www.activiti.org/
5. Bonitasoft: Bonita Process Engine, https://www.bonitasoft.com/
6. Cohn, D., Hull, R.: Business artifacts: A data-centric approach to modeling business operations and processes. IEEE Data Eng. Bull. 32(3), 3–9 (2009)
7. Damaggio, E., Hull, R., Vaculín, R.: On the equivalence of incremental and fixpoint semantics for business artifacts with guard-stage-milestone lifecycles. Inf. Syst. 38(4), 561–584 (2013)
8. Dori, D.: Object-Process Methodology. Springer (2002)
9. Eshuis, R., Van Gorp, P.: Synthesizing Object Life Cycles from Business Process Models. In: Atzeni, P., Cheung, D., Ram, S. (eds.) ER 2012 Main Conference 2012. LNCS, vol. 7532, pp. 307–320. Springer, Heidelberg (2012)
10. Künzle, V., Reichert, M.: PHILharmonicFlows: Towards a Framework for Object-aware Process Management. J. Softw. Maint. Evol.R 23(4), 205–244 (2011)
11. Küster, J., Ryndina, K., Gall, H.: Generation of Business Process Models for Object Life Cycle Compliance. In: Alonso, G., Dadam, P., Rosemann, M. (eds.) BPM 2007. LNCS, vol. 4714, pp. 165–181. Springer, Heidelberg (2007)
12. Lanz, A., Reichert, M., Dadam, P.: Robust and flexible error handling in the aristaflow bpm suite. In: Soffer, P., Proper, E. (eds.) CAiSE Forum 2010. LNBIP, vol. 72, pp. 174–189. Springer, Heidelberg (2011)
13. Liu, R., Wu, F.Y., Kumaran, S.: Transforming activity-centric business process models into information-centric models for soa solutions. J. Database Manag. 21(4), 14–34 (2010)
14. Meyer, A., Pufahl, L., Fahland, D., Weske, M.: Modeling and Enacting Complex Data Dependencies in Business Processes. Tech. Rep. 74, HPI at the University of Potsdam (2013)
15. Müller, D., Reichert, M., Herbst, J.: Data-driven modeling and coordination of large process structures. In: Meersman, R., Tari, Z. (eds.) OTM 2007, Part I. LNCS, vol. 4803, pp. 131–149. Springer, Heidelberg (2007)
16. Nigam, A., Caswell, N.: Business artifacts: An Approach to Operational Specification. IBM Systems Journal 42(3), 428–445 (2003)
17. OMG: Business Process Model and Notation (BPMN), Version 2.0 (2011)
18. OMG: Unified Modeling Language (UML), Version 2.4.1 (2011)
19. Redding, G., Dumas, M., ter Hofstede, A.H.M., Iordachescu, A.: A flexible, object-centric approach for business process modelling. In: SOCA 2010, vol. 4(3), pp. 191–201 (2010)
20. Reichert, M., Rinderle-Ma, S., Dadam, P.: Flexibility in process-aware information systems. In: Jensen, K., van der Aalst, W.M.P. (eds.) ToPNoC II. LNCS, vol. 5460, pp. 115–135. Springer, Heidelberg (2009)
21. Silberschatz, A., Korth, H.F., Sudarshan, S.: Database System Concepts, 4th edn. McGraw-Hill Book Company (2001)
22. Vanderfeesten, I.T.P., Reijers, H.A., van der Aalst, W.M.P.: Product-based workflow support. Inf. Syst. 36(2), 517–535 (2011)
23. Wang, J., Kumar, A.: A Framework for Document-Driven Workflow Systems. In: van der Aalst, W.M.P., Benatallah, B., Casati, F., Curbera, F. (eds.) BPM 2005. LNCS, vol. 3649, pp. 285–301. Springer, Heidelberg (2005)
24. Wang, Z., ter Hofstede, A.H.M., Ouyang, C., Wynn, M., Wang, J., Zhu, X.: How to Guarantee Compliance between Workflows and Product Lifecycles? Tech. rep., BPM Center Report BPM-11-10 (2011)

Event Stream Processing Units in Business Processes

Stefan Appel, Sebastian Frischbier, Tobias Freudenreich, and Alejandro Buchmann

TU Darmstadt, Germany
`lastname@dvs.tu-darmstadt.de`

Abstract. The Internet of Things and Cyber-physical Systems provide enormous amounts of real-time data in form of streams of events. Businesses can benefit from the integration of this real-world data; new services can be provided to customers, or existing business processes can be improved. Events are a well-known concept in business processes. However, there is no appropriate abstraction mechanism to encapsulate event stream processing in units that represent business functions in a coherent manner across the process modeling, process execution, and IT infrastructure layer. In this paper we present Event Stream Processing Units (SPUs) as such an abstraction mechanism. SPUs encapsulate application logic for event stream processing and enable a seamless transition between process models, executable process representations, and components at the IT layer. We derive requirements for SPUs and introduce a BPMN extension to model SPUs. We present a runtime infrastructure that executes SPUs and supports implicit invocation and completion semantics. We illustrate our approach using a logistics process as running example.

1 Introduction

Business process modeling and execution is widely adopted in enterprises. Processes are modeled by business experts and translated into executable workflow representations. They are executed inside IT infrastructures, e.g., Service-oriented Architectures (SOAs) or workflow management systems. With the adoption of the Internet of Things and Cyber-physical Systems, huge amounts of information become available that reflect the state of the real world. The integration of this up-to-date information with business processes (BPs) allows quick reactions on unforeseen situations as well as offering new services to customers, e.g., monitoring of environmental conditions during transport of goods and handling exceeded thresholds.

A common paradigm for the representation of information from sources like the Internet of Things or Cyber-physical Systems are streams of events. The notion of a *stream* illustrates that new events occur over time, e.g., continuous temperature sensor readings. In such event-based systems, event producers do not necessarily know the event consumers, or whether the events will be consumed at all. This independence is intrinsic to the event-based approach [4]. The decoupling of event producers and consumers as well as the arrival of an indefinite number of events over time requires an appropriate event dissemination mechanism. Commonly, publish/subscribe systems are used; they allow asynchronous communication between fully decoupled participants.

Event consumers specify their interest in events in form of *subscriptions*; event producers specify the type of events they may publish in *advertisements*.

While single events are a well known and established concept in BPs [25,20], event stream processing lacks an appropriate abstraction for the seamless integration across the process modeling, process execution, and IT infrastructure layer. In collaboration with Software AG[1], a leader in business process management, we developed *Event Stream Processing Units* (SPUs) as such an integration concept.

In this paper we present SPUs. We analyze BP modeling, BP execution, and the IT infrastructure, and derive requirements for SPUs at the modeling, execution, and IT infrastructure layer. We address the decoupled nature of event-based systems and provide process modelers with an appropriate representation of SPUs that can be mapped to executable workflow representations and the IT infrastructure seamlessly. SPUs encapsulate event stream processing logic at the abstraction level of business functions and hide implementation details. At the IT layer, SPUs are manageable components that are conceptually equivalent to services in a SOA. SPUs contain, for example, complex event processing (CEP) functionality.

The paper is structured as follows: we introduce a logistics scenario as running example; we then derive requirements for the integration of event streams with BPs at the modeling, execution, and IT infrastructure layer. In Section 3, we introduce Event Stream Processing Tasks (ESPTs), a BPMN 2.0 extension to model SPUs. We present a mapping of ESPTs to BPEL as well as a runtime environment for SPUs. In Section 4, we discuss related work; we summarize our findings in Section 5.

Scenario. We illustrate our concept of SPUs by means of an order-to-delivery process. The processing of an order consists of multiple process steps: an order is received, the invoice for the order is prepared and the payment is processed. With SPUs, data generated during the physical transport can now be integrated with this process. An event stream that provides monitoring data related to the shipment can be used to detect, e.g., temperature threshold violations. An SPU can represent such a monitoring task and integrate it at the BP modeling, BP execution, and IT infrastructure layer. A shipment monitoring SPU is *instantiated* with the shipment of an order. The SPU *completes* after delivery. Throughout the paper, we illustrate our approach on the basis of such a monitoring SPU.

2 Event Stream Integration Requirements

Business process models describe workflows in companies in a standardized way. They document established business procedures with the goal of making complex company structures manageable. This encompasses the business perspective as well as the IT perspective. For the modeling and execution of processes, an appropriate level of abstraction is crucial to hide irrelevant details to the process modeler. Building blocks for BP modeling, BP execution, and IT infrastructure should encapsulate business functions in a self-contained way, e.g., like services in a SOA [22]. The BP model describes interactions between these building blocks.

---

[1] www.softwareag.com

The implementation of BPs in enterprises involves three layers: the modeling layer, the execution layer, and the IT infrastructure layer (see Figure 1). During design time, business experts create models, e.g., using the Business Process Modeling Notation (BPMN) [20]. The model is then transformed into an executable workflow expressed, e.g., with the Business Process Execution Language (BPEL) [19]. Typically, the workflow execution requires IT support, which is provided by a SOA and workflow management systems.

	BPM Transition Process		Examples of Abstraction	
			low coherence	high coherence
Design Time	[diagram]	Model (e.g., BPMN 1/2, EPC)	Accounting (Invoice & Billing)	Billing by Credit Card
	[code snippet]	Executable Workflow (e.g., BPMN 2.0, BPEL)	Invoke *Invoice* Service and *Billing* Service	Invoke *Billing by Credit Card* Service
Run Time	[diagram]	IT Infrastructure (e.g., SOA, EDA)	Billing Service (different methods); Invoice Service	Billing by Credit Card Service

Fig. 1. Transition steps between process modeling, process execution, and IT infrastructure layer

The transition process from a BP model to, e.g., SOA service interactions is not trivial and requires expertise from the business perspective as well as from the IT perspective. To enable the seamless implementation of modeled processes, the abstraction of business functions should have the same granularity at each layer; a coherent abstraction across the layers minimizes the transition effort [21]. The example in Figure 1 illustrates this: the *low coherence* case requires a refinement with each transition step (a single BPMN task maps to multiple services) while the *high coherence* case allows a one-to-one transition between the business function representations available at each layer (e.g., BPMN tasks, BPEL invocations, and SOA services). In the following, we derive requirements for SPUs as business function abstractions. With the encapsulation of event stream processing in SPUs, a high coherence between the different layers is achieved; this supports a seamless transition between process model, executable workflow, and IT infrastructure.

2.1 Business Process Modeling Layer

Process models are typically created by business experts that have a good knowledge about the company structure and established workflows. These process models describe interactions between business functions [22]. For a clear separation of concerns between the business perspective and the IT perspective, it is necessary to encapsulate event stream processing logic in SPUs that hide technical details at the modeling layer. SPUs are the abstract representation of business functions that process event streams. SPUs require at least one event stream as input and may output event streams or single events. An important characteristic of SPUs is the demand for continuous processing of event streams; rather than in single request/reply interactions, SPUs process new events as they arrive, e.g., a shipment monitoring SPU receives new monitoring data continuously.

Requirements. For the integration of event streams, the modeling notation has to provide *elements or patterns to express SPUs (R_1)*. While the actual event-processing functionality is encapsulated inside SPUs, event streams should be accessible by the modeler. Integrating event streams during modeling simplifies the transition to an executable workflow. Thus, the modeling notation has to provide *means to express event streams as input/output to/from SPUs (R_2)*. Finally, the model notion must allow *SPUs to run continuously and in parallel to other tasks (R_3)*. This includes *appropriate execution semantics adapted to event-based characteristics (R_4)*.

2.2 Workflow Execution Layer

The execution of BP models requires a transition from the, often graphical, model notation to a formal process representation. The interactions between the different process tasks are formalized in a workflow description, e.g., using BPEL. This workflow description contains, e.g., service invocations and defines the input data for services. Like traditional BP tasks can be mapped to human tasks or service invocations, SPUs need to be mapped from the model to the IT infrastructure.

Requirements. To support SPUs at the workflow execution layer, the execution notation has to *support the instantiation of the SPUs provided by the IT infrastructure (R_5)*. It further needs means to *define streams of events as input and output of SPUs (R_6)*. The *instantiation and completion of SPUs needs to be configurable with respect to event-based characteristics (R_7)*.

2.3 IT Infrastructure Layer

The IT infrastructure holds the technical representations of SPUs. It is responsible for the execution of the encapsulated event stream processing logic. In contrast to SOA services, SPUs follow the event-based paradigm. While services are invoked explicitly, SPUs behave reactively on streams of events. Services encapsulate business functions in a pull manner (reply is requested); SPUs encapsulate reactive business functions that are defined on event streams pushed into the system.

Requirements. The IT infrastructure has to *provide a runtime environment for SPUs that respects event-based characteristics, e.g., implicit instantiation (R_8)*. It must *provide containers for SPUs that represent business functions (R_9)*. Just like services, these *SPU containers must be manageable and capable of receiving the required data in form of event streams (R_{10})*.

3 Event Stream Processing Units

To support SPUs at the BP modeling, BP execution, and IT infrastructure layer, we suggest mechanisms at each layer. At the modeling layer, we introduce *Event Stream*

Processing Tasks (ESPTs) to represent SPUs in BPMN process models. At the IT infrastructure layer, we adapt *Eventlets* [1] for the implementation of SPUs. The execution layer is responsible for the mapping between ESPTs and Eventlets. This is shown in Figure 2: like services form a SOA, SPUs form an event-driven architecture (EDA). At the execution layer, service tasks in a model are mapped to, e.g., web services. Equally, ESPTs are mapped to Eventlets.

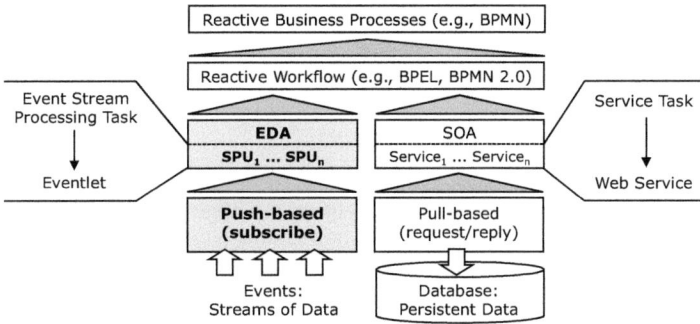

Fig. 2. Stream Processing Units (SPUs) as building blocks of an event-driven architecture (EDA)

3.1 Modeling Layer

BPMN 2.0 is widely adopted in industry and has a broad tool support. From a technological perspective, processes can be modeled in different granularities with BPMN. From a semantical perspective, the single building blocks (BPMN tasks) of a process model should reflect business functions and hide technical details. We extend BPMN with building blocks that represent SPUs. The extension of BPMN is necessary to address the characteristics of SPUs determined by the streaming nature of event data. SPUs exhibit the following specific properties that cannot be expressed completely with existing BPMN elements:

- *Execution semantics:* After the instantiation, SPUs can run indefinitely; events arrive and are processed continuously, e.g., temperature measurements during the shipment transport. The completion semantics differ from service-like request/reply interactions where the reply triggers the process control flow to proceed. In contrast, completion of SPUs has to be triggered - either implicitly or explicitly. In either case, the completion indicates a clean shutdown. *Implicit completion* requires the specification of a condition that determines when the SPU should complete. Examples are a timeout in case no new events arrive, the detection of a certain event pattern, or dedicated events, e.g., shipment arrival. *Explicit completion* triggers the completion of an SPU externally. For example, when a process reaches a point where the processing of an event stream is not required anymore, e.g., shipment arrival has been confirmed.
- *Signaling:* The continuous processing inside of SPUs requires support to trigger concurrent actions, e.g., triggering exception handling in case of a temperature threshold violation without stopping the shipment monitoring SPU.

– *Event stream input and output:* The inputs for SPUs are event streams. An event stream is specified by a subscription to future events, e.g., temperature measurements for a certain shipment. The output is specified by an advertisement that describes the events producible by an SPU.

Our extensions to BPMN are shown in Figure 3. We introduce *Event Stream Specifications* (ESSs) that reflect input data and output data in form of event streams. Further, we introduce *Event Stream Processing Tasks* (ESPTs) to model SPUs.

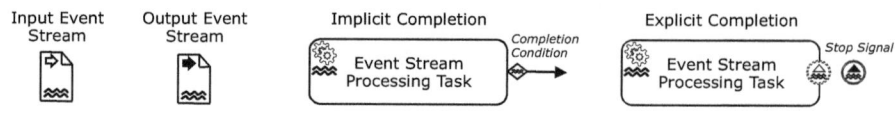

Fig. 3. Extensions to BPMN: Event Stream Specifications (ESSs) and Event Stream Processing Tasks (ESPTs)

Definition 1. *An **Event Stream Specification (ESS)** ($\rightarrow R_2$) references a stream of events and their parameters. ESSs can be used as input and output of ESPTs. An ESS used as input determines the subscription an ESPT has to issue. An ESS used as output determines the advertisement that describes the event output stream of an ESPT.*

Definition 2. *An **Event Stream Processing Task (ESPT)** ($\rightarrow R_1, R_3, R_4$) requires at least one ESS as input. It may have output ESSs. When the control flow reaches an ESPT, it is activated with the specified ESS as input. The transition from the active state to the completing state (see BPMN task lifecycle [20, p. 428]) is triggered implicitly or explicitly ($\rightarrow R_5$). The implicit completion of an ESPT is realized with a modified conditional sequence flow; the condition determines when the ESPT completes. The explicit completion is realized with a dedicated signal. It is attached as non-interrupting signal to the boundary of the ESPT. Upon completion, either implicitly or explicitly, the ESPT stops processing, performs a clean shutdown, and passes on the control flow. To trigger concurrent actions, ESPTs can activate outgoing sequence flow elements while remaining in the active state.*

Related BPMN Concepts. Events are part of the BPMN specification. However, events in BPMN are meant to affect the control flow in a process [20, p. 233]. Events modeled as ESS do not exhibit this property; they are rather a source of business-relevant information that is exploited within the process. Thus, due to the different semantics, events in the sense of the BPMN standard are not appropriate to model SPUs.

To avoid unnecessary extensions of BPMN, we evaluated different BPMN task types as alternatives to ESPTs. From the task types contained in the BPMN 2.0 standard, service tasks, business rule tasks, loop service tasks, and multiple instance service tasks share properties with SPUs.

Service Tasks are containers for business functions that are implemented as SOA services. The execution semantics for service tasks state, that data input is assigned to the service task upon invocation; upon completion output data is available. For SPUs, this separation is not feasible; input data arrives continuously and output data can be available during task execution in form of output streams. Therefore, service tasks are no appropriate representation for SPUs. In *Business Rule Tasks*, event stream processing can be used to check conformance with business rules. However, event stream processing supports a wider application spectrum than conformance checking, e.g., real-time shipment tracking. Further, output in form of event streams is not part of business rule tasks; their purpose is to signal business rule evaluation results. *Loop Service Tasks* perform operations until a certain stop condition is met. However, the whole loop task is executed repeatedly, i.e., a repeated service call. This repeated execution of a business function depicts a different level of abstraction compared to continuous processing inside an SPU; SPUs perform continuous processing to complete a single business function. To use loop tasks for event stream processing, the process model would have to define the handling of single events rather than the handling of event streams. This conflicts with the abstraction paradigm of business functions and degrades coherence across the layers. *Multiple Instance Service Tasks* allow the execution of a task in parallel, i.e., parallel service calls. However, like loop tasks, this would require one task per event which conflicts with the intention to encapsulate business functions in tasks. In addition, the number of task instances executed in parallel is static and determined at the beginning of the task. This is not suitable for event processing since the number of events is not known a priori.

In general, BPMN tasks have no support for triggered completion required in event processing. In addition, event streams cannot be represented as input to and output from tasks. Thus, we extend BPMN with ESPTs. ESPTs support implicit and explicit completion, an essential part of SPU execution semantics. Further, we introduce ESSs as input to and output from ESPTs in the form of event streams.

Example: Shipment Monitoring. To illustrate the application of our BPMN extensions, we model the monitoring of environmental conditions in the order process introduced in Section 1. Figures 4 and 5 show two variants with different completion strategies. The shipment monitoring is an SPU that receives monitoring events as input stream. This shipment monitoring SPU is modeled as an ESPT in BPMN; the monitoring events are assigned as an input ESS. The monitoring task can send a message event (as concurrent action) to indicate a violation of environmental conditions, e.g., temperature threshold exceeded. The message event can activate a task or trigger a different process for handling the exception; this exception handling is omitted here for brevity.

In Figure 4, the shipment monitoring is modeled with explicit completion semantics. As soon as the shipment has arrived, the monitoring is not required anymore. Thus, the monitoring task completion is triggered by sending the stop signal.

In Figure 5, the shipment monitoring is modeled with implicit completion semantics. This requires the definition of a completion condition. In our example, we specify the shipment arrival: when the location of the shipment matches the destination address, the monitoring is completed. Other implicit completion conditions could be dedicated arrival events, e.g., arrival scans of shipment barcodes, or timeouts, e.g., no new monitoring events for the shipment arrive. The condition needs to be evaluated inside the SPU, thus support for different condition types depends on the technical infrastructure that executes SPUs.

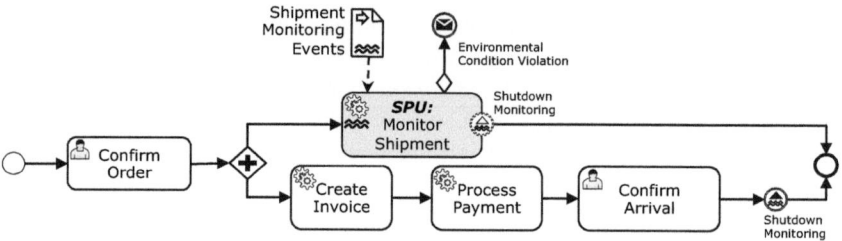

Fig. 4. Shipment monitoring SPU that is stopped explicitly. The data input/output of the service tasks omitted.

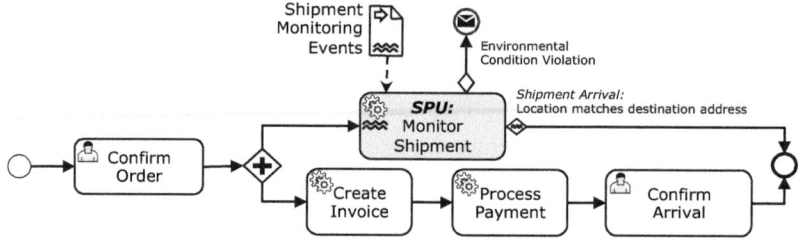

Fig. 5. Shipment monitoring SPU that is stopped implicitly. The data input/output of the service tasks omitted.

3.2 Workflow Execution Layer

The support of BPs by an IT infrastructure requires a transition from the graphical process notation to an executable format. With this technical representation, tasks of a process model can be executed by technical components of the IT infrastructure. The BPMN 2.0 standard itself specifies such a technical representation of the graphical model. The standard also provides examples for the mapping between BPMN and BPEL. Independent of the concrete technical representation format, the goal is to bridge the semantic gap between graphical notation and interfaces of IT components so that the process can be executed automatically. The transition from a graphical model towards a technical representation requires adding additional technical information necessary for the execution.

For different task types and control flow components, execution languages provide executable representations. When the mapping of graphical process task and process control flow elements is complete and all necessary data is specified, the process execution engine is able to execute instances of the process. Each instance reflects a concrete business transaction, e.g., processing of Order No. 42. For each process instance, the execution engine orchestrates the different tasks, passes on task input and output data, and evaluates conditions specified in the control flow. Examples are the execution of BPMN service tasks and human tasks: a service task can be executed by calling a web service. For this, the execution engine needs the service address as well as the input data to send to a service and the format of the expected output data from this service. For the execution of human tasks, process execution engines typically provide a front end to perform the work necessary to complete the task.

At the execution layer we define the technical details that allow ESPTs to be mapped to IT components. The mapping mechanism has to take into consideration, that events arrive indefinitely and are not known when the control flow reaches an ESPT. Thus, the data input must be specified as a *subscription* for desired events that arrive during the execution period of an ESPT. During process execution, this subscription has to partition the event stream in process instance specific sub streams: when a process instance is created for a certain business task, e.g., processing of Order No. 42, the event stream has to be partitioned in sub streams of events relevant for the different order process instances. This is shown in Figure 6: a monitoring task must be active for each process instance. This task instance has to receive all monitoring events for the shipment that is handled in this process instance. Given that each event carries a shipment ID, each monitoring task instance can issue a subscription for the appropriate events using the shipment ID as filter. When the process instance ID correlates with the shipment ID, the subscription can also be derived by the process execution engine on the basis of the process instance ID.

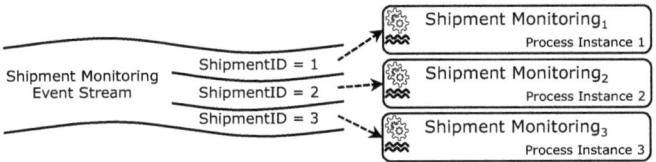

Fig. 6. Process execution: Event Stream Processing Tasks (ESPTs) receive sub streams of events

The subscription parameters are essential for the instantiation of an ESPT. Like the input data passed on to a service during a service call, the subscription is part of the input data during an ESPT instantiation. Further, when the ESPT is modeled with an implicit completion, the completion condition is part of the input data required for the instantiation. As for ESPT completion, different ESPT instantiation strategies are possible. The push-based nature of stream processing allows an implicit creation of ESPT instances upon the arrival of appropriate events. In addition, ESPT instances can also be created explicitly by the process execution engine. When switching from explicit to implicit instantiation, the responsibility of instantiation moves from the process execution engine to the IT infrastructure. Implicit instantiation is useful when the moment of instantiation cannot be determined by the execution engine. It is also the more natural approach with respect to the characteristics of event streams; application logic is executed as soon as appropriate events are available. We support both instantiation schemes to allow for a high flexibility ($\rightarrow R_8$). Independent of the instantiation scheme, a subscription does not guarantee the availability of events, e.g., that events for Shipment No. 42 are published. Explicitly instantiated ESPTs can use a timeout to detect such an absence of events. With implicit instantiation, ESPT instances are not created in this case; the execution environment can detect and report this.

ESPT Instantiation and Completion. The execution of a BPs leads to process instances that may run in parallel. Each ESPT in the model has corresponding ESPT instances that are created during process execution. Each ESPT instance processes the event streams relevant for a particular process instance (see Figure 6). The process execution engine can create an ESPT instance explicitly during the execution of a process instance. The subscription parameters required for the explicit instantiation must be derived per process instance; they define the sub stream of events that has to be processed by a particular ESPT instance, e.g., monitoring events for Shipment No. 42. The *explicit instantiation* is specified as follows ($\rightarrow R_6, R_7, R_8$):

EsptInstantiate(EsptName, EventStreamFilter, SubStreamAttribute,
    SubStreamId [, CompletionCondition])

For the monitoring example, the explicit instantiation of a monitoring task for Shipment No. 42 without and with completion condition is:

EsptInstantiate(MonitorShipment, MonitoringEvent,
    ShipmentId, 42)

EsptInstantiate(MonitorShipment, MonitoringEvent,
    ShipmentId, 42, timeout(120sec))

An ESPT is referenced by name: EsptName, e.g., Monitor Shipment. The subscription parameter has three parts: First, a general filter for events of interest that applies to all ESPT instances is specified as EventStreamFilter, e.g., monitoring events. Second, the SubStreamAttribute defines the part of the event data that partitions the event stream with respect to ESPT instances, e.g., the shipment ID; both are static expressions and derived based upon the ESS used in the model. Third, the SubStreamId defines the concrete event sub stream for which an ESPT instance should be created, e.g., Shipment No. 42. The SubStreamId is dynamic and derived per process instance by the execution engine at run time, e.g., based on the process instance ID. The optional CompletionCondition can be specified for implicit completion, e.g., defining a time out.

With implicit instantiation, the process execution engine only registers a static subscription pattern for an ESPT once, e.g., with the registration of the process. Since events arise in a push-style manner, the IT infrastructure is able to create ESPT instances implicitly at run time. The *implicit instantiation* is specified as follows ($\rightarrow R_6, R_7, R_8$):

EsptRegister(EsptName, EventStreamFilter,
    SubStreamAttribute [, CompletionCondition])

For the shipment monitoring example, the ESPT registration is:

EsptRegister(MonitorShipment, MonitoringEvent, ShipmentId)

In contrast to explicit instantiation, the execution engine is not responsible for the dynamic subscription part anymore. Rather, the IT infrastructure ensures, that an ESPT instance is created for each distinct value of the SubStreamAttribute, e.g., for each shipment ID.

For the explicit completion of an ESPT instance, the process execution engine has to advise the IT infrastructure to perform a shutdown of particular ESPT instances, e.g., the shipment monitoring of Shipment No. 42. The completion command is specified as follows ($\rightarrow R_8$):

EsptComplete(EsptName, SubStreamId)

The `SubStreamId` identifies the ESPT instance that should be completed. In the monitoring example for Shipment No. 42, the following completion command is issued after the arrival confirmation task:

`EsptComplete``(MonitorShipment,42)`

Although ESPTs have different execution semantics than BPMN service tasks, the control commands to register, instantiate, and complete ESPTs follow a request/reply pattern. Thus, our integration approach of event streams with BPs can be mapped to web service invocations. Web service invocation capabilities are part of most process execution engines so that ESPTs can be registered, instantiated, or completed; the ESPT name as well as further subscription and completion parameters are specified as variables in the service invocation. In addition to service invocation mechanisms, it might be necessary to implement a back channel for control flow purposes. Implicitly completing ESPT instances might have to notify the process execution engine about completion. This is the case when the control flow waits for a completion of an ESPT, e.g., when an ESPT is used before a BPMN AND-Join.

ESPT Mapping in BPEL. Business process models that contain ESPTs can be mapped to BPEL. However, the BPEL standard [19] does not support all concepts required for a complete mapping of the different instantiation and completion strategies. ESPTs with explicit instantiation and explicit completion can be mapped to standard BPEL: the explicit instantiation is realized as web service call. The return from this call is blocked by the IT infrastructure until the ESPT instance is explicitly stopped by a `EsptComplete` service invocation. Explicit instantiation and completion in BPEL are as follows:

```
<invoke partnerLink="EsptWebService" operation="EsptInstantiate"
    inputVariable="explicitInstantiateParams"
    outputVariable="completed"/>

<invoke partnerLink="EsptWebService" operation="EsptComplete"
    inputVariable="explicitCompletionParams"/>
```

With implicit instantiation, single ESPT instances are transparent to the process execution engine. The registration of ESPTs has to be performed once with the registration of a process; the ESPT instances are then created automatically. The BPEL standard does not support hooks for service invocation upon the registration of new processes. Thus, a BPEL execution engine has to be extended with these capabilities to support implicit instantiation of ESPTs. The hook for execution at process registration can be part of the BPEL code itself; when a new process is registered and checked, this part of the process is executed only once:

```
<atRegistration><invoke partnerLink="EsptWebService" operation=
    "EsptRegister" inputVariable="implicitInstantiateParams"/>
</atRegistration>
```

When an ESPT is invoked implicitly, there is no BPEL web service invocation in each process instance. Thus, a blocking service invocation cannot be used to interrupt the control flow until completion of an ESPT instance. Rather, the process execution engine has to be notified externally about the completion of an ESPT instance so that the control flow can proceed. Extensions to BPEL engines to react on such external triggers have been proposed, e.g., in [14] and [12]. The ESPT can be mapped to a barrier that is released when the ESPT instance signals its completion.

3.3 IT Infrastructure Layer

SPUs require a technical representation at the IT infrastructure layer. In [1] we present a suitable component model and runtime infrastructure to encapsulate event stream processing. We introduce event applets, in short *Eventlets*, as service-like abstraction for event stream processing. Our model benefits from concepts known from services; it hides application logic so that Eventlets represent business functions. We extend the runtime environment presented in [1] to allow for the integration with BP execution engines. We now introduce the main concepts of Eventlets to make this paper self-contained; we then present the extensions to the Eventlet middleware. We adapt the more general Eventlet nomenclature of [1] to fit the terminology of this paper.

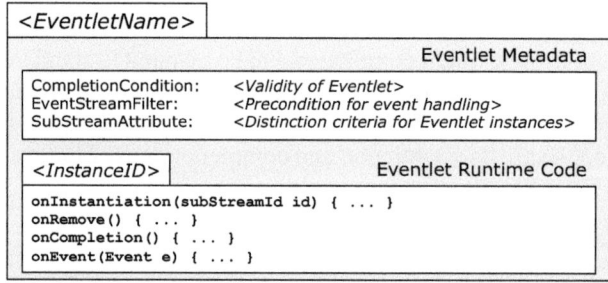

Fig. 7. Eventlet structure: Eventlet metadata and Eventlet runtime methods

Eventlets encapsulate event stream processing logic with respect to a certain entity, e.g., shipments ($\rightarrow R_{10}$). An Eventlet instance subscribes to events of a certain entity instance, e.g., Shipment No. 42 ($\rightarrow R_{11}$). The basic structure of an Eventlet is shown in Figure 7. The grouping attribute to define the sub stream of events associated with a certain entity instance is specified as Sub Stream Attribute[2] in the Eventlet metadata, e.g., the shipment ID. Further, the metadata holds the Completion Condition[3], e.g., a timeout, as well as the Event Stream Filter[4] as a general subscription filter applied by all Eventlet instances, e.g., monitoring event. Eventlet instances are created implicitly or explicitly ($\rightarrow R_9$). With implicit instantiation the middleware ensures that an Eventlet instance is active for each distinct value of the sub stream attribute, e.g., for each shipment in transport. With explicit instantiation, Eventlet instances are created manually by

---
[2] Referred to as Instantiation Expression in [1].
[3] Referred to as Validity Expression in [1].
[4] Referred to as Constant Expression in [1].

specifying a concrete sub stream attribute value, e.g., Shipment No. 42. The completion of Eventlet instances is triggered implicitly by the completion condition or explicitly by a command ($\rightarrow R_9$). Eventlet instances run in a distributed setting and have a managed lifecycle; application logic can be executed upon instantiation, removal, completion, and upon event arrival ($\rightarrow R_{11}$).

In our monitoring example, an Eventlet holds application logic to detect temperature violations. This can involve a lookup in a database at instantiation to retrieve the temperature threshold for a certain shipment. It can also involve issuing complex event processing (CEP) queries to rely on the functionality of a CEP engine for temperature violation detection. An evaluation of CEP queries encapsulated in Eventlets is presented in [1]. The semantics of ESPT execution (cf. Section 3.2) are implemented by the Eventlet middleware. The `EsptInstantiate` and `EsptRegister` invocations provide the Eventlet middleware with the metadata to explicitly or implicitly create Eventlet instances. For implicit instantiation, the middleware creates a so-called Eventlet Monitor; it analyzes the event stream and detects the need to create Eventlet instances as soon as events of a new entity instance, e.g., a new shipment, occur. Like services, Eventlets are managed in a repository and identified via the `EsptName`.

Eventlet Middleware Extension. The Eventlet middleware infrastructure uses the Java Message Service (JMS) for event dissemination. JMS supports publish/subscribe communication with event content sensitive subscriptions. Our implementation supports events in attribute-value and XML representation. For attribute-value events, the Event Stream Filter is specified as JMS message selector in a SQL-like syntax. The Sub Stream Attribute is the name of an attribute, e.g., shipmentID. For XML events, Event Stream Filter and Sub Stream Attribute are specified as XPath expressions on the event content. For implicit completion of Eventlet instances, timeouts are supported.

We extended the Eventlet middleware in [1] to support ESPT execution. As shown in Figure 8, the Eventlet middleware is configured and controlled using a command bus. This command bus is realized as a set of JMS queues and topics to which all middleware components connect. We added a web service interface to the Eventlet Manager; the new interface accepts service invocations as described in Section 3.2 and uses the internal command bus to start or stop Eventlet Monitors and Eventlet instances. The web service interface is implemented as Java Enterprise application. The Eventlet

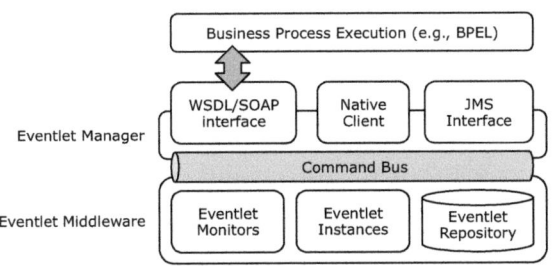

Fig. 8. Eventlet middleware access via web service

middleware can be deployed on multiple application servers and use a JMS infrastructure in place. It is designed for scalability: Eventlet instances can run on arbitrary machines.

4 Related Work

Events are part of various BP modeling notations like BPMN 2.0 and event-driven process chains (EPCs) [13,25]; they trigger functions/tasks and influence the process control flow. The incorporation of (complex) events leads to more reactive and dynamic processes. This is a core concept in event-driven architectures (EDA) [6,18] or event-driven SOA [16]. However, event streams do not have explicit representations in BPMN or EPCs. Currently, event streams have to be modeled explicitly as multiple events, e.g., using loops that process events. Such explicit modeling of complex events and event processing is for example presented in [2,3,5,9,26]. The problem is, that process models are often created by business experts without detailed knowledge about technical details of event processing. Further, to make models intuitively understandable, modelers should use as few elements as possible with self-explaining activity labels [17]. Thus, activities should represent business functions. Services are a successful abstraction mechanism to support this. Services represent business functions and exhibit a data input/output interface [22]. Process models do not (and should not) contain the application logic of a service; this is left to service developers who can use more appropriate modeling notations to describe the technical details. Thus, the approach in this work confers basic service concepts [7] to event stream processing and introduces SPUs as an appropriate abstraction.

At the execution layer, Juric [12] presents extensions to BPEL that allow service invocations by events. In [23], Spiess et al. encapsulate event sources as services. Both approaches do not address event streams as input/output to/from components; rather than a stream of events, single events are understood as business relevant.

At the technical layer, event streams are well known. CEP is supported by a variety of tools, e.g., the Esper CEP engine [8]. CEP is also part of BP execution environments like JBoss jBPM/Drools [11]. In [15], BP modeling techniques are used to express CEP queries. Event stream processing is integrated bottom-up; CEP queries and rules are specified at the technical layer. In contrast, we propose a top-down approach where business entity-centric event streams are visible as input/output of ESPTs at the modeling layer. Event streams can be as business relevant as, e.g., input/output data of services. Thus, like service task input/output is explicit in models, event streams are explicit at the modeling layer in our approach.

The event stream processing application logic inside Eventlets can be simple rules, CEP queries, or complex event processing networks as described in [10]. While event stream processing queries can run centralized, e.g., a single CEP query processes monitoring data of all shipments, our middleware instantiates Eventlets for each entity instance, e.g., one CEP query per shipment. This encapsulation of event stream processing logic is related to *design by units* described in [24]. It improves scalability and fosters elasticity; in [1] we show the scalability benefits of CEP query encapsulation in Eventlets. The more process instances require entity-centric stream processing, the more Eventlets are instantiated and vice versa.

5 Conclusion

In collaboration with Software AG, we identified the need to integrate event streams with BP modeling and execution. Rather than single events, event streams are considered as business-relevant units in this context. We developed an approach for this integration at the modeling, execution, and IT infrastructure layer. Our approach introduces SPUs: a consistent abstraction for event stream processing across the layers. Like services, SPUs encapsulate business functions; they use event streams as business-relevant data sources. This allows intuitive modeling from the business perspective. The abstraction paradigm of SPUs leads to a high coherence across the layers. This minimizes the transition effort from the graphical model notation to the executable process description and from the executable process description to the IT infrastructure. Our approach is a clear separation of concerns; SPUs are declarative, the (imperative) application logic resides solely at the technical layer inside Eventlets.

The contributions of this paper are: 1) SPUs as abstraction to encapsulate event stream processing as business functions, 2) an extension of BPMN 2.0 with ESPTs and ESSs to model SPUs, 3) a mapping of ESPTs and ESSs to an executable process description, and 4) an extension of our Eventlet middleware to interface with BP execution engines. We take semantics of event processing into account and support implicit as well as explicit instantiation and completion strategies. Event stream processing techniques, like CEP, are widely adopted. Our approach encapsulates them and makes event stream processing available coherently across the BP modeling, BP execution, and IT infrastructure layer. We illustrate our approach with the running example of a shipment monitoring SPU inside an order-to-delivery process.

In ongoing work we are enhancing our Eventlet middleware. We implement support for more types of completion conditions and investigate complex expressions as triggers for the instantiation of Eventlets. We are also working on extensions to the event-driven process chain (EPC) notation to support SPUs in EPCs.

Acknowledgements. We thank Dr. Walter Waterfeld, Software AG, Germany, for the valuable feedback and insights into process modeling practice. Funding by German Federal Ministry of Education and Research (BMBF) under research grants 01IS12054, 01IC12S01V, and 01IC10S01. The authors assume responsibility for the content.

References

1. Appel, S., Frischbier, S., Freudenreich, T., Buchmann, A.: Eventlets: Components for the integration of event streams with SOA. In: SOCA, Taiwan, (2012)
2. Barros, A., Decker, G., Grosskopf, A.: Complex events in business processes. In: Abramowicz, W. (ed.) BIS 2007. LNCS, vol. 4439, pp. 29–40. Springer, Heidelberg (2007)
3. Biörnstad, B., Pautasso, C., Alonso, G.: Control the flow: How to safely compose streaming services into business processes. In: SCC, USA (2006)
4. Buchmann, A., Appel, S., Freudenreich, T., Frischbier, S., Guerrero, P.E.: From calls to events: Architecting future bpm systems. In: Barros, A., Gal, A., Kindler, E. (eds.) BPM 2012. LNCS, vol. 7481, pp. 17–32. Springer, Heidelberg (2012)
5. Caracaş, A., Kramp, T.: On the expressiveness of BPMN for modeling wireless sensor networks applications. In: Dijkman, R., Hofstetter, J., Koehler, J. (eds.) BPMN 2011. LNBIP, vol. 95, pp. 16–30. Springer, Heidelberg (2011)

6. Chakravarty, P., Singh, M.: Incorporating events into cross-organizational business processes. IEEE Internet Computing 12(2), 46–53 (2008)
7. Elfatatry, A.: Dealing with change: components versus services. Communications of the ACM 50(8), 35–39 (2007)
8. EsperTech Inc. Esper Complex Event Processing Engine (2013)
9. Estruch, A., Heredia Álvaro, J.A.: Event-driven manufacturing process management approach. In: Barros, A., Gal, A., Kindler, E. (eds.) BPM 2012. LNCS, vol. 7481, pp. 120–133. Springer, Heidelberg (2012)
10. Etzion, O., Niblett, P.: Event processing in action. Manning Publications Co. (2010)
11. JBoss.com. Drools - The Business Logic integration Platform (2013)
12. Juric, M.B.: WSDL and BPEL extensions for event driven architecture. Information and Software Technology 52(10), 1023–1043 (2010)
13. Keller, G., Scheer, A.-W., Nüttgens, M.: Semantische Prozeßmodellierung auf der Grundlage "Ereignisgesteuerter Prozeßketten (EPK)". Inst. für Wirtschaftsinformatik (1992)
14. Khalaf, R., Karastoyanova, D., Leymann, F.: Pluggable framework for enabling the execution of extended BPEL behavior. In: ICSOC/WESOA, Austria (2007)
15. Kunz, S., Fickinger, T., Prescher, J., Spengler, K.: Managing complex event processes with business process modeling notation. In: Mendling, J., Weidlich, M., Weske, M. (eds.) BPMN 2010. LNBIP, vol. 67, Springer, Heidelberg (2010)
16. Levina, O., Stantchev, V.: Realizing event-driven SOA. In: ICIW, Italy (2009)
17. Mendling, J., Reijers, H., van der Aalst, W.: Seven process modeling guidelines (7pmg). Information and Software Technology 52(2), 127–136 (2010)
18. Michelson, B.M.: Event-driven architecture overview. Patricia Seybold Group (2006)
19. OASIS Web Services Business Process Execution Language (WSBPEL) TC. Web services business process execution language (BPEL), version 2.0 (April 2007)
20. Object Management Group (OMG). Business process model and notation (BPMN), version 2.0 (January 2011)
21. Ouyang, C., Dumas, M., van der Aalst, W., ter Hofstede, A., Mendling, J.: From business process models to process-oriented software systems. ACM Transactions on Software Engineering and Methodology 19(1), 2:1–2:37 (2009)
22. Papazoglou, M.: Service-oriented computing: concepts, characteristics and directions. In: WISE, Italy (2003)
23. Spiess, P., Karnouskos, S., Guinard, D., Savio, D., Baecker, O., Souza, L., Trifa, V.: SOA-based integration of the internet of things in enterprise services. In: ICWS, USA (2009)
24. Tai, S., Leitner, P., Dustdar, S.: Design by units: Abstractions for human and compute resources for elastic systems. IEEE Internet Computing 16(4), 84–88 (2012)
25. van der Aalst, W.: Formalization and verification of event-driven process chains. Information and Software Technology 41(10), 639–650 (1999)
26. Wieland, M., Martin, D., Kopp, O., Leymann, F.: SOEDA: A method for specification and implementation of applications on a service-oriented event-driven architecture. In: Abramowicz, W. (ed.) BIS 2009. LNBIP, vol. 21, pp. 193–204. Springer, Heidelberg (2009)

Predicting the Quality of Process Model Matching

Matthias Weidlich[1], Tomer Sagi[1], Henrik Leopold[2], Avigdor Gal[1], and Jan Mendling[3]

[1] Technion - Israel Institute of Technology, Technion City, 32000 Haifa, Israel
{weidlich,stomers7}@tx.technion.ac.il, avigal@ie.technion.ac.il
[2] Humboldt-Universität zu Berlin, Unter den Linden 6, 10099 Berlin, Germany
henrik.leopold@wiwi.hu-berlin.de
[3] Wirtschaftsuniversität Wien, Augasse 2-6, A-1090 Vienna, Austria
jan.mendling@wu.ac.at

Abstract. *Process model matching* refers to the task of creating correspondences among activities of different process models. This task is crucial whenever comparison and alignment of process models are called for. In recent years, there have been a few attempts to tackle process model matching. Yet, evaluating the obtained sets of correspondences reveals high variability in the results. Addressing this issue, we propose a method for predicting the quality of results derived by process model matchers. As such, prediction serves as a case-by-case decision making tool in estimating the amount of trust one should put into automatic matching. This paper proposes a model of prediction for process matching based on both process properties and preliminary match results.

1 Introduction

Process models have been widely established as a tool to manage business operations. They may be created for different purposes, such as process documentation or workflow implementation and in different contexts, e.g., for different organisational units or at different points in time. Many use cases require the comparison and alignment of process models, for instance, the validation of a technical process implementation against a business-centred specification model [1] or clone detection within a process model repository [2]. The need for comparing process models fostered research on *process model matching*, which refers to the task of creating correspondences among activities of different process models.

Recently, there have been a few attempts to tackle process model matching [1,3,4,5]. Typically, the developed matchers relied on the rich literature of schema and ontology matching [6,7] with emphasis on string comparison and graph matching. Evaluating the outcome of these works shows that the empirical quality is subject to high variability even within a single dataset. While matchers yield high precision and recall for some matching tasks, they entirely fail for others. This raises the question of *how to distinguish matching tasks for which matchers yield high quality matches from those for which results are poor.*

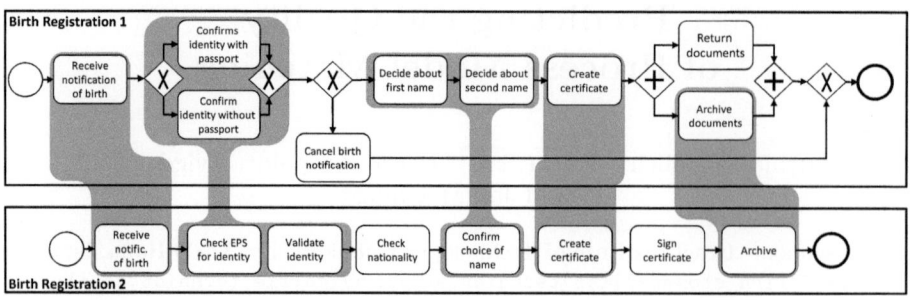

Fig. 1. Example of two business process models and their correspondences

In this work, we offer preliminary observations on how to use matching prediction [8] to tackle this question. We observe that both properties of process models and the similarity between their characteristics impact the accuracy of a specific match task. In particular, differences in syntactic and semantic aspects of labels as well as structure and behaviour of the models can be taken into account. Based on such process properties and similarity characteristics, we develop a statistical model to predict the quality of a match result for a given task.

The rest of the paper is organized as follows. Section 2 introduces the process model matching problem and the state-of-the-art in schema matching prediction. Our approach to prediction for process model matching is detailed in Section 3. Section 4 reviews related work, before Section 5 concludes the paper.

2 Background

This section first reviews the matching problem for process models, before explaining the background of schema matching prediction.

The Matching Problem. For two process models with A_1 and A_2 as their sets of activities, process model matching aims at identifying activity correspondences that represent the same behaviour in both models. Following Gal [6], we subdivide the matching process into first and second line matching. A *first line matcher* operates on the process models, compares some of their attributes such as activity labels or the process structure, and produces a similarity matrix $M(A_1,A_2)$ over activities with $|A_1|$ rows and $|A_2|$ columns. A *second line matcher* works on one or more similarity matrices, e.g., by thresholding or combining them. Certain second line matchers create a binary similarity matrix $M'(A_1,A_2)$ with entries being either 0 or 1, the latter represents correspondences.

Figure 1 illustrates the matching problem with two processes for registering a newborn. Although both processes are similar, the lower process slightly deviates from the upper one. Considering the highlighted correspondences between both models, it becomes apparent that some matches are more easily identified than others. A straightforward correspondence is the one between *Receive notification of birth* and *Receive notific. of birth* as measures for first line matching, e.g., the Levenshtein distance, indicate high values in a similarity matrix. However, to identify complex correspondences involving sets of activities, like the one between *Decide about first name* and *Decide about second name* with *Confirm choice of name*, the usage of semantic knowledge and the model structure is required. For instance, lexical databases can help to identify that words such as *decide* and *confirm* are close in their meaning. Other differences relate to models in their properties. The upper process contains three splits, whereas the lower one represents a plain sequence of tasks. Hence, we anticipate that there may be several complex correspondences that are generally harder to identify.

Schema Matching Prediction. Our approach relies on recent results on *schema matching prediction* [8]. In the absence of a ground truth, matchers perform a "best effort" matching without any indication of the prospective success of their efforts. Schema matching prediction provides an assessment mechanism that supports schema matchers in this context. Predictors foretell the success of a matcher in identifying correct correspondences by analysing the matcher's pair-wise similarity scores.

Sagi and Gal [8] argue for the importance of *tunability* to support prediction of different qualities, putting emphasis, e.g., on precision or recall. Thus, prediction models compose various, loosely correlated predictors into a statistical model. The weights of participating predictors are tuned, so that the combined prediction correlates well with the desired quality criterion. To accommodate for tunable prediction models, our work leverages a set of matrix evaluation functions, termed *matrix predictors* [8]. These predictors encode different assumptions on how a particular value distribution in a similarity matrix indicates the likelihood of a successful match. Each predictor is applied to a similarity matrix $M(A_1,A_2)$ obtained by a first line matcher and yields a non-binary prediction value. Here, we give two examples for such predictors.

- An entry (a_i, a_j) in $M(A_1,A_2)$ is dominant, if it has the highest value in the respective row and column of the matrix. The *Dominants* matrix predictor measures the ratio of dominant values and $k = \min\{|A_1|, |A_2|\}$.
- The *Binary Matrix* predictor measures the distance between $M(A_1,A_2)$ and the closest ideal matrix $M'(A_1,A_2)$ in a vector space, where $M'(A_1,A_2)$ is required to be a binary matrix (with the entries being either 0 or 1).

3 Prediction for Process Model Matching

This section introduces our approach to predicting the quality of process model matching. Figure 2 illustrates the major components of the proposed prediction architecture. Given a pair of process models, prediction may either be based solely on process properties (top) or on a similarity measure (bottom). In the first case, properties of both process models are extracted and process property predictors derive a score for the model pair. In the second case, we obtain a set of similarity matrices over the activities of the processes. Then, matrix predictors exploit characteristics of these matrices to obtain a prediction score per model pair and similarity measure.

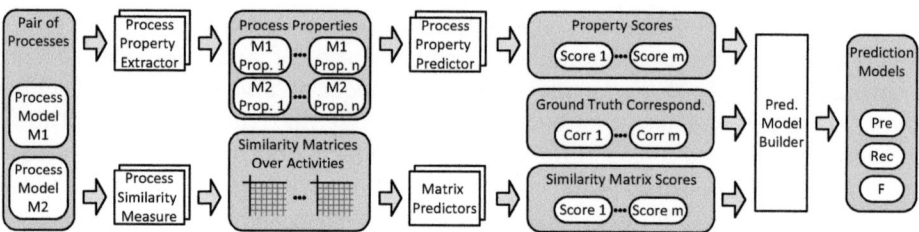

Fig. 2. Overview of the prediction architecture

The prediction scores are combined into a prediction model, predicting a certain quality measure, such as precision, recall, or their harmonic mean, the F-score. To this end, a stepwise (multi-valued) regression is performed over the whole set of predictors in the presence of a ground truth, i.e., a set of correspondences that are known to hold true. Depending on the origin of the prediction scores, the prediction model generalises in different dimensions, e.g., it is relative to process properties (if only scores per process pair are considered) or to process properties and characteristics of similarity measures.

Below, we instantiate this architecture with strategies for prediction based on process properties (Section 3.1) and process similarity measures (Section 3.2). Then, Section 3.3 discusses how prediction is used to answer the question of how to identify matching tasks for which matchers yield high quality results.

3.1 Prediction Based on Process Properties

Below, we present several examples of property predictors, each taking a certain process property and implementing an evaluation measure.

Avg Length of Labels (ALL). An example of a property referring to the textual syntax is the average length of activity labels. It can be expected to yield insights on the suitability of textual similarity measures. With avg_1 and avg_2 as the average lengths of activity labels in two processes, we define two predictors.

- ALLR is the relative difference between the properties, i.e., the prediction score is $p_{ALLR} = 1$ if $\max\{avg_1, avg_2\} = 0$ and $p_{ALLR} = 1 - (|avg_1 - avg_2|/\max\{avg_1, avg_2\})$ otherwise.
- ALLA is the arithmetic average of the smoothed absolute deviation of the property values from a label length l (e.g., $l = 20$), i.e., $p_{ALLA} = (1 - \max\{0, 1 - 0.01(avg_1 - 20)^2\})/2 + (1 - \max\{0, 1 - 0.01(avg_2 - 20)^2\})/2$.

Number of Labels with Action in a Lexical Database (NLALD). To take semantic textual features into account, we consider the number of activity labels for which the action can be found in a lexical database, e.g. WordNet [9] for English. Therefore, all activity labels are annotated with their semantic components using the approach presented by Leopold et al. [10]. Then, a lookup in a lexical database is performed. If the lookup is successful in many cases, we expect good results of textual similarity measures. With act_1 and act_2 as the numbers of activities of two process models and $actAction_1$ and $actAction_2$ as the number of these activities with labels for which the lookup succeeded, a predictor uses the arithmetic average of the ratio of labels for which actions have been found as an evaluation function, i.e., $p_{NLALD} = (actAction_1/act_1)/2 + (actAction_2/act_2)/2$.

Number of Nodes in Cycles (NNC). Focussing on structural features of a process model, we consider the number of nodes in control flow cycles. A large difference in the values of this property for two process models hints at different control flow structures and, thus, lower chances of achieving a good match result. Our predictor, thus, applies a relative comparison. With $inCycle_1$ and $inCycle_2$ as the number of nodes in two process models that are part of a control flow cycle, the prediction score is $p_{NNC} = 1$ if $\max\{inCycle_1, inCycle_2\} = 0$ and $p_{NNC} = 1 - (|inCycle_1 - inCycle_2|/\max(inCycle_1, inCycle_2))$ otherwise.

Depth of the RPST (DRPST). Another structural property of a process model is the depth of a decomposition tree, e.g., defined by the Refined Process Structure Tree (RPST) [11]. The depth of this tree provides a means to assess the complexity of the control flow structure. Complex control flow structures in either model as well as large differences in this complexity can be expected to have a negative impact on process model matching. With $depth_1$ and $depth_2$ as the depths of the RPSTs of two process models, we define two predictors.

- DRPSTR measures the relative difference, i.e., $p_{DRPSTR} = 1 - (|depth_1 - depth_2|/\max\{depth_1, depth_2\})$.
- DRPSTA measures the arithmetic average of a smoothed absolute depth, i.e., $p_{DRPSTA} = (1 - \max\{0, 1 - 0.02(depth_1 - 1)^2\})/2 + (1 - \max\{0, 1 - 0.02(depth_2 - 1)^2\})/2$.

Size of the Concurrency Relation (SCR). The size of the concurrency relation is an example for a behavioural property. The concurrency relation contains all pairs of activities that may be enabled concurrently in some reachable state of the process, cf., [12]. Since its size provides insights on behavioural complexity, high absolute values and large relative differences for two process models may lower the result quality of process model matchers. Let $conc_1$ and $conc_2$ be the sizes of the concurrency relation of two process models with act_1 and act_2 as the number of activities, respectively. Then, we define two predictors.

- SCRR measures the relative difference, i.e., $p_{SCRR} = 1$ if $\max\{conc_1, conc_2\} = 0$ and $p_{SCRR} = 1 - (|conc_1 - conc_2|/\max\{conc_1, conc_2\})$ otherwise.
- SCRA measures the arithmetic average of the ratio of concurrent activities, i.e., $p_{SCRA} = (conc_1/act_1^2)/2 + (conc_2/act_2^2)/2$.

3.2 Prediction Based on Similarity Measures

Most matchers use textual similarity measures for deriving match candidates and consider structural and behavioural features for selecting correspondences. Hence, below, we focus on textual similarity measures and, for each of them, apply one of the matrix predictors (Section 2) to obtain a prediction score.

Optimal String Edit Distance over Activity Labels (OSEDAL). A first syntactical similarity measure is the optimal string edit distance over tokenised activity labels. First, string preprocessing techniques, such as stop word removal and stemming, are applied to all terms. For the remaining, preprocessed terms $\{t_1, \ldots, t_n\}$ and $\{t'_1, \ldots, t'_m\}$ of two activity labels, we seek an optimal term alignment $\sim \subseteq \{t_1, \ldots, t_n\} \times \{t'_1, \ldots, t'_m\}$ that (1) relates one term t to at most one term t' and (2) maximises the string edit distance similarity $seds(t, t') = lev(t, t')/ \max\{|t|, |t'|\}$ (with lev as the Levenshtein Distance and $|\cdot|$ as the term length) over the aligned pairs. Then, the similarity measure for the two activities is defined as $s_{OSEDAL} = \sum_{t \sim t'} seds(t, t')/ \max\{n, m\}$.

Virtual Docs Distance Set (VDDS). As another syntactical similarity measure, we define a measure that first groups activities in either process and then assesses their similarity based on virtual documents. We follow the heuristics of the Distance Doc Searcher of the ICoP framework [4] for grouping activities: Given a base activity, we group activities based on their distance in the flow graph according to predefined patterns, e.g., a join (activities from which the base activity can be reached within a certain distance). For these groups, we derive virtual documents as the union of terms of all activity labels. For two virtual documents d and d', a vector space is created and the Cosine similarity $cos(d, d')$ is used to assess their similarity, cf., [13]. For each pair of activities a_1 and a_2, the similarity score is defined as $s_{VDDS} = \max\{cos(d_1, d'_1), \ldots, cos(d_n, d'_m)\}$ with $d_1, \ldots, d_n$ and $d'_1, \ldots, d'_m$ as documents representing groups that include a_1 and a_2, respectively.

Number of (Common) Semantic Components of Activity Labels (N(C)SCAL). Turning to semantic features, we compute a similarity based on the common semantic components of activity labels. Again, we annotate activity labels to obtain their semantic components a^{ac} (the action), a^{bo} (the object), and a^{ad} (an additional part) for the activity label a [10]. Let $comp_a \subseteq \{ac, bo, ad\}$ denote the type of the components found for activity a. Then, we define two similarity measures:

- Similarity in the number of semantic components $comp_1$ and $comp_2$ for two activities a_1 and a_2 is considered by the measure defined as $s_{NSCAL} = 1 - |((| comp_{a_1} | - | comp_{a_2} |)/3)|$.
- Similarity in the types of semantic components is considered by an adapted measure, defined as $s_{NCSCAL} = 1 - (| comp_{a_1} \cap comp_{a_2} | /3)$.

Lin Distance between Activity Labels (LDAL). A fine-grained similarity measure for semantic features, is the semantic distance among the activity labels. Given the semantic components of two labels, we assess their semantic distance with the Lin metric [14] (denoted by lin). For two activities a_1 and a_2 with a_1^{ac}, a_1^{bo}, a_1^{ad}, and a_2^{ac}, a_2^{bo}, a_2^{ad} as their semantic components, we define the similarity score as $s_{LDAL} = (lin(a_1^{ac}, a_2^{ac}) + lin(a_1^{bo}, a_2^{bo}) + lin(a_1^{ad}, a_2^{ad}))$.

3.3 Assessing the Confidence in Match Results

Predictions are used to determine the confidence that is associated with a match result. Because of their high result variability, existing matchers are rarely applicable in a setting that requires unsupervised matching, e.g., similarity search in process model repositories. Further, even if applied as a semi-automated technique, a process expert has to review all match results including those that have high quality and could directly have been processed further, as well as those that have poor quality and should thus be neglected. Using the prediction architecture, we address this issue following a machine learning approach:

(1) In a training phase, prediction models are created for a sample of process models for which some ground truth is available.
(2) In an application phase, the prediction models are applied to further matching tasks, i.e., pairs of process models, for which the ground truth is not available.

The score obtained by a prediction model is interpreted as the confidence in the match result. Prediction models should generalise for different process model matchers. They are defined relative only to process properties and characteristics of some basic similarity measures, such that the predicted score, the confidence in the match result, holds independent of any concrete matcher.

Since prediction models are geared towards a quality criterion, they can be selected for the envisioned setting of process model matching. For instance, a recall-oriented prediction qualifies for computation of match confidence when conducting process model clone detection, in order not to miss potential clones for manual evaluation. For matching in automated similarity search over process models, in turn, precision-oriented prediction may be a better option.

4 Related Work

Recently, various approaches addressed the problem of process model matching [1,3,4,5]. These works typically combine a measure for textual similarity applied for first line matching with a measure for structural or behavioural similarity that guides the second line matching. Our prediction architecture considers both and, thus, can be seen as a first step towards integrating matchers that have different strengths for certain types of matching tasks.

As for basic similarity measures, we focussed on those commonly used for process model matching. Yet, additional measures may be considered. For instance, a large number of string distance metrics, as reviewed by Cohen et al. [15], has been presented for assessing syntactic, textual similarity. Besides, a large body of structural and behavioural similarity measures are available for process models, e.g., [16,17,18]. Recent surveys of these techniques have been presented by Dijkman et al. [19] and Becker and Laue [20]. These measures can be integrated in our architecture to broaden the basis of prediction.

5 Conclusion

The presented approach addresses the issue of variability in the results obtained by process model matchers. We showed how prediction models for the quality of match results are created based on predictors that refer to process properties and characteristics of similarity measures. Such prediction models allow for assigning a confidence value to a match result.

In future work, we aim at conducting prediction on a more fine-granular level, i.e., for individual correspondences. Also, we want to exploit prediction not only for post-matching analysis, but also for improving the actual matching.

References

1. Castelo Branco, M., Troya, J., Czarnecki, K., Küster, J., Völzer, H.: Matching business process workflows across abstraction levels. In: France, R.B., Kazmeier, J., Breu, R., Atkinson, C. (eds.) MODELS 2012. LNCS, vol. 7590, pp. 626–641. Springer, Heidelberg (2012)
2. Ekanayake, C.C., Dumas, M., García-Bañuelos, L., Rosa, M.L., ter Hofstede, A.H.M.: Approximate clone detection in repositories of business process models. [21], pp. 302–318
3. Dijkman, R.M., Dumas, M., García-Bañuelos, L., Kääarik, R.: Aligning business process models. In: EDOC, pp. 45–53. IEEE Computer Society (2009)
4. Weidlich, M., Dijkman, R., Mendling, J.: The iCoP framework: Identification of correspondences between process models. In: Pernici, B. (ed.) CAiSE 2010. LNCS, vol. 6051, pp. 483–498. Springer, Heidelberg (2010)
5. Leopold, H., Niepert, M., Weidlich, M., Mendling, J., Dijkman, R.M., Stuckenschmidt, H.: Probabilistic optimization of semantic process model matching. [21], pp. 319–334
6. Gal, A.: Uncertain Schema Matching. Morgan & Claypool Publishers (2011)
7. Bellahsene, Z., Bonifati, A., Rahm, E. (eds.): Schema Matching and Mapping. Springer (2011)
8. Sagi, T., Gal, A.: Schema matching prediction with applications to data source discovery and dynamic ensembling. Technical Report IE/IS-2013-02, Technion (March 2013), http://ie.technion.ac.il/tech_reports/1364134687_Prediction_v7.pdf
9. Miller, G.A.: WordNet: A lexical database for English. Commun. ACM 38(11), 39–41 (1995)
10. Leopold, H., Smirnov, S., Mendling, J.: On the refactoring of activity labels in business process models. Inf. Syst. 37(5), 443–459 (2012)
11. Vanhatalo, J., Völzer, H., Koehler, J.: The refined process structure tree. Data Knowl. Eng. 68(9), 793–818 (2009)
12. Kovalyov, A., Esparza, J.: A polynomial algorithm to compute the concurrency relation of free-choice signal transition graphs. In: WODES, Edinburgh, Scotland, UK. IEE Society (1996)
13. Salton, G., Wong, A., Yang, C.S.: A vector space model for automatic indexing. Commun. ACM 18(11), 613–620 (1975)
14. Lin, D.: An information-theoretic definition of similarity. In: Proceedings of the 15th International Conference on Machine Learning, pp. 296–304. Morgan Kaufmann (1998)
15. Cohen, W.W., Ravikumar, P.D., Fienberg, S.E.: A comparison of string distance metrics for name-matching tasks. In: IIWeb, pp. 73–78 (2003)
16. Wombacher, A., Li, C.: Alternative approaches for workflow similarity. In: IEEE SCC, pp. 337–345. IEEE Computer Society (2010)
17. Corrales, J.C., Grigori, D., Bouzeghoub, M.: BPEL processes matchmaking for service discovery. In: Meersman, R., Tari, Z. (eds.) OTM 2006. LNCS, vol. 4275, pp. 237–254. Springer, Heidelberg (2006)
18. Kunze, M., Weidlich, M., Weske, M.: Behavioral similarity – A proper metric. In: Rinderle-Ma, S., Toumani, F., Wolf, K. (eds.) BPM 2011. LNCS, vol. 6896, pp. 166–181. Springer, Heidelberg (2011)
19. Dijkman, R.M., Dumas, M., van Dongen, B.F., Kääarik, R., Mendling, J.: Similarity of business process models: Metrics and evaluation. Inf. Syst. 36(2), 498–516 (2011)
20. Becker, M., Laue, R.: A comparative survey of business process similarity measures. Computers in Industry 63(2), 148–167 (2012)
21. Barros, A., Gal, A., Kindler, E. (eds.): BPM 2012. LNCS, vol. 7481. Springer, Heidelberg (2012)

Increasing Recall of Process Model Matching by Improved Activity Label Matching

Christopher Klinkmüller[1,2], Ingo Weber[2,3], Jan Mendling[4], Henrik Leopold[5], and André Ludwig[1]

[1] Information Systems Institute, University of Leipzig, Leipzig, Germany*
{klinkmueller,ludwig}@wifa.uni-leipzig.de
[2] Software Systems Research Group, NICTA, Sydney, Australia**
ingo.weber@nicta.com.au
[3] School of Computer Science & Engineering, University of New South Wales
[4] Wirtschaftsuniversität Wien, Augasse 2-6, A-1090 Vienna, Austria
jan.mendling@wu.ac.at
[5] Humboldt-Universität zu Berlin, Unter den Linden 6, 10099 Berlin, Germany
henrik.leopold@wiwi.hu-berlin.de

Abstract. Comparing process models and matching similar activities has recently emerged as a research area of business process management. However, the problem is fundamentally hard when considering realistic scenarios: e.g., there is a huge variety of terms and various options for the grammatical structure of activity labels exist. While prior research has established important conceptual foundations, recall values have been fairly low (around 0.26) – arguably too low to be useful in practice. In this paper, we present techniques for activity label matching which improve current results (recall of 0.44, without sacrificing precision). Furthermore, we identify categories of matching challenges to guide future research.

Keywords: BPM, process similarity, process model matching.

1 Introduction

Business process models support analysis, redesign, and implementation projects in enterprises. In various situations, correspondences between different process models have to be found, e.g. when similar processes of recently merged companies have to be identified. The major challenge in such scenarios is the efficient and effective identification of same or similar activities in heterogeneous models.

Recent research has approached the problem of automatically matching activities between process models by adopting techniques from schema and ontology

---

* The work presented in this paper was partly funded by the German Federal Ministry of Education and Research under the projects LSEM (BMBF 03IPT504X) and LogiLeit (BMBF 03IPT504A).
** NICTA is funded by the Australian Government as represented by the Department of Broadband, Communications and the Digital Economy and the Australian Research Council through the ICT Centre of Excellence program.

matching [15,9]. However, the few studies in this area reveal an issue with recall. This is a serious problem since process matching is usually utilized as decision support. As such it aims to show users an extensive set of potential matches from which they de-select false positives [4]. A prerequisite for applying matching in such a way is a high recall and a big share to be true matches.

This paper contributes to the area of process model matching in a twofold way. First, we present label matching techniques that aim to improve the recall without weakening precision. These techniques are evaluated using established benchmark samples, and yield statistically significant improvements. The source code for the techniques and for the evaluation is publicly available[1]. Second, we conduct a qualitative study towards identifying categories of issues that impede matching performance. Our work not only has implications for process matching research, but also for consistent process modeling altogether.

The paper is structured as follows. Section 2 summarizes prior research and section 3 introduces the techniques for improving recall. Evaluation results and a qualitative analysis are presented in section 4. Section 5 concludes the paper.

2 Prior Research on Process Model Matching

The use of heterogeneous terminology and labels with different levels of details as well as different grammatical structure are challenges, not only to process matching research, but also to practice [1]. The foundations for research in process model matching can be found in various works on process model similarity and ontology matching. Such process similarity techniques exploit different sources of information such as text [3,7], model structure [6,2], or execution semantics [8,16]. Approaches on process model matching directly build on such techniques and combine them in different ways. For example, the ICoP framework defines a generic architecture for assembling and combining different matchers [15]. It, for instance, integrates the graph-based matcher from [2] and the Levenshtein distance [11]. The semantic matcher proposed in [9] relies on Markov logic networks and on an approach to derive semantic match hypotheses from model pairs. Therefore, they apply a label decomposition approach [10] to annotate each activity with action, business object, and additional fragment. Based on the semantic comparison of these components with techniques from ontology matching [5], such as the Lin metric [12], semantic match hypotheses are computed. These hypotheses then serve as input for the Markov model. Although these approaches include several similarity measures and apply complex mechanisms to compute the best matching constellation, they only achieve low recall values of around 0.26.

3 Activity Label Similarity

We now discuss techniques for matching activities based on their labels. Therefore, we introduce a basic process matching algorithm. Subsequently, we describe two variations of this algorithm called *Bag-of-Words* and *Label Pruning*.

---

[1] http://code.google.com/p/jpmmt/

Basic Process Matching Algorithm. Algorithm 1 presents our basic procedure to compute activity matches between two process models p_1, p_2. As we do not consider structural properties of process models for process matching, we simply refer to a process model as a set of activities $p \in \mathcal{P}(A)$. Furthermore, each activity is given a label which is returned by the function $\lambda : A \to \mathcal{L}$.

First, the function *createSimilarityMatrix* calculates similarity scores of all activity pairs as $sim.\lambda(a_1, a_2)$, where $a_1 \in p_1$, $a_2 \in p_2$. $sim.\lambda = 0$ implies complete dissimilarity, $sim.\alpha = 1$ means that the two words are identical, and in between are degrees of similarity. Next, the algorithm selects all activity pairs whose similarity score is above a threshold, and proposes them as matches.

Algorithm 1. Basic process matching algorithm (pseudocode)

```
map(Process p1, Process p2, double threshold) {
  SimilarityMatrix sim = createSimilarityMatrix(p1,p2);
  MatchList matches = emptyMatchList();
  while (highestScore(sim) >= threshold) {
    ActivityPair match = getPairWithHighestScore(sim);
    addMatch(matches, match);
    removeMatchFromMatrix(sim, match);
  }
  return matches;
}
```

Bag-of-Words. The first variant adopts the bag-of-words technique, where we treat each label as a set of words – and do not further consider the structure of the label. The rationale for neglecting label structure is that the brevity of labels makes it hard to deduce information like word forms. In this way, we aim to offer a means to find matches like "prepare online application" vs. "apply online".

In order to define the bag-of-words similarity, a *tokenize* function is introduced as $tok : \mathcal{L} \to \mathcal{P}(\mathcal{W})$, from the set of labels, $\mathcal{L}$, to the powerset of words $\mathcal{P}(\mathcal{W})$. This function splits a label into its individual words, and removes common *stop words* like "the", "if", and "to". Then, the label similarity $sim.\lambda$ is computed by comparing the tokenized words of both labels, using a word similarity function $sim.\omega : (\omega_1, \omega_2) \to [0..1]$ which has the same properties as *actsim*. Note that we evaluate concrete implementations of $sim.\omega$ in section 4. In the basic variant, $sim.\lambda_b$, we aggregate these values by determining the maximum similarity score for each word and calculating the mean over these values.

Definition 1 (Basic bag-of-words similarity). Let p_1, p_2 be two processes, and $a_1 \in p_1$, $a_2 \in p_2$ be two activities. We define $\Omega^1 := tok(\lambda_1(a_1))$, $\Omega^2 := tok(\lambda_2(a_2))$ as tokenized lists of words contained in the labels. The basic bag-of-word similarity $sim.\lambda_b(a_1, a_2)$ is then defined as:

$$sim.\lambda_b(a_1,a_2) := \frac{\sum_{i=1}^{|\Omega^1|} max_{j=1}^{|\Omega^2|}(sim.\omega(\omega_i^1,\omega_j^2)) + \sum_{j=1}^{|\Omega^2|} max_{i=1}^{|\Omega^1|}(sim.\omega(\omega_i^1,\omega_j^2))}{|\Omega^1| + |\Omega^2|}$$

Label Pruning. The second technique for label similarity builds on $sim.\lambda_b$, but attempts to better capture activity labels with a strong difference in specificity.

This extension called $sim.\lambda_p$ prunes words from the longer label. Thus, in cases where $|\Omega^1| > |\Omega^2|$ (without loss of generality), e.g. "rank application on scale of 1 to 10" vs. "rank case", $sim.\lambda_p$ only considers $|\Omega^2|$-many words of Ω^1.

First, we introduce a generic function $pru : \mathcal{P}(\mathcal{W}) \times \mathcal{P}(\mathcal{W}) \to \mathcal{P}(\mathcal{W})$. It returns a set of words extracted from its first input: $pru(\Omega^1, \Omega^2)$ is Ω^1 iff $|\Omega^1| \leq |\Omega^2|$, or a subset of Ω^1 of size $|\Omega^2|$ otherwise. Criteria for choosing the words to prune from Ω^1 are introduced below the generic definition of $sim.\lambda_p$.

Definition 2 (Bag-of-words similarity with label pruning). *Let p_1, p_2 be two processes, $a_1 \in p_1$, $a_2 \in p_2$ two activities, and $\Omega^1 := tok(\lambda_1(a_1))$, $\Omega^2 := tok(\lambda_2(a_2))$ tokenized lists of words contained in the labels. Further, $pr_1 = pru(\Omega^1, \Omega^2)$ and $pr_2 = pru(\Omega^2, \Omega^1)$ are the pruned lists of words. The bag-of-words similarity with label pruning $sim.\lambda_p(a_1, a_2)$ is then defined as:*

$$sim.\lambda_p(a_1, a_2) := \frac{\sum_{i=1}^{|\Omega^1|} max_{j=1}^{|\Omega^2|}(sim.\omega(pr_1^i, pr_2^j)) + \sum_{j=1}^{|\Omega^2|} max_{i=1}^{|\Omega^1|}(sim.\omega(pr_1^i, pr_2^j))}{2 \times min(|\Omega^1|, |\Omega^2|)}$$

We consider three variants of pru. The first variant, pru_{max}, calculates the similarity scores for all word pairs, as well as the maximal score for each word in $|\Omega^1|$. $pru_{max}(\Omega^1, \Omega^2)$ returns the $|\Omega^2|$-top-scoring words from Ω^1. The second and the third variant rely on the occurrence of a term t in a collection of documents $\mathcal{D}$, called *document frequency* (df). The df measure is defined as $\frac{f_t}{|\mathcal{D}|}$, where f_t is the number of documents containing t. In our context, an activity label is considered a document, but we provide two variants for determining which documents are considered part of the collection. One variant takes all activity labels of all models in the model collection as part of the document pool. This variant is called pru_{coll}. In the other variant, only the activity labels of the two models being compared form the document pool. This variant is called pru_{2p}. In both cases the $|\Omega^2|$ words from Ω^1 with the highest df are selected. Applying df, we consider words occuring more often as more important for activity matching.

4 Evaluation

In this section, we evaluate the introduced matching techniques. First, we describe the evaluation's setup including the data set and parameter sampling. Then, the results are presented with focus on precision and recall. Next, we provide a qualitative result analysis. Finally, the findings are discussed.

Setup. In order to achieve comparability, we used the data set from [9] containing a *process model collection* of nine admission processes of German universities which are publicly available[2]. The other part of the evaluation data is a *process matching standard* which was also used in [9]. It defines normative 1:1 activity matches for all 36 possible pairs in the collection.

---
[2] http://www.mendling.com/Admission_Processes_BPM2012_Leopold_et_al.zip

To evaluate the quality of a matching technique, each 1:1 match found by the technique can be classified as true-positive (TP), true-negative (TN), false-positive (FP), or false-negative (FN) – with respect to the standard. Based on this classification the standard measures of *precision (P)* (TP/(TP+FP)), *recall (R)* (TP/(TP+FN)), and F_1 *measure* as harmonic mean between P and R ($2 \times P \times R/(P+R)$) can be computed for each model pair. We measure overall quality for a given technique as the mean and standard deviation of these three values over the set of process pairs.

In the evaluation, we examined different parameter configurations for the basic process matching algorithm and both label similarity scores. We sampled *threshold* over the interval [0..1] in steps of 0.05. Furthermore, we employed the following variants for $sim.\omega$:

1. Levenshtein ($sim.\omega_{lev}$): based on the Levenshtein distance [11]
2. Lin ($sim.\omega_{lin}$): a semantic notion [12] based on WordNet [14]
3. Levenshtein-Lin-Max ($sim.\omega_{max}$) the maximum of $sim.\omega_{lev}$ and $sim.\omega_{lin}$
4. Stemmed versions of the former ($sim.\omega_{s.lev}$, $sim.\omega_{s.lin}$, $sim.\omega_{s.max}$): which apply word stemming [13] and in particular the stemming algorithm in the state-of-the-art tool *MIT Java Wordnet Interface*[3] to their stems.

Results. Table 1 summarizes the evaluation results. The first two rows list the results from [9] whereby *ICoP* refers to a matching approach based on the ICoP framework and *Markov* to the one relying on Markov Logic (cf. Section 2).

The next two rows outline the results for the basic process matching algorithm in combination with the basic bag-of-words similarity. The first row shows the best parameter configuration when applying word similarity functions without stemming, while the second row presents the best stemming variant. Note, that "best" refers to the highest F_1 value obtained using the parameter sampling explained above. There are two important observations. First, the variant without stemming outperformed Markov and ICoP regarding precision (0.748), recall (0.299) and F_1 (0.363). Second, the application of stemming helped to improve the F_1 value (0.372) due to higher precision (0.808) and recall (0.304).

The last three rows represent the best results for the basic process matching algorithm in combination with each of the three pruning variants. All pruning variants yield higher F_1 measures than the best basic bag-of-words variants. The best F_1 measure (0.409) was yielded by the document frequency variant using the whole model collection (pru_{coll}). This variant also yielded the highest recall (0.450), while the variant based on the maximal similarity scores yielded the highest precision (0.735).

Qualitative Analysis: Matching Challenges. To identify challenges in matching activity labels we conducted, a qualitative analysis based on data collected during the evaluation. For the admission data set, we considered all matches found by the best configuration as well as all matches contained in the gold standard – a total of 912 matches comprising 223 true positives (TP), 381

---
[3] http://projects.csail.mit.edu/jwi/

Table 1. Evaluation results for variants of bag-of-words similarity

variant	precision	stddev.	recall	stddev.	F_1	stddev.	threshold	$sim.\omega$	prune
Markov	0.421	0.217	0.263	0.170	0.315	0.182	-	-	-
ICoP	0.506	0.309	0.255	0.282	0.294	0.253	-	-	-
$sim.\lambda_b$	0.748	0.254	0.299	0.282	0.363	0.249	0.75	max	-
$sim.\lambda_b$	0.808	0.241	0.304	0.281	0.372	0.247	0.75	$s.lev$	-
$sim.\lambda_p$	0.735	0.235	0.331	0.279	0.393	0.245	0.75	$s.lev$	max
$sim.\lambda_p$	0.468	0.253	0.450	0.256	0.409	0.179	0.70	$s.lin$	$coll$
$sim.\lambda_p$	0.689	0.259	0.356	0.287	0.407	0.242	0.80	$s.lev$	$2p$

false positives (FP) and 308 false negatives (FN). In an iterative process of manual coding and clustering, we derived a list of *matching challenge categories*. This process involved three researchers in clustering reasons and resolving different opinions in discussions. We explain the four major categories below – specificity of labels, wording, term semantics and process structure.

1. Different specificity in labels: This class refers to the degree of information provided by a label. We found a difference in the *detail of information*, a.o., when one of the activities is described in more detail than the other. There are problems with *implicit objects*, i.e. when the object of consideration is assumed to be known from the context of an activity, and thus omitted. There are also *higher-level activity* challenges, where one activity in the first process corresponds to multiple activities in the second process, or activities in both processes refer to the same higher-level activity. Finally, *action/object combinations* are challenging when one of the activities contains a list of actions or objects.
2. Other wording challenges: Challenges in this class refer to words. The *domain specificity* can be a problem. Second, *abbreviations* are sometimes used in labels. Third, the action is the same but *different conditions* might apply. Fourth, similar issues are expressed with similar words but different *sentence structure*. Fifth, one of the labels may be the *inverse* of the other.
3. Challenges from term semantics: The comparison of labels depends on the meaning of words. We identified several problems regarding the interpretation of words. A concept can be expressed by a *compound word*. A word might have *spelling errors*. There exist *semantic relations* between the concepts represented by words, like homonyms and antonyms.
4. Process structure-related challenges: Control flow characteristics may challenge activity matches. First, activities with similar labels may appear at different *control flow positions*. Second, activities may be performed by *different roles* that are not modeled. Third, processes use non-consensual *case differentiation*.

The results of the analysis are summarized in Table 2. For each challenge the table shows how often it was identified (#) and the relative appearance in false positive (FP) and false negative (FN) matches – note that a match can pose

Table 2. Matching challenge classification, ordered by number of occurrences (#)

class	challenge	#	FP	FN	class	challenge	#	FP	FN
1	detail of information	463	0.35	0.51	4	different roles	75	1.00	0.00
3	compound words	412	0.59	0.26	4	case differentiation	59	0.24	0.49
1	implicit object	290	0.38	0.48	2	abbreviations	27	0.11	0.82
2	different conditions	249	0.48	0.36	2	domain specificity	25	0.40	0.56
1	higher-level activity	223	0.05	0.87	3	spelling errors	21	0.29	0.57
3	semantic relation	136	0.22	0.54	2	sentence structure	17	0.77	0.00
4	control flow position	120	1.00	0.00	2	inverse	9	0.67	0.33
1	action/object combinations	99	0.37	0.46					

multiple challenges. The most striking problems are apparently *detail of information* and *compound words*. Overall, challenges regarding the label specificity appear to constitute the biggest source of errors, while challenges related to the process structure and other wording issues seem to occur least often.

Discussion. The evaluation shows that we were able to outperform the results of the two state-of-the-art approaches from previous research by applying our label based matching techniques. Most of the gains in recall can be attributed to the general design decision to employ a bag-of-words technique. This is in contrast to prior research where the label structure is explicitly utilized [9]. Disregarding the label structure alone already yielded improvements in our evaluation, with word stemming and pruning providing further gains.

Our post-hoc analysis of false positive and false negative match proposals provides a good basis for future innovations in process model matching. Detail of information and compound words are difficult problems, in particular as their resolution has to rely on less semantic context and text structure as in general natural language processing. There are also problems that are apparently specific to process models. The identification of implicit objects and roles may offer opportunities for further improvements.

However, the validity of our results is clearly restricted by the size of the data set used in the evaluation. Linked thereto is the threat to validity that we did not distinguish between training and evaluation data. A clear separation of data for development and evaluation purposes prevents the development of techniques well suited for a certain data set. Thus, enlarging the evaluation data set is an important step to substantiate our findings in future work.

5 Conclusion

In this paper, we presented techniques for improving process activity matching. In particular, our focus is on activity labels, so as to increase recall of matches when applied to realistic process model collections. Our comparative evaluation shows that we achieved significant improvements: recall increased by around 0.2 to 0.445. Driven by this outcome, we analyzed what makes activity matching hard, and categorized the challenges into 4 classes over 15 categories in total.

In future work, we plan to pursue two directions regarding the improvement of process matching: investigating additional techniques for considering process structure, both from literature and new approaches, as well as further improving label matching. To substantiate our findings we will also work on an enlarging our evaluation data set.

References

1. Castelo Branco, M., Troya, J., Czarnecki, K., Küster, J., Völzer, H.: Matching business process workflows across abstraction levels. In: France, R.B., Kazmeier, J., Breu, R., Atkinson, C. (eds.) MODELS 2012. LNCS, vol. 7590, pp. 626–641. Springer, Heidelberg (2012)
2. Dijkman, R., Dumas, M., García-Bañuelos, L.: Graph matching algorithms for business process model similarity search. In: Dayal, U., Eder, J., Koehler, J., Reijers, H.A. (eds.) BPM 2009. LNCS, vol. 5701, pp. 48–63. Springer, Heidelberg (2009)
3. Dijkman, R., Dumas, M., van Dongen, B., Käärik, R., Mendling, J.: Similarity of business process models: Metrics and evaluation. Inf. Syst. 36(2), 498–516 (2011)
4. Duchateau, F., Bellahsene, Z., Coletta, R.: A flexible approach for planning schema matching algorithms. In: COOPIS 2008 (2008)
5. Euzenat, J., Shvaiko, P.: Ontology Matching. Springer (2007)
6. Grigori, D., Corrales, J.C., Bouzeghoub, M.: Behavioral Matchmaking for Service Retrieval. In: IEEE ICWS (2006)
7. Koschmider, A., Blanchard, E.: User assistance for business process model decomposition. In: IEEE RCIS (2007)
8. Kunze, M., Weidlich, M., Weske, M.: Behavioral similarity – A proper metric. In: Rinderle-Ma, S., Toumani, F., Wolf, K. (eds.) BPM 2011. LNCS, vol. 6896, pp. 166–181. Springer, Heidelberg (2011)
9. Leopold, H., Niepert, M., Weidlich, M., Mendling, J., Dijkman, R., Stuckenschmidt, H.: Probabilistic optimization of semantic process model matching. In: Barros, A., Gal, A., Kindler, E. (eds.) BPM 2012. LNCS, vol. 7481, pp. 319–334. Springer, Heidelberg (2012)
10. Leopold, H., Smirnov, S., Mendling, J.: On the refactoring of activity labels in business process models. Inf. Syst. 37(5), 443–459 (2012)
11. Levenshtein, V.I.: Binary codes capable of correcting deletions, insertions and reversals. Soviet Physics Doklady 10(8), 707–710 (1966)
12. Lin, D.: An information-theoretic definition of similarity. In: ICML (1998)
13. Lovins, J.B.: Development of a stemming algorithm. Mechanical Translation and Computational Linguistics 11, 22–31 (1968)
14. Miller, G.A.: Wordnet: a lexical database for english. Commun. ACM 38(11), 39–41 (1995)
15. Weidlich, M., Dijkman, R., Mendling, J.: The iCoP framework: Identification of correspondences between process models. In: Pernici, B. (ed.) CAiSE 2010. LNCS, vol. 6051, pp. 483–498. Springer, Heidelberg (2010)
16. Zha, H., Wang, J., Wen, L., Wang, C., Sun, J.: A workflow net similarity measure based on transition adjacency relations. Computers in Industry 61(5), 463–471

A Visualization Approach for Difference Analysis of Process Models and Instance Traffic

Simone Kriglstein[1], Günter Wallner[2], and Stefanie Rinderle-Ma[3]

[1] SBA Research, Vienna, Austria
skriglstein@sba-research.at
[2] University of Applied Arts, Institute of Art and Technology, Vienna, Austria
guenter.wallner@uni-ak.ac.at
[3] University of Vienna, Faculty of Computer Science, Vienna, Austria
stefanie.rinderle-ma@univie.ac.at

Abstract. Organizations are often confronted with the task to identify differences and commonalities between process models but also between the instance traffic that presents how instances have progressed through the model. The use cases range from comparison of process variants in order to identify redundancies and inconsistencies between them to the analysis of instance traffic for the (re)design of models. Visualizations can support users in their analysis tasks, e.g., to see if and how the models and their instance traffic have changed. In this paper we present a visualization approach to highlight the differences and commonalities between two models and – if available – their instance traffic.

Keywords: Visualization, Control Flow Analysis.

1 Introduction

In the last years, the interest to develop approaches in order to support users in analyzing process models and their instances with regard to their differences and commonalities has increased. This could be partly caused by the need to manage the increasing number of process models and their instances that can accumulate in organizations over the years (cf. [12]). Therefore different ways to compare process models have been developed. One way is the use of similarity checks (see, e.g., [8,17]) for checking commonalities. Another way is to check explicitly for the differences between the process models (e.g., [7]).

According to van der Aalst [2], there exist only a few techniques (e.g., [1,9,11]) for detecting differences in process models, but because of the importance it needs more attention. For example, in addition to the analysis of process models, it is also of interest to find techniques to analyze the instance traffic (based on the executable logs or simulation data) that reflects how instances have progressed through the model in order to, e.g., see the distribution of instances over the different paths through the process model. Understanding the flow of instances helps to distinguish well-designed models from models that require modifications (e.g., to identify redundant paths because of changed conditions). Furthermore, the analysis of the differences between the instance traffic helps to identify trends across multiple process instances or time periods. Moreover, it allows to see if and how the traffic has changed, e.g., to detect more or less visited paths or to follow the consequences of changes in process models with respect to the execution of instances.

In this paper we present a visualization approach to highlight the difference information between process models and – if available – between the instance traffic in a single graph. The differences between the two input models and their instance traffic are visualized as difference model that merges the two input models in such a way that it allows users to visually see differences and commonalities between the two models. With the presented visualization approach, users have the possibility to analyze two models and their instance traffic to support the following tasks: 1) comparison of two process models, 2) comparison of instance traffic between two process models and 3) comparison of instance traffic of one model at different points in time.

2 Related Work

Comparing artifacts in order to detect their differences plays an important role in many application domains. For example, detecting differences in models is an essential operation in software development including version and change management, software evolution etc. in order to find problems or to detect discrepancies between the models (see, e.g., [3,13,14,16]). Especially for business processes, delta analysis is used in order to compare the differences between two models. For example, various approaches were developed that use delta analysis to compare predefined process models with discovered models derived from event logs (e.g., [1,9,11]).

For the representation of differences, color-coding is often used to highlight which nodes and edges were added or removed from a graph (see, e.g., [5,6,10,13,14]). In contrast, Andrews et al. [4] use color-coding in such a way that each of the two input models is associated with a single color. The difference model is a superposition of the two input models in order to highlight differences and commonalities between both models. The coloring of the nodes in the calculated difference model depicts in which input model the node is present. If a node is present in both input models the node is two colored. In contrast to our approach, their approach requires to specify node similarities a priori before the difference model can be calculated.

3 Basic Concepts

In this paper, we focus on a visualization concept for directed connected graphs in order to provide a basis for existing business process modeling and execution notations such as Event-driven Process Chains (EPC), UML Activity Diagrams, and the Business Process Modeling Notation (BPMN). For special concepts of certain languages corresponding extensions might become necessary.

At this point we should also emphasize that we are looking at the processes from the control flow perspective.

3.1 Difference Model

We define a process model as a directed connected graph $PM = (N, E \subseteq N \times N)$, where N is a set of nodes and E is a set of directed control edges. Each node $n \in N$ is described by a 3-tuple (id, l, t) where id is a unique identifier, l is the label and t is the type of the node. Different business modeling languages like BPMN or EPC distinguish between different types of nodes. For example, BPMN differentiates between activity nodes, event nodes, and gateway nodes for the control flow graph. For the sake of simplicity, we restrict the following discussion to activity and gateway nodes.

A process model contains one start node and one end node. Nodes are connected in such a way that each node is on a path from the start point to the end point. The start node has no incoming edge and the end node has no outgoing edge. Let $PM_1 = (N_1, E_1)$ and $PM_2 = (N_2, E_2)$ be the two process model to be compared, then the *difference model*[1] can be defined as

$$DM = PM_2 - PM_1 := (N_d, E_d, M_{N_d}, M_{E_d}) = \\ = (N_2 \cup N_1, E_2 \cup E_1, M_{N_d}, M_{E_d}) \quad (1)$$

where M_{N_d} and M_{E_d} describe the node and edge markings of DM with $M_{N_d} : N_d \mapsto \{-1, 0, 1\}$ and $M_{E_d} : E_d \mapsto \{-1, 0, 1\}$. For a node $n \in N_d$ its marking is determined as follows:

$$m_n = \begin{cases} 0, & \text{if } n \in N_1 \wedge n \in N_2. \\ 1, & \text{if } n \in N_2 \wedge n \notin N_1. \\ -1, & \text{otherwise.} \end{cases} \quad (2)$$

The same applies for the marking of a control edge $e \in E_d$:

$$m_e = \begin{cases} 0, & \text{if } e \in E_1 \wedge e \in E_2. \\ 1, & \text{if } e \in E_2 \wedge e \notin E_1. \\ -1, & \text{otherwise.} \end{cases} \quad (3)$$

The markings are used to distinguish between *add* and *delete* change operations. The markings also indirectly cover some other change operations like *move* (moving a node will remove it from the old location and add it at a new location in the model), but currently we do not account for them explicitly in the visualization.

3.2 Instance Traffic

If the control flow of process instances – either on the same process model or two different process models – should be compared the above concept can be extended by considering how often control edges have been executed by individual

---

[1] Mathematically, this can be considered as merging PM_1 and PM_2. However, with the term *difference model* we want to emphasize that the merged model reflects the *differences* between PM_1 and PM_2.

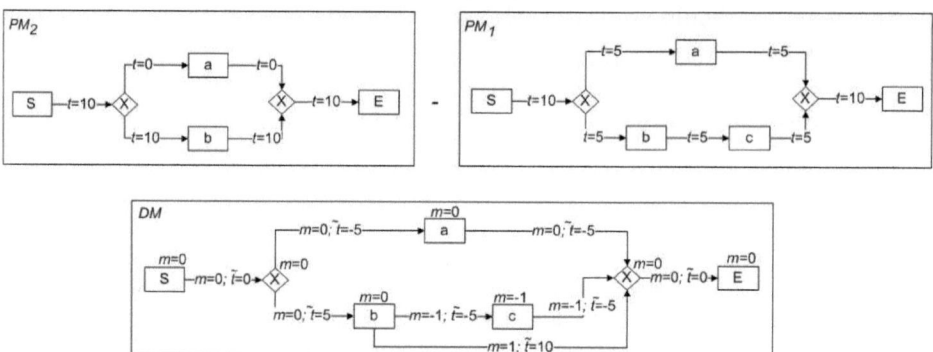

Fig. 1. An example to illustrate the instance traffic for PM_1 with $k_1 = 10$ and PM_2 with $k_2 = 10$ and the relative traffic for DM with its corresponding marking information

instances (in the following referred to as *instance traffic*) to observe the distribution of instances over the different paths through the process model. For a given process model $PM = (N, E)$ with a set of instances $\mathcal{I}$, $|\mathcal{I}| = k$ executed on PM, the instance traffic $t(e)^{PM}$ for a control edge $e \in E$ is given by the number of instances which passed e during the execution. Please note that $t(e)^{PM}$ can be greater than k if there are loops in PM which may cause an instance to pass e several times.

However, when comparing two sets of instances $\mathcal{I}_1$ executed on PM_1 and $\mathcal{I}_2$ executed on PM_2 usually $|\mathcal{I}_1| \neq |\mathcal{I}_2|$ will be different. Calculating the difference directly from the traffic values of the individual process models would therefore skew the result in favor of one of the two process models being compared. We therefore equalize the traffic by weighting the traffic of PM_2 with $\delta = k_1/k_2$. The *relative* traffic $\tilde{t}(e)^{DM}$ of $e \in E_d$ in the difference model DM is then given by

$$\tilde{t}(e)^{DM} = \delta t(e)^{PM_2} - t(e)^{PM_1} \qquad (4)$$

where $t(e)^{PM_1} = 0$ if $e \notin E_1$, $t(e)^{PM_2} = 0$ if $e \notin E_2$.

To illustrate these concepts the example in Figure 1 shows the instance traffic for two input models and the relative traffic in the corresponding difference model ($k = 10$ for both input models) with the corresponding marking information. The node S is the start point and the node E is the end point. In this example, the difference between PM_1 and PM_2 is the node c and the edges from b to c, c to gateway node x, and b to x. The instance traffic in PM_1 shows that the instances split into two halves after the XOR split (presented by the gateway node x), but in PM_2 all instances go across b. The difference model DM allows to observe these changes of the instance traffic between PM_1 and PM_2 in a single graph. For instance, the relative traffic in the difference model shows that the traffic has decreased for the path via a and increased for the path x→b→x.

Table 1. Description of the visual elements which can occur in the difference model

	Meaning	Short Description
Representation of Activities/Gateways/Edges		
□ ◇ →	No Change	Black is used to highlight all nodes $n \in N_d$ where the marking $m_n = 0$. The same applies for an edge $e \in E_d$ with $m_e = 0$.
□ ◇ →	Only in PM_2	Green is used to present all $n \in N_d$ where $m_n = 1$. The same applies for an edge $e \in E_d$ with $m_e = 1$.
□ ◇ →	Only in PM_1	Gray is used to visualize all $n \in N_d$ where $m_n = -1$. The same applies for an edge $e \in E_d$ with $m_e = -1$.
Representation of Instance Traffic between Activities/Gateways		
⇒	No Change	Blue is used to present the instance traffic between nodes if the traffic $t(e)^{PM_1} = \delta t(e)^{PM_2}$ of $e \in E_d$.
⇒	Increased Traffic	Green is used if the traffic $\delta t(e)^{PM_2} > t(e)^{PM_1}$ of $e \in E_d$.
⇒	Increased Traffic (New Edge)	Light green is used if the traffic $\delta t(e)^{PM_2} > 0 \wedge e \in E_2 \wedge e \notin E_1$ to highlight that the instance traffic increased due to the addition of e.
⇒	Decreased Traffic	Red is used to highlight the instance traffic if the traffic $\delta t(e)^{PM_2} < t(e)^{PM_1}$ of $e \in E_d$.
⇒	Decreased Traffic (Removed Edge)	Orange is used if the traffic $t(e)^{PM_1} > 0 \wedge e \in E_1 \wedge e \notin E_2$ to highlight that instance traffic decreased due to the removal of e.

4 Visualization Design and Implementation

For the visualization of the two input models and the difference model, we use a node-link representation. For the left-to-right arrangement of the nodes a Sugiyama-style layouter [15] is used. Activities are displayed as rectangular nodes and gateways as diamond shaped nodes. Color-coding is used to highlight the changes between the process models and between their instance traffic (cf. Table 1).

The thickness d of an arrow depicting the instance traffic in an input model along edge e is given by $\Delta d \cdot t(e)^{PM}$ where Δd is a user-changeable parameter. However, in case of the difference model we have to take care of the special case that $\tilde{t}(e)^{DM} = 0$ due to the adjusted instance traffic being equal in both input models. To be able to distinguish this case (and to highlight this fact in the visualization) from the case where the difference is zero because no traffic occurred along e in PM_1 as well as PM_2, the thickness in the difference model is given by

$$d = \begin{cases} d_{min} & \text{if } t(e)^{PM_1} = \delta t(e)^{PM_2} \\ \Delta d \cdot \tilde{t}(e)^{DM} & \text{otherwise.} \end{cases} \quad (5)$$

As proof of concept, we implemented a C# prototype (see Figure 2) which allows the user to load two process models that should be compared in .xml format.

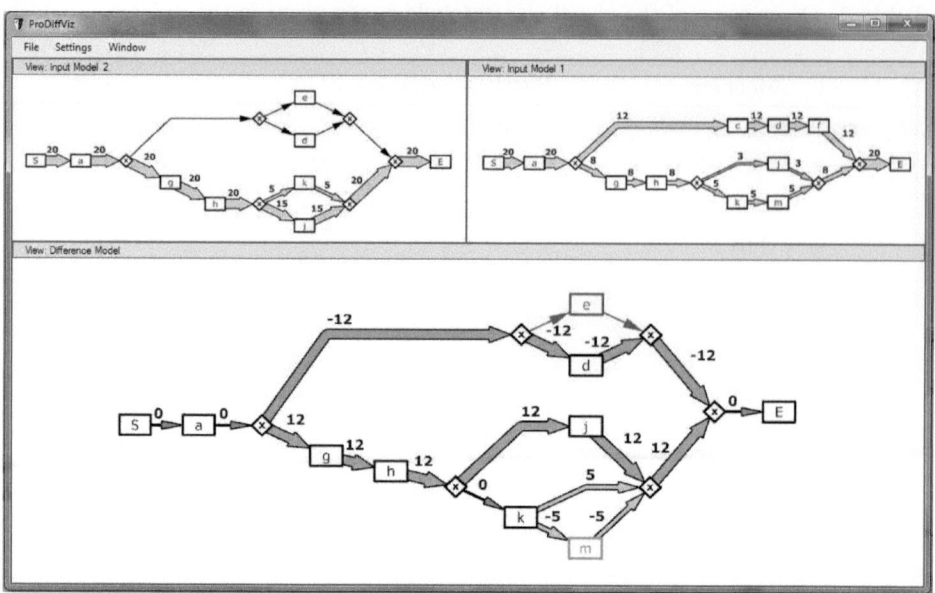

Fig. 2. Interface of the prototype. The two input models are shown on the top and the difference model at the bottom.

Multiple views are used to present the two input models and their difference model at the same time. Furthermore, users have the possibility to simulate the execution of a certain number of instances on a process model. If instances are simulated, this information is automatically considered when calculating the difference model. Options for filtering allow the user to hide or show the different types of edges (e.g., only showing edges which have been added or removed). This can be useful to reduce visual clutter especially for larger process models.

5 Use Case

Organizations are often confronted with the need to adapt their business process to react to new or changed environmental conditions (e.g., requirements of customers changed). The comparison of the different process versions and their instance traffic helps to analyze the impact of such changes. For example, the process model in Figure 3 on the right side shows that only the lower path of the process was executed whereas the upper path was never executed. A simulation of the changed process model shows the new distribution of instances over the different paths (cf. Figure 3, left side). The difference model highlights how the instance traffic changed between the two process versions. For example, the instance traffic increased for the upper path but decreased for the lower one. A reason is that the path with the increased instance traffic, has never been executed in the old version. The decreased instance traffic was caused by a different distribution of instances. A reason could be that some of the activities

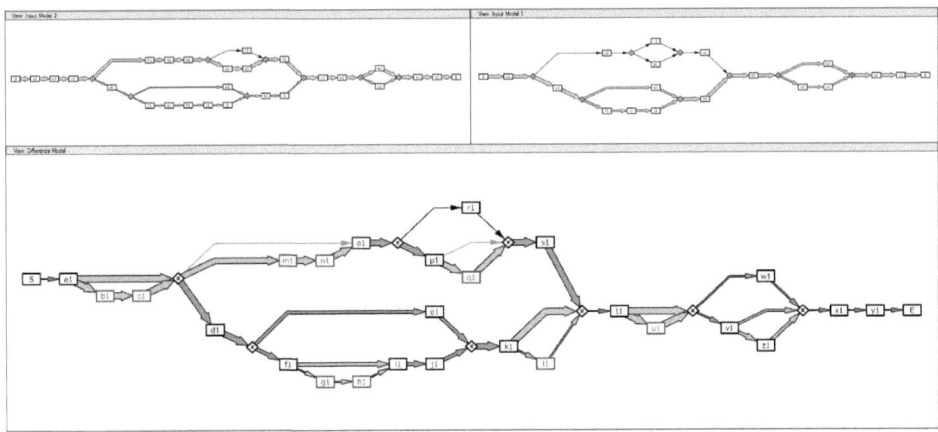

Fig. 3. Use Case: Comparison of instance traffic between two process versions

may not be well-suited for the adapted process model anymore. The difference visualization of instance traffic makes the effects of the changes visible and can support users in their design decisions (e.g., if a redesign of the process model is necessary or not).

6 Conclusion

The interest to develop approaches for the identification of differences and commonalities between process models and instances has increased in the last years. In this paper we presented a visualization approach with the goal to highlight differences but also commonalities to support the following tasks: comparison of two process models, the comparison of instance traffic between two process models and the comparison of instance traffic of one model at different points in time.

Acknowledgements. The research was funded by COMET K1, FFG - Austrian Research Promotion Agency.

References

1. van der Aalst, W.M.P.: Business alignment: Using process mining as a tool for delta analysis and conformance testing. Requir. Eng. 10(3), 198–211 (2005)
2. van der Aalst, W.M.P., Weijters, A.J.M.M.: Process mining: a research agenda. Comput. Ind. 53(3), 231–244 (2004)
3. Alanen, M., Porres, I.: Difference and union of models. In: Stevens, P., Whittle, J., Booch, G. (eds.) UML 2003. LNCS, vol. 2863, pp. 2–17. Springer, Heidelberg (2003)
4. Andrews, K., Wohlfahrt, M., Wurzinger, G.: Visual graph comparison. In: Proc. of the 13th Int. Conf. Information Visualisation, pp. 62–67. IEEE (2009)

5. Archambault, D.: Structural differences between two graphs through hierarchies. In: Proc. of Graphics Interface, pp. 87–94. GI, Canadian Information Processing Society (2009)
6. van den Brand, M., Protić, Z., Verhoeff, T.: Generic tool for visualization of model differences. In: Proc. of the 1st Int. Workshop on Model Comparison in Practice, pp. 66–75. ACM Press (2010)
7. Delugach, A., de Moor, H.: Difference graphs. In: Meersman, R., Tari, Z. (eds.) Proc. of Common Semantics for Sharing Knowledge: Contributions to the 13th Int. Conf. on Conceptual Structures, pp. 41–53. ICCS (2005)
8. Dijkman, R., Dumas, M., van Dongen, B., Käärik, R.R., Mendling, J.: Similarity of business process models: metrics and evaluation. Information Systems 36(2), 498–516 (2011)
9. Esgin, E., Senkul, P.: Delta analysis: A hybrid quantitative approach for measuring discrepancies between business process models. In: Corchado, E., Kurzyński, M., Woźniak, M. (eds.) HAIS 2011, Part I. LNCS, vol. 6678, pp. 296–304. Springer, Heidelberg (2011)
10. Geyer, M., Kaufmann, M., Krug, R.: Visualizing differences between two large graphs. In: Brandes, U., Cornelsen, S. (eds.) GD 2010. LNCS, vol. 6502, pp. 393–394. Springer, Heidelberg (2011)
11. Kleiner, N.: Delta analysis with workflow logs: aligning business process prescriptions and their reality. Requirements Engineering 10, 212–222 (2005)
12. La Rosa, M., Dumas, M., Uba, R., Dijkman, R.: Merging business process models. In: Meersman, R., Dillon, T.S., Herrero, P. (eds.) OTM 2010. LNCS, vol. 6426, pp. 96–113. Springer, Heidelberg (2010)
13. de Moor, H., Delugach, A.: Software process validation: comparing process and practice models. In: Proc. of the 11th Int. Workshop on Exploring Modeling Methods for Systems Analysis and Design (EMMSAD 2006) held in conjunction with the 18th Conf. on Advanced Information Systems (CAiSE 2006), pp. 533–540 (2006)
14. Ohst, D., Welle, M., Kelter, U.: Differences between versions of UML diagrams. In: Proc. of the 9th European Software Engineering Conf. held jointly with 11th ACM SIGSOFT Int. Symposium on Foundations of Software Engineering, ESEC/FSE, pp. 227–236. ACM Press (2003)
15. Sugiyama, K., Tagawa, S., Toda, M.: Methods for visual understanding of hierarchical system structures. IEEE Trans. Systems, Man and Cybernetics 11(2), 109–125 (1981)
16. Treude, C., Berlik, S., Wenzel, S., Kelter, U.: Difference computation of large models. In: Proc. of the the 6th Joint meeting of the European Software Engineering Conf. and the ACM SIGSOFT Symposium on the Foundations of Software Engineering, ESEC-FSE, pp. 295–304. ACM Press (2007)
17. Yan, Z., Dijkman, R., Grefen, P.: Fast business process similarity search. Distributed and Parallel Databases 30, 105–144 (2012)

Business Process Architectures with Multiplicities: Transformation and Correctness

Rami-Habib Eid-Sabbagh, Marcin Hewelt, and Mathias Weske

Hasso Plattner Institute at the University of Potsdam
{rami.eidsabbagh,marcin.hewelt,mathias.weske}@hpi.uni-potsdam.de

Abstract. Business processes are instrumental to manage work in organisations. To study the interdependencies between business processes, Business Process Architectures (BPA) have been introduced. These express trigger and message flow relations between business processes. When we investigate real world business process architectures we find complex interdependencies, involving multiple process instances. These aspects have not been studied in detail so far, especially concerning correctness properties. In this paper, we propose a modular transformation of BPAs to open nets for the analysis of behavior involving multiple business processes instances with multi-communication.

1 Introduction

In today's organisations, business processes play a key role to manage work. Business Process Architectures (BPAs) have been introduced in [1] to represent the interdependencies between related processes. Real-world scenarios show that complex relationships between business processes are rather the rule than the exception. This involves the repeated execution of processes as well as multi-communication. By this we mean communication between multiple instances of several processes, instead of one-to-one correspondence between instances. It is desirable to analyse the behavior of interacting processes and to assure certain correctness criteria.

Consider the scenario of applying for a construction permit, illustrated as BPA in Fig. 1. Depending on the type of construction, the application is forwarded to between two and five experts instantiating an appropriate number of "create expert report" processes. On termination, each instance returns a message to the "examine application" instance that waits for the according number of messages, then terminates, returning the decision to the applicant. Business process modeling approaches which allow to express these types of multiplicity do not offer formal analysis. Formal methods based on Petri nets have been successfully applied to model and analyse workflows, services and their composition as well as process choreographies. However, those elaborated analysis methods do not explicitly deal with multiple instances of processes. Our aim is to

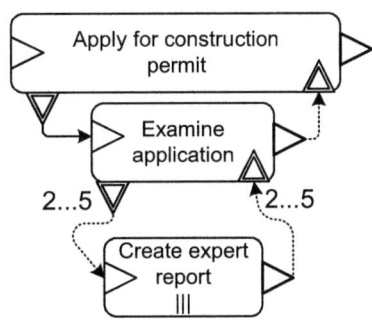

Fig. 1. Exemplary BPA

analyse BPAs with multiple instances and multi-communication. We propose a transformation from BPAs with multiplicities into open nets and introduce intermediary nets to represent and analyse multiple instances and multi-communication in this formalism.

This paper is structured as follows: Section 2 presents current research. Section 3 introduces the foundations of BPAs and open nets. Section 4 presents the transformation of BPAs into open nets, followed by the conclusion in Section 5. A detailed version of this paper containing an evaluation is published as technical report in [2].

2 Related Work

Research in the field of BPM evolved from modeling of single processes to modeling the behavior of interacting processes and choreographies, e.g. [3, 4], and analysis of their correctness [5–8]. To facilitate the modeling of process interaction existing languages were extended, e.g. BPMN with Choreography diagrams, or new notations were proposed, e.g. Let's dance. However, none of those approaches provide both means to express and formally analyse interactions between multiple process instances and multi-message communication. Most of the proposed solutions address interactions between two processes and assuming messages to be sent once to only one receiver.

Going a step further, BPMN choreographies also depict the message exchange between two or more processes but do not provide means for correctness analysis. In [3] Proclets are presented to model multi-instance communication by multicast messages via ports and associated cardinalities between different business processes. Both methodologies lack formal analysis techniques.

In contrast to that, Petri net based techniques, e.g. open nets or interaction Petri nets are used to verify correct interaction behavior, compatibility, controllability, and local enforceability [5–8]. Common patterns of service interaction between two processes were described and examined by [7, 9]. Barros et al. [9] propose three multi-transmission patterns among their basic service interaction patterns. Aalst et al. [7] look at multi-instance correlation in one to one correspondences and provide means for verification of process interaction, but they mainly deal with service refinement, replacement and integration.

Similar to their approach our solution builds on the open nets formalism to analyse process interaction behavior. It extends the current research by combining the capabilities of BPAs to express interactions between multiple processes with several process instances as well as multi-communication, with an adapted open net formalism to analyse such interactions.

3 Foundations

3.1 Business Process Architectures

Business Process Architectures capture all business processes of an organisation together with their interdependencies, expressed as message and trigger flow relations. In contrast to other approaches, BPAs provide means to model *multiplicities*, a term subsuming the sending and receiving of variably many messages to and from multiple process instances of several processes. In the model this is expressed by assigning multiplicity specifications to the events in the BPA. When external requests are grouped into scenarios, non-disjoint subsets of all processes can be identified that are responsible for handling the scenario. Such a BPA subset realizes a service or creates a product of an organisation. In the following we focus our inquiry to subsets of a BPA.

Definition 1 (Business Process Architecture (based on [1,10])). A Business Process Architecture is a tuple $(E, V, L, I, \mu, =)$, in which:
- E is a set of events, partitioned in start events, E^S, end events E^E, intermediate throwing events E^T, and intermediate catching events E^C
- V is a partition of E representing a set of business processes
- $v \in V$ is a sequence of events, $v = \langle e_1, ..., e_n \rangle$ such that $e_1 \in E^S$ is a start event, $e_n \in E^E$ an end event, and $e_i \in E^C \cup E^T$ for $1 < i < n$ are intermediate events
- $L \subseteq (E^T \cup E^E) \times E^C$ is a message flow relation.
- $I \subseteq (E^T \cup E^E) \times E^S$ is a trigger relation.
- $\mu : E \to \mathcal{P}(\mathbb{N}_0)$ denotes the multiplicity set of an event.
- $= \subseteq (E^T \times E^C) \cup (E^C \times E^T)$ is an equivalence relation between events of the same process, demanding they send resp. receive the same number of messages

The multiplicity set μ contains all valid numbers of messages or trigger signals an event can send or receive. $\mu(e) = \{1\}$ is called *trivial* and is omitted in graphical representation. The set $\bullet e = \{e' \in E^E \cup E^T | (e', e) \in I \cup L\}$, called *preset of* e, contains the events with an outgoing relation to $e \in E$. The set $e\bullet = \{e' \in E^S \cup E^C | (e, e') \in I \cup L\}$, called *postset of* e, consists of the events with an incoming relation from $e \in E$ [1].

Business Process Architecture Run. On instance level we define the notion of a *BPA run*, which describes how many instances of each process are instantiated and in which order they interact. By assigning to each event one element from its multiplicity set, the BPA run also determines how many messages or trigger signals an event sends or receives. Hence each run consists of a fixed number of process instances, which run in parallel or sequentially. The assignment of multiplicity elements to events must conform to the equivalence specification $=$.

A BPA run is started by an initial stimulus that activates all those business processes that are not triggered within the BPA, for instance the desire of a citizen to build a house in Fig. 1. The start events of those processes are considered external [1]. All other start events occur and instantiate their process when they receive the amount of assigned trigger signals from another process in the same BPA run. All events require to receive or emit the number of trigger signals or messages assigned to them by that BPA run.

BPA Correctness Criteria. As BPA subsets generally describe the interaction of many processes, the notion of soundness which was introduced for single processes is too restrictive. We propose to use the following BPA correctness criteria to decide whether a given BPA is correct.

Every BPA run initially instantiates all those processes whose start events have no incoming triggers ($\bullet b = \emptyset$). A BPA run is called *terminating* if it guarantees for all processes, that the end event of a process will occur eventually once its start event occurred.

Hence all processes that are instantiated in a terminating run also terminate. The weaker notion of *lazy termination* allows BPA runs with pending messages or left-behind process instances, if at least one instance of every process, which was instantiated by a run, terminates.

However a BPA run might also fail to terminate, if for a process of a BPA subset one or more occurrences of its start event are part of the run, but its end event is not. Such a BPA run is called a *deadlock*. Similarly, *livelocks* are BPA runs, which are infinite due to business processes triggering each other in a cyclic fashion. A BPA run need not instantiate all business processes of the BPA subset. A process in a BPA is called *dead* if no run instantiates it.

Definition 2 (Correctness Criteria for BPA Subsets). A BPA subset is correct if it complies to the following rules:
1. The BPA subset has at least one (lazily) terminating run.
2. The BPA subset is free from dead processes.
3. The BPA subset contains no livelocks.

A BPA is correct if all its subsets are correct.

3.2 Open Nets

The open nets formalism is an extension of classical Petri nets by interface places and final markings. We employ the definition and composition rules from [8,11].

For a set X we denote with $MS : X \to \mathbb{N}$ the multiset over X, where each element of X can occur multiple times (i.e. $x \in X$ occurs $MS(x)$ times). We write multisets as a formal sum of their elements e.g. $2 \cdot p_1 + p_2$ for the multiset containing two exemplars of p_1 and one of p_2. The empty multiset is denoted as 0.

Definition 3 (Open Net). An open net is a tuple $N = (P, T, F, M_0, \Omega)$ in which P is a finite set of places that is partitioned into pairwise disjoint sets of internal places P^N, incoming places P^I, and outgoing places P^O, T is a finite set of transitions, disjoint with P, $F : (P \times T) \cup (T \times P) \to \mathbb{N}$ is the flow relation assigning weights to arcs. $M : P \to \mathbb{N}$ denotes the marking of a place P, M_0 denotes the initial marking of the net, Ω the set of final markings. •t is called the preset, t• the postset of a transition $t \in T$. $t \in T$ is activated in a marking M, denoted by $m \xrightarrow{t}$ if $\forall p \in P : M(p) \geq$ •$t(p)$ i.e. if there are enough token on p for t to consume. Firing an activated transition t leads to a follower marking M' defined by $M' = M -$ •$t + t$•

Definition 4 (Composition of Open Nets). Two open nets N_1 and N_2 are called *composable* if no input place p of one net is also input place of the other net, and vice versa. If the nets are composable, composition yields open net $N = N_1 \oplus N_2$ with
- $P = P_1 \cup P_2$ and $T = T_1 \cup T_2$
- $P^I = (P_1^I \cup P_2^I) \setminus (P_1^O \cup P_2^O)$ and $P^O = (P_1^O \cup P_2^O) \setminus (P_1^I \cup P_2^I)$
- $P^N = P_1^N \cup P_2^N \cup (P_1^I \cap P_2^O) \cup (P_1^O \cap P_2^I)$
- $M_0 = M_{0_1} + M_{0_2}$
- $\Omega = \{M_1 + M_2 \mid M_1 \in \Omega_1 \land M_2 \in \Omega_2\}$

and F being defined as $F(x,y) = F_1(x,y)$ if $(x,y) \in (P_1 \times T_1) \cup (T_1 \times P_1)$ and $F_2(x,y)$ otherwise. Note that fused places become internal places in the composed net.

4 Transformation of BPA Multiplicities

4.1 Multiplicity in BPA

Business Process Architectures exhibit two kinds of multiplicity: a) multiple instances of a business process and b) sending and receiving multiple messages or trigger signals. These were described as patterns in [1] but so far not covered by the transformation proposed in [10].

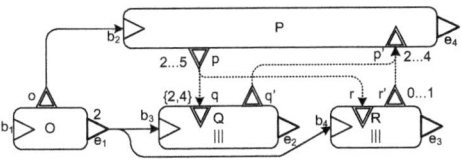

Fig. 2. BPA multiplicity concepts

A particular run of a BPA subset can comprise multiple instances of its business processes. The number of times a process is instantiated depends on the number of trigger signals it receives compared to the number assigned by its multiplicity specification in this particular run. Start events can be in trigger relation with several other events ($b \in E^S : |\bullet b| > 1$). In such a case each trigger signal from one of the predecessors causes one instance of the process to be created. If the multiplicity set of the start event is non-trivial, it needs to receive the amount of trigger signals assigned by the run, before it can occur and instantiate the process.

Sending and receiving multiple messages. Throwing events can send messages to multiple receiving processes, while catching events can receive messages from multiple sending processes according to the multiplicity assigned to them. In the first case the same amount of messages is delivered to each receiver, while in the second case messages from various senders are collected before being consumed according to the multiplicity specification. Zero is a valid value in the multiplicity set of a throwing event, meaning that a message (or trigger signal) is not sent at all. At the same time zero is forbidden in the multiplicity for catching events for the following reasons. Optional start events could instantiate an unbounded number of process instances without receiving a trigger signal, while optional receiving events would exhibit the undesired behavior of ignoring incoming messages. If the multiplicity set of an end event contains a zero, this does not mean that the process might not terminate, but rather that it terminates and optionally sends a message or trigger signal. The BPA in Fig. 2 illustrates those concepts.

Relating event multiplicity specifications. Often the number of messages a process sends is closely related to the number it expects to receive, e.g. in Fig. 1. This relation between two events is captured in the =-relation, to which all BPA runs need to conform, hence reducing the amount of possible BPA runs. Runs which assign numbers contradicting the =-relation are considered invalid and can be omitted in the state space of a BPA subset. If the =-relation is not used, all possible runs are valid and the complete state space has to be explored during analysis.

4.2 Transforming Business Process Architectures

For the analysis of BPAs, we employ a transformation into open nets [11], which have been successfully applied to study the composition of services and its correctness. Due to the definition of open net composition we cannot directly express the triggering resp.

sending or receiving of an varying amount of instances resp. messages with open nets. Events that are in trigger or message flow relation with several other events are also not directly covered. To overcome these limitations we adopt the approach of inserting intermediary nets from [10] and extend it with net constructs for multi-communication.

The transformation is conducted in a modular fashion: Each of the BPA's processes is first transformed independently into an open net. As a second step intermediary open nets are created that capture the trigger and message relations and interconnect the process's open nets. In the last step intermediary and process's nets are composed into one p/t-net and analysed with the model checker LoLA [12].

Transforming Business Processes. The transformation of a single business process is defined as follows.

Definition 5 (BPA Process Transformation). Given a BPA, let $\langle e_1 e_2 \ldots e_n \rangle$ be the sequence of events belonging to the business process $v \in V$ then the process's open net is defined as $N_v = (P_v, T_v, F_v, M_{0_v}, \Omega_v)$, where
- $T_v = \{t_{e_i} | e_i \in v\}, P_v = P_v^N \cup P_v^O \cup P_v^I$,
- $P_v^N = \{p'_{e_i} | e_i \in v \land 1 \leq i < n\}$,
- $P_v^O = \{p_{e_i} | e_i \in (E^E \cup E^T) \cap v\} \setminus \{p_{e_n} | e_n \bullet = \emptyset\}$,
- $P_v^I = \{p_{e_i} | e_i \in (E^S \cup E^C) \cap v\} \setminus \{p_{e_1} | \bullet e_1 = \emptyset\}$,
- $F = \{(t_{e_i}, p'_{e_i}), (p'_{e_i}, t_{e_{i+1}}) | t_{e_i} \in T_v \land p'_{e_i} \in P_v^N\} \cup \{(t_{e_i}, p_{e_i}) | t_{e_i} \in T_v \land p_{e_i} \in P_v^O\} \cup \{(p_{e_i}, t_{e_i}) | t_{e_i} \in T \land p_{e_i} \in P_v^I\}$,
- $M_{0_v} = \emptyset$ if there exists $(t, e_1) \in I$ and p_{e_1} otherwise
- $\Omega_v = \{\}$ if there exists $(e_n, t) \in I \cup L$ and $\{p_{e_n}\}$ otherwise

The sets P_v^I of input and P_v^O of output places depend partially on the trigger relation I. Only if an start event e_1 is triggered the place p_{e_1} is an input place, otherwise it is an initially marked internal place. Equivalently p_{e_n} is an output place only if e_n has a non-empty postset, otherwise it is internal and part of the final marking. As in [10] we resort to indicating the number of business process instances as black tokens in open net.

Multicast and multireceive net. Depending on the multiplicity of a throwing event it emits a different number of messages or trigger signals. To capture this in the open nets formalism, we propose to use an intermediary open net called *multicast net*. It is a net schema, because each multiplicity specification entails a different multicast net, consisting of one input place, one output place, and one transition for each element in the multiplicity set of the event. Note, that the same construct is used for triggering multiple instances as well as sending multiple messages. Fig. 3(a) presents an exemplary multicast net.

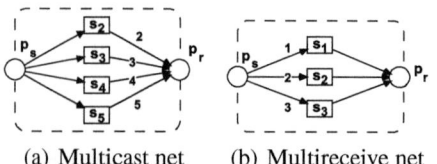

(a) Multicast net (b) Multireceive net

Fig. 3. Open net constructs to represent multi-communication

Definition 6 (Multicast Net). Given a BPA the multicast net for a message or trigger flow $(s, r) \in L \cup I$ is defined as $N_{s,r} = (P_{s,r}, T_{s,r}, F_{s,r}, 0, \{0\})$ where $P_{s,r} = P_{s,r}^N \cup P_{s,r}^I \cup P_{s,r}^O$ and $P_{s,r}^I = \{p_s\}, P_{s,r}^O = \{p_r\}, P^N = \emptyset, T_{s,r} = \{s_i | i \in \mu(s)\}$, $F_{s,r}(p_s, s_i) = 1, F_{s,r}(s_i, p_r) = i$ where $i \in \mu(s)$. Note that the multicast net has the empty multiset as initial and as only final marking.

The *multireceive net* which is a slightly adapted version of the multicast net, expresses that a process instance needs a certain number of messages or trigger signals before it can continue resp. is instantiated only. Formally we have $F_{s,r}(p_s, s_i) = i$, $F_{s,r}(s_i, p_r) = 1$ where $i \in \mu(s)$ for the multireceive net, while the rest stays the same. The resulting open net construct is depicted in Fig. 3(b).

Splitter and collector net. Processes can not only trigger multiple instances of one process, but also instances of multiple processes. The same is true for sending and receiving messages. In Fig. 2 for example, process P sends messages to both processes Q and R. Formally we have $p\bullet = \{q, r\}$ two events in the postset of throwing event p. Note, that it only matters that the preset resp. postset is non-singleton and not in which relation those events are. Therefore the following definitions for open nets, adapted from [10] apply to both messaging and triggering.

Definition 7 (Splitter and Collector Net). Given a BPA, a throwing or end event $e \in E^T \cup E^E$ and a catching or start event $e' \in E^S \cup E^C$. Then the open net $N_e = (P_e, T_e, F_e, 0, \{0\})$ is called the *splitter net for* e, where $P_e = P_e^N \cup P_e^I \cup P_e^O$, $P_e^N = \emptyset$, $P_e^I = \{p_e\}$, $P_e^O = \{p_b \mid b \in e\bullet\}$, $T_e = \{t_e\}$, $F_e(p, t_e) = F_e(t_e, p) = 1 \; \forall p \in P_e$. The initial marking is the empty multiset, the only final marking as well.
The *collector net for* e' is defined similarly except that $P_{e'}^I = \{p_e \mid e \in \bullet e'\}$, $P_{e'}^O = \{p_{e'}\}$ and $T_{e'} = \{t_e \mid e \in \bullet e'\}$.

4.3 Composition and Analysis

Before the analysis, the open nets resulting from the transformation have to be composed according to Def. 4. This composition relies on the names of interface places. For each pair of events in trigger or message flow relation at least one intermediary net is created. Those are defined to provide the complementary interface places and make the nets composable. If not for the intermediary nets, the composition would yield unconnected nets leaving all places unfused.

In some cases additional care has to be taken to avoid wrong composition, e.g. for events that have both a non-trivial multiplicity set $|\mu(e)| \neq \{1\}$ *and* a non-singleton postset $|e\bullet| > 1$. In such cases multiple intermediary nets are necessary, which per default would have interface places with identical names, thus making the nets non-composable. But since such situations can be derived from the relations, the problem can be circumvented by renaming those places. Details and the renaming algorithm can be found in the technical report [2].

Analysis with LoLA. To analyse the correctness of a BPA subset, several of LoLAs built-in verification tasks are applied to the composed open net. For this purpose we express the BPA correctness criteria as CTL formulae or state predicates and apply model checking to determine if they can be satisfied. A *terminating* BPA run is characterized by the final place or places of the net being marked with one or more tokens and any other place in the net being unmarked. If such a state is reachable in the state space, the BPA subset has a terminating run and is thus correct. *Lazy termination* of a BPA run can be concluded if there is a path in the state space leading to a final marking, such that each process terminates at least once, if it is instantiated at all. In lazy terminating BPA runs unterminated instances and pending messages might stay behind. If a final marking is not reachable, the BPA subset contains only deadlocks and infinite BPA runs (livelocks). Those can automatically be detected by LoLA. *Dead* processes are found by searching the state space for all those initial places, that are always unmarked. If the transformed open net successfully passes all the verification tasks the BPA subset is correct.

5 Conclusion

Business Process Architectures provide means to model and analyse multi-communication between multiple instances of interacting business processes. In this contribution we introduced the concept of a BPA run and elaborated on correctness criteria for BPAs. Our main contribution is the introduction of intermediary nets to capture BPA multiplicities inside the frame of open nets. The resulting open net allows analysis with established verification tools.

Future work will deal with extending BPAs with the ability to model alternative behaviour as well as focus on introducing correlation concepts. A BPA analysis tool for the extraction of BPAs from process model collections and their large scale analysis is currently under development.

References

1. Eid-Sabbagh, R.-H., Dijkman, R., Weske, M.: Business process architecture: Use and correctness. In: Barros, A., Gal, A., Kindler, E. (eds.) BPM 2012. LNCS, vol. 7481, pp. 65–81. Springer, Heidelberg (2012)
2. Eid-Sabbagh, R.H., Hewelt, M., Weske, M.: Business Process Architectures with Multiplicities: Transformation and Correctness. Technical Report 77, Hasso-Plattner-Institut (2013)
3. van der Aalst, W., Barthelmess, P., Ellis, C., Wainer, J.: Proclets: A Framework for Lightweight Interacting Workflow Processes. Int. J. Cooperative Inf. Syst. 10(04), 443–481 (2001)
4. Decker, G., Zaha, J.M., Dumas, M.: Execution semantics for service choreographies. In: Bravetti, M., Núñez, M., Zavattaro, G. (eds.) WS-FM 2006. LNCS, vol. 4184, pp. 163–177. Springer, Heidelberg (2006)
5. Martens, A.: Analyzing web service based business processes. In: Cerioli, M. (ed.) FASE 2005. LNCS, vol. 3442, pp. 19–33. Springer, Heidelberg (2005)
6. Decker, G., Weske, M.: Local Enforceability in Interaction Petri Nets. In: Alonso, G., Dadam, P., Rosemann, M. (eds.) BPM 2007. LNCS, vol. 4714, pp. 305–319. Springer, Heidelberg (2007)
7. van der Aalst, W.M.P., Mooij, A.J., Stahl, C., Wolf, K.: Service interaction: Patterns, formalization, and analysis. In: Bernardo, M., Padovani, L., Zavattaro, G. (eds.) SFM 2009. LNCS, vol. 5569, pp. 42–88. Springer, Heidelberg (2009)
8. Weinberg, D.: Efficient Controllability Analysis of Open Nets. In: Bruni, R., Wolf, K. (eds.) WS-FM 2008. LNCS, vol. 5387, pp. 224–239. Springer, Heidelberg (2009)
9. Barros, A., Dumas, M., ter Hofstede, A.H.M.: Service Interaction Patterns. In: van der Aalst, W.M.P., Benatallah, B., Casati, F., Curbera, F. (eds.) BPM 2005. LNCS, vol. 3649, pp. 302–318. Springer, Heidelberg (2005)
10. Eid-Sabbagh, R.-H., Weske, M.: In: Salinesi, C., Norrie, M.C., Pastor, Ó. (eds.) CAiSE 2013. LNCS, vol. 7908, pp. 208–223. Springer, Heidelberg (2013)
11. Massuthe, P., Serebrenik, A., Sidorova, N., Wolf, K.: Can I find a partner? Undecidability of partner existence for open nets. Information Processing Letters 108(6), 374–378 (2008)
12. Schmidt, K.: LoLA: A Low Level Analyser. In: Nielsen, M., Simpson, D. (eds.) ICATPN 2000. LNCS, vol. 1825, pp. 465–474. Springer, Heidelberg (2000)

Optimal Resource Assignment in Workflows for Maximizing Cooperation

Akhil Kumar[1], Remco Dijkman[2], and Minseok Song[3]

[1] Smeal College of Business, Penn State University, University Park, PA 16802, USA
AkhilKumar@psu.edu
[2] Eindhoven University of Technology, P.O. Box 513, 5600 MB Eindhoven,
The Netherlands
r.m.dijkman@tue.nl
[3] Ulsan National Institue of Science and Technology, UNIST-GIL 50,
Ulsan 689-798, South Korea
msong@unist.ac.kr

Abstract. A workflow is a team process since many actors work on various tasks to complete an instance. Resource management in such workflows deals with assignment of tasks to workers or actors. In team formation, it is necessary to ensure that members of a team are compatible with each other. When a workflow instance of, say, an insurance claim (or a surgery) process is performed, the handoffs between successive tasks are often *soft* as opposed to *hard*, and actors who perform successive tasks in this process instance must cooperate. If they cooperate well, it can improve quality and increase throughput of the instance. In general, the degree of required cooperation between a pair of tasks varies and this should be captured by a model. This paper develops a model to capture the compatibility between actors while assigning tasks in a workflow to a group of actors. The model is tested through a simulation and the results from a greedy algorithm are compared with optimal results. A technique for computing the compatibility matrix is given and used for an empirical validation from a real execution log. We argue that workflow resource models should recognize soft handoffs and provide support for them.

1 Introduction

"We found that patients whose surgical teams exhibited less teamwork behaviors were at a higher risk for death or complications." [10]

Much work within organizations takes place in teams whether it is performing surgery (as in the quotation above), designing a car, or processing a customer's insurance claim application. Naturally, it is very important that members of a team, in addition to having the requisite qualifications, also be compatible with one another in order to ensure smooth execution and flow of the work. Of course, in a team of *n* workers or actors, it is not necessary that every pair of members must be fully compatible with each other, but the goal in general would be to maximize overall compatibility particularly across actors whose roles require considerable collaboration and cooperation. Non-cooperation can result in loss of productivity. In a similar vein, the need for optimization also arises in business processes. In a typical insurance claim process, several tasks must be done by different roles in a certain order. After a worker or actor completes her task she hands off the process workflow to the next actor. In a *hard handoff* no further interaction between the two actors may be required. But in a *soft handoff*, the two actors may still need to interact later for queries and clarifications even though the process definition may not reflect it. Thus, in practice "there is a series of *overlapping* and *nested* roles and responsibilities."[8] In general, an actor doing a later task in a workflow may need to refer back to consult with an actor who did a previous task for the same case. Hence, cooperation is necessary between the two actors of successive tasks so that the workflow can proceed smoothly.

Workflow management systems can be viewed from various perspectives such as: control flow, data flow and resource modeling. The control flow describes the ordering relationships between various tasks, and the data flow its data inputs and outputs. The resource model [7,19,18] refers to the roles and specific actors who are qualified to perform various tasks. Most resource assignment algorithms consider issues like suitability, urgency, conformance and availability [6, 11] while allocating tasks to actors. However, they fail to recognize the interactions among the actors performing different tasks in a workflow instance, say for insurance claim processing. In practice, there is need for such interaction.

The execution of a process instance, in general, is really a team effort involving multiple handoffs and the handoff should be as smooth as possible. The Free Dictionary (http://www.thefreedictionary.com) defines compatible as: "capable of existing or performing in harmonious, agreeable, or congenial combination with another." Thus, *compatibility* is a measure of the degree to which actors cooperate with one another in a workflow. Hence, compatibility between actors should be considered while assigning tasks to actors. Current approaches only consider suitability of an actor for a task in isolation of her compatibility with actors of others tasks in an instance. We propose a model that allows us to specify compatibilities among actors in compatibility matrix, and also the required degree of desired cooperation among tasks through a cooperation matrix. In general, compatibility between two actors may be task-specific, but for now we will assume that it is the same for all tasks.

As noted above, the medical domain is another area where multiple roles must work together in order to achieve a positive outcome, and compatibility and smooth coordination and handoffs between various personnel involved (such as surgeons, anesthesiologists, nurses, lab technicians, etc.) is very important [1,10]. In this paper we show how to model compatibility between actors while making work assignments so as to achieve a high degree of overall compatibility for the process. Section 2 gives a basic framework and preliminaries. Then, Section 3 describes our model for maximizing compatibility. Next, Section 4 gives a greedy heuristic and experimental results for its performance against an optimal solution. Sections 5 and 6 show how to compute the compatibility matrix and provide empirical validation respectively. Section 7 presents several directions for extending this approach. Finally section 8 gives a discussion along with related work and we conclude with Section 9.

2   Basic Framework

Consider an example of a medical insurance claim process model shown in BPMN in Figure 1. In this process, a claim is received, and then checked by a reviewer who verifies that it is a valid claim. Next, it is examined by an evaluator who determines the amount of the settlement. A manager must approve the claim, and finally the accounts officer issues a payment for it. Thus, the key steps or tasks, the roles that perform each step, the actors in the roles and their respective locations, in this process are:

Receive claim (role: customer service rep; actors: John, Mary; location: call center 1)
Review, validate, assign claim (role: reviewer; actors: Beth, Sue; location: call center 2)
Evaluate and determine settlement (role: evaluator; actors: Mike, Jim; location: client city)
Approve payment (role: manager; actors: Jen, Pat; location: regional office)
Make payment (role: accounts officer; actors: Mark, Lin; location: headquarters)

Notice that the roles for each task are geographically dispersed. This makes the need for cooperation even greater. As depicted by the dotted arrows in Figure 1, roles performing different tasks may need to interact. For example, after a claim is received, the reviewer might need to refer back to the customer service representative for clarification about certain missing information on the claim (say, the exact location or time of an accident is missing). Similarly, the evaluator may need to consult with the reviewer for additional details. Finally, the manager could seek clarifications with the evaluator regarding the payment amount before approving it.

Thus, even though formal representations for workflow processes may not show it, there is often a need for such referrals. But formal modeling approaches tend to neglect this issue. Our goal is to capture notions of compatibility between actors who will perform tasks where soft handoffs are important. Hence, a metric for compatibility is required.

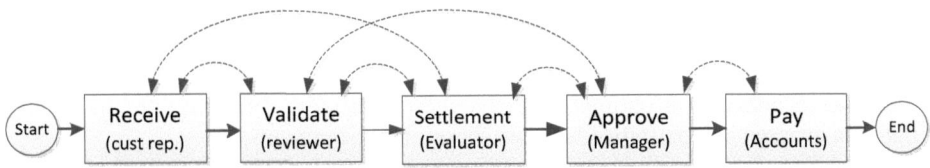

Fig. 1. A simplified insurance claim process with several tasks and roles
(Dashed lines show the need for cooperation among actors of pairs of tasks)

Our metrics for compatibility within a team or a process workflow are:

$$Total\ Compatibility = \sum_{\forall (u1,u2,t1,t2)} fit_{u1,u2,t1,t2} * coop_{t1,t2} * cweight_{u1,u2}$$

$$Average\ Compatibility = \frac{Total\ Compatibility}{\sum_{t1,t2} coop_{t1,t2}}$$

Where $fit_{u1,u2,t1,t2}: \begin{cases} 1\ if\ actor\ u1, u2\ perform\ tasks\ t1, t2\ respectively \\ 0, otherwise \end{cases}$

$$coop_{t1,t2}: \begin{cases} 1, if\ cooperation\ required\ between\ tasks\ t1\ and\ t2 \\ 0, otherwise \end{cases}$$

$cweight_{u1,u2}$: *compatibilty of actors $u1, u2$ on a continuous scale of 01*

The fit and cooperation values are stored in two matrices. Table 1 is an actor-actor compatibility matrix with values on a scale of 0 to 1 (from low to high compatibility). Table 2 gives a binary cooperation matrix for all pairs of tasks, where a '0' means cooperation between a pair of tasks is not required, and '1' that it is. We assume that cooperation is reciprocal; hence the matrices are symmetric. The start and end tasks are not shown in the tables because they are not performed by humans. The diagonal entries in the table are 1.0 to represent that an actor is fully compatible with herself. Here we assume that compatibility between actors is not task-specific, but to make it task specific, $cweight_{u1,u2}$ can be modified in the above formulation to $cweight_{u1,u2,t}$ where the new subscript t represent a task. Later we will show how this model is modified to allow non-discrete values of cooperation between actors.

Example 1: (Partial Cooperation) Below we calculate average compatibilities using the values in Tables 1 and 2. There are five main tasks in this instance. Moreover, as per Table 2 there are only 6 interactions where cooperation is required; hence it is a case of partial cooperation. Clearly, several combinations of actor assignments are possible here. Let us look at two examples.

Assignment 1 (random):
cust. rep: John ; Reviewer: Sue; Evaluator: Jim; Manager: Pat; accounts officer: Mark

Average compatibility = (0.1 + 0.3 + 0.6 + 0.6 + 0.1 + 0.1)/6 = 0.3

Assignment 2 (optimal):
cust rep: Mary; Reviewer: Beth; Evaluator: Jim; Manager: Jen; accounts officer: Mark

Average compatibility = (0.3 + 0.8 + 0.8 + 0.7 + 0.8 + 0.7)/6 = 0.683

The first assignment is made simply by randomly assigning a task to a qualified actor, while the second one is optimal. Clearly, there is a large difference (of more than 100%) in average compatibility between these two assignments.

Table 1. Actor-Actor Compatibility matrix (*cweight*)

Role > (Task) >	Cust. Rep (receive)		Reviewer (validate)		Evaluator (settle)		Manager (approve)		Accounts (pay)	
	John	Mary	Beth	Sue	Mike	Jim	Jen	Pat	Mark	Lin
John	1.0	0.9	0.8	0.1	0.8	0.3	0.9	0.3	0.4	0.2
Mary	0.9	1.0	0.3	0.7	0.2	0.8	0.9	0.2	0.1	0.8
Beth	0.8	0.3	1.0	0.8	0.3	0.8	0.7	0.3	0.2	0.9
Sue	0.1	0.7	0.8	1.0	0.9	0.6	0.4	0.6	0.8	0.4
Mike	0.8	0.2	0.3	0.9	1.0	0.9	0.3	0.9	0.8	0.1
Jim	0.3	0.8	0.8	0.6	0.9	1.0	0.8	0.1	0.3	0.9
Jen	0.9	0.9	0.7	0.4	0.3	0.8	1.0	0.8	0.7	0.3
Pat	0.3	0.2	0.3	0.6	0.6	0.9	0.8	1.0	0.1	0.8
Mark	0.4	0.1	0.2	0.8	0.8	0.3	0.7	0.1	1.0	0.9
Lin	0.2	0.8	0.9	0.4	0.1	0.9	0.3	0.8	0.9	1.0

Example 2:(Full Cooperation) Next consider a variation of the above example. Instead of assuming that cooperation between some pairs of participants is necessary, let us assume that all participants who work on an instance of a process must cooperate with each other. The corresponding cooperation matrix is shown in Table 3. The solutions from the random assignment and the optimal assignment are as follows.

Table 2. Cooperation matrix (*partial* cooperation required)

	Receive	Validate	Settle	Approve	Pay
Receive	–	1	1	0	0
Validate	1	–	1	1	0
Settle	1	1	–	1	0
Approve	0	1	1	–	1
Pay	0	0	0	1	–

Assignment 3 (random):
cust rep: Mary ; Reviewer: Sue; Evaluator: Jim; Manager: Jen; accounts officer: Lin
Average compatibility =
(0.7 + 0.8 + 0.9 + 0.8 + 0.6 + 0.4 + 0.4 + 0.8 + 0.9 + 0.3)/10= 0.66

Assignment 4 (optimal):
cust rep: Mary; Reviewer: Beth; Evaluator: Jim; Manager: Jen; accounts officer: Lin
Average compatibility =
(0.3 + 0.8 + 0.9 + 0.8 + 0.8 + 0.7 + 0.9 + 0.8 + 0.9 + 0.3)/10= 0.72

Table 3. Cooperation matrix (*full* cooperation required)

	Receive	Validate	Settle	Approve	Pay
Receive	–	1	1	1	1
Validate	1	–	1	1	1
Settle	1	1	–	1	1
Approve	1	1	1	–	1
Pay	1	1	1	1	–

In this example, the difference in average compatibility between the optimal and random assignments is much smaller than in Example 1. The improvement through an optimal reassignment of tasks in the full cooperation case is less because, in general, perhaps few actors cooperate well with all other actors in a process.

We have considered two scenarios involving different levels of cooperation. In general, the cooperation matrix could vary, and the best assignment will also be different accordingly. Next we describe our model for finding an optimal solution so as to maximize cooperation within the team.

3 Model – Optimal Work Assignment (OWA)

The objective of this model shown in Figure 2 is to maximize total (or average) *compatibility*. However, we express our objective function so as to minimize total *incompatibility* and the reason for this is explained shortly. Our notion of overall compatibility is as an aggregate of all pair-wise compatibilities between actors who are involved in task-pairs of a process that require cooperation. Since pair-wise actor-actor compatibility ranges between 0 and 1, *incompatibility=(1− compatibility)*.

Model OWA

$$\text{Minimize} \sum_{u1,u2,t1,t2} fit_{u1,u2,t1,t2} * (1 - cweight_{u1,u2})$$

Subject to:

$$\sum_u does_{u,t} = 1, \forall t \quad (1)$$

$$does_{u,t} \leq cando_{u,t} \quad (2)$$

$$does_{u1,t1} + does_{u2,t2} - fit_{u1,u2,t1,t2} \leq 1, \forall\, t1, t2 \text{ where } coop(t1, t2) = 1 \quad (3)$$

Where:

$$fit_{u1,u2,t1,t2} = \begin{cases} 1 \text{ if actors } u1, u2 \text{ perform tasks } t1, t2 \text{ respectively} \\ 0, otherwise \end{cases}$$

$$does_{u,t} = \begin{cases} 1, if \text{ actor } u \text{ is assigned to perform task } t \\ 0, otherwise \end{cases}$$

$$cando_{u,t} = \begin{cases} 1, if \text{ actor } u \text{ is qualified to performtask } t \\ 0, otherwise \end{cases}$$

$$coop_{t1,t2} = \begin{cases} 1, if \text{ cooperation is needed between } t1 \text{ and } t2 \\ 0, otherwise \end{cases}$$

$cweight_{u1,u2}$: compatibilty between actors $u1, u2$

Fig. 2. Model OWA for optimal work assignment

By constraint 1 of the OWA model, every task must be assigned to exactly one actor. The second constraint requires that the actor u who is assigned to perform task $t (does_{u,t})$ must be qualified to do it ($cando_{u,t}$). The third constraint forces the fit variable between two actors doing tasks that have a soft handoff between them to 1. Thus, the fit variable $fit_{u1,u2,t1,t2}$ must be 1. The model in Figure 2 is called an integer programming (IP) formulation which is known to be NP-complete [2]. Hence solving the OWA is an NP-complete problem too. It can be solved with a tool like CPLEX [4]. The solution of the model gives the optimal assignment by finding the values for the variable $does_{u,t}$ for all u,t. Additional constraints can be added to this basic model to enforce minimum (maximum) limits on number of tasks assigned to any actor. Note that the objective function assumes that overall compatibility is linear in individual actor-pair compatibility.

Now, the reason the objective function minimizes total incompatibility is as follows: If we try to maximize compatibility then the *fit* variables are all forced to 1 resulting in an incorrect formulation. However, if we express the objective as minimizing incompatibility this error does not occur, and a fit variable $fit_{u1,u2,t1,t2}$ assumes a 1 value only when actor *u1* does task *t1* and actor *u2* does task *t2*.

To construct the OWA model, we only need to know the data in the coop, cweight and cando matrices. The complexity of this problem is $O(t^u)$, where t is number of tasks and u is number of actors per task. In the next section we develop a heuristic to solve this problem.

4 A Greedy Heuristic and Results

Here we describe a greedy heuristic to solve the actor assignment problem. The main steps are shown in Figure 3. The coop, cweight and cando arrays are taken directly from the model described above. For each successive task $t1$ (line 1), we consider each actor $u1$ (line 2) who can do $t1$. Then, for each actor $u1$ and for every other task $t2$ (line 3) such that cooperation between $t1$ and $t2$ is required (line 4), we find the maximum compatibility actor with actor $u1$ from the cweight array and accumulate the compatibility in a variable *score*. This is repeated for every task $t2$ that requires cooperation with $t1$ and in this way a score is computed for each actor who can perform task $t1$. Finally, the actor with the maximum score is assigned the task $t1$ (line 7) and corresponding actor to other tasks that need cooperation with t1. This is repeated until all actors are assigned. The algorithm returns the assign array.

```
Algorithm Greedy_Coop
        Input: coop[][],cweight[][], cando[][]
        Output: assign[]
1       for each (task t1 = 1,…, num_tasks)
2          for each (u1 ∈ cando[t1])
3             for each (task t2 = t1+1,…, num_tasks)
4       if (coop(t1,t2)&& not(assign[t1])&& not(assign[t2]):
        score(u1)=score(u1) + max(cweight(u1,u2),
                                        ∀ u2∈cando[t2])
5          end for
6       end for
7       assign[t1] = u*,
           s.t. score[u*],u*= max(score[u], u∈cando[t1])
8       for each (task t2 = t1+1,…,num_tasks)
9       if (coop(t1,t2)&& not(assign[t2]):
        assign[t2] = u2*, s.t.
           cweight[u*,u2*]=max(cweight[u*,u2], u2∈cando[t2])
10      end for
11      return(assign[])
```

Fig. 3. A greedy heuristic for actor assignment

This is a greedy algorithm. At each successive step, we assign actors to a task based on the best compatibility for this particular assignment without optimizing across all tasks. Next, we compare the greedy heuristic results against the optimal solution to see how much improvement is possible by using the optimal approach.

We conducted experiments to compare the greedy heuristic with the optimal solution. The greedy heuristic was implemented in Python language, while the optimal solution was found by solving the model using CPLEX software [4]. We used a simulation first to create the data for the experiments, and the parameters of the simulation are given in Table 4. In particular there are 10 tasks in the process and 20 actors. Each task can be done by either 2 or 3 actors. First, we select the number of qualified actors for each task (2 or 3, with equal probability), and then pick the actual actors at random. Our cooperation model assumes that:

(1) task i must cooperate with the next task $i+1$ with probability 1.0
(2) tasks in the pairs $(i,i+1)$ and $(i,i+2)$ must cooperate with probability 0.5

Finally an actor-actor compatibility matrix is generated where compatibility values of 0.1, 0.2, …, 0.9 are randomly assigned. If the same actor performs two tasks, then her compatibility with herself is 0.99 (i.e. close to 1). In these experiments we assumed availability of all actors was 1, i.e. they were all available.

Table 4. Parameters used in the simulation experiment

Parameter	Description	value
# tasks	Number of tasks	10, 20
Total # actors	Number of actors	20, 40
Task- actor assignment	For each task, assign actors who can perform the task	Pick 2 or 3 actors at random
Cooperation requirement	Between tasks i and $i+1$ with prob. 1, and between i, and, $i+2$ and $i+3$, with prob. 0.5	
Compatibility weight	Weight between 0 and 1 to measure degree of fit between two actors where handoff is important	0.1,0.2, … 0.9
Availability	Extent of availability of an actor (0.0,…1.0)	1.0

In Table 5 (a) we summarize the results for 10 cases with 10 tasks and 20 actors in each case. The actual actor assignments produced by the heuristic are not shown. In case 1, the heuristic produces an assignment where task 1 is assigned to actor 19, task 2 to actor 10, and so on. For this case the heuristic assignment is very surprisingly close to the optimal solution. In fact 9 out of 10 actor assignments are the same except that task 9 is assigned to actor 10 in the heuristic instead of actor 7. We also report the average compatibility, i.e. the average of the compatibility values across the '1' entries in the cooperation matrix, along with the percentage gap between the optimal and the heuristic solutions. In case 1, the heuristic is worse than the optimal by just about 6%, but in other cases, the gap is larger, even as high as 40% in case 9. Overall, across all 10 cases the average gap is about 19%.

Similarly, the results for a second experiment with 20 tasks and 40 actors are given in Table 5 (b). Now there is an average gap of 17% between the performance of the optimal and the heuristic, and it lies between 8% (case 3) and 23% (case 7). In case 3, 6 out of 10 actor assignments are the same, while in case 7, 5 out of 10 are the same.

The results clearly show that the greedy algorithm is useful but suboptimal. The main problem observed in both sets of experiments with the greedy algorithm is that if it makes a bad assignment early on, this effect gets magnified with successive task assignments. Thus, it can lead to a very inferior final solution since there is no backtracking in the greedy algorithm. The assignment of actors to tasks can be done dynamically rather than making a static assignment at the start of the process instance. Thus, in a dynamic mode an initial assignment is made at the start, and after each successive task is completed, the algorithm is rerun to make the next assignment based on availability of actors.

The experiments were carried out on a typical desktop PC (Intel dual core CPU at 2.40 GHz with 3.25 GB RAM) running CPLEX. The running times to find the solutions were in fractions of a second for the problems above. Thus, for problems of

Table 5. Results for average compatibility: heuristic vs. optimal solutions

(a) 10 tasks, 20 actors

Case	Avg. Compat. Greedy	Avg. Compat. Opt.	% gap
1.	0.656	0.700	6.29
2	0.650	0.759	14.36
3.	0.669	0.760	11.97
4.	0.653	0.785	16.82
5.	0.591	0.740	20.14
6.	0.615	0.737	16.55
7.	0.461	0.597	22.78
8.	0.550	0.761	27.73
9.	0.466	0.780	40.26
10.	0.615	0.730	15.75
Avg.	0.593	0.735	19.32

(b) 20 tasks, 40 actors

Case	Avg. Compat. Greedy	Avg. Compat. Opt.	% gap
1.	0.615	0.684	10.09
2	0.568	0.717	20.78
3.	0.557	0.607	8.24
4.	0.605	0.759	20.29
5.	0.608	0.712	14.61
6.	0.596	0.771	22.70
7.	0.567	0.734	22.75
8.	0.556	0.718	22.56
9.	0.570	0.691	17.51
10.	0.619	0.720	14.03
Avg.	0.586	0.711	17.36

medium size one can find optimal solutions but for larger problems heuristic methods may be more appropriate.

5 Automatically Computing the Compatibility Matrix

To fully benefit from optimal work assignment with the compatibility matrix, a compatibility matrix must be determined that corresponds to the manner in which actors work together in practice. While this matrix can be designed in a traditional manner, e.g. based on interviews with the actors, this is not ideal. In particular, because it is unlikely that the interviewees will accurately report on their cooperation with others, due to political considerations. Therefore, we propose an approach in which we derive the compatibility matrix automatically based on an execution log that contains for each execution trace: the executed tasks, the actor executing each task and the total throughput time.

The basic idea is that if, in cases where two actors u_1 and u_2 cooperate, the throughput time is lower on average than in the general case, these actors can be assumed to have a higher compatibility. Conversely, if the throughput time is higher on average, the actors can be assumed to have a lower compatibility. Based on this assumption, we can use a sigmoid function to derive the actors' compatibility from the throughput times as follows. Given two actors u_1 and u_2, the average throughput time t of the process, and the average throughput time tc of the process for execution traces in which u_1 and u_2 collaborated,

$$cweight_{u1,u2} = \frac{1}{1 + e^{-k(t-tc)}}$$

Figure 4 illustrates the relation between t, tc and $cweight$ for $k = 1$. In this function k is a parameter that we can vary to obtain better results. In particular, if the variance in throughput time is high k should be smaller to be more sensitive to these variances, similarly, if the variance is low, *k* should be greater. A suggestion is, to choose *k* such that the sigmoid is most sensitive for *tc* from the first to the third quartile of the throughput times domain (see Figure 4). Given the first quartile is *q1*, the third quartile *q3* and the average *t*, $k = 10/(q3-q1)$.

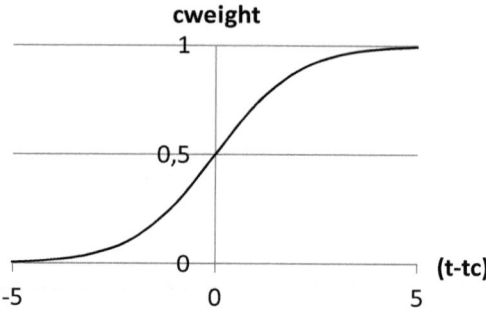

Fig. 4. Relation between $(t- tc)$ and *cweight* in a collaboration

Alternatives to the sigmoid function, such as a simple linear function, and alternative values of k can also be used to compute the compatibility matrix. We experimented with some different values for k during the evaluation (see Section 6), but did not evaluate alternatives exhaustively. In future work, we aim to investigate alternative functions and determine the parameter settings (a value for *k* in case of the sigmoid function) and a function that produces the best result.

Figure 5 shows an example of the automated computation of the compatibility matrix from an execution log. The average throughput time of the execution traces is 9 and the average throughput times for traces where a particular combination of actors appears is shown in Figure 5 (b). For example, the average throughput time for execution traces in which John and Mary work together is 8.5, for traces where John and Beth work together it is 10. Figure 5 (c) shows a compatibility matrix computed based on the throughput times using the sigmoid function. For example, the *cweight*

(a) execution traces

Trace	Receive	Validate	Settlement	t
1	John	Mary	Mike	8
2	John	Beth	Mike	10
3	John	Mary	Mike	9

(b) average throughput times

	John	Mary	Beth	Mike
John	9	8.5	10	9
Mary	8.5	9	–	8.5
Beth	10	–	9	10
Mike	9	8.5	10	9

(c) compatibility matrix

	John	Mary	Beth	Mike
John	0.5	0.6	0.3	0.5
Mary	0.6	0.5	–	0.6
Beth	0.3	–	0.5	0.3
Mike	0.5	0.6	0.3	0.5

Fig. 5. Example of automated computation of the compatibility matrix

for the collaboration between John and Mary is $1/(1 + e^{-(9-8.5)}) \approx 0.6$, i.e.: John and Mary are slightly more compatible than the average, which is 0.5, and certainly more compatible than John and Beth, who have compatibility $1/(1 + e^{-(9-10)}) \approx 0.3$.

In the next section, we will apply the automatic computation of the compatibility matrix, as it is explained here, to an execution log from practice.

6 Empirical Evaluation

We evaluated the technique described in this paper using an execution log of a doctor's consultation process in Seoul National University Bundang Hospital, South Korea. The log was manually constructed from data that was extracted from the software systems that are used in the various process steps. The process involved five steps: reserving a room for the consultation; the actual consultation; planning follow-up appointments; making payment; and issuing a prescription. The first and second steps are performed by the same role (the doctor), which has 174 possible actors. The third step is performed by a secretary, which has 74 possible actors. The fourth and fifth steps are again performed by the same role (an administrator) and had 38 possible actors. We had 4,446 execution traces.

First, we empirically validated that collaborations between actors did indeed have an effect on the throughput time. Because of the large number of unique collaborations, we focused on a subset of collaborations that occurred more than 20 times, and disregarded other collaborations as insignificant (in fact, many occurred only once). We also focused on collaborations in the third, fourth and fifth steps of the process. These steps involved administrative tasks around the consultation: making the next appointment, receiving a prescription and paying for the appointment. It was felt that these steps were more likely to be affected by compatibility and less likely to be affected by other factors, such as complexity of the medical case. This selection resulted in 35 pairs of collaborations, associated with 1,717 execution traces. The data was analyzed in SPSS. We determined whether the throughput times for the collaborations were normally distributed, using a Shapiro-Wilk test. The test showed that the data was *not* normally distributed. Consequently, we used a Kruskal-Wallis test (instead of ANOVA) to determine whether the collaborations differed significantly, which was found to be the case at a 0.05 significance level. Therefore, we conclude that there are significant differences in throughput times between collaborations.

Second, we evaluated the theoretical improvement that the technique described in this paper can achieve in work assignments. We did so by determining the compatibility matrix for the case and subsequently determining the optimal work assignment for this compatibility matrix. We used the sigmoid function to determine *cweight* with the parameter k set such that the function was most sensitive in the second and third quartiles of the throughput times. Figure 6 shows a part of the compatibility matrix for the case, showing the actors in the process and their compatibility. The actors are represented by codes such as EIC, CDCJJ, etc. to ensure anonymity. Due to the large number of actors involved in the case, the full compatibility matrix has 286 x 286 cells. The optimal work assignment computed from the compatibility matrix leads to an average throughput time of 6 minutes, which is a strong improvement over the overall average throughput time of 42.9 minutes. However, this average is based on *cweights* computed from only one execution trace for illustration of an extreme case.

Focusing on assignments that were based on at least 10 execution traces, the best work assignment leads to an average throughput time of 23.7 minutes, still a strong improvement over the overall average throughput times. Interestingly, in this case the third-best work assignment is actually better at an average of 19.7 minutes. The best assignment based on at least 20 execution traces has an average throughput time of 26.9 minutes.

	EIC	CDCJJ	CHBAB	CEFGG	...
EIC	0.50	0.99	–	–	...
CDCJJ	0.99	0.50	0.25	0.75	...
CHBAB	–	0.25	0.50	–	...
CEFGG	–	0.75	–	0.50	...
...	...	...	...	...	...

Fig. 6. Part of the compatibility matrix of the case

Although our results on throughput were not tested for statistical significance, we believe these differences are too large to be explained by differences in worker competence alone, especially given that the tasks involved are of low complexity. Hence, our initial evidence points to varying levels of cooperation among actors.

7   Further Extensions

In this section we consider some variants of the basic model. The first one allows us to model varying degrees of cooperation between actors instead of just 0-1 binary cooperation. The second extension considers how to find an optimal assignment when multiple paths exist in the process. Finally, the last variant includes cost in the model as a constraint or an objective.

7.1   Varying Degrees of Required Cooperation

In the discussion thus far, the coop matrix only contained discrete 0-1 entries for pairs of tasks, where a 0 indicated cooperation was not required between the actors performing two tasks, and a 1 indicated it was required. In general, varying degrees of cooperation may be required between actors of different pairs of tasks. For example, in the process of Figure 2, a high degree of cooperation (say, 0.9) may be necessary between the evaluator and the manager, the need for cooperation between the manager and the accounts officer may be less (say, 0.3). This can be captured by associating a continuous parameter between 0 and 1 to denote the strength of cooperation required between the performers of two tasks. Thus, the cooperation matrix would contain $coop_{t1,t2}$ entries that are values between 0 and 1, and not binary values. These values would be determined subjectively by somebody with knowledge about the process. Again, the objective function would also be modified as follows:

$$Minimize \sum_{\forall u1,u2,t1,t2} coop_{t1,t2} fit_{u1,u2,t1,t2} * (1 - cweight_{u1,u2})$$

The rest of the formulation would remain unchanged.

7.2 Multiple Paths in a Process

The process described in Figure 1 is linear. Now, consider a modified version of that process as shown in Figure 4 with two alternative branches after the *validate* step, the lower branch being taken when the claim is rejected outright on initial review, say if it is not covered by the policy. To handle this situation, we modify the objective function by introducing a new parameter $p_{t1,t2}$ for the transition probability between two tasks t1, t2. An example of a transition probability matrix is shown in Table 6. The $p_{t1,t2}$ values are also shown on the edges in Figure 7. The revised objective function is a weighted sum of the probability of path π_i being taken and the incompatibility along that path. The probability $P(\pi_i)$ of a path being taken is computed as the product of probabilities along all the edges on the path from the start node to t2. The constraints, however, remain the same as before. Thus, the new objective function is:

$$\text{Minimize} \sum_{\pi_i \in Paths} P(\pi_i) \sum_{u1,u2,t1,t2} fit_{u1,u2,t1,t2} * (1 - cweight_{u1,u2})$$

In a process model with loops the compatibility matrix is created as before by considering the activities in a loop and the compatibility requirements for them. An estimate is used for the average number of loop repetitions, so the pairs of activities within the loop can be weighted by this factor in the objective function.

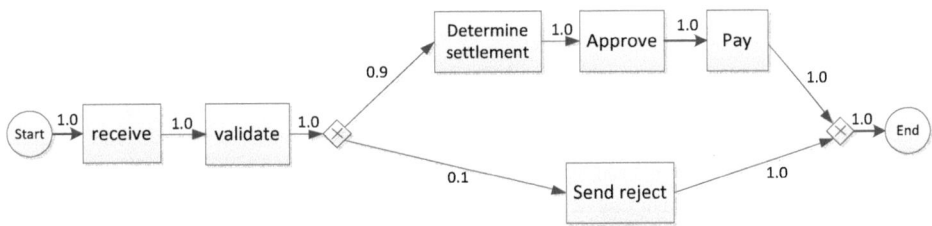

Fig. 7. A revised process (labels on arcs show transition probabilities)

Table 6. A task-task transition probability matrix for the process in Figure 4

	Receive	Validate	Settle	Approve	Pay	Reject
Receive	0	1	0.9	0.9	0.9	0.1
Validate	0	0	0.9	0.9	0.9	0.1
Settle	0	0	0	1	1	0
Approve	0	0	0	0	1	0
Pay	0	0	0	0	0	0

7.3 Optimization of Cost, Time, Resource

Model OWA in Section 3 has been formulated to minimize incompatibility, or equivalently, to maximize compatibility. However, in some actor assignment scenarios an additional objective is to minimize cost, time or another resource. Given an actor-task cost matrix, where $cost_{u,t}$ is the cost of actor u performing one instance of task t, the model can be modified easily. In such a case it is possible to incorporate cost into our model as an additional constraint such as:

$$\sum_{u,t} cost_{u,t} does_{u,t} < cost_{max}$$

Where, $cost_{max}$ is the maximum allowable cost for the assignment.

Another alternative is to convert the objective function and add it as a constraint into a cost optimization model. Then the constraint is expressed as:

$$\sum fit_{u1,u2,t1,t2} * (1 - cweight_{u1,u2}) > 1 - compat_{min}$$

where $compat_{min}$ is a minimum desired compatibility threshold.

In a similar way, it is possible to further extend the formulation by adding availability, throughput and resource consumption constraints.

8   Discussion and Related Work

Research has shown that cooperative behavior is reciprocal [14] as we assume here, and it affects service quality and performance [17]. Therefore, a workflow framework should incorporate cooperation by providing suitable constructs for modeling compatibility between actors. This means that a process designer should be able to model soft handoffs between tasks and the degree of cooperation. This information can be used in making resource assignments to enable a smoother flow of work.

In general, the time to perform a task consists of two elements: the intrinsic capability of an actor(u_i) to perform task t based on skill and experience, and her compatibility(u_i,u_j) with other actors (u_j) of related tasks of an instance. Thus,

Avg. time for task t by actor u_i = f(capability(u_i,t), compatibility(u_i, u_j))

Although we do not model the output quality of a process instance in this paper, it is reasonable to assume that given qualified actors, better compatibility among them will lead to higher quality and greater customer satisfaction. Further work is needed to develop a more elaborate model that can capture quality and tease out the role of the capability and compatibility elements. The approach described here can be implemented with a push-pull hybrid strategy. Actors would be offered a list of new tasks based on their compatibility, and then they may accept tasks from it.

In recent years there has been a surge of interest in modeling, connecting, scheduling and optimizing business processes both within and across organizations [16,18,19]. All such processes involve actors interacting in a collaborative manner. Techniques for organizational mining to discover organizational models and social networks are discussed in [15]. These models can assist in improving the underlying processes and provide insights for resource assignment. When many actors or workers collaborate on a team or on an instance of a running workflow, several factors can influence the overall performance. In [12], based on an extensive empirical study it was shown that there is a positive effect on performance of workflow instances when actors are located geographically close together. This study has implications for assignment of work to distributed actors, and in relation to our work it suggests that geographical distribution of actors may affect cooperation adversely.

The issue of cooperation among actors also has implications for best practices in business process redesign [9]. In a cooperative setting, a process may be designed in such a way that the boundaries between tasks are flexible. In a non-cooperative environment the interfaces between tasks must be rigid. In [13] it is shown that asymmetry in task size of tasks in a process, knowledge intensity levels and required customization needs of tasks have an impact on throughput times and are factors to consider in process redesign. When knowledge intensity and level of customization are high, effective communication becomes critical in ensuring a smooth handoff, and hence compatibility between the actors carrying out the handoff is important. It can also be helpful to develop handoff protocols for better performance of a process as was shown for the case of nursing shift handoffs in critical care [1].

There is related work as well on assignment of tasks to actors. Wolf [18] describes a constraint programming approach for modeling and scheduling clinical pathways. An IP formulation with the objective to minimize cost for assigning medical personnel is discussed in [3]. Another approach for assigning work in emergency situations [11] is based on *threshold models* consisting of two components, threshold and stimulus. As stimulus associated with a task increases, even actors who have a high threshold for performing the task respond. Since cooperation plays an important role in emergencies, compatibility should be a factor in deciding the stimulus.

9 Conclusions

In this paper we have highlighted the importance of compatibility among actors for resource assignments in workflows. In practice, the actors who participate in a workflow instance are part of a collaborative team. Empirical evidence from an execution log of a doctor's consultation process in a hospital was given to show that throughput times can vary considerably when resource assignments change. Thus, there is a need to adequately model soft handoffs between tasks. Such situations are frequent in practice and this issue has received little attention in research literature. We developed a novel approach for such scenarios using the notion of compatibility between tasks, and built a formal model to describe assignments of actors to tasks so as to maximize overall compatibility across an end-to-end workflow instance. The optimal solution for this model performed 20% better than a heuristic greedy algorithm. For medium size problems the optimal solution could be found very fast. A technique for discovering compatibility matrices from logs was described, but it needs further validation. Other non-greedy heuristics for task assignment would also be worth exploring.

We argue for new constructs for modeling of soft handoffs that allow cooperation among actors and sharing of responsibility across tasks in a workflow. Future work should examine ways to model such cooperation more accurately, and also study its impact on throughput and other metrics of performance. More research is also needed to understand and better model factors that affect cooperation.

Acknowledgement. Song was supported by the Basic Science Research Program through the National Research Foundation of Korea (NRF) funded by the Ministry of Education, Science and Technology (No. 2011-0010561).

References

1. Berkenstadt, H., Haviv, Y., Tuval, A., et al.: Improving handoff communications in critical care: Utilizing simulation-based training toward process improvement in managing patient risk. CHEST 134(1), 158–162 (2008)
2. Garey, M.R., Johnson, D.S. (eds.): Computers and Intractability: A Guide to the Theory of NP-Completeness. W.H. Freeman, San Francisco (1979)
3. Grunow, M., Günther, H.-O., Yang, G.: Development of a decision support model for scheduling clinical studies and assigning medical personnel. Health Care Management Science 7(4), 305–317 (2004)
4. ILOG: Ilog CPLEX software, Version 11.010 (2008)
5. Jablonski, S., Bussler, C.: Workflow Management: Modeling Concepts, Architecture and Implementation. Thomson Computer Press, London (1996)
6. Kumar, A., van der Aalst, W.M.P., Verbeek, H.M.W.: Dynamic work distribution in workflow management systems: How to balance quality and performance. Journal of Management Information Systems 18(3), 157–193 (2002)
7. Kumar, A., Wang, J.: A framework for designing resource driven workflow systems. In: Rosemann, M., vom Brocke, J. (eds.) The International Handbook on Business Process Management, pp. 419–440. Springer (2010)
8. Leach, L., Myrtle, R., Weaver, F., Dasu, S.: Assessing the performance of surgical teams. Health Care Manage Rev. 34(1), 29–41 (2009)
9. Mansar, S., Reijers, H.: Best practices in business process redesign: validation of a redesign framework. Computers in Industry 56(5), 457–471 (2005)
10. Mazzocco, K., Petitti, D.B., Fong, K.T., Bonacum, D., Brookey, J., Graham, S., Lasky, R., Sexton, J., Thomas, E.: Surgical team behaviors and patient outcomes. The American Journal of Surgery 197(5), 678–685 (2009)
11. Reijers, H.A., Jansen-Vullers, M.H., Zur Muehlen, M., Appl, W.: Workflow management systems + swarm intelligence = dynamic task assignment for emergency management applications. In: Alonso, G., Dadam, P., Rosemann, M. (eds.) BPM 2007. LNCS, vol. 4714, pp. 125–140. Springer, Heidelberg (2007)
12. Reijers, H.A., Song, M., Jeong, B.: Analysis of a collaborative workflow process with distributed actors. Information System Frontiers 11(3), 307–322 (2008)
13. Seidmann, A., Sundararajan, A.: The effects of asymmetry on business process redesign. International Journal of Production Economics 50, 117–128 (1997)
14. Sen, S.: Reciprocity: a foundational principle for promoting cooperative behavior among self-interested actors. In: Proceedings of the Second International Conference on Multiactor Systems, pp. 322–329. AAAI Press, Menlo Park (1996)
15. Song, M., van der Aalst, W.M.P.: Towards comprehensive support for orga-nizational mining. Decision Support Systems 46(1), 300–317 (2008)
16. Sun, S., Kumar, A., Yen, J.: Merging workflows: A new perspective on connecting business processes. Decision Support Systems 42(2), 844–858 (2006)
17. Tjosvold, D., Moy, J., Sasaki, S.: Co-operative teamwork for service quality in East Asia. Managing Service Quality 9(3), 209–216 (1999)
18. Wolf, A.: Constraint-based modeling and scheduling of clinical pathways. In: Larrosa, J., O'Sullivan, B. (eds.) CSCLP 2009. LNCS, vol. 6384, pp. 122–138. Springer, Heidelberg (2011)
19. ZurMühlen, M.: Organizational management in workflow applications – Issues and perspectives. Information Technology and Management 5(3-4), 271–291 (2004)

Accelerating Collaboration in Task Assignment Using a Socially Enhanced Resource Model

Rong Liu[1], Shivali Agarwal[2], Renuka R. Sindhgatta[2], and Juhnyoung Lee[1]

[1] IBM T.J. Watson Research Center, New York, USA
[2] IBM Research – India, Bangalore, India
{rliu,jyl}@us.ibm.com,
{shivaaga,renuka.sr}@in.ibm.com

Abstract. Knowledge-intensive business processes require knowledge workers to collaborate on complex activities. Social network analysis is increasingly being applied in organizations to understand the underlying interaction patterns between teams and foster meaningful collaboration. The social positions of a worker, i.e. the role played in working with others, can be identified through analyzing process logs to assist effective collaboration. In this paper, we present a novel resource model that incorporates the concepts of resource communities and social positions. We demonstrate our resource model through a real industry process - IT incident management process. This socially enhanced resource model is also used to accelerate the collaboration between various work groups by dedicating collaborative units in the task of incident resolution.

Keywords: BPM, resource model, social network, social compute unit.

1 Introduction

Social networking has become a powerful paradigm in enabling people to work together. Participation in a business process is "social" in nature [10]. Particularly, knowledge workers interact with each other, share ideas, and build knowledge to execute complex activities in knowledge-intensive processes. For such processes, it is critical to provide knowledge workers with an appropriate social supporting structure for effective task execution. For example, in IT Service Management (ITSM), support teams troubleshoot IT issues that are formally referred to as *IT incidents*. Due to the complexity of IT environment, incidents regarding enterprise applications (e.g. SAP), often require on-demand collaboration across teams, e.g., middleware or operation system teams. However, traditional process technologies often have difficulties in supporting such collaboration that usually cannot be prescribed before runtime [10].

There is a strong call for injecting social computing technologies into business process management (BPM) framework for a higher level of flexibility and efficiency [1,11,15]. A Social Compute Unit (SCU) [6,15] is dynamically and virtually formed as a loosely coupled team of skilled (human) resources to execute a specific task. An ITSM example is provided in [15] where an SCU is created based on IT component dependencies involved in an incident. Although such intrinsic dependencies within a task mandate collaboration to a degree, social positions of workers are also a critical factor in successful collaboration. Moreover, often such dependencies need to be explored as part of task execution. In this paper, we propose a new method to study social networks formed during process execution, identify different social positions, and utilize these social positions to dynamically form SCUs.

A resource is an entity assigned to a process activity during runtime to perform work. In this paper, we focus on human resources. Traditional resource models often consider organizational aspects of resources [3,12,14], not social connections among resources. However, resources, especially, knowledge workers, form various social communities and take different social positions while participating in business processes. In this paper, we enhance a traditional resource model with a set of social networking features to facilitate collaboration. Also, we provide a new resource assignment method that utilizes the social networking features. To illustrate this model, we study a real-world ITSM process to discover the social networks among knowledge workers and incorporate their social features into resource assignment.

The remainder of this paper is organized as follows: Section 2 introduces the enhanced resource model. Section 3 provides a case study to illustrate this model and use it in task assignment. Section 4 compares our work with related approaches and concludes this paper with a brief description of our future work.

2 Socially Enhanced Resource Model

In this paper, we adapt Muehlen's resource model in [12] to accommodate resource social positions as shown in Figure 1. In the traditional model, each human resource (i.e., *person*) owns some *roles* and occupies *positions* in *organization units*. Often, we refer to an organization unit as a *work group* that specializes in a particular domain, e.g., a finance work group. These elements specify basic competency requirements for resource assignment. When collaboration is mandatory, in addition to the basic requirements, a dynamic supporting team (i.e. SCU) comprised of a set of relevant resources will greatly improve the execution efficiency. In the extended model, each person is interested in some *topics*. A topic can be represented as a bag of keywords [5]. Also, topics may be related to each other through overlapping keywords. A resource belongs to one or more *communities* and has a degree of social power. The social power is reflected in the resource's social positions, the roles played in connecting groups [8]. We are interested in three social positions within a community: *key contributor*, *influencer* and *coordinator*. A key contributor is an active resource, e.g., constantly executing a fair number of tasks. Usually, we identify *group key contributors* for each work group. An influencer has high influence power over a community. This influence power is often interpreted as leadership. A proper measure of influence is *eigenvector centrality* [13]. A coordinator (see Figure 2(a)) within a community connects others and thus can be measured by *betweenness centrality*. Moreover, a community is formed by a group of people who have common interest on certain topics. Thus, a community often focuses on a collection of related topics.

People within a community often interact with other communities. Figure 2 illustrates "brokerage" social positions [8]. A resource may act as a *representative* of a community, which directly connects to other communities and is on most outgoing paths from this community to others, while a *gatekeeper* of a community is a resource to which other communities often directly connect for communication going to this community. These social positions often play critical roles during resource collaboration across communities. In the next section, we will use a real-world example to illustrate how to create such an enhanced resource model.

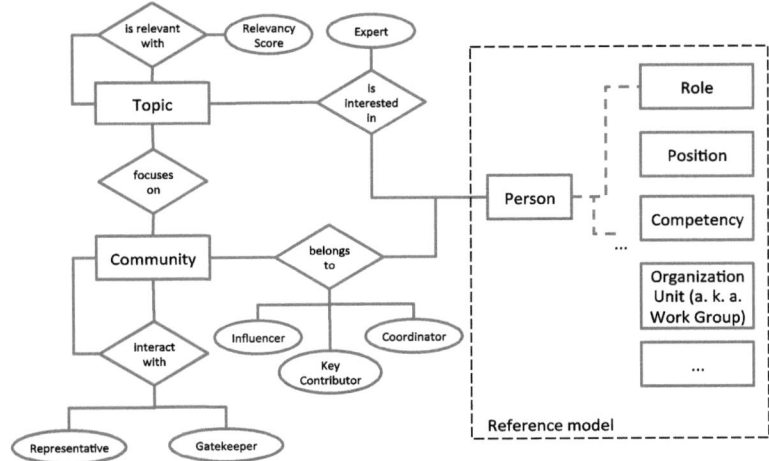

Fig. 1. Socially enhanced resource model (extended from resource meta model [12])

Fig. 2. Four different "brokerage" social positions [8] of Resource B: (a) Coordinator, (b) Gatekeeper of Blue Community, and (c) Representative of Red Community

3 Case Study – IT Incident Management

3.1 IT Incident Management Process

As a common practice, many enterprises outsource the management of their IT systems to specialized service providers. Business users of the IT systems submit incidents when they face issues with the systems. Resources from the service provider resolve the issues within timelines as defined in a service level agreement. The process starts when a business user reports in a ticketing tool and records the issue typically in a free-text form. Then the incident is assigned to a specific work group based on the problem description by a dispatcher. The incident is then picked up by an available resource within the group. The resource starts the resolution process. The resource analyzes the problem in the ticket, communicates to the business user for more input if needed, and resolves the problem. The business user validates the restoration of service and the incident is closed. Note that the resolution stage in this process is *iterative* because: (1) the incident may be misrouted due to insufficient information, (2) the assigned resource may be unavailable, and/or (3) for the complex nature of issues involved in the incident, multiple resources with different specialties may be required. Currently, an incident is assigned to one resource at a time. When necessary, the assigned resource works with a team lead and *transfers* the ticket to another suitable resource. An *incident transfer* reflects the need for collaboration.

3.2 Resource Social Network, Communities, and Social Positions

We analyzed 1,563 incidents along with 23,123 task execution logs from a client in the travel and entertainment industry. We built a network of 154 nodes and 220 edges based on incident transfer logs, as shown in Figure 3. In this network, each node is a resource and a direct link indicates incident transferred from the source to the target with the number of transferred incidents as the weight. We applied Girvan and Newman's algorithm [9] to detect communities in this network. This algorithm returns 21 communities as shown by different colors in Figure 3. Clearly, there are four major interconnected communities (A-D). Some communities are aligned with resource work group structures, while others spread across work groups. For example, among the 28 resources in Community B, there are 10 resources from HR Payroll work group, 7 from Security, and 3 from Travel and Expense group. We also discovered main topics from the incidents handled by Communities A-D using Latent Dirichlet Allocation [5]. As shown in Table 1, tickets processed by Community A are about four major topics, including *Purchasing*, *Payment*, *Invoice*, and *Web Method Integration*, with sample keywords shown in Table 1. The topics of each community can be considered as an affinity bond among the resources. Communities may have overlapping topics, but each community should have at least one unique topic.

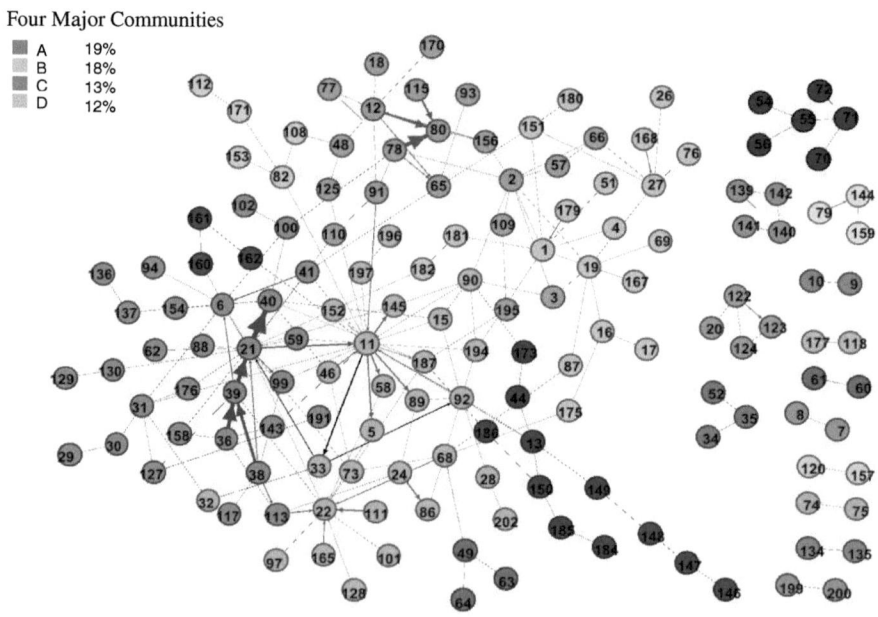

Fig. 3. The resource social network consists of communities highlighted in different colors

Table 1. Topics of Communities A, B, C, and D

Community	Size	Group Mix	Topics
A	29	Procure to Pay, Web Methods Application, Custom Application	*Purchasing*: purchasing order, shopping cart, goods movement, buyer, process *Payment*: payment, vendor, approval, transaction, *Invoice*: invoice, item, line, code *Web Methods Integration*: Hub, Request
B	28	Security, Travel and Expense, HR Payroll	*User Password*: User ID, user locked, password reset *Access*: authentication, connection, access, role, applicable, portal, self service, registration *HR Expense / Payroll*: employee, time, trip, deposit
C	20	Planned Transport Charges (PTC), Business Reports	PTC: ledger, session, task abended, printing failure *Reports*: source, error, report, filename
D	19	Business Reports, Security	*Reporting*: report, file, excel, attachment, record, pdf, accessing, absence, transport

Furthermore, we identified a number of interesting social positions as shown in Table 2. For each community, we identified coordinators by betweenness centrality, which measures the number of shortest paths that pass through a node [13]. For example, in Community A, Resource 21 has the highest betweenness centrality score, 87. In ITSM domain, coordinators are often IT architects, or managers responsible for coordinating groups. Influencers are identified through eigenvector centrality. This metric assigns relative scores to all nodes based on the concept that connections to high-scoring nodes weigh more than those to low-scoring nodes [13]. In Community A, Resource 36 has the highest score. In addition, we also identify group key contributors by the degree centrality, i.e., the number of edges of a node.

Table 2. Coordinator, Influencer, and Group Key Contributor

Community	Coordinator		Influencer		Key Contributor		
	Resource	Betweenness	Resource	Eigenvector	Resource	Workgroup	Degree
A	21	87	36	0.46	21	procure to pay	37
	40	24	39	0.39	39	custom application	28
	6	27	38	0.37	40	procure to pay	21
	31	18	21	0.35	36	web methods application	12
B	11	265	90	0.47	11	security	26
	92	206	11	0.39	22	HR travel and expense	15
	22	152	15	0.34	92	HR Payroll	9
	68	151	92	0.30	33	security	7

Communities may interact with each other through representatives and gatekeepers. Representatives typically correspond to leads or managers, and gatekeepers can be considered as points of contact within a community. To identify these positions, we studied the sub-network formed by only the links cutting across each pair of communities and measured indegree/outdegree centrality score (the number incoming/outgoing links of a node). A node with a high indegree score is recognized as a gatekeeper, and that with a high outdegree score is identified as a representative. For example, for community pair (A, B) shown in Figure 3, Resource 21 is a representative of Community A and Resource 11 acts as a gatekeeper of B.

3.3 Using Resource Model in Task Assignment

In this section, we provide an algorithm that augments the traditional incident assignment approach [4] with a social compute unit (SCU). This algorithm is not specific to ITSM and may be applicable to task assignment in other knowledge-intensive processes as well. For each high priority incident, a primary owner is assigned and a group of resources are formed as an SCU in anticipation of collaboration. The SCU leverage their broad knowledge and social power to advice the task owner resolution strategies and recommend suitable resources to collaborate. A formally assigned SCU is especially useful in a situation where a resource has not developed his own collaborative network. Figure 4 shows the outline of the proposed task assignment algorithm. Assuming that resource social networks have been analyzed, communities are well formulated, and different social positions are identified using the approach described above, this algorithm is triggered upon a new incident arrives. Traditional approaches, for example, the predictive learning model [4], can be used to recommend a workgroup and determine the task owner. Then, the following steps are taken to recommend resources forming an SCU:

1) Associate the incident with communities that are most relevant to it based on the keywords present in task description. There are two cases:

   Case A: The incident is matched with one community
   i. Choose an *influencer* node and a *coordinator* node from the matching community to the SCU. In case there are multiple influencers/coordinators, choose the one with best availability and least load. Preference is given to a resource qualified as both a coordinator and an influencer.
   ii. If the matching community consists of multiple work groups, choose a *key contributor* to the SCU from each group based on load and availability. If a selected influencer/coordinator is also a key contributor for a workgroup, then there is no need to pick another from that work group.

   Case B: The incident is matched with multiple communities
   i. Complete all steps in Case A for each community.
   ii. Choose a *representative* and a *gatekeeper* to the SCU from each pair of matching communities in case they are not already chosen in the capacity of their other social positions.

2) Notify the task owner and SCU of the incident.
3) If needed, members from the SCU can be added or removed, and task ownership can be transferred to a member in the SCU.

Figure 5 gives an incident to illustrate this algorithm. The text of this incident has references to keywords "goods movement" and "authorization", which match with the topics associated with both Communities B and A. Following the algorithm, two possible SCUs suggested are also shown in Figure 5. From the actual incident logs, we find the incident was transferred between Communities A & B as follows: 21 (A) → 40 (A) → 46 (B) → 11 (B) → 187 (B) → 40 (A) → 15 (B) →11 (B) → 145 (B) →21 (A). This case clearly indicates that the transfer is caused by collaboration. It can be seen from the logs that the key social positions do get involved and the transfers typically are originate from these powerful positions.

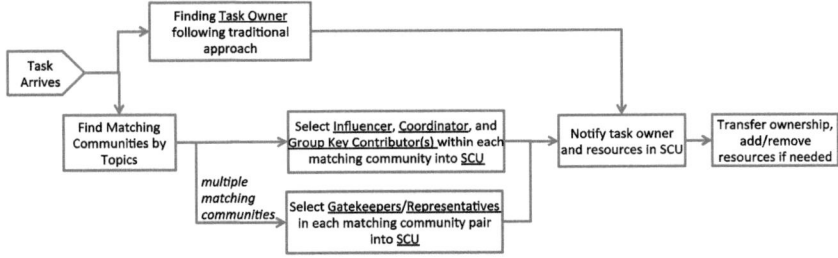

Fig. 4. Task Assignment Outline

Incident ID: INC1 Priority: High
Open time: 8/23/2010 2:02:16 PM Close Time: 7/28/2010 6:34:41 PM
Had system reimaged a few months ago, has not been able to perform *goods movement*, had previous incident opened (INCx) to report *authorization* issue, but is still unable to complete work, referring back to appropriate parties at higher severity. Please help to check.

Two possible SCUs:
i) *Community A*: 21 (coordinator, key contributor, gatekeeper, and representative), 36 (influencer, key contributor), 39 (key contributor)
   Community B: 92 (coordinator, influencer, key contributor), 11 (gatekeeper, key contributor), 33 (representative), 22 (key contributor)
ii) *Community A*: 21 (coordinator, gatekeeper, and representative), 36 (influencer, key contributor), 40 (key contributor), 39 (key contributor)
   Community B: 90 (influencer), 11 (coordinator, key contributor, and gatekeeper), 22 (key contributor), 33 (representative), 92 (key contributor).

Fig. 5. An Incident Example

4 Related Work and Conclusion

Technologies developed for BPM have had a tremendous success in the past two decades [2]. Resource modeling has been an important part of BPM. In [12], Muehlen describes a generic resource meta-model where a set of attributes may be associated with workflow participants. In [14], Russell et al present a collection of resource patterns in the context of process-aware information systems. A team-enabled workflow reference model is introduced in [3]. An SCU can be considered as a dynamically formed team on demand. In general, all of the above work focused on modeling of static features of resources but not the social aspect of resources.

Another challenge of BPM comes from its flexibility in handling processes that cannot be well defined before execution [2]. Social computing is considered as a natural remedy to this issue. General introduction to social computing and network analysis can be found in [13]. There is growing interest in integrating social computing with BPM (a. k. a. Social BPM) [7,11]. The studies in Social BPM propose the integration of different social tools, e.g., Wikis, discussion forums, to engage stakeholders in designing process models or collaborating on task execution, but not on analytical approaches to understanding resource social structures and utilizing the social structures in process execution, as presented in our work. Moreover, recent work also analyzed process execution logs to understand resource social behaviors. [1] introduces a systematic approach and also a tool called MiSoN that creates social networks based on task execution logs. Our work moves a step further to identify different resource social positions and use them to create SCUs for collaborative task execution. In addition, our paper proposed an approach to forming SCUs, which differs from previous work [15] in that SCUs are recommended based on social positions but not on dependencies involved in a task.

In summary, we have presented a resource model for process execution augmented with social characteristics of resources. This model brings together social concepts such as communities, topics, and various social positions along with traditional concepts such as roles and work groups, to support knowledge-intensive processes. Also, we provided a new approach to suggesting Social Compute Unit, a dynamic collaborative team, to execute a task in an efficient manner. We plan to work on a pilot of the new socially enhanced task assignment approach and will evaluate it by appropriate business measures such as reduced task execution time.

References

1. van der Aalst, W.M.P., Song, M.S.: Mining Social Networks: Uncovering Interaction Patterns in Business Processes. In: Desel, J., Pernici, B., Weske, M. (eds.) BPM 2004. LNCS, vol. 3080, pp. 244–260. Springer, Heidelberg (2004)
2. van der Aalst, W.M.P.: Business Process Management: A Comprehensive Survey. ISRN Software Engineering (2013)
3. van der Aalst, W.M.P., Kumar, A.: A reference model for team-enabled workflow management systems. Data Knowl. Eng. 38(3), 335–363 (2001)
4. Agarwal, S., Sindhgatta, R., Sengupta, B.: SmartDispatch: enabling efficient ticket dispatch in an IT service environment. In: KDD 2012 (2012)
5. Blei, D., Ng, A., Jordan, M.: Latent Dirichlet allocation. Journal of Machine Learning Research 3, 993–1022 (2003)
6. Dustdar, S., Bhattacharya, K.: The Social Compute Unit. IEEE Internet Computing 15(3), 64–69 (2011)
7. Erol, S., Granitzer, M., Happ, S., Jantunen, S., Jennings, B., Johannesson, P., Koschmider, A., Nurcan, S., Rossi, D., Schmidt, R.: Combining BPM and social software: contradiction or chance? Journal of Software Maintenance and Evolution 22, 449–476 (2010)
8. Fernandez, R.M., Gould, R.V.: A Dilemma of State Power: Brokerage and Influence in the National Health Policy Domain. American Journal of Sociology 99, 1455–1491 (1994)
9. Girvan, M., Newman, M.E.J.: Community structure in social and biological networks. Proc. of National Academy of Sciences of USA 99, 7821–7826 (2002)
10. Khan, R.: Social Networking and BPM of the Future. BPTrends (2009)
11. Koschmider, A., Song, M., Reijers, H.A.: Social software for modeling business processes. In: Ardagna, D., Mecella, M., Yang, J. (eds.) BPM 2008 Workshops. LNBIP, vol. 17, pp. 666–677. Springer, Heidelberg (2009)
12. Muehlen, M.: Organizational Management in Workflow Applications – Issues and Perspectives. Information Technology and Management Archive 5(3-4), 271–291 (2004)
13. Newman, M.E.J.: Networks: An Introduction. Oxford University Press, Oxford (2010)
14. Russell, N., van der Aalst, W.M.P.: Work Distribution and Resource Management in BPEL4People: Capabilities and Opportunities. In: Bellahsène, Z., Léonard, M. (eds.) CAiSE 2008. LNCS, vol. 5074, pp. 94–108. Springer, Heidelberg (2008)
15. Sengupta, B., Jain, A., Bhattacharya, K., Truong, H.-L., Dustdar, S.: Who do you call? Problem resolution through social compute units. In: Liu, C., Ludwig, H., Toumani, F., Yu, Q. (eds.) ICSOC 2012. LNCS, vol. 7636, pp. 48–62. Springer, Heidelberg (2012)

Splitting GSM Schemas: A Framework for Outsourcing of Declarative Artifact Systems

Rik Eshuis[1,*], Richard Hull[2,**], Yutian Sun[3,***], and Roman Vaculín[2]

[1] School of Industrial Engineering, Eindhoven University of Technology, Netherlands
[2] IBM T J Watson Research Center, USA
[3] Department of Computer Science, UC Santa Barbara, USA

Abstract. Case Management is emerging as an important paradigm for Business Process Management. The Guard-Stage-Milestone (GSM) model is a recent case management approach that substantially influences OMG's emerging Case Management Modeling Notation standard. We study the problem of outsourcing part of a GSM schema to another party, and develop a framework that supports splitting and outsourcing of GSM schemas. One element of the framework focuses on restructuring the GSM schema to facilitate outsourcing while preserving the semantics of the original schema; the second focuses on locking protocols that define how the distributed parties should operate. Additionally, the framework allows parties to keep local parts of their GSM subschema private without affecting the outcomes of the global execution. The rules restructuring developed here enables a crisp separation of concerns, which allows reuse of existing GSM (and thus Case Management) engines for executing the subschemas.

1 Introduction

Nowadays, cloud-computing is a key enabler of business process outsourcing. Collaboration in an outsourcing relationship is typically organized around business objects or business artifacts, like Order or Product, that are continually modified during the collaboration. This has a natural fit with data-centric BPM and case management [2,23], recent BPM paradigms that organize processes around business artifacts and cases [7].

In this paper we study outsourcing of portions of case management models. The business process modeling approach we use is the Guard-Stage-Milestone (GSM) model [12,6], which supports a declarative specification of case lifecycles, also known as "artifact lifecycles". GSM has substantially influenced the forthcoming OMG Case Management Model and Notation (CMMN) standard [3,18].

To support outsourcing of parts of a GSM schema, we propose a solution in which each collaborating party has its own artifact-centric system, and the GSM schema (original schema) is split into parts (essentially, subschemas) that are hosted by the respective parties. This allows a party to use its own GSM engine for performing its work. To simplify the discussion, we focus on the two party scenario (client and provider), but the technical results can be extended to an arbitrary number of parties.

---

[*] Performed some of this research while visiting the IBM T.J. Watson Research Center.
[**] Supported in part by NSF grant IIS-0812578, and in part by the European Community Seventh Framework Programme FP7/2007-2013 under grant agreement number 257593 (ACSI).
[***] Supported in part by NSF grant IIS-0812578. Performed part of the research as a summer intern at the IBM T.J. Watson Research Center.

An obvious naive way to achieve a split of a GSM schema is to simply partition it into subschemas that are to be executed by the parties. However, this can cause two kinds of challenges. First, because of the declarative, rule-based nature of GSM (and CMMN), processing (incorporating) a new event can lead to a long propagation of rule firings, which could involve arbitrarily long and inefficient back-and-forth interaction between the two parties. Second, if multiple incoming events are to be processed in the distributed setting, race conditions may break the equivalence between the original schema and the pair of split subschemas. To mitigate the race conditions introduced by the naive splitting approach, the underlying GSM engines would need to be extended to incorporate transactional mechanisms in the heart of the rule propagation logic.

To addresses these concerns, we propose an alternative technique for restructuring (the rules of) the original GSM schema into the two subschemas, so that the rule propagation caused by an incoming event can be achieved in 3 steps: incorporating the event into one subschema, sending a single message (event) to the other subschema, and then incorporating the event into the other subschema. Also, we propose a light-weight distributed 2-phase locking protocol to avoid race conditions. This construction enables a separation of concerns, allowing the core GSM algorithm (and engine) to remain unchanged and layering the outsourcing and locking protocol above it. These two elements combine into a formal framework that covers both the design-time (splitting GSM schemas) and run-time aspects (locking protocol) of outsourcing GSM schemas.

The basic restructuring assumes that every part of the GSM schema is public and, therefore, that any part can be placed with either party. In practice, the parties may want to keep certain parts of the GSM schema private, meaning that other parties should not be able see it. For instance, a business rule that explains under what conditions a credit request is rejected might be considered confidential. To address privacy requirements, we extend the framework to allow hiding of private elements of a GSM schema behind newly created anonymizing events, which can be processed as normal events.

Although left as future work, we anticipate that the techniques developed here can be extended to other declarative, rules-driven approaches to data-centric business process management, including OMG's CMMN [3] and the model of [2]. Also, the approach here can be used with artifact-centric interoperation hubs [13] (see Section 6).

The remainder of this paper is organized as follows. Section 2 introduces GSM schemas by means of a real-world example, and also shows the issues that arise from naive GSM schema partitioning to support outsourcing. Section 3 formally introduces the GSM model used in this paper. Section 4 defines the outsourcing framework, in particular the restructuring and splitting of GSM schemas and a locking protocol. Section 5 extends the framework to deal with privacy. Section 6 discusses related work and Section 7 offers conclusions.

Because of space limitations the exposition in this paper is succinct, with a focus on the main intuitions and techniques used. Full details are provided in [8].

2 Motivating Example

We introduce the problem of outsourcing GSM artifact schemas by means of an example from the processes used by IBM Global Financing (IGF) [4], which is the largest IT financier in the world. IGF finances hardware, software, and services in the IT industry. First, we explain a simplified portion of a GSM schema for IGF processes. Then, we discuss the problem of outsourcing parts of this GSM schema to other parties.

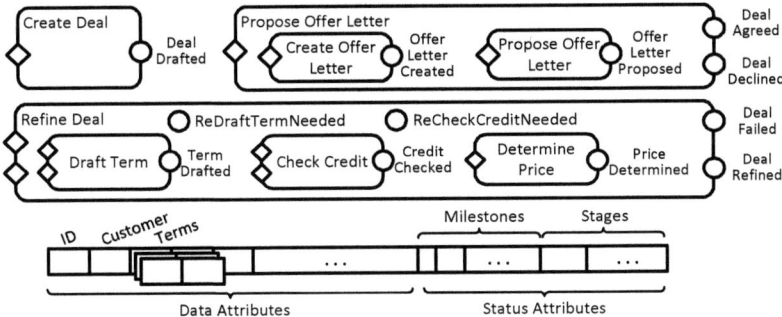

Fig. 1. GSM schema of the simplified part of the IGF business process: the Deal artifact

2.1 The Guard-Stage-Milestone Model of IGF

The main business process of IGF is arranging financial deals with clients. First, a draft deal is created. Next, a deal offer is sent to the client. If the client accepts, the deal is refined and signed by both parties. We focus on deal refinement process and three of its main activities: drafting the terms of the deal, checking the credit level of the client, and determining the price. The price can only be determined if the term has been drafted and the credit checked. A complicating factor is that the result of drafting terms might be that the credit check needs to be redone. For instance, if the risk is high the requirements on the client's credit are more strict. Conversely, the outcome of the credit check might be that more strict terms are needed, requiring the terms to be redrafted. (In the actual IGF process there are about 10 interrelated activities needed before determining price.)

As in other artifact-centric models, in GSM the business process is represented as interaction of key business artifacts, with each artifact consisting of a data schema and a lifecycle schema. Figure 1 shows a simplified GSM schema of part of the IGF business process, organized around the key artifact Deal. The information part (bottom half of Figure 1) consists of data attributes specific to the deal, and status attributes that record the full state of the artifact lifecycle. In GSM, the lifecycle includes *stages* (rounded rectangles), which represent the business activities. The Deal lifecycle includes three main stages. Stages are composite (i.e., contain other substages, e.g. RefineDeal) or atomic (i.e., stages that encapsulate a task, e.g. CheckCredit). Tasks correspond to external service invocations (manual or automated), and when completed they typically update data attributes. Each stage has one or more *guards*, or *opening sentries* (diamonds), which are expressions specifying when stages open, and one or more *terminators*, or *terminating sentries*, which specify when stages close. *Milestones* (circles) represent important business objectives or conditions. Milestones can be attached to a stage to represent the goal reached when the stage has completed, or can be standalone to represent an important business condition that is not directly the result of any stage.

Informally, a *sentry* is an expression that may get triggered by an *event* and/or a Boolean condition. A *rule* is a sentry along with an internal action, namely opening/closing (terminating) a stage or achieving/invalidating a milestone. Figure 2 shows the opening and terminating sentries for the three atomic stages in composite stage RefineDeal. Some sentries reference *internal events* that correspond to status changes of stages or milestones. For instance, if stage RefineDeal is opened, internal event +RefineDeal is generated. Closing RefineDeal generates internal event −RefineDeal.

Stages	Guards (Opening sentries)	Terminating sentries
DraftTerm	r_1: **on** +RefineDeal	r_3: **on** +TermDrafted
	r_2: **on** +ReDraftTermNeeded **if** RefineDeal	r_4: **on** −RefineDeal
CheckCredit	r_5: **on** +RefineDeal	r_7: **on** +CreditChecked
	r_6: **on** +ReCheckCreditNeeded **if** RefineDeal	r_8: **on** −RefineDeal
DeterminePrice	r_9: **if** TermDrafted ∧ CreditChecked ∧ RefineDeal	r_{10}: **on** +PriceDetermined
		r_{11}: **on** +DraftTerm
		r_{12}: **on** +CheckCredit
		r_{13}: **on** −RefineDeal

Fig. 2. Guards and terminators of IGF schema

Milestones	Achieving sentries	Invalidating sentries
TermDrafted	r_{14}: **on** C:DraftTerm **if** RefineDeal	r_{15}: **on** +DraftTerm
		r_{16}: **on** +ReDraftTermNeeded
CreditChecked	r_{17}: **on** C:CheckCredit **if** RefineDeal	r_{18}: **on** +CheckCredit
		r_{19}: **on** +ReCheckCreditNeeded
PriceDetermined	r_{20}: **on** C:DeterminePrice **if** RefineDeal	r_{21}: **on** +DraftTerm **if** ReDraftTermNeeded
		r_{22}: **on** +CheckCredit **if** ReCheckCreditNeeded
		r_{23}: **on** +DeterminePrice
ReDraftTermNeeded	r_{24}: **on** E:RegulationChange **if** RefineDeal	r_{26}: **on** +TermDrafted
	r_{25}: **if** credit_level>100,000 ∧ RefineDeal	
ReCheckCreditNeeded	r_{27}: **if** risk_level > 4 ∧ RefineDeal	r_{28}: **on** +CreditChecked

Fig. 3. Milestones with achieving and invalidating sentries of IGF schema

The opening sentries containing internal event +RefineDeal, namely r_1 and r_5, state that if +RefineDeal occurs, stages DraftTerm and CheckCredit are opened. Similarly, a stage is closed when one of its terminating sentries becomes true, e.g., r_4 indicates that if RefineDeal closes then so does DraftTerm. A substage can open only if its parent is open, e.g., r_2, r_6, r_9 all include the conjunct RefineDeal used here as a Boolean status attribute which is true when the stage is open (in practice inclusion of such conjuncts can be omitted and inferred by the underlying system).

Figure 3 shows the achieving and invalidating sentries for several milestones in RefineDeal; these specify when a milestone should become true or false. For example, milestone CreditChecked is achieved (sentry r_{17}) when task *CheckCredit* completes, denoted by C:CheckCredit, a task *completion event*. Also, milestone TermDrafted gets invalidated (sentry r_{16}) when milestone ReDraftTermNeeded is achieved.

The GSM execution semantics is driven by *incoming events*, including external events, such as E:RegulationChange, and task completion events, such as C:DraftTerm; these are processed in sequence. An incoming event can result in one or more *internal events*, i.e., changes in status attributes. Such changes may have cascading effects by triggering other internal events. The full effect of incorporating one incoming event is called a *business step* or *B-step*. To ensure that each incoming event has "maximal effect", sentries are evaluated in an order so that modifications of all status attributes occurring in the sentry have been performed before the sentry is evaluated (see Section 3).

Example 2.1. Consider a *snapshot* (or instance) of the IGF schema in which milestones TermDrafted and ReCheckCreditNeeded are true (have been achieved), stages

RefineDeal and CheckCredit are open, and task *CheckCredit* is in progress. Suppose that task *CheckCredit* completes and this results in an incoming task completion event C:CheckCredit which has as its payload a value 200,000 for credit_level. This incoming event initiates a B-step which involves the following steps:
1: (a) milestone CreditChecked is achieved, which causes (b) stage CheckCredit to close
2: (a) milestone ReDraftTermNeeded gets achieved and (b) opens stage DraftTerm, which causes (c) TermDrafted to be invalidated
3: since TermDrafted becomes invalidated, stage PriceDetermined stays closed. ∎

2.2 Outsourcing GSM Schemas and Maintaining Privacy

In this subsection we examine two outsourcing scenarios for IGF. Outsourcing will involve dividing or splitting the GSM schema of Figure 1 into two parts that can execute on the GSM engines of the two different parties. For each scenario we show that naive splitting results in problematic behavior. In Sections 4 and 5 we revisit the outsourcing scenarios to illustrate how the proposed framework resolves the identified problems.

Example 2.2. (*Outsourcing Scenario 1.*) IGF hires a specialized Law Office (LO) to draft the terms of each contract and outsources stage DraftTerm (with its embedded task of the same name) and milestones TermDrafted and ReDraftTermNeeded in the GSM schema (in Figure 1) to LO. Several splits of the GSM schema are possible.

A naive split creates a LO subschema (called IGF_{LO}) that only contains stage Draft-Term plus its embedded task and milestones TermDrafted and ReDraftTermNeeded, together with the corresponding sentries. All other stages and milestones with their sentries remain in the subschema IGF_{MAIN} that is maintained by the IGF organization. It turns out, that to preserve the behavior of the original GSM schema, the two subschemas require an intricate synchronization to guide their interactions. Consider for instance the situation in Example 2.1, where event C:CheckCredit triggers three sequential steps as denoted by the bullet points 1–3 there. With the stage DraftTerm and milestones TermDrafted and ReDraftTermNeeded outsourced to the LO, step (2) needs to be processed at LO and LO needs to wait until step (1) is finished, which is processed by IGF. Similarly, when step (2) is under processing at LO, IGF cannot start processing step (3) until LO informs IGF about finishing of step (2). Without such a synchronization, given the situation in Example 2.1, IGF might inadvertently open stage DeterminePrice, as it might conclude that both milestones CreditChecked and TermDrafted are true at a certain moment. Thus, for a naive split a complex synchronization mechanism is required that needs to be built into the GSM engines of the two parties. ∎

In contrast, the framework presented in this paper splits GSM schemas in such a way that both parties can reuse their GSM engines and use a simple locking protocol to coordinate their execution. For the situation of Example 2.2, the framework restructures the schema into subschemas that support the following behaviors. If event C:CheckCredit arrives at IGF, then IGF first performs all relevant processing on its subschema IGF_{MAIN}, and then sends an event to LO, which performs all relevant processing on its subschema. To ensure the behavior of the original schema is preserved, the framework duplicates certain status attributes and sentries from IGF_{LO} subschema into IGF_{MAIN} subschema. This enables, for example, IGF to determine whether or not DeterminePrice should open without waiting for LO to do its part of the processing (see Example 4.1).

A more complicated synchronization problem arises when two incoming events arrive at the two parties simultaneously (this is illustrated in Example 4.3).

We now illustrate how our framework can maintain privacy.

Example 2.3. (*Outsourcing Scenario 2.*) IGF outsources stages CheckCredit and DraftTerm with their tasks, their milestones CreditChecked and TermDrafted, and the corresponding sentries to an Administration Company (AC). All other milestones, in particular ReDraftTermNeeded, are kept at IGF. Consider again that event C:CheckCredit with credit_level $= 200,000$ occurs. According to the approach for restructuring described above, an attribute for tracking the status of milestone ReDraftTermNeeded is created at AC and the achieving sentry r_{25} (see Figure 3) of the milestone is included into AC.

However, IGF might consider the logic that determines ReDraftTermNeeded to be confidential, and want to keep the sentry r_{25} private. A private sentry should not be moved to another party, so the split we used before is not possible. To solve this problem, we introduce "anonymizing events" that hide private sentries. As explained in Section 5, a refinement of our restructuring approach can be used to preserve the privacy of a set of status attributes, and preserve the behavior of the original GSM schema. ∎

3 The Formal GSM Model

This section presents the formalism underlying the GSM model. (Further details are presented in [8].) To simplify exposition, the model used in this paper is a variation of the models defined in [6,22], and it incorporates features that simplify technical aspects of how rules are fired when processing incoming events. The core properties of GSM, including the equivalence of the incremental and fixpoint semantics [6] hold in this variant. For the technical development we focus on GSM schemas with a single artifact type, and assume that there is no interaction between artifact instances. Generalization to multiple artifact types and instances is left as future work.

Definition 3.1. A (single artifact type) *GSM schema* is a tuple $\Gamma = (\mathcal{A}, \mathcal{E}, \mathcal{H}, \mathcal{R})$, where

- $\mathcal{A} = (\mathcal{A}_D, \mathcal{A}_S, \mathcal{A}_M)$ is a family of three disjoint sets of symbols, called *data*, *stage*, and *milestone attributes*, respectively. The data attributes have types including scalars, records, and sets. The elements of $\mathcal{A}_{status} = \mathcal{A}_S \cup \mathcal{A}_M$ are called *status attributes*, and have Boolean values (always initialized to be false). The stage and milestone attributes correspond to the stages and milestones in the schema.
- $\mathcal{E} = \mathcal{E}_{inc} \cup \mathcal{E}_{gen}$, where $\mathcal{E}_{inc}$ is the set of incoming event types that can be received by snapshots (i.e., instances) of Γ, and $\mathcal{E}_{gen}$ is the set of event types that can be generated by snapshots of Γ. Each event type has the form $E(a_1, \ldots, a_n)$, where E is the event type name and $\{a_1, \ldots, a_n\} \subseteq \mathcal{A}$ is the payload, with the restriction that for $E \in \mathcal{E}_{inc}$, the payload must be in $\mathcal{A}_D$, i.e., data attributes. Generated events draw their payload from the attribute values in the snapshot; incoming events update snapshot attributes according to the payload.
- $\mathcal{H} = (Substage, Task, Submilestone)$ is the *hierarchy schema*, that specifies the relationships between stages, tasks, and milestones in Γ. In particular:
    - *Substage* is a function from $\mathcal{A}_S$ to finite subsets of $\mathcal{A}_S$. The relation $\{(S, S') | S' \in Substage(S)\}$ creates a forest.

- *Task* is a function from the atomic stages in $\mathcal{A}_S$ to tasks (i.e., external services). The event type associated with the invocation (completion) of a task of type T is denoted by *Invoke(T)* (*Compl(T)*).
- *Submilestone* defines a function from $\mathcal{A}_S$ to finite subsets of $\mathcal{A}_M$, such that $Submilestone(S) \cap Submilestone(S') = \emptyset$ for $S \neq S'$.
- $\mathcal{R}$ is a set of Event-Condition-Action (ECA) *rules* formed over $\mathcal{A} \cup \mathcal{E}$ (see below).

For a GSM schema Γ as above, a *snapshot* is an assignment Σ of values for the attributes.

We assume a standard condition language $\mathcal{C}$ with the following characteristics. Atomic terms include symbols in $\mathcal{A}_S \cup \mathcal{A}_M \cap \mathcal{E}_{inc}$, and $pred(x_1, \ldots, x_n)$, where *pred* is a supported predicate (e.g., $=$, $<$, and set membership) and where each x_i is either a constant, an attribute, or a variable. The variables are used in quantification (e.g., if a data attribute has set type). $\mathcal{C}$ also permits terms that are *polarized status attributes*, i.e., expressions of the form $+\sigma$ and $-\sigma$ where $\sigma \in \mathcal{A}_S \cup \mathcal{A}_M$; intuitively, $+\sigma$ (or $-\sigma$) is true if σ has become true (or false), during a B-step (defined below).

The truth value of a formula φ in $\mathcal{C}$ is defined relative to triples of the form (Σ, e, Σ') where Σ, Σ' are snapshots of Γ and e is an event with type in $\mathcal{E}$. Intuitively, Σ corresponds to the initial snapshot of a B-step, e corresponds to the incoming event that triggers the B-step, and Σ' corresponds to a snapshot that is constructed during the computation that incorporates e into Σ. (So, Σ' might be the result of updating the data attributes according to e, or might correspond to some snapshot computed during incremental firing of ECA rules). The triple (Σ, e, Σ') *satisfies* expression $pred(x_1, \ldots, x_n)$, denoted $(\Sigma, e, \Sigma') \models pred(x_1, \ldots, x_n)$, if $\Sigma' \models pred(x_1, \ldots, x_n)$. For terms $E \in \mathcal{E}_{inc}$, $(\Sigma, e, \Sigma') \models E$ if e has type E. For polarized status attributes, the triple $(\Sigma, e, \Sigma') \models +\sigma$ if $\Sigma \models \neg\sigma$ and $\Sigma' \models \sigma$, and analogously for $(\Sigma, e, \Sigma') \models -\sigma$. The notion of $(\Sigma, e, \Sigma') \models \varphi$ for other formulas in $\mathcal{C}$ is defined recursively in the usual manner.

We define a *sentry* as an expression ξ of form "on δ if φ", "on δ" or "if φ", where δ is an event expression, φ is an expression in $\mathcal{C}$ with no free variables. An *event expression* is a conjunction holding zero or one incoming event types and any number of polarized status attributes. A *rule* over GSM schema Γ is an expression ρ of form "ξ then $\odot\sigma$", where ξ is a sentry, $\odot \in \{+, -\}$ and $\odot\sigma$ is a polarized status attribute.

In this paper we use the *newly-true* semantics when testing the truth condition of a sentry ψ of form "if φ" (i.e., no incoming event and no polarized attributes). In this case, we define $(\Sigma, e, \Sigma') \models \varphi$ if $\Sigma \not\models \varphi$ and $\Sigma' \models \varphi$. The intuition is that a rule of form "if φ then $\odot\sigma$" will be applicable, and will cause a change in the value of σ, only if the value of φ has changed from false to true during the B-step being computed.

Suppose now that ψ is a sentry, $\rho =$ "ψ then $\odot\sigma$" is a rule, and (Σ, e, Σ') is a triple as above. Then ρ is *applicable* to (Σ, e, Σ') if $(\Sigma, e, \Sigma') \models \psi$ and $\odot\sigma$ can be applied to Σ' (i.e., either $\odot = +$ and $\Sigma' \models \neg\sigma$ or $\odot = -$ and $\Sigma' \models \sigma$).

The application of event e to snapshot Σ, denoted $apply(\Sigma, e)$ is the result of updating the attributes of Σ according to the payload of e. Event e is *applicable* to Σ in Γ if the sentry of at least one rule in Γ is true for $(\Sigma, e, apply(\Sigma, e))$.

Following [6], the operational semantics of GSM is based on the notion of *B-steps*:

Definition 3.2. Let $\Gamma = (\mathcal{A}, \mathcal{E}, \mathcal{H}, \mathcal{R})$ be a GSM schema, Σ, Σ' snapshots of Γ, e an event with type in $\mathcal{E}$ that is applicable to Σ, and $\mathcal{G}$ a set of events whose type corresponds to task invocations for tasks in $\mathcal{H}$. The tuple $(\Sigma, e, \Sigma', \mathcal{G})$ is a *B-step* of Γ if there is a sequence $\Sigma_0 = \Sigma, \Sigma_1 = apply(\Sigma, e), \Sigma_2, \ldots, \Sigma_n = \Sigma'$ of snapshots of Γ, where Σ_i

is the result of applying a rule in $\mathcal{R}$ to Σ_{i-1} for each $i \in [2..n]$ and $\mathcal{G}$ is the set of events corresponding to the tasks invoked because of atomic stages S whose value is false in Σ and true in Σ'. (The order of rule firing must be compatible with the Event-relativized Polarized Dependency Graph, defined below.) The set of B-steps for a GSM schema Γ is denoted as $Bstep(\Gamma)$.

Finally, we describe two "healthiness" conditions on GSM schemas. Both of these rely on graphs formed from Γ that capture the relationships between the rules in Γ.

Let $\Gamma = (\mathcal{A}, \mathcal{E}, \mathcal{H}, \mathcal{R})$ be a GSM schema and $E \in \mathcal{E}$. The *Event-relativized Polarized Dependency Graph* (*erPDG*) of Γ for E, denoted $PDG_\Gamma(E)$, is a directed graph whose set of nodes is a subset of $\{E\} \cup \mathcal{A}_D \cup \bigcup_{\sigma \in \mathcal{A}_{status}} \{+\sigma, -\sigma\}$ that describes the dependencies among E, the payload attributes of E, and selected polarized status attributes of Γ. (The detailed definition is in [8].) Essentially, an edge is included in an erPDG from one polarized attribute, say $+\tau$, to another one, say $-\sigma$, if some rule for $-\sigma$ has $+\tau$ in its "on" part or τ in its "if" part. If there is such an edge in the erPDG, then all the rules that might toggle τ to true should be considered, and fired if appropriate, before any rules that might toggle σ to be false. (If τ is in the "if" part of a rule for $-\sigma$, then both $(+\tau, -\sigma)$ and $(-\tau, -\sigma)$ are included in the erPDG.) Further, if an event type E (or a data attribute a in the payload of E) occurs in the sentry of $-\sigma$, edge $(E, -\sigma)$ (or $(a, -\sigma)$) should be included. Finally, if a is in the payload of E, edge (E, a) is included.

Example 3.3. Figure 4 shows an event-relativized polarized dependency graph with respect to event C:CheckCredit based on the GSM schema in Figure 1 and the rules in Figures 2 and 3. Some sentries are labeled on edges to illustrate the why these edges are included. For example, there is an edge from +ReDraftTermNeeded to −TermDrafted, because one of the sentries of −TermDrafted is r_{16} = "on +ReDraftTermNeeded". ∎

Due to declarative nature of GSM, a designer may accidentally create a family of rules that, in some circumstances, has conflicting effects on a status attribute, i.e., where there exists a single B-step that leads to both a request to make some status attribute σ true and a request to make σ false. To prevent this, we introduce the concept of *pathwise consistency*. (See [8] for further details.) Intuitively, an erPDG for an event type E is pathwise consistent, if for each status attribute σ, if there is a path from E to $+\sigma$ and a path from E to $-\sigma$, then the sentry ψ on an edge of one of these paths is "blocked" by the other path, i.e., the conjunction of sentries on the other path implies $\neg\psi$. As discussed in [8], if the underlying logic is decidable then determining pathwise consistency is also decidable. If the underlying logic is undecidable, then decidable modified versions of "pathwise consistent" can be used.

Definition 3.4. A GSM schema $\Gamma = (\mathcal{A}, \mathcal{E}, \mathcal{H}, \mathcal{R})$ is *well-formed* if for each event type $E \in \mathcal{E}$, $PDG_\Gamma(E)$ has no directed cycles and is pathwise consistent.

If Γ is a well-formed GSM schema, then the incremental semantics in Definition 3.2 is equivalent to both the incremental and fixpoint semantics defined in [6] (see [14]).

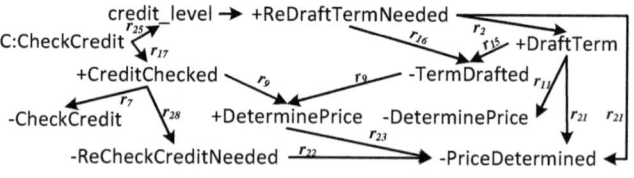

Fig. 4. Event-relativized PDG for C:CheckCredit

4 GSM Splitting

This section presents the formal framework for splitting a GSM schema into two subschemas (the approach can be generalized to n subschemas), so that each B-step of the original schema can be simulated using a B-step of the one subschema followed by a B-step of the other subschema. The first part of the subsection considers situation where there is only one event that is being processed; and the second part develops a framework based on locking to achieve transactional consistency when multiple concurrent incoming events are processed. Further details are presented in [8].

4.1 Splitting a Single B-Step

Let $\Gamma = (\mathcal{A} = (\mathcal{A}_D, \mathcal{A}_S, \mathcal{A}_M), \mathcal{E} = (\mathcal{E}_{inc} \cup \mathcal{E}_{gen}), \mathcal{H}, \mathcal{R})$ be a well-formed GSM schema. To support outsourcing of a portion of a GSM schema Γ, we use a form of "splitting", to create two GSM schemas $\Gamma^1 = (\mathcal{A}^1, \mathcal{E}^1, \mathcal{H}^1, \mathcal{R}^1)$ and $\Gamma^2 = (\mathcal{A}^2, \mathcal{E}^2, \mathcal{H}^2, \mathcal{R}^2)$. (In this case, Γ^1 can be thought of as the client that owns the overall process and Γ^2 as the server that supports the outsourced portion of the process. However, Γ^1 and Γ^2 are symmetric in the mathematical framework developed in this paper.) The splitting of Γ is specified by partitioning the attribute set $\mathcal{A}$ of Γ into a pair of disjoint sets $Base^1_{att}$ and $Base^2_{att}$ (possibly including both data and status attributes). Intuitively Γ^1 includes the data attributes, stages, and milestones corresponding to $Base^1_{att}$, and also each task that is contained in an atomic stage in $Base^1_{att}$, and similarly for Γ^2. The set $\mathcal{A}^1$ will typically be formed as the union of $Base^1_{att}$ along with some additional attributes from $Base^2_{att}$, and similarly for $\mathcal{A}^2$, as explained below.

When specifying Γ^1 and Γ^2, we also specify $Base^1_{inc}$ and $Base^2_{inc}$ as a partition of $\mathcal{E}_{inc}$ corresponding to the incoming event types that can be received by Γ^1 and Γ^2 respectively. To simplify exposition, assume that for $i \in \{1, 2\}$ and each event type $E \in Base^i_{inc}$, the payload of E is entirely contained within $Base^i_{att}$. Moreover, if atomic stage $S \in Base^i_{att}$ holds task T, then the payload of completion event type $Compl(T)$ is contained in $Base^i_{att}$. (These assumptions can be dropped without substantially altering the framework or results.)

Let Γ be a well-formed GSM schema, Γ^1 and Γ^2 be a splitting of Γ, and e as an incoming event of Γ, our construction ensures that the B-step triggered by e of Γ is equivalent to a B-step triggered by e of Γ^1 followed by a B-step triggered by $\widehat{e}$ of Γ^2 (where $\widehat{e}$ will be introduce later).

There are four primary elements in the framework for splitting GSM schemas to achieve the above property. The first three relate to the construction of Γ^1 and Γ^2.

1. **Duplication of selected attributes:** This involves identifying an "extension" set $Ext^1 \subseteq Base^2_{att}$ that will be duplicated in Γ^1, and similarly, identifying a set $Ext^2 \subseteq Base^1_{att}$ that will be duplicated in Γ^2. Let the attribute set $\mathcal{A}^i$ of Γ^i be $Base^i_{att} \cup Ext^i$ for $i \in \{1, 2\}$. The duplicated attributes are needed so that the first host that computes part of a B-step against Γ can perform a complete B-step without reference to the other host.
2. **Rules allocation:** The set of rules in Γ are allocated to Γ^1 and Γ^2 in such a way that each rule fired in a given subschema (i.e., in Γ^1 or in Γ^2) has the information needed without referring to the other subschema. In some cases, a rule for a status attribute $\sigma \in Ext^2$ (i.e., a status attribute in $Base^2_{att}$ that is duplicated in Γ^1) will be

allocated to $\mathcal{R}^1$, and visa-versa. In other cases the same rule may be allocated to both Γ^1 and Γ^2

3. **Event transformation:** This aspect involves creating, for each incoming event type $E \in Base^1_{inc}$, and for each event e of type E, an event type $\widehat{E}$, along with event $\widehat{e}$ that are applied to snapshots of Γ^2, and visa-versa. Let the event set $\mathcal{E}^1$ of Γ^1 be $Base^1_{inc} \cup \{\widehat{E} \mid E \in Base^2_{inc}\}$, and similarly for $\mathcal{E}^2$.
4. **B-step Simulation Protocol:** Finally, a protocol is specified for communication between the hosts of Γ^1 and Γ^2, that enables simulation of multiple B-steps against Γ by pairs of B-steps against Γ^1 and Γ^2 that do not "interfere" with each other.

We first discuss the construction of Γ^1 and Γ^2 from the perspective of the first three elements. The core definitions are in the context of a single incoming event type E. In particular, we will define Ext^i_E and $\mathcal{R}^i_E$ for $i \in \{1,2\}$; then $Ext^i = \bigcup_{E \in \mathcal{E}} Ext^i_E$ and $\mathcal{R}^i = \bigcup_{E \in \mathcal{E}} \mathcal{R}^i_E$. We use example event C:CheckCredit, abbreviated as CC, to illustrate the core definitions. To simplify the definitions, we use the following auxiliary notions.

1. The *range* of E in Γ is $range^{att}_\Gamma(E) = payload(E) \cup \{\sigma \in \mathcal{A}_{status} \mid \text{for some } \odot \in \{+,-\}, \text{there is a directed path from } E \text{ to } \odot\sigma \text{ in } PDG_\Gamma(E)\}$. Intuitively, this holds all data attributes and status attributes in Γ that might be affected by an incoming event e of type E. For example, the range of CC contains all the data and (unpolarized) status attributes shown in Figure 4.
2. The *rule range* of E in Γ is $range^{rule}_\Gamma(E) = \{\rho \in \mathcal{R} \mid \text{either } E \text{ or some } a \in range^{att}_\Gamma(E) \text{ occurs in the sentry of } \rho\}$. Intuitively, this holds all rules that might fire because of an incoming event e of type E.
3. The *support* of a status attribute $x \in range^{att}_\Gamma(E)$ is $Supp^E_\Gamma(x) = \{y \in \mathcal{A} \mid \text{for some } z \in range^{att}_\Gamma(E) \cap \mathcal{A}_{status} \text{ and } \rho \in range^{rule}_\Gamma(E), y \text{ occurs in the sentry of } \rho, z \text{ occurs in the "then" part of } \rho \text{ and there is a (possibly zero-length) path from } z \text{ to } x \text{ in } PDG_\Gamma(E)\}$. Intuitively, y is in the support of x for E if the value of y (or a change in value of y) is referred to by some rule in $range^{rule}_\Gamma(E)$ that influences if x toggles. For example, the support of DeterminePrice for CC is {credit_level, RefineDeal, CreditChecked, ReDraftTermNeeded, DraftTerm, TermDrafted}.
4. For $X \subseteq range^{att}_\Gamma(E)$, $Supp^E_\Gamma(X) = \bigcup_{x \in X} Supp^E_\Gamma(x)$. We note that for $X \subseteq range^{att}_\Gamma(E)$, the set $Margin^E_\Gamma(X) = Supp^E_\Gamma(X) - range^{att}_\Gamma(E)$ may be nonempty. Intuitively, this is the set of attributes that a rule in $range^{rule}_\Gamma(E)$ might refer to, but whose value will not be affected by events of type E. For example, given CC and the range set of CC, the margin set is {RefineDeal}.

For notational convenience, we set $Base^i_{status} = Base^i_{att} \cap \mathcal{A}_{status}$ for $i \in \{1,2\}$.

Suppose that E is associated with Γ^1 and that $\sigma \in Base^1_{status}$. (The construction for E associated with Γ^2 is symmetrical.) Intuitively, if $y \in Supp^E_\Gamma(\sigma)$, then the value of y is needed by the host of Γ^1, in order to determine whether σ should toggle in a B-step launched by an E event. In particular, set $Ext^1_E = Supp^E_\Gamma(Base^1_{status} \cap range^{att}_\Gamma(E)) - Base^1_{att}$, i.e., the extension in Γ^1 needed for E is all attributes not already in $Base^1_{att}$ (i.e., that are in $Base^2_{att}$) that are used to determine the value of an attribute in $Base^1_{status}$. We also set $\mathcal{R}^1_E = \bigcup_{\sigma \in (Base^1_{att} \cup Ext^1_E) \cap \mathcal{A}_{status}} \mathcal{R}(\sigma) \cap range^{rule}_\Gamma(E)$, i.e., a rule is included into Γ^1 if it may be triggered by an event of type E and it governs a status attribute in $Base^1_{att}$ or its extension for E.

For Γ^2, the extension set of E, $Ext_E^2 = Supp_\Gamma^E(Base_{status}^2 - Ext_E^1) - Base_{att}^2$, i.e., include duplicates in Γ^2 for support attributes of those status attributes that are in $Base_{att}^2$ and not included in Ext_E^1. (Because E is assumed to be associated with Γ^1 for this development, the status attributes in Ext_E^1 will be computed by Γ^1 and then passed to Γ^2 by an $\widehat{E}$ event.) For the rules, use $\mathcal{R}_E^2 = \bigcup_{\sigma \in Base_{status}^2 - Ext_E^1} \{\widehat{\rho} \mid \rho \in \mathcal{R}(\sigma) \cap range_\Gamma^{rule}(E)\}$ where $\widehat{\rho}$ is constructed from ρ by replacing "E" by "$\widehat{E}$", if "E" occurs in ρ; otherwise $\widehat{\rho} = \rho$.

Example 4.1. Consider schemas IGF$_{\text{MAIN}}$ and IGF$_{\text{LO}}$ in Section 2. We have $Ext_{\text{CC}}^{\text{IGF}_{\text{MAIN}}} = \{\text{TermDrafted}, \text{ReDraftTermNeeded}, \text{DraftTerm}\}$ and $\mathcal{R}_{\text{CC}}^{\text{IGF}_{\text{MAIN}}} = \{r_2, r_7, r_9, r_{11}, r_{15}, r_{16}, r_{17}, r_{21}, r_{22}, r_{23}, r_{25}, r_{28}\}$. Although status attribute RefineDeal occurs in r_2 and r_{25}, these rules toggle status attributes in $Ext_{\text{CC}}^{\text{IGF}_{\text{MAIN}}}$, hence $Ext_{\text{CC}}^{\text{IGF}_{\text{LO}}} = \emptyset = \mathcal{R}_{\text{CC}}^{\text{IGF}_{\text{LO}}}$.

Let abbreviation RC denote E:RegulationChange, which arrives at LO. We have $Ext_{\text{RC}}^{\text{IGF}_{\text{LO}}} = \{\text{RefineDeal}\}$ and $\mathcal{R}_{\text{RC}}^{\text{IGF}_{\text{LO}}} = \{r_2, r_{15}, r_{16}, r_{24}\}$. For IGF, $Ext_{\text{RC}}^{\text{IGF}_{\text{MAIN}}} = \{\text{TermDrafted}, \text{DraftTerm}, \text{ReDraftTermNeeded}\}$ and $\mathcal{R}_{\text{RC}}^{\text{IGF}_{\text{MAIN}}} = \{r_9, r_{11}, r_{21}\}$. ∎

The remaining aspects of the construction is presented informally (the formal construction is in [8]); namely, (a) specifying the payloads of the event types $\widehat{E}$, and (b) describing how the events of type $\widehat{E}$ are generated. For (a), if E is associated with Γ^1, then events of type $\widehat{E}$ will send all attributes of $range_E^{att}$ that are in $\mathcal{A}^1$ and also in $\mathcal{A}^2$. Intuitively, these attributes are computed in Γ^1, and should be sent to Γ^2 to avoid recomputation. For (b), a new atomic stage is added to Γ^1, which is triggered only after all other processing for E in Γ^1 is completed. This stage includes a task that generates a message of type $\widehat{E}$ with payload from the (newly updated) attributes of Γ^1.

Given a snapshot Σ of a well-formed GSM schema Γ, a pair Γ^1, Γ^2 a splitting of Σ, and $i \in \{1,2\}$, denote $\theta^i(\Sigma)$ to be a snapshot of Γ^i, such that $\theta^i(\Sigma)$ and Σ agree on the values of the same attributes in Γ and Γ^i (including the duplicated ones), and for each event type E of Γ^i, S_E is false. The following lemma (whose detailed proof is in [8]) states that the pair Γ^1 and Γ^2 can faithfully simulate the behavior of Γ.

Lemma 4.2. Let $\Gamma, \Gamma^1, \Gamma^2$ as above, $\mathcal{G}$ a set of outgoing events of Γ, Σ, Σ' are snapshots of Γ, and e an event of type $E \in Base_{inc}^1$. Then the following two are equivalent: (1) $(\Sigma, e, \Sigma', \mathcal{G})$ is a B-step of Γ, and (2) there exist an event $\widehat{e}$ of type $\widehat{E}$ and a partition $\mathcal{G}^1, \mathcal{G}^2$ of $\mathcal{G}$, such that $(\theta^1(\Sigma), e, \theta^1(\Sigma'), \mathcal{G}^1 \cup \{\widehat{e}\})$ is a B-step of Γ^1, and $(\theta^2(\Sigma), \widehat{e}, \theta^2(\Sigma'), \mathcal{G}^2)$ is a B-step of Γ^2.

4.2 Splitting with Multiple B-Steps

This subsection considers the management of multiple B-steps. In general, problems with the simulation may arise if two events, e of type E arriving for Γ^1 and f of type F arriving for Γ^2, are processed almost simultaneously. In particular, there may be a race condition, as illustrated in the following example.

Example 4.3. We continue with Example 4.1. Suppose now that stage CheckCredit is open, stages DraftTerm and DeterminePrice are closed, and milestone CreditChecked is not achieved. Suppose events E:RegulationChange and +C:CheckCredit with payload credit_level = 50,000 arrive at LO and IGF respectively at almost the same time. Then, consider this scenario: first, the B-step triggered by +C:CheckCredit (at IGF) will achieve milestone CreditChecked and open stage DeterminePrice; then the B-step triggered by E:RegulationChange (at LO) opens stage DraftTerm and sends an event to IGF to report the status change; upon receving the event, IGF marks DraftTerm as open. In this case, both DraftTerm and DeterminePrice are open, which is impossible based on the rules in Figure 2 and 3. Intuitively, the problem arises because the simulation of the second B-step modifies attributes before the simulation of the first B-step completes. ∎

We prevent such race conditions by using a protocol borrowed from distributed database management that guarantees a form of serializability. More specifically, the B-step Simulation Protocol is based on a form of distributed 2-phase commit [10]. It is assumed that communication between the hosts is reliable, and also that if a host states that it will perform an activity, then it will eventually complete that activity.

Let Γ be a well-formed GSM schema, E an event type, Γ^1 and Γ^2 be a splitting of Γ as described above, and $E \in Base^i_{inc}$ for $i \in \{1, 2\}$. Intuitively, the *write lock set* and *read lock set* for E in Γ^i, denoted as $write^i(E)$ and $read^i(E)$ respectively, are the set of attributes that might be written and read (resp.) in Γ^i when processing E. (The detailed definitions of $write^i(E)$ and $read^i(E)$ are in [8].)

To prevent dead locks, for each $i \in \{1, 2\}$ and each $E \in Base^i_{inc}$, assume that the priority to process an event of type $\widehat{E}$ is higher than each event of a type in $Base^{3-i}_{inc}$.

The **B-step Simulation Protocol** that is for simulating a B-step triggered by event e of type $E \in Base^1_{inc}$, is stated as follows.

1. The host of Γ^1 attempts to lock $write^1(E)$ and $read^1(E)$, and requests that the host of Γ^2 lock $write^2(E)$ and $read^2(E)$. If the locks can be obtained then proceed to step (2); otherwise, the host of Γ^1 waits and tries again later.
2. The host of Γ^1 performs B-step triggered by the event e, sends the event $\widehat{e}$ to the host of Γ^2, and then releases locks $write^1(E)$ and $read^1(E)$.
3. The host of Γ^2 performs B-step triggered by the event $\widehat{e}$ and then releases locks $write^2(E)$ and $read^2(E)$.

Let SYS be a system with a host for Γ^1 and a host for Γ^2. The following theorem (whose formal statement and proof is in [8]) states that based on the B-step Simulation Protocol, the B-steps processed under the two hosts will not interfere with each other.

Theorem 4.4. (*Informal*) Let SYS, Γ, Γ^1, and Γ^2 be as above. Suppose that the B-step Simulation Protocol is followed, Σ is a snapshot of Γ, and $\mu = e_1, \ldots, e_n$ is a sequence of events for Γ. Then the overall effect of applying $e_1, \ldots, e_n$ on $(\theta^1(\Sigma), \theta^2(\Sigma))$ in SYS is equivalent, in terms of the final snapshots and the set of outgoing events, to the effect of some permutation μ' of μ applied to Σ, where μ' is a shuffle of the Γ^1 events in μ (in order) with the Γ^2 events in μ (in order).

5 Outsourcing with Hidden Rules

The framework for hiding status attribute rules has two main aspects. First, given GSM schema Γ and set H of status attributes to be hidden, a new schema $\overline{\Gamma} = hide(\Gamma, H)$ is constructed. Second, $\overline{\Gamma}$ is split into $\overline{\Gamma}^1, \overline{\Gamma}^2$ according to the construction of Section 4. For the latter aspect, the B-step Simulation Protocol is modified.

Suppose that status attribute σ is owned by $host^1$ (which is holding Γ^1), and its rules are to be "hidden" from $host^2$ ($host^2$ may be allowed to see value of σ). To hide the rules governing σ two new anonymizing event types, and two new stages are introduced that provide a level of indirection between the rules of σ and the actual toggling of σ. Specifically, two new stages $Toggle^{STG}(+\sigma)$ and $Toggle^{STG}(-\sigma)$ are included into $\overline{\Gamma}$; these will be held by $host^1$. In the simulation of a B-step of Γ, the stage $Toggle^{STG}(+\sigma)$ in $\overline{\Gamma}$ is triggered by the sentries that cause $+\sigma$ in Γ (and similarly for $Toggle^{STG}(-\sigma)$). Also, stage $Toggle^{STG}(+\sigma)$ will invoke a task that generates a new anonymizing incoming event $Toggle^{EVT}(+\sigma)$. This event will cause a separate B-step in the simulation. In that B-step σ will toggle to true, and rules propagation based on $+\sigma$ will occur. The rules that trigger $Toggle^{STG}(+\sigma)$ (i.e., the rules causing $+\sigma$) will be held by $host_1$ and are not duplicated in $host_2$. In this sense, $Toggle^{STG}(+\sigma)$ "anonymizes" the event $+\sigma$, and similarly for $-\sigma$.

The simulation of one B-step of Γ typically involves a *cluster* of B-steps of $hide(\Gamma, H)$, essentially the cluster starts with the original B-step and it adds one extra B-step for each hidden status attribute. It is important to prevent "interference" from other incoming events while performing this cluster. In our framework, the interference is prevented by the mechanisms for managing incoming events; the GSM engines of the hosts do not need to be modified.

The exposition in this section is terse; further details are presented in [8].

5.1 Hidden Rules in a Centralized GSM Schema

We illustrate the construction of $hide(\Gamma, H)$ by extending Example 2.3 for IGF, which focuses on the desire to hide the rules for ReDraftTermNeeded, denoted here as RDTN. We describe here some of the rules restructuring used to build $hide$(IGF, {RDTN}). We focus on the rewriting used in connection with incoming event type C:CheckCredit, denoted here as CC; similar rewritings are needed for each incoming event type.

An incoming event of type CC might cause +RDTN but not −RDTN according to Figure 4. We thus focus exclusively on the former for CC of $hide$(IGF, {RDTN}).

To hide the rules of RDTN, a new stage $Toggle^{STG}_{CC}(+RDTN)$ will be introduced, which holds a task that generates an event of type $Toggle^{EVT}_{CC}(+RDTN)$; these are the "anonymizing" events to indicate that RDTN should be toggled to true. In the rewriting relevant to CC, the new sentry of +RDTN is simply "**on** $+ Toggle^{EVT}_{CC}(+RDTN)$". Relative to CC, the sentries of $Toggle^{STG}_{CC}(+RDTN)$ in $hide$(IGF, {RDTN}) are essentially the sentries of +RDTN in IGF, although a transform will have to be applied (see below). In this example there will be one sentry for $Toggle^{STG}_{CC}(+RDTN)$ stemming from CC, namely a transform of r_{25}. (r_{24} is triggered by a different event, so not relevant to CC.)

In the framework we also need an event type $NoToggle^{EVT}_{CC}(+RDTN)$ (sent by a task in a new atomic stage), used to indicate that RDTN is *not* toggled to true in the original B-step (needed for the simulation to know when the B-steps cluster for CC is finished).

In this example, the simulation of a CC event in Γ involves two B-steps, the first one triggered by a CC event and the second triggered by a $Toggle^{EVT}_{CC}(+RDTN)$ or $NoToggle^{EVT}_{CC}(+RDTN)$ event. In the second B-step it is important that sentries to be evaluated are "aware of" which status attributes were toggled in the first B-step.

To address this, for each status attribute $\odot\sigma$ that may get toggled in the first B-step we introduce in $hide$(IGF, {RDTN}) a new milestone $Toggle^{MST}_{CC}(\odot\sigma)$ with achieving sentry "**on** $\odot\sigma$", and we transform rules by replacing $\odot\sigma$ by $Toggle^{MST}_{CC}(\odot\sigma)$.) Such milestones have the function of "remembering" the toggling of the status attributes, and are invalidated at the end of the simulation of the CC B-step.

The construction involves two more steps for CC, namely: (i) Ensure that rules fire in the correct B-step of the simulation, accomplished by introducing additional milestones that track which B-steps have occurred so far, and (ii) "Clean up" the milestones that record which status attributes have toggled during the simulation, accomplished by a new stage $EndOfSim_{CC}^{EVT}$ that opens during the final B-step in the simulation to occur.

To summarize, we state the following.

Lemma 5.1. (*Informal*) Let Γ be a well-formed GSM schema and H a set of status attributes in Γ. Then $\overline{\Gamma} = hide(\Gamma, H)$ is a well-formed GSM schema such that (a) the sentries in $\overline{\Gamma}$ of each attribute in H are of form "**on** E" for some new incoming event type E, and (b) each B-step of Γ is faithfully simulated by a cluster of B-steps of $\overline{\Gamma}$.

5.2 Hidden Rules in a Split GSM Schema

As noted above, a single B-step of Γ is simulated by a cluster of B-steps of $\overline{\Gamma} = hide(\Gamma, H)$. The generalized B-step Simulation Protocol ensures that there is no "interference" between the simulation of one Γ-level B-step and another one.

Suppose now that SYS is a system with two hosts, one for $\overline{\Gamma}^1$ and the other for $\overline{\Gamma}^2$. As with the B-step Simulation Protocol of Section 4, to simulate a Γ-level B-step of event e with type E, the generalized version first obtains read and write locks at both hosts (this time relative to $\overline{\Gamma}$ rather than Γ). The hosts maintain the read and write locks during the simulation of the entire cluster of B-steps against $\overline{\Gamma}$ that correspond to the single B-step for e in Γ. The hosts will "know" when the simulation is completed, because of the generated event $EndOfSim_E^{EVT}$, which can be shared with both hosts.

We summarize the development with the following.

Theorem 5.2. Let $SYS, \Gamma, H, \overline{\Gamma} = hide(\Gamma, H), \overline{\Gamma}^1, \overline{\Gamma}^2$ be as above, Σ a snapshot of Γ, and $\mu = e_1, \ldots, e_n$ a sequence of events for Γ. Let $\overline{\Sigma}$ correspond to Σ in $\overline{\Gamma}$, and let $\theta^1(\overline{\Sigma}), \theta^2(\overline{\Sigma})$ correspond to $\overline{\Sigma}$ in $\overline{\Gamma}^1, \overline{\Gamma}^2$. Then the overall effect of applying $e_1, \ldots, e_n$ on $\theta^1(\overline{\Sigma}), \theta^2(\overline{\Sigma})$ in SYS will correspond to the effect of some permutation μ' of μ applied to Σ, where μ' is a shuffle of the Γ^1 events in μ (in order) with the Γ^2 events in μ (in order).

6 Related Work

There has been quite some work that studies how part of a procedural workflow without data can be outsourced to another party [1,15,20,11] without changing the original behavior. The race conditions tackled in this paper are specific to data-centric workflows; therefore the framework developed in this paper is radically different from these works.

To tackle the issue of privacy in procedural workflows, the notion of view [5,9,17,21] has been proposed. A process view hides certain internal details of the procedural workflow, similar to the way a database view hides a conceptual database schema. If two activities owned by two different views collaborate, then the activities are required to be public [5,9]. In contrast, the framework of the current paper allows that shared business logic like a sentry is marked as private and therefore gets hidden, without affecting the overall outcome. Yongchareon et al. [25] uses a similar style of views to model inter-organizational artifact-centric business processes, but do not address runtime aspects.

To the best of our knowledge, outsourcing has not been studied previously for data-centric or artifact-centric processes. A closely related work is [24], which develops a formal framework for several algebraic operations on GSM schemas, including the notion of "tear" which is similar to splitting. Also somewhat related are artifact-centric interoperation hubs [13], which enable multiple parties to collaborate on a single artifact-based business process (state-machine-based or GSM) that is maintained by the centralized hub using an underlying centralized GSM engine. However, the work on artifact-centric hubs does not consider outsourcing a part of the global schema to another hub or GSM engine of another participant. Recent work [16] addresses some aspects of privacy and information hiding, but the underlying artifact schema runs entirely in the hub, rather than being distributed between the hub and a participant. The research described in the current paper could extend [16] by enabling such distribution, and also enabling a participant to hide some of its logic from the interoperation hub.

The GSM approach is based on the Event-Condition-Action (ECA) approach (e.g., [19]) for providing declarative semantics to data-centric system, and so the formal techniques used in this paper build on those from the ECA literature. Importantly, GSM adds structure to classical ECA approaches; this structure is exploited to achieve the protocol and privacy results obtained in this paper.

7 Conclusions

The main contribution of this paper is a formal framework that supports the outsourcing of GSM schemas by splitting them. Race conditions prohibit the use of a direct split on the orginal schema. The framework avoids race conditions by restructuring GSM schemas as well as using locking protocols that ensure serializability of multiple event occurrences. Restructuring a GSM schema does not change its behavior of the GSM schema, but allows for a dramatic simplification of the locking protocols.

Key feature of the framework is that it allows reuse of existing GSM centralized engines for executing the split subschemas. Moreover, the framework supports hiding of parts of a GSM schema that are private, without affecting the outcomes of the global execution. The framework is proven to preserve the behavior of the original GSM schema.

There are several directions for future work. We plan to apply the framework to OMG's CMMN [3]. Also, we plan to extend framework by considering multi-party outsourcing and multiple interacting artifact types.

References

1. van der Aalst, W.M.P., Weske, M.: The P2P approach to interorganizational workflows. In: Dittrich, K.R., Geppert, A., Norrie, M. (eds.) CAiSE 2001. LNCS, vol. 2068, pp. 140–156. Springer, Heidelberg (2001)
2. Aalst, W., Weske, M., Grünbauer, D.: Case handling: a new paradigm for business process support. Data Knowl. Eng. 53(2), 129–162 (2005)
3. BizAgi, et al.: Case Management Model and Notation (CMMN), FTF Beta 1, OMG Document Number dtc/2013-01-01, Object Management Group (January 2013), http://www.omg.org/spec/CMMN/1.0/Beta1/
4. Chao, T., et al.: Artifact-Based Transformation of IBM Global Financing. In: Dayal, U., Eder, J., Koehler, J., Reijers, H.A., et al. (eds.) BPM 2009. LNCS, vol. 5701, pp. 261–277. Springer, Heidelberg (2009)

5. Chebbi, I., Dustdar, S., Tata, S.: The view-based approach to dynamic inter-organizational workflow cooperation. Data Knowl. Eng. 56(2), 139–173 (2006)
6. Damaggio, E., Hull, R., Vaculín, R.: On the equivalence of incremental and fixpoint semantics for business artifacts with guard-stage-milestone lifecycles. Information Systems 38, 561–584 (2013)
7. de Man, H.: Case management: A review of modeling approaches. BP Trends (January 2009), http://www.bptrends.com
8. Eshuis, R., Hull, R., Sun, Y., Vaculín, R.: Splitting GSM schemas: A framework for outsourcing of declarative artifact systems with privacy guarantees (in preparation, 2013)
9. Eshuis, R., Norta, A.: A framework for service outsourcing using process views. In: Proc. EDOC 2010, pp. 99–108. IEEE Computer Society (2010)
10. Gray, J., Reuter, A.: Transaction Processing: Concepts and Techniques. Morgan Kaufmann, Burlington (1993)
11. Grefen, P., et al.: CrossFlow: Cross-organizational Workflow Management in Dynamic Virtual Enterprises. Intl. J. of Computer Systems, Science, and Engineering 15(5), 277–290 (2000)
12. Hull, R., et al.: Business artifacts with guard-stage-milestone lifecycles: Managing artifact interactions with conditions and events. In: ACM Intl. Conf. on Distributed Event-based Systems, DEBS (2011)
13. Hull, R., Narendra, N.C., Nigam, A.: Facilitating workflow interoperation using artifact-centric hubs. In: Baresi, L., Chi, C.-H., Suzuki, J. (eds.) ICSOC-ServiceWave 2009. LNCS, vol. 5900, pp. 1–18. Springer, Heidelberg (2009)
14. Hull, R., Sun, Y., Vaculín, R.: Equivalence on Variants of Guard-Stage-Milestone Artifact Models (in preparation, 2013)
15. Khalaf, R., Kopp, O., Leymann, F.: Maintaining data dependencies across bpel process fragments. Int. J. Cooperative Inf. Syst. 17(3), 259–282 (2008)
16. Limonad, L., et al.: A generic business artifacts based authorization framework for cross-enterprise collaboration. In: SRII Global Conference, pp. 70–79 (2012)
17. Liu, D.-R., Shen, M.: Workflow modeling for virtual processes: an order-preserving process-view approach. Inf. Syst. 28(6), 505–532 (2003)
18. Marin, M., Hull, R., Vaculín, R.: Data centric BPM and the emerging case management standard: A short survey. In: La Rosa, M., Soffer, P. (eds.) BPM Workshops 2012. LNBIP, vol. 132, pp. 24–30. Springer, Heidelberg (2013)
19. McCarthy, D.R., Dayal, U.: The architecture of an active data base management system. In: Proc. ACM SIGMOD Intl. Conf. on Mgmnt of Data (SIGMOD), pp. 215–224 (1989)
20. Muth, P., et al.: From centralized workflow specification to distributed workflow execution. Journal of Intelligent Information Systems 10(2), 159–184 (1998)
21. Schulz, K., Orlowska, M.: Facilitating cross-organisational workflows with a workflow view approach. Data Knowl. Eng. 51(1), 109–147 (2004)
22. Sun, Y., Hull, R., Vaculín, R.: Parallel processing for business artifacts with declarative lifecycles. In: Proc. of Intl. Conf. on Cooperating Information Systems (CoopIS); OTM Conferences (1), pp. 433–443 (2012)
23. Swenson, K.D.: Mastering the Unpredictable: How Adaptive Case Management will Revolutionize the Way that Knowledge Workers Get Things Done. Meghan-Kiffer, FL (2010)
24. Vaculín, R., Chee, Y.-M., Oppenheim, D.V., Varshney, L.R.: Work as a service meta-model and protocol for adjustable visibility, coordination, and control. In: SRII Global Conference, San Jose, California, pp. 90–99. IEEE Computer Society (July 2012)
25. Yongchareon, S., Liu, C., Zhao, X.: An artifact-centric view-based approach to modeling inter-organizational business processes. In: Bouguettaya, A., Hauswirth, M., Liu, L. (eds.) WISE 2011. LNCS, vol. 6997, pp. 273–281. Springer, Heidelberg (2011)

Composing Workflow Activities on the Basis of Data-Flow Structures

Han van der Aa[1], Hajo A. Reijers[1,2], and Irene Vanderfeesten[3]

[1] Dept. of Mathematics and Computer Science, Eindhoven University of Technology,
PO Box 513, 5600MB Eindhoven, The Netherlands
[2] Perceptive Software, Piet Joubertstraat 4, 7315AV Apeldoorn, The Netherlands
[3] School of Industrial Engineering, Eindhoven University of Technology,
PO Box 513, 5600MB Eindhoven, The Netherlands

Abstract. The proper composition of activities is important for the efficient execution of a workflow process. In this paper, an approach is presented that utilizes the data-flow underlying a workflow process to determine the importance and semantic relatedness of the various, elementary data-processing steps. Based on these aspects, fundamental guidelines are proposed to drive and objectify the task of activity composition in the context of workflow design.

1 Introduction

The bulk of business processes in the service domain pursue the production of an informational product, such as a mortgage contract, a decision on a damage claim, or a commercial offer. We will refer to these processes as *workflows*. When designing a workflow, one should carefully consider how to properly design its *activities* (or *tasks*). An activity is a *logical piece of work* within a workflow, which may comprise a number of elementary data processing steps. For example, the activity of calculating a mortgage amount may consist of entering the current interest rate, choosing the discount rate negotiated by the customer, and calculating the amortized amount of debt.

The focus of attention in this paper is on the grouping of elementary data processing steps into activities. We will refer to this act as *activity composition*. Proper composition can result in activities that have a proper size, i.e. are of a right *granularity*. They provide a balance between an increased number of work hand-overs that result from many small activities against the reduced flexibility caused by too many large activities [1]. Secondly, activity composition can be used to increase the meaningfulness of activities for employees executing these [2].

This paper introduces fundamental design guidelines for activity composition by exploiting the structural data-flow relations in a workflow. To make our ideas operational, we will assume that such relations are captured in a Product Data Model (PDM). However, the guidelines can be easily transferred to comparable data-flow specifications, e.g. the data flow matrices of [3]. The PDM that we build on stems from Product Based Workflow Design (PBWD), a method for the radical redesign of workflows [4]. It is proposed here that data-flow relations in the form of a PDM can be used to determine the *semantic relatedness* as well as the *relative importance* of its elements. These two notions are used to propose guidelines on activity composition, which form the main contribution of this paper.

This work extends the state of the art in several ways. The interaction between the steps in a process and the data being processed is at the basis of a wide range of research efforts, e.g. [3,5]. Yet, their exclusive focus is on the detection of data-flow errors. While we agree that it is important to ensure that a workflow works correctly, they leave open the issue of designing granular, meaningful tasks. The job design literature does address these issues [2,6], but we noted that the provided guidance is rather abstract and does not rest on a detailed understanding of the data-flow perspective in a specific process. Earlier, we proposed metrics to evaluate the quality of activity compositions on the basis of job design insights [7], but these can only be retrospectively applied on activities already composed. The guidelines we provide ensure a correct data processing through its reliance on a PDM, while they additionally lead to concrete and proper compositions of activities.

In the remainder of this paper, Sect. 2 provides an example to motivate the goal of activity composition and introduces some important notions. Sect. 3 proposes our solution: three guidelines that objectify activity composition. Finally, Sect. 4 concludes the paper with a discussion and directions for future research.

2 Motivating Example

To motivate the application of activity composition in a workflow process, this section presents the design of activities for an example case. The example, introduced in [8], considers the process that deals with requests for governmental student grants in the Netherlands. The presented process is a simplified version of the actual procedure as implemented by the "Dienst Uitvoering Onderwijs" (DUO)[1], the governmental agency in the Netherlands responsible for the assessment of student grant requests.

2.1 Product Data Model

Fig. 1 presents the PDM of the *student grants* example. A PDM contains a set of *data elements*, which are depicted as labelled circles. The top element $i42$, referred to as the *root* element, resembles the total student grant assigned to an applicant. The other data elements in the PDM are data elements that are relevant for the computation of $i42$, the ultimate goal of this workflow. A description of all data elements is provided in Table 1. The values for data elements for a specific case are computed by executing *operations* on data elements.

---

[1] See http://www.duo.nl

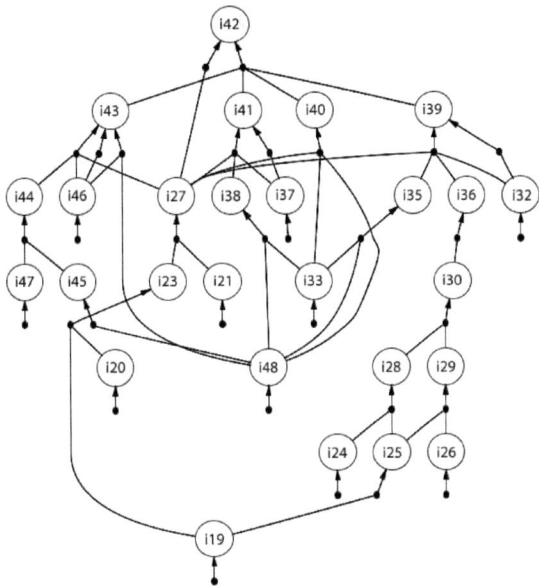

Fig. 1. Product Data Model of the student grants example

Operations are depicted as black dots in the figure. Each operation requires a set of input elements, and produces a single output data element. For example, Fig. 1 expresses that a value for $i42$ can be computed based on the values for data elements $i39$, $i40$, $i41$, and $i43$. These four elements represent the four types of student grant an applicant may be eligible to receive: (i) a basic grant ($i40$), (ii) a supplementary grant ($i39$), (iii) a loan ($i41$), and (iv) any credit for tuition fees ($i43$). A value for $i42$ can also be computed via a second operation, which has $i27$ as its only input element. This input element represents an applicant's eligibility to receive a grant[2]. The second operation is enabled when the value of $i27$ is negative, i.e. the applicant is not entitled to receive a grant. Hence, the execution of this operation means that an application is rejected. We refer to distinct operations that can produce a value for the same data element, as *alternative operations*; they provide alternative routings through a workflow. Finally, the figure shows operations that do not have input elements. These operations are referred to as *leaf operations*. Leaf operations produce values for *leaf elements*, i.e. data that is received from outside the process. In this example, the leaf elements contain the data that is provided by the applicant, such as $i20$, the applicant's date of birth. For a more detailed description of the case, the interested reader is referred to [8, p.193].

---

[2] An applicant must have the Dutch nationality (stored in $i21$) and may not be older than thirty ($i23$) in order to be eligible to receive a grant.

Table 1. Description of data elements present in the student grants example

ID	Description	ID	Description
i19	Date of request	i36	Parental contribution
i20	Birth date of applicant	i37	Requested amt. of loan
i21	Nationality of applicant	i38	Max. amt. of loan
i23	Age of applicant	i39	Amt. of supplementary grant assigned
i24	Social Security Number of father	i40	Amt. of basic grant assigned
i25	Reference year for tax authority	i41	Amt. of loan assigned
i26	Social Security Number of mother	i42	Total amt. of student grant assigned
i27	Applicant has the right to receive grant	i43	Amt. of tuition credit assigned
i28	Income of father of applicant	i44	Max. amt. of credit for tuition fees
i29	Income of mother of applicant	i45	Tuition fees of educational institution
i30	Income of parents of applicant	i46	Has requested credit for tuition fees
i32	Has requested a supplementary grant	i47	Tuition fees declared by law
i33	Living situation of applicant	i48	Kind of education of applicant
i35	Max. amt. of supplementary grant		

2.2 Activity Design

In PBWD, the task of activity design is to group the operations in a PDM into activities that form logical pieces of work [8]. As introduced in Sect. 1, activity composition can influence the efficiency of workflow execution [1], as well as the meaningfulness of activities for workflow users [2].

Fig. 2 presents a workflow design for the student grant example based on a proposed set of eight activities. Each activity, depicted in Fig. 3, is designed such that it results in the computation of a data element that directly affects the total amount of student grant an applicant receives, e.g. activity B determines the eligibility of an applicant to receive a grant. Each activity thus represents a significant step during the workflow's execution. The non-atomic activities furthermore encompass distinct sub-processes in the workflow, in which all underlying operations have a similar meaning or subject, e.g. all operations in activity D are related to a student's tuition credit. The proposed design shows that it is possible to partition a PDM into activities that form meaningful tasks in a workflow. The issue of how to design these activities, however, still remains open. Section 3 addresses this by defining objective guidelines for this purpose.

3 Activity Composition

The main contribution in this paper consists of three activity composition guidelines. The guidelines consider the semantic aspects of workflow design. Semantics are those properties that relate to the meaning of PDM elements. These properties are often inferred from the context, rather than explicitly defined in a PDM. Despite this lack of explicitness, it is here proposed that such semantics can be partly derived from the structure of a PDM. This section introduces design

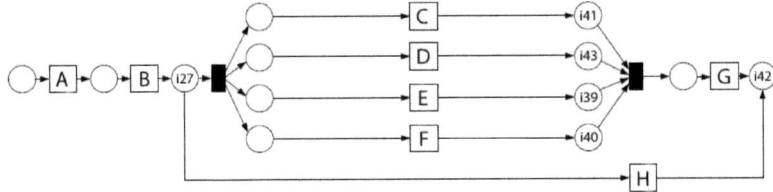

Fig. 2. Process model based on the proposed activity design

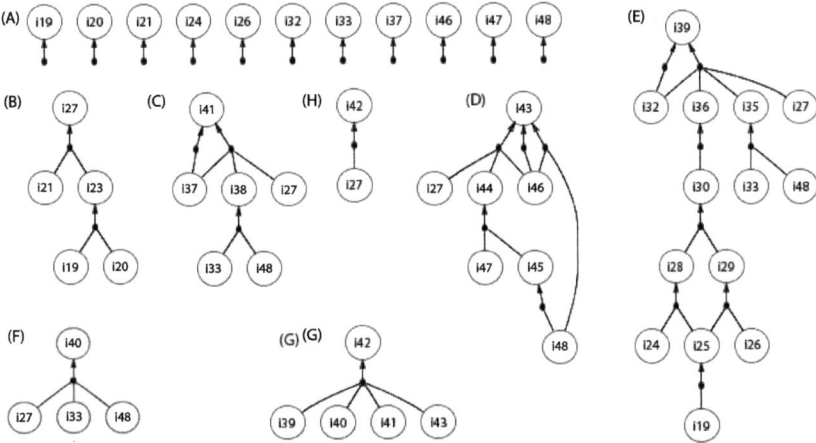

Fig. 3. Non-atomic activities in the process model

guidelines that exploit the proposed relation between semantics and structure. The guidelines are purposefully designed to be independent of context, or any data beyond the structure of a PDM. The proposed guidelines result in activities that work towards the production of an important data element on the one hand and of which the operations are semantically related on the other. This concept is, amongst others, based on the notions of *task identity* and *task significance*, two determinants of *experienced meaningfulness* in the widely used Job Characteristics Model of Hackman & Oldman [2].

This section comprises two parts. Sect. 3.1 considers patterns that imply relative importance of data elements. Secondly, Sect. 3.2 regards the identification of semantically related operations based on structural properties. The guidelines are motivated by referring to the student grants example. However, the propositions are designed to apply to PDMs and PDM-like structures in general.

3.1 Data Element Importance

All data elements in a PDM are to some degree required to produce a value for the root data element. Nonetheless, it is clear that not all data elements are equally important. For example, in the students grants case, data element $i27$, an applicant's right to receive a grant, is certainly more important than $i28$, the income of the applicant's father. The semantic importance of $i27$ is clear, because it fully determines acceptance or rejection. This section proposes that different types of semantically important data elements (IDEs) can be identified based on five structural patterns. The proposed patterns have been found by analysing manual activity designs in [7,8,9] and through utilization of best modelling practices.

Pattern 1 (Root Data). *The root data element is the single data element that is not used as input for any operations.*

Pattern 1 identifies the first type of IDE, namely the root element of a PDM. This element is straightforwardly the most important data element in a PDM, as it represents the final outcome of a workflow. For example in the student grants case, this is the total amount of student grant assigned to an applicant ($i42$).

Pattern 2 (Leaf Data). *A leaf data element is a data element that is produced by an operation without input elements.*

Leaf elements represent the second type of IDEs. These are the data elements that are provided as input to a workflow; the values for these elements are retrieved from outside the process. In the student grants example, the leaf elements represent the data that is retrieved from a student's application, e.g. $i19$, $i24$ and $i26$.

Pattern 3 (Conditional Data). *A conditional data element is a data element that can be produced by multiple alternative operations.*

Pattern 3 identifies *conditional data elements*. These data elements can be produced by multiple alternative operations. Four such elements exist in the student grants example: the root element $i42$, and the data elements $i39$, $i41$, and $i43$. The latter data elements represent three out of the four types of grant that applicants may be eligible to receive. These grants directly affect the value of the root element and are therefore clearly important in this process.

Pattern 4 (Equal Level Data). *An equal level data element is an input data element to an operation that also requires conditional data as input.*

By considering conditional data, three out of the four types of grant are identified as goals. The fourth type of grant is the amount of basic grant assigned to an applicant ($i40$). Without additional context information, there is no reason why this fourth grant is less important than the other types of grant; $i40$ is hence also considered to be of importance. In this case, an important element is thus identified based on its adjacent elements. It is proposed that this transitive notion can be applied in a generic fashion to uncover the fourth type of IDEs: *equal level data*. These elements are revealed by considering the operations that require conditional data as input elements, as defined in Pattern 4.

Pattern 5 (Reference Data). *A reference data element is a data element that is an input element to multiple operations that are, directly or indirectly, involved in the computation of different important data elements.*

Recall that $i27$, the eligibility to receive a grant, is arguably an important data element. $i27$ is important from a structural perspective, because the data element is required to produce multiple other IDEs. Such data elements shall be referred to as *reference data elements*, the final type of IDE.

The five types of IDEs represent those structural patterns that are proposed to predict the significance of data elements. This results in Proposition 1.

Proposition 1 (Important Data Elements). *Root, leaf, conditional, equal level and reference data elements represent important data elements in a PDM.*

3.2 Semantic Relatedness

Semantic relatedness considers the degree to which the meaning of elements is similar. It is here proposed that operations with similar meaning can, to a certain extent, be identified based on structural properties of a PDM. The underlying intuition is that each operation can be associated with the computation of a single IDE. Operations that are associated with the same goal are then considered to be semantically related. Definition 1 defines how operations are associated with a unique IDE[3].

Definition 1 (Associated Element). *The associated element of an operation is the unique IDE for which there exists a path in the PDM from the operation to that IDE, such that this path does not contain any other IDEs.*

Since operations that are associated to the same element are considered to be semantically related, it is proposed that such operations can be grouped into a semantically coherent activity. This proposition is extended with the notion that leaf operations can be grouped together into *leaf activities*. This notion is based on the premise that the values for multiple leaf elements are often retrieved from the same data source. For example, as seen in Sect. 2.1, all leaf elements in the student grants case are derived from a student's application. By grouping leaf operations, the workflow design enforces the retrieval of multiple data elements at once, which is often desirable [11].

Proposition 2 (Semantically Coherent Activities). *A semantically coherent activity is an activity that consists of a set of operations that are associated with the same IDE.*

Proposition 1 and Proposition 2 together form the means to compose activities that result in activities that work towards a goal and of which the operations are semantically related. Finally, it is proposed that an activity composition that conforms to both aforementioned propositions results in well-designed activities.

---

[3] Due to the way the IDEs, especially reference data elements, are defined in Sect. 3.1, each operation is associated with exactly one IDE. [10] provides a formal proof for this.

Proposition 3 (Well-Designed Activities). *The set of operations in an activity should work towards the production of a relatively important data element and be semantically related to each other.*

4 Conclusions

This paper introduces fundamental guidelines for the objective composition of activities in workflow settings. The proposed guidelines pose that activities should work towards a goal, and should consist of semantically related operations. It has been shown that these properties can be identified based on structural data-flow relations. Hence, the guidelines can be applied objectively.

While this paper emphasizes the motivation for the activity composition problem as well as the development of guidelines, follow-up work has been carried out that does not fit the constraints of this paper. Specifically, an automation of the task of composing activities has been undertaken and a thorough validation of the guidelines has taken place. We intend to report on these in a future publication.

References

1. Seidmann, A., Sundararajan, A.: The effects of task and information asymmetry on business process redesign. International Journal of Production Economics 50(2), 117–128 (1997)
2. Hackman, J.R., Oldham, G.R.: Motivation through the design of work: Test of a theory. Organizational Behavior and Human Performance 16(2), 250–279 (1976)
3. Sun, S.X., Zhao, J.L., Nunamaker, J.F., Sheng, O.R.L.: Formulating the data-flow perspective for business process management. Information Systems Research 17(4), 374–391 (2006)
4. Reijers, H.A., Limam, S., Van der Aalst, W.M.P.: Product-based workflow design. Journal of Management Information Systems 20(1), 229–262 (2003)
5. Trčka, N., van der Aalst, W.M.P., Sidorova, N.: Data-flow anti-patterns: Discovering data-flow errors in workflows. In: van Eck, P., Gordijn, J., Wieringa, R. (eds.) CAiSE 2009. LNCS, vol. 5565, pp. 425–439. Springer, Heidelberg (2009)
6. Robbins, S.P., Judge, T.A., et al.: Organizational behaviour. Pearson Education, Inc., New Jersey (2007)
7. Vanderfeesten, I., Reijers, H.A., Van der Aalst, W.M.P.: Evaluating workflow process designs using cohesion and coupling metrics. Comput. Ind. 59(5), 420 (2008)
8. Vanderfeesten, I.: Product-Based Design and Support of Workflow Processes. PhD thesis, Eindhoven University of Technology (2009)
9. Reijers, H.A.: Design and control of workflow processes: business process management for the service industry. Springer-Verlag (2003)
10. Van der Aa, J.H.: Composing workflow activities. Master's thesis, Eindhoven University of Technology (2013)
11. Reijers, H.A., Mansar, S.L.: Best practices in business process redesign: an overview and qualitative evaluation of successful redesign heuristics. Omega 33(4), 283–306 (2005)

Mixing Paradigms
for More Comprehensible Models

Michael Westergaard[1,2,*] and Tijs Slaats[3,4]

[1] Department of Mathematics and Computer Science,
Eindhoven University of Technology, The Netherlands
[2] National Research University Higher School of Economics,
Moscow, 101000, Russia
[3] IT University of Copenhagen
Rued Langgaardsvej 7, 2300 Copenhagen, Denmark
[4] Exformatics A/S, Lautrupsgade 13, 2100 Copenhagen, Denmark
m.westergaard@tue.nl, tslaats@itu.dk

Abstract. Petri nets efficiently model both data- and control-flow. Control-flow is either modeled explicitly as flow of a specific kind of data, or implicit based on the data-flow. Explicit modeling of control-flow is useful for well-known and highly structured processes, but may make modeling of abstract features of models, or processes which are highly dynamic, overly complex. Declarative modeling, such as is supported by Declare and DCR graphs, focus on control-flow, but does not specify it explicitly; instead specifications come in the form of constraints on the order or appearance of tasks. In this paper we propose a combination of the two, using colored Petri nets instead of plain Petri nets to provide full data support. The combined approach makes it possible to add a focus on data to declarative languages, and to remove focus from the explicit control-flow from Petri nets for dynamic or abstract processes. In addition to enriching both procedural processes in the form of Petri nets and declarative processes, we also support a flow from modeling only abstract data- and control-flow of a model towards a more explicit control-flow model if so desired. We define our combined approach, and provide considerations necessary for enactment. Our approach has been implemented in CPN Tools 4.

1 Introduction

Petri nets provide a powerful formalism for specifying many real-life systems, including business processes. Petri nets excel by having a duality between data and events, yielding a very powerful tool for specifying how data flows though a system. Control-flow of a Petri net model is often modeled explicitly as flow of a specific kind of data, similar to a program counter in traditional programming. Alternatively, the control-flow is not modeled at all, and just manifests as a consequence of the data-flow. As such, we call a Petri net model a procedural model

---

[*] Support from the Basic Research Program of the National Research University Higher School of Economics is gratefully acknowledged.

as the control-flow when disregarding data is close to procedural programming languages: modelers specify *how* to solve a problem. An example where such a language is useful, is classical filling of forms, such as a patient registration process at a hospital.

Declarative specification of processes is an emerging trend for specifying especially business processes, but it has not seen massive use in practice. Declarative models often focus primarily on flow of control, but instead of explicitly modeling control-flow as a program counter, constraints between the different events are described. Declarative languages resemble declarative programming languages: modelers specify what the *intention* of the control-flow is, but not how to achieve that. An example where such languages are useful, is a patient treatment process at a hospital; here, many tests need to be run and many treatments are possible. There is no strict order of tests and treatments, but some treatments are incompatible with each other, and some treatments need follow-up treatments.

Declarative processes are typically better at describing highly dynamic environments, where actions can take place in many different orders, or early in the design, where the exact order of events is unknown. On the other hand, Petri nets are far better at modeling data-flow, and the strict control-flow model makes it easier to model processes with a strict and well-understood control-flow, which also makes it much easier to extract experiences from the model to an eventual implementation [10]. In this paper, we propose to merge two declarative approaches, Declare [15,19] and DCR graphs [7,13], with a high-level Petri nets formalism, colored Petri nets [9], to obtain a formalism that offers the best of both worlds. We aim to do so in a manner that makes it possible to use all three formalisms completely independently of each other or to mix all three formalisms in a single model. This makes it also possible to initially construct a purely declarative model, optionally with data, and during refinement make it more procedural as applicable. If we consider a hospital, this allows us to make a single model comprising both patient registration, diagnosis, and treatment. The reason for using both DCR graphs and Declare for the declarative parts is that the languages have different focus areas: Declare provides higher level primitives, often resulting in more comprehensible models, but DCR graphs do not suffer from the computational overhead of detecting conflicts necessary to ensure correct execution of Declare models.

We introduce our combined approach in Sect. 2, including pointers on how to allow analysis of combined models and our implementation in CPN Tools 4 [17]. In Sect. 3, we sum up our conclusions and compare with related work.

2 Combined Models

In this section we informally introduce our hybrid model and its semantics, and provide analysis considerations important for implementation. Actual implementation details are deferred to the next section.

The idea behind the hybrid approach is to identify transitions of CP-nets with tasks of Declare models and events of DCR graphs and then allow places and arcs (with annotations) from CP-nets, constraints from Declare models, and the relations from DCR graphs to be added to the model to constrain the possible executions.

The reason for including these three languages is that CP-nets is a widely used procedural formalism with a strong theoretical background. It provides great support for data flow, both theoretically and practically in the form of tool support. We also prefer to use both Declare and DCR graphs for specifying the declarative parts of the model. We choose these two languages because they are on the surface very similar, yet they have different focus areas.

Declare offers a large set of contraints which have been identified as commonly used in business processes, making it well-suited to the BPM domain. DCR Graphs on the other hand aim to provide a formal language for describing processes in general, containing only 4 basic constrains while still being formally more expressive than LTL.

By providing both languages, we can use pre-existing tools and techniques to analyze our combined models, automatically switching from one kind of analysis to the other as needed.

An execution is considered accepting if it is accepting for all three underlying models. In other words, the execution should be accepting for the CP-net that one gets when removing all Declare constraints and DCR Graph relations, it should be accepting for the Declare model one gets by removing all places, arcs and DCR Graph relations and it should also be accepting for the DCR Graph model that one gets by removing all places, arcs and Declare constraints. Formally, we can define the semantics of all three languages in terms of transition systems, and the semantics of the combined language is just the synchronization of the three transition systems we get from the individual semantics by projecting the combined model onto each of the three languages.

2.1 Analysis

We would like to provide a step-wise semantics for combined models. This is necessary for efficient simulation. For CP-nets isolated, this is easy because every state is accepting, so if a binding element sequence is enabled, the execution will inevitably end in an accepting state. For Declare models and DCR graphs, this is possible using a preprocessing step: we simply compute the prefix automaton, which is possible as they both have a semantics yielding finite automata, and only allow a transition if it leads to an accepting state in the prefix automaton. For the combined models, however, this is not in general decidable. While we can construct the transition system product of the 3 automata on the fly, we cannot employ any of the techniques to ensure we can end up in an accepting state: as not all states of Declare models and DCR graphs are accepting, not all states of the product are necessarily accepting, so we cannot just execute any enabled binding element sequence and be sure to end in an accepting state. As the transition system we get from a CP-net is not necessarily finite, neither is the product, so we cannot compute the prefix automaton. If either the CP-net model is bounded (yielding a finite state space), or the Declare model automaton and the DCR graph automaton only have accepting states, we can use the fact that these properties are preserved by transition system product and use the appropriate technique. Otherwise, we must settle for weaker guarantees.

When talking about runtime verification of Declare models [12], each constraint can be in not just the two states *satisfied* and *violated*, but also in two weaker states, where a constraint is only temporarily satisfied or violated, but future execution may violate or satisfy it. Only when the execution is terminated, is it possible to collapse possible satisfied/violated constraints into their (permanently) satisfied/violated counterparts.

For DCR Graphs we do not keep track of the state of individual constraints, instead we have a current marking and on execution check that the executed event is enabled and calculate the new marking. If a marking contains no pending included responses, the DCR Graph is in an accepting state and the process can terminate. Feedback to the user consists of showing which events have occured before, are enabled and need to occcur.

Simple Simulation. As demonstrated in [18], even if Declare is decidable, constructing the automaton for the full system can be very time and memory consuming – it is exponential in the number of constraints. To avoid this overhead, we can instead create an automaton for each individual constraint. If we do so, we can avoid ever violating individual constraints, while retaining fast simulation (we can update the model in the initial state in constant time). CPN Tools offers a mixed mode, where simulation and editing are interleaved. This is useful for testing and debugging, but requires that the simulation can resume very quickly, so performing an operation that is exponential in the size of the model may be undesirable (at least for large models). By constructing the individual automata, we can avoid ever (permanently) violating constraints, and for some constraints, e.g., init, this is sufficient. For other constraints, this provides a best-effort but fast simulation mode (we can update the model in constant time in the initial state). We call this the *simple simulation* approach. The simple simulation approach for DCR Graphs comes down to doing basic runtime verification as described previously: checking that an event is enabled in the current marking and calculating a new marking can be done in constant time.

Smart Simulation. As shown in [11] some Declare constraints can be in a conflicted state: they are not violated, but also cannot all be (possibly) satisfied at the same time. We can only catch this if we construct the automaton for the full Declare model. By making the product explicit, we can compute the prefix automaton. Unfortunately, the product of the prefix automata is not sufficient. As demonstrated in [18], this can still be fairly fast for moderately-sized models (in the order of seconds for models with 30-50 constraints). We call this *smart simulation*: we avoid executing any transition that would lead to a conflicted state. We can also do *smart simulation* of the DCR Graph constraints by building the finite automaton that corresponds to the graph and only allowing the execution of events that can lead to an accepting state (i.e., the DCR Graph does not contain any deadlocks). The efficiency of this approach has not been investigated structurally yet, but for the models that we have considered to date the state space tends to be modest. We can compute the product of the automata from the underlying Declare model and the underlying DCR Graph model to ensure that the two kinds of declarative constraints cannot conflict with other as well.

Data-Aware Simulation. When combining declarative models with CP-nets, we get an additional type of conflicts: a declarative constraint might require some task to be executed, while the the CP-net model blocks its execution (f.e. because of a missing token). Smart simulation cannot catch this on its own as it only looks at the declarative (and computable) parts of the model. To handle such situations we need constraints that yield automata which only have accepting states, which severely limits the usability, or that the state-space is finite. Thus, *data-aware simulation* is as hard as state space analysis.

For simple examples with small domains, we can just generate the state-space and perform the synchronization, typically in minutes or hours. If the state-space is larger but still finite, we can perform many simulations using smart simulation and discard any not ending in an accepting state, similar to how simulation is used for bug-finding until a final verification often is used. After computing the synchronization, it can be stored efficiently (often only few states are conflicted). If we deal with large domains, it is sufficient if we can generate an equivalence-reduced state-space. This is for example the case if all types are integers or reals, and we only compare all tokens with integers, similarly to region or zone reduction for timed automata.

2.2 Implementation

We have implemented our combined models in CPN Tools 4 [5,17]. CPN Tools 4 adds support for *simulator extensions* [17], a mechanism which makes it possible to extend CPN Tools using Java code. Each extension can add operations to CPN Tools and also modify existing operations. The integration comprises 4 parts: GUI extension, syntax check extension, enabling restriction, and analysis. In Fig. 1, we see how combined models look and are constructed in CPN Tools.

3 Conclusion

In this paper we have introduced a new approach to modelling workflows combining the procedural formalism colored Petri nets, and the two declarative formalisms, Declare and DCR graphs. The combined formalism can be seen as adding declarative control-flow to CP-nets or as adding data-flow to declarative formalisms. Declarative approaches are typically better for abstract descriptions or highly dynamic processes, where procedural approaches are better for well-known and structured processes. Combining the two allows us the best of both

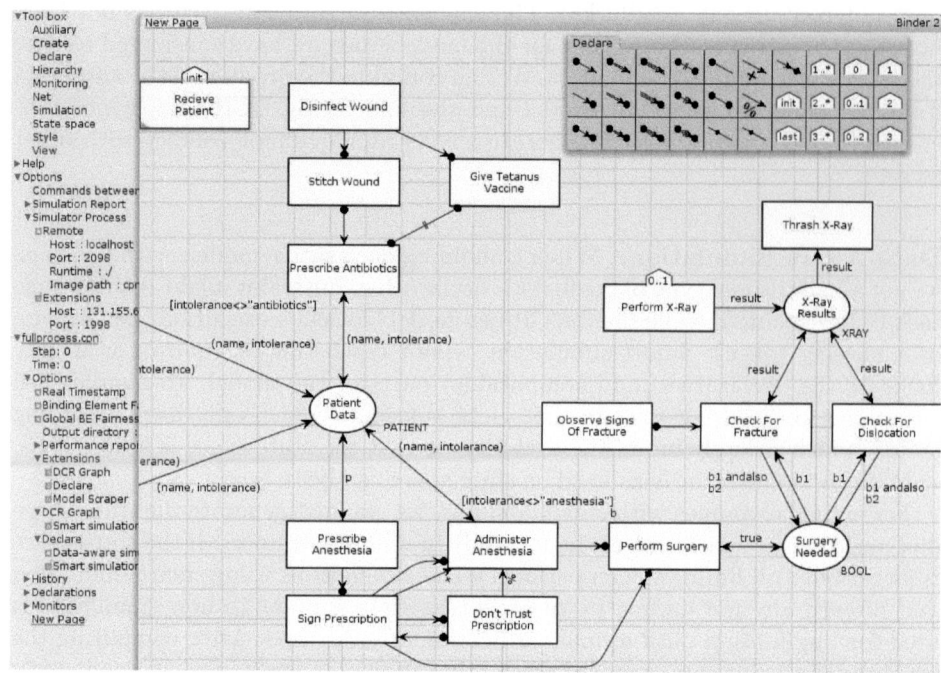

Fig. 1. Declare and DCR graphs in CPN Tools 4

worlds and allows declarative processes to also deal with data. We have considered what is needed to provide simulation that avoids future conflicts in efficient ways, and introduce three modes of simulation: simple, smart, and data-aware, where the simple mode only avoids individual conflicts, smart avoids conflicts not related to data, and data-aware makes sure that even in the presence of data, all executions can terminate successfully. We have briefly introduced our implementation in CPN Tools.

3.1 Related Work

The *Guard-Stage-Milestone* (GSM) model [8] by Hull et al, which originated from the work on artifact-centric business processes [3], takes an approach to modelling business processes where a process consists of a number of (possibly nested) stages, which in turn contain a number of tasks. A stage also has guards and milestones; it is activated by satisfying its guards and through performing the tasks in the stage its milestones can become enabled, which can then in turn satisfy the guards of other stages. We see the GSM model as a hybrid model combining procedural and declarative structures in a single language, whereas our approach is based on combining existing procedural and declarative languages. In [14] the authors introduce a declarative version of the Computer-Interpretable Guidelines (CIG) language for modelling clinical guidelines, they conclude that because both the procedural and declarative languages have their disadvantages it would be best to combine them into a single model, but leave this for future work. In [16] the authors have examined the understanding of procedural and declarative process models by users. In their conclusions they note that while it appears that procedural models are more comprehensible, it remains uncertain to what extent this is caused by participants being skewed towards procedural models because of their general acceptance and availability. They do not consider a hybrid approach using both procedural and declarative concepts. In [6] Fahland bridges the gap between declarative and procedural workflow approaches by proposing a general compositional mechanism for translating declarative workflow models to procedural workflow models. He exemplifies the general approach by giving a translation from Declare to Petri nets. The main difference to our approach is that while in [6] a declarative model is translated to a procedural version to facilitate using existing modeling, analysis and management techniques, we aim to combine the declarative and procedural approaches and provide tools and techniques for the hybrid approach.

3.2 Future Work

Here we have assumed that a user creates and refines a model. Another approach is to have the tool do that. For example, a precedence(A, B) constraint is trivially modeled using a single place of type boolean, initially marked by false. Then A changes the value indiscriminately to true and B checks that the value on the place is true. not co-existence(A, B) can be implemented using a place with three possible values: {A,B,UNDECIDED}. init(A) is less elegant, but can be implemented using, e.g., inhibitor arcs. This will not catch conflicts, but we can do that (and translate all constraints in a uniform way) by constructing the finite automaton either just equate the states of the automaton with new places or use a (not data-aware) process mining algorithm [1] or the theory of regions [4] to construct a Petri net for the control flow. Future work includes investigating the best way to make such a translation (semi-)automatically.

The current approach works as long as we describe a single run of a single process. That is, our example in the figures handles one treatment of one patient. It would be interesting to investigate multiple instances, which would essentially be a folding of the current model. We could also have multiple processes communicate, e.g., like Proclets [2], resulting in a more artifact-driven result. Using a translation from declarative constraints would essentially result in process-partitioned CP-nets in the sense of [10], which means it would be possible to automatically derive code from the resulting model. It would also be interesting to look into making a proper notion of a process in CP-net models, where instances cannot just terminate in any state. This would also include adding a notion of instances to the declarative languages.

References

1. van der Aalst, W.M.P.: Process Mining: Discovery, Conformance and Enhancement of Business Processes. Springer (2011)

2. van der Aalst, W.M.P., Barthelmess, P., Ellis, C.A., Wainer, J.: Workflow Modeling using Proclets. In: CoopIS 2000. LNCS, pp. 198–209. Springer, Heidelberg (2000)
3. Bhattacharya, K., Gerede, C., Hull, R., Liu, R., Su, J.: Towards formal analysis of artifact-centric business process models. In: Alonso, G., Dadam, P., Rosemann, M. (eds.) BPM 2007. LNCS, vol. 4714, pp. 288–304. Springer, Heidelberg (2007)
4. Carmona, J.A., Cortadella, J., Kishinevsky, M.: A Region-Based Algorithm for Discovering Petri Nets from Event Logs. In: Dumas, M., Reichert, M., Shan, M.-C. (eds.) BPM 2008. LNCS, vol. 5240, pp. 358–373. Springer, Heidelberg (2008)
5. CPN Tools webpage, http://cpntools.org
6. Fahland, D.: Towards analyzing declarative workflows. In: Autonomous and Adaptive Web Services. Dagstuhl Seminar Proceedings, vol. 07061, p. 6. Internationales Begegnungs- und Forschungszentrum fuer Informatik, IBFI (2007)
7. Hildebrandt, T., Mukkamala, R.R.: Declarative event-based workflow as distributed dynamic condition response graphs. In: Post-Proc. of PLACES 2010 (2010)
8. Hull, R., Damaggio, E., Fournier, F., Gupta, M., Terry, H.,I.F., Stacy, H., Mark, L., Sridhar, M., Anil, N., Piyawadee, S., Roman, V.: Introducing the guard-stage-milestone approach for specifying business entity lifecycles. In: Proc. of WS-FM 2010, pp. 1–24. Springer, Heidelberg (2011)
9. Jensen, K., Kristensen, L.: Coloured Petri Nets – Modelling and Validation of Concurrent Systems. Springer (2009)
10. Kristensen, L.M., Westergaard, M.: Automatic Structure-Based Code Generation from Coloured Petri Nets: A Proof of Concept. In: Kowalewski, S., Roveri, M. (eds.) FMICS 2010. LNCS, vol. 6371, pp. 215–230. Springer, Heidelberg (2010)
11. Maggi, F.M., Westergaard, M., Montali, M., van der Aalst, W.M.P.: Runtime Verification of LTL-Based Declarative Process Models. In: Khurshid, S., Sen, K. (eds.) RV 2011. LNCS, vol. 7186, pp. 131–146. Springer, Heidelberg (2012)
12. Maggi, F.M., Montali, M., Westergaard, M., van der Aalst, W.M.P.: Monitoring Business Constraints with Linear Temporal Logic: An Approach Based on Colored Automata. In: Rinderle-Ma, S., Toumani, F., Wolf, K. (eds.) BPM 2011. LNCS, vol. 6896, pp. 132–147. Springer, Heidelberg (2011)
13. Mukkamala, R.R.: A Formal Model For Declarative Workflows - Dynamic Condition Response Graphs. Ph.D. thesis, IT University of Copenhagen (March 2012)
14. Mulyar, N., Pesic, M., van der Aalst, W.M.P., Peleg, M.: Declarative and procedural approaches for modelling clinical guidelines: Addressing flexibility issues. In: ter Hofstede, A.H.M., Benatallah, B., Paik, H.-Y. (eds.) BPM 2007 Workshops. LNCS, vol. 4928, pp. 335–346. Springer, Heidelberg (2008)
15. Pesic, M.: Constraint-Based Workflow Management Systems: Shifting Controls to Users. Ph.D. thesis, Beta Research School for Operations Management and Logistics, Eindhoven (2008)
16. Pichler, P., Weber, B., Zugal, S., Pinggera, J., Mendling, J., Reijers, H.A.: Imperative versus declarative process modeling languages: An empirical investigation. In: Proc. of ER-BPM 2011, pp. 383–394 (2011)
17. Westergaard, M.: CPN Tools 4: Multi-formalism and Extensibility. In: Colom, J.-M., Desel, J. (eds.) PETRI NETS 2013. LNCS, vol. 7927, pp. 400–409. Springer, Heidelberg (2013)
18. Westergaard, M.: Better Algorithms for Analyzing and Enacting Declarative Workflow Languages Using LTL. In: Rinderle-Ma, S., Toumani, F., Wolf, K. (eds.) BPM 2011. LNCS, vol. 6896, pp. 83–98. Springer, Heidelberg (2011)
19. Westergaard, M., Maggi, F.: Declare: A Tool Suite for Declarative Workflow Modeling and Enactment. In: Business Process Management Demonstration Track (BPMDemos 2011). CEUR Workshop Proceedings, vol. 820, CEUR-WS.org (2011)

An Agile BPM Project Methodology

Christian Thiemich and Frank Puhlmann

Bosch Software Innovations GmbH
D-10785 Berlin, Germany
{christian.thiemich,frank.puhlmann}@bosch-si.com

Abstract. Business Process Management (BPM) has become one of the most important management disciplines in recent years. In reality, however, many technical process improvement projects failed in the past and the expected benefits could not be established. In the meantime, the agile software development movement made massive progress in contrast to classic waterfall approaches which are still the foundational methodologies for many BPM projects. This paper investigates the combination of a traditional BPM methodology and agile software development to overcome the limitations of existing BPM methodologies. The main focus is on projects that cover the technical realization of processes based on modern Business Process Management Systems (BPMS).

1 Motivation

Business Process Management (BPM) helps companies focusing on value-adding end-to-end processes and supporting them with IT systems. Hence, it focusses on implementing process-based, long-running and wide-reaching business applications with a specific set of tools (Business Process Management System, abbr. BPMS). Additionally, it supports the organizational change management which is required to successfully roll-out these changes throughout the company.

In some of our projects, however, we discovered that the process implementation the business departments got is precisely what they once required, but not what they need anymore as the requirements changed over time. Traditional software engineering were faced with the same problems but came up with solutions to closely link the customers (e.g. the requirement providers) with the engineers who actually build the systems. The solutions are based around the principles of agile software development, such as "satisfy the customer through early and continuous delivery of valuable software", "Welcome changing requirements, even late in development", or "Deliver working software frequently" (see [3]).

To gain the benefits of the agile principles for BPM projects, we developed a new approach for the realization of BPM projects which is based on the principles of the agile software development manifesto. Therefore we classify the existing artifacts and methods of an existing BPM methodology with a traditional waterfall project execution (named IBPM, see [12]) and reframe the generic parts into an agile development methodology based on Scrum. The derived framework

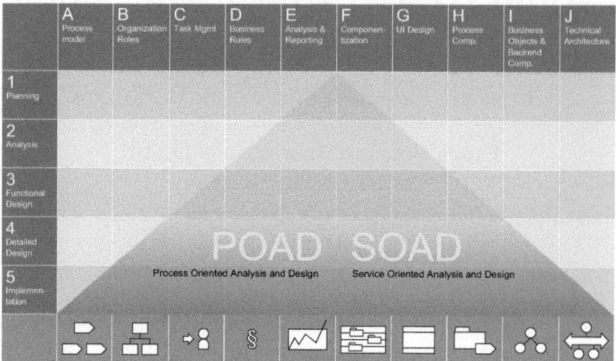

Fig. 1. The Integrated BPM Project Methodology Framework according to [12]

builds the foundation for an agile BPM methodology that provides guidance from early BPM project initiatives to the final implementation.

The paper is structured as follows. We start with an overview of the preliminaries in section 2, in particular IBPM as well as Scrum. Section 3 discusses the foundations of agile BPM projects. Besides providing an adaption of the agile principles to BPM, it also provides a guideline whether a BPM project should be implemented with the usage of the traditional lifecycle or by an agile methodology. Section 4 provides the core concepts of the agile BPM methodology, including a formal meta model, the agile lifecycle and key artifacts and methods.[1] Section 5 introduces a practical experience with the application of the agile methodology. We discuss related work in section 6 and conclude in section 7.

2 Preliminaries: IBPM and Scrum

This section introduces the basics of the Integrated BPM Project Methodology (IBPM) [12] and the Scrum software development framework. Both approaches have different purposes. While IBPM has a strong focus on analysis and design, Scrum delivers a holistic approach of how to get requirements implemented. IBPM furthermore provides best practices and artifacts to capture and discuss business requirements.

2.1 The Integrated BPM Project Methodology

The Integrated BPM Project Methodology enables BPM projects to be accomplished in a structured manner. The authors introduce different characteristics

---

[1] A complete description of the agile BPM methodology has been published as a Master Thesis (In German), available online at http://frapu.de/pdf/thiemich2012.pdf

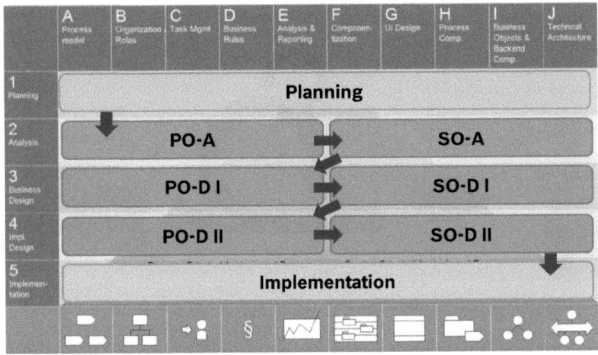

Fig. 2. IBPM Project Approach according to [12]

of BPM projects that are distinct to pure software development projects. BPM projects are to a large degree organizational projects. The challenge is to separate process flow and decision logic from software development aspects such as functions, thus establishing a well aligned and loosely coupled service-oriented architecture.

The motivation behind IBPM was a desire to increase quality and efficiency as well as to reduce risks and costs by enabling people to ask the right questions and deliver the right artifacts at the right time. For this purpose IBPM uses best practices and consists of the following three core components: IBPM Framework, IBPM Pattern Catalogue, IBPM Project Approach.

Preliminary 1 (IBPM Framework). The IBPM Framework, shown in figure 1, defines ten thematic pillars, which combine the most important aspects from the process-oriented and the service-oriented perspective in a BPM project. Both perspectives are represented by five columns. Given that the process model is based on BPMN, it is the leading artifact for the process-oriented perspective. Additional pillars include Organization and Roles (B), User Tasks (C), Business Rules (D) as well as Process Monitoring (E). The same idea can be applied to the pillars in the service perspective. The Componentization (F) contains the leading artifact represented as an SOA-Map as well as four more refining pillars. The Framework is additionally based on five different levels of detail (Planning, Analysis, Business Design, Implementation Design and Implementation). The resulting matrix allows the structured discussion of artifacts and corresponding requirements.

Preliminary 2 (IBPM Pattern Catalogue). The IBPM Pattern Catalogue is based on best practices and provides project conventions for eight different aspects with predefined patterns. The patterns include BPMN modeling guidelines, UI templates, or patterns covering change management.

Preliminary 3 (IBPM Project Approach). The IBPM Project Approach (figure 2) is based on a waterfall approach and introduces different project phases

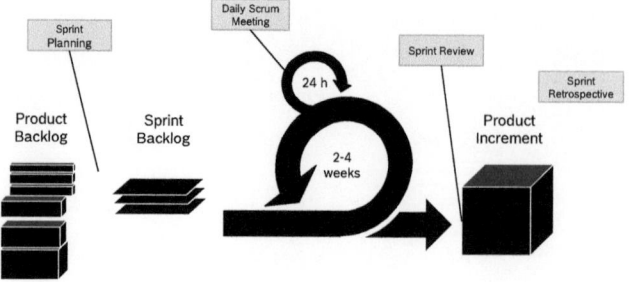

Fig. 3. The Scrum Development Process

(Planning, Analysis, Business Design, Implementation Design, Implementation) and working packages, focusing either on Processes or Services with a strong emphasis on the Analysis and Design of a BPM project. IBPM splits the design phase into the Business Design and the Implementation Design. Comparing IBPM to generic project approaches, IBPM adds value by defining BPM-specific tasks, roles and artifacts.

2.2 The Scrum Software Development Framework

Scrum (see e.g. [10],[15]) is a lightweight development framework, which is easy to understand and provides defined roles and processes. Even though the framework was born the early 1990s for software development purposes, other disciplines, including general management, have adapted it more and more [4]. It represents the Agile Manifesto[2] and the associated principles by focusing on collaboration and interaction to satisfy the customer. Scrum is based on empirical process control theory and utilizes an iterative, incremental approach to control risks and optimize predictability. The main goal is to develop potentially releasable product increments in short, consistent and time-boxed iterations, so-called sprints.

Scrum is based around three roles (Product Owner, Scrum Master, Team), four meetings (Sprint Planning, Daily Scrum, Sprint Review and Sprint Retrospective) and three artifacts (Product Backlog, Sprint Backlog, Product Increment). We introduce the product backlog, followed by the other artifacts and roles based on the meetings as shown in figure 3.

Preliminary 4 (Product Backlog). A "Product Backlog" describes the requirements for a product prioritized by their business values. In addition each entry in a Backlog is estimated (according to an abstract effort metrics based on "Story Points") and has a set of acceptance criteria.

Preliminary 5 (Sprint Planning). Within the first part of a "Sprint Planning" the "Product Owner" presents his goal for the following sprint and his priorities. The team will estimate the presented items and depending on the

---

[2] See http://agilemanifesto.org/

velocity (e.g. how many "Story Points" a team can currently implement in a predefined time frame), a certain amount of "Backlog Items" are selected for the sprint. In the second part of the "Sprint Planning" those requirements are broken down into "Tasks" which result as entries in the "Sprint Backlog".

Preliminary 6 (Daily Scrum). Over a predefined length of a sprint (usually 2-4 weeks) the Team will meet daily for the "Daily Scrum" to synchronize the current work and especially the problems (so-called impediments). The "Scrum Master" is responsible for solving those impediments as quickly as possible.

Preliminary 7 (Sprint Review). At the end of a "Sprint" the "Team", the "Scrum Master" and the "Product Owner" will meet again for the "Sprint Review". Based on the requirements and their predefined acceptance criteria the "Product Owner" will approve the requirements in the live system.

Preliminary 8 (Sprint Retrospective). The last meeting of a "Sprint" is the "Retrospective" where the "Team" and the "Scrum Master" (sometimes including the "Product Owner") reflect the result of the "Sprint" and define tasks to improve their Scrum process.

Scrum has a number of variants with additional steps or artifacts like Backlog Grooming, a Definition of Ready and a Definition of Done. The Backlog Grooming establishes a new meeting that helps the Product Owner to maintain his Product Backlog. He can get the assistance of the Team to make sure that the items in his Product Backlog are ready corresponding to the Definition of Ready. The Definition of Done is used to define general criteria which are needed in order for each requirement to be approved by the Product Owner.

3 Foundations of Agile BPM Projects

This section discusses selected agile principles and how they affect BPM projects. We start by introducing the foundation of agile BPM projects by comparing the idea of BPM and the definition of a project. The idea behind BPM is to provide sustainable and continuous improvements, whereas projects are intended to be unique and to have defined goals.

From our experience, most BPM improvements are motivated by a project and are not continuous at all. BPM aims to make the business processes flexible and to improve them continuously. Even though agile projects are still projects, they have certain advantages in combination with BPM. They lead to an inevitable flexibility for BPM projects which embraces and welcomes changes. Additionally, when most projects start, their goal is often not exactly defined at a detailed levels. Agile approaches cut off the overhead of a multiple-month analysis and design phase and deliver visible results in early phases of the project.

Best Practice 1 (Motivate the Different Approaches Using the "Magic Triangle"). Use the "Magic Triangle", shown in figure 4, to explain the idea of the paradigm shift that accompanied an agile development approach. While the classic waterfall approach has a fixed project scope, it only delivers assumptions

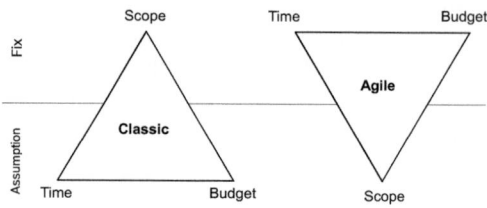

Fig. 4. Comparing the magic triangle

on time and budget. Turning the triangle to agile, in contrast, offers a fixed time and budget, but no limitation or restriction on the scope.

Until recently, a project without a clearly defined scope was not acceptable. Nowadays it is recognized that long-running projects with a fixed scope are often not successful and do not lead to end-user acceptance. To overcome this issue, the foundation of agile BPM projects is based on an adaption of the Agile Manifesto and its principles. In the following, the most relevant principles behind the Agile Manifesto are reflected from the perspective of a BPM project. We cite the principles according to [5]:

Principle 1. *Our highest priority is to satisfy the customer through early and continuous delivery of valuable software.*

A number of BPM projects have a long analysis and design phase, including late presentation of visible results. Thus, the customer is not able to realign the direction of the project at appropriate times, leading to no continuous delivery at all. BPM projects are often accompanied by coarse-grained requirements. Since BPM and the agile approaches have similar preconditions, further research is necessary on how they fit together. Again, the idea of BPM is that of a sustainable improvement and support of the business' processes and not the accomplishment of a single project. This is a significant problem that is addressed via agile BPM projects.

Principle 2. *Welcome changing requirements, even late in development. Agile processes harness change for the customer's competitive advantage.*

Why do companies engage in BPM? They expect competitive advantages and want to reduce the time-to-market of their innovations and improvements. Our experience has shown that BPM projects are often delayed due to changing requirements. Agile methods welcome changes to satisfy customer requirements, which have evolved over time. This refines the process implementation, channeling it into the direction to help fulfill the customer's needs.

Principle 3. *Deliver working software frequently, from a couple of weeks to a couple of months, with a preference towards the shorter timescale.*

This principle raises the question, 'what does working software mean for a BPM project?' Is it only the "living" process running in the BPMS or does it mean we have rolled out the process throughout the company, including training and

Fig. 5. Project parameters

documentation? A complete rollout cannot be achieved in one single sprint. In case of a technical BPM project we need to deliver a working process in our BPMS frequently. Depending on the project, we might have multiple releases every 5–10 sprints. In this case it is important to insure that the whole lifecycle of a process has been completed (incl. test/rollout/training).

Principle 4. *Business professionals and developers must work together on a daily basis throughout the project.*

One of the major benefits of agile software development approaches is that they are run in short and frequent iterations. This enables a higher transparency for both sides. Problems become visible earlier than in classic approaches and can be addressed directly. Business professionals are often working on multiple projects at the same time. This leads to a problem regarding their availability and focus on one single project. In BPM projects, the business professionals need to be closely integrated, since the project is not only about changing software but also about organizational changes.

Principle 5. *Continuous attention to technical excellence and good design enhances agility.*

Besides needing a well-designed architecture, the technical implementation of a business process might differ from the business processes model. Therefore synchronization is needed. At this point, discussions often arise as to whether the process model or the (existing) technical implementation is leading. From our point of view, the process model should be the leading artifact. Nevertheless, to succeed with agile BPM projects it is necessary to focus on architecture first. An advantage of using modern BPMS is that there is a common base on which reference architectures can be used as a starting point for new projects.

Principle 6. *Simplicity—the art of maximizing the amount of work not done—is essential.*

When business people and IT people work together, it is important to keep it simple. The focus should always be on a minimum valuable process. That means

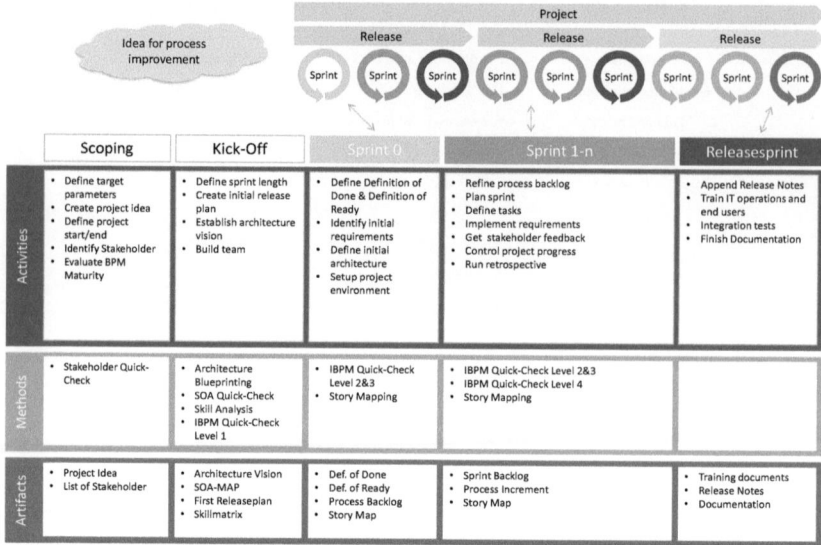

Fig. 6. Agile BPM Framework Overview

that the details are only needed for the requirements that will be implemented in the next 2–3 sprints. By doing so, the approach stays conform to the agile principles that value generating business value over documentation.

All discussed principles have their impact on a BPM project. In most cases, it is not possible to stay conform to all of them.

Best Practice 2 (Parameters for Agile or Classic Project Approaches). Evaluate the parameters shown in figure 5 to decide whether you should tend towards executing your project in an agile or more classic (waterfall)-oriented approach.

4 An Agile BPM Methodology

Since IBPM and Scrum are suitable methods for their purpose, the missing link is a value-adding combination of both frameworks. The goal of the current section is to combine BPM and Scrum to introduce a flexible framework for agile BPM projects. The proposed framework consists of three core aspects: "Project approach", "Artifacts", and "Methods". It enhances the reflected adaption of agile principles in BPM projects. Our focus is on the technical implementation of process-centric projects that are realized based on BPMS.

Agile BPM projects can be divided into the phases and types of sprints shown in figure 6. As discussed, we differentiate between artifacts, methods, and activities in each phase. Before a project starts, it must be scoped. Afterwards, the project kick-off starts the project and is followed by an adjustable number of

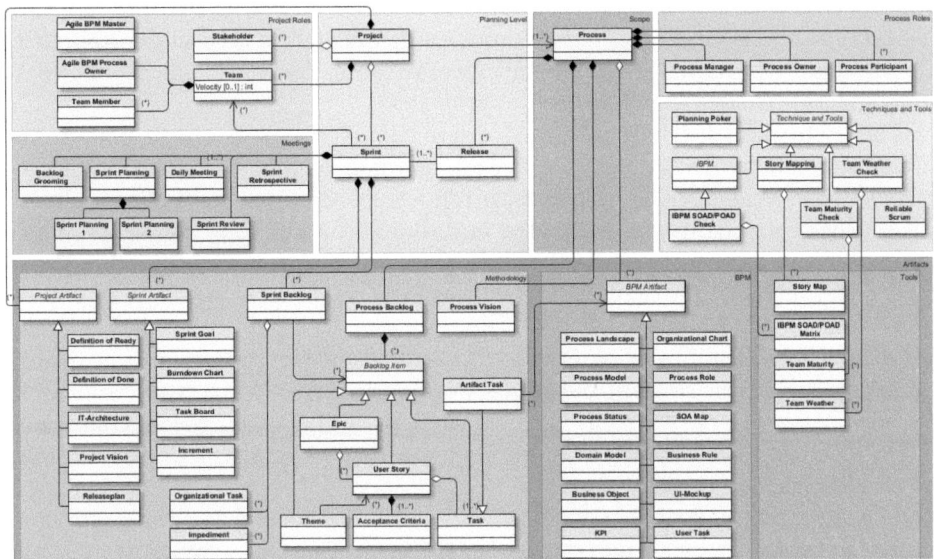

Fig. 7. Agile BPM Meta Model

sprints, until the project goal is achieved. Depending on the project, the number of releases will vary.

At customer sites, the agile life cycle often leads to a discussion regarding modeling vs. implementation. This is one of the central differences between traditional agile software development projects and BPM projects. So, how does the documentation and modeling of business processes fit into the idea of agile software development? Though it is obvious that the code itself is a kind of documentation, how can we argue the value of business process models? Since a BPM project is mostly running on different abstraction levels (from management, business professionals and IT), we need to clarify a language that is understood by both worlds. A process model helps to communicate the needs of the business people to the IT. Furthermore, a modern BPMS allows the implementation of the processes based on their models.

Best Practice 3 (Clarify Modeling vs. Implementation). We believe that in a BPM project, both—the process model and the implementation—generate business value. Furthermore, BPM projects are often connected with organizational change that is based and communicated using the different models.

4.1 Agile BPM Meta Model

Given that a process model is adding value to the project and needs to be specified before the process can be implemented, we generate additional dependencies that have to be managed. A common problem in a software development project using Scrum and User Stories is that the big picture or strategic fit is often lost.

The combination of IBPM and Scrum in an agile BPM project helps to keep this big picture. Therefore several of methods and artifacts are used in our approach. In the following paragraphs, we will give an overview and some examples to highlight the linkage between both approaches.

The meta model of our proposed approach, shown in figure 7, depicts the different artifacts, methods and activities, and indicates how they are connected with the processes. Not all relations are shown at the given level of granularity. As can be seen, the model is divided into different main subjects, according to figure 6. From the BPM perspective, we assume that a process has a manager, an owner and multiple participants. Processes exist in different releases. A process improvement will be initiated with a new project, where a project has different roles. It always has Stakeholders and depending on the project size, a project might consist of one or multiple teams working together. Each team, aligned to the idea of Scrum, has its Agile BPM Master, an Agile BPM Process Owner and a 3–5 member team. We chose a different wording to highlight that those roles need additional competencies.

The Agile BPM Process Owner is responsible for identifying the customer's needs. He has to extract and transfer them into appropriate requirements in the process backlog. The prioritization and estimation of the backlog is also his responsibility. Besides that, he is accountable for the Return on Invest of the project. It is necessary that he is always available for the team, in case questions and problems arise during a sprint. The Agile BPM Master takes care of the compliance to the Agile BPM Methodology, the project approach and different responsibilities. He is familiar to BPM as well as agile principles and approaches. Particularly in the early phases of the project he is the trainer and mentor for the whole project team and moderates the meetings. He is the first contact person in case of any ambiguity and for problems that may threaten the target achievements. The team has the same role it has in Scrum. Since it is a BPM project, the required skills are different to those in software development projects. Projects have multiple sprints and these sprints are associated to releases of the appropriate processes. Every sprint is run the same way. At this point our approach is very similar to Scrum. We decided to establish the Backlog Grooming as a mandatory activity within our projects, since we discovered out that most of the projects use something similar to help the product owner to prepare the backlog for the next sprints.

4.2 Tools and Techniques

We identified a set of tools and techniques that support us in delivering successful BPM projects. In the following we describe an excerpt of these tools and techniques as best practices.

Given that we work with user stories in our process backlog, we developed three IBPM Quick Check Levels based on the IBPM Matrix (see figure 1) for different purposes and phases (see figure 6). They establish the big picture and help to identify the BPM artifacts needed to achieve the defined targets and goals. The goal of those different Quick Checks is to ask the right questions depending on the detail level and project approach, e.g.

An Agile BPM Project Methodology 301

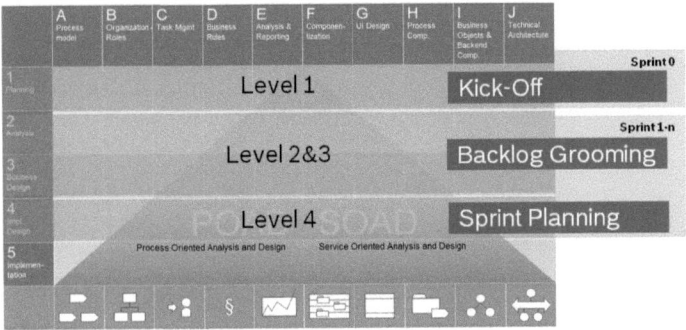

Fig. 8. IBPM Quick Check Level

- "Do we need a UI? If so, how should it look like?"
- "Are there any business rule candidates within the process?"
- "Which non-functional requirements have to be considered?"

Best Practice 4 (Use the IBPM Story Check). You should use the IBPM Story Check (see figure 9) in the early phase of a new user story to identify which subjects and dependencies the specific story will generate. The goal is to classify new requirements and to identify the relevant IBPM pillars. Even though it is a very simple enhancement to a story card, it helped in our projects to handle dependencies and to maintain the big picture. Lets say we have a story card that says: *"As a purchasing agent I want to create a new purchase requisition to initiate the purchase process"*. This story will get a priority and some acceptance criterias. In our framework, we additionally map this story into a specific process step. In this case it is *"Create purchase requisition"*. This process step can be found directly in our process model. Doing this for each user story will help us to keep track of our end-to-end processes. A best practice is to offer three options for the relevance of a specific pillar: Existing artifacts, Artifacts needed, Not needed. Based on this information we can derive specific tasks and artifacts that have to be delivered before we can put the story into a specific sprint. We highly recommend to tie this method into the Definition Of Ready.

Best Practice 5 (Use IBPM Quick Checks). Use the different IBPM Quick Checks levels shown in figure 10 to decide on important steps within a Sprint. Since the IBPM Quick Check Level 1 is only used within the project kickoff, the other three are used within the preparation of the next sprints. The Backlog Grooming is supported by the Level 2 and 3. The goal is to make the requirements achievable for the team. Therefore it is necessary to identify the missing BPM artifacts. If there are any required artifacts missing, they have to be addressed within the next sprint. Since IBPM specifies a lot of artifacts, it is not mandatory to deliver all of them. In agile BPM projects, the associated user story is used as guideline, which artifacts should be considered. The team defines which of the artifacts generate value for the business and IT alignment.

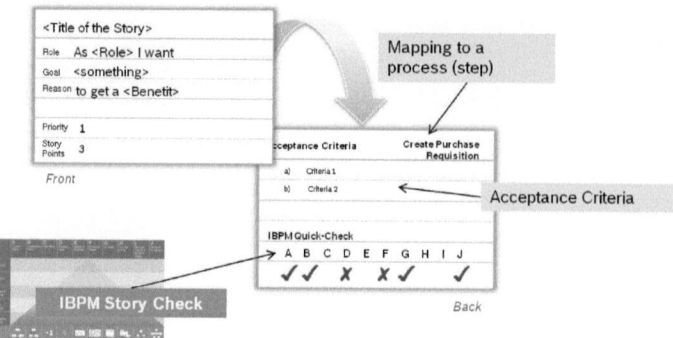

Fig. 9. IBPM Story Check

All of these checks generate a broad set of artifacts. The artifacts are linked to either a process, the project or methods. To handle the complexity and to understand their relations, we use the meta model shown in the beginning of this section.

Best Practice 6 (Customize the Framework). Take the time to think about a project-specific customization carefully. Depending on specific problems or questions there are ways to solve issues by adapting some of our best practices. One point that sometimes leads to questions is the feasibility of requirements within one sprint. To make sure that any requirement that gets into a sprint can be achieved successfully, the "Definition of Ready" defines what needs to be delivered prior to the realization. It is a best practice to establish the Backlog Grooming to identify the information demand for the next one or two sprints. In case the team and the Agile BPM Process Owner identifies a missing BPM artifact, there is enough time to gather or create the required information.

Best Practice 7 (Use Interleaved Teams for Business and Technical Perspectives If Needed). Use interleaved parallel teams to generate "ready" backlog items with an offset of one sprint if the stories become too complex. One team represents the business perspective and shapes the requirements which will then be implemented by the second team. This approach collides with the agile principles, but sometimes helps to get at least some of the concepts into a project. [14]

Best Practice 8 (Adjust Stories from Horizontal to Vertical as the Project Progresses). From the product development perspective, user stories have to be vertical (e.g. one feature/activity in depth). Otherwise they can't produce any benefit. In contrast, BPM projects are not about product development. We recognized that there are often horizontal user stories which are predominantly at the beginning of a project (e.g. a click-dummy of the process). They help people understand how their process will look and feel like. Afterwards it is much easier to identify which aspects must be considered vertically. Adjust the splitting of the user stories from horizontal to vertical as the project progresses.

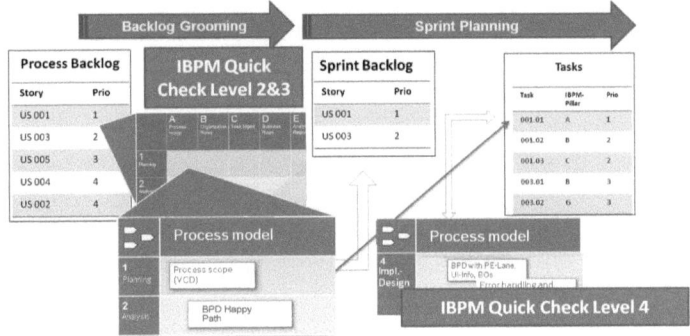

Fig. 10. Sprint preparation with IBPM Quick Checks

5 Experience

In our professional experiences, we have analyzed multiple projects and their lessons learned. Most of the less successful projects suffer from the same problems. Waterfall oriented approaches were not able to use the benefits of modern BPMS. The time between the initial planning, the analysis, design phase and the final implementation causes a reduced end-user acceptance, a lack of management attention and often changed business requirements.

The first practical experiences of applying the presented framework are very promising. We had several projects that were successfully accomplished based on the described framework. We observed that the classification of the project environment is one of the key issues for successful BPM projects (see best practice 2). In projects where agile approaches are used for the wrong reasons, for example to only seem state-of-the-art, we recognized that they were neither successful, nor did they emphasize the agile principles. Talking to project members clarified that it only left '"scorched earth"'. One of our goals is to establish guidelines that help BPM projects to decide between agile and classic approaches. In the following we introduce one of our recent projects that highlights how the sketched framework can be adapted for specific requirements.

5.1 Service Portal Project

In September 2012, our company set up a project to build a remote service portal based on our core products. Before the project started, we considered the parameters that would influence the project. The outcome of our classification (based on figure 5) stated that it matched our expectations of an agile environment. The project was defined by a fixed timeline and the allocated resources. Since the project was based on our core products, the technical architecture was also well defined in the early stage of this project. Another important aspect was fuzzy requirements at the project start which often resembled more a vision than concrete issues. The basic parameters of the project can be summarized as follows. We had one single team which was cross-functional and international but had no former experience with agile methodologies. In this project we began by coaching the team and filled the position of the Agile BPM Master. Additionally we supported the Agile BPM Product Owner by getting the stories ready according to our definition. Since the team had neither experience in IBPM nor in Scrum, we chose to start with a reduced set of artifacts to begin with. Besides a lack of experience in the Agile BPM area, we had to face cultural differences. The people who formed the team were from Singapore, USA and Germany. Nevertheless, we passed through the defined phases (see figure 6), which helped the team to structure their work several times, especially in the initial workshops and sprints.

The team chose to start with a sprint length of one week. They started with this high frequency for several reasons. First of all, they wanted to learn more about the Agile BPM approach and expected a faster adaption. On the other hand they had fuzzy requirements and wanted to remain flexible in the face of a highly changing process backlog. At the end of the project, their decision has proven of value. During the project the stakeholders were highly satisfied by the results and the project approach. Before the project started there was a certain suspiciousness among the stakeholders. They were doubtful how a newly formed and international team should produce any usable outcome in a short running project like this. The results from our project have shown that most of the issues can be overcome, based on the application of the agile principles explained earlier.

5.2 Lessons Learned

We have learned that a clearly defined process for collaboration accelerates the knowledge transfer and the efficiency. From our experience we know that it works well to start with agile projects in smaller scopes. The most important thing to start with agile approaches is to find a project initiative that matches the requirements for an agile approach. Do not try and implement the agile approach in a project just to say that you are doing so; in most cases this will not work out well.

We additionally found out that IT departments often think in short terms. Unfortunately, in a lot of cases, the business departments are not ready to think this way yet. Their organization does not support early and frequent feedback since they are working in many different projects and can not devote their full attention to one project. At this point our approach can not deliver a general recommendation, since every company is differently organized. We can only demand that the stakeholders from the business departments must have at least half of their time available for a particular project, since otherwise it will not be possible to align the pulse of business and IT. Also keep in mind, that one of the most important things is to keep it simple. It is not about following our framework in a dogmatic way but rather about finding a pragmatic, customized path. When we start working with our approach, we consider the people and their knowledge and then successively bring in methods, tools, and artifacts.

6 Related Work

BPM methodologies can be clustered based on their focus (e.g. enterprise, process, or project level) or purpose (e.g. business process redesign or continuous process improvements). Enterprise-BPM [12] has a focus on the enterprise-wide establishment of BPM. It helps to identify project initiatives, to manage complex application landscapes and to improve BPM based on a risk-oriented approach. Six-Sigma' DMAIC, the RummlerBrache Methodology [11], or Jeston and Nelis [9] are focussing on the process level. In addition to those methodologies , there are a number of other approaches. Nevertheless, most focus on the process level and help to identify possible process improvements. Existing BPM methodologies that focus on the project level, such as the Integrated BPM Methodology (IBPM) [12], help business departments to precisely state their requirements as process models and corresponding artifacts. The traditional BPM-lifecycle (model, implement, execute, analyze) [1] defines how to hand over the documented requirements to the IT department for implementation.

Evaluating the agile methods and approaches, we focussed on the most popular methods, e.g. Scrum and Kanban [13][6][2]. Scrum is originally a framework for developing complex software products. We chose Scrum in this approach, because it fits very well with the IBPM approach.

During the last year, we recognized a stronger interest in this topic in the academic sector and the industry as well. Parallel to the thesis on which this paper is based on, there had been some investigations into the subject. One of them is a study confirming that agile approaches are progressively adapted to process centric projects[6]. Wauch and Meyer illustrate an approach to establish an agile BPM organization within the company in their conference paper[14]. Another topic is the current rise of cloud services and their combination with BPM and agile methods [8][7].

7 Conclusions

This paper introduced an agile BPM project methodology that has been based upon an existing BPM methodology and an agile software development framework. In contrast to existing BPM methodologies, the proposed agile methodology focuses on the customer needs first, by tightly integrating them into the process implementation.

As a result, the first two steps of the traditional BPM lifecycle (e.g. modeling and implementation) are merged together, resulting in "better" processes, since the business departments iterate in close cycles together with the IT departments to implement the processes that are really needed. Since the business gets a better understanding of what they really want in each iteration, the fuzziness of the to-be processes is cleared up in early stages. Due to the high frequency of feedback cycles and the daily synchronization of the progress, we discovered that the agile approaches establish a very transparent project environment.

While the first practical results are very encouraging, in our ongoing research we will analyze more agile BPM projects and investigate the results to come up with recommendations on how to handle those difficulties. If needed, the proposed framework will be adapted to a more fine-grained support of different project causalities.

References

1. van der Aalst, W.M.P., ter Hofstede, A.H.M., Weske, M.: Business process management: A survey. In: van der Aalst, W.M.P., ter Hofstede, A.H.M., Weske, M. (eds.) BPM 2003. LNCS, vol. 2678, pp. 1–12. Springer, Heidelberg (2003)
2. Anderson, D.J.: Kanban: Evolutionäres Change Management für IT-Organisationen. dpunkt, Heidelberg and Neckar, 1st edn (2011)
3. Beck, K., Jeffries, R., Highsmith, J., Grenning, J., Martin, R.C., Schwaber, K., Cunningham, W., Sutherland, J., Mellor, S., Thomas, D.: Manifesto for agile software development (2001), http://agilemanifesto.org/
4. Denning, S.: The Leader's Guide to Radical Management. John Wiley and Sons, San Francisco (2010)
5. Beck, K., et al.: Twelve Principles of Agile Software (2001), http://agilemanifesto.org/principles.html
6. Komus, A.: Studie: Status Quo Agile: Verbreitung und Nutzen agiler Methoden (2012)
7. Kruba, S., Baynes, S., Hyer, R.: Bpm, agile, and virtualization combine to create effective solutions. CoRR abs/1208.3887 (2012)
8. Krumeich, J., Werth, D., Loos, P.: Knowledge management and business processes learning on the job; a conceptual approach and its prototypical implementation. In: Malzahn, D. (ed.) eKNOW 2013, The Fifth International Conference on Information, Process, and Knowledge Management, Nizza, France, pp. 1–7. International Academy, Research, and Industry Association (IARIA), ThinkMind (2013)
9. Nelis, J. (ed.): Business Process Management: Practical Guidelines to Successful Implementations. Taylor & Francis (2008)
10. Pichler, R.: Agile product management with Scrum: Creating products that customers love. Addison-Wesley, Upper Saddle River (2010)
11. Rummler, G.A., Brache, A.P.: Improving Performance: How To Manage the White Space on the Organization Chart. The Jossey-Bass Management Series. ERIC (1995)
12. Slama, D., Nelius, R., Breitkreuz, D.: Enterprise BPM: Erfolgsrezepte für unternehmensweites Prozessmanagement, 1st edn. dpunkt-Verlag, Heidelberg (2011)
13. VersionOne: State of agile survey 2011: The state of agile development: 6th annual (2011)
14. Wauch, F., Meyer, S.: Agilität als Wegbereiter für lebende Prozesse. In: Engstler, M., Oestereich, B. (eds.) IT-Projektmanagement 2012+ im Spagat zwischen Industrialisierung und Agilität?, pp. 49–62. dpunkt-Verlag, Heidelberg (2012)
15. Woodward, E., Surdek, S., Ganis, M.: A practical guide to distributed Scrum. IBM Press, Upper Saddle River (2010)

Declarative Modeling–An Academic Dream or the Future for BPM?

Hajo A. Reijers[1,2], Tijs Slaats[3,4], and Christian Stahl[1]

[1] Department of Mathematics and Computer Science, Technische Universiteit Eindhoven, P.O. Box 513, 5600 MB Eindhoven, The Netherlands
{H.A.Reijers,C.Stahl}@tue.nl
[2] Perceptive Software, Piet Joubertstraat 4, 7315 AV Apeldoorn, The Netherlands
[3] IT University of Copenhagen, Rued Langgaardsvej 7, 2300 Copenhagen, Denmark
TSlaats@itu.dk
[4] Exformatics A/S, Lautrupsgade 13, 2100 Copenhagen, Denmark

Abstract. Declarative modeling has attracted much attention over the last years, resulting in the development of several academic declarative modeling techniques and tools. The absence of empirical evaluations on their use and usefulness, however, raises the question whether practitioners are attracted to using those techniques. In this paper, we present a study on *what practitioners think of declarative modeling*. We show that the practitioners we involved in this study are receptive to the idea of a *hybrid approach* combining imperative and declarative techniques, rather than making a full shift from the imperative to the declarative paradigm. Moreover, we report on requirements, use cases, limitations, and tool support of such a hybrid approach. Based on the gained insight, we propose a *research agenda* for the development of this novel modeling approach.

1 Introduction

Imperative modeling is currently the most prominent modeling paradigm in BPM. Imperative modeling techniques are implemented in almost every modeling tool, and many imperative modeling languages have been developed, most prominently, Event-Driven Process Chains (EPCs) and Business Process Modeling Notation. Imperative models take an *"inside-out"* approach; that is, every possible execution sequence must be modeled explicitly. As a consequence, imperative modeling may lead to over-specification and lack of flexibility, making it difficult to defer decisions at runtime and to change existing process models [21,2].

To overcome these shortcomings, *declarative modeling* approaches have been proposed [3]. In contrast to imperative approaches, declarative models take an *"outside-in"* approach. Instead of describing how the process has to work exactly, only the essential characteristics are described. To this end, constraints are specified that restrict the possible execution of activities.

Research on declarative modeling has gained increasing interest over the last years. Declarative languages, such as Declare [3] (formerly known as DecSerFlow), DCR Graphs [12] and SCIFF [14], have been developed. These languages have been integrated in academic and industrial modeling tools [24].

Beside the development of declarative techniques, also empirical research has been conducted to study the relation between imperative and declarative approaches [8,9,22,20]. It is well understood how to specify properties of a business process, but it is still not clear how to define a business process modeling languages that is understandable [8] on the one hand, and enables maintainability [9], expressiveness and modeling comfort, on the other hand.

To the best of our knowledge, there does not exist any studies that reflect on the question whether declarative techniques can be used in practise from a practitioner's standpoint. This raises a question, which has not been answered yet: *Do practitioners see opportunities to use declarative techniques?*

The contribution of this paper is to present *what practitioners think of declarative modeling*. In that way, we close the gap between research on declarative techniques and empirical investigations on declarative modeling. Our results are based on a workshop on declarative modeling with ten professionals from industry, including both consultants involved in modeling projects and developers of industrial modeling tools. During the workshop, we introduced declarative modeling techniques, performed two modeling assignments, and discussed the prospects of a declarative approach. The evaluation, both qualitative and quantitative, shows that practitioners see good opportunities for a *hybrid approach combining imperative and declarative techniques* while they are skeptical regarding a purely declarative approach. With the gained insight from the discussion, we present requirements on such a hybrid approach, use cases, limitations, and requirements concerning tool support. Shifting the focus from imperative and declarative modeling to a hybrid approach raises many research questions. Therefore, we propose a *research agenda* for the BPM community to make the hybrid approach work.

We continue with a brief introduction to Declare and DCR Graphs, two declarative approaches we used throughout the workshop. In Sect. 3, we describe the outline of the workshop and our evaluation method. The quantitative evaluation is described in Sect. 4, and Sect. 5 reports on the qualitative evaluation. In Sect. 6, we present our research agenda. We close with a conclusion and directions for future work.

2 Declare and DCR Graphs by Example

In this section, we briefly introduce two declarative modeling approaches, Declare [3,24] and DCR Graphs [12], using the following example of a document management system. To simplify the presentation, we restrict ourselves to the control flow dimension and do not consider data or resources.

Example 1. Every case of the document management system is initially *created* and eventually *closed*. For a created case, an arbitrary number of documents can

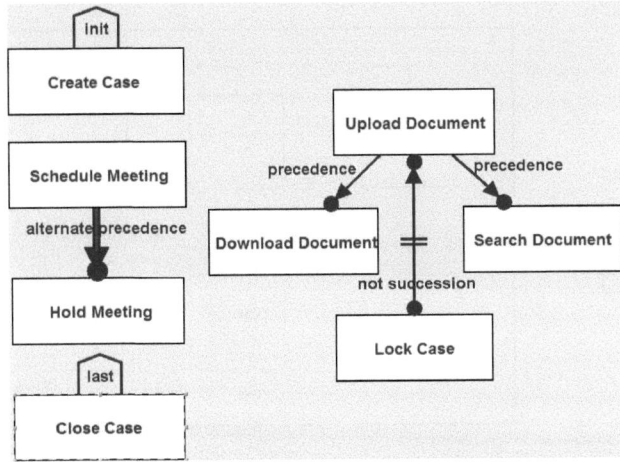

Fig. 1. Declare model of the document management system

be *uploaded*. An uploaded document can be *downloaded* or *searched*. At any time, a case can be *locked*. After locking a case, it is not possible to upload a document; still, uploaded documents can be downloaded and searched. Furthermore, in every case, meetings can be *held*. To hold a meeting, it has to be *(re-)scheduled*. Meetings can be rescheduled arbitrarily often, but it is not possible to schedule more than one meeting in advance.

2.1 Declare

A Declare model consists of activities and constraints. An activity is depicted as a rectangle and a constraint as a hyper-arc (i.e., a constraint connects one or more activities). From the specification, we identify eight activities which are highlighted in the description. Figure 1 shows the Declare model of the example. The *init* symbol on top of activity *Create Case* specifies that every case of the document management system starts with activity *Create Case*. Likewise, the *last* symbol on top of activity *Close Case* specifies that the final activity of every case of the document management system is *Close Case*.

There are three types of arcs in Fig. 1. Each arc type specifies one type of constraint. The precedence constraint, modeled as an arc from *Upload Document* to *Download Document* specifies that a document has to be uploaded before it can be downloaded. Likewise, we can only search a document once it has been uploaded (arc from *Upload Document* to *Search Document*). The second type of constraint is the not-succession constraint, which is modeled by an arc from *Lock Case* to *Upload Document*. It specifies that after a case has been locked, we cannot upload new documents. The third type of constraint, alternate precedence, is the arc from *Schedule Meeting* to *Hold Meeting*. It means that a meeting can only be held after it has been (re-)scheduled at least once. Moreover,

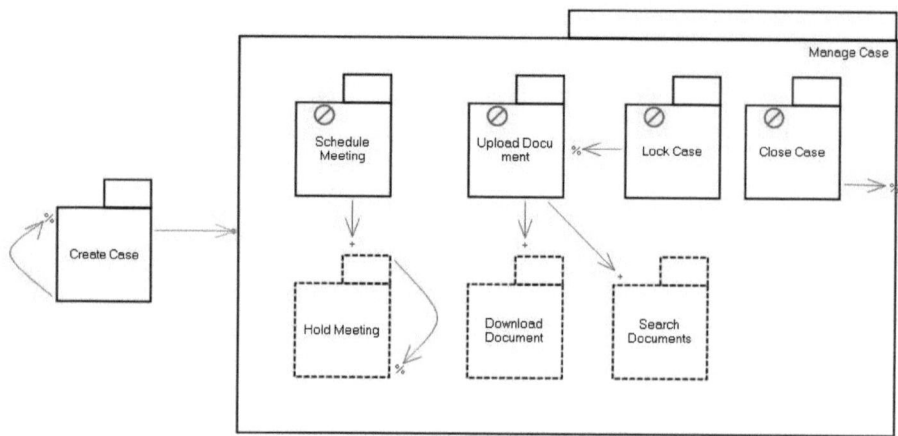

Fig. 2. DCR Graph model of the document management system

after a meeting has been held, the next meeting has to be (re-)scheduled before it can be held (i.e., activity *Hold Meeting* has to be followed by *Schedule Meeting* before *Hold Meeting* can be executed again).

As mentioned in the introduction, a declarative model only describes the essential characteristics of a process rather than how the process has to work exactly. For example, holding and (re-)scheduling meetings is independent from handling documents. Therefore the respective activities are not connected by arcs; that is, no constraint restricts their interplay. To execute the model in Fig. 1, one has to determine which activities are enabled by evaluating all constraints. Initially, it is the start activity, *Create Case*. After this activity is executed, any of the activities *Schedule Meeting*, *Upload Document*, *Lock Case* and *Close Case* can occur. A Declare model can be enacted and executed. The tool then computes the enabled transitions for every state [24].

2.2 DCR Graphs

A DCR Graph model consists of activities, relations, and a runtime marking. Activities are depicted as rectangles with an "ear" that can contain the roles which can execute the activity. Activities can be nested under super-activities, depicted by drawing an activity inside the rectangle of another activity, in which case any relation that applies to the super-activity, applies to all its sub-activities. Only the atomic activities (that do not contain any sub-activities of their own) are executable. The relations are drawn as arrows between activities.

Figure 2 shows the DCR model of the example. The first activity is *Create Case*, which should occur before all other activities can occur. We model this behaviour by the yellow *condition relation* from *Create Case* to the super-activity *Manage Case*, containing all other activities. The condition relation states that the second activity (in this case any sub-activity of *Manage Case*) can not occur before the first activity (in this case *Create Case*). We also require that *Create Case* happens only once, which we model through the *dynamic exclusion relation* drawn as a red arrow with a percentage sign at the end. Through this relation *Create Case* excludes itself from the workflow when it is executed, meaning that it can not be executed anymore afterward. The next two activities are *Schedule Meeting* and *Hold Meeting*. We should always schedule a meeting before we can hold a meeting, but it might be the case that a meeting is rescheduled before it is held. We model this in the following way: *Hold Meeting* is *initially excluded*, meaning that at the start of the workflow it can not be executed before it is included. *Hold Meeting* is included by doing *Schedule Meeting*, modelled by the *dynamic inclusion relation*, drawn as a green arrow with a plus sign in the end. *Hold Meeting* excludes itself meaning that it can not be executed again before there has been a new occurrence of *Schedule Meeting*. The next three activities are *Upload Document*, *Download Document*, and *Search Documents*. We can not download or search documents before at least one document has been uploaded, therefore those activities are initially excluded and will be included by *Upload Document*. The case can also be locked through the activity *Lock Case*, which makes it impossible to upload further documents, therefore *Lock Case* excludes *Upload Document*. Finally we can close the case by executing the activity *Close Case*. We model this by having *Close Case* exclude the super-activity *Manage Case*. Because all activities are nested under *Manage Case*, *Close Case* will exclude all activities from the workflow.

The final two relations of DCR Graphs are not used in the example. First there is the response relation which states that one activity requires another activity to happen in the future, when this occurs we say that the second activity is a *pending response* and annotate it with an exclamation mark. A workflow is in an accepting state while there are no *included pending responses*, in case there are included pending responses these should be executed before the workflow can be closed. The second relation that is not shown is the milestone relation, it captures this accepting condition on the level of activities by stating that while some activity is a pending response, some other activity can not be executed.

We represent the runtime of a DCR Graph by showing which activities have been executed at least once before by drawing them with a green check-mark, showing which activities are pending responses by drawing them with a red exclamation mark and showing which activities are currently excluded by drawing them with a dashed line instead of a solid line. We call these three sets of activities the *marking* of the DCR Graph. Based on the marking we can determine which activities are enabled: Activities which are excluded (drawn with a dashed line) are not enabled and activities that are blocked by a condition and/or milestone relation are also not enabled. In the latter case, we show this by drawing a red stop-mark on the activity. In Fig. 2, one can see that the only initially enabled activity is *Create Case*. All other activities are either excluded (drawn with dashed lines) or blocked through the condition relation (drawn with a red stop-mark). We distinguish between being excluded and blocked by a condition/milestone relation because we consider these two as essentially different states of the activity: When it is blocked it is still a part of the workflow, but being stopped from executing. When it is excluded it is not considered as a part of the workflow at that time. This is also why only *included* pending responses will block the workflow from being closed.

2.3 Comparison

Figures 1 and 2 clearly illustrate the idea behind declarative modeling. The main difference between DCR Graphs and Declare is that the DCR Graph approach allows to define any constraint using the five basic relations, while one has to define many more constraint for Declare (some of them are logical combinations of simpler constraints). Also, Declare represents the runtime of a workflow by showing the state of the individual constraints—that is, which constraints are (possibly) satisfied, and which constraints are (possibly) violated. DCR Graphs, by contrast, represents the runtime of a workflow by showing which tasks have been executed at least once before, which tasks are pending as a response and should be done some time in the future, and which tasks are currently included in the workflow. While on infinite traces DCR Graphs are strictly more expressive than Declare, this has no impact on practical business process modeling: The processes under consideration typically produce finite traces.

3 Method

For our evaluation, we worked together with Perceptive Software, a provider of enterprise content management and BPM technologies. We invited both consultants, who engage with clients to model their processes and implement BPM suites using such models, and professionals who contribute to the development of the toolsets. We planned a single workshop that went through the four phases, as depicted in Fig. 3.

In the first phase (*Introduction*), we provided the participants with the motivation for organizing the workshop and gave them a generic introduction to declarative principles. After this phase, we split the groups into two sub-groups of equal size. We first randomly assigned half of the consultants to group 1 and the other half to group 2. We did the same for the developers after that. In this way, we ensured an even distribution of consultants and developers over the groups.

The second phase was specific for each group and consisted of a tutorial on the techniques under consideration (*Explanation*). In other words, one group received the tutorial on DCR Graphs and the other on Declare. The tutorials were provided by separate moderators for each group. Each moderator had deep expertise in the technique that he explained. The tutorials were synchronized beforehand between the moderators to guarantee a similar level of depth and the same duration.

Following up on the tutorials, each group received two assignments. These assignments were the same for both groups and required the participants to

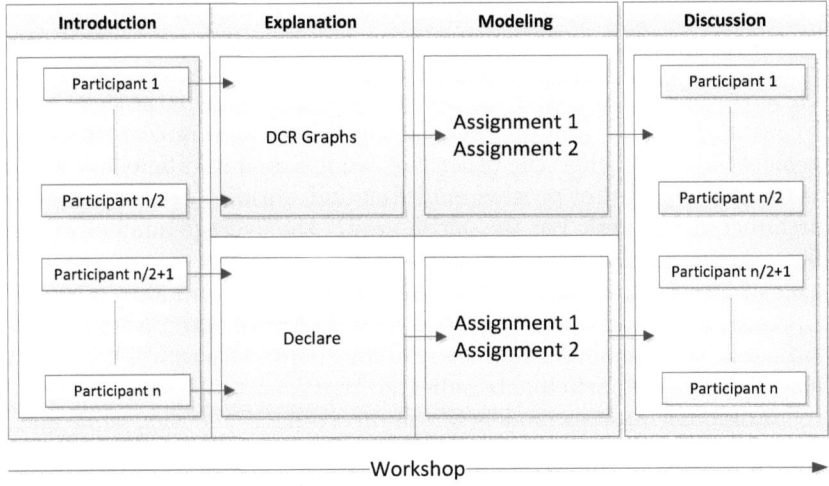

Fig. 3. Organization of the workshop

translate the assignment material into process models (*Modeling*). Clearly, the sub-group who received the tutorial on DCR Graphs used this technique; the other sub-group used Declare. The assignments can be found back at http://www.win.tue.nl/ais/doku.php?id=research:declare:bpm2013. As we were not so much interested in checking the correctness of the solutions but in transferring knowledge on the techniques to the participants, we encouraged them to work in pairs within each sub-group.

The final phase re-united the sub-groups (*Discussion*). During this phase, we first had the participants fill out a questionnaire on usefulness, ease of use, and intent to use as proposed by Moody [17]. The questionnaire can be used to get a broad-brush insight into the perceived quality of an IS design method, building on the concepts known from the Technology Acceptance Model as proposed by Davis [6]. We extended the questions with some more to gather demographic data on the group. The used questions can also be found at http://www.win.tue.nl/ais/doku.php?id=research:declare:bpm2013. After the questionnaire, we engaged in a semi-structured discussion with the group. This discussion was moderated by one of the authors, while the other authors took notes. The independently taken notes were used to reach consensus on how the participants reflected on the questions.

The insights that we gathered during the last phase of the evaluation with the questionnaire will be referred to as the *quantitative evaluation*, because the design of Davis' list allows for measuring the strength of the perceptions on ease of use, usefulness, and intent to use. Our insights on the modeling phase and the open part of the discussion phase will be dealt with as the *qualitative evaluation*, as they add a qualifying lens on the results. These respective evaluations will be discussed next.

4 Quantitative Evaluation

4.1 Demographics

Overall, ten professionals participated in the workshop. Of these, five are active as consultants, modeling processes at client sites and implementing process management software, while the other five are involved in different roles associated to the development of process modeling and workflow tools (product manager/architect/developer). For the entire group, the average number of years of experience in the BPM domain was more than 11 years. Of the ten participants, on a scale of 1 to 5, three considered themselves to have an intermediate expertise in process modeling (level=3), three to have an advanced level of expertise (level=4), and the remaining four people considered themselves to be experts (level=5). Finally, the participants indicated that on average they had each read close to 15 different process models in the preceding 12 months, while each had created or updated nearly four models on average in the same period. We are aware that the number of professionals is rather low. However, within a given time frame, we were choosing the day for which most professionals indicated their availability.

4.2 Validity and Reliability

Prior to performing an in-depth analysis of the data that had been gathered through the questionnaire, the validity and reliability of the empirical indicators were checked. We determined all correlations between the responses for questions that were used to measure to same construct (inter-item correlations) and identified no item that displayed a low convergent validity. In other words, the questions and their grouping to measure the constructs appeared valid. Next, we used Cronbach's alpha to test the reliability of the items to measure the various constructs. This is a test to check internal consistency of the questions. While there is no authoritative level for Cronbach's alpha, it is generally assumed that levels above 0.7 point at a good reliability of the items [18]. Adequate levels were established for *Perceived Usefulness* (0.743) and *Perceived Ease of Use* (0.826). However, *Intention to Use* scored too low (0.600). For this reason, we removed the latter construct from our main analysis and will only report on the mean scores of the items. Note that it was the only construct measured using just two items—an approach to be reconsidered in future applications of the questionnaire.

4.3 Results

Our main analysis then focused on this question: Are the considered techniques, DCR Graphs vs. Declare, perceived differently by the groups? To select the appropriate technique, we established with the Shapiro-Wilk test that the respondent answers were normally distributed. We could, therefore, proceed with applying a one-way ANOVA test with Perceived Usefulness and Perceived Ease

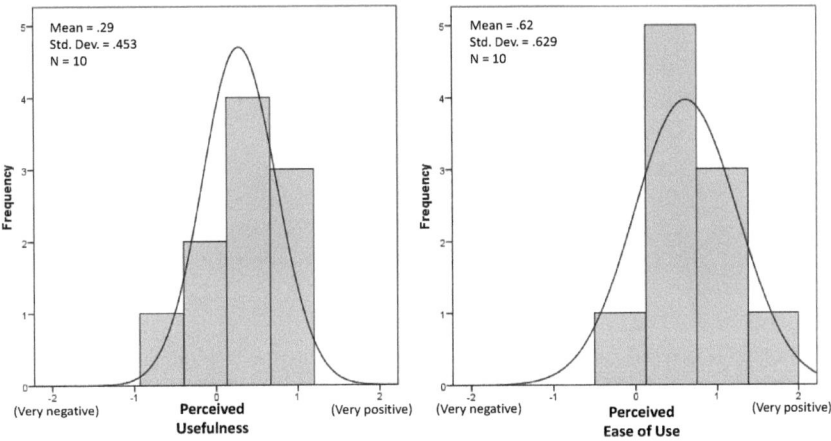

Fig. 4. Histograms for Perceived Usefulness and Perceived Ease of Use

of Use as dependent variables and the technique employed as factor. The test generated p-values of 0.116 and 0.939 for Perceived Usefulness and Perceived Ease of Use, respectively. By maintaining a confidence level of 95%, both of these values exceed the 0.05 threshold. In other words, any differences in perception between the used techniques are not statistically significant. Therefore, we must reject the idea that people perceive the techniques as different in either their usefulness or their ease of use.

This first important insight allows us to aggregate the responses received from both groups to determine a view on the usefulness and ease of use of declarative techniques on a more general level. Figure 4 shows the histograms for the two constructs under consideration, Perceived Usefulness and Perceived Ease of Use, aggregating the responses from all ten respondents. Also displayed is the fitted normal distribution for both constructs.

The histograms display the frequencies of the scores on a scale of -2.0 (very negative) to +2.0 (very positive). The 0 value indicates the neutral stance (not negative, not positive). What can be seen is that the averages of the distributions for both constructs are positive, hinting at a receptive mood toward declarative techniques in terms of both constructs. Note that the mean values for the two items under consideration for Intention to Use are 0.00 and 1.00. Second, Perceived Ease of Use seems to be more positively evaluated than Perceived Usefulness, with respective mean values of 0.62 and 0.29.

To determine whether the optically favorable outcomes are indeed statistically significant, we applied one sample t-tests. Like in our previous test, we used a confidence level of 95%, which means that we will only treat p-values below 0.05 as statistically significant. The outcomes of the t-tests are that the positive mean score for Perceived Ease of Use is significantly different from zero (p=0.013), but that this is—just—not the case for Perceived Usefulness (p=0.076). In other words, one can trust that the positive stance toward the ease of use is not a matter of chance. However, this cannot be ruled out for usefulness, despite its closeness to the cut-off value. Apparently, the involved respondents can easily use the method, despite the limited amount of training received. They were not similarly outspoken about the usefulness of a declarative technique, albeit certainly not negative either.

We finally checked whether the years of experience, the level of expertise, the type of role (consultant vs. non-consultant), or the modeling intensity in terms of models read or created had any relation to the outcomes. Interestingly, we could see that the most negative responses on Perceived Usefulness came from those respondents who assessed their own level of process modeling expertise as relatively low. While on average the three respondents with an intermediate expertise assessed the usefulness of the declarative techniques as negative (-0.208), the advanced modelers and the experts were positive (0.417 and 0.563, respectively). Tukey's HSD (Honestly Significant Difference) confirmed that the self-assessed level of expertise was a significant factor to explain differences in scores on Perceived Usefulness ($p=0.042$). In other words, the higher the level of expertise, the more merit a participant saw in the declarative techniques. The other factors had no noticeable effects on the scores.

5 Qualitative Evaluation

In this section, we present the qualitative evaluation of the workshop. In particular, we report on the results of the modeling assignment and of the discussion with the professionals.

5.1 Modeling Assignment

As reported in Sect. 3, we split the ten professionals into two groups of five. One group got an introduction to Declare and the other group to DCR Graphs. After this introduction of about 30 minutes, each group was asked to work on two small modeling assignments. One assignment was the document management system, which we used to illustrate Declare and DCR Graphs in Sect. 2. The second assignment was a hospital process of similar size and level of difficulty. The professionals worked in groups of two and three on the two assignments. Each assignment took less than 15 minutes, after which we presented and discussed our solution. All four groups came up with a correct solution for each of the two assignments.

The way we organized the assignment does not allow us to derive overly strong conclusions. Still, we gained two interesting insights. First, the result of the assignment shows that it is possible to teach declarative modeling to practitioners. Although it was difficult for the professionals to get used to the declarative way of modeling and to the graphical notations of the techniques, they came up with correct models in reasonable time. Second, we were told that the graphical notation of Declare and DCR Graphs are too academic and for practitioners neither convincing nor intuitive. Moreover, also the informal description, which we provided for each introduced constraint, did not help them to easily identify the constraint they needed. These comments hold for both techniques, DCR Graphs and Declare. This comes, indeed, not as a surprise as both formalisms have an academic background. However, we expected DCR Graphs to be more comprehensible and easier to use than Declare because DCR Graphs only consist of five relations, whereas Declare requires to learn a larger set of constraints.

5.2 Opportunities for a Declarative Approach

In the subsequent discussion with the professionals, we tried to figure out whether they see opportunities for a declarative modeling approach. Clearly, such a question is difficult to answer given the the short tutorials and only taking two assignments. The participants did indicate that there are probably processes that can be modeled most naturally using the imperative approach, while others would fit better with the declarative approach. For example, a clearly well-structured process of registering a newborn at a townhall can be modeled most naturally in an imperative way whereas the document management system of Sect. 2 is an example of a process that can be modeled most natural in a declarative way. In addition, in almost all processes the professionals came across, there were always at least parts or subprocesses where an imperative approach seems most natural. So, the conclusion to this question is that a purely declarative approach seems less attractive than a *hybrid approach*, which combines imperative and declarative modeling aspects.

5.3 Requirements Concerning a Declarative/Hybrid Approach

In the previous section, we showed that practitioners see opportunities for a hybrid approach. Next, we report on the practitioners' requirements concerning the specification, the constraints, the process, and tool support.

The consensus was that the efficient design of a declarative model (or of the declarative part of a hybrid model) will require a declarative specification. The reason is that it can be nontrivial to derive constraints from an imperative specification. We received one comment that it might be difficult to get a declarative specification at all, but we are not that pessimistic. Based on our experience, it depends on how one formulates questions to domain experts; that is, asking about the relationship between two activities (i.e., declarative) rather than which steps can be performed in a certain state (i.e., imperative) will allow one to come up with a declarative specification.

Other requirements concern the constraints. The involved professionals brought forward that too many constraints may negatively influence the quality of a declarative model. For example, many constraints affecting few activities may result in an unreadable model. Furthermore, they assumed the completeness of the constraints to be crucial, although that is similar to the completeness of the branching conditions in an imperative model.

Looking at the process model or the specification to identify "candidate" parts that may benefit from a declarative modeling approach, the professionals suggested to identify parts that have many dependencies (e.g., spaghetti-like parts). Although such parts seem good candidates, it is unclear whether a declarative way of modeling results in a better model. Another suggestion was to identify those parts where much modeling freedom is; for example, a set of concurrent activities (that preferably occur more than once) with only few dependencies may result in a simpler declarative model than their imperative counterpart.

Finally, also proper tool support is a hard requirement. Here, in particular, the professionals saw deficits in the usability of the academic techniques when used in a pen-and-paper fashion. We shall discuss tool support in Sect. 5.6 in more detail.

5.4 Use Cases for a Declarative/Hybrid Approach

In this section, we list use cases for the declarative approach as identified during the discussion.

Process evolution [21] was mentioned as the main use case by the involved professionals—that is, manage processes along the various changes it encounters. Having a set of constraints rather than a graph-based model seems to be beneficial to visualize changes over time, on the one hand and to actually change a process model, on the other hand. This is, in fact, one of the claimed advantages of declarative modeling [3,15]. The "outside-in" approach of declarative models allows for a higher level of abstraction than an imperative process model. Therefore, it is often simpler to add or remove constraints than changing a BPMN model, for instance.

The discussion also suggested that the use case for declarative models is tied to model purpose. Process models serve different purposes—for example, as a medium to communicate with stakeholders (i.e., communication model) or to execute a process (i.e., executable model). Especially with respect to the communication aspect, the professionals saw good opportunities for using declarative techniques. Communication models are rather imprecise (e.g., exceptions may be left out), and business analysts do not tend to stick to model conventions. Instead, they may prefer to use short hands to illustrate behavior in a simplified way, for instance. Here, a hybrid approach looks promising as the business analyst is provided with a lot of different ways to present the model. Again, this follows from the higher level of abstraction of declarative models. In contrast, there was no common agreement on a declarative approach being useful for specifying executable models. As an executable model contains all behavior, a hybrid approach will only be beneficial if it allows for designing more readable or simpler models.

Another interesting aspect mentioned was that a hybrid approach may result in fewer errors in the model than using a purely imperative approach. This may lead to shorter development cycles. We think that this is also a consequence of the higher level of abstraction in declarative modeling. A modeler has to identify the constraints rather than encode it in terms of control flow. However, no experience report or empirical results exist that confirm this assumption.

5.5 Limitations of a Declarative/Hybrid Approach

In this section, we report on limitations of a declarative/hybrid approach concerning the specification, the modeling paradigm, and the usability.

The main concern regarding the specification is that currently all specifications are imperative (e.g., "we first do this, then that"), and it seems to be very difficult to produce a declarative model for such a specification. As discussed in Sect. 5.3, we think that it is possible to receive declarative specifications.

There has been a paradigm shift in system development from monolithic systems to component-based systems that are distributed within and across organizational boundaries. One prominent computing paradigm that implements this trend is service-oriented computing (SOC) [19]. We received concerns that in this setting declarative modeling techniques may be less applicable compared to imperative techniques. The reason for this concern lies in the fact that certain constraints affect activities of an individual component, whereas other constraints affect activities of different components. Declarative techniques have, however, been successfully applied in the service-oriented setting [14,15], and it has been studied how a declarative cross-organizational workflow containing global constraints can be projected to its individual localized components [11], so we are convinced that this concern is unsubstantiated.

Another limitation concerns the usability of existing techniques and tools. Current tool support is mainly academic by nature and seems, therefore, not overly concerned with usability issues. Moreover, the declarative paradigm also requires a different way of thinking, making it perhaps difficult for practitioners to understand declarative models. Here, more research is required to make declarative techniques more comprehensible.

5.6 Requirements Concerning Tool Support

In this section, we report on feedback we received concerning Declare and DCR Graphs and general requirements concerning tool support.

Several requirements on tools that were discussed deal with the specification and visualization of *constraints*. As mentioned earlier in Sect. 5.1, the professionals mentioned that working with constraints was relatively difficult for them. The graphical notations used in Declare and DCR Graphs were not always that intuitive. Moreover, specifying constraints in plain English is not always helpful either, because it is often nontrivial to identify the differences between two constraints. Therefore, the professionals proposed that constraints should be automatically derived from an informal textual specification. This problem has indeed been investigated in the field of computer-aided verification, for instance. Different approaches have been proposed, for example [7,5], but none of them could solve the problem entirely.

A given set of constraints makes it necessary to check for conflicting constraints. This is a feature which has been implemented in most declarative modeling tools [24], but has also been investigated in the context of compliance rules [4], for instance. Another important feature is to generate a model from a given set of constraints and to identify missing features. This problems is related to scenario-based programming [10]. In case an implementation and recorded event logs exist, process mining techniques to automatically derive missing constraints from the logs are required. First attempts at dealing with this topic exist, see [13].

Besides modeling support, tools should preferably also provide operational support. For example, event logs may be exploited to provide at runtime the best possible next step. Such features are implemented in recommender systems.

Finally, usability plays an important role. Specification of constraints, their graphical representation and the complete interplay between the tool and an end user must be on an abstraction level that is adequate to the task at hand.

6 Research Agenda

In this section, we pick up the results from the discussion with the professionals as presented in the previous section. We propose a research agenda for the development of a hybrid modeling approach that combines imperative and declarative techniques. The aim is thereby to point out necessary steps for developing and actually using a hybrid technique rather than a complete research agenda.

Model guidelines. In order to apply the hybrid approach, a modeler has to know when to model in an imperative and when in a declarative way. In other words, we need to identify modeling guidelines to guide modelers through the modeling process. This requires rules for identifying imperative and declarative "candidate" parts on the level of an existing (imperative) process model (e.g., for process redesign), on the level of event logs (e.g., for process discovery), and on the level of (informal) specifications (e.g., for designing a new model).

Identify the hybrid technique. Modeling in a hybrid way requires a well-suited modeling language. It needs to be investigated whether we can combine existing imperative and declarative languages or whether a new language has to be designed. For instance, we can integrate a declarative part as a subprocess into an imperative model (e.g., as a hierarchical transition in a Petri net or subprocess task in BPMN) or we can allow declarative and imperative constructs to coexist within a single subprocess. The modeling language must in any case support hierarchy. In the latest version of CPN Tools [23], Westergaard integrated DCR Graphs and Declare into Colored Petri nets. It turned out that defining the semantics of such models is nontrivial.

Beside that, it needs to be settled which constraints are relevant for practise and, thus, what the expressiveness of the declarative part of the language is. Empirical research has shown [8,9] that certain declarative constructs may be more difficult to understand. Thus, we think the language should not contain too many declarative constructs, but this needs further empirical investigation.

Also, the graphical representation of hybrid models must be investigated. Different graphical notations exist, for example, compare DCR Graphs and Declare. Insights from [16] may aid the design of a hybrid notation.

Analysis of hybrid models. The novel modeling approach needs analysis techniques including the verification of models, performance analysis, and property-preserving abstraction and refinement techniques. Also, process mining techniques [1] are needed—for example, checking the conformance of an event log and a hybrid model and discovering a hybrid model from a given event log.

Tool support. To show the applicability of the hybrid modeling technique, tool support is a *sine qua no*. As reported in Sect. 5.6, research has to be performed to simplify the use of declarative techniques, for example, finding a way to derive constraints from informal specifications that can be used by business analysts without requiring knowledge about temporal logics.

7 Conclusion

We reported on a workshop on declarative modeling given to professionals from industry. The goal of this workshop was to gain insight into what practitioners think about declarative modeling and what opportunities they see to use this technique. Our quantitative evaluation showed that they were mostly positive and open to this modeling paradigm. In particular, the techniques were rather easy to learn. The qualitative evaluation showed that the practitioners did single out the use of declarative techniques in the context of a hybrid approach, which combines imperative and declarative modeling. Although our study is only based on a small group of practitioners, we are convinced that practise can benefit from such a hybrid modeling approach. To arrive at such an approach, we proposed a research agenda for the development of a hybrid approach.

In our ongoing research, we plan to work on the development of modeling guidelines. We will investigate techniques to identify "candidate" parts of a model for which a declarative way of modeling seems most natural. Also, we plan to study event logs and process models and try to use the results to identify constraints that frequently occur. In a second branch of research, we will investigate what a hybrid technique may look like, thereby using Declare, DCR Graphs and CPN Tools as starting points for our studies.

References

1. van der Aalst, W.M.P.: Process Mining: Discovery, Conformance and Enhancement of Business Processes. Springer (2011)
2. van der Aalst, W.M.P.: Business process management: A comprehensive survey. ISRN Software Engineering (2013)
3. van der Aalst, W.M.P., Pesic, M., Schonenberg, H.: Declarative workflows: Balancing between flexibility and support. Computer Science - R&D 23(2), 99–113 (2009)
4. Awad, A., Weidlich, M., Weske, M.: Consistency checking of compliance rules. In: Abramowicz, W., Tolksdorf, R. (eds.) BIS 2010. LNBIP, vol. 47, pp. 106–118. Springer, Heidelberg (2010)
5. Cobleigh, R.L., Avrunin, G.S., Clarke, L.A.: User guidance for creating precise and accessible property specifications. In: SIGSOFT FSE, pp. 208–218. ACM (2006)

6. Davis, F.D.: Perceived usefulness, perceived ease of use, and user acceptance of information technology. MIS Q. 13(3), 319–340 (1989)
7. Dwyer, M.B., Avrunin, G.S., Corbett, J.C.: Patterns in property specifications for finite-state verification. In: ICSE 1999, pp. 411–420. ACM (1999)
8. Fahland, D., Lübke, D., Mendling, J., Reijers, H., Weber, B., Weidlich, M., Zugal, S.: Declarative versus imperative process modeling languages: The issue of understandability. In: Halpin, T., Krogstie, J., Nurcan, S., Proper, E., Schmidt, R., Soffer, P., Ukor, R. (eds.) BPMDS 2009. LNBIP, vol. 29, pp. 353–366. Springer, Heidelberg (2009)
9. Fahland, D., Mendling, J., Reijers, H.A., Weber, B., Weidlich, M., Zugal, S.: Declarative versus imperative process modeling languages: The issue of maintainability. In: Rinderle-Ma, S., Sadiq, S., Leymann, F. (eds.) BPM 2009. LNBIP, vol. 43, pp. 477–488. Springer, Heidelberg (2010)
10. Harel, D.: Come, let's play - scenario-based programming using LSCs and the play-engine. Springer (2003)
11. Hildebrandt, T., Mukkamala, R.R., Slaats, T.: Safe distribution of declarative processes. In: Barthe, G., Pardo, A., Schneider, G. (eds.) SEFM 2011. LNCS, vol. 7041, pp. 237–252. Springer, Heidelberg (2011)
12. Hildebrandt, T., Mukkamala, R.R.: Declarative event-based workflow as distributed dynamic condition response graphs. In: PLACES 2010. EPTCS, vol. 69, pp. 59–73 (2010)
13. Maggi, F.M., Bose, R.P.J.C., van der Aalst, W.M.P.: Efficient discovery of understandable declarative process models from event logs. In: Ralyté, J., Franch, X., Brinkkemper, S., Wrycza, S. (eds.) CAiSE 2012. LNCS, vol. 7328, pp. 270–285. Springer, Heidelberg (2012)
14. Karpinski, M.: Specification and Verification of Declarative Open Interaction Models - A Logic-Based Approach. LNBIP, vol. 56. Springer (1977)
15. Montali, M., Pesic, M., van der Aalst, W.M.P., Chesani, F., Mello, P., Storari, S.: Declarative specification and verification of service choreographiess. TWEB 4(1) (2010)
16. Moody, D.: The physicsof notations: toward a scientific basis for constructing visual notations in software engineering. IEEE Transactions on Software Engineering 35(6), 756–779 (2009)
17. Moody, D.L.: The method evaluation model: a theoretical model for validating information systems design methods. In: ECIS 2003, pp. 1327–1336 (2003)
18. Nunnally, J.C.: Psychometric theory. McGraw-Hill, New York (1978)
19. Papazoglou, M.: Web Services - Principles and Technology. Prentice Hall (2008)
20. Pichler, P., Weber, B., Zugal, S., Pinggera, J., Mendling, J., Reijers, H.A.: Imperative versus declarative process modeling languages: An empirical investigation. In: Daniel, F., Barkaoui, K., Dustdar, S. (eds.) BPM Workshops 2011, Part I. LNBIP, vol. 99, pp. 383–394. Springer, Heidelberg (2012)
21. Reichert, M., Weber, B.: Enabling Flexibility in Process-Aware Information Systems. Springer (2012)
22. Weber, B., Reijers, H.A., Zugal, S., Wild, W.: The declarative approach to business process execution: An empirical test. In: van Eck, P., Gordijn, J., Wieringa, R. (eds.) CAiSE 2009. LNCS, vol. 5565, pp. 470–485. Springer, Heidelberg (2009)
23. Westergaard, M.: CPN Tools 4: Multi-formalism and Extensibility. In: Colom, J.-M., Desel, J. (eds.) PETRI NETS 2013. LNCS, vol. 7927, pp. 400–409. Springer, Heidelberg (2013)
24. Westergaard, M., Maggi, F.M.: Declare: A tool suite for declarative workflow modeling and enactment. In: BPM (Demos) 2011. CEUR Workshop Proceedings, vol. 820, CEUR-WS.org (2011)

Investigating Clinical Care Pathways Correlated with Outcomes

Geetika T. Lakshmanan, Szabolcs Rozsnyai, and Fei Wang

IBM T.J. Watson Research Center, Hawthorne, NY, USA
{gtlakshm,srozsny,fwang}@us.ibm.com

Abstract. Clinical care pathway analysis is the process of discovering how clinical activities impact patients in their care journeys, and uses the discovered knowledge for various applications including the redesign and optimization of clinical pathways. We present an approach for mining clinical care pathways correlated with patient outcomes that involves a combination of clustering, process mining and frequent pattern mining. Our approach is implemented as a set of interactive tools in the business process insight (BPI) platform, a a collaborative software as a service platform, that provides an event-driven process-aware analytics toolset. After interactively utilizing the individual clustering, process mining, and frequent pattern mining capabilities in BPI, users can overlay frequent patterns, ranked according to their correlation with a particular patient outcome, on a mined model of the patient population with that outcome. We have tested our approach for mining care pathways correlated with outcomes on electronic medical record data obtained from a US based healthcare provider on congestive heart failure (CHF) patients. Experimental results show that the tools we have developed and implemented can provide new insights to facilitate the improvement of existing clinical care pathways.

Keywords: Care pathway, clustering, frequent pattern mining, process mining.

1 Introduction

A clinical pathway, guided by clinical practice guidelines, is a standardized therapy pattern and procedure for a specific disease that follows contemporary clinical experts' experiences [14,16]. Researchers in medical informatics and process-aware analytics have paid significant attention to the analysis of clinical care pathways [36,15,8]. Clinical pathway analysis is the process of discovering how clinical activities impact patients in their care journeys, and uses the discovered knowledge for various applications including clinical pathway redesign, clinical pathway optimization, clinical decision support, and medical deviation detection [14]. In this paper we address the problem of mining clinical care pathways correlated with patient outcomes from healthcare data. Among other things, this could allow a healthcare professional to determine whether the pathway is compliant with care pathway guidelines for a particular disease, and identify which additional or lack of activities beyond the care pathway guidelines contributed to positive or negative patient outcomes.

Healthcare processes are dynamic, complex and ad-hoc [32]. Process changes occur due to a variety of reasons including new administrative procedures, technological developments, or drug discovery. The complexity arises from many factors such as complex medical decision processes, large amounts of data, and the unpredictability of patients and treatments. Healthcare depends significantly on human collaboration, and participants have the expertise and autonomy to decide their own procedures [25,21]. As demonstrated in recent work [25,32,26,20], process mining and clustering are useful tools to address these challenges in healthcare data, and can be used to mine clinical care pathways.

In this paper, we provide users with an interactive set of tools to extract and visualize clinical care pathway related insight from healthcare data. The tools include trace clustering, process mining, frequent pattern mining, and the ability to overlay frequent patterns on the mined model. Many existing studies on healthcare data [32,25,36,14] use data that is available from healthcare information systems, and therefore the data contains activity events such as *scan abdomen*, *CT scan brain*, *follow-up visit* etc. The data used in our study, however, is electronic medical record (EMR) data. Such EMR data consists of events including diagnoses, medication orders, laboratory reports and vital statistics for a given patient.

Extracting and visualizing care pathways correlated with outcomes is challenging particularly on EMR data. Such data typically contains a large proportion of events occurring on the same day. In addition there is incredible diversity in the range of event names. In this paper we describe some data pre-processing strategies and an algorithm to collapse same day events to address these issues. Due to their dynamic, complex, and ad-hoc nature, healthcare process instances are disparate and there may be a plethora of treatment pathways correlated with positive or negative patient outcomes. We describe an algorithm to mine clinical care pathways using frequent pattern mining, and rank the frequent patterns according to the degree of their correlation with a patient outcome. An individual care pathway mined from real patient event data in the form of a frequent pattern may contain a small subset of the overall possible set of events that could be applied to treat a particular disease. Healthcare professionals need some context with which to interpret a frequent pattern care pathway. We describe an interactive tool to overlay each individual frequent pattern, representing a single care pathway, on a mined process model of all care pathways of a segment of the patient population. The patient population is segmented by outcome where the outcome criteria is established on our dataset with the help of an expert physician. The overlay capability provides healthcare professionals with some context with which to interpret a frequent pattern care pathway with respect to the overall set of treatment events for a disease. We also describe a trace clustering algorithm to eliminate outliers in the patient data.

We have implemented the tools introduced in this paper in an existing collaborative platform called business process insight (BPI) [33] that provides process-aware analytics tools in a software as a service (SaaS) environment. Process mining is an existing capability BPI. Clustering, frequent pattern mining, and the ability to overlay frequent patterns on a mined process model have been developed and implemented as additional features of BPI during the course of this work. We report on the use of these tools to investigate clinical care pathways correlated with outcomes on real EMR data collected from 4096 patients diagnosed with congestive heart failure (CHF) belonging to a US-based healthcare provider. The utility of the tools was validated with the help of an expert physician with 20+ years of experience in treating CHF patients.

2 Related Work

There is considerable existing work on the application of process mining, clustering and frequent pattern mining on healthcare data. In this section we survey state of the art work in each of these fields and outline differences between existing works and our approach. The uniqueness of our contribution stems from the combination of these three techniques in a single interactive toolset.

Process mining has been applied extensively in healthcare. HeuristicsMiner, social network analysis, and dotted chart analysis are used for obtaining insights into care flow data in [25]. A methodology for analyzing business processes in a healthcare environment using sequence clustering and process mining is presented in [32]. The use of fuzzy mining and trace alignment for investigating clinical pathway data is proposed by [7]. The applicability of various mining techniques to healthcare data by adopting both a department and treatment based focus is discussed in [8]. The benefits of both a drill up and drill down perspective on the data relying on control-flow discovery with the Fuzzy Miner and networked graph visualizations are presented in [36]. The effectiveness of several process mining algorithms on Magnetic Resonance Imaging (MRI), ultrasound and X-ray appointments within a Radiology workflow has been explored in [20]. Hidden Markov Models in combination with process mining techniques are used to investigate care pathways for breast cancer patients in [30]. Use of process mining and clustering to discover patient journeys has been examined in [29]. A new process mining approach is introduced in [14] to discover temporal orders of medical behaviors in clinical pathways. Data mining techniques inspired by process mining are applied to detect time dependency patterns in clinical pathways in [23].

There is a significant amount of work on clustering techniques for business processes. A method to group process instances based on similar behavior is presented in [6,35]. They use methods to determine transitions between activities to derive the underlying process model and relate instances to that shared common behavioral model. Some work has been devoted to organize, group and cluster process models based on similarities such as structure and contained data (organizations, activity names, etc) [31]. These techniques are based on defined static process models not on process execution footprints. This problem and the solutions are different from the trace clustering method applied in this paper. Evaluating different similarity measures for clustering process instances using a density based clustering algorithm for evaluation (DBSCAN) is done in [18]. While we also use a density based clustering algorithm for clustering process instances, we use a different representation for process instances and distance metrics. In the clustering approach discussed in [17] processes are represented as weighted graphs and similarity measures are based on graph vectors that are estimated based on activity and transition frequencies. Similarly in [34] clustering is based on computing graph similarity. Improving process mining techniques by hierarchical clustering of execution traces is presented in [13] in which each trace is viewed as a point in a properly identified space of features. Another approach for optimizing mined process models using clustering is presented in [2], where process models (not instances such as in our work) are translated into string representations representing all possible execution permutations.

There is a significant amount of work on the application of frequent pattern mining techniques to healthcare data. A technique to mine discriminative dyadic sequential patterns is presented in [24]. It cannot handle sequences with same-day concurrent events. A tree based algorithm for identifying discriminative patterns is presented in [9]. It does not however use a pattern based representation for events, and cannot handle sequences with same-day concurrent events. A statistical approach for summarizing and visualizing temporal associations between the prescription of a drug and the occurrence of a medical event is presented in [28]. This is quite different from the use of frequent patterns in our work. Another approach for temporal pattern discovery is presented in [27] that requires a predefined temporal grammar and logic with prior knowledge. A visual interface [11] for finding temporal patterns in multivariate temporal clinical data is used in [4] for searching for temporal patterns in patient histories and requires users to specify the structure of the pattern.

3   Identifying Care Pathways Correlated with Outcomes

In order to identify care pathways correlated with outcomes several steps are performed as outlined in Fig 1. The patient population is first segmented by patient outcomes, and events are pre-processed. Irrelevant events are removed and raw event names are replaced by hierarchical category names. EMR data typically has a lot of same day events. We designed and implemented a same day concurrent event collapse algorithm to address this problem. After pre-processing, users of BPI can either mine frequent patterns from patient events or perform patient trace clustering or mine a process model from traces created from the data. We conduct trace clustering first in order to remove outliers from the patient pool before performing frequent pattern mining and process mining on a set of clustered traces. Next, each frequent pattern can be overlaid on the mined process model, or users can choose a different cluster or do clustering again with different parameters. This section describes the details of the data

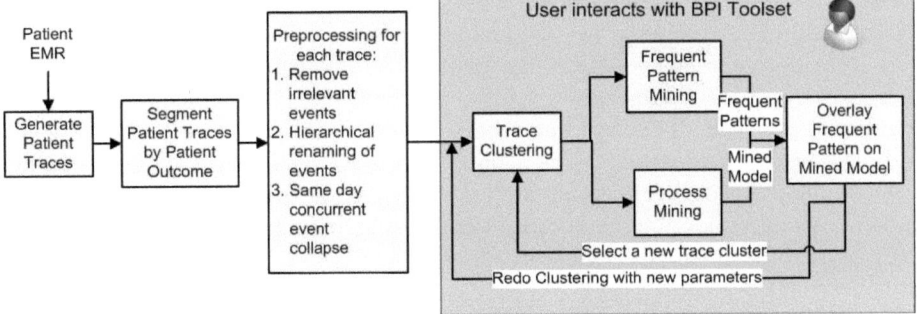

Fig. 1. An overview of our end to end approach

pre-processing steps, and the algorithms applied for clustering, frequent pattern mining and overlaying frequent patterns on a mined model.

3.1 Segmenting Patients by Outcome and Hierarchical Renaming of Events

We tested our methodology on data belonging to 4096 patients already diagnosed with CHF in ambulatory care (i.e. outpatient setting) consisting of EMR data containing diagnoses, prescribed medications, labs and vital signs recorded over several years from a US healthcare provider. With the help of the CHF expert physician we defined criteria for positive and negative outcomes, and segmented the patient population according to this criteria. Patients hospitalized within one year of being diagnosed with CHF are classified as negative outcome patients. Patients not hospitalized up to one year or more after being diagnosed with CHF are classified as positive outcome patients. There were a total of 2197 patients with positive outcomes in our data set. In the expert physician's opinion, one year is a sufficiently large enough time period to extract care pathways correlated with a positive outcome. For each negative outcome patient, events are collected up to their first hospital admission date. For each positive outcome patient, events are collected up to one year of the patient being diagnosed with CHF.

The EMR data we received contained many redundancies in event names. For example, 40 different medication names all corresponded to renal failure medication. Using publicly available medical vocabularies, we developed a set of hierarchical category names to replace each individual event name in the medications, labs, and diagnoses event classes. The expert physician provided guidance to identify the level of granularity at which to perform this transformation in each event class. For medications we used publicly available pharmacy subclass names to identify medications with different names that served the same purpose. We also concatenated the level of CHF treated by the pharmacy subclass with the pharmacy subclass name (e.g. AntianginalAgents4 represents Antianginal agents used to treat CHF level 4). This resulted in a total of 9 different kinds of medication events. All medication events not related to the treatment of CHF were discarded. For diagnoses, we used publicly available DXGroup names to rename and classify individual diagnosis names, and discarded diagnoses events that were not related to CHF. This resulted in a total of 11 different kinds of diagnoses events. For labs, we restricted events to labs performed specifically in connection to CHF. This resulted in a total of 30 different kinds of lab events, and we discarded all other types of labs. For each set of vital signs (e.g. heart rate, blood pressure etc), we created a single *Vital* event type, and gave it a timestamp corresponding to the date coinciding with the recording of a set of vital signs for a given patient.

3.2 Same Day Concurrent Event Collapse

An issue that affects the efficiency of temporal pattern mining and the quality of process mining is when many events happen simultaneously. This is particularly true when the time granularity of the patient EMR is low resolution. Typical to many EMRs (especially outpatient records), the finest time resolution is a *day*, and during a day, multiple medical events may occur to a patient. For example, the patient may have multiple lab tests performed, diagnoses made, and medications prescribed on the same day that the patient visits their primary care physician.

Algorithm 1. Breaking Down a SDCE

Require: A SDCE S to be broken down, Pre-detected Clinical Event Packages (CEP)
 1: Sort the detected CEPs into buckets according to their cardinalities (number of events contained), such that the packages within the same bucket have the same cardinality.
 2: Sort the packages within the same bucket with their appearance frequencies in the patient traces.
 3: $\mathcal{O} = \emptyset$
 4: **for** Every bucket $\mathcal{B}$ **do**
 5:   **if** length($\mathcal{B}$) <length($\mathcal{S}$) **then**
 6:     **for** Every CEP $\mathcal{E}$ in $\mathcal{B}$ **do**
 7:       **if** $\mathcal{E}$ is a subset of s **then**
 8:         Add $\mathcal{E}$ to $\mathcal{O}$, Set $\mathcal{S} = \mathcal{S}\backslash\mathcal{E}$
 9:         **if** $\mathcal{S} == \emptyset$ **then**
10:           **Return** $\mathcal{O}$
11:         **else**
12:           Return to Step 4
13:         **end if**
14:       **end if**
15:     **end for**
16:   **end if**
17: **end for**

Such data characteristics yield a great challenge for frequent pattern mining algorithms, as they detect patterns with all possible combinations of events and subsets of events occurring at the same time. For instance, if we have A;B-->A;C as a frequent pattern, then A-->A, A-->C, A;B-->A, A;B-->C, A-->A;C, B-->A;C are all frequent patterns (a semicolon connotes events occurring at the same time). If there are even more concurrent events, the number of detected frequent patterns increases dramatically. We refer to this phenomenon as *pattern explosion*. An explosion of same timestamp events are also a challenge for process mining algorithms as the mining algorithm cannot extract a causal ordering between the events, and therefore the mined model representation of such events may not be reliable.

To alleviate these problems, we pre-process patient traces before feeding them to the frequent pattern miner. The goal is to reduce the number of events happening at the same time. There are many *Same Day Concurrent Events* (SDCEs) contained in patient EMRs, thus we first detect the frequent *Clinical Event Packages* (CEPs) that are frequent subsets of SDCEs. If we treat each SDCE in every patient trace as a *transaction*, then the problem of detecting those CEPs is equivalent to the problem of *frequent itemset mining* [1], and each detected CEP can be used as a *super event*. Then, a greedy approach is applied based on *Two-Way Sorting* to break down each SDCE as a combination of regular and super events, such that the number of events contained in each SDCE is greatly reduced.

Algorithm 1 summarizes the main procedure of breaking down a specific SDCE. After the sorting procedure (line 1), all the CEP buckets are ordered from the largest cardinality to the lowest. After step 2, all CEPs within each bucket are ordered from the highest frequency to the lowest. The enumeration process of all buckets and CEPs in lines 4 and 6 is according to this order.

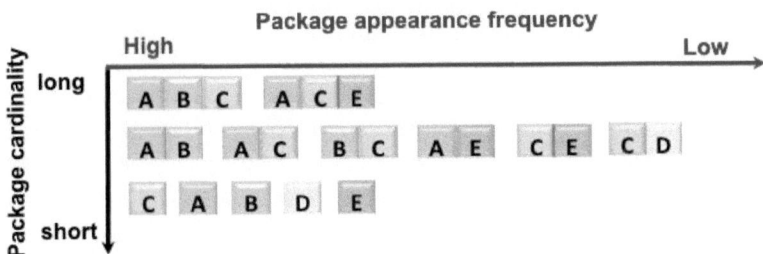

Fig. 2. A graphical illustration of how the two-way sorting procedure works. Mined clinical packages are first sorted according to their cardinalities. Next, packages with the same cardinality are sorted according to their frequency.

To illustrate the process of breaking down SDCEs, we provide an example: Suppose we have an SDCE ABCDE and we wish to break it down using the detected CEPs, shown in the central area of Figure 2. The algorithm then sorts the packages according to a two-way sorting strategy as shown in Figure 2. It first sorts the packages according to their cardinalities (length). Then, for packages with the same cardinality, they are sorted with respect to their appearance frequency. To breakdown ABCDE, the algorithm first finds the *longest* clinical packages that are subsets of ABCDE. In this example, ABC and ACE are the longest packages which are subsets of ABCDE. Then, because ABC occurs more frequently than ACE, ABC is selected as a super event contained in ABCDE. Besides ABC, the rest of the events are DE. The procedure is applied again to break down ABCDE as ABC,D, E. There are only 3 super events in ABCDE with our technique, as opposed to 5 events.

After conducting same day event collapse on the data according to this algorithm, users can either mine frequent patterns, or perform clustering after generating patient traces. In the next section (3.3) we provide details of the frequent pattern mining algorithm. In section 3.4 we provide details of the clustering algorithm we employed in order to remove patient traces that are outliers.

3.3 Frequent Pattern Mining

We first detect frequent patterns using SPAM (Sequential Pattern Mining with bitmap representation)[5], where we specified the support threshold as 15% meaning that a pattern must occur in at least 15% of the input patient traces. Next the patterns are collected into a dictionary and a *Bag-of-Pattern* (BoP) representation for each patient trace is constructed. Suppose the pattern dictionary size is m, then the BoP vector for each patient is an m-dimensional vector, such that the value on the ith dimension represents the frequency of the ith pattern in the corresponding patient trace. When counting pattern frequency, the bitmap representation of patient trace is applied, as done by SPAM, and pattern matching is done bit by bit. After a match is detected, we examine its validity by checking whether the duration of the match is shorter than a pre-specified threshold. Ultimately, the pattern frequency is the number of valid matches.

After BoP representation, all patient traces are represented as an $n \times m$ matrix $\mathbf{X}$, with X_{ij} indicating the frequency of the jth pattern in the ith patient's trace, and n is the number of patients. Suppose each patient has an outcome, which can be either discrete (e.g., hospitalized or not hospitalized) or continuous (e.g., HbA1c value for diabetes patients), we can construct an n-dimensional patient outcome vector $\mathbf{y}$. Let $\mathbf{x}_i$ be the ith column of $\mathbf{X}$, which characterizes the appearance frequency distribution of the ith pattern in different patient traces. We can now compute correlation statistics between each $\mathbf{x}_i$ ($i = 1, 2, \cdots, m$) and $\mathbf{y}$, and identify patterns with high correlation with patient outcomes. Specifically, we compute the *Information Gain*, $IG(\mathbf{x}_i, \mathbf{y})$, between a pattern x_i and an outcome y as follows[1]:

$$IG(\mathbf{x}_i, \mathbf{y}) = H(\mathbf{x}_i) - H(\mathbf{x}_i|\mathbf{y}) \qquad (1)$$

where

$$H(\mathbf{x}_i) = -\sum_\alpha P(x_{i_j} = \alpha) \log(P(x_{i_j} = \alpha)) \qquad (2)$$

---

[1] http://en.wikipedia.org/wiki/Information_gain_in_decision_trees

where $P(x_{i_j} = \alpha)$ is the probability that the j-th variable of x_i equals α, and

$$H(\mathbf{x}_i|\mathbf{y}) = - \sum_{\beta=\{-1,+1\}} P(y_i = \beta) \sum_{\alpha} P(x_{i_j} = \alpha | y_i = \beta) \log(P(x_{i_j} = \alpha | y_i = \beta)) \tag{3}$$

where $P(x_{i_j} = \alpha | y_i = \beta)$ is the conditional probability that the j-th variable of pattern x_i is α while its outcome is β.

$H(\cdot)$ is the entropy of a variable. For example, $H(\mathbf{x}_i|\mathbf{y})$ is the entropy of pattern x_i with respect to outcome y. We also compute the P-value [12] of $IG(\mathbf{x}_i, \mathbf{y})$ in order to check whether it is statistically significant.

3.4 Clustering

We apply the DBScan [10] clustering algorithm and use a custom string-based distance metric to determine the distance between process traces. The goal of this clustering method is to group process traces together based on, what we refer to as, *execution footprint*. Many existing clustering techniques [2,13,18,31,34] are based on process models rather than process execution footprints. As opposed to existing clustering methods, we do not take into account underlying process model, structure (e.g. transitions between events), event payloads or attribute data belonging to traces into account. We represent the sequence of events within a trace as a String where the position of characters within that String represents the temporal occurrence of events within a trace.

For all patients, all events related to a patient are grouped into a trace so that they reflect a given process instance. Each event contains a payload (i.e. timestamp etc). The events in a trace must be ordered corresponding to their temporal occurrence. This is achieved by having either a defined order of their occurrence or a timestamp. Each event type is uniquely mapped to a single digit unicode character. In case event names exceed the space of available Unicode characters, digits may be added to ensure a unique mapping. Every given trace is then transformed to a String representation, where the mapped Unicode character replaces the event type. The order of the Unicode characters within the String is determined by the order of the events within the process trace (i.e. through timestamp or defined order). We show a simple example of the mapping. The first step is to take all known event types and map them to Unicode characters as follows: $Heartfailure \to A$, $Diuretics \to B$, $AntianginalAgents \to C$, $Creatinine \to D$, $Vital \to E$. Each event in each trace $(T_1, T_2, ..., T_n)$ is then replaced by the corresponding mapped character as shown in table 1. As events within a trace are ordered (typically by time), the resulting character representation of a trace resembles that order. Each trace in its string representation $(T_n Mapped)$ is now equivalent to a point. DBScan computes clusters of such traces. By default most DBScan implementations rely on the Euclidean Distance and a point requires a numeric representation. In our case each point is a sequence of characters. Rather than Euclidean Distance, we use the Levenshtein distance [22]. The Levenshtein distance measures the amount of difference

Table 1. An example of traces and their corresponding string representations

T_1	Heartfailure → Diuretics → AntianginalAgents → Creatinine → Vital
$T_1 Mapped$	ABCDE
T_2	Heartfailure → Diuretics → AntianginalAgents → Diuretics → AntianginalAgents → ...
$T_2 Mapped$	ABCBC...

between two sequences (not necessarily of the same length) and allows determination of the number of operations required to transform one string into another. Thus, Levenshtein provides a good measure of similarity for our goal of finding similar execution patterns. DBScan requires two parameters to be initialized:

1. **MinPts**: Determines the minimum number of points required to form a cluster. In our setup this parameter is 1, which means that for every trace a cluster is created. This also means that a cluster containing 1 trace can be considered an outlier.
2. ϵ: represents the distance threshold between two points that can be considered to be similar.

Finding the optimal offset of ϵ can be achieved through experiments (by users) in combination with subjective expectations of what should correspond to a cluster. Depending on the user's preference, sometimes finer and sometimes more coarse-grained clusters are expected. In order to aid the user with this task, we implemented a utility to provide a suggestion for the offset by calculating the median Levenshtein distance between a sample set of all available traces. Calculating the median distance over all traces would take too long on a large set of traces. Experiments on data from various domains have shown that taking $\frac{1}{16}$th of the median distance provides an offset that produces clusters with finer granularity that is perceived by users to be a good starting point for the threshold. The clustering algorithm outputs groups of traces that share a similar execution sequence (based on Levenshtein string distance metric), the distance between individual clusters, and the size of clusters.

3.5 Overlaying Frequent Patterns on a Mined Process Model

To enable process mining, the well known HeuristicsMiner [3] algorithm is implemented and integrated into BPI. We choose HeuristicsMiner because it is robust to noise and incomplete trace sets [19], and therefore well suited for mining healthcare data [20,25]. The overlay algorithm first identifies every node in the frequent pattern that occurs in the mined process model and highlights the color of that node. For every two consecutive nodes, a and b in the frequent pattern, if an edge from a to b exists in the mined process model, that edge is highlighted. If an edge does not exist from a to b, we run Dijkstra's shortest path algorithm to determine the shortest path from a to b in the mined process model, and highlight that path. This procedure is repeated for every consecutive pair of nodes in the frequent pattern. For example, suppose *Cardiotonics4* → *Vital* → *Heartfailure* is a frequent pattern to be overlaid on a mined process model. Thus nodes Cardiotonics4, Vital, and Heartfailure in the process model are highlighted by a color, and either an edge or a path of edges from Cardiotonics4 to Vital, and Vital to Heartfailure are highlighted.

4 Results and Discussion

We have implemented the clustering, process mining, frequent sequence mining and overlay tools as part of the BPI platform [33]. BPI uses Cloud-based storage built on HBase. Each tool in BPI is implemented as a server-side library with a full Java API, and a web-based user interface (UI) implemented using the Google Web Toolkit.

Data is loaded in BPI as events after performing same day concurrent event collapse (algorithm 1 in section 3.2). BPI has the ability to generate patient traces, where all the events for a given patient are correlated by patientID. As a result of the same day concurrent event collapse algorithm, we found that a large majority of same day concurrent events that were collapsed consisted of individual lab tests. For example, labs *BUN, AST, ALT, HDL* were determined as a frequently occurring set of same day concurrent events. At the request of the expert physician, such events were collapsed into a single event denoted as *LabPanel{i}*, where i is a single character (e.g. LabPanelA). In addition, identical events that occurred consecutively for a given patient were collapsed into a single event denoted as Repeat$\{e\}$, where e is an event name (e.g. RepeatVital). Both of these techniques contributed to providing easier to interpret mined process models. Differentiating between a *Vital* and a *RepeatVital* event is particularly important. In the CHF expert physician's opinion, a recurring *Vital* event denoted as *RepeatVital* indicates regular visits to a primary care physician, where as a singular *Vital* event indicates the need for a checkup in response to particular symptoms.

Figure 3 shows an example of the clusters resulting from executing clustering on patient traces containing EMR events of CHF patients, while using a suggested epsilon value of 2.75. As shown in the figure, the largest cluster has 204 traces, the second largest cluster has 10 traces, and many clusters have only 1 trace indicating that they are outliers. Users can right click on a cluster in order to mine a process model out of it using the HeuristicsMiner algorithm.

Fig. 4 shows an example of a model mined from a cluster of 204 patients with positive outcomes. Discussions of the mined models with an expert physician allowed us to better understand the insight showcased by the mined models. For example, from Fig. 4 the following insight was extracted for three of the many clinical care pathways depicted in the mined model. **Pathway 1:** Start → AntianginalAgents4 → Vital → Cardiotonics4 → LabPanelL → Digoxin → Magnesium → NatureticPeptide → HeartFailure → Vital. Antianginal agents are prescribed for CHF level 4 for someone at risk of heart attack. Once this medication is given, vitals are checked. Cardiotonics are prescribed if abnormal

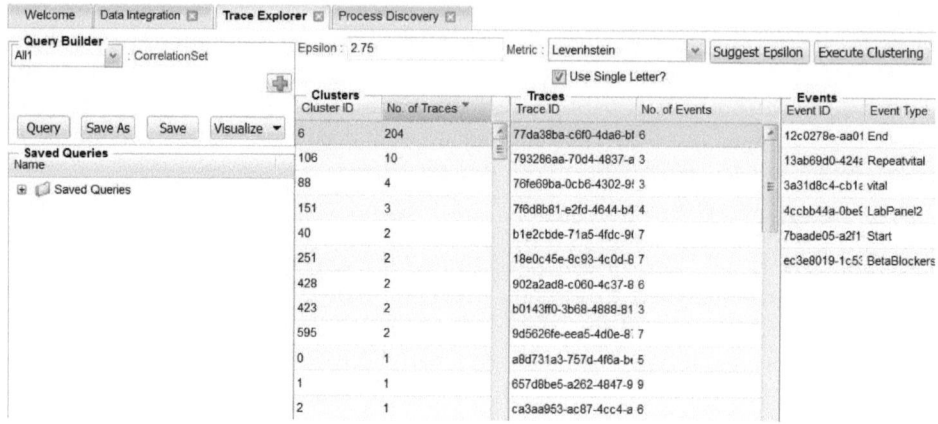

Fig. 3. A set of patient trace clusters. The largest cluster has 204 traces.

pumping of the heart is detected. Next, labs including LabPanelL (a panel of labs), as well as individual labs such as Digoxin and Magnesium are conducted followed by a NatureticPeptide test. A positive result of this test leads to a diagnosis of exacerbated heart failure. It serves as a confirmation of the patient's heart failure diagnosis.

Pathway 2: Vital → Diuretics3 → Vital → as well as Vital → Diuretics3 → Vital → LabPanelK → Diuretics3 → Vital. If vitals indicate fluid overload, Diuretics for the appropriate CHF level (in this case level 3) are prescribed to reduce fluid overload. Upon taking Diuretics3 the patient will immediately undergo weight-loss and Vitals are rechecked to determine how the patient is responding. An additional a set of labs (LabPanelK) are conducted to monitor the patient's mineral levels. This explains the loop between Diuretic3, Vital and LabPanelK.

Pathway 3: Vital → Potassium → LabPanelC → FO2HBArterial → O2SArterial → PCO2Arterial → PHArterial → POArterial → PulseOx → Vital. These labs serve as direct measures for diagnosing respiratory distress. They serve as follow up tests after managing the patient's condition with either Antianginal Agents or after managing a patient's condition with Diuretics. This explains why pathways 1 and 2 merge into Vital which allows the connection to pathway 3.

Table 2 shows an example of frequent patterns ranked by their information gain that were extracted for the congestive heart failure patients using the algorithm described in section 3.3. The overlay feature is enabled via an *Overlay Pattern* button in BPI. Figure 5 shows an example of a frequent pattern overlaid on a mined model of the patients with positive outcomes. In this experiment we also collapsed all individual lab and lab panel events in to a single event called LabTest which significantly simplified the model in the expert physician's opinion and allowed him to view the overlaid pattern clearly in the context of the other pathways. Discussions with the expert physician made it apparent that this pattern is correlated with positive outcomes because taking Cardiotonics

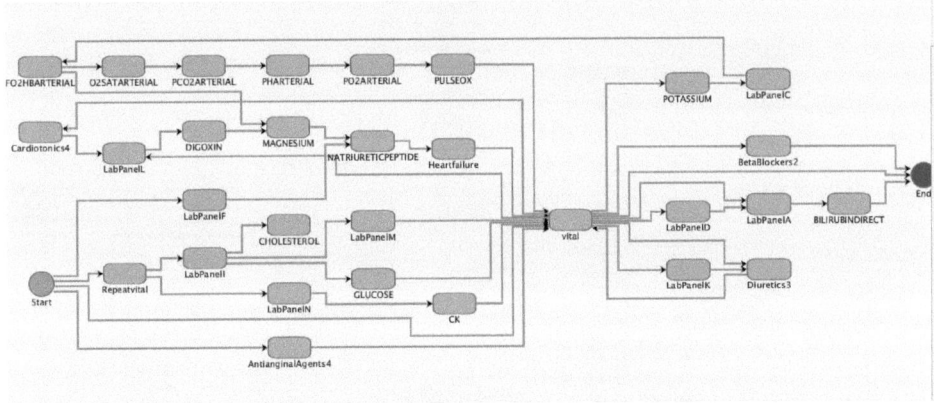

Fig. 4. A process model mined from a cluster of 204 positive outcome patients using the HeuristicsMiner algorithm

Table 2. A sample of frequent patterns ordered by information gain corresponding to the patient population in Fig 4

Frequent Pattern	Information Gain
Diuretics3 → Vital	0.142934165
AntianginalAgents4 → Vital	0.127046503
Vital → Beta Blockers2	0.108907065
Vital → Cardtiotonics4 → Digoxin	0.101768006
Repeatvital → Diuretics3 → Repeatvital	0.07780386

for CHF level 4 control's a patient's acute CHF condition, and Diuretics for CHF level 4 manages their electrolytes. This overall reduces a patient's risk of hospitalization by reducing the risk of their heart failure exacerbation. Next vital signs are checked (in the Vital event) immediately after taking Diuretics to check the patient's response to the medications.

Experimental validation allowed us to identify several limitations which we intend to address in future work:

- The frequent pattern generation algorithm is governed by a *support* threshold that controls how frequently a pattern may be found. Similarly, the HeuristicsMiner algorithm has threshold parameters for edge and node frequencies. While it is possible that frequent patterns mined from a dataset can be placed on the process model mined from the same data set, this is not guaranteed. This is because the parameters for the HeuristicsMiner and the FPMiner algorithm need to be synchronized to guarantee placement of frequent patterns on the mined model.
- While replacing raw event names with publicly available hierarchical category names (section 3.1) helped eliminate redundancies in event names, it may have led to loss of useful event information.

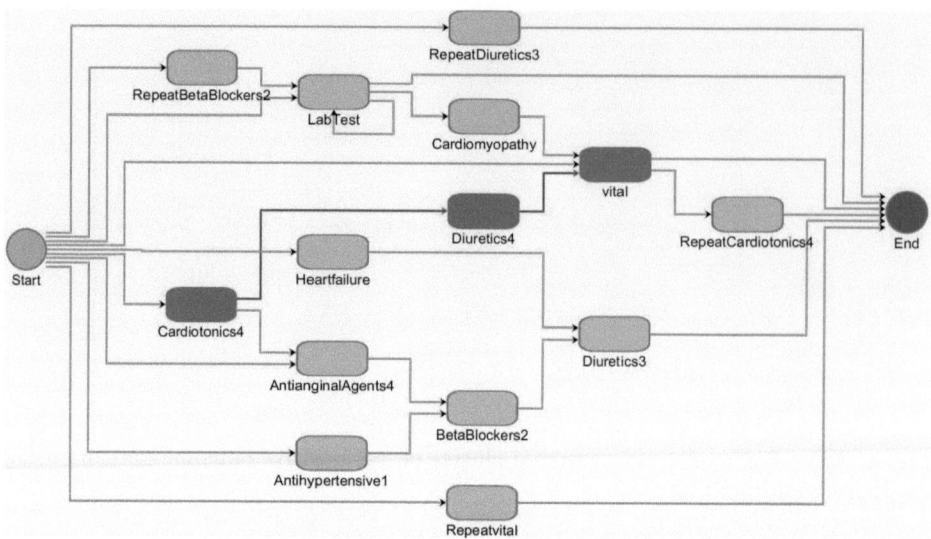

Fig. 5. Frequent pattern $Cardiotonics4 \rightarrow Diuretics4 \rightarrow Vital$ overlaid on a mined model of a cluster of the data

- Although overlaying a frequent pattern on a mined model of the patient EMR data was useful to the expert physician in terms of understanding how the care pathway represented by the pattern fit with respect to other care pathways in the mined model, the utility of the toolset needs to be validated with a larger set of users. Depending upon their individual objectives, the utility of the toolset to individual users may vary dramatically.

5 Conclusions

Process mining has been applied extensively to extract insight from healthcare data [8,14,20,25,26,36] with promising results. In this paper we have applied process mining in combination with frequent pattern mining to investigate clinical care pathways correlated with outcomes on traces of congestive heart failure patients, where the traces are first clustered to remove outliers. These techniques are provided as tools in a collaborative SaaS environment called BPI [33]. Trace clustering, frequent pattern mining and overlay of frequent patterns on a mined model are implemented as new features in BPI as a result of our work. We also implemented a same day concurrent event collapse algorithm to address situations with events occurring within the same time window. Unlike many existing studies on the application of process mining to healthcare data [8,14,20,25,26,36], we have evaluated the effectiveness of these tools on CHF patient EMR data from a healthcare provider. Activity level data was not available. Experimental results discussed with an expert physician allowed us to evaluate the utility of these tools in extracting clinical care pathway insight from EMR data. In future work we plan to enhance the interactive capabilities of the toolset while experimenting with EMR data from other providers.

Acknowledgments. We thank Dr. Robert Sorrentino M.D. and Dr. Jianying Hu at IBM T. J. Watson Research Center for valuable discussions.

References

1. Agrawal, R., Srikant, R.: Fast algorithms for mining association rules in large databases. In: VLDB 1994, San Francisco, CA, USA (1994)
2. Aiolli, F., Burattin, A., Sperduti, A.: A business process metric based on the alpha algorithm relations. In: Daniel, F., Barkaoui, K., Dustdar, S. (eds.) BPM Workshops 2011, Part I. LNBIP, vol. 99, pp. 141–146. Springer, Heidelberg (2012)
3. Weijters, A.J.M.M., van der Aalst, W., de Medeiros, A.A.: Process mining with the heuristics miner-algorithm. BETA Working Paper (2006)
4. C.P., et al.: Searching electronic health records for temporal patterns in patient histories: A case study with microsoft amalga. In: AMIA Annual Symposium, pp. 601–605 (2008)
5. Ayres, J., Gehrke, J., Yiu, T., Flannick, J.: Sequential pattern mining using a bitmap representation. In: KDD, pp. 429–435. ACM Press (2002)
6. Bose, R.P.J.C., van der Aalst, W.M.P.: Context aware trace clustering: Towards improving process mining results. In: SDM, pp. 401–412 (2009)
7. Jagadeesh Chandra Bose, R.P., van der Aalst, W.: Trace alignment in process mining: Opportunities for process diagnostics. In: Hull, R., Mendling, J., Tai, S. (eds.) BPM 2010. LNCS, vol. 6336, pp. 227–242. Springer, Heidelberg (2010)
8. Caron, F., Vanthienen, J., De Weerdt, J., Baesens, B.: Advanced care-flow mining and analysis. In: Daniel, F., Barkaoui, K., Dustdar, S. (eds.) BPM 2011 Workshops, Part I. LNBIP, vol. 99, pp. 167–168. Springer, Heidelberg (2012)
9. Cheng, H., Yan, X., Han, J., Yu, P.S.: Direct discriminative pattern mining for effective classification. In: ICDE, pp. 169–178 (2008)
10. Ester, M., Kriegel, H.P., Sander, J., Xu, X.: A density-based algorithm for discovering clusters in large spatial databases with noise. Computer (6), 226–231 (1996)
11. Fails, J.A., Karlson, A.K., Shahamat, L., Shneiderman, B.: A visual interface for multivariate temporal data: Finding patterns of events across multiple histories. In: IEEE VAST, pp. 167–174 (2006)
12. Goodman, S.N.: Toward evidence-based medical statistics. 1: The p value fallacy. Annals of Internal Medicine 130, 995–1004 (1999)
13. Greco, G., Guzzo, A., Pontieri, L., Saccá, D.: Mining expressive process models by clustering workflow traces. In: Dai, H., Srikant, R., Zhang, C. (eds.) PAKDD 2004. LNCS (LNAI), vol. 3056, pp. 52–62. Springer, Heidelberg (2004)
14. Huang, Z., Lu, X., Duan, H.: On mining clinical pathway patterns from medical behaviors. Artif. Intell. Med. 56(1), 35–50 (2012)
15. Huang, Z., Lu, X., Duan, H.: Using recommendation to support adaptive clinical pathways. Journal of Medical Systems 36(3), 1849–1860 (2012)
16. Ireson, C.L.: Critical pathways: Effectiveness in achieving patient outcomes. Nursing Administration 27(6), 16–23 (1997)
17. Jung, J.-Y., Bae, J.: Workflow clustering method based on process similarity. In: Gavrilova, M.L., Gervasi, O., Kumar, V., Tan, C.J.K., Taniar, D., Laganá, A., Mun, Y., Choo, H. (eds.) ICCSA 2006. LNCS, vol. 3981, pp. 379–389. Springer, Heidelberg (2006)

18. Kastner, M., Wagdy Saleh, M., Wagner, S., Affenzeller, M., Jacak, W.: Heuristic methods for searching and clustering hierarchical workflows. In: Moreno-Díaz, R., Pichler, F., Quesada-Arencibia, A. (eds.) EUROCAST 2009. LNCS, vol. 5717, pp. 737–744. Springer, Heidelberg (2009)
19. Lakshmanan, G., Khalaf, R.: Leveraging process mining techniques to analyze semi-structured processes. IT Professional PP (99), 1–1 (2012)
20. Lang, M., Bürkle, T., Laumann, S., Prokosch, H.U.: Process mining for clinical workflows: Challenges and current limitations. In: MIE, pp. 229–234 (2008)
21. de Leoni, M., Adams, M., van der Aalst, W.M.P., ter Hofstede, A.H.M.: Visual support for work assignment in process-aware information systems: Framework formalisation and implementation. Decision Support Systems 54(1), 345–361 (2012)
22. Levenshtein, V.I.: Binary codes capable of correcting deletions, insertions and reversals. Soviet Physics Doklady 10, 707–710 (1966)
23. Ren Lin, F., Chao Chou, S.: Mining time dependency patterns in clinical pathways. International Journal of Medical Informatics, 11–25 (2001)
24. Lo, D., Cheng, H.: Lucia: Mining closed discriminative dyadic sequential patterns. In: International Conference on Extending Database Technology, pp. 21–32 (2011)
25. Mans, R.S., Schonenberg, H., Song, M., van der Aalst, W.M.P., Bakker, P.J.M.: Application of process mining in healthcare - a case study in a dutch hospital. In: BIOSTEC (Selected Papers), pp. 425–438 (2008)
26. Mans, R., van der Aalst, W.M.P., Vanwersch, R.J.B., Moleman, A.J.: Process mining in healthcare: Data challenges when answering frequently posed questions. In: ProHealth/KR4HC, pp. 140–153 (2012)
27. Moskovitch, R., Shahar, Y.: Medical temporal-knowledge discovery via temporal abstraction. In: AMIA Annual Symposium, pp. 452–456 (2009)
28. Norén, G.N., Bate, A., Hopstadius, J., Star, K., Edwards, I.R.: Temporal pattern discovery for trends and transient effects: its application to patient records. In: SIGKDD, pp. 963–971. ACM (2008)
29. Perimal-Lewis, L.: Gaining insight from patient journey data using a process-oriented analysis approach. In: HIKM 2012, vol. 129, pp. 59–66 (2012)
30. Poelmans, J., Dedene, G., Verheyden, G., Van der Mussele, H., Viaene, S., Peters, E.: Combining business process and data discovery techniques for analyzing and improving integrated care pathways. In: Perner, P. (ed.) ICDM 2010. LNCS, vol. 6171, pp. 505–517. Springer, Heidelberg (2010)
31. Qiao, M., Akkiraju, R., Rembert, A.J.: Towards efficient business process clustering and retrieval: Combining language modeling and structure matching. In: Rinderle-Ma, S., Toumani, F., Wolf, K. (eds.) BPM 2011. LNCS, vol. 6896, pp. 199–214. Springer, Heidelberg (2011)
32. Rebuge, Á., Ferreira, D.R.: Business process analysis in healthcare environments: A methodology based on process mining. Inf. Syst. 37(2), 99–116 (2012)
33. Rozsnyai, S., Lakshmanan, G.T., Muthusamy, V., Khalaf, R., Duftler, M.J.: Business process insight: An approach and platform for the discovery and analysis of end-to-end business processes. In: SRII Global Conference, pp. 80–89 (2012)
34. Silva, V., Fernando Chirigati, K.M.A.O., de Oliveira, D., Braganholo, V., Murta, L., Mattoso, M.: Similarity-based workflow clustering. Journal of Computational Interdisciplinary Sciences 2(1), 23–35 (2011)
35. Song, M., Günther, C.W., van der Aalst, W.M.P.: Trace clustering in process mining. In: Ardagna, D., Mecella, M., Yang, J. (eds.) BPM 2008 Workshops. LNBIP, vol. 17, pp. 109–120. Springer, Heidelberg (2009)
36. Weerdt, J.D., Caron, F., Vanthienen, J., Baesens, B.: Getting a grasp on clinical pathway data: An approach based on process mining. In: PAKDD Workshops, pp. 22–35 (2012)

Exformatics Declarative Case Management Workflows as DCR Graphs

Tijs Slaats[1,2], Raghava Rao Mukkamala[1],
Thomas Hildebrandt[1], and Morten Marquard[2,*]

[1] IT University of Copenhagen,
Rued Langgaardsvej 7, 2300 Copenhagen, Denmark
{hilde,rao,tslaats}@itu.dk
http://www.itu.dk
[2] Exformatics A/S,
Lautrupsgade 13, 2100 Copenhagen, Denmark
{mmq,ts}@exformatics.com
http://www.exformatics.com

Abstract. Declarative workflow languages have been a growing research subject over the past ten years, but applications of the declarative approach in industry are still uncommon. Over the past two years Exformatics A/S, a Danish provider of Electronic Case Management systems, has been cooperating with researchers at IT University of Copenhagen (ITU) to create tools for the declarative workflow language Dynamic Condition Response Graphs (DCR Graphs) and incorporate them into their products and in teaching at ITU. In this paper we give a status report over the work. We start with an informal introduction to DCR Graphs. We then show how DCR Graphs are being used by Exformatics to model workflows through a case study of an invoice workflow. Finally we give an overview of the tools that have been developed by Exformatics to support working with DCR Graphs and evaluate their use in capturing requirements of workflows and in a bachelor level course at ITU.

Keywords: workflows, declarative specifications, tools, teaching, case study.

1 Introduction

Declarative workflow modelling [8,9,16] is an emerging field in both academia and industry which offers a new paradigm that supports flexibility and adaptability in business processes. Traditional imperative workflow languages describe *how* a process is carried out as a procedure with explicit control flow. This often leads to rigid and overspecified process descriptions, that fails to capture *why* the activities must be done in the given order. Declarative workflow languages on the other hand specify processes by the constraints describing *why* activities can or must be executed in a particular order, and not how the the process is to be executed, i.e. activities can be executed in any order and any number of times, as long as not prohibited by a constraint [15,19]. This may lead to under specified process descriptions and make it difficult to perceive the path from

---
* This research is supported by the Danish Research Agency through an industrial PhD Grant.

start to end, but captures the reason for the ordering of activities and leaves flexibility in execution.

An example a constraint between activities is the response constraint [4, 16] (e.g. $A \bullet\!\!\rightarrow B$), which requires that an execution of one task (A) is eventually followed by an execution of another task (B), but it does not put any further limits on the number of times and order in which the tasks are executed. For example, it would be perfectly valid if the second task occurs first, as long as it also occurs after the first task. In other words, $B, AB, BAB, AAB, \ldots$ are all valid runs, where as $A, BA, BBA, \ldots$ are not valid runs, as they fail to satisfy the constraint by having an occurence of A that is not followed by an occurence of B.

Examples of processes that require more flexibility are commonly found in the healthcare [5] and case management [1] domains. In those processes, the work is being carried out by knowledge workers who typically have the experience and expertise needed to deal with the complexity of a process whose requirements may vary from case to case. For this reason, knowledge-intensive processes require flexible workflow systems that support the users in their work (instead of dictating them what to do) and allow them to make their own choices as long as they do not break those constraints that do need to be strictly followed in all cases (e.g. laws or organizational policies).

Over the last decade, several declarative languages for business processes have been proposed in academic literature. The first of these languages is Declare [15, 19] which gave a number of common workflow constraints formalized in Linear-time Temporal Logic (LTL). More recently, DCR Graphs [4] have been developed as a generalization of event structures [21], where processes are described as a graph of events related by only 4 basic constraints. A simple operational semantics based on markings of the process graph makes it possible to clearly visualize the runtime state. Furthermore, the Guard-Stage-Milestone [10] has been developed, which is a *data-centric* workflow model with declarative elements for modeling life cycles of business artifacts.

Even though by now these techniques have become well known in academia, their application in the industry is relatively uncommon. Over the last two years Exformatics A/S, a Danish provider of Electronic Case Management(ECM) systems, has been collaborating with researchers of IT University of Copenhagen (ITU), to develop tools for the declarative workflow language DCR Graphs with the aim to apply and evaluate the use of DCR Graphs on real world scenarios in the case management domain and in teaching at ITU.

The goal of the present paper is to give a status report, presenting and evaluating the tools developed so far. As the first step, the core DCR Graphs model were used by Exformatics A/S in a case study to capture some of the requirements in the design phase of a cross-organizational case management system [1]. The case study led to the further development of the DCR Graphs model by adding support for *hierarchical* modelling using nested events and a (*milestone*) constraint [6], making it possible to concisely specify that some event(s) must not be pending in order for some event to happen. It also encouraged developing a graphical design, simulation and verification tool [18] which is being used successfully in further case studies with industry and in teaching at ITU.

In the remainder of this paper we will first introduce DCR Graphs informally in Sec. 2, in Sec. 3 we will explain how they are used as the underlying formalism for workflows within the Exformatics ECM system and in Sec. 4 we will give an overview of the tools for managing DCR Graphs that have been developed by Exformatics. We evaluate and describe related work in Sec. 5 and conclusions and future work in Sec. 7.

2 DCR Graphs by Example

This section describes DCR Graphs informally by giving an overview of the declarative nature of the language and its graphical modeling notation. (All figures shown are produced in the developed graphical editor and simulation tool [18]). The formal semantics of DCR Graphs are given in [4, 6, 12].

A DCR Graph specifies a process as a set of *events*, typically representing the (possibly repeated) execution of activities in the workflow process, changes to a dataset or timer events. The events are represented graphically as rectangular boxes with zero or more *roles* in a small box on top of the event as depicted in Fig. 1, showing an excerpt of an invoice workflow with three events: Recieve Invoice, Enter Invoice Data and Responsible Approval and two roles: Administration (Adm), representing the administration office of a company and Responsible (Res), the person responsible for the invoice. The administation office has access to the tasks Recieve Invoice and Enter Invoice Data and the responsible has access to the task Responsible Approval.

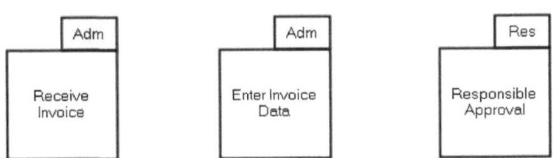

Fig. 1. DCR Graphs: Tasks and Roles

The concrete principals/actors (either human or automated) are typically not shown in the graphical notation, but will at runtime be assigned one or more of the roles and can then execute any of the events that are assigned to one of these roles.

The events in a DCR Graph can happen any number of times and in any order, unless prevented by a constraint relation. The graph in Fig. 1 has no constraints, so it would be valid to e.g. just receive an invoice and do nothing else, or to receive an invoice and then approve the invoice twice. Constraints are defined using five different kinds of relations between the events, named the *condition, response, milestone, inclusion* and *exclusion* relation respectively.

Fig. 2(a) gives an example of a condition relation (depicted graphically as →•) between Recieve Invoice and Enter Invoice Data, which states that before Enter Invoice Data can happen, the event Recieve Invoice must first have happened. In other words, we have to receive an invoice before we can enter the details of the invoice into the system. The DCR Graph shown in Fig. 2(a) allows possible runs such as Recieve Invoice.Enter Invoice Data or Recieve Invoice.Enter Invoice Data.Recieve Invoice or Recieve Invoice.Recieve Invoice.Enter Invoice Data, but it does not allow e.g. Enter Invoice Data. Recieve Invoice as it invalidates the condition constraint. As a help for the user, the graphical editor shows a "no entry" sign at the event Enter Invoice Data to indicate that it is not enabled.

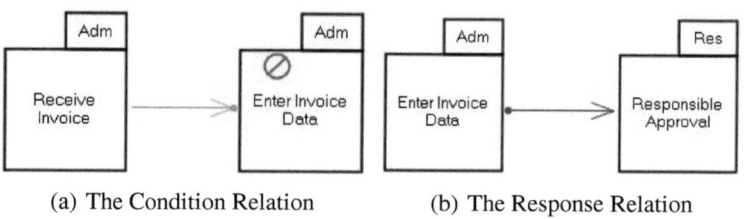

(a) The Condition Relation   (b) The Response Relation

Fig. 2. The Condition and Response relations

In Fig. 2(b) is given an example of the response relation (depicted graphically as •→), which states that if Enter Invoice Data happens, Responsible Approval eventually has to happen in order for the workflow to be completed. Note that this relation is not counting, i.e., it is not required to execute Responsible Approval once for each execution of Enter Invoice Data. In other words, the response relation offers the flexibility of approving one to many invoices just by executing Responsible Approval once. Examples of completed runs in the process represented by the graph in Fig. 2(b) are: Enter Invoice Data.Responsible Approval, and Enter Invoice Data.Enter Invoice Data.Responsible Approval. An example of a run which is possible, but not completed is Enter Invoice Data.Responsible Approval.Enter Invoice Data as the last Enter Invoice Data is not (yet) followed by Responsible Approval.

In [6] we extended DCR Graphs to allow *nested* events as shown in Fig. 3. Nesting both acts as a logical grouping and as a shorthand notation for having the same relation between many events. For instance, the response relation from Enter Invoice Data in Fig. 3 represents a response relation from Enter Invoice Data to all three sub events of the super event Approval.

Adding nesting to the model, made it apparant, that it is useful to be able of express, that an event can not happen when a nested subgraph is not in an accepting state. We call this relation the milestone relation (depicted graphically as →⋄), and is exemplified shown in Fig. 3 from the Approval super event to Pay Invoice. The meaning is, that after doing Enter Invoice Data, we will have a pending response on each approval task and therefore we can't execute Pay Invoice until each of these tasks has been done. Note that in contrast to the condition relation, by using a combination of the response and milestone relations we can require approval again after it was already given.

Finally, the exclude relation (depicted graphically as →%) and its dual the include relation (depicted graphically as →+) allows for dynamically respectively exclude and include events from the workflow. Fig. 4(a) shows a typical example of the use of the dynamic include and exclude relations to model *exclusive choice* between events: The

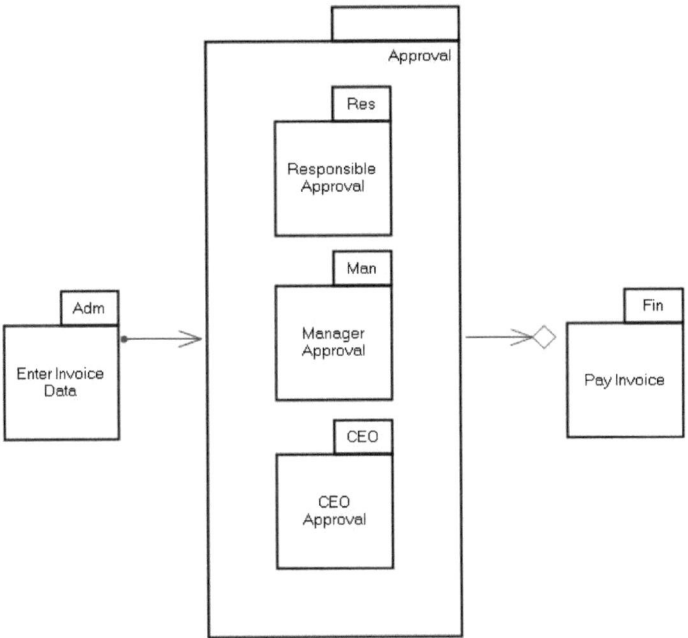

Fig. 3. Example of Nesting and the Milestone Relation

responsible may choose between approving or request a change to the invoice. The choice is modelled by letting the two events mutually exclude each other. If a change is requested, the administration is required to enter data again (because of the response relation from **Request Change** to **Enter Invoice Data**), and when data is entered again, the two events nested under the *Approval* super event is included again because of the include relation from **Enter Invoice Data** to **Approval**. This example illustrates the flexible nature of DCR Graphs in process modeling, as compared to the typical BPMN procedural model in Fig. 4(b). In the DCR Graph, invoice data can be entered any number of times before approval, and changes can also be requested any number of times before data is entered again, while the BPMN process only allows every task to be executed once for each cycle in the loop. It is of course possible to model the more flexible execution in BPMN, but not in a natural way.

2.1 Execution Semantics

The runtime state of a DCR Graph is defined by a *marking* of the graph, formally given by 3 finite sets of events representing respectivly which events are *executed* (at least once), *pending responses* and *included*. By keeping track of which events have been executed at least once in the *executed* set, we can determine which conditions have been satisfied. The *pending responses* set keeps track of which events need to be executed before the workflow is in a completed state. Finally, the *included* set keeps track of the currently included events. An event is enabled for execution if it is currently included

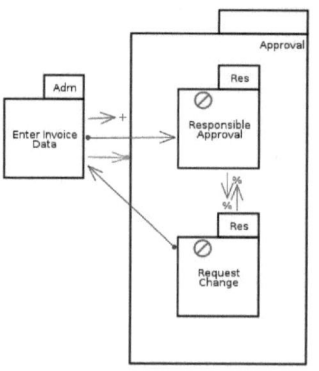 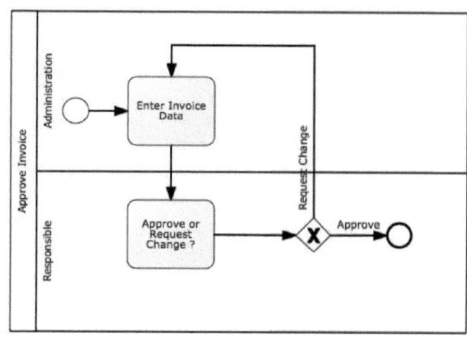

(a) Modeling choice with include and exclude   (b) Imperative BPMN model

Fig. 4. Declarative DCR Graph and imperative BPMN model of invoice approval

(i.e. part of the included set in the current marking) and all of its conditions are either executed or excluded (i.e all condition events that are currently included should be part of the executed events set) and no event related to it by the milestone relation is included and a pending response. A (finite or infinite) execution is defined to be accepting, when no event from some point stays included and as a pending response forever without eventually being executed.

The excluded events are graphically depicted by a dashed border, the executed events by a green checkmark at the event, and pending response events by a red exclamation mark. This is shown in Fig. 5, where Enter Invoice Data and Request Change are executed, and thereby Responsible Approval is a pending response, but it is also excluded and Enter Invoice Data is a pending response too.

A DCR Graph contains an initial marking defined as part of the graph. For example, a graph may have a number of initial pending responses (representing tasks that are required to be executed mandatorily for the workflow to be considered finished), or initially excluded events.

2.2 DCR Graphs with Global Data

In one of the more recent extensions to DCR Graphs [12], we have introduced the concept of global data. In DCR Graphs, data is modelled as a global store that contains a number of named variables. The variables are mapped to events so that we can specify which events can read/write to specific variables. Furthermore, *guards* are defined as boolean expressions over the values of variables. Guards can be placed on both events and relations. If a guard is assigned to an event, then as long as the guard does not evaluate to true, the event is blocked from execution. On the other hand, having a guard on a relation means that the relation is only evaluated when the guard evaluates to true, in other words the condition constraint only needs to hold and an event is only recorded as a response while the guard holds.

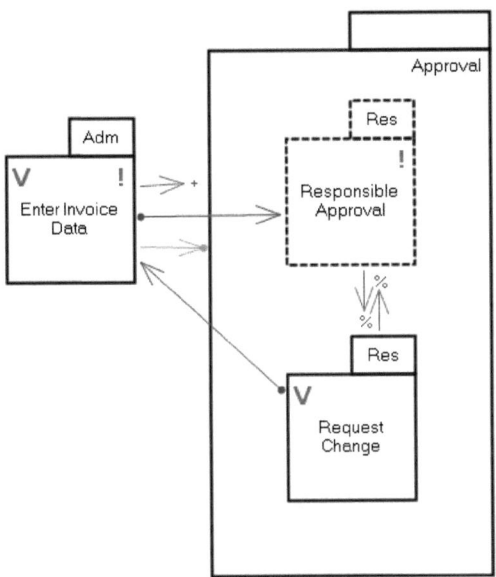

Fig. 5. Example marking after executing Enter Invoice Data followed by Request Change

For example, the response between Enter Invoice Data and Manager Approval in Fig 6 is only recorded when the amount of the invoice is equal or larger than 1000 euro, if the amount is lower than 1000 euros, executing Enter Invoice Data will not make Manager Approval a pending response.

3 Exformatics Workflows as DCR Graphs

Before the introduction of (Nested) DCR Graphs, the Exformatics workflow model consisted of tasks grouped under phases. There was always one active phase, which could be changed manually by the user, tasks belonging to that phase were then enabled. When introducing DCR Graphs we chose to map tasks to events and to maintain the phase model, mapping it to a single-level nesting structure. We removed the practice that tasks were enabled when their phase was active and allowed the active phase to be changed automatically through the execution of certain tasks. In the new model, the active phase no longer controls the workflow but instead just gives a general indication of the state that the case is in. We introduced all five relations of DCR Graphs as ways of constraining the flow of tasks. One distinction from the traditional DCR Graph approach is that tasks in the Exformatics system are normally only done once. As a result, when a task is executed, it is not shown in the list of tasks that need to be done anymore. However, unless it is exlicitely excluded through the exclude relation it remains possible to open the task again manually and do it again, so the execution semantics remains faithful to the DCR Graphs semantics.

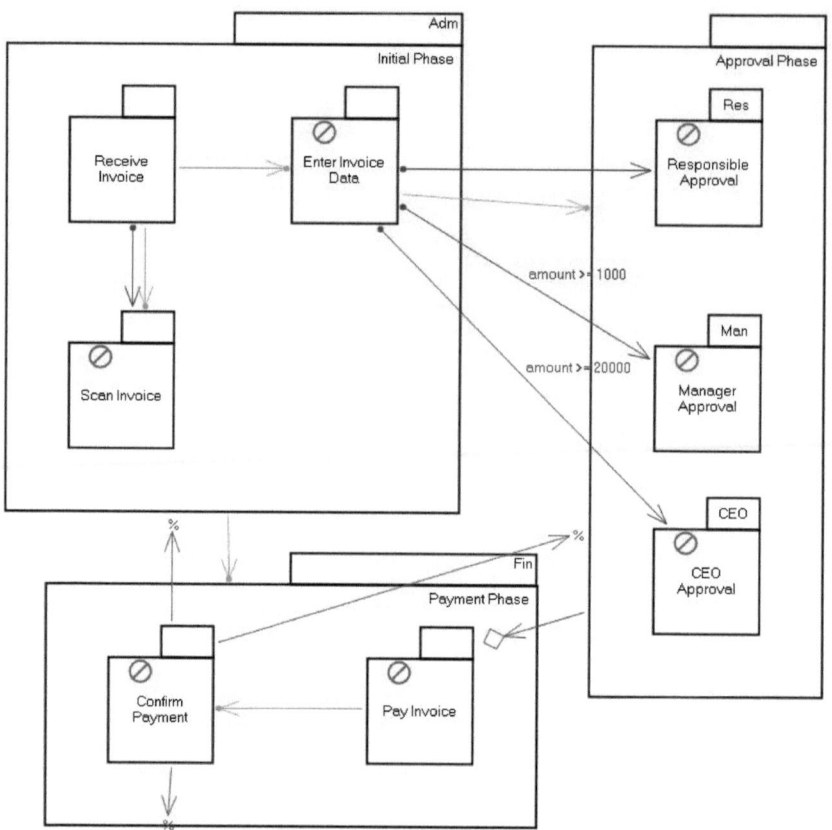

Fig. 6. Exformatics Invoice Workflow as a DCR Graph

Fig. 6 shows a workflow that is being used internally by Exformatics and has been modelled using DCR Graphs. It describes how to handle the process of receiving invoices.

The workflow contains five roles: 1) the administration department (**Adm**), which is responsible for receiving the invoice, scanning it and creating an invoice case . 2) The invoice responsible (**Res**), which is responsible for the invoice, usually because they are the person that bought the items that the invoice concerns, they are expected to check and approve the invoice. 3) The manager of the responsible (**Man**), whose approval may be needed in certain circumstances. 4) The CEO (**CEO**) who may also need to give approval in certain exceptional cases. And finally 5) the finance department (**Fin**), which takes care of paying the invoice and confirming that payment has succeeded. The tasks are divided into three phases, the **Initial Phase** which contains the tasks of the administration department, the **Approval Phase** which consists of the approval tasks and the **Payment Phase** which contains the tasks that handle the payment of the invoice.

The process starts when an invoice is received by the administration department, because Exformatics wants to keep all their documents in an electronic format it is required (through the response relation from **Receive Invoice** to **Scan Invoice**) that the invoice is scanned. The administration department is also required to decide if the invoice should be entered into the system (sometimes fake or wrong invoices are received which can be easily filtered out at first sight, for example because they are addressed to a non-existent employee). If they decide that the invoice appears legit then they enter all relevant data into the system, in particular the amount the invoice is for, which is used by the workflow system to determine whose approval is needed for the invoice. The responsible for the invoice should always approve the invoice (modelled by an unguarded response relation), if the amount of the invoice is higher then 1000 euros, approval from the responsible's manager is required as well (modelled by a response relation with the guard **amount** $\geq$ **1000**). In special cases where the amount is higher then 20000 euros, approval from the CEO of the company is required as well.

It is possible that data is entered again, for example because a mistake was made by the administration department, or because a correction on the invoice was received, in this case new approvals will be required. When all necessary approvals have been received the invoice can be paid, this is modelled through the milestone relation from the **Approval Phase** to the task **Pay Invoice**, which means that **Pay Invoice** can not be done while there are pending responses in the **Approval Phase**. Once payment is confirmed, the invoice case should be closed, modelled through an exclusion relation from **Confirm Payment** to all three phases. There are five conditions in the workflow: first of all, **Receive Invoice** is required before the administration department can execute **Enter Invoice Data** or **Scan Invoice**. **Enter Invoice Data** is required before any approval can be given and all of the tasks in the **Initial Phase** should be done before any of the tasks in the **Payment Phase** can be done. Finaly, we have to pay the invoice before we can confirm payment.

4 Tool Support

Several tools have been developed at Exformatics to design and execute DCR Graphs internally or externally when presenting DCR Graphs at seminars or when interacting with customers. First of all, to facilitate the exchange of process descriptions between the tools developed by Exformatics and the tools being developed at IT University of Copenhagen, we defined a common XML format, which we will show in the first subsection. Secondly we developed a set of webservices that provide functionality for the execution, verification, storage and visualization of DCR Graphs, we named this set of services the *Process Engine*. Finally, as already mentioned above, we developed a standalone graphical editor to support the visual modelling and simulation of DCR Graphs, called the *DCR Graphs Editor*, which has also been used for teaching at a bachelor level course on Business Processes and IT at the IT University of Copenhagen.

Fig. 7 gives an overview of these tools and how they interact with eachother and the Exformatics ECM. The Process Engine is central to our tools and is used by the ECM to execute, verify and visualize workflows. The DCR Graphs Editor allows for execution of single steps by itself, but also uses the Process Engine for verification

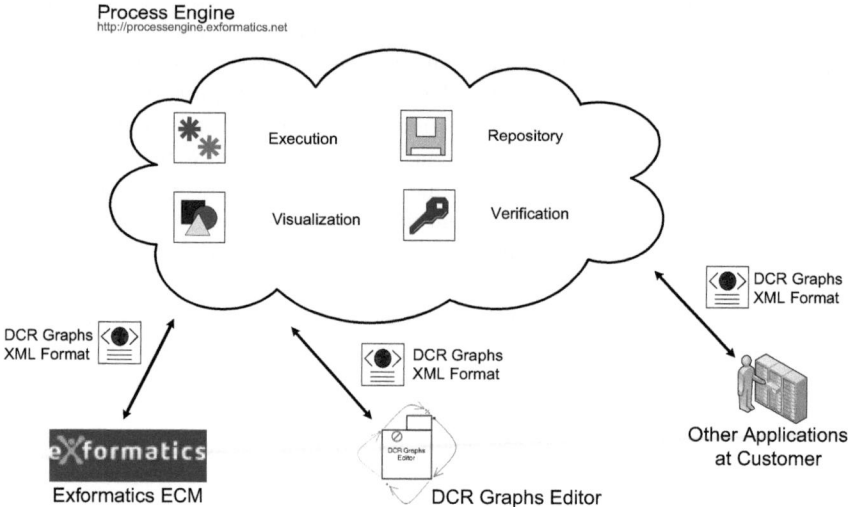

Fig. 7. Overview of the Exformatics DCR Graphs Tools

of DCR Graphs. Finally the purpose of the Process Engine is to be easily plugged in to other case management solutions as well, so that we may provide only workflow functionalities such as execution, verification, visualization and storage to customers without them being required to adopt the full Exformatics ECM package.

4.1 DCR Graphs XML Format

In listing 1 we give an example of the XML format for describing DCR Graphs.

The xml file consists of two main parts: the specification of the DCR Graph and the runtime state of the DCR Graph. The specification is split up into a section decribing resources and section describing constraints. The resource section contains subsections for events (possibly nested), labels, a mapping from labels to events, variables, expressions and variable acccess rights. The constraint section contains five subsections for the DCR Graph relations. The runtime section contains a subsection for the marking, containing the set of executed events, pending responses and included events, and a subsection for the state of the globalstore, which contains the values assigned to the variables in the current state.

Listing 1. Overview of DCR Graph XML Format

```
<?xml version = "1.0" encoding = "utf 8"?>
<dcrgraph>
    <specification>
        <resources>
            <events>
                <event id="Initial Phase">
                    <event id="Enter Invoice Data"/>
                    ...
                </event>
```

```xml
            ...
        </events>
        <labels>
            <label id="CEO Approval"/>
            ...
        </labels>
        <labelMappings>
            <labelMapping eventId="CEO Approval" labelId="CEO Approval"/>
            ...
        </labelMappings>
        <variables>
            <variable id="amount" value="0"/>
        </variables>
        <expressions>
            <expression id="gte1000" value="amount >= 1000"/>
            ...
        </expressions>
        <variableAccesses>
            <readAccesses>
                <readAccess eventId="Enter Invoice Data" variableId="amount"/>
                ...
            </readAccesses>
            <writeAccesses>
                <writeAccess eventId="Enter Invoice Data" variableId="amount"/>
            </writeAccesses>
        </variableAccesses>
    </resources>
    <constraints>
        <conditions>
            <condition sourceId="Receive Invoice" targetId="Scan Invoice"/>
            ...
        </conditions>
        <responses>
            <response sourceId="Enter Invoice Data" targetId="Manager Approval" expressionId="gte1000"/>
            ...
        </responses>
        <excludes>
            <exclude sourceId="Confirm Payment" targetId="Approval Phase"/>
            ...
        </excludes>
        <includes/>
        <milestones>
            <milestone sourceId="Approval Phase" targetId="Pay Invoice"/>
        </milestones>
    </constraints>
</specification>
<runtime>
    <marking>
        <executed/>
        <included>
            <event id="Approval Phase"/>
            ...
        </included>
        <pendingResponses/>
    </marking>
    <globalStore>
        <variable id="amount" value="0"/>
    </globalStore>
</runtime>
</dcrgraph>
```

Next to the standard elements described above, it is possible to insert *custom* elements at all nodes of the XML tree. This allows one to add additional data for specific tools that is not required for the formal definition of a DCR Graph. Examples of these are the roles (they are not a part of the formal model as they are not necesairily interesting for applications in other domains than BPM) and the location of events when drawn in the visual editor as shown in listing 2.

Listing 2. Example of how custom data can be insterted into the XML format

```
<?xml version="1.0" encoding="utf 8"?>
<event id="CEO Approval">
    <custom>
        <visualization>
            <location xLoc="449" yLoc="123"/>
        </visualization>
            <roles>
                <role>CEO</role>
            </roles>
    </custom>
</event>
```

4.2 Process Engine

Currently the Process Engine consists of three main webservices: the first for execution, the second for storage of DCR Graphs and the third for visualization of DCR Graphs. The execution service contains methods for executing and verifying DCR Graphs. The execution methods support the global data model, verification consists of checking for deadlock and livelock, but only for standard DCR Graphs without data. In the future we plan to extend the verification aspect and move it to its own service. The repository service for storage of DCR Graphs is currently very limited and mainly a proof of concept, it is planned to extend this in the future so it can be used to support sharing of workflows between cooperating organizations. The visualization service can be used to automatically layout and draw DCR Graphs, currently limited to the basic model without guards on data. All of these services are used by the Exformatics ECM for modelling and executing workflows.

4.3 DCR Graphs Editor

The DCR Graphs Editor is a graphical editor for modelling and simulating DCR Graphs. There are two main screens in the tool: in the Process Model screen one can design DCR Graphs by drawing events, changing the name, label and initial marking, adding roles and adding relations between events. In he Process Simulation Screen one can simulate DCR Graphs by clicking on the events that one wants to execute, the tool will give feedback on the current trace of executed events, which events can be executed and if the DCR Graph is in an accepting state. The tool can also interact with the verification methods of the Process Engine to check DCR Graphs for deadlock and livelock. It currently supports nested DCR Graphs including the milestone relation and work is underway to also add support for the global data model. All the images of DCR Graphs in this paper come directly from the editor.

5 Related Work

As mentioned in the introduction Declare [15, 19] was the first serious attempt at creating a declarative notation for describing business processes. Tool support for Declare consists of a design tool, a server and corresponding user client for executing Declare processes. The designer is similar to the DCR Graphs Editor, allowing modellers to draw and verify Declare models (including a notion of data) by using a graphical user interface. The server is similar to the execution webservices contained in the Process Engine, allowing execution of Declare models by client programs. Finally the user client is somewhat comparable to the simulation part of the DCR Graphs Editor, although it offers more features to support the user in the execution of the process. These tools have been in development since the inception of the Declare language and therefor have seen a fair amount of iterations and reached a high level of maturity. The DCR Graphs tools on the other hand can be seen as being an advanced prototype version (with the most mature parts, such as the execution engine, currently being brought into production), where new features are still frequently being added. Both Declare and DCR Graphs are being included as extensions to the newest version of CPN Tools [20], for Declare it is the intention that this will become the main vehicle for further developments on the language and that no further features will be added to the previously mentioned tools. Declare also offers extensive support for analysis of Declare logs through ProM and support for process mining through the Declare Miner [11]. At the moment nothing comparable exists for DCR Graphs, however there is an interest in investigating process mining on running instances of DCR Graphs, particularly in the context of adaptive processes, with the goal of identifying common adaptation patterns. DCR Graphs also offer extended tool support for verification, allowing users to specify properties to be verified as a DCR Graph and then verifying processes modelled as DCR Graphs against these properties [13]. These tools are being developed at the IT University of Copenhagen and are therefor not described in detail this paper, however since these tools use the common XML format described in sec. 4.1, the Exformatics tools can easily interact with them.

The business artifacts [14] model developed by IBM Research combines both data and process aspects in a holistic manner. An artifact type contains both an information model (data for business objects) and a lifecycle model, which describes the possible ways a business entity might progress through and responds to events and external activities. A declarative approach using *Guard-Stage-Milestone* (GSM model) [9] based on ECA(Event Condition Action)-like rules for specification of life cycles on business artifacts has been developed in the recent years. Compared to DCR Graphs, the GSM-model has a richer support for data, but also a more complex semantics that does not capture acceptance criteria for infinite executions.

6 Evaluation

This work provides an initial report on tools being developed at Exformatics A/S examplified by a use-case being used internally within the company itself. As such no concrete quantitative evaluation of the usefulness and commercial viabilty of the tools exists yet. However, DCR Graphs as a modelling paradigm and the Exformatics tools themselves have already seen both commercial and academic use. As a modelling paradigm, DCR Graphs were applied in a commercial project involving Exformatics and *Landsorganisationen i Danmark (LO)*, the umbrella organisation for Danish unions. During this project DCR Graphs were used to model the IT system that Exformatics developed for LO [1], but the lack of tool support for design and simulation limited its use. In [5] we showed how DCR Graphs can be used to model a distributed healthcare process encountered in a Danish hospital. DCR Graphs and the tools are currently employed in a project jointly with a danish research foundation for modelling the case management process for handling funding applications from submission to descission. All of these cases have been demonstrated for industry at seminars with positive feedback resulting in several requests for follow up meetings. Finally, Exformatics has recently started a commercial project for the Danish Cancer Society, including the development of an invoice approval solution based on the example used in this paper and using the Process Engine for execution of the workflows in the solution.

In the recent paper [17] we give the first empirical evaluation on what practitioners think of declarative modelling based on a study performed at a Dutch provider of ECM software. During the study some of those participating were presented Declare, while others were presented DCR Graphs. While the overall results of the study point in the direction of a hybrid model combining the imperative and declarative paradigms, it was also clear that the declarative paradigm by itself was percieved as useful for the right application domains.

In the Spring 2012 and 2013, the DCR Graphs model has been introduced in a bachelor course in IT and Business Process Modelling at the IT University of Copenhagen [2]. Each year, the course was followed by about 40 students, and the DCR Graph model was introduced for capturing process requirements, along with BPMN 2.0 for modelling processes imperatively. The students worked in groups, modelling their own processes identified in a field study performed in a previous course. They first modelled the process in BPMN and subsequently were asked to model the requirements in DCR Graphs and compare the models. They all experienced that the initial BPMN was good at describing a procedure of *how* to carry out the process. However, when turning to the DCR Graph model, they also realized that in most cases their BPMN model only described a fairly rigid, happy path through the process. In most cases it took the group two iterations to change their mindset to model requirements instead of the procedure. This may however be influenced by the fact, that they did no longer have access to the company in which they had performed the field study. Only in 2013, the DCR Graphs editor was available, and we experienced that it made it much easier for the students to learn the notation and semantics, and to appreciate its use for modelling process requirements. However, it was also clear that it still could be difficult for some of the students to visualize the possible paths of the process specified as DCR Graphs.

7 Conclusion

In this paper, we have given an informal introduction to DCR Graphs and briefly described current tool support, and how DCR Graphs and the tools are being used by Exformatics and in teaching at ITU university to model workflows.

Even though the uses in practice and teaching so far is limited, it has been very encouraging. At presentations for industry the models have generally been appreciated and easily understood. At the course the students were able to apply DCR Graphs to model processes obtained from their own field studies in a previous course. They reported back that using the simulation facility in the tool was a great help to understand both the constraints of their own process and DCR Graphs as a model language.

As part of the future work, we plan to further develop the tools, making them more easily accessible and user-friendly to process modelers, based on the usability studies and feedback from students and clients of Exformatics. Furthermore, we also intend to upgrade the tools to support some of the latest extensions on DCR Graphs such as time [7], a distributed data model and more advanced verification techniques. Similarly, we are also working on extending the theory of DCR Graphs to provide a behavioral type system for cross-organizational workflows as initiated in [3]. In the future we also want to research the challenge of developing business processes for knowledge-intensive and adaptive case management processes as initiated in [13], which require more focus on evolutionary process data and adaptability of the process during execution.

References

1. Hildebrandt, T., Mukkamala, R.R., Slaats, T.: Designing a cross-organizational case management system using dynamic condition response graphs. In: 2011 15th IEEE International Enterprise Distributed Object Computing Conference (EDOC), October 2-September 2, pp. 161–170 (2011)
2. Hildebrandt, T.: It and business process modelling course. IT University of Copenhagen (2013), https://blog.itu.dk/BIMF-F2013/
3. Hildebrandt, T., Carbone, M., Slaats, T.: Rsvp: Live sessions with responses. In: Proceedings of BEAT 2013, 1st International Workshop on Behavioural Types (2013)
4. Hildebrandt, T., Mukkamala, R.R.: Declarative event-based workflow as distributed dynamic condition response graphs. In: Post-Proceedings of PLACES 2010 (2010)
5. Hildebrandt, T., Mukkamala, R.R., Slaats, T.: Declarative modelling and safe distribution of healthcare workflows. In: International Symposium on Foundations of Health Information Engineering and Systems, Johannesburg, South Africa (August 2011)
6. Hildebrandt, T., Mukkamala, R.R., Slaats, T.: Nested dynamic condition response graphs. In: Arbab, F., Sirjani, M. (eds.) FSEN 2011. LNCS, vol. 7141, pp. 343–350. Springer, Heidelberg (2012)
7. Hildebrandt, T., Mukkamala, R.R., Slaats, T., Zanitti, F.: Contracts for cross-organizational workflows as timed dynamic condition response graphs. Journal of Logic and Algebraic Programming, JLAP (May 2013), http://dx.doi.org/10.1016/j.jlap.2013.05.005
8. Hildebrandt, T.T., Mukkamala, R.R.: Declarative event-based workflow as distributed dynamic condition response graphs. In: Honda, K., Mycroft, A. (eds.) PLACES. EPTCS, vol. 69, pp. 59–73 (2010)
9. Hull, R.: Formal study of business entities with lifecycles: Use cases, abstract models, and results. In: Bravetti, T., Bultan, M. (eds.) 7th International Workshop on Web Services and Formal Methods. LNCS, vol. 6551, Springer, Heidelberg (2001)
10. Hull, R., Damaggio, E., Fournier, F., Gupta, M., Heath III, F.T., Hobson, S., Linehan, M., Maradugu, S., Nigam, A., Sukaviriya, P., Vaculin, R.: Introducing the guard-stage-milestone approach for specifying business entity lifecycles. In: Proc. of WS-FM 2010, pp. 1–24. Springer, Heidelberg (2011)

11. Maggi, F.M., Mooij, A.J., van der Aalst, W.M.P.: User-Guided Discovery of Declarative Process Models. In: 2011 IEEE Symposium on Computational Intelligence and Data Mining, IEEE (2011)
12. Mukkamala, R.R.: A Formal Model For Declarative Workflows - Dynamic Condition Response Graphs. PhD thesis, IT University of Copenhagen (March 2012) (forthcomming)
13. Mukkamala, R.R., Hildebrandt, T., Slaats, T.: Towards trustworthy adaptive case management with dynamic condition response graphs. In: Proceedings of the 17th IEEE International EDOC Conference, EDOC 2013 (2013)
14. Nigam, A., Caswell, N.S.: Business artifacts: An approach to operational specification. IBM Syst. J. 42, 428–445 (2003)
15. Pesic, M., Schonenberg, M.H., Sidorova, N., Van Der Aalst, W.M.P.: Constraint-based workflow models: change made easy. In: Meersman, R., Tari, Z. (eds.) OTM 2007, Part I. LNCS, vol. 4803, pp. 77–94. Springer, Heidelberg (2007)
16. Pesic, M., van der Aalst, W.M.P.: A declarative approach for flexible business processes management. In: Eder, J., Dustdar, S. (eds.) BPM Workshops 2006. LNCS, vol. 4103, pp. 169–180. Springer, Heidelberg (2006)
17. Reijers, H.A., Slaats, T., Stahl, C.: Declarative Modeling — An Academic Dream or the Future for BPM? In: Daniel, F., Wang, J., Weber, B. (eds.) BPM 2013. LNCS, vol. 8094, pp. 307–322. Springer, Heidelberg (2013)
18. Slaats, T.: Dcr graphs wiki. IT University of Copenhagen (2013), http://www.itu.dk/research/models/wiki/index.php/DCR_Graphs_Editor
19. van der Aalst, W.M.P., Pesic, M., Schonenberg, H.: Declarative workflows: Balancing between flexibility and support. Computer Science - R&D 23(2), 99–113 (2009)
20. Westergaard, M., Slaats, T.: Mixing Paradigms for More Comprehensible Models. In: Daniel, F., Wang, J., Weber, B. (eds.) BPM 2013. LNCS, vol. 8094, pp. 283–290. Springer, Heidelberg (2013)
21. Winskel, G.: Events in Computation. PhD thesis, Edinburgh University (1980)

Author Index

Agarwal, Shivali   251
Appel, Stefan   187

Baeyens, Tom   10
Baier, Thomas   17
Bose, Rantham Prabhakara Jagadeesh Chandra   97
Buchmann, Alejandro   187
Buijs, Joos C.A.M.   33

Carmona, Josep   130
Carrera, David   65
Contractor, Noshir   1

de Leoni, Massimiliano   113
Dijkman, Remco   235
Dumas, Marlon   49, 81

Eid-Sabbagh, Rami-Habib   227
Ekanayake, Chathura C.   49
Eshuis, Rik   259

Fahland, Dirk   171
Fdhila, Walid   146
Freudenreich, Tobias   187
Frischbier, Sebastian   187

Gal, Avigdor   203
Gao, Xiang   4
García-Bañuelos, Luciano   49, 81

Hewelt, Marcin   227
Hildebrandt, Thomas   339
Hull, Richard   259

Khalaf, Rania   65
Klinkmüller, Christopher   211
Knuplesch, David   146
Kriglstein, Simone   219
Kumar, Akhil   235

Lakshmanan, Geetika T.   323
La Rosa, Marcello   49
Lee, Juhnyoung   251
Leopold, Henrik   203, 211

Liu, Rong   251
Ludwig, André   211

Maggi, Fabrizio Maria   81, 97
Marquard, Morten   339
Mendling, Jan   17, 203, 211
Meyer, Andreas   171
Montali, Marco   81, 155
Mukkamala, Raghava Rao   339
Munoz-Gama, Jorge   130
Muthusamy, Vinod   65

Nutt, Werner   155

Poggi, Nicolas   65
Pufahl, Luise   171
Puhlmann, Frank   291

Razniewski, Simon   155
Reichert, Manfred   146
Reijers, Hajo A.   275, 307
Rinderle-Ma, Stefanie   146, 219
Rozsnyai, Szabolcs   323

Sagi, Tomer   203
Sindhgatta, Renuka R.   251
Slaats, Tijs   283, 307, 339
Song, Minseok   235
Stahl, Christian   307
Sun, Yutian   259

Thiemich, Christian   291

Vaculín, Roman   259
van der Aa, Han   275
van der Aalst, Wil M.P.   33, 97, 113, 130
Vanderfeesten, Irene   275
van Dongen, Boudewijn F.   33

Wallner, Günter   219
Wang, Fei   323
Weber, Ingo   211
Weidlich, Matthias   203
Weske, Mathias   171, 227
Westergaard, Michael   283

MIX
Papier aus verantwortungsvollen Quellen
Paper from responsible sources
FSC® C105338

If you have any concerns about our products,
you can contact us on
ProductSafety@springernature.com

In case Publisher is established outside the EU,
the EU authorized representative is:
Springer Nature Customer Service Center GmbH
Europaplatz 3, 69115 Heidelberg, Germany

Printed by Libri Plureos GmbH
in Hamburg, Germany